PHILOSTRATUS

EUNAPIUS

LCL 134

PHILOSTRATUS

LIVES OF THE SOPHISTS

EDITED AND TRANSLATED BY

GRAEME MILES

EUNAPIUS

LIVES OF PHILOSOPHERS AND SOPHISTS

EDITED AND TRANSLATED BY

HAN BALTUSSEN

HARVARD UNIVERSITY PRESS
CAMBRIDGE, MASSACHUSETTS
LONDON, ENGLAND
2023

LOEB CLASSICAL LIBRARY® is a registered trademark
of the President and Fellows of Harvard College

Library of Congress Control Number 2022039364
CIP data available from the Library of Congress

ISBN 978-0-674-99753-0

*Composed in ZephGreek and ZephText by
Technologies 'N Typography, Merrimac, Massachusetts.
Printed on acid-free paper and bound by
Maple Press, York, Pennsylvania*

CONTENTS

PREFACE

Philostratus is a challenging author to translate, not only
(and not even primarily) due to his many linguistic foibles
(to which Schmid dedicated the entire fourth volume of
his *Der Atticismus*) but rather due to his reworkings and
evocations of a broad span of literature, and to the subtlety
of his shifts of tone and mood. It is not difficult to observe
the catty humor in his character sketches or his love of a
great one-liner, but there is also a certain pathos in his
work and a spectrum of subtle and not-so-subtle ironies.
In translating the text I began again from scratch, though
I did on occasion borrow a phrase from Wilmer Cave
Wright's previous Loeb edition or a short note where this
appeared to me to give in a few words the information that
a reader might want. Wright was a true pioneer, and by all
accounts a remarkable person. I hope that our work in this
volume will refresh rather than erase her memory, even
when we invariably disagree with her on many occasions.

When we took on this project, Han Baltussen and I felt
that the time was right for new translations of both Philostratus' and Eunapius' texts. Nearly a hundred years had
elapsed since Wright's Loeb was published, and it had
been dated by changes in our understanding of, and appreciation for, the Greek literature of the Roman era, as

well as by changes in styles of translation. I have endeavored to translate with an eye to the large amount of excellent scholarly work that has been produced on this text in the last few decades in particular. It is desirable in a translation like this one to cite only a small portion of that scholarship. The publication of a new critical edition by Rudolf S. Stefec was also a prompt to undertake a new translation of the *Lives of the Sophists*, since it provided a firm foundation that had not previously existed. I have almost always concurred with Stefec's text, and have naturally indicated the few passages where I have preferred another reading.

My family (Ali, Angus, and Freya) have as always been supportive of me as I undertook this work. They would probably like now to hear fewer sophistic anecdotes. It has been a great pleasure to collaborate with Han Baltussen. Meeting by videoconference to tease out puzzles in our respective texts was a highlight in grim and uncertain times: a consolation of philology. Thanks as well to my colleagues in Classics at the University of Tasmania: Jonathan Wallis, Jayne Knight, Charlotte Dunn, Dirk Baltzly, and Jonathan West. I am grateful to Kai Brodersen for sending me a copy of his text and German translation of the *Lives of the Sophists*, and for the collegial support of the broader community of scholars of Greek literature of the Roman Empire and later, especially my fellow Philostrateans: Kristoffel Demoen, Danny Praet, Wannes Gyselinck, Jaap-Jan Flinterman, Gerard Boter, Patrick Robiano, Owen Hodkinson, Jaś Elsner, and Ewen Bowie, all of whom have shared papers and thoughts. It has been a great pleasure to work with the editors of the

Loeb Classical Library, Jeffrey Henderson and Michael B. Sullivan, whose patient and methodical help has been invaluable.

G. M.

The present work offers a thoroughly revised and updated text and translation of Wilmer Cave Wright's 1921 Loeb Eunapius, a new Introduction, and its correct title, *Lives of Philosophers and Sophists* (*VPS*). The text has been revised in light of the excellent new critical edition of R. Goulet (Édition Budé, 2014, 2 vols.), which I follow in almost all textual corrections (any deviations are marked in the notes to the Greek text), and by consulting the principal manuscript online (on which more below). I have adopted Goulet's numbering system (using Arabic numerals as is standard in Loeb volumes, i.e., IV.4 has been converted to 4.4, etc.). Another outstanding resource was Becker's German translation and extensive commentary (2013). These two works assisted greatly in many decisions on textual and interpretive issues.

I would like to thank Graeme Miles for his equanimity, collegiality, and assistance during our collaboration on the volume. While the Covid-19 pandemic made face-to-face meetings impossible, we made good use of videoconferencing software to discuss the project and much else (*omne tulit punctum . . .*). Questions on papers presented to audiences in Auckland, Brisbane, Leuven, Melbourne, Toronto, Dunedin, and Adelaide encouraged me to revisit certain choices in translation. I acknowledge the assistance of the University of Adelaide, which granted me a sabbatical semester in 2020 under difficult circumstances. I also owe a debt of gratitude to Dirk Baltzly, Bert van den

ix

PREFACE

Berg, Matthew Crawford, Greg Horsley, Mark Masterson, Arthur Pomeroy, Jan Stenger, and Edward Watts for their willingness to review a section of the first draft of the translation and for offering many useful suggestions. I am most grateful to Managing Editor Michael B. Sullivan and General Editor Jeffrey Henderson for their forbearance and patient editorial help with the preparations, questions, and online editing system of the Loeb Classical Library. Last but certainly not least, I thank my wife, Angélique, for her support and patience, while I indulged in another long-term project that may at times have seemed without end.

H. B.

PHILOSTRATUS

INTRODUCTION

THE LIVES OF THE SOPHISTS

Philostratus' *Lives of the Sophists* gives a series of sketches of the lives, activities, and rhetorical styles of a succession of fifty-nine figures whom its author classes as "sophists" or in some cases "philosopher-sophists." These *bioi*[1] range in length from a dismissive few lines to approximately seventeen Teubner pages, in the case of the longest, being that of Herodes Atticus. It is in the introductory sections of this text that Philostratus coined the phrase "Second Sophistic" (δευτέρα σοφιστική, VS 481). Though this term has come, in the scholarship of the twentieth and twenty-first centuries, to denote in a very broad sense Hellenic literature and culture of the high Roman Empire, especially of the second and early third centuries AD, this is a significant widening of Philostratus' use of the term.[2]

---

[1] I have preferred the term *bios* to biography because these short accounts, largely due to their brevity and selectiveness, are distinct from larger scale ancient biographies, let alone modern biography.

[2] The capacious sense of the term "Second Sophistic" in contemporary scholarship is evident, for example, in the range of authors and topics treated in Richter and Johnson 2017.

INTRODUCTION

For Philostratus, as the recorder and historian of the sophistic movements, there are two sophistics: the first, which he terms the "Ancient Sophistic," was characterized by "rhetoric doing philosophy" (ῥητορικὴ φιλοσοφοῦσα, VS 480). Though the sophists of this movement, Philostratus states, treated the same kinds of topics as philosophers, they did not approach these topics as philosophers do, through painstaking reasoning and an acceptance of uncertainty, but rather on the basis of an assumption of knowledge that verged on claiming omniscience. His "Second Sophistic," by contrast, specializes in the assumption of characters, whether historical individuals or stock types, and handles more concrete themes (VS 481).[3] In the course of the text it will indeed be this type of rhetorical activity, and the archaizing language in which it is conducted, that emerges as the highest cultural attainment. The sophists, as they live in Philostratus' *Lives*, are glamorous, eloquent, often egotistical, and petty. At their best they are embodiments of the traditions of rhetoric and literature to which they dedicate their intellects, ambassadors from their cities to the emperors, teachers and performers of an imagined past. The narrating voice of this text is itself a sophistic and eloquent one, exemplifying a learned, Atticizing style without falling into the "hyper-

---

[3] The First (or Ancient) Sophistic is made up of the sophists of the fifth and fourth centuries BC, beginning from Gorgias (ca. 480–ca. 380). Philostratus' Second Sophistic ranges from Aeschines (390s BC to ca. 322 or 315 BC) to the time of writing the text in the 230s AD.

Atticism" that is on occasion criticized in this and other Philostratean texts.[4]

In the *Lives of the Sophists*, the word "sophist" is invariably a term of praise.[5] The series of biographies as a whole provides a composite image of sophistic excellence in which repetition emphasizes the most important characteristics. This idealizing of the sophist runs contrary, of course, to an opposing current in Greek thought descending from Plato, which saw in sophistry only false claims to knowledge and the unscrupulous pursuit of wealth.[6] Philostratus' practice in this regard was certainly not universal for his era: Aelius Aristides, whom Philostratus plainly admired (*VS* 581–85), vigorously rejected the name of sophist, preferring the less loaded *rhētōr* ("rhetorician" or "orator").

In reality, the line between sophists and other kinds of intellectuals had never been clear cut, which raised for Philostratus some problems of definition. Part of his response to this difficulty is the identification (or creation) of a class of "philosopher-sophists" who belong to some extent to both groups. These, he tells us, were "philosophers who made their arguments with fluency" and therefore had a reputation as sophists (*VS* 484). Of this

[4] See *VS* 503 on Critias.

[5] This is generally the case in Philostratus' other surviving works too, though in the *Life of Apollonius* he is careful to distinguish Apollonius' speech as a philosopher from that of the sophists. Nonetheless, Apollonius too is made to resemble a sophist. See Billault 1993.

[6] See, for instance, Plato's definition of the sophist as a hunter of wealthy young men (*Soph.* 223b, 231d).

class he gives eight examples, separating them from the broadly chronological sequence of those who "were correctly called sophists" that follows (VS 492). The longest *bioi* in this group are those of Dio Chrysostom and Favorinus of Arles (VS 486–92). Philostratus professes that he does not know how to describe Dio, given the range of his abilities as philosopher and as sophist (VS 486). For Philostratus, the differing sides of Dio's character and work simultaneously coexist; he does not subscribe to a narrative of "conversion" from sophistry to philosophy like the one for which Synesius of Cyrene would later argue, and which until relatively recently dominated scholarship on Dio's work.[7] In the case of Favorinus, Philostratus is confident that he is indeed a philosopher, despite his extraordinary eloquence (VS 480).

Having completed his short sequence of philosopher-sophists, Philostratus begins his account of sophists properly so-called, commencing with the "Ancient Sophistic" and the foundational figure of Gorgias, who was to sophistry what Aeschylus was to tragedy (VS 492). This brief account of Gorgias introduces several themes that will characterize later sophists: "he initiated for the sophists the energetic style and paradoxical expression and inspired impressiveness and speaking in the grand style of great themes, and the habit of breaking off clauses and making sudden transitions, by all of which a speech becomes more pleasurable and more distinguished. And he clothed his speech in poetic words for the sake of ornament and dig-

---

[7] For Synesius' developmental view, see his *Dio*. For an overview of some trends in the interpretation of Dio, see Jackson 2017.

5

nity" (*VS* 492). The style of Gorgias is clearly a particular interest of Philostratus, who claims in his letter to Julia Domna (*Letter* 73) that Plato himself imitated the Gorgianic style. In his *bios* of Gorgias he also notes the civic and religious duties that Gorgias performed (*VS* 493–94), his apparent omniscience and fluency at improvisation, and his continued vigor to the end of his life. All of these features reappear in accounts of later sophists, which look back to Gorgias as an exemplar for both sophistics.

After his account of the philosophizing sophists of the Ancient Sophistic, Philostratus comes to his main subject, the account of the Second Sophistic, which will occupy the remainder of the text. Here the foundational figure is Aeschines, who brings further definition to the sophistic ideal, which continues to be developed in composite form through the *bioi* of other sophists. Other than Favorinus, whose ongoing quarrel with Polemo of Laodicea was mentioned in the excursus on philosopher-sophists, Aeschines is the first sophist in whose life Philostratus identifies a feud with a rival as a major point of reference. This is the famous enmity between Aeschines and Demosthenes, which Philostratus attributes both to their differing political factions and to their differing characters (*VS* 507); the sociable and affable Aeschines clashed, he says, with the austere Demosthenes. Such clashes, driven by temperament, ambition, politics, or a combination of all of these factors, will figure prominently in the lives of later sophists.[8] Like Gorgias, Aeschines too is praised for his fluency

[8] On professional quarrels among sophists, see Bowersock 1969, 89–100; Bowie 2006.

in improvisation (*VS* 509). This *bios* also reinforces the quasi-religious force of some sophistic performance, since Aeschines introduced "the divinely inspired manner" of speaking (τὸ θείως λέγειν, *VS* 509). He is also, paradoxically, both an example to be imitated and impossible to imitate (*VS* 510). In this respect too, the account of Aeschines raises a tension that will reappear: between the achievement of sophistic excellence by hard work and by innate, natural talent, or even by divine inspiration.

In arguing for Aeschines as the foundational figure of the Second Sophistic, Philostratus of course wishes to stretch back to classical antiquity, establishing the cultural current to which he belongs as a respectably ancient one rather than newer and therefore less prestigious. This raises, however, a chronological problem, in that he is unable to point to any first-rate sophists between Aeschines (who was born between 430 and 420 BC and died after 376/5 BC) and Nicetes of Smyrna, who flourished in the mid- to late first century AD. The highpoint of Philostratus' Second Sophistic is undeniably in the second century AD, with some earlier antecedents and some of the later figures still active in his own time in the first decades of the third century. Philostratus' picture of sophistic vitality during this period is borne out by the epigraphic record.[9] In terms of the geographic frame of the text, while Philo-

---

[9] As Puech notes in her meticulous study of these inscriptions, of the fifty-three individuals whom she discusses, two were active in the first century, forty-one in the second or third, five are of unknown date, and five lived in the fourth century or the first half of the fifth: Puech 2002, 6.

stratus' interest in Athens, Smyrna, Ephesus, and Rome does also accord with the spread of inscriptions, he does less than justice, as Puech observes, to Aphrodisias and Pergamum.[10]

The problems that Philostratus faces in these opening parts of the *Lives* are partly of his own making, but it is clear that they follow from pursuit of his purpose. He wishes to establish that sophistry is distinct from and at least equal to philosophy, and that the sophistic practice of his time is genuinely ancient and truly Hellenic. To do this he relies on some sleight-of-hand when negotiating the lines between sophists and philosophers, and on some chronological telescoping to draw in the precedent of Aeschines. We need not be too surprised nor too critical of Philostratus on these grounds: genealogies, after all, invariably work from the bottom upward, establishing the legitimacy and importance of those who create them.

The long series of *bioi* that form the bulk of the text and that give a partial history (in every sense) of Greek rhetorical activity in the high Roman empire, are the fullest surviving account of sophistic teaching, performance, and political intervention in this period. Philostratus' approach is anecdotal, partly due no doubt to the nature of his primarily oral sources, but also partly because it serves the needs of his imagined audience. As Goldhill has argued, the anecdotes can be readily extracted and retold as needed in the display of culture, serving in this regard the same purpose as the miscellanies that were also popular

10 Puech 2002, 21.

at this time.[11] Each life also offers some comments on the sophist's style, the length being in proportion to the perceived interest and importance of each. These passages of evaluation cumulatively offer an education to readers in how one speaks about and critiques rhetorical performance. The text demonstrates, through the depiction of sophists interpreting and criticizing one another's work, the hazards of criticism as well as of performance: when Sceptus of Corinth, for instance, says of a declamation by Alexander the Clay Plato that he has found the clay but not the Plato, Herodes Atticus quickly puts him in his place (*VS* 572). Increasingly as the text goes on, it also offers its readers the opportunity to practice evaluating sophists for themselves, giving more extended quotations from their works. Onomarchus of Andros, for instance, whose work appears to have been something of a guilty pleasure, being neither astonishing nor contemptible, and perhaps a little juvenile, receives a long quotation (*VS* 598–99) from his speech in the character of a man in love with a statue. Others are quoted in order to demonstrate their rhythm (e.g., *VS* 580 on Philagrus of Cilicia, *VS* 602 on the rhythms of Apollonius of Naucratis).[12]

Though Philostratus adopts the tone of the neutral historian, the account that he offers is a highly selective one.

[11] On anecdotes in the Second Sophistic, see Goldhill 2009. The style of miscellanies of the period are best illustrated by reading works like Aulus Gellius' *Attic Nights* or Aelian's *On the Nature of Animals*.

[12] The best discussion of sophistic rhythms remains Norden 1923.

It is clear from the epigraphic evidence that there were many individuals who were prominent as rhetoricians whom Philostratus does not mention at all. As Eshleman has shown, the central figure for Philostratus is Herodes Atticus, and sophists without any connection to him do not figure in Philostratus' narrative.[13] The focus is also squarely on the spoken performance of sophists and only secondarily on their written work. The resulting omissions can be striking: Philostratus' silence on Lucian has often been remarked but need be due to nothing more than his relatively low profile as a performer as opposed to a writer.[14] Similarly, in the long life of Polemo there is no mention of his writings on physiognomics, though it is clear that Philostratus knew them and was influenced by them. His concern in this life is rather to discuss, as ever, the performances, the feuds, and the political activities of his protagonist. There is, however, an oblique reference to Polemo's physiognomics in his cameo appearance in the life of Marcus of Byzantium (VS 528–29), where Polemo fails to read correctly the character of the notoriously scruffy Marcus. The narrating voice, however, guides us to the correct physiognomic signs and their interpretation.[15]

13 See Eshleman 2008; Puech 2002. On Philostratus' preference for elaborate rhetorical work over the more straightforward, see Guast 2019.

14 It is clear from Philostratus' work that he did read Lucian. See Miles 2018, 92–93, on Philostratus' response to Lucian's *Imagines*.

15 On Polemo's physiognomics, see Swain 2007. On Philostratus' use of physiognomics in the VS, see Miles 2018, 130–32.

INTRODUCTION

Sophistic performance, especially improvised performance, is Philostratus' central concern in this text. Within
this concern he shows an interest more specifically in vocal
performance. It is telling that musical analogies occur on
several occasions,[16] and it is clear that the musicality of a
speaker's performance is an important feature, yet one
that can be taken too far, as is evident in Philostratus'
criticism of Favorinus (VS 491–92). The rhythmic and
more broadly musical aspects of declamation are closely
related to its emotive force; Theophrastus had long ago
remarked that for this reason these aspects tend to emerge
most clearly at the ends of speeches.[17] Here, indeed, is
where Favorinus most tended to emotional and musical
excess, as Philostratus tells us (VS 491). This close connection of musicality and emotion, particularly the possibility
of what Philostratus (and no doubt some other observers)
considered excessive emotion, is also responsible for the
moral judgments that Philostratus makes about rhetorical
rhythms. In the case of Onomarchus of Andros (VS 598–
99), for instance, the rhythm of his speeches seem to have
been felt to verge on self-indulgence. And yet Philostratus
finds himself sufficiently drawn to those rhythms that he
quotes one of Onomarchus' speeches at some length (VS
599). The speaker needed, in short, to tread a fine line,
aiming to strike just the right amount of emotion without
falling into immoral excess.[18]

[16] See, for instance, the image of the bridge of a lyre used to
describe Dio's mixing of styles (VS 487).

[17] The testimonium is in Plutarch, Quaest. Conv. 623a–c.

[18] See Quintillian, Inst. 1.8.2, for just this sentiment. On the
possibility of an "immoral" music in rhetoric, see Philostratus'
dismissal of Varus of Laodicea (VS 620).

It is easy to forget in reading Philostratus' vivid sketches of the great figures of the Second Sophistic, such as Polemo and Herodes, that he knew them only through what he had heard about them and what he had read of their work. In some instances we can flesh out these sketches by ourselves through reading their surviving work. There remain, for instance, considerable corpora from Dio Chrysostom and Aelius Aristides, and there are scanter remnants of Favorinus and Polemo. It is an irony of history that in the case of Herodes Atticus, Philostratus' ideal of Hellenic eloquence, we can hear his words only through the Latin of Aulus Gellius (*NA* 19.12). Indeed, Gellius' *Attic Nights* is a further invaluable source for some of the central figures, especially Favorinus as well as Herodes himself, providing as it does an eyewitness account. Gellius often differs in important ways from Philostratus: while the famously self-immolating cynic Peregrinus Proteus is for Philostratus (as for Lucian) contemptible, Gellius, who had visited Peregrinus in his hut outside Athens, rates him highly as a philosopher (*NA* 12.11). More subtly, while Philostratus contrasts the intense grief of Herodes Atticus with the Stoic control of Marcus Aurelius (*VS* 561), Gellius reports a speech of Herodes in which he directly responded to his Stoic critics, arguing that their goal of freedom from affect (*apatheia*) was emotionally and cognitively damaging, destroying a person's best qualities as well as the painful emotions that the Stoic sought to control (*NA* 19.12).

As the *Lives of the Sophists* approaches its end, the narrative does indeed come down to figures of Philostratus' own day. At *VS* 602–4 he tells us of one of his own teachers, Proclus of Naucratis. The last sophist to receive a *bios*, Aspasius of Ravenna, held the chair of rhetoric at Rome in Philostratus' own time, and had an ongoing feud with the author's nephew, Philostratus of Lemnos (*VS* 627–28). The text ends, however, not so much with Aspasius as with the figures about whom Philostratus chooses not to speak in case he appears to be unduly favoring his friends: Nicagoras of Athens, Apsines the Phoenician, and Philostratus of Lemnos (*VS* 628). This ending reminds us once more that our guide to the sophistic life has himself been in the thick of things. It also attempts to show that the Second Sophistic is still flourishing in its author's present day.

FLAVIUS PHILOSTRATUS

The author of the *Lives of the Sophists* is, as he tells us (*VS* 570), the same Philostratus who wrote the *Life of Apollonius of Tyana*, the sprawling, genre-crossing biography of a wandering Pythagorean holy man of the first century AD. As it is practically certain that the *Heroicus*,[19] a dialogue concerning hero cult and Homeric rewriting, was also written by this Philostratus, that work too can be ascribed to our author. The scholarly consensus ascribes, in fact, almost all of the works of the *Corpus Philostrateum* to the author of the *Lives of the Sophists*, with the exception of the second set of *Imagines* and one letter, wrongly categorized by Kayser as a *dialexis*,[20] which is almost cer-

---

[19] See Solmsen 1940.
[20] See Miles 2018, 9, with further bibliography.

tainly the letter on epistolary style by Philostratus of Lemnos mentioned in the closing chapters of the *Lives of the Sophists* (*VS* 628). In other words, our Philostratus was probably also the author of the *Imagines* (descriptions of a series of paintings in a probably imaginary gallery on the bay of Naples), the *Gymnasticus* (a guide to athletic training), a series of love letters, a *dialexis* on the ancient topic of the relationship of *nomos* and *physis*, and a brief dialogue, *Nero*, which comes down to us wrongly attributed to Lucian.[21] Though untangling the details of the Philostrati as recorded in the *Suda* is difficult,[22] it is certain that other works have been lost. Nonetheless, what survives gives a sense of his wide-ranging interests, energetic engagement with the Hellenic tradition, and his verve and playfulness as an author and stylist of Greek prose.

The chronology of Philostratus' life and work is far from certain. In the prologue to the *Life of Apollonius*, he mentions his sometime patron, Julia Domna, in the past tense, which places this work after her death in AD 217. The intellectual "circle" of Julia Domna, to which Philostratus says that he belonged, once attracted a great deal of speculation, but it must be admitted that we really know nothing else about it.[23] The dates of other texts remain a matter of conjecture, beyond two references to the Olympic victory of the athlete Helix in 213 or 217.[24] Three in-

---

[21] For discussion of this brief text, see Whitmarsh 1999.

[22] See *Suda* ϕ 421–23, with de Lannoy 1997 and Bowie 2009.

[23] See on this Whitmarsh 2007, 31–34.

[24] See Bowie 2009, 30–31; Münscher 1907, 497–98, 553–54; Jüthner 1909, 87–89. On the date of the *VS* and *VA*, see most recently Kemezis 2014, 294–97.

14

scriptions attest an L. Flavius Philostratus who was "hoplite general" at Athens between AD 200–201 and 210–211. This role, which had once been a military one, was by this time concerned with food and water supplies, as Philostratus himself tells us in the *Lives of the Sophists* (*VS* 526).

We have already noted Philostratus' fondness in the *Lives of the Sophists* for the stylish anecdote and his assemblage of shorter, related pieces to create a composite whole. This too is a characteristic of other Philostratean texts, for instance, in the *Imagines* and the *Letters*. The former text builds up a composite ideal of how one should view art, moving in Newby's apt phrase from "erudition" to "absorption" and back.[25] The *Letters* work with a similarly deliberate casualness through the tropes of amatory persuasion.[26] This tendency to catalog and accumulate, while at the same time avoiding any order that could be described as systematic, is closely related to the evident desire to assemble and to preserve Hellenic culture, to give some overarching sense of what that culture is and has been. This artfully casual ordering, like the anecdotal form itself, recalls the manner of the miscellanists. For all of these texts the answer to the broader question of the nature of Hellenism is that it is primarily a matter of *paideia*, of education in the language, literature, and thought of the past, and the creative reinterpretation of this inheritance in the present.[27] I have argued elsewhere that a

[25] Newby 2009.

[26] On the letters, see Rosenmeyer 2001, 322–38; Goldhill 2009b; Schmitz 2017; Miles 2018, 137–48; Robiano 2021.

[27] See, among much else, Whitmarsh 2001 and 2007; Goldhill 2001; Borg 2004; Richter and Johnson 2017.

key part of this engagement with Hellenic traditions is a concern with how one interprets, and in particular with pursuing an ideal of an interpreter who is free and creative in treating inherited material, yet sufficiently knowledgeable in and respectful of those traditions that their broad lines continue.[28]

Philostratus plays freely with fiction and fact, with the details of traditional myths, and with the tropes of contemporary rhetorical practice. In all of these reworkings and reimaginings of the Hellenic past, however, it is not a matter of "anything goes." The traditions themselves have their own established lines, which he can bend and to a degree alter but which always largely retain their inherited form. In the corpus as a whole we can see its author traversing certain ground repeatedly, and always endeavoring to make the Hellenic past live in the Roman present.

TRANSLATION

My translation draws occasionally on Wright's 1921 Loeb where a turn of phrase struck me as a particularly apt way of capturing the Greek. Wright's translation was groundbreaking in its day, but the language has become dated in the intervening hundred years. Philostratus' Greek was, of course, archaizing in his own time, but translating into an archaizing idiom in English would produce a very different effect from that made by the text on its contemporaries in its own day. In the second and third centuries this archaizing was itself part of a contemporary, learned style.

[28] Miles 2018.

I have aimed to retain something of the grace of Philostratus' style, though it is difficult, indeed likely impossible, to sense the rhythms of Greek prose of this era with the immediacy with which Philostratus and his contemporaries sensed them. It is, however, within the realm of possibility to bring over into English such features as his occasional striking similes, the vividness with which he sketches his characters and their actions, and his shifts of emotion from wit to pathos. It is no accident that the elegant and subtle poet Cavafy was a reader of Philostratus.[29] I have attempted to be as consistent as possible in the treatment of technical and semitechnical terms. Like Wright before me, I have placed a Rhetorical Glossary at the end of the volume, but I have generally altered her entries and have also added many of my own. In particular, I have added a number of terms that relate to the sounds and effects of rhetorical performance, these being among Philostratus' main interests when assessing the work of sophists.

It must be emphasized that we now have a much better critical edition, in Stefec's Oxford Classical Text,[30] than was previously available.[31] This is a great advance on the editions of Kayser, on which Wright had to depend, and which was until recently all that was available; cumulatively, the many small (and sometimes not so small) im-

[29] See, for instance, the poems "Apollonios of Tyana in Rhodes," "But the Wise Perceive Things About To Happen," "Herodes Attikos," and "If Actually Dead."

[30] Stefec 2016.

[31] Kayser 1844, 1849, and 1870/71.

provements that Stefec has made constitute a substantial improvement,[32] and there is no doubt that it will be the standard for the foreseeable future. With very few exceptions I have followed Stefec's text.

It has been possible, after a further century of scholarship, to improve in many instances on Wright's notes on the content and context of the *Lives of the Sophists*. Although it was true, for example, that nothing more was known of certain sophists in 1921, we have often been able to add references to further evidence that fills out our picture of the sophists and their world, especially by drawing upon the epigraphic record. The notes do not aim to interpret the text, nor to be exhaustive, but to produce the kind of background that should assist readers in approaching it.

HISTORY AND CONSTITUTION OF THE TEXT

As Stefec observes in the introduction to his edition, the transmission of the *Lives of the Sophists* is a relatively good one, consisting of twenty-five manuscripts, of which ten are independent witnesses. There are two families (named by Stefec α and β), the earliest members of which date respectively to the beginning of the tenth century and probably the early fourteenth century.[33]

We have adopted Stefec's sigla[34] for the convenience of

[32] See further below on the text and the nature of my textual notes.

[33] Stefec 2016, v–vi.

[34] Stefec 2016, xi–xii.

those who wish to refer to his full edition, and in order to avoid textual notes that would otherwise either be vague ("most manuscripts read . . .") or unduly long, naming all of the manuscripts that contain a particular reading. As is customary in Loeb editions, the textual notes are not intended to be used as a full *apparatus criticus*: textual notes are offered only when there is a significant, unresolved uncertainty that has a bearing on the translation or the meaning. Readers who want further information should turn to Stefec's Oxford Classical Text. We provide paragraph and section numbers but cite the text in our notes by reference to the pagination of Olearius' edition of 1709, which remains the standard method of citation in the current scholarship on Philostratus.

SIGLA

Manuscripts

α   Stefec's first family of manuscripts, containing four independent witnesses. The first three offer large parts of the text but none complete: Vat. gr. 99 (beginning of tenth century), Laur. Plut. 59.15 (late tenth century) and Vat.gr.140 (beginning of fourteenth century). Only complete text in this family Marc. gr. 391 (second half of fifteenth century), probably supplemented from manuscripts outside the α family.

β   Second family of manuscripts, "represented by six independent witnesses and a short fragment," the earliest of which is probably, according to Stefec, Par. gr. 1696, "written partially by the same anonymous scribe who is responsible for one part of the famous Paris manuscript of Xenophon, dated 1320 (Par. gr. 1640)."

χ   This is the consensus of Mq, Ab (see below) and Esc. Ψ. IV.1 (middle of the fifteenth century), Guelferbyt. Gud. Gr. 25 (fifteenth century), and Par. gr. 3059 (before 1474).

ω   The archetype, according to Stefec's reconstruction.

Ab   Abros. T 122 sup. (end of fifteenth century)

L   Laru. Plut. 59.15 (end of fifteenth century)

Mq   Mosq. Synod. Gr. 239 (beginning of fourteenth century)

V   Vat. gr. 96 (before 1152)

Va   Vat. gr. 99 (beginning of tenth century)

Vb   Vat. gr. 140 (second half of fourteenth century)

L   Laur. Plut. 59.15 (end of tenth century)

M   Marc. gr. 391 (middle of fifteenth century)

P   Par. gr. 1696 (fourteenth century)

P²   Second hand in P (Ioannes Catrarius)

REFERENCES

SCHOLARS

Boter
: G. J. Boter's conjectures are reported in Stefec's edition from correspondence.

Brodersen
: Edition and German translation by K. Brodersen: Brodersen, K., ed. *Philostratos. Leben der Sophisten. Zweisprachige Ausgabe.* Wiesbaden, 2014.

Callistus
: Andronicus Callistus in Comensis 1.3.19, a manuscript of the fifteenth century.

Catrarius
: Ioannes Catrarius' in Par. gr. 1696 (see P above)

Citti
: Citti, V. "Filostrato, *Vit. Soph.* 1.11." *Prometheus* 14 (1988): 219–20.

Cobet
: Cobet, C. G. "Miscellanea philologica et critica IV. Ad Philostrati Vitas sophistarum et Heroica." *Mnemosyne* n.s.1 (1873): 209–32.

Damilas
: Demetrius Damilas (beginning of sixteenth century) in Haun. Fabr. 60.4o.

Diels   Diels, H. *Die Fragmente der Vorsokra-*
        tiker. Griechisch und deutsch von
        H. Diels. Herausgegeben von W.
        Kranz. 12th ed. Dublin–Zürich,
        1966.

Engelmann   Engelmann, H. "Philostrat und Ephe-
        sos." *ZPE* 108 (1995): 77–87.

Eugenicus   Ioannes Eugenicus (died after 1454) in
        codex Guelferbyt. Gud. Gr. 82.

Hesseling   Hesseling, D. C. "On Philostratus'
        Lives of the Sophists I.24." *Classical*
        Review 44 (1930): 59–61.

Jacobs   Jacobs, F. "Lectiones memorabiliores in
        Phi lostrati Vitas Sophistarum ex.
        Cod. Guelph. 25 additis nonnullis ex
        Parisino 1696." *Neue Jahrbücher für*
        Philologie und Paedagogik. Supple-
        mentband 1.2 (1832): 325–43.

Jahn   Jahn, A. *Symbolas ad emendandum et*
        illustrandum Philostrati librum De
        vitis sophistarum. Bern, 1837.

Jones   C. P. Jones' conjectures are reported
        in Stefec's edition from correspon-
        dence.

Jüttner   Jüttner, H. *De Polemonis rhetoris vita*
        operibus arte. Breslau, 1898.

Lucarini   Lucarini, C. M. "A proposito di una
        nuova traduzione e commento a
        Filostrato, Vite dei sofisti." *Rivista*
        degli studi orientali 76 (2002): 215–
        20.

REFERENCES

Nesselrath   H.-G. Nesselrath's conjectures are re-
                ported in Stefec's edition from corre-
                spondence.

Richards   Richards, H. "Notes on the Philostrati."
                Classical Quarterly 3 (1909): 104–9.

Reiske   Notes in codex Hauniensis NKS 111,
                reported in Stefec's edition.

Schmid   Schmid, W. *Der Atticismus in seinen
                Hauptvertretern von Dionysius von
                Halikarnass bis auf den zweiten Phi-
                lostratus.* Stuttgart, 1887–1897.

Schröder   S. Schröder's conjectures are reported
                in Stefec's edition from correspon-
                dence.

Stefec   Stefec, R. "Zur Überlieferung und Text-
                kritik der Sophistenviten Philostrats."
                Wiener Studien 123 (2010): 63–93
                and Stefec, R. "Die Handschriften
                der Sophistenviten Philostrats."
                Römische Historische Mitteilungen
                55 (2014): 137–206.

Valckenaer   Schenkl, K. "Valkenarii animadversio-
                nes in Philostratos." *Wiener Studien*
                14 (1892): 267–77.

Valesius   Henricus Valesius (Henri Valois) (18th-
                century scholar): see *Henrici Valesii
                Militis, D'Orcé, Consiliarii, et Histo-
                riographi Regii, Emendationum Libri
                Quinque et de Critica Duo* (ed. Petrus
                Burmannus). Amsterdam: Apud Salo-
                monem Schouten, 1740.

van Wulfften Palthe

van Wulfften Palthe, C. B. *Dissertatio litteraria continens observationes grammaticas et criticas in Philostratum, habita impris vitae Apollonii ratione.* Diss., Leiden, 1887.

EDITIONS

Morel

Philostrati Lemnii Opera quae exstant. Philostrati Iunioris Imagines et Callistrati Ecphrases, item Eusebii Caesariensis Episcopi Liber Contra Hieroclem (1608 edition and Latin translation).

Olearius

Olearius, Gottfried, ed. and trans. ΤΑ ΤΩΝ ΦΙΛΟΣΤΡΑΤΩΝ ΛΕΙΠΟΜΕΝΑ ΠΑΝΤΑ/*PHILOSTRATORUM QUAE SUPERSUNT OMNIA.* Leipzig, 1709.

Kayser

Kayser, C. L. ed. *Flavii Philostrati Quae Super sunt. Philostrati Iunioris Imagines. Callistrati De scriptiones.* Leipzig, 1844, 1849, and 1870/71. (Kayser revised his text with each edition, so it is on occasion necessary to report his readings and notes from each.)

Westermann

Westermann, A., ed. *Philostratorum et Callistrati Opera Recognovit Antonius Westermann.* Paris, 1849.

REFERENCES

Wright   Wright, Wilmer Cave, ed. and trans. *Philostratus: Lives of the Sophists. Eunapius: Lives of the Sophists*. Cambridge, MA, 1921.

Stefec   Stefec, Rudolf C. *Flavii Philostrati Vitas Sophistarum*. Oxford, 2016.

GENERAL BIBLIOGRAPHY

Alcock, S. E. *Graecia Capta: The Landscapes of Roman Greece*. Camridge: Cambridge University Press, 1996.

Avotins, I. "The Holders of the Chairs of Rhetoric at Athens." *HSPh* 79 (1975): 313–24.

Billault, A. "The Rhetoric of a 'Divine Man': Apollonius of Tyana as Critic of Oratory and as Orator According to Philostratus." *Philosophy & Rhetoric* 26 (1993): 227–35.

Borg, B. E., ed. *Paideia: The World of the Second Sophistic.* Berlin: De Gruyter, 2004.

Bowersock, G. W. *Greek Sophists in the Roman Empire.* Oxford: Oxford University Press, 1969.

Bowie, E. L. "The Importance of Sophists." *YClS* 27 (1982): 29–59.

———. "Greek Sophists and Greek Poetry in the Second Sophistic." *ANRW* 33.1 (1989): 209–58.

———. "Portrait of the Sophist as a Young Man." In *The Limits of Ancient Fiction*, edited by B. McGing and J. Mossman, 141–53. Swansea: Classical Press of Wales, 2006.

———. "Philostratus: The Life of a Sophist." In Bowie and Elsner, *Philostratus*, 19–32. Cambridge: Cambridge University Press, 2009.

Bowie, E. L., and J. Elsner, eds. *Philostratus.* Cambridge: Cambridge University Press, 2009.

Burnet, J. *Plato's Euthyphro, Apology of Socrates and Crito*. Oxford: Oxford University Press, 1924.

Côté, D. "L'Héracles d'Hèrode: héroïsme et philosophie dans la sophistique de Philostrate." In *Perceptions of the Second Sophistic and its Times / Regards sur la Seconde Sophistique et son Époque*, edited by T. Schmidt and P. Fleury, 36–62. Toronto: University of Toronto Press, 2011.

Demoen, K., and D. Praet, eds. *Theios Sophistes: Essays on Flavius Philostratus' Vita Apollonii*. Leiden: Brill, 2009.

Eshleman, K. "Defining the Circle of Sophists: Philostratus and the Construction of the Second Sophistic." *Classical Philology* 103.4 (2008): 395–413.

———. *The Social World of Intellectuals in the Roman Empire: Sophists, Philosophers, and Christians*. Cambridge: Cambridge University Press, 2012.

Fant, J. C. "The Choleric Roman Official of Philostratus, *Vitae Sophistarum*." *Historia* 30 (1981): 240–43.

Furley, W. D. "Antiphon der Athener: ein Sophist als Psychotherapeut?" *Rh.M* 135 (1992): 198–216.

Gaines, R. N. "A Note on Rufus' ΤΕΧΝΗ ΡΗΤΟΡΙΚΗ." *RhM.* 129 (1986): 90–92.

Geagan, D. J. "A Family of Marathon and Social Mobility in Athens of the First Century BC." *Phoenix* 46 (1992): 29–44.

Gleason, M. *Making Men: Sophists and Self-Presentation in Ancient Rome*. Princeton, NJ: Princeton University Press, 1995.

———. "Making Space for Bilingual Identity: Herodes Atticus Commemorates Regilla." In *Local Knowledge and Microidentities in the Imperial Greek World*, edited by T. Whitmarsh, 125–162. Cambridge: Cambridge University Press, 2010.

Goldhill, S., ed. *Being Greek Under Rome: Cultural Identity, the Second Sophistic and the Development of Empire*. Cambridge: Cambridge University Press, 2001.

———. "The Anecdote: Exploring the Boundaries Between Oral and Literate Performance in the Second Sophistic." In *Ancient Literacies: The Culture of Reading in Greece and Rome*, edited by W. A. Johnson and H. N. Parker, 96–113. Oxford: Oxford University Press, 2009a.

———. "Constructing Identity in Philostratus 'Love Letters.'" In Bowie and Elsner, *Philostratus*, 287–308. Cambridge: Cambridge University Press, 2009b.

Groag, E. "Prosopographische Einzelheiten." *Wiener Studien* 55 (1879): 319–24.

Guast, W. "Greek Declamation Beyond Philostratus' Second Sophistic." *Journal of Hellenic Studies* 139 (2019): 172–86.

Hinck, H., ed. *Polemonis Declamationes quae extant duae*. Berlin: De Gruyter, 1873.

Hodkinson, O. *Authority and Tradition in Philostratus' Heroikos*. Lecce: Pensa Multimedia, 2011.

Holford-Strevens, L. *Gellius: An Antonine Scholar and His Achievement*. Oxford: Oxford University Press, 2003.

Ioppolo, A. M. "The Academic Position of Favorinus of Arelate." *Phronesis* 38 (1993): 182–213.

Jackson, C. R. "Dio Chrysostom." In Richter and Johnson, *Oxford Handbook of the Second Sophistic*, 217–32. Oxford: Oxford University Press, 2017.

Jones, C. P. "Two Enemies of Lucian." *GRBS* 13 (1972): 475–87.

———. "Philostratus and the Gordiani." *Mediterraneo Antico* 5 (2002): 759–67.

Jüthner, J. *Philostratos über Gymnastik*. Leipzig: Teubner, 1909.

Keil, J. "Die Bibliothek." *Jahreshefte des Österreichisches Archäologischen Institutes in Wien* (1953): 219–53.

Kemezis, A. M. *Greek Narratives of the Roman Empire Under the Severans: Cassius Dio, Philostratus and Herodian*. Cambridge: Cambridge University Press, 2014.

Kokolakis, M. "Zeus' Tomb. An Object of Pride and Reproach." *Kernos* 8 (1995): 123–38.

de Lannoy, L. "Le Problème des Philostrate (État de la question)." *ANRW* 2.34.3 (1997): 2362–449.

Meritt, B. G., A. G. Woodhead, and G. A. Stamires. "Greek Inscriptions." *Hesperia* 26 (1957): 220, number 78.

Miles, G. "Music and Immortality: The Afterlife of Achilles in Philostratus' *Heroicus*." *Ancient Narrative* 4 (2005): 66–78.

———. "Incarnating Proteus in Philostratus' *Life of Apollonius of Tyana*." *Ancient Narrative* 13 (2016): 139–57.

———. *Philostratus: Interpreters and Interpretation*. London: Routledge, 2018.

Moles, J. "The Career and Conversion of Dio Chryostom." *Journal of Hellenic Studies* 98 (1978): 79–100.

Morgan, J. R. "The Emesan Connection: Philostratus and Heliodorus." In Demoen and Praet, *Theios Sophistes*, 263–81. Leiden: Brill, 2009.

Münscher, K. "Die Philostrate." *Philologus Supplementum* 10 (1907): 467–558.

Newby, Z. "Absorption and Erudition in Philostratus' 'Imagines.'" In Bowie and Elsner, *Philostratus*, 322–42. Cambridge: Cambridge University Press, 2009.

Norden, E. *Die Antike Kunstprosa vom VI. Jahrhundert v. Chr. bis in die Zeit der Renaissance*. Stuttgart: Teubner, 1923.

Penella, R. J. "Scopelianus and the Eretrians in Cissia." *Athenaeum* 52 (1974): 295–300.

Puech, B. *Orateurs et sophistes grecs dans les inscriptions d'époque impériale*. Paris: Vrin, 2002.

Richter, D. S., and W. A. Johnson, eds. *The Oxford Handbook of the Second Sophistic*. Oxford: Oxford University Press, 2017.

Rife, J. L. "The Burial of Herodes Atticus: Élite Identity, Urban Society, and Public Memory in Roman Greece." *Journal of Hellenic Studies* 128 (2008): 92–127.

Robert, Jeanne, and Louis Robert. "Bulletin épigraphique." *Revue des études grecques* 84 (1971): 397–540.

Robiano, P. "Une identité rhétorique entre personne et personage: Le <<je>> des Lettres d'amour de Philostrate livre-t-il des indices autobiographiques?" *Revue des Études Grecques* 134.1 (2021): 121–41.

Rosenmeyer, P. *Ancient Epistolary Fictions: The Letter in Greek Literature*. Cambridge: Cambridge University Press, 2001.

Rusten, J., and J. König, eds. and trans. *Philostratus. Heroicus. Gymnasticus. Discourses 1 and 2*. Cambridge, MA: Harvard University Press, 2014.

Sánchez Hernández, J. P. "Scopelianus and the Homerids. Notes on Philostratus' *Lives of the Sophists* (VS 1.21.518)." *Mnemosyne* 64 (2011): 455–63.

Schmitz, T. A. *Bildung und Macht: Zur sozialen und poli-*

tischen Funktion der zweiten Sophistik in der grie-schischen Welt der Kaiserzeit. München: Beck, 1997.

——. "The Rhetoric of Desire in Philostratus's Letters." *Arethusa* 50.2 (2017): 257–79.

Solmsen, F. "Some Works of Philostratus the Elder." *Transactions of the American Philological Association* 71 (1940): 556–72.

Swain, S. "Introduction." In *Severan Culture*, edited by S. Swain, S. Harrison, and J. Elsner, 1–28. Cambridge: Cambridge University Press, 2007.

Thompson, Homer A. "The Odeion in the Athenian Agora." *Hesperia* 19 (1950): 31–141.

Whitmarsh, T. "Greek and Roman in Dialogue: The Pseudo-Lucianic Nero." *Journal of Hellenic Studies* 119 (1999): 142–60.

——. *Greek Literature and the Roman Empire: The Politics of Imitation.* Oxford: Oxford University Press, 2001.

——. "Prose Literature and the Severan Dynasty." In *Severan Culture*, edited by S. Swain, S. Harrison, and J. Elsner, 29–51. Cambridge: Cambridge University Press, 2007.

ΦΙΛΟΣΤΡΑΤΟΥ
ΒΙΟΙ ΣΟΦΙΣΤΩΝ

ΤΩΙ ΛΑΜΠΡΟΤΑΤΩΙ ΥΠΑΤΩΙ
ΑΝΤΩΝΙΩΙ ΓΟΡΔΙΑΝΩΙ
ΦΛΑΟΥΙΟΣ ΦΙΛΟΣΤΡΑΤΟΣ

(1) Τοὺς ἐν δόξῃ τοῦ σοφιστεῦσαι φιλοσοφήσαντας
καὶ τοὺς οὕτω κυρίως προσρηθέντας σοφιστὰς ἐς δύο
βίβλους ἀνέγραψά σοι, γιγνώσκων μέν, ὅτι καὶ γένος
ἐστί σοι πρὸς τὴν τέχνην ἐς Ἡρώδην τὸν σοφιστὴν
ἀναφέροντι, μεμνημένος δὲ καὶ τῶν κατὰ τὴν Ἀντιόχειαν σπουδασθέντων ποτὲ ἡμῖν ὑπὲρ σοφιστῶν ἐν
τῷ τοῦ Δαφναίου ἱερῷ. πατέρας δὲ προσέγραψα, μὰ
Δί᾿, οὐ πᾶσιν, ἀλλὰ τοῖς ἀπ᾿ εὐδοκίμων· οἶδα γὰρ δὴ
καὶ Κριτίαν τὸν σοφιστὴν οὐκ ἐκ πατέρων ἀρξάμενον,[1] ἀλλὰ Ὁμήρου δὴ μόνου σὺν τῷ πατρὶ ἐπιμνη-

---

[1] ἀρξάμενον add. Richards

---

[1] It remains a topic of debate whether Philostratus addresses
this work to Gordian I, II, or III. Gordian I was born ca. AD 159;
suffect consul, ca. 223; Proconsul of Africa, 237/8; and Caesar,
March–April 238. Gordian II (son of the I), was born ca. 192,
proclaimed emperor with his father in 238, and died in battle

PHILOSTRATUS
LIVES OF THE SOPHISTS

TO THE MOST ILLUSTRIOUS CONSUL 479
ANTONIUS GORDIANUS,[1]
FROM FLAVIUS PHILOSTRATUS

(1) I have recorded for you in two books both those who practiced philosophy and had a reputation for sophistry and those who were properly designated sophists, since I am aware that you trace back your ancestry in the art to the sophist Herodes, and because I remember the earnest   480
discussions about sophists that we once had in Antioch, in the temple of Daphnaean Apollo.[2] I have not, by Zeus, added the fathers of all of them, but only for those whose fathers were eminent. I know indeed that the sophist Critias did not begin from his subjects' fathers, but mentioned the father in the case of Homer alone, since he was

---

after their brief joint rule. Gordian III, his grandson, was Caesar from 238 to 244. See de Lannoy 1997, 2366, 2387–89; Jones 2002 (arguing for Gordian III); and Kemezis, 2014, 294–97 (arguing for I or II).

[2] On the famous temple of Apollo in the suburb of Daphne in Antioch, cf. Julian. *Mis.* 33.16, and more fully Philostr. *VA* 1.16, where Apollonius is highly critical of what he sees as the low cultural standards of Apollo's famous sanctuary.

σθέντα, ἐπειδὴ θαῦμα δηλώσειν ἔμελλε πατέρα Ὁμήρου ποταμὸν εἶναι. καὶ ἄλλως οὐκ εὐτυχὲς τῷ
βουλομένῳ πολλὰ εἰδέναι πατέρα μὲν τοῦ δεῖνος ἐξ-
επίστασθαι καὶ μητέρα, τὰς δὲ περὶ αὐτὸν ἀρετάς τε
καὶ κακίας οὐ γιγνώσκειν, μηδ᾽ ὅ τι κατώρθωσέ τε
οὗτος καὶ ἐσφάλη ἢ τύχῃ ἢ γνώμῃ. τὸ δὲ φρόντισμα
τοῦτο, ἄριστε ἀνθυπάτων, καὶ τὰ ἄχθη σοι κουφιεῖ
τῆς γνώμης, ὥσπερ ὁ κρατὴρ τῆς Ἑλένης τοῖς Αἰ-
γυπτίοις φαρμάκοις. ἔρρωσο Μουσηγέτα.

A´

(2) Τὴν ἀρχαίαν σοφιστικὴν ῥητορικὴν ἡγεῖσθαι χρὴ
φιλοσοφοῦσαν· διαλέγεται μὲν γὰρ ὑπὲρ ὧν οἱ φιλο-
σοφοῦντες, ἃ δὲ ἐκεῖνοι τὰς ἐρωτήσεις ὑποκαθήμενοι
⟨κα⟩τὰ σμικρὰ[2] τῷ ζητουμένῳ προβιβάζοντες[3] οὔπω
φασὶ γιγνώσκειν, ταῦτα ὁ παλαιὸς σοφιστὴς ὡς εἰδὼς λέγει. προοίμια γοῦν ποιεῖται τῶν λόγων τὸ
"οἶδα" καὶ τὸ "γιγνώσκω" καὶ "πάλαι διέσκεμμαι" καὶ
"βέβαιον ἀνθρώπῳ οὐδέν." ἡ δὲ τοιαύτη ἰδέα τῶν
προοιμίων εὐγένειάν τε προηχεῖ τῶν λόγων καὶ

---

²⟨κα⟩τὰ σμικρὰ Reiske   ³προβιβάζοντες LMq

---

3 It is not clear which of the works of Critias (ca. 460–403 BC)
Philostratus cites. He alludes, in any case, to the tradition that
Homer's father was the river Meles, which is the topic of one of
the *Imagines* (2.8).

4 The reference to Hom. *Od.* 4.220 is also used of Apollonius'
consolation to his fellow prisoners at *VA* 7.22, and by Julian. *Or.*

going to reveal a wonder: that Homer's father was a river.[3] In other cases it is no great good fortune for one who wants to be well informed to know well the father and mother of somebody, but to be ignorant of his virtues and vices, and of what he accomplished or failed to accomplish, either by chance or by judgment. This literary work of mine, best of proconsuls, will lighten the burdens on your mind, just as Helen's mixing bowl did with its Egyptian drugs.[4] Farewell, leader of the Muses.[5]

BOOK I

(2) One must consider the Ancient Sophistic to be rhetoric doing philosophy, since it discusses the same things as do those philosophizing, but whereas they lie in wait for their questions and advance little by little to the subject of inquiry and do not yet say that they know, the ancient sophist speaks about these things as if he knows.[6] At any rate they preface their discussions with expressions like "I know" and "I recognize" and "I have long considered" and "nothing is certain for a human being." This type of introduction resounds with nobility of expression and intelli-

---

8 (240c). Gorgias' conception of rhetoric as a drug (*pharmakon*) may also have influenced Philostratus: see Pl. *Grg.* 456b–c; Gorg. *Hel.* 14.

5 The title ascribed to Gordian here ("leader of the Muses") is generally a title of Apollo.

6 The Greek ὡς εἰδώς may mean either "on the grounds that he knows" or "as if he knows." Philostratus is subtly evasive, especially in this prologue, as to whether his sophists' claims to knowledge are grounded in real knowledge.

φρόνημα καὶ κατάληψιν σαφῆ τοῦ ὄντος. ἥρμοσται
481 δὲ ἡ μὲν τῇ ἀνθρωπίνῃ μαντικῇ, ἣν Αἰγύπτιοί τε καὶ
Χαλδαῖοι καὶ πρὸ τούτων Ἰνδοὶ ξυνέθεσαν, μορίοις[4]
ἀστέρων στοχαζόμενοι τοῦ ὄντος, ἡ δὲ τῇ θεσπιῳδῷ
τε καὶ χρηστηριώδει· καὶ γὰρ δὴ καὶ τοῦ Πυθίου
ἀκούειν ἐστὶν

οἶδα δ᾽ ἐγὼ ψάμμου τ᾽ ἀριθμὸν καὶ μέτρα
    θαλάσσης

καὶ

τεῖχος Τριτογενεῖ ξύλινον διδοῖ εὐρύοπα Ζεύς

καὶ

Νέρων Ὀρέστης Ἀλκμαίων μητροκτόνοι

καὶ πολλὰ τοιαῦτα, ὥσπερ σοφιστοῦ, λέγοντος.
(3) Ἡ μὲν δὴ ἀρχαία σοφιστικὴ καὶ τὰ φιλοσο-
φούμενα ὑποτιθεμένη διῄει αὐτὰ ἀποτάδην καὶ ἐς
μῆκος· διελέγετο μὲν γὰρ περὶ ἀνδρείας, διελέγετο δὲ
περὶ δικαιότητος, ἡρώων τε πέρι καὶ θεῶν καὶ ὅπη
ἀπεσχημάτισται ἡ ἰδέα τοῦ κόσμου. ἡ δὲ μετ᾽ ἐκείνην,
ἣν οὐχὶ νέαν, ἀρχαία γάρ, δευτέραν δὲ μᾶλλον προσ-
ρητέον, τοὺς πένητας ὑπετυπώσατο καὶ τοὺς πλου-
σίους καὶ τοὺς ἀριστέας καὶ τοὺς τυράννους καὶ τὰς

4 Reading μορίοις ἀστέρων ("signs of the zodiac") with
Stefec rather than μυρίοις ἀστέρων ("tens of thousands of
stars"). Cf. Ptolemy, *Tetrabiblos* 3.13.8bis.9, for this technical
term of ancient astrology.

gence and clear apprehension of reality. The first method is in harmony with human prophetic art, which both the Egyptians and Chaldeans and before them the Indians constructed, aiming at the truth by means of the signs of the zodiac, and the second with divinely inspired and oracular prophecy. And in fact one can hear the Pythian oracle say

481

> I know the number of the sand and the measures of the sea[7]

and

> Wide-seeing Zeus gives a wooden wall to Tritogenes[8]

and

> Nero Orestes Alcmaeon matricides[9]

and many similar things, speaking like a sophist.

(3) The Ancient Sophistic proposed philosophical themes and discussed them diffusely and at length. It discussed courage, and it discussed justice, and both heroes and gods, and in what form the cosmos was fashioned. But the sophistic following that one, which we must not call new, for it is ancient, but rather second, depicted poor men and rich and the noble and the tyrants and themes

[7] Hdt. 1.147; *VA* 6.11.

[8] I.e., Athena, whose city, Athens, is protected by the wooden wall of her navy.

[9] Suet. *Ner.* 39; *VA* 4.38. Philostratus often likens rhetoric to the language of oracles. See also, for instance, Apollonius speaking "as if from the Delphic tripod" (*VA* 1.17).

37

ἐς ὄνομα ὑποθέσεις, ἐφ᾽ ἃς ἡ ἱστορία ἄγει. ἦρξε δὲ
τῆς μὲν ἀρχαιοτέρας Γοργίας ὁ Λεοντῖνος ἐν Θετταλοῖς, τῆς δὲ δευτέρας Αἰσχίνης ὁ Ἀτρομήτου τῶν μὲν
Ἀθήνησι πολιτικῶν ἐκπεσών, Καρίᾳ δὲ ἐνομιλήσας
καὶ Ῥόδῳ. καὶ μετεχειρίζοντο τὰς ὑποθέσεις οἱ μὲν
<ἀπὸ Αἰσχίνου>[5] κατὰ τέχνην, οἱ δὲ ἀπὸ Γοργίου
κατὰ τὸ δόξαν.

482   (4) Σχεδίων δὲ πηγὰς λόγων οἱ μὲν ἐκ Περικλέους
πρώτου ῥυῆναι φασίν. ὅθεν καὶ μέγας ὁ Περικλῆς
ἐνομίσθη τὴν γλῶτταν, οἱ δὲ ἀπὸ τοῦ Βυζαντίου
Πύθωνος, ὃν Δημοσθένης μόνος Ἀθηναίων ἀνασχεῖν
φησι θρασυνόμενον καὶ πολὺν ῥέοντα, οἱ δὲ Αἰσχίνου
φασὶ τὸ σχεδιάζειν εὕρημα, τοῦτον γὰρ πλεύσαντα
ἐκ Ῥόδου παρὰ τὸν Κᾶρα Μαύσωλον σχεδίῳ αὐτὸν
λόγῳ ἦσαι. ἐμοὶ δὲ πλεῖστα μὲν ἀνθρώπων Αἰσχίνης
δοκεῖ σχεδιάσαι πρεσβεύων τε καὶ ἀποπρεσβεύων
συνηγορῶν τε καὶ δημηγορῶν, καταλιπεῖν δὲ μόνους
τοὺς συγγεγραμμένους τῶν λόγων, ἵνα τῶν Δημοσθένους φροντισμάτων μὴ πολλῷ λείποιτο, σχεδίου δὲ
λόγου Γοργίας ἄρξαι—παρελθὼν γὰρ οὗτος ἐς τὸ
Ἀθηναίων θέατρον ἐθάρρησεν εἰπεῖν "προβάλλετε"
καὶ τὸ κινδύνευμα τοῦτο πρῶτος ἀνεφθέγξατο, ἐνδεικνύμενος δήπου πάντα μὲν εἰδέναι, περὶ παντὸς δ᾽ ἂν
εἰπεῖν ἐφιεὶς[6] τῷ καιρῷ—τοῦτο δ᾽ ἐπελθεῖν τῷ Γοργίᾳ

5 ἀπὸ Αἰσχίνου Stefec
6 Olearius' ἑαυτόν makes things clearer. This must be
understood in any case. Cf. below, VS 483.7.

relating to named characters, to which history leads the way. Gorgias of Leontini began the more Ancient Sophistic in Thessaly, while Aeschines the son of Atrometus began the second, when he was exiled from political activity at Athens, and had become acquainted with Caria and Rhodes. Some, influenced by Aeschines, handled their themes according to method, while others, influenced by Gorgias, handled them however seemed best to them.

(4) As to the springs of improvised speeches, some say 482 that they flowed first from Pericles, which is in fact the reason that he was considered a great man in eloquence, but others say that they flowed from Python of Byzantium, whose vehemence and flow of words Demosthenes said that he alone of the Athenians could overcome.[10] Others say that improvisation was Aeschines' discovery, because when he had sailed from Rhodes to the court of Mausolus the Carian he delighted him with an improvised speech. Aeschines seems to me to have improvised most of all men, both serving as an ambassador and reporting as one, both pleading in court and speaking before the people, and to have left behind only the carefully written of his speeches, so that he would not seem to be left far behind the thoughtful compositions of Demosthenes. But Gorgias seems to have begun improvised speaking. When he came forward in the theater of the Athenians he was bold enough to say, "propose a theme," and was the first to issue this dangerous challenge, evidently demonstrating that he knew everything, throwing himself into speaking about each thing as suited the present moment. And this idea

[10] Dem. *De cor.* 136; the same account is given by Philostr. *VA* 7.37. Python came to Athens as the agent of Philip of Macedon.

διὰ τόδε· Προδίκῳ τῷ Κείῳ συνεγέγραπτό τις οὐκ
ἀηδὴς λόγος· ἡ ἀρετὴ καὶ ἡ κακία φοιτῶσαι παρὰ τὸν
Ἡρακλέα ἐν εἴδει γυναικῶν, ἐσταλμέναι ἡ μὲν ἀπα-
τηλῷ τε καὶ ποικίλῳ, ἡ δὲ ὡς ἔτυχε, καὶ προτείνουσαι
τῷ Ἡρακλεῖ νέῳ ἔτι ἡ μὲν ἀργίαν καὶ τρυφήν, ἡ δὲ
αὐχμὸν καὶ πόνους· καὶ τοῦ ἐπὶ πᾶσι διὰ πλειόνων
ξυντεθέντος, τοῦ λόγου ἔμμισθον ἐπίδειξιν ἐποιεῖτο
Πρόδικος περιφοιτῶν τὰ ἄστη καὶ θέλγων αὐτὰ τὸν
Ὀρφέως τε καὶ Θαμύρου τρόπον, ἐφ᾽ οἷς μεγάλων μὲν
ἠξιοῦτο παρὰ Θηβαίοις, πλειόνων δ᾽ ἐν Λακεδαίμονι,
ὡς ἐς τὸ συμφέρον τῶν νέων ἀναδιδάσκων ταῦτα· ὁ
δὴ Γοργίας ἐπισκώπτων τὸν Πρόδικον, ὡς ἕωλά τε
καὶ πολλάκις εἰρημένα ἀγορεύοντα, ἐπαφῆκεν ἑαυτὸν
τῷ καιρῷ. οὐ μὴν φθόνου γε ἥμαρτεν· ἦν γάρ τις
Χαιρεφῶν Ἀθήνησιν, οὐχ ὃν ἡ κωμῳδία πύξινον
ἐκάλει, ἐκεῖνος μὲν γὰρ ὑπὸ φροντισμάτων ἐνόσει τὸ
αἷμα, ὃν δὲ νυνὶ λέγω, ὕβριν ἤσκει καὶ ἀναιδῶς
ἐτώθαζεν. οὗτος ὁ Χαιρεφῶν τὴν σπουδὴν τοῦ Γορ-
γίου διαμασώμενος, "διὰ τί," ἔφη "ὦ Γοργία, οἱ κύαμοι
τὴν μὲν γαστέρα φυσῶσι, τὸ δὲ πῦρ οὐ φυσῶσιν;" ὁ
δὲ οὐδὲν ταραχθεὶς ὑπὸ τοῦ ἐρωτήματος, "τουτὶ μὲν,"
ἔφη, "σοὶ καταλείπω σκοπεῖν, ἐγὼ δὲ ἐκεῖνο πάλαι
οἶδα, ὅτι ἡ γῆ τοὺς νάρθηκας ἐπὶ τοὺς τοιούτους
φύει."

483

---

11 For this story, see Xen. *Mem.* 2.1.21. Philostratus mentions
it again at VS 496.

occurred to Gorgias as follows. There was a certain speech, not without charm, written by Prodicus of Ceos:[11] virtue and vice came to Heracles in the form of women, one dressed in a deceptive and elaborate way, the other haphazardly, and one held out to Heracles, who was still young, ease and luxury, and the other dusty labor and toils. Adding to the story a summary of its meaning, Prodicus employed it in demonstrations for paying audiences, traveling around the cities and charming them like Orpheus and Thamyrus.[12] He was greatly esteemed in Thebes and even more so in Lacedaemon, since he taught things that were useful for the young. But Gorgias mocked Prodicus for saying stale and much repeated things, and launched himself into the present moment. Yet he did not escape envy. There was a certain Chaerephon at Athens, not the one whom comedy used to call boxwood,[13] because he had an illness of the blood from excessive thinking, but I mean a different one, who used to practice insolence and mocked others without respect. This latter Chaerephon, sinking his teeth into the seriousness of Gorgias said, "why is it, Gorgias, that beans blow up my stomach, but they don't blow up the fire?" Not at all disturbed by the question he said, "I'll leave this for you to investigate, but I have long known that the earth produces canes for your kind."

483

[12] An echo of Pl. *Prt.* 315a, where it is said of Protagoras.

[13] Chaerephon appeared frequently in Old Comedy: see schol. ad. Ar. *Vesp.* 1408, *Nub.* 496, as well as Eup. fr. 253 K-A (cited by Stefec). Burnet (1924, 169–70) observed that Chaerephon appeared to come from the Pythagorean end of Socrates' circle.

41

(5) Δεινότητα δὲ οἱ Ἀθηναῖοι περὶ τοὺς σοφιστὰς
ὁρῶντες ἐξεῖργον αὐτοὺς τῶν δικαστηρίων, ὡς ἀδίκῳ
λόγῳ τοῦ δικαίου κρατοῦντας καὶ ἰσχύοντας παρὰ τὸ
εὐθύ, ὅθεν Αἰσχίνης καὶ Δημοσθένης προὔφερον μὲν
αὐτὸ ἀλλήλοις, οὐχ ὡς ὄνειδος δέ, ἀλλὰ ὡς διαβε-
βλημένον τοῖς δικάζουσιν, ἰδίᾳ γὰρ ἠξίουν ἀπ᾽ αὐτοῦ
θαυμάζεσθαι. καὶ Δημοσθένης μέν, εἰ πειστέα⁷ Αἰσχίνῃ, πρὸς τοὺς γνωρίμους ἐκόμπαζεν, ὡς τὴν τῶν
484 δικαστῶν ψῆφον πρὸς τὸ δοκοῦν ἑαυτῷ μετάγων, Αἰσχίνης δὲ οὐκ ἄν μοι δοκεῖ πρεσβεῦσαι παρὰ Ῥοδίοις, ἃ μήπω ἐγίγνωσκον, εἰ μὴ καὶ Ἀθήνησιν αὐτὰ
ἐσπουδάκει.

(6) Σοφιστὰς δὲ οἱ παλαιοὶ ἐπωνόμαζον οὐ μόνον
τῶν ῥητόρων τοὺς ὑπερφωνοῦντάς τε καὶ λαμπρούς,
ἀλλὰ καὶ τῶν φιλοσόφων τοὺς ξὺν εὐροίᾳ ἑρμηνεύοντας, ὑπὲρ ὧν ἀνάγκη προτέρων λέγειν, ἐπειδὴ οὐκ
ὄντες σοφισταί, δοκοῦντες δὲ παρῆλθον ἐς τὴν ἐπωνυμίαν ταύτην.

(7) 1. αʹ. Εὔδοξος μὲν γὰρ ὁ Κνίδιος τοὺς ἐν Ἀκαδημίᾳ
λόγους ἱκανῶς ἐκφροντίσας ὅμως ἐνεγράφη τοῖς σοφισταῖς ἐπὶ τῷ κόσμῳ τῆς ἀπαγγελίας καὶ τῷ σχεδιάζειν εὖ, καὶ ἠξιοῦτο τῆς τῶν σοφιστῶν ἐπωνυμίας
καθ᾽ Ἑλλήσποντον καὶ Προποντίδα κατά τε Μέμφιν

---

⁷ πειστέα Schmid

(5) The Athenians, seeing the power[14] associated with sophists, debarred them from the law courts, on the grounds that they made the unjust argument more powerful than the just and were stronger than direct expression. Thereupon Aesechines and Demosthenes brought this as an accusation against each other, not as a real reproach, but since it was a slander in the eyes of those acting as jurors; in their private activity they laid claim to wonder as sophists. And Demosthenes, if one may believe Aeschines, used to boast to his friends that he led the vote of the jurors toward his own opinion. But it does not seem to me that Aeschines would have given prime importance among the Rhodians to the subject, which they did not know before, if he had not already seriously studied it at Athens.

484

(6) The ancients used to give the name of sophist not only to those rhetors who were most eloquent and famous, but also to those philosophers who made their arguments with fluency. It is necessary then to speak of these men first since, though they were not sophists, they appeared to be, and they came to have that title.

(7) 1. Eudoxus of Cnidus, who was well acquainted with the arguments current in the Academy, was nevertheless listed among the sophists due to the good order of his expression and his skill at improvisation, and he was deemed worthy of the name of sophist in the Hellespont and Propontis and at Memphis and in Egypt beyond

---

[14] On δεινότης, here translated "power," and other technical terms, see the Rhetorical Glossary.

καὶ τὴν ὑπὲρ Μέμφιν Αἴγυπτον, ἣν Αἰθιοπία τε ὁρίζει
καὶ τῶν ἐκείνῃ σοφῶν οἱ Γυμνοί.

485
(8) 2. β′. Λέων δὲ ὁ Βυζάντιος νέος μὲν ὢν ἐφοίτα
Πλάτωνι, ἐς δὲ ἄνδρας ἥκων σοφιστὴς προσερρήθη
πολυειδῶς ἔχων τοῦ λόγου καὶ πιθανῶς τῶν ἀποκρίσεων. Φιλίππῳ μὲν γὰρ στρατεύοντι ἐπὶ Βυζαντίους
προαπαντήσας "εἰπέ μοι, ὦ Φίλιππε," ἔφη "τί παθὼν
πολέμου ἄρχεις;" τοῦ δὲ εἰπόντος, "ἡ πατρὶς ἡ σὴ
καλλίστη πόλεων οὖσα ὑπηγάγετό με ἐρᾶν αὐτῆς καὶ
διὰ τοῦτο ἐπὶ θύρας τῶν ἐμαυτοῦ παιδικῶν ἥκω," ὑπο-
λαβὼν ὁ Λέων, "οὐ φοιτῶσιν," ἔφη, "μετὰ ξιφῶν ἐπὶ
τὰς τῶν παιδικῶν θύρας οἱ ἄξιοι τοῦ ἀντερᾶσθαι, οὐ
γὰρ πολεμικῶν ὀργάνων, ἀλλὰ μουσικῶν οἱ ἐρῶντες
δέονται." καὶ ἠλευθεροῦτο τὸ Βυζάντιον Δημοσθένους
μὲν πολλὰ πρὸς Ἀθηναίους εἰπόντος, Λέοντος δὲ
ὀλίγα πρὸς αὐτὸν τὸν Φίλιππον. καὶ πρεσβεύων δὲ
παρ᾽ Ἀθηναίοις ὁ Λέων οὗτος, ἐστασίαζε μὲν πολὺν
ἤδη χρόνον ἡ πόλις καὶ παρὰ τὰ ἤθη ἐπολιτεύετο,
παρελθὼν δ᾽ εἰς τὴν ἐκκλησίαν προσέβαλεν αὐτοῖς
ἀθρόον γέλωτα ἐπὶ τῷ εἴδει, ἐπειδὴ πίων ἐφαίνετο καὶ
περιττὸς τὴν γαστέρα, ταραχθεὶς δὲ οὐδὲν ὑπὸ τοῦ
γέλωτος, "τί," ἔφη, "ὦ Ἀθηναῖοι, γελᾶτε; ἢ ὅτι παχὺς

---

[15] Philostratus appears to have been the first author to move
the Gymnosophists (Naked Sages) from India to Ethiopia (*VA*
6.5), followed by Heliodorus (Morgan 2009, 272–78). This brief

Memphis, upon which borders Ethiopia and where dwell the naked sages.[15]

(8) 2. Leon of Byzantium, when he was young, at-   485
tended the classes of Plato, but when he came to manhood he was called by the name of sophist since he was varied and inventive in speech and persuasive in his answers to others. For instance when he met with Philip, who was waging a campaign against the Byzantines he said, "Tell me, Philip. What wrong have you suffered that you begin this war?" And when he said, "Because your city is the most beautiful in the world it has overcome me with desire for it, and so I have come to my beloved's door," Leon replied, "those who are worthy of being loved in return do not come to their beloved's door with swords, because lovers do not need instruments of war, but of music." And so Byzantium was liberated when Demosthenes had spoken a great deal to the Athenians, but Leon had said just a few words to Philip himself. And when this Leon spoke as an ambassador before the Athenians, when the city had been divided by factional strife for a long time and it was governed contrary to its customs, he came before the assembly and caused a flood of laughter because he was fat and had an enormous paunch, he was not at all flustered by the laughter but said, "Why do you laugh, Athenians? Is it because I am as fat and large as I am? I have a wife

account of Eudoxus' is typical of Philostratus' interests, focusing on rhetoric and the connection with the Gymnosophists but leaving out Eudoxus' considerable achievements as mathematician.

ἐγὼ καὶ τοσοῦτος; ἔστι μοι καὶ γυνὴ πολλῷ παχυ-
τέρα, καὶ ὁμονοοῦντας μὲν ἡμᾶς χωρεῖ ἡ κλίνη, δια-
φερομένους δὲ οὐδὲ ἡ οἰκία," καὶ ἐς ἓν ἦλθεν ὁ τῶν
Ἀθηναίων δῆμος ἁρμοσθεὶς ὑπὸ τοῦ Λέοντος σοφῶς
ἐπισχεδιάσαντος τῷ καιρῷ.

(9) 3. γ΄. Δίας δὲ ὁ Ἐφέσιος τὸ μὲν πεῖσμα τῆς
ἑαυτοῦ φιλοσοφίας ἐξ Ἀκαδημίας ἐβέβλητο, σοφιστὴς δὲ ἐνομίσθη διὰ τόδε· τὸν Φίλιππον ὁρῶν χαλεπὸν ὄντα τοῖς Ἕλλησιν ἐπὶ τὴν Ἀσίαν στρατεύειν
486 ἔπεισε, καὶ πρὸς τοὺς Ἕλληνας διεξῆλθε λόγον,[8] ὡς
δέον ἀκολουθεῖν στρατεύοντι, καλὸν γὰρ εἶναι καὶ τὸ
ἔξω δουλεύειν ἐπὶ τῷ οἴκοι ἐλευθεροῦσθαι.

(10) 4. δ΄. Καὶ Καρνεάδης δὲ ὁ Ἀθηναῖος ἐν σοφισταῖς ἐγράφετο, φιλοσόφως μὲν γὰρ κατεσκεύαστο
τὴν γνώμην, τὴν δὲ ἰσχὺν τῶν λόγων ἐς τὴν ἄγαν
ἤλαυνε δεινότητα.

(11) 5. ε΄. Οἶδα καὶ Φιλόστρατον τὸν Αἰγύπτιον
Κλεοπάτρα μὲν συμφιλοσοφήσαντα[9] τῇ βασιλίδι,
σοφιστὴν δὲ προσρηθέντα, ἐπειδὴ λόγου ἰδέαν πανη-
γυρικὴν ἥρμοστο καὶ ποικίλην, γυναικὶ ξυνών, ᾗ καὶ
αὐτὸ τὸ φιλολογεῖν τρυφὴν εἶχεν, ὅθεν καὶ παρῳδοῦν
τινες ἐπ᾽ αὐτῷ τόδε τὸ ἐλεγεῖον·

---

[8] Reading διεξῆλθε λόγον (the consensus of the α branch)
with Stefec rather than διεξῆλθε λέγων (the consensus of the β
branch, adopted by Wright and Kayser). The construction of δι-
έρχομαι with πρός is awkward.

[9] συμφιλοσοφοῦντα VaL

who is much fatter, and when we are getting along our bed is big enough for us, but when we argue even the house is not large enough." So the Athenian people came together, brought into harmony by Leon, who improvised cleverly to suit the moment.

(9) 3. Dias[16] of Ephesus had moored his own philosophy to the Academy, but was considered a sophist for the following reason: when he saw that Philip was treating the Greeks harshly, he persuaded him to lead his army against Asia, and he related a speech to the Greeks, arguing that they must follow him in the expedition. For it was a fine thing, he said, to slave abroad in order to gain freedom at home.

486

(10) 4. Carneades of Athens was also enrolled among the sophists. While he prepared his ideas with philosophical precision, he drove the force of his words to great power.

(11) 5. I know as well of Philostratus the Egyptian, who philosophized in company with the queen Cleopatra, but was called a sophist. This was because he composed a form of speech that was panegyrical and full of novelty, since he kept company with a woman for whom even literary study tended to indulgent luxury. For this reason certain people made this elegiac parody against him:

[16] Possibly Delios, as Stefec notes ad loc. Cf. Plut. *Mor.* 1126d.

πανσόφου ὀργὴν ἴσχε Φιλοστράτου, ὃς
    Κλεοπάτρᾳ
    νῦν προσομιλήσας τοῖος ἰδεῖν πέφαται.[10]

(12) 6. ϛʹ. Καὶ Θεόμνηστον δὲ τὸν Ναυκρατίτην
ἐπιδήλως φιλοσοφήσαντα ἡ περιβολὴ τῶν λόγων ἐς
τοὺς σοφιστὰς ἀπήνεγκεν.

(13) 7. ζʹ. Δίωνα δὲ τὸν Προυσαῖον οὐκ οἶδ' ὅ τι
χρὴ προσειπεῖν διὰ τὴν ἐς πάντα ἀρετήν, Ἀμαλθείας
487   γὰρ κέρας ἦν, τὸ τοῦ λόγου, ξυγκείμενος μὲν τῶν
ἄριστα εἰρημένων τοῖς ἀρίστοις, βλέπων δὲ πρὸς τὴν
Δημοσθένους ἠχὼ καὶ Πλάτωνος, ᾗ, καθάπερ αἱ μα-
γάδες τοῖς ὀργάνοις, προσήχει ὁ Δίων τὸ ἑαυτοῦ ἴδιον
ξὺν ἀφελείᾳ ἐπεστραμμένη. ἀρίστη δὲ ἐν τοῖς Δίωνος
λόγοις καὶ ἡ τοῦ ἤθους κρᾶσις· ὑβριζούσαις τε γὰρ
πόλεσι πλεῖστα ἐπιπλήξας οὐ φιλολοίδορος οὐδὲ ἀηδὴς ἔδοξεν, ἀλλ' οἷον ἵππων ὕβριν χαλινῷ καταρτύων

---

[10] Reading πέφαται or πέφανται with Stefec rather than the
aorist which Wright brings in, following Cobet, from the Theognis
poem, which these lines parody (Thgn. 1.215–6). The original
poem urges its addressee, Thymus, to be as changeable as the
octopus, camouflaging itself against the rocks. It became proverbial, as Wright observed: Ath. 317; Julian, *Mis.* 349d.

---

[17] Reading πέφαται or πέφανται with Stefec rather than the
aorist, which Wright brings in from the Theognis poem that these
lines parody (Thgn. 1.215–16). The original poem urges its addressee, Thymus, to be as changeable as the octopus, camouflaging itself against the rocks. It became proverbial, as Wright observed: Ath. 317; Julian. *Mis.* 349d.

[18] The "horn of plenty," or Cornucopia, was proverbial for an

Adopt the temperament of the wise Philostratus, who
    kept company
  with Cleopatra just now and has taken on her
    appearance.[17]

(12) 6. While Theomnestus of Naucratis was plainly a
philosopher, the expansiveness of his speeches brought
him into the ranks of the sophists.

(13) 7. About Dio of Prusa I do not know what one
should say, because of his excellence at everything. For he
was a horn of Amaltheia,[18] as the proverb says, constituted   487
of what has best been said by the best writers. He looked
to the resonant style[19] of Demosthenes and Plato, employing it like the bridge on a musical instrument, to re-echo
his own voice, with an earnest simplicity. The blending of
rhetorical personae[20] in Dio's speeches is excellent: though
he very often chastised cities that were behaving inso-
lently, he seemed neither like someone who takes pleasure
in insults nor disagreeable, but like one disciplining the
violence of horses with a bridle rather than a whip. When

inexhaustible source (Stefec aptly cites Zen. 2.48). Amaltheia was
the name of the goat on whose milk the nymphs fed the infant
Zeus when he was hidden away on Mount Ida. When Zeus transformed the goat into the constellation of the Goat, he gave its
horn of plenty to the nymphs, who in turn passed it on to Ache-
lous.   [19] The word for style here, $\mathring{\eta}\chi\acute{\omega}$, is a standard rhetorical term: see the Rhetorical Glossary. $\pi\rho o\sigma\acute{\eta}\chi\epsilon\iota$ in the following line ascribes a specifically echoing aesthetic to Dio, who was
able to incorporate these canonical models into his own voice.
The image of the bridge on the lyre also indicates this orderly
articulation of influences.

  [20] The term $\mathring{\mathring{\eta}}\theta o\varsigma$ here has its rhetorical sense of the character
that the speaker projects.

μᾶλλον ἢ μάστιγι, πόλεών τε εὐνομουμένων ἐς ἐπαίνους καταστὰς οὐκ ἐπαίρειν αὐτὰς ἔδοξεν, ἀλλ' ἐπι-
στρέφειν μᾶλλον ὡς ἀπολουμένας, εἰ μεταβαλοῖντο.
ἦν δὲ αὐτῷ καὶ τὸ τῆς ἄλλης φιλοσοφίας ἦθος οὐ
κοινὸν οὐδ' εἰρωνικόν, ἀλλὰ ἐμβριθῶς μὲν ἐγκείμενον,
κεχρωσμένον δέ, οἷον ἡδύσματι, τῇ πρᾳότητι. ὡς δὲ
καὶ ἱστορίαν ἱκανὸς ἦν ξυγγράφειν, δηλοῖ τὰ Γετικά,
καὶ γὰρ δὴ καὶ ἐς Γέτας ἦλθεν, ὁπότε ἠλᾶτο. τὸν δὲ
Εὐβοέα καὶ τὸν τοῦ ψιττακοῦ ἔπαινον καὶ ὁπόσα οὐχ
ὑπὲρ μεγάλων ἐσπούδασται τῷ Δίωνι, μὴ μικρὰ ἡγώμεθα, ἀλλὰ σοφιστικά, σοφιστοῦ γὰρ τὸ καὶ ὑπὲρ
τοιούτων σπουδάζειν.

(14) Γενόμενος δὲ κατὰ χρόνους, οὓς Ἀπολλώνιός
488 τε ὁ Τυανεὺς καὶ Εὐφράτης ὁ Τύριος ἐφιλοσόφουν,
ἀμφοτέροις ἐπιτηδείως εἶχε καίτοι διαφερομένοις
πρὸς ἀλλήλους ἔξω τοῦ φιλοσοφίας ἤθους. τὴν δὲ ἐς
τὰ Γετικὰ ἔθνη πάροδον τοῦ ἀνδρὸς φυγὴν μὲν οὐκ
ἀξιῶ ὀνομάζειν, ἐπεὶ μὴ προσετάχθη αὐτῷ φυγεῖν,
οὐδὲ ἀποδημίαν, ἐπειδὴ τοῦ φανεροῦ ἐξέστη κλέπτων
ἑαυτὸν ὀφθαλμῶν τε καὶ ὤτων καὶ ἄλλα ἐν ἄλλῃ γῇ
πράττων δέει τῶν κατὰ τὴν πόλιν τυραννίδων, ὑφ' ὧν
ἠλαύνετο φιλοσοφία πᾶσα. φυτεύων δὲ καὶ σκάπτων
καὶ ἐπαντλῶν βαλανείοις τε καὶ κήποις καὶ πολλὰ

---

21 This work is lost.
22 The *Euboean Oration*, one of Dio's surviving works, has
attracted considerable debate. See for further bibliography Jackson 2017, 220–22. Synesius (*Dio* 2.5–6) criticizes Philostratus'

he came to praise cities that were governed by good laws, he did not seem to exalt them, but rather to guide their attention to the fact that they would be destroyed if they should change. And the character of the rest of his philosophy was not common nor ironic. Rather, although it was delivered with severity, it was seasoned with gentleness, as if with a sauce. The fact that he was also capable of writing history is demonstrated by his work *On the Getae*.[21] What is more he traveled to the Getae, when he went into exile. And as to his *Euboean Oration*[22] and his *Encomium of a Parrot* and all such writings in which Dio gave serious attention to trivial topics, let us not consider them minor, but sophistic. For it is characteristic of a sophist to devote serious study even to things like these.

(14) He lived at the time when both Apollonius of Tyana and Euphrates of Tyre were practicing philosophy, and he was on friendly terms with both of them, although they quarreled with one another in a manner inappropriate for philosophers.[23] I do not think it right to call the man's journey to the Getic tribes exile, since he had not been ordered to go into exile, nor merely travel abroad, because he vanished, hiding himself out of sight and hearing, and doing different things in different lands, out of fear of the tyranny in the capital, by which all philosophy had been driven out.[24] Although he planted and dug and drew water for baths and gardens and performed many

488

view that this is a sophistic work, asserting that it conveys a serious moral message, directed to rich and poor alike.

[23] See Philostratus' telling of this story in his *VA* 5.33 and 37. The younger Pliny took a very different view of Euphrates (*Ep.* 1.10).   [24] See *VA* 7.4. The driving out of philosophers is a trope in the representation of the so-called bad emperors.

PHILOSTRATUS

τοιαῦτα ὑπὲρ τροφῆς ἐργαζόμενος οὐδὲ τοῦ σπουδάζειν ἠμέλει, ἀλλ᾽ ἀπὸ δυοῖν βιβλίοιν ἑαυτὸν ξυνεῖχε·
ταυτὶ δὲ ἦν ὅ τε Φαίδων ὁ τοῦ Πλάτωνος καὶ Δημοσθένους ὁ κατὰ τῆς πρεσβείας. θαμίζων δὲ ἐς τὰ
στρατόπεδα, ἐν οἷσπερ εἰώθει τρύχεσι,[11] καὶ τοὺς
στρατιώτας ὁρῶν ἐς νεώτερα ὁρμῶντας ἐπὶ Δομετιανῷ
ἀπεσφαγμένῳ οὐκ ἐφείσατο ἀταξίαν ἰδὼν ἐκραγεῖ-
σαν, ἀλλὰ γυμνὸς ἀναπηδήσας ἐπὶ βωμὸν ὑψηλὸν
ἤρξατο τοῦ λόγου ὧδε·

αὐτὰρ ὁ γυμνώθη ῥακέων πολύμητις Ὀδυσσεύς,

καὶ εἰπὼν ταῦτα καὶ δηλώσας ἑαυτόν, ὅτι μὴ πτωχός,
μηδὲ ὃν ᾤοντο, Δίων δὲ εἴη ὁ σοφός, ἐπὶ μὲν τὴν
κατηγορίαν τοῦ τυράννου πολὺς ἔπνευσεν, τοὺς δὲ
στρατιώτας ἐδίδαξεν ἄμεινον φρονεῖν τὰ δοκοῦντα
Ῥωμαίοις πράττοντας. καὶ γὰρ ἡ πειθὼ τοῦ ἀνδρὸς
οἵα καταθέλξαι καὶ τοὺς μὴ τὰ Ἑλλήνων ἀκριβοῦν-
τας· Τραιανὸς γοῦν ὁ αὐτοκράτωρ ἀναθέμενος αὐτὸν
ἐπὶ τῆς Ῥώμης ἐς τὴν χρυσῆν ἅμαξαν, ἐφ᾽ ἧς οἱ βα-
σιλεῖς τὰς ἐκ τῶν πολέμων πομπὰς πομπεύουσιν,
ἔλεγε θαμὰ ἐπιστρεφόμενος πρὸς τὸν Δίωνα, "τί μὲν
λέγεις, οὐκ οἶδα, φιλῶ δέ σε ὡς ἐμαυτόν."

(15) Σοφιστικώταται δὲ τοῦ Δίωνος αἱ τῶν λόγων
εἰκόνες, ἐν αἷς εἰ καὶ πολύς, ἀλλὰ καὶ ἐναργὴς καὶ
τοῖς ὑποκειμένοις ὅμοιος.

[11] τρύχεσθαι archetype; τρύχεσι Cobet

52

such tasks for a living, he did not disregard study, but sustained himself with two books. These were the *Phaedo* of Plato and Demothenes' *On the False Embassy*. He used to go often to the army camps in the rags that he was accustomed to wear, and when he saw the soldiers beginning to mutiny since Domitian had been murdered, he did not hold back, seeing disorder breaking out, but stripping off his rags he leaped up onto a high altar and began his speech with the line:

Then wily Odysseus stripped off his rags.[25]

And saying this, and showing that he was not a beggar, nor what they believed him to be, but rather Dio the wise, he gave a vehement condemnation of the tyrant, and taught the soldiers that they would act more wisely by following the will of the Roman people. And in fact the man's power of persuasion was such that it charmed even those who were not well versed in Greek literature. For example the emperor Trajan in Rome set him in the golden chariot in which the emperors ride in procession when they triumph in war, and often turned to Dio and said, "I do not know what you are saying, but I love you like myself."[26]

(15) The images in Dio's speeches are entirely in the sophistic manner, and though he employs them frequently, he is nonetheless both vivid and suited to his subject matter.

[25] Hom. *Od.* 22.1.

[26] This incident is not otherwise attested, with the exception of Photius and the *Suda*, both of which presumably draw on Philostratus. On the probability that Trajan did in fact know Greek, Wright cited Cass. Dio 68.3, 68.7 and Plin. *Pan.* 47.1.

PHILOSTRATUS

489   (16) 8. ηʹ. Ὁμοίως καὶ Φαβωρῖνον τὸν φιλόσοφον
ἡ εὐγλωττία ἐν σοφισταῖς ἐκήρυττεν. ἦν μὲν γὰρ τῶν
ἑσπερίων Γαλατῶν οὗτος, Ἀρελάτου πόλεως, ἣ ἐπ'
Ἠριδανῷ¹² ποταμῷ ᾤκισται, διφυὴς δὲ ἐτέχθη καὶ ἀν-
δρόθηλυς, καὶ τοῦτο ἐδηλοῦτο μὲν καὶ παρὰ τοῦ εἴδους, ἀγενείως γὰρ τοῦ προσώπου καὶ γηράσκων εἶχεν, ἐδηλοῦτο δὲ καὶ τῷ φθέγματι, ὀξυηχὲς γὰρ
ἠκούετο καὶ λεπτὸν καὶ ἐπίτονον, ὥσπερ ἡ φύσις τοὺς
εὐνούχους ἥρμοκε. θερμὸς δὲ οὕτω τις ἦν τὰ ἐρωτικά,
ὡς καὶ μοιχοῦ λαβεῖν αἰτίαν ἐξ ἀνδρὸς ὑπάτου. διαφορᾶς δὲ αὐτῷ πρὸς Ἀδριανὸν βασιλέα γενομένης
οὐδὲν ἔπαθεν, ὅθεν ὡς παράδοξα ἐπεχρησμῴδει τῷ
ἑαυτοῦ βίῳ τρία ταῦτα· Γαλάτης ὢν ἑλληνίζειν, εὐνοῦχος ὢν μοιχείας κρίνεσθαι, βασιλεῖ διαφέρεσθαι
καὶ ζῆν. τουτὶ δὲ Ἀδριανοῦ ἔπαινος ἂν εἴη μᾶλλον, εἰ
βασιλεὺς ὢν ἀπὸ τοῦ ἴσου διεφέρετο πρὸς ὃν ἐξῆν
ἀποκτεῖναι. βασιλεὺς δὲ κρείττων,

    ὅτε χώσεται ἀνδρὶ χέρηι,

ἢν ὀργῆς κρατῇ, καὶ

¹² ἐπὶ Ῥοδανῷ Salmasius

---

27 Philostratus sees Dio's activities as sophist and as philosopher as simultaneous and linked, whereas Synesius (in his *Dio*)
initiates the reading of Dio, which treats his exile as the point of
conversion from sophistry to philosophy. Contemporary scholarship on Dio has, broadly speaking, moved closer to Philostratus'
position. See Moles 1978 and Jackson 2017.

54

(16) 8. Similarly to Dio, Favorinus the philosopher was 489
heralded as a sophist by his eloquence.[27] This man was
from among the Gauls of the west, from the city of Arelate,
which is built on the river Eridanus,[28] but he was double-
natured and androgynous,[29] and this was obvious even
from his appearance, because even when he was growing
old he had a beardless face, and it was obvious too from
his voice: for it sounded high-pitched and delicate and
strained, with the sound that nature gives to eunuchs.[30]
Yet he so burned with desire that he was even charged
with adultery by a man of consular rank. And when he had
a disagreement with the emperor Hadrian he suffered no
harm, for which reason he used to speak in oracular style
about these three paradoxes of his life: he was a Gaul who
Hellenized, a eunuch who was tried for adultery, and he
had quarreled with an emperor and lived. But this would
really be more to the credit of Hadrian if, although he was
emperor, he quarreled from a position of equality with one
whom he could have killed. And a king is greater if he
masters his anger,

when he is angry with a lesser man,[31]

and

[28] That is, from Arles on the Rhône.

[29] On the "double-natured and androgynous" appearance of
Favorinus, see Gleason 1995, esp. 131–58.

[30] Lucian's much more hostile account of Favorinus also remarks on his voice: *Eunuch* 10.

[31] Hom. *Il.* 1.80. As Wright observed, Philostratus interprets
κρείσσων as "morally superior," whereas in the original it simply
means "stronger."

θυμὸς δὲ μέγας ἐστὶ διοτρεφέος βασιλῆος,[13]

ἢν λογισμῷ κολάζηται. βέλτιον γὰρ ταῦτα ταῖς τῶν
ποιητῶν δόξαις προσγράφειν τοὺς εὖ τιθεμένους τὰ
τῶν βασιλέων ἤθη.

490   (17) Ἀρχιερεὺς δὲ ἀναρρηθεὶς εἰς τὰ οἴκοι πάτρια
ἐφῆκε μὲν κατὰ τοὺς ὑπὲρ τῶν τοιούτων νόμους, ὡς
ἀφειμένος τοῦ λειτουργεῖν, ἐπειδὴ ἐφιλοσόφει, τὸν δὲ
αὐτοκράτορα ὁρῶν ἐναντίαν αὑτῷ θέσθαι διανοούμε-
νον, ὡς μὴ φιλοσοφοῦντι, ὑπετέμετο αὐτὸν ὧδε· "ἐνύ-
πνιόν μοι," ἔφη, "ὦ βασιλεῦ, γέγονεν, ὃ καὶ πρὸς σὲ
χρὴ εἰρῆσθαι· ἐπιστὰς γάρ μοι Δίων ὁ διδάσκαλος
ἐνουθέτει με ὑπὲρ τῆς δίκης λέγων, ὅτι μὴ ἑαυτοῖς
μόνον, ἀλλὰ καὶ ταῖς πατρίσι γεγόναμεν· ὑποδέχομαι
δή, ὦ βασιλεῦ, τὴν λειτουργίαν καὶ τῷ διδασκάλῳ
πείθομαι." ταῦτα ὁ μὲν αὐτοκράτωρ διατριβὴν ἐπε-
ποίητο, καὶ διῆγε τὰς βασιλείους φροντίδας ἀπο-
νεύων ἐς σοφιστάς τε καὶ φιλοσόφους, Ἀθηναίοις δὲ
δεινὰ ἐφαίνετο καὶ ξυνδραμόντες αὐτοὶ μάλιστα οἱ ἐν
τέλει Ἀθηναῖοι χαλκῆν εἰκόνα κατέβαλον τοῦ ἀνδρὸς
ὡς πολεμιωτάτου τῷ αὐτοκράτορι· ὁ δέ, ὡς ἤκουσεν,
οὐδὲν σχετλιάσας οὐδὲ ἀγριάνας ὑπὲρ ὧν ὕβριστο,
"ὤνητ᾽ ἂν," ἔφη, "καὶ Σωκράτης εἰκόνα χαλκῆν ὑπ᾽
Ἀθηναίων ἀφαιρεθεὶς μᾶλλον ἢ πιὼν κώνειον."

---

13 διοτρεφέων βασιλήων VaL

---

32 Hom. *Il.* 2.196. Here again, Philostratus takes in a moral
sense a statement that is not of this kind in Homer. In this Iliadic
line, Odysseus is urging the Achaeans not to leave Troy, since he

great is the anger of god-nurtured kings[32]

if it is disciplined by reason. It would be better for those who try to guide the character of kings to add these words to the advice from the poets.

(17) When he was appointed high priest, he appealed   490
to the inherited customs of his birthplace that in accordance with the laws governing such things, he was exempt from public service, since he was a philosopher. But when he saw that the emperor intended to vote against him, because he did not believe that he was a philosopher, he cut him short in the following way. "I had a dream," he said, "emperor, which I must tell you. Dio, my teacher, stood beside me and instructed me about this case, saying that we are born not for ourselves alone, but for our native land.[33] Therefore I receive, emperor, the public service, and I obey my teacher." While the emperor had spent time on these matters as a diversion, and he used to shift his mind from imperial business to both sophists and philosophers, the Athenians took them very seriously, and those who held office gathered together and cast down a bronze statue of the man, considering him the emperor's worst enemy. But Favorinus, when he heard, did not complain nor was he angry at these outrageous acts, but he said, "It would have been better for Socrates if he had been deprived of a bronze statue by the Athenians, rather than drinking hemlock."

says that Agamemnon is testing them, and the anger of a king should not be lightly provoked. Philostratus varies the line to say that the anger of kings is great (i.e., powerful and useful) if governed by reason.   [33] An echo of Dem. *De cor.* 205, and perhaps also of Pl. *Cri.* 50.

(18) Ἐπιτηδειότατος μὲν οὖν Ἡρώδη τῷ σοφιστῇ ἐγένετο διδάσκαλόν τε ἡγουμένῳ καὶ πατέρα καὶ πρὸς αὐτὸν γράφοντι, "πότε σε ἴδω καὶ πότε σου περιλείξω τὸ στόμα;" ὅθεν καὶ τελευτῶν κληρονόμον Ἡρώδην ἀπέφηνε τῶν τε βιβλίων, ὁπόσα ἐκέκτητο, καὶ τῆς ἐπὶ τῇ Ῥώμῃ οἰκίας καὶ τοῦ Αὐτοληκύθου. ἦν δὲ οὗτος Ἰνδὸς μὲν καὶ ἱκανῶς μέλας, ἄθυρμα δὲ Ἡρώδου τε καὶ Φαβωρίνου, ξυμπίνοντας γὰρ αὐτοὺς διῆγεν ἐγκαταμιγνὺς Ἰνδικοῖς Ἀττικὰ καὶ πεπλανημένη τῇ γλώττῃ βαρβαρίζων.

(19) Ἡ δὲ γενομένη πρὸς τὸν Πολέμωνα τῷ Φαβωρίνῳ διαφορὰ ἤρξατο μὲν ἐν Ἰωνίᾳ προσθεμένων αὐτῷ τῶν Ἐφεσίων, ἐπεὶ τὸν Πολέμωνα ἡ Σμύρνα ἐθαύμαζεν, ἐπέδωκε δὲ ἐν τῇ Ῥώμῃ, ὕπατοι γὰρ καὶ παῖδες ὑπάτων οἱ μὲν τὸν ἐπαινοῦντες, οἱ δὲ τόν, ἦρξαν αὐτοῖς φιλοτιμίας, ἣ πολὺν ἐκκαίει καὶ σοφοῖς ἀνδράσι τὸν πόλεμον.[14] συγγνωστοὶ μὲν οὖν τῆς φιλοτιμίας, τῆς ἀνθρωπείας φύσεως τὸ φιλότιμον ἀγήρων ἡγουμένης,[15] μεμπτέοι δὲ τῶν λόγων, οὓς ἐπ᾽ ἀλλήλους ξυνέθεσαν, ἀσελγὴς γὰρ λοιδορία, κἂν ἀληθὴς τύχῃ, οὐκ ἀφίησιν αἰσχύνης οὐδὲ τὸν ὑπὲρ τοιούτων εἰπόντα. τοῖς μὲν οὖν σοφιστὴν τὸν Φαβωρῖνον καλοῦσιν ἀπέχρη ἐς ἀπόδειξιν καὶ αὐτὸ τὸ σο-

491

---

[14] φθόνον σοφοῖς ἀνδράσι Catrarius; φθόνον καὶ σοφοῖς ἀνδράσι M
[15] κεκτημένης Cobet

(18) He was a close associate of the sophist Herodes, who regarded him as his teacher and father, and wrote to him: "when will I see you and when will I lick the honey from your mouth?"[34] Accordingly when Favorinus died he made Herodes heir both of all the books that he owned and of his house in Rome and of Autolecythus.[35] He was an Indian and entirely black, and was the plaything of Herodes and Favorinus. For he used to entertain them when they were drinking together, by mixing up Attic words with Indian, and speaking barbarously with a stammering tongue.

(19) And the quarrel that arose between Favorinus and Polemo began in Ionia, with the Ephesians allying themselves to Favorinus, while Smyrna was in awe of Polemo. But it escalated in Rome, when consuls and sons of consuls praised one or the other, and began a rivalry for honor between them, which ignites warfare even among wise men. They should be forgiven for this rivalry, because human nature holds that the love of honor is unaging,[36] but they should be blamed for the speeches that they composed against each other. Brutal personal abuse, even if it happens to be true, does not spare from shame the one who speaks of such things. For those who called Favorinus a sophist, the fact that he had quarreled with a sophist

491

34 An echo of Ar. fr. 231, preserved in Dio Chrys. *Or.* 52 Arnim.

35 *Pace* Wright, the Indian Autolecythus, a slave of Herodes, is clearly not the same person as Memnon (on whom see *VS* 558–59), Herodes' foster child or student (τρόφιμος).

36 An echo of Thuc. 2.44.

φιστῇ διενεχθῆναι αὐτόν· τὸ γὰρ φιλότιμον, οὗ ἐπεμνήσθην,[16] ἐπὶ τοὺς ἀντιτέχνους φοιτᾷ.

(20) Ἥρμοστο δὲ τὴν γλῶτταν ἀνειμένως μέν, σοφῶς δὲ καὶ ποτίμως. ἐλέγετο δὲ καὶ σὺν εὐροίᾳ σχεδιάσαι. τὰ μὲν δὴ εἰς Πρόξενον μήτ᾽ ἂν ἐνθυμηθῆναι
τὸν Φαβωρῖνον ἡγώμεθα μήτ᾽ ἂν ξυνθεῖναι, ἀλλ᾽ εἶναι
αὐτὰ μειρακίου φρόντισμα μεθύοντος, μᾶλλον δὲ
ἐμοῦντος, τὸν δὲ ἐπὶ τῷ λήρῳ[17] καὶ τὸν ὑπὲρ τῶν μο-
νομάχων καὶ τὸν ὑπὲρ τῶν βαλανείων γνησίους τε
ἀποφαινώμεθα[18] καὶ εὖ ξυγκειμένους, καὶ πολλῷ μᾶλλον τοὺς φιλοσοφουμένους αὐτῷ τῶν λόγων, ὧν ἄριστοι οἱ Πυρρώνειοι· τοὺς γὰρ Πυρρωνείους ἐφεκτι-
κοὺς ὄντας οὐκ ἀφαιρεῖται καὶ τὸ δικάζειν δύνασθαι.

(21) Διαλεγομένου δὲ αὐτοῦ κατὰ τὴν Ῥώμην με-
στὰ ἦν σπουδῆς πάντα, καὶ γὰρ δὴ καὶ ὅσοι τῆς
Ἑλλήνων φωνῆς ἀξύνετοι ἦσαν, οὐδὲ τούτοις ἀφ᾽
ἡδονῆς ἡ ἀκρόασις ἦν, ἀλλὰ κἀκείνους ἔθελγε τῇ τε
ἠχῇ τοῦ φθέγματος καὶ τῷ σημαίνοντι τοῦ βλέμμα-
492   τος καὶ τῷ ῥυθμῷ τῆς γλώττης. ἔθελγε δὲ αὐτοὺς τοῦ
λόγου καὶ τὸ ἐπὶ πᾶσιν, ὃ ἐκεῖνοι μὲν ᾠδὴν ἐκάλουν,

---

[16] ἐμνήσθην a

[17] The reading here is uncertain between ἐπὶ τῷ λήρῳ (On
Trash or On Nonsense) and ἐπὶ τῷ ἀώρῳ (On One Untimely
Dead). The former, the reading of the a group, is printed by
Stefec, the latter, the reading of the rest (β), by Kayser.

[18] ἀποφαινόμεθα χ; ἀποφαινοίμεθα a

provided clear evidence, since the rivalry of which I have spoken arises between practitioners of the same craft.[37]

(20) He composed his language in a leisurely way, but cleverly and pleasantly. And he was said to improvise with fluency.[38] Let us not consider that the speeches *On Proxenus* could have been conceived or written by Favorinus, but that they are the work of a drunken youth, or rather of one vomiting.[39] Let us declare genuine and well composed, however, the speech *On Trash*, and the one *On the Gladiators*, and *On the Baths*,[40] and much more so his philosophical works, of which the best were those on Pyrrho.[41] Although the followers of Pyrrho suspend judgment, he does not take away from them even the ability to judge in a court of law.

(21) When he engaged in dialogue in Rome, the whole city was full of enthusiasm, so much so that even those who did not understand the Greek language heard him with pleasure, and he charmed them with the sound of his voice, the expression of his gaze and the rhythm of his tongue. He used to charm them too with the endings of   492

[37] Hes. *Op.* 25.

[38] On εὐροία, see the Rhetorical Glossary.

[39] Philostratus appears to have been fond of this image. Cf. the saying of Aristides below, *VS* 583.

[40] None of these works survive.

[41] Favorinus had a clear interest in skepticism but is sometimes described as an Academic and sometimes a Pyrrhonian. For a discussion of the inconclusive evidence, see Ioppolo 1993, and for Favorinus as an Academic skeptic, Holford-Strevens 2003, 110–11, 116, and 269.

ἐγὼ δὲ φιλοτιμίαν, ἐπειδὴ τοῖς ἀποδεδειγμένοις ἐφυμνεῖται. Δίωνος μὲν οὖν ἀκοῦσαι λέγεται, τοσοῦτον δὲ ἀφέστηκεν, ὅσον οἱ μὴ ἀκούσαντες.

(22) Τοσαῦτα μὲν ὑπὲρ τῶν φιλοσοφησάντων ἐν δόξῃ τοῦ σοφιστεῦσαι. οἱ δὲ κυρίως προσρηθέντες σοφισταὶ ἐγένοντο οἵδε·

(23) 9. θ'. Σικελία Γοργίαν ἐν Λεοντίνοις ἤνεγκεν, ἐς ὃν ἀναφέρειν ἡγώμεθα τὴν τῶν σοφιστῶν τέχνην, ὥσπερ εἰς πατέρα· εἰ γὰρ τὸν Αἰσχύλον ἐνθυμηθείημεν, ὡς πολλὰ τῇ τραγῳδίᾳ ξυνεβάλετο ἐσθῆτί τε αὐτὴν κατασκευάσας καὶ ὀκρίβαντι ὑψηλῷ καὶ ἡρώων εἴδεσιν ἀγγέλοις τε καὶ ἐξαγγέλοις καὶ οἷς ἐπὶ σκηνῆς τε καὶ ὑπὸ σκηνῆς χρὴ πράττειν, τοῦτο ἂν εἴη καὶ ὁ Γοργίας ἐν τοῖς ὁμοτέχνοις. ὁρμῆς τε γὰρ τοῖς σοφισταῖς ἦρξε καὶ παραδοξολογίας καὶ πνεύματος καὶ τοῦ τὰ μεγάλα μεγάλως ἑρμηνεύειν, ἀποστάσεών τε καὶ προσβολῶν, ὑφ' ὧν ὁ λόγος ἡδίων ἑαυτοῦ καὶ σοβαρώτερος, περιεβάλλετο δὲ καὶ ποιητικὰ ὀνόματα ὑπὲρ κόσμου καὶ σεμνότητος. ὅπως μὲν οὖν καὶ ῥᾷστα ἀπεσχεδίαζεν, εἴρηταί μοι κατὰ ἀρχὰς τοῦ λόγου, διαλεχθεὶς δὲ Ἀθήνησιν ἤδη γηράσκων εἰ μὲν ὑπὸ τῶν πολλῶν ἐθαυμάσθη, οὔπω θαῦμα, ὁ δέ, οἶμαι, καὶ τοὺς ἐλλογιμωτάτους ἀνηρτήσατο, Κριτίαν μὲν

---

[42] Though Philostratus often remarks with approval on the rhythmic and musical qualities of the sophists' performances, he is critical of what he sees as excessive musicality. A similar sentiment from Isaeus the Assyrian is quoted below (VS 513). Aelius

his discourses, which they used to call the Ode,[42] but which I call ostentation, since he chanted this upon the points already proven. And it is said that he was a student of Dio, but he differs as much from him as do those who never studied with him.

(22) Enough then about those who practiced philosophy while having a reputation as sophists. Those were correctly called sophists were the following.

(23) 9. Sicily produced Gorgias in Leontini, and let us attribute the art of the sophists to him as if to a father. If we should think of Aeschylus, and of how many things he contributed to tragedy, since he equipped it with appropriate costumes and high buskins and the images of heroes, and with messengers from elsewhere and from within the house, and established what should be done on and off stage, Gorgias achieved the same among his fellow craftsmen. For he initiated for the sophists the energetic style and paradoxical expression and inspired impressiveness and speaking in the grand style of great themes, and the habit of breaking off clauses and making sudden transitions,[43] by all of which a speech becomes more pleasurable and more distinguished. And he clothed his speech in poetic words for the sake of ornament and dignity. How fluently he improvised, I have said at the beginning of my narrative.[44] When he spoke at Athens, being already an old man, it is no wonder if he was wondered at by the crowd. But he also, I believe, won over to him the most eminent

Aristides was more consistently critical of such practices associated with Asianism (*Or.* 34.45–47, 48, 55).

[43] For these terms (ἀπόστασις and προσβολή), see the Rhetorical Glossary.　　[44] See above, *VS* 482.

493 καὶ Ἀλκιβιάδην νέω ὄντε, Θουκυδίδην δὲ καὶ Περικλέα ἤδη γηράσκοντε. καὶ Ἀγάθων δὲ ὁ τῆς τραγῳδίας ποιητής, ὃν ἡ κωμῳδία σοφόν τε καὶ καλλιεπῆ
οἶδε, πολλαχοῦ τῶν ἰαμβείων γοργιάζει.

(24) Ἐμπρέπων δὲ καὶ ταῖς τῶν Ἑλλήνων πανη-
γύρεσι τὸν μὲν λόγον τὸν Πυθικὸν ἀπὸ τοῦ βωμοῦ
ἤχησεν, ἐφ' οὗ καὶ χρυσοῦς ἀνετέθη, ἐν τῷ τοῦ Πυθίου ἱερῷ, ὁ δὲ Ὀλυμπικὸς λόγος ὑπὲρ τοῦ μεγίστου
αὐτῷ ἐπολιτεύθη. στασιάζουσαν γὰρ τὴν Ἑλλάδα
ὁρῶν ὁμονοίας ξύμβουλος αὐτοῖς ἐγένετο τρέπων ἐπὶ
τοὺς βαρβάρους καὶ πείθων ἆθλα ποιεῖσθαι τῶν
ὅπλων μὴ τὰς ἀλλήλων πόλεις, ἀλλὰ τὴν τῶν βαρβάρων χώραν. ὁ δὲ Ἐπιτάφιος, ὃν διῆλθεν Ἀθήνησιν,
εἴρηται μὲν ἐπὶ τοῖς ἐκ τῶν πολέμων πεσοῦσιν, οὓς
Ἀθηναῖοι δημοσίᾳ ξὺν ἐπαίνοις ἔθαψαν, σοφίᾳ δὲ
ὑπερβαλλούσῃ ξύγκειται· παροξύνων τε γὰρ τοὺς
Ἀθηναίους ἐπὶ Μήδους τε καὶ Πέρσας καὶ τὸν αὐτὸν
νοῦν τῷ Ὀλυμπικῷ ἀγωνιζόμενος ὑπὲρ ὁμονοίας μὲν
τῆς πρὸς τοὺς Ἕλληνας οὐδὲν διῆλθεν, ἐπειδὴ πρὸς
Ἀθηναίους ἦν ἀρχῆς ἐρῶντας, ἣν οὐκ ἦν κτήσασθαι
μὴ τὸ δραστήριον αἱρουμένους, ἐνδιέτριψε δὲ τοῖς τῶν
Μηδικῶν τροπαίων ἐπαίνοις, ἐνδεικνύμενος αὐτοῖς,

---

45 Though the *Suda* (possibly following Philostratus) also reports that Gorgias influenced Pericles, Olearius (1709, 493n14)
already noted the impossibility, since Pericles died two years before Gorgias arrived at Athens.

men: Critias and Alcibiades, who were then young, and
Thucidides and Pericles who were already old.[45] And Ag-   493
athon the tragic poet, whom comedy knows as wise and
eloquent,[46] often wrote in Gorgias' style in his iambics.

(24) Moreover he played a distinguished part at the
festivals of the Greeks and declaimed his *Pythian Oration*
from the altar, for which reason a golden statue of him was
dedicated in the temple of the Pythia.[47] His *Olympian
Oration* dealt with a theme of the highest political importance. Seeing that Greece was divided by factional strife,
he counseled concord, trying to urge them against the
barbarians and to persuade them not to consider one another's cities, but rather the land of the barbarians, as the
prizes of their arms. And the *Funeral Oration*, which he
delivered at Athens, was spoken in honor of those who had
fallen in the wars, whom the Athenians buried with praise
and public funerals, and the speech itself is composed with
surpassing wisdom. For he sharpened the Athenian re-
solve against the Medes and Persians and argued the same
opinion as he had in the *Olympian Oration*. But while he
said nothing about concord with the Greeks, since he was
speaking to Athenians who craved empire, which they
could not possess except by adopting a bold position, he
dwelt upon their victories over the Medes, demonstrating

[46] Ar. *Thesm.* 49, 60. Plato, *Symp.* 195 ff., with satirical intention, makes Agathon speak in the style of Gorgias.

[47] Plato mentions this fact in the *Gorgias*, as does Cic. *De or.*
3.22 and Val. Max. 8.45. All agree that the statue was dedicated
by the will of all the Greeks, though the elder Pliny says that
Gorgias dedicated the statue to himself (*HN* 33.24).

494 ὅτι τὰ μὲν κατὰ τῶν βαρβάρων τρόπαια ὕμνους ἀπαι-
τεῖ, τὰ δὲ κατὰ τῶν Ἑλλήνων θρήνους.

(25) Λέγεται δὲ ὁ Γοργίας ἐς ὀκτὼ καὶ ἑκατὸν ἐλά-
σας ἔτη μὴ καταλυθῆναι τὸ σῶμα ὑπὸ γήρως, ἀλλ᾽
ἄρτιος καταβιῶναι καὶ τὰς αἰσθήσεις ἡβῶν.

(26) 10. ιʹ. Πρωταγόρας δὲ ὁ Ἀβδηρίτης σοφιστὴς
μὲν καὶ Δημοκρίτου ἀκροατὴς οἴκοι ἐγένετο, ὡμίλησε
δὲ καὶ τοῖς ἐκ Περσῶν μάγοις κατὰ τὴν Ξέρξου ἐπὶ
τὴν Ἑλλάδα ἔλασιν. πατὴρ μὲν γὰρ ἦν αὐτῷ Μαίαν-
δριος[19] πλούτῳ κατεσκευασμένος παρὰ πολλοὺς τῶν
ἐν τῇ Θρᾴκῃ, δεξάμενος δὲ τὸν Ξέρξην οἰκίᾳ τε καὶ
δώροις τὴν ξυνουσίαν τῶν μάγων τῷ παιδὶ παρ᾽
αὐτοῦ εὕρετο. οὐ γὰρ παιδεύουσι τοὺς μὴ Πέρσας
Πέρσαι μάγοι, ἢν μὴ ὁ βασιλεὺς ἐφῇ. τὸ δὲ ἀπορεῖν
φάσκειν, εἴτε εἰσὶ θεοί, εἴτε οὐκ εἰσί, δοκεῖ μοι Πρωταγόρας ἐκ τῆς Περσικῆς παιδεύσεως παρανομῆσαι·
μάγοι γὰρ ἐπιθειάζουσι μὲν οἷς ἀφανῶς δρῶσι, τὴν
δὲ ἐκ φανεροῦ δόξαν τοῦ θείου καταλύουσιν οὐ βουλόμενοι δοκεῖν παρ᾽ αὐτοῦ δύνασθαι. διὰ μὲν δὴ τοῦτο
πάσης γῆς ὑπὸ Ἀθηναίων ἠλάθη, ὡς μέν τινες, κριθείς, ὡς δὲ ἐνίοις δοκεῖ, ψήφου ἐπενεχθείσης μὴ
κριθέντι. νήσους δὲ ἐξ ἠπείρων ἀμείβων καὶ τὰς
Ἀθηναίων τριήρεις φυλαττόμενος πάσαις θαλάτταις
ἐνεσπαρμένας κατέδυ πλέων ἐν ἀκατίῳ μικρῷ.

[19] Μαίανδρ‹ι›ος Olearius on basis of Diog. Laert. 9.50

to them that while victories over the barbarians called for 494
hymns, those over Greeks called for laments.

(25) Though Gorgias is said to have lived to one hundred and eight, his body was not broken by old age, but he was fit to the end of his life and he was youthful in his senses.

(26) 10. Protagoras, the sophist from Abdera, was in his home city a student of Democritus, but also enjoyed the company of the Persian magi,[48] at the time of Xerxes' expedition against Hellas. For his father was Maeandrius, who was more wealthy than most of those in Thrace, and he entertained Xerxes in his home and, by giving gifts, obtained permission from him for his son to keep company with the magi. The Persian magi do not educate those who are not Persian, unless the king should command it. It seems to me that Protagoras took from his Persian education his unlawful assertion of doubt as to whether there are gods or whether there are not, since although the magi call upon the gods in their secret rites, they oppose a public belief in divinity, because they do not wish to seem to draw their power from it. It was for this reason that he was driven from the whole land by the Athenians, either having been judged guilty, as some believe, or else when a vote had been taken against him, without him being judged. He traveled from the mainland to the islands, watching for the Athenian triremes that were scattered through every sea, and drowned sailing in a small boat.

[48] Diogenes Laertius tells this story of Democritus, not of Protagoras. As we do not have the sources on which either are drawing, it seems impossible to determine who is in error.

(27) Τὸ δὲ μισθοῦ διαλέγεσθαι πρῶτος εὗρε, πρῶτος
δὲ παρέδωκεν Ἕλλησι πρᾶγμα οὐ μεμπτόν, ἃ γὰρ
σὺν δαπάνῃ σπουδάζομεν, μᾶλλον ἀσπαζόμεθα τῶν
προῖκα. γνοὺς δὲ τὸν Πρωταγόραν ὁ Πλάτων σεμνῶς
495 μὲν ἑρμηνεύοντα, ἐνυπτιάζοντα δὲ τῇ σεμνότητι καί
που καὶ μακρολογώτερον τοῦ ξυμμέτρου, τὴν ἰδέαν
αὐτοῦ μύθῳ μακρῷ ἐχαρακτήρισεν.

(28) 11. ια΄. Ἱππίας δὲ ὁ σοφιστὴς ὁ Ἠλεῖος τὸ μὲν
μνημονικὸν οὕτω τι καὶ γηράσκων ἔρρωτο, ὡς καὶ
πεντήκοντα ὀνομάτων ἀκούσας ἅπαξ ἀπομνημονεύειν
αὐτὰ καθ᾽ ἣν ἤκουσε τάξιν, εἰσήγετο δὲ εἰς τὰς διαλέξεις γεωμετρίαν ἀστρονομίαν μουσικὴν ῥυθμούς, διελέγετο δὲ καὶ περὶ ζωγραφίας καὶ ἀγαλματοποιίας.
ταῦτα μὲν[20] ἑτέρωθι, ἐν Λακεδαίμονι δὲ γένη τε διῄει
πόλεων καὶ ἀποικίας καὶ ἔργα, ἐπεὶ οἱ Λακεδαιμόνιοι
διὰ τὸ βούλεσθαι ἄρχειν τῇ ἰδέᾳ ταύτῃ ἔχαιρον.
ἔστιν δὲ αὐτῷ καὶ Τρωικὸς διάλογος, οὗ[21] λόγος· ὁ
Νέστωρ ἐν Τροίᾳ ἁλούσῃ ὑποτίθεται Νεοπτολέμῳ τῷ
Ἀχιλλέως, ἃ χρὴ ἐπιτηδεύοντα ἄνδρ᾽ ἀγαθὸν φαίνεσθαι. πλεῖστα δὲ Ἑλλήνων πρεσβεύσας ὑπὲρ τῆς
Ἤλιδος οὐδαμοῦ κατέλυσε τὴν ἑαυτοῦ δόξαν δημηγορῶν τε καὶ διαλεγόμενος, ἀλλὰ καὶ χρήματα πλεῖστα ἐξέλεξε καὶ φυλαῖς ἐνεγράφη πόλεων μικρῶν τε
καὶ μειζόνων. παρῆλθε καὶ ἐς τὴν Ἴνυκον ὑπὲρ χρη-

[20] μέν Nesselrath   [21] Adopting with Stefec the correction,
proposed by Andronicus Callistus in MS Comensis 1.3.19, of οὗ
for οὐ. Stefec ascribes the error to the archetype.

(27) He was the first to discover charging fees for discourses, and the first who handed down to the Greeks a custom that should not be criticized, because we value more highly the pursuits on which we spend money than those that are free. Plato, knowing that Protagoras spoke in a grand style but rested upon that very grandiloquence   495
and was more longwinded than was proportionate,[49] impersonated his style in a long myth.[50]

(28) 11. The sophist Hippias of Elis had such strength in the art of memory, even in his old age, that if he once heard fifty names he could remember them in the order in which he heard them. He introduced into his discourses geometry, astronomy, music, rhythms, and he conversed also about painting and the art of sculpture. These were his subjects in other places, but in Sparta he related the types of cities and their colonies and actions, since the Spartans enjoyed this topic because of their desire to rule. And there is extant by him a Trojan dialogue, of which this is the subject: Nestor, in the captured city of Troy, instructs Neoptolemus the son of Achilles what habits of life one must practice to appear to be a good man. For Elis he went on more embassies than any other Greek, and never damaged his reputation, both when making speeches and when conversing, and he made a very great deal of money and was enrolled in the tribes of cities small and greater. He went even to Inycus for money, which is a small town

[49] This is implied in Plato's *Protagoras*, where the great sophist's eagerness to speak at length is in tension with Socrates' desire to engage him in dialogue.

[50] 320c–22d. This is the myth of Prometheus and Epimetheus in the *Protagoras*.

μάτων, τὸ δὲ πολίχνιον τοῦτο Σικελικοί εἰσιν, οὓς ὁ
Πλάτων ἐν τῷ Γοργίᾳ[22] ἐπισκώπτει. εὐδοκιμῶν δὲ καὶ
496 τὸν ἄλλον χρόνον ἔθελγε τὴν Ἑλλάδα ἐν Ὀλυμπίᾳ
λόγοις ποικίλοις καὶ πεφροντισμένοις εὖ. ἑρμήνευε δὲ
οὐκ ἐλλιπῶς, ἀλλὰ περιττῶς καὶ κατὰ φύσιν, ἐς ὀλίγα
καταφεύγων τῶν ἐκ ποιητικῆς ὀνόματα.

(29) 12. ιβ′. Προδίκου δὲ τοῦ Κείου ὄνομα τοσοῦτον
ἐπὶ σοφίᾳ ἐγένετο, ὡς καὶ τὸν Γρύλλου ἐν Βοιωτοῖς
δεθέντα ἀκροᾶσθαι διαλεγομένου, καθιστάντα ἐγγυη-
τὴν τοῦ σώματος. πρεσβεύων δὲ παρὰ Ἀθηναίοις
παρελθὼν ἐς τὸ βουλευτήριον ἱκανώτατος ἔδοξεν ἀνθρώπων, καίτοι δυσήκοον καὶ βαρὺ φθεγγόμενος.
ἀνίχνευε δὲ οὗτος τοὺς εὐπατρίδας τῶν νέων καὶ τοὺς
ἐκ τῶν βαθέων οἴκων, ὡς καὶ προξένους κεκτῆσθαι
ταύτης τῆς θήρας, χρημάτων τε γὰρ ἥττων ἐτύγχανε
καὶ ἡδοναῖς ἐδεδώκει. τὴν δὲ Ἡρακλέους αἵρεσιν τὸν
τοῦ Προδίκου λόγον οὗ κατ᾽ ἀρχὰς ἐπεμνήσθην, οὐδὲ
Ξενοφῶν ἀπηξίωσε μὴ οὐχὶ ἑρμηνεῦσαι. καὶ τί ἂν

---

[22] Restoring τῷ Γοργίᾳ, which Kayser cut in his second
edition, followed without comment by Wright. Citti plausibly
defends the MS reading as a lapse by Philostratus due to quotation
from memory. Stefec also retains the phrase and adds ἐν, the
conjecture of Diels. Olearius' correction to τῷ Ἱππίᾳ amends
Philostratus' lapse to the correct reference, *Hippias Major* 282e,
where Hippias says that at Inycus he made more than twenty
minae.

in Sicily, whose people Plato mocks in the *Gorgias*. He was
highly esteemed at other times and especially charmed   496
Greece at Olympia with speeches that were ornate and
well thought out.[51] And his style was never inadequate, but
copious and natural, taking refuge in few words drawn
from poetry.

(29) 12. The name of Prodicus of Ceos for wisdom
was so great that even the son of Gryllus, when he was
imprisoned in Boeotia, listened to his discourses, when he
secured a guarantor for himself.[52] When he went as an
ambassador to the Athenians and appeared before the
council, he seemed the most capable of men, although he
spoke in a voice that was hard to hear and deep.[53] He used
to hunt out wellborn youths and those from wealthy
houses,[54] so much that he even had assitants to help him
in the hunt, because he had a weakness for money and was
addicted to pleasures. But not even Xenophon deemed
unworthy of telling the *Choice of Heracles*,[55] the speech
of Prodicus that I mentioned at the beginning. And why

[51] See Pl. *Hp. mi.* 231; Cic. *De or.* 3.32.

[52] The "son of Gryllus" is Xenophon. Kayser wished to add the
name, but identifying such a well-known figure by patronymic
alone is very much in Philostratus' style. In *Letter* 73 (to Julia
Domna), Philostratus uses the same phrase in speaking about
Xenophon's admiration for Prodicus: ὁ τοῦ Γρύλλου φιλοτιμεῖται
πρὸς τὸν τοῦ Προδίκου Ἡρακλέα (*Ep.* 73.15–16). There is no
other evidence for Xenophon's imprisonment, though Wright
speculates that "it may have occurred in 412 when the Boeotians
took Oropus," citing Thuc. 8.60.

[53] Probably an echo of Pl. *Prt.* 316a.   [54] Cf. Pl. *Soph.*
231d on the sophist as a hunter of wealthy youths.

[55] Xen. *Mem.* 2.1.21. See above, *VS* 482–83.

χαρακτηρίζοιμεν τὴν τοῦ Προδίκου γλῶτταν, Ξενο-
φῶντος αὐτὴν ἱκανῶς ὑπογράφοντος;

497   (30) 13. ιγ΄. Πῶλον δὲ τὸν Ἀκραγαντῖνον Γοργίας
σοφιστὴν ἐξεμελέτησε πολλῶν, ὥς φασι, χρημάτων,
καὶ γὰρ δὴ καὶ τῶν πλουτούντων ὁ Πῶλος. εἰσὶ δ᾽ οἳ
φασι καὶ τὰ πάρισα καὶ τὰ ἀντίθετα καὶ τὰ ὁμοιοτέλευτα Πῶλον εὑρηκέναι πρῶτον, οὐκ ὀρθῶς λέγοντες, τῇ γὰρ τοιᾷδε ἀγλαΐᾳ τοῦ λόγου Πῶλος εὑρη-
μένῃ κατεχρήσατο, ὅθεν ὁ Πλάτων διαπτύων αὐτὸν
ἐπὶ τῇ φιλοτιμίᾳ ταύτῃ φησίν· "ὦ λῷστε Πῶλε, ἵνα
προσείπω σε κατὰ σέ."

(31) 14. ιδ΄. Οἱ δὲ καὶ Θρασύμαχον τὸν Καλχη-
δόνιον ἐν σοφισταῖς γράφοντες δοκοῦσί μοι παρα-
κούειν Πλάτωνος ταὐτὸν εἶναι φάσκοντος λέοντα ξυ-
ρεῖν καὶ συκοφαντεῖν Θρασύμαχον· δικογραφίαν γὰρ
αὐτῷ προφέροντός ἐστι δήπου ταῦτα καὶ τὸ ἐν δικαστηρίοις συκοφαντοῦντα τρίβεσθαι.

498   (32) 15. ιε΄. Ἀντιφῶντα δὲ τὸν Ῥαμνούσιον οὐκ οἶδ᾽
εἴτε χρηστὸν δεῖ προσειπεῖν εἴτε φαῦλον. χρηστὸς
μὲν γὰρ προσειρήσθω διὰ τάδε· ἐστρατήγησε πλεῖστα, ἐνίκησε πλεῖστα, ἑξήκοντα τριήρεσι πεπληρωμέ-
ναις ηὔξησεν Ἀθηναίοις τὸ ναυτικόν, ἱκανώτατος ἀνθρώπων ἔδοξεν εἰπεῖν τε καὶ γνῶναι· διὰ μὲν δὴ ταῦτα

56 Pl. *Grg.* 467b. In the Greek, the sentence contains two
jingles of sound like those that Polus and his school employed. Cf.
Pl. *Symp.* 185.

should I describe the language of Prodicus, when Xenophon has given so complete a sketch of it?

(30) 13. Polus of Agrigentum was trained as a sophist ⟨497⟩
by Gorgias at great expense, so they say, and in fact Polus
came from a wealthy family. There are some who say that
Polus was the first to discover balancing clauses and antitheses and homioteleuta, but they are mistaken. Polus
merely abused this kind of ornament of speech that had
already been discovered. For this reason Plato, spitting
upon him because of this affectation, says, "O polite Polus,
to address you in your own style."[56]

(31) 14. Those who enlist Thrasymachus of Chalcedon
among the sophists seem to me not to listen to Plato,
who says that shaving a lion is the same thing as bringing
false charges against Thrasymachus.[57] Saying this clearly
amounts to reproaching him for writing legal speeches and
spending his time in the courts contriving false accusations.

(32) 15. As for Antiphon of Rhamnus, I do not know ⟨498⟩
whether one should call him a good man or bad. Let him
be declared good for the following reasons: he very often
held military commands, was victorious very often, increased the Athenian fleet by sixty fully equipped triremes, seemed the most capable of men at speaking and
at inventing themes. For these reasons he seems to me

---

57 Pl. *Resp.* 341c. Despite Philostratus' assertion, Cicero himself enlisted Thrasymachus among the sophists, who praises him
highly as the *princeps inveniendi* (*Orator* 52), as Olearius already
noted (1709, 497n3). See this same note for further evidence of
Thrasymachus' standing as a sophist/*rhētor*.

ἐμοί τε ἐπαινετέος καὶ ἑτέρῳ. κακὸς δ' αὖ²³ εἰκότως διὰ
τάδε· κατέλυσε τὴν δημοκρατίαν, ἐδούλωσε τὸν Ἀθηναίων δῆμον, ἐλακώνισε κατ' ἀρχὰς μὲν ἀφανῶς,
ὕστερον δ' ἐπιδήλως, τυράννων τετρακοσίων σμῆ-
νος²⁴ ἐπαφῆκε τοῖς Ἀθηναίων πράγμασιν.

(33) Ῥητορικὴν δὲ τὸν Ἀντιφῶντα οἱ μὲν οὐκ οὖσαν
εὑρεῖν, οἱ δ' εὑρημένην αὐξῆσαι, γενέσθαι τε αὐτὸν οἱ
μὲν αὐτομαθῶς σοφόν, οἱ δὲ ἐκ πατρός. πατέρα δὴ
αὐτῷ Σόφιλον διδάσκαλον ῥητορικῶν λόγων, ὃς ἄλλους τε τῶν ἐν δυνάμει καὶ τὸν τοῦ Κλεινίου ἐπαίδευσε. πιθανώτατος δὲ ὁ Ἀντιφῶν γενόμενος καὶ
προσρηθεὶς Νέστωρ ἐπὶ τῷ περὶ παντὸς εἰπὼν ἂν
πεῖσαι νηπενθεῖς ἀκροάσεις ἐπήγγειλεν, ὡς οὐδὲν
οὕτω δεινὸν ἐρούντων ἄχος, ὃ μὴ ἐξέλοι τῆς γνώμης.
499 καθάπτεται δὲ ἡ κωμῳδία τοῦ Ἀντιφῶντος ὡς δεινοῦ
τὰ δικανικὰ καὶ λόγους κατὰ τοῦ δικαίου ξυγκειμένους ἀποδιδομένου πολλῶν χρημάτων αὐτοῖς μάλιστα τοῖς κινδυνεύουσιν. τουτὶ δὲ ὁποίαν ἔχει φύσιν,
ἐγὼ δηλώσω· ἄνθρωποι κατὰ μὲν τὰς ἄλλας ἐπι-
στήμας καὶ τέχνας τιμῶσι τοὺς ἐν ἑκάστῃ αὐτῶν
προὔχοντας καὶ θαυμάζουσι μὲν τῶν ἰατρῶν τοὺς

---

²³ αὖ Reiske   ²⁴ δῆμον ω; σμῆνος Nesselrath

⁵⁸ This account of Antiphon as the contriver of the whole
scheme of the oligarchic revolution, and of his rhetorical ability,
is probably derived from Thuc. 8.68.   ⁵⁹ Alcibiades.
⁶⁰ Νηπενθής is an epic word, and the reference is to the
φάρμακον νηπενθές used by Helen (Hom. Od. 4.221). The no-

worthy of praise and to any other. But he could reasonably be declared bad for these reasons: he destroyed the democracy,[58] he enslaved the Athenian people, he sided with Sparta, secretly at first but later openly, he let loose on the public life of Athens the swarm of the Four Hundred Tyrants.

(33) Some say that Antiphon discovered rhetoric, which did not exist before, others that he extended it when it had already been discovered, and some say that his wisdom was self-taught, while others say he learned from his father. They say that his father was Sophilus the teacher of rhetorical speeches, who taught both many other powerful people and the son of Cleinias.[59] Antiphon was the most persuasive speaker and was nicknamed Nestor because he could persuade his hearers when he spoke on any topic. And he proclaimed Speeches to Quell Pain,[60] saying that no one could tell a grief so terrible that he could not take it from the mind.[61] Comedy latches onto Antiphon because he was cunning in legal matters and provided, for a great deal of money, speeches that were contrary to justice for those whose cases were especially precarious. What the nature of the charge is, I shall demonstrate: in the case of the other sciences and arts, people honor those who are outstanding in each of them. They marvel, for instance, more at physicians who are more skillful than at

499

---

tion of language as a drug to cure pain occurs several times in Philostratus (see *VS* 480 above, and *VA* 7.26). On these occasions Philostratus likely draws the idea ultimately from Antiphon and from Gorg. *Hel.* 14. Pseudo-Plutarch (*Vit. Antiph.* 833c) states that he practiced an art of dispelling grief (τέχνη ἀλυπίας) in Corinth. See Furley 1992.

[61] A paraphrase of Eur. *Or.* 1–3.

μᾶλλον παρὰ τοὺς ἧττον, θαυμάζουσι δ' ἐν μαντικῇ
καὶ μουσικῇ τὸν σοφώτερον, τὴν αὐτὴν καὶ περὶ
τεκτονικῆς καὶ πασῶν βαναύσων τιθέμενοι ψῆφον,
ῥητορικὴν δ' ἐπαινοῦσι μέν, ὑποπτεύουσι δὲ ὡς παν-
οῦργον καὶ φιλοχρήματον καὶ κατὰ τοῦ δικαίου ξυγ-
κειμένην. γιγνώσκουσι δ' οὕτω περὶ τῆς τέχνης οὐχ
οἱ πολλοὶ μόνον, ἀλλὰ καὶ τῶν σπουδαίων οἱ ἐλλογι-
μώτατοι· καλοῦσι γοῦν δεινοὺς ῥήτορας τοὺς ἱκανῶς
μὲν συνιέντας, ἱκανῶς δὲ ἑρμηνεύοντας, οὐκ εὔφημον
ἐπωνυμίαν τιθέμενοι τῷ πλεονεκτήματι. τούτου δὲ φύσιν τοιαύτην ἔχοντος οὐκ ἀπεικὸς ἦν, οἶμαι, γενέσθαι
καὶ τὸν Ἀντιφῶντα κωμῳδίας λόγον αὐτὰ μάλιστα
κωμῳδούσης τὰ λόγου ἄξια.

(34) Ἀπέθανε μὲν οὖν περὶ Σικελίαν ὑπὸ Διονυσίου
τοῦ τυράννου, τὰς δ' αἰτίας, ἐφ' αἷς ἀπέθανεν, Ἀντιφῶντι μᾶλλον ἢ Διονυσίῳ προσγράφωμεν.[25] διεφαύ-
λιζε γὰρ τὰς τοῦ Διονυσίου τραγῳδίας, ἐφ' αἷς ἐκεῖνος ἐφρόνει μεῖζον ἢ ἐπὶ τῷ τυραννεῖν. σπουδάζοντος
δὲ τοῦ τυράννου περὶ εὐγενείας χαλκοῦ καὶ ἐρομένου
τοὺς παρόντας, τίς ἤπειρος ἢ νῆσος τὸν ἄριστον χαλ-
κὸν φύει, παρατυχὼν ὁ Ἀντιφῶν τῷ λόγῳ, "ἐγὼ ἄριστον," ἔφη, "οἶμαι[26] τὸν Ἀθήνησιν, οὗ γεγόνασιν αἱ
Ἁρμοδίου καὶ Ἀριστογείτονος εἰκόνες." ἐπὶ μὲν δὴ
τούτοις ἀπέθανεν, ὡς ὑφέρπων τὸν Διονύσιον καὶ τρέπων ἐπ' αὐτὸν τοὺς Σικελιώτας. ἥμαρτε δὲ ὁ Ἀντιφῶν

500

____

[25] προσγράφομεν ω; προσγράφωμεν Kayser
[26] οἶμαι Jones (post Ἀθήνησιν); οἶδα Callistus

76

those who are less so, and marvel more at the one who is more expert in divination and music, and in the case of carpentry and all of the mechanical skills they cast their vote in the same way. But in the case of rhetoric they praise it yet are suspicious of it, considering it shifty and greedy and established contrary to justice. And it is not only the crowd who think this way about the art, but also the most educated of serious people. At any rate they call those who are capable at inventing and in interpreting themes "cunning rhetoricians," giving to their achievement a name that is far from flattering. Seeing that such conditions exist, it was not unlikely, I think, that Antiphon like others would become a subject for comedy, which chooses to laugh at things worth speaking about.

(34) He was put to death in Sicily by the tyrant Dionysius,[62] but let us ascribe the reasons for which he died to Antiphon more than to Dionysius, because he used to say that the tragedies of Dionysius were worthless, on which he prided himself more than on his power as tyrant. When the tyrant was intent on learning the best source of bronze and asked those present, "what land or island produces the best bronze?," Antiphon happened to be present at the conversation and said, "I think the best is at Athens, from which the statues of Harmodius Aristogeiton are made."[63] So for these reasons he was put to death, on the grounds that he was stealthily plotting against Dionysius and turning the Sicilians against him. Antiphon was in the wrong

500

---

[62] Philostratus confuses the orator Antiphon with a tragic poet of the same name, who was put to death by Dionysius (Arist. *Rh.* 1385a).   [63] Who overthrew the tyrants at Athens.

77

πρῶτον μὲν τυράννῳ προσκρούων, ὑφ' ᾧ ζῆν ᾔρητο
μᾶλλον ἢ οἴκοι δημοκρατεῖσθαι, ἔπειτα Σικελιώτας
μὲν ἐλευθερῶν, Ἀθηναίους δὲ δουλούμενος. καὶ μὴν
καὶ τοῦ τραγῳδίαν ποιεῖν ἀπάγων τὸν Διονύσιον ἀπῆγεν αὐτὸν τοῦ ῥᾳθυμεῖν. αἱ γὰρ τοιαίδε σπουδαὶ
ῥᾴθυμοι, καὶ οἱ τύραννοι δὲ αἱρετώτεροι τοῖς ἀρχομένοις ἀνιέμενοι μᾶλλον ἢ ξυντείνοντες, εἰ γὰρ ἀνήσου-
σιν, ἧττον μὲν ἀποκτενοῦσιν, ἧττον δὲ δράξονταί τε
καὶ ἁρπάσονται, τύραννος δὲ τραγῳδίαις ἐπιτιθέμε-
νος ἰατρῷ εἰκάσθω νοσοῦντι μέν, ἑαυτὸν δὲ θεραπεύ-
οντι. αἱ γὰρ μυθοποιίαι καὶ αἱ μονῳδίαι καὶ οἱ ῥυθμοὶ
τῶν χορῶν καὶ ἡ τῶν ἠθῶν μίμησις, ὧν ἀνάγκη τὰ
πλείω χρηστὰ φαίνεσθαι, μετακαλεῖ τοὺς τυράννους
τοῦ ἀπαραιτήτου καὶ σφοδροῦ, καθάπερ αἱ φαρμακο-
ποσίαι τὰς νόσους. ταῦτα μὴ κατηγορίαν Ἀντιφῶντος, ἀλλὰ ξυμβουλίαν εἰς πάντας ἡγώμεθα τοῦ μὴ
ἐκκαλεῖσθαι τὰς τυραννίδας, μηδὲ ἐς ὀργὴν ἄγειν
ἤθη ὠμά.

(35) Λόγοι δ' αὐτοῦ δικανικοὶ μὲν πλείους, ἐν οἷς ἡ
δεινότης καὶ πᾶν τὸ ἐκ τέχνης ἔγκειται, σοφιστικοὶ δὲ
καὶ ἕτεροι μέν, σοφιστικώτερος δὲ ὁ ὑπὲρ τῆς ὁμονοίας, ἐν ᾧ γνωμολογίαι τε λαμπραὶ καὶ φιλόσοφοι
σεμνή τε ἀπαγγελία καὶ ἐπηνθισμένη ποιητικοῖς ὀνόμασι καὶ τὰ ἀποτάδην ἑρμηνευόμενα παραπλήσια
τῶν πεδίων τοῖς λείοις.

501   (36) 16. ιϛ'. Κριτίας δὲ ὁ σοφιστὴς εἰ μὲν κατέλυσε
τὸν Ἀθηναίων τὸν δῆμον, οὔπω κακός—καταλυθείη
γὰρ ἂν καὶ ὑφ' ἑαυτοῦ δῆμος οὕτω τι ἐπηρμένος, ὡς

firstly because he came into conflict with a tyrant under whom he chose to live, rather than live under a democracy at home. Then there is the fact that he tried to free the Sicilians, but to enslave the Athenians. What is more, by trying to lead Dionysius away from writing tragedies he drew him away from being easygoing. For such undertakings are relaxing, and tyrants who are relaxed are preferable to their subjects to those who are tense. If they will relax they will put fewer people to death, they will lay hold of fewer and plunder less. A tyrant applying himself to tragedies should be compared to a doctor who is ill, but is treating himself. This is because the writing of myths and the monodies and the rhythms of the chorus and the imitation of characters, the majority of whom must represent good morals, all call tyrants back from their merciless and vehement temper, just as taking medicine affects diseases. Let us consider these points not as a case against Antiphon, but as counsel to everyone not to provoke tyrants nor to lead savage characters to anger.

(35) Very many of his legal speeches are extant, in which his rhetorical power and every aspect of the art are evident. But there are sophistic speeches too, both some others and especially his speech *On Concord*, in which are brilliant philosophical aphorisms and an elevated eloquence adorned with the flowers of poetic vocabulary, and their extended style makes them seem like the smooth plains.

(36) 16. The sophist Critias, even if he did bring the Athenian democracy to an end, was not necessarily a bad man for that reason, for the democracy would have been

501

μηδὲ τῶν κατὰ νόμους ἀρχόντων ἀκροᾶσθαι—ἀλλ'
ἐπεὶ λαμπρῶς μὲν ἐλακώνισε, προυδίδου δὲ τὰ ἱερά,
καθήρει δὲ διὰ Λυσάνδρου τὰ τείχη, οὓς δ' ἤλαυνε
τῶν Ἀθηναίων τὸ στῆναί ποι τῆς Ἑλλάδος ἀφῃρεῖτο
πόλεμον Λακωνικὸν προειπὼν²⁷ ἐς πάντας, εἴ τις τὸν²⁸
Ἀθηναῖον φεύγοντα δέξαιτο, ὠμότητι δὲ καὶ μιαιφο-
νίᾳ τοὺς τριάκοντα ὑπερεβάλλετο βουλεύματός τε
ἀτόπου τοῖς Λακεδαιμονίοις ξυνελάμβανεν, ὡς μηλό-
βοτος ἡ Ἀττικὴ ἀποφανθείη τῆς τῶν ἀνθρώπων
ἀγέλης ἐκκενωθεῖσα, κάκιστος ἀνθρώπων ἔμοιγε φαίνεται ξυμπάντων, ὧν ἐπὶ κακίᾳ ὄνομα. καὶ εἰ μὲν
ἀπαίδευτος ὢν ἐς τάδε ὑπήχθη, ἔρρωτο ἂν ὁ λόγος
τοῖς φάσκουσιν ὑπὸ Θετταλίας καὶ τῆς ἐκείνῃ ὁμιλίας
παρεφθορέναι αὐτόν, τὰ γὰρ ἀπαίδευτα ἤθη εὐπαρά-
γωγα πάντως ἐς βίου αἵρεσιν· ἐπεὶ δὲ ἄριστα μὲν ἦν
πεπαιδευμένος, γνώμας δὲ πλείστας ἑρμηνεύων, ἐς
Δρωπίδην δ' ἀναφέρων, ὃς μετὰ Σόλωνα Ἀθηναίων
ἦρξεν, οὐκ ἂν διαφύγοι παρὰ τοῖς πολλοῖς αἰτίαν τὸ
μὴ οὐ κακίᾳ φύσεως ἁμαρτεῖν ταῦτα. καὶ γὰρ ἂν
κἀκεῖνο ἄτοπον Σωκράτει μὲν τῷ Σωφρονίσκου μὴ
ὁμοιωθῆναι αὐτόν, ᾧ πλεῖστα δὴ συνεφιλοσόφησε
σοφωτάτῳ τε καὶ δικαιοτάτῳ τῶν ἐφ' ἑαυτοῦ δόξαντι,

27 <ἀν>ειπών Kayser; <προ>ειπών Stefec
28 τόν ω; τιν' Boter

64 Plato remarks upon the "disorder and lack of discipline"
(ἀταξία καὶ ἀκολασία) of the Thessalians (Cri. 53d).

80

destroyed from within, since it had become so swollen up
with pride that it would not listen to those ruling in accordance with the laws. But since he conspicuously took
the side of Sparta, and betrayed the holy sanctuaries, and
pulled down the walls by the agency of Lysander, and he
deprived those whom he had exiled from Athens of any
place of rest in Greece, by proclaiming that Sparta would
wage war on anyone who harbored an Athenian exile, and
in savagery and bloodthirstiness he surpassed the Thirty
Tyrants, and he shared an insane plan with the Spartans,
to make Attica look like a sheep pasture, by emptying it of
its human flock—for all these reasons he seems to me the
most evil of all men who possess a reputation for evil. If
he had been led into these actions because he lacked education, there would be some force to the argument of
those who allege that he had been corrupted by Thessaly
and the company he kept there,[64] since uneducated characters are easily led to choose any way of life at all. But
since he was educated to the highest level, and framed
many philosophical aphorisms, and traced his ancestry
back to Dropides, who was archon at Athens after Solon,
he could not be acquitted of the charge in most people's
eyes that he committed these crimes out of innate evil. It
would otherwise be a strange thing that he did not come
to resemble Socrates, son of Sophroniscus, with whom he
philosophized most of all, and who was reputed to be both
the wisest and the most just man of his time,[65] but rather

[65] Philostratus suggests, but does not quite echo, the last
words of Plato's *Phaedo*: τῶν τότε ὧν ἐπειράθημεν ἀρίστου καὶ
ἄλλως φρονιμωτάτου καὶ δικαιοτάτου (*Phd.* 118a16–17).

81

Θετταλοῖς δ' ὁμοιωθῆναι, παρ' οἷς ἀγερωχία κατὰ
κράτος²⁹ καὶ τυραννικὰ ἐν οἴνῳ σπουδάζεται. ἀλλ'
ὅμως οὐδὲ Θετταλοὶ σοφίας ἠμέλουν, ἀλλ' ἐγοργία-
ζον ἐν Θετταλίᾳ μικραὶ καὶ μείζους πόλεις ἐς Γοργίαν
502 ὁρῶσαι τὸν Λεοντῖνον, μετέβαλον δ' ἂν καὶ ἐς τὸ κρι-
τιάζειν, εἴ τινα τῆς ἑαυτοῦ σοφίας ἐπίδειξιν ὁ Κριτίας
παρ' αὐτοῖς ἐποιεῖτο. ὁ δὲ ἠμέλει μὲν τούτου, βαρυ-
τέρας δ' αὐτοῖς ἐποίει τὰς ὀλιγαρχίας διαλεγόμενος
τοῖς ἐκεῖ δυνατοῖς καὶ καθαπτόμενος μὲν δημοκρατίας
ἁπάσης, διαβάλλων δ' Ἀθηναίους, ὡς πλεῖστα ἀνθρώπων ἁμαρτάνοντας, ὥστε ἐνθυμουμένῳ ταῦτα Κριτίας
ἂν εἴη Θετταλοὺς διεφθορὼς μᾶλλον ἢ Κριτίαν Θετ-
ταλοί.

(37) Ἀπέθανε μὲν οὖν ὑπὸ τῶν ἀμφὶ Θρασύβουλον,
οἳ κατῆγον ἀπὸ Φυλῆς τὸν δῆμον, δοκεῖ δ' ἐνίοις ἀνὴρ
ἀγαθὸς γενέσθαι παρὰ τὴν τελευτήν, ἐπειδὴ ἐνταφίῳ
τῇ τυραννίδι ἐχρήσατο· ἐμοὶ δὲ ἀποπεφάνθω μηδένα
ἀνθρώπων καλῶς δὴ ἀποθανεῖν ὑπὲρ ὧν οὐκ ὀρθῶς
εἵλετο, δι' ἅ μοι δοκεῖ καὶ ἡ σοφία τοῦ ἀνδρὸς καὶ τὰ
φροντίσματα ἧττον σπουδασθῆναι τοῖς Ἕλλησιν· εἰ
γὰρ μὴ ὁμολογήσει ὁ λόγος τῷ ἤθει, ἀλλοτρίᾳ
γλώττῃ δόξομεν φθέγγεσθαι, ὥσπερ οἱ αὐλοί.

(38) Τὴν δὲ ἰδέαν τοῦ λόγου δογματίας ὁ Κριτίας
καὶ πολυγνώμων σεμνολογῆσαί τε ἱκανώτατος οὐ τὴν

---

²⁹ κατὰ κράτος Jahn; καὶ ἄκρατος ω

came to resemble the Thessalians, who are arrogant in their use of power and tyrannical in their wine drinking. Nevertheless not even the Thessalians used to neglect wisdom, but cities small and great in Thessaly Gorgianized, looking to Gorgias of Leontini, but would have Critianized, if Critias had made any display of his own wisdom among them.[66] He neglected this, but instead made the oligarchs more oppressive of the people, by conversing with those in power there and attacking democracy in general, and slandering the Athenians, saying that they committed more crimes than any other people. For one who bears these things in mind, Critias would be the one who corrupted the Thessalians, rather than the Thessalians Critias.

502

(37) He died at the hands of the followers of Thrasybulus, who restored the democracy from Phyle. He seems to some to have become a good man at the end, since his tyranny became his shroud.[67] But let me declare that no one dies nobly for a cause that he was wrong to choose. For this reason it seems to me that the wisdom of the man and his intellectual works are less esteemed by the Greeks. If speech does not align with character, we will seem to speak with a tongue not our own, like auloi.[68]

(38) Regarding the style of his oratory, Critias was fond of brief and sententious sayings, and was highly capable in

[66] Philostratus also mentions the Thessalian love of Gorgias in his letter to Julia Domna (*Letter* 73) and in the life of Scopelian below, *VS* 521.　　[67] That is, he lost his life in its cause. For this favorite figure, cf. *VS* 590 and *Gymn.* 34; it is derived from Isoc. *Arch.* 45.　　[68] An echo of Aeschin. *In Ctes.* 623; cf. 1 Cor. 13:1: "I am become as sounding brass or a tinkling cymbal."

διθυραμβώδη σεμνολογίαν, οὐδὲ καταφεύγουσαν ἐς
503 τὰ ἐκ ποιητικῆς ὀνόματα, ἀλλ' ἐκ τῶν κυριωτάτων
συγκειμένην καὶ κατὰ φύσιν ἔχουσαν. ὁρῶ τὸν ἄνδρα
καὶ βραχυλογοῦντα ἱκανῶς καὶ δεινῶς καθαπτόμενον
ἐν ἀπολογίας ἤθει, ἀττικίζοντά τε οὐκ ἀκρατῶς οὐδὲ
ἐκφύλως—τὸ γὰρ ἀπειρόκαλον ἐν τῷ ἀττικίζειν βάρβαρον—ἀλλ' ὥσπερ ἀκτίνων αὐγαὶ τὰ Ἀττικὰ ὀνόματα διαφαίνεται τοῦ λόγου. καὶ τὸ ἀσυνδέτως δὲ
χωρίῳ προσβαλεῖν Κριτίου ὥρα, καὶ τὸ παραδόξως
μὲν ἐνθυμηθῆναι, παραδόξως δ' ἀπαγγεῖλαι Κριτίου
ἀγών, τὸ δὲ τοῦ λόγου πνεῦμα ἐλλιπέστερον μέν, ἡδὺ
δὲ καὶ λεῖον, ὥσπερ ἡ τοῦ Ζεφύρου αὔρα.

(39) 17. ιζ'. Ἡ δὲ Σειρὴν ἡ ἐφεστηκυῖα τῷ Ἰσοκράτους τοῦ σοφιστοῦ σήματι, ἐφέστηκε δὲ καὶ οἷον
ᾄδουσα, πειθὼ κατηγορεῖ τοῦ ἀνδρός, ἣν συνεβάλετο
ῥητορικοῖς νόμοις καὶ ἤθεσι, πάρισα καὶ ἀντίθετα
καὶ ὁμοιοτέλευτα οὐχ εὑρὼν πρῶτος, ἀλλ' εὑρημένοις
εὖ χρησάμενος, ἐπεμελήθη δὲ καὶ περιβολῆς καὶ
ῥυθμῶν[30] καὶ συνθήκης καὶ κρότου. ταυτὶ δ' ἡτοίμασέ
504 που καὶ τὴν Δημοσθένους γλῶτταν· Δημοσθένης γὰρ
μαθητὴς μὲν Ἰσαίου, ζηλωτὴς δὲ Ἰσοκράτους γενόμενος ὑπερεβάλετο αὐτὸν θυμῷ καὶ ἐπιφορᾷ καὶ πε-

---

[30] ῥυθμοῦ Callistus

an elevated style, but it was not the elevation of dithyramb nor one resorting to poetic words, but composed from the most appropriate ones and in accordance with nature. I   503
see the man also as capable in concise speaking and he could be powerful in attack, even in the character appropriate to a defense speech. And he did not Atticize excessively nor using bizarre words (because excess in Atticizing is truly barbarous),[69] but the Attic words shone through his speech like rays of sunlight. The beauty particular to Critias leaps without connectives from one part of a speech to another,[70] and he aims for the unexpected in thought and also in expression. But the energy of his speech was rather lacking, though it was pleasant and gentle, like the breath of Zephyrus.

(39) 17. The Siren that stands on the tomb of the sophist Isocrates—and it stands as though singing—declares the man's power of persuasion, which he combined with the conventions and customs of rhetoric. He was not the first to discover balancing clauses and antitheses and homioteleuta, but he employed well these things that had already been discovered. He also practiced hard at rhetorical amplification[71] and rhythms and structure and a percussive effect. These techniques also developed, I suppose, the speech of Demosthenes, because Demosthenes   504
was a student of Isaeus, but it was Isocrates he imitated, and he surpassed him in passion and impetuosity, in am-

[69] Philostratus praises the style of Apollonius of Tyana in very similar terms, similarly emphasizing his avoidance of hyper-Atticizing (VA 1.17).   [70] See the Rhetorical Glossary for the practice of προσβολαί.   [71] For amplification (περιβολή) and a percussive effect (κρότος), see the Rhetorical Glossary.

ριβολῇ καὶ ταχυτῆτι λόγου τε καὶ ἐννοίας. σεμνότης
δ᾽ ἡ μὲν Δημοσθένους ἐπεστραμμένη μᾶλλον, ἡ δὲ
Ἰσοκράτους ἁβροτέρα τε καὶ ἡδίων. παράδειγμα δὲ
ποιώμεθα τῆς μὲν Δημοσθένους σεμνότητος· "πέρας
μὲν γὰρ ἅπασιν ἀνθρώποις ἐστὶ τοῦ βίου θάνατος,
κἂν ἐν οἰκίσκῳ τις αὑτὸν καθείρξας τηρῇ, δεῖ δὲ τοὺς
ἀγαθοὺς ἄνδρας ἐγχειρεῖν μὲν ἅπασιν ἀεὶ τοῖς καλοῖς
τὴν ἀγαθὴν προβαλλομένους ἐλπίδα, φέρειν δέ, ἃ ἂν
ὁ θεὸς διδῷ, γενναίως." ἡ δὲ Ἰσοκράτους σεμνότης
ὧδε κεκόσμηται· "τῆς γὰρ γῆς ἁπάσης τῆς ὑπὸ τῷ
κόσμῳ κειμένης δίχα τετμημένης, καὶ τῆς μὲν Ἀσίας,
τῆς δὲ Εὐρώπης καλουμένης, τὴν ἡμίσειαν ἐκ τῶν
συνθηκῶν εἴληφεν, ὥσπερ πρὸς τὸν Δία τὴν χώραν
νεμόμενος."

505   (40) Τὰ μὲν οὖν πολιτικὰ ὤκνει καὶ ἀπεφοίτα τῶν
ἐκκλησιῶν διά τε τὸ ἐλλιπὲς τοῦ φθέγματος, διά τε
τὸν Ἀθήνησιν φθόνον ἀντιπολιτευόμενον αὐτοῖς μάλιστα τοῖς σοφώτερόν τι ἑτέρου ἀγορεύσουσιν. ὅμως δ᾽
οὐκ ἀπεσπούδαζε τῶν κοινῶν· τόν τε γὰρ Φίλιππον,
ἐν οἷς πρὸς αὐτὸν ἔγραφεν, Ἀθηναίοις δήπου διωρθοῦτο, καὶ οἷς περὶ τῆς εἰρήνης συνέγραφεν, ἀνεσκεύ-
αζε τοὺς Ἀθηναίους τῆς θαλάττης, ὡς κακῶς ἐπ᾽[31]
αὐτῇ ἀκούοντας. ὁ Πανηγυρικός τε αὐτῷ λόγος, ὃν
διῆλθεν Ὀλυμπίασι τὴν Ἑλλάδα πείθων ἐπὶ τὴν
Ἀσίαν στρατεύειν παυσαμένους τῶν οἴκοι ἐγκλη-

[31] ἐπ᾽ Jones; ἐν ω

plification, and in speed of both language and thought. The grand style of Demosthenes is more vehement, but that of Isocrates is more graceful and more pleasant. Let us give an example of the grand style of Demosthenes: "The limit of life for all people is death, even if one should close himself in a tiny room, but good men must always try their hands at all noble deeds, setting their good hope before them, but bear whatever god gives, nobly."[72] By contrast the grand style of Isocrates was adorned like this: "Since the whole earth that lies under the heavens has been divided in two, part called Asia, and part Europe, he has taken half by the treaty, as if dividing the land with Zeus."[73]

(40) He shrank from politics and avoided assemblies   505
because of the inadequacy of his voice, and because of the envious opposition in Athenian political life, directed especially at those who were cleverer than the next person at speaking.[74] Nevertheless, he took a keen interest in public affairs. For instance, in the letters that he wrote to Philip he tried to reconcile him with the Athenians, and in the his writings about peace, he tried to shift the Athenians from their focus on the sea, since it was bad for their reputation. Then there is the *Panegyric Oration* that he delivered at Olympia, attempting to persuade Greece to make war against Asia and to cease from domestic squab-

[72] Dem. *De cor.* 97. This is a favorite passage with the rhetoricians; cf. Lucian, *Dem.* 5; Hermog. *Id.* 222 Walz.

[73] *Paneg.* 179. Note the similar endings of the participles.

[74] This may once more recall Plato's *Protagoras*, where the sophist claims that the envy aroused by the art of sophistry has often led its practitioners to conceal themselves (*Prt.* 316d).

μάτων. οὗτος μὲν οὖν εἰ καὶ κάλλιστος λόγων, αἰτίαν
ὅμως παραδέδωκεν ὡς ἐκ τῶν Γοργίᾳ σπουδασθέντων
ἐς τὴν αὐτὴν ὑπόθεσιν ξυντεθείς. ἄριστα δὲ τῶν Ἰσοκράτους φροντισμάτων ὅ τε Ἀρχίδαμος ξύγκειται καὶ
ὁ Ἀμάρτυρος, τοῦ μὲν γὰρ διήκει φρόνημα Λακεδαι-
μονίους³² τῶν Λευκτρικῶν ἀναφέρον καὶ οὐκ ἀκριβῆ
μόνον τὰ ὀνόματα, ἀλλὰ καὶ ἡ ξυνθήκη λαμπρά, ἐναγώνιος δὲ ὁ λόγος, ὡς καὶ τὸ μυθῶδες αὐτοῦ μέρος,
τὸ περὶ τὸν Ἡρακλέα καὶ τὰς βοῦς, σὺν ἐπιστροφῇ
ἡρμηνεῦσθαι, ὁ δὲ Ἀμάρτυρος ἰσχὺν ἐνδείκνυται κε-
κολασμένην ἐς ῥυθμούς, νόημα γὰρ ἐκ νοήματος ἐς
περιόδους ἰσοκώλους τελευτᾷ.

506   (41) Ἀκροαταὶ τοῦ ἀνδρὸς τούτου πολλοὶ μέν, ἐλλογιμώτατος δ᾽ Ὑπερείδης ὁ ῥήτωρ, Θεόπομπον γὰρ
τὸν ἐκ Χίου καὶ τὸν Κυμαῖον Ἔφορον οὔτ᾽ ἂν δια-
βάλοιμι οὔτ᾽ αὖ θαυμάσαιμι. οἱ δὲ ἡγούμενοι τὴν κω-
μῳδίαν καθάπτεσθαι τοῦ ἀνδρός ὡς αὐλοποιοῦ ἁμαρ-
τάνουσιν· πατὴρ μὲν γὰρ αὐτῷ Θεόδωρος ἦν, ὃν
ἐκάλουν αὐλοποιὸν Ἀθήνησιν, αὐτὸς δὲ οὔτε αὐλοὺς

³² Λακεδαιμονίους Eugenicus; Λακεδαιμονίοις ω; del.
³Kayser

75 This is the subtitle of the speech *Against Euthynous*, and
was so called because the plaintiff had no evidence to produce
and depended on logical argument.   76 The tenth labor of
Heracles was to carry off the oxen of Geryon. See Apollod. *Bibl.*
2.5.10. It was also the subject of Stesichorus' *Geryoneis*.

77 Despite Hypereides' standing as an orator in ancient judg-

bles—this, although it was the finest of speeches, has given rise to the charge that it was put together from Gorgias' teachings on the same subject. The best of Isocrates' compositions are the *Archidamus* and *Without Witnesses*.[75] In the former of these he conveyed the intention of lifting up the Spartans from the defeat at Leuctra, and it was not only exact in its choice of words, but the composition also was brilliant, and the speech as a whole full of combative energy, so that even the mythic portion of it, that concerning Heracles and the oxen,[76] was developed with intensity. The speech *Without Witnesses* shows power restrained into rhythm, as one idea follows another into periods of equal length.

(41) The students of this man were many, but the most 506 famous was Hypereides the orator.[77] I would neither deride nor marvel at Theopompus of Chios and Ephorus of Cumae.[78] Those who believe that comedy attacks the man as an aulos maker are wrong.[79] In fact it was his father Theodorus whom they used to call "aulos maker" in Athens, but he himself neither knew about auloi nor about

ments, we have only large fragments of surviving speeches. He appears not to have been a major point of reference for Philostratus, who mentions him on only one further occasion, as part of a topic for a declamation at VS 588.   [78] These two, along with Anaximenes of Lampsacus, were the main practitioners of a Hellenistic rhetorical history of which very little remains.

[79] [Plut.] *Vit. Dec. Orat.* 836e states that Isocrates' father was of the middle class and owned slaves who made *auloi*. A comic fragment (Strattis frag. 712 Kock) refers to Isocrates as "the *aulos* borer." Despite the continuing habit of translators to render aulos as "flute," it was an ancient reed instrument, with emotive and sympotic associations.

ἐγίγνωσκεν οὔτε ἄλλο τι τῶν ἐν βαναύσοις, οὐδὲ γὰρ
ἂν οὐδὲ τῆς ἐν Ὀλυμπίᾳ εἰκόνος ἔτυχεν, εἴ τι τῶν
εὐτελῶν εἰργάζετο. ἀπέθανε μὲν οὖν Ἀθήνησιν ἀμφὶ
τὰ ἑκατὸν ἔτη, ἕνα δὲ αὐτὸν ἡγώμεθα τῶν ἐν πολέμῳ
ἀποθανόντων, ἐπειδὴ μετὰ Χαιρώνειαν ἐτελεύτα μὴ
καρτερήσας τὴν ἀκρόασιν τοῦ Ἀθηναίων πταίσματος.

507   (42) ιη΄. Περὶ δὲ Αἰσχίνου τοῦ Ἀτρομήτου, ὃν φαμεν
τῆς δευτέρας σοφιστικῆς ἄρξαι, τάδε χρὴ ἐπεσκέ-
φθαι· ἡ Ἀθήνησι δημαγωγία διειστήκει πᾶσα, καὶ οἱ
μὲν βασιλεῖ ἐπιτήδειοι ἦσαν, οἱ δὲ Μακεδόσιν, ἐφέροντο δὲ ἄρα τὴν πρώτην τῶν μὲν βασιλεῖ χαριζο-
μένων ὁ Παιανιεὺς Δημοσθένης, τῶν δὲ ἐς Φίλιππον
ὁρώντων ὁ Κοθωκίδης Αἰσχίνης, καὶ χρήματα παρ᾽
ἀμφοῖν ἐφοίτα σφίσι, βασιλέως μὲν ἀσχολοῦντος δι᾽
Ἀθηναίων Φίλιππον τὸ μὴ ἐπὶ Ἀσίαν ἐλάσαι, Φιλίππου δὲ πειρωμένου διαλύειν τὴν Ἀθηναίων ἰσχὺν, ὡς
ἐμπόδισμα τῆς διαβάσεως.

Διαφορᾶς δ᾽ ἦρξεν Αἰσχίνῃ καὶ Δημοσθένει καὶ
αὐτὸ μὲν τὸ ἄλλον ἄλλῳ βασιλεῖ πολιτεύειν, ὡς δ᾽
ἐμοὶ φαίνεται, τὸ ἐναντίως ἔχειν τῶν ἠθῶν· ἐξ ἠθῶν
γὰρ ἀλλήλοις ἀντιξόων φύεται μῖσος αἰτίαν οὐκ ἔχον.
ἀντιξόω δ᾽ ἤστην διὰ τάδε· ὁ μὲν Αἰσχίνης φιλο-
πότης ἐδόκει καὶ ἡδὺς καὶ ἀνειμένος καὶ πᾶν τὸ
ἐπίχαρι ἐκ Διονύσου ἡρηκώς, καὶ γὰρ δὴ καὶ τοῖς
βαρυστόνοις ὑποκριταῖς τὸν ἐν μειρακίῳ χρόνον ὑπε-

---

80 Demosthenes (*De cor.* 262) relishes the story of Aeschines
playing third actor (tritagonist) to the "deeply groaning"

anything else practiced by craftsmen. He would not have achieved having his statue at Olympia if he had worked at any lowly trade. He died at Athens at about a hundred years of age, but let us consider him one of those who died in war, because he died after Chaironeia, unable to bear hearing about the Athenians' fall.

(42) 18. Regarding Aeschines the son of Atrometus, 507 whom we say began the Second Sophistic, one must consider the following points. The political leadership at Athens as a whole was divided into two parties, one of which was friendly to the Persian king, the other to the Macedonians. The leader of the faction favoring the king was Demosthenes of the deme Paeania, and the leader of those who looked to Philip was Aeschines of the deme Cothocidae. And money came frequently from both parties: from the king because he used the Athenians to keep Philip too busy to drive his forces into Asia, and from Philip because he was trying to break down the power of the Athenians since it was an impediment to his crossing into Asia.

The disagreement between Aeschines and Demosthenes arose for this reason, namely that one was working in the interests of one king and one of another, but also, it seems to me, because they had opposing characters. Between opposing characters hatred naturally arises without any cause. And the pair were opposed for the following reasons. Aeschines was reputed to be fond of drinking, pleasant and relaxed and possessing all the charm that comes from Dionysus. Moreover he played minor parts with bellowing tragic actors while he was still a youth.[80]

($\beta\alpha\rho\acute{\upsilon}\sigma\tau\upsilon\upsilon\iota$) Simylus and Socrates, and enduring great risks as a thief from nearby orchards and in front of unimpressed audiences.

508 τραγῴδησεν· ὁ δ᾽ αὖ συννενοφώς[33] τε ἐφαίνετο καὶ
βαρὺς τὴν ὀφρὺν καὶ ὕδωρ πίνων, ὅθεν δυσκόλοις τε
καὶ δυστρόποις ἐγράφετο,[34] καὶ πολλῷ πλέον, ἐπειδὴ
πρεσβεύοντε ξὺν ἑτέροις παρὰ τὸν Φίλιππον καὶ ὁμο-
διαίτω ὄντε ὁ μὲν διακεχυμένος τε καὶ ἡδὺς ἐφαίνετο
τοῖς συμπρέσβεσιν, ὁ δὲ κατεσκληκώς τε καὶ ἀεὶ
σπουδάζων. ἐπέτεινε δὲ αὐτοῖς τὴν διαφορὰν ὁ ὑπὲρ
Ἀμφιπόλεως ἐπὶ τοῦ Φιλίππου λόγος, ὅτε δὴ ἐξέπεσε
μὲν τοῦ λόγου ὁ Δημοσθένης, ὁ δ᾽ Αἰσχίνης ... οὐδὲ
τῶν ἀποβεβληκότων[35] ποτὲ τὴν ἀσπίδα, ἀλλ᾽ ἐνθυμούμενος τὸ ἐν Ταμύναις ἔργον,[36] ἐν ᾧ Βοιωτοὺς
ἐνίκων Ἀθηναῖοι. ἀριστεῖα τούτου δημοσίᾳ ἐστεφα-
νοῦτο τά τε ἄλλα καὶ χρησάμενος ἀμηχάνῳ τάχει
περὶ τὰ εὐαγγέλια τῆς νίκης. διαβάλλοντος δὲ αὐτὸν
Δημοσθένους ὡς αἴτιον τοῦ Φωκικοῦ πάθους ἀπέγνω-
σαν Ἀθηναῖοι τὴν αἰτίαν, ἐπὶ δὲ τῷ καταψηφισθέντι
Ἀντιφῶντι ἥλω μὴ κριθείς, καὶ ἀφείλοντο αὐτὸν οἱ ἐξ
Ἀρείου πάγου τὸ μὴ οὐ συνειπεῖν σφισιν ὑπὲρ τοῦ
ἱεροῦ τοῦ ἐν Δήλῳ. καὶ μὴν καὶ πυλαγόρας ἀναρρη-

---

[33] Following ³Kayser's συννενοφώς, a *hapax legomenon* if
correct, which is also adopted by Wright and Stefec. MSS are
divided between συννενηφώς (LVP²) and νενηφως (VbMβ).

[34] ἐπεγράφετο α; ἐγράφετο β (adopted by Stefec); ἐνεγρά-
φετο Kayser

[35] ἀποβεβλημένων α

[36] Some words seem to have been omitted here, making the
construction, though not the sense, unclear. The various cases of
ἐνθυμούμενος in the MSS look like attempts to fix the problem.
I have followed Stefec's reconstruction.

Demosthenes by contrast appeared clouded over and   508
heavy in his brows and a water drinker, and so was enlisted
among the ill-tempered and surly, and especially so when
both men went along with others as ambassadors to Philip
and lived together. One seemed relaxed and pleasant to
his fellow ambassadors, the other seemed rigid and always
serious. And their disagreement was intensified by the
discussion concerning Amphipolis in the presence of
Philip, when Demosthenes broke down in his speech,[81]
but Aeschines was not one of those who ever throw away
the shield, but remembered the battle of Tamynae,[82] when
the Athenians defeated the Boeotians. As a reward for his
part in this he was crowned by the state, both for his other
activities and because he announced the victory with exceptional speed. When Demosthenes accused him of being responsible for the Phocian disaster, the Athenians
acquitted him of the charge, but just as Antiphon was
condemned without a trial, Aeschines was found guilty
without a trial, and the members of the Areopagus council
prevented him from speaking for the temple on Delos.[83]
In addition, after he had been nominated as a representa-

[81] The incident is described by Aeschines, *On the False Embassy* 34.

[82] The Athenian general Phocion won the battle of Tamynae
in Euboea in 354 in an attempt to recover the cities that had revolted from Athens; cf. Aeschines, *On the False Embassy* 139.

[83] The Athenians were defending their right to control the
sanctuary of Apollo on Delos. On Antiphon's death, see above, *VS*
499–500.

θεὶς οὐδ' οὕτω[37] παρὰ τοῖς πολλοῖς διαπέφευγε τὸ μὴ
509 οὐκ αὐτὸς Ἐλατείᾳ ἐπιστῆσαι τὸν Φίλιππον τὴν Πυ-
λαίαν συνταράξας εὐπροσώποις λόγοις καὶ μύθοις.
Ἀθηνῶν δ' ὑπεξῆλθεν οὐχὶ φεύγειν προσταχθείς, ἀλλ'
ἀτιμίᾳ ἐξιστάμενος, ᾗ ὑπήγετο ὑπὸ Δημοσθένει καὶ
Κτησιφῶντι ἐκπεσὼν τῶν ψήφων. ἡ μὲν δὴ ὁρμὴ τῆς
ἀποδημίας αὐτῷ παρὰ τὸν Ἀλέξανδρον ἦν, ὡς αὐτίκα
ἥξοντα ἐς Βαβυλῶνά τε καὶ Σοῦσα, καθορμισθεὶς δ'
ἐς τὴν Ἔφεσον καὶ τὸν μὲν τεθνάναι ἀκούων, τὰ δὲ
τῆς Ἀσίας αὐτῷ ξυγκεκλυσμένα πράγματα, Ῥόδου
εἴχετο ἡ δὲ νῆσος ἀγαθὴ ἐνσπουδάσαι, καὶ σοφιστῶν
φροντιστήριον ἀποφήνας τὴν Ῥόδον αὐτοῦ διῃτᾶτο
θύων ἡσυχίᾳ τε καὶ Μούσαις καὶ Δωρίοις ἤθεσιν
ἐγκαταμιγνὺς Ἀττικά.

(43) Τὸν δὲ αὐτοσχέδιον λόγον ξὺν εὐροίᾳ καὶ
θείως διατιθέμενος τὸν ἔπαινον τουτονὶ πρῶτος ἠνέγ-
κατο. τὸ γὰρ θείως λέγειν οὔπω μὲν ἐπεχωρίασε σοφιστῶν σπουδαῖς, ἀπ' Αἰσχίνου δ' ἤρξατο θεοφορήτῳ
ὁρμῇ ἀποσχεδιάζοντος, ὥσπερ οἱ τοὺς χρησμοὺς
ἀναπνέοντες. ἀκροατὴς δὲ Πλάτωνός τε καὶ Ἰσοκράτους γενόμενος πολλὰ καὶ παρὰ τῆς ἑαυτοῦ φύ-
510 σεως ἠγάγετο. σαφηνείας τε γὰρ φῶς ἐν τῷ λόγῳ καὶ

---

[37] οὐδ'οὕτω is Reiske's conjecture for the MSS' οὔπω

---

[84] Demosthenes, *De cor.* 143, brings this charge; Philostratus
borrows freely from this speech in his account of the political life
of Aeschines.

tive at Pylae, he did not escape the suspicion with the people that he himself prompted Philip to attack Elateia, throwing matters into confusion at Pylae with his fair-seeming arguments and myths.[84] And he escaped secretly from Athens, not because he had been ordered into exile, but because he had lost his citizen rights, when he failed to reach the number of votes he needed in his suit against Demosthenes and Ctesiphon. His goal when he set out into exile was to go to Alexander, since he was about to arrive at Babylon and Susa. But when he had traveled as far as Ephesus and heard that he had died,[85] and so all of Asia was in confusion, he stayed on Rhodes. The island was an excellent place for his studies, and making Rhodes known as a school for sophists, he lived there, making sacrifice to peace and the Muses, and blending Attic ways with Doric habits.

(43) He composed improvised speeches with fluency and divine inspiration, and was the first to win praise for it. The divinely inspired manner had not yet come to be at home in the studies of the sophists, but began from Aeschines, who improvised with a divine impulse, like those who exhale oracles.[86] Though he was a student of Plato and Isocrates,[87] he drew much of his ability from his own nature. The light of clarity in his speech and its seduc-

509

510

[85] Philostratus ignores the fact that seven years elapsed between the departure of Aeschines from Athens in 330 and the death of Alexander in 323. [86] Wright suggested that this might be an echo of [Longinus] *Sub.* 13.2. This is possible, and if true would be significant for that dating of that text, but Philostratus is fond in any case of expressions involving πνέω and its compounds. [87] There is no other evidence for this assertion.

ἁβρὰ σεμνολογία καὶ τὸ ἐπίχαρι σὺν δεινότητι καὶ
καθάπαξ ἡ ἰδέα τοῦ λόγου κρείττων ἢ μιμήσει ὑπ-
αχθῆναι.

(44) Λόγοι δ' Αἰσχίνου τρεῖς,[38] κατ' ἐνίους δὲ καὶ
τέταρτός τις, Δηλιακὸς καταψευδόμενος τῆς ἐκείνου
γλώττης. οὐ γὰρ ἄν ποτε τοὺς μὲν περὶ τὴν Ἄμφισ-
σαν λόγους, ὑφ' ὧν ἡ Κιρραία χώρα καθιερώθη, εὐ-
προσώπως τε καὶ ξὺν ὥρᾳ διέθετο κακὰ βουλεύων
Ἀθηναίοις, ὥς φησι Δημοσθένης, ἐπὶ δὲ τοὺς Δηλια-
κοὺς μύθους, ἐν οἷς θεολογία τε καὶ θεογονία καὶ ἀρ-
χαιολογία, φαύλως οὕτως ὥρμησε καὶ ταῦτα προαγωνιζόμενος Ἀθηναίων οὐ μικρὸν ἀγώνισμα ἡγουμένων
τὸ μὴ ἐκπεσεῖν τοῦ ἐν Δήλῳ ἱεροῦ. τρισὶ δὴ λόγοις
περιωρίσθω ἡ Αἰσχίνου γλῶττα· τῷ τε κατὰ Τιμάρ-
χου καὶ τῇ ἀπολογίᾳ τῆς πρεσβείας καὶ τῇ τοῦ Κτησιφῶντος κατηγορίᾳ. ἔστι δὲ καὶ τέταρτον αὐτοῦ
φρόντισμα, ἐπιστολαί, οὐ πολλαὶ μέν, εὐπαιδευσίας
δὲ μεσταὶ καὶ ἤθους. τοῦ δὲ ἠθικοῦ καὶ Ῥοδίοις ἐπίδειξιν ἐποιήσατο· ἀναγνοὺς γάρ ποτε δημοσίᾳ τὸν
κατὰ Κτησιφῶντος οἱ μὲν ἐθαύμαζον, ὅπως ἐπὶ
τοιούτῳ λόγῳ ἡττήθη, καὶ καθήπτοντο τῶν Ἀθηναίων
ὡς παρανομούντων,[39] ὁ δὲ "οὐκ ἄν," ἔφη, "ἐθαυμάζετε,
εἰ Δημοσθένους λέγοντος πρὸς ταῦτα ἠκούσατε," οὐ
μόνον εἰς ἔπαινον ἐχθροῦ καθιστάμενος, ἀλλὰ καὶ
τοὺς δικαστὰς ἀφιεὶς αἰτίας.

[38] τρεῖς Reiske
[39] Reading παρανομούντων with Stefec and Olearius. Wright
reads παρανοούντων (the reading of the a group).

tive elevation and grace along with power and, in general, his whole form of eloquence defy imitation.

(44) There are three orations of Aeschines, though some ascribe to him a fourth, the *Delian Oration*, which is false and unworthy of his eloquence. When he had composed with such apparent plausibility and beautifully the speeches about Amphissa, by whose people the plain of Cirrha was consecrated, when he spoke in his hostility to the Athenians, as Demosthenes says, he would not have handled so poorly the myths of Delos, concerned as they are with the nature and birth of the gods and with ancient times. And this is especially true as he argued in a cause that the Athenians deemed far from trivial: maintaining their presence in the temple on Delos.[88] So let the eloquence of Aeschines be defined by three speeches: *Against Timarchus*, *In Defense of the Embassy* and *Against Ctesiphon*. And he has a fourth composition, his letters, which are not numerous, but are full of erudition and character.[89] He displayed this character to the Rhodians too: once, when was publicly reading the speech *Against Ctesiphon*, they were astonished that he had been defeated after a speech like that, and were criticizing the Athenians as criminals, but he said, "You would not be astonished, if you had heard Demosthenes speaking in response." He not only praised an enemy, but also acquitted the jurors of the charge.

[88] This speech is in any case no longer extant.

[89] The twelve surviving letters under Aeschines' name are generally considered spurious. On character ($\mathring{\eta}\theta o\varsigma$) as a desirable trait in letter writing, see Book 2, note 35.

97

(45) 19. ιθ'. Ὑπερβάντες δ' Ἀριοβαρζάνην τὸν
511 Κίλικα καὶ Ξενόφρονα τὸν Σικελιώτην καὶ Πειθα-
γόραν τὸν ἐκ Κυρήνης, οἳ μήτε γνῶναι ἱκανοὶ ἔδοξαν,
μήθ' ἑρμηνεῦσαι τὰ γνωσθέντα, ἀλλ' ἀπορίᾳ γεν-
ναίων σοφιστῶν ἐσπουδάσθησαν τοῖς ἐφ' ἑαυτῶν
Ἕλλησιν, ὅν που τρόπον τοῖς σίτου ἀπορῦσιν οἱ
ὄροβοι, ἐπὶ Νικήτην ἴωμεν τὸν Σμυρναῖον. οὗτος γὰρ
παραλαβὼν τὴν ἐπιστήμην εἰς στενὸν ἀπειλημμένην
ἔδωκεν αὐτῇ παρόδους πολλῷ λαμπροτέρας ὧν αὐτὸς
τῇ Σμύρνῃ ἐδείματο, συνάψας τὴν πόλιν ταῖς ἐπὶ τὴν
Ἔφεσον πύλαις καὶ διὰ μέγεθος ἀντεξάρας λόγοις
ἔργα. ὁ δὲ ἀνὴρ οὗτος τοῖς μὲν δικανικοῖς ἀμείνων
ἐδόκει τὰ δικανικά, τοῖς δὲ σοφιστικοῖς τὰ σοφιστικὰ
ὑπὸ τοῦ περιδεξίως τε καὶ πρὸς ἅμιλλαν ἐς ἄμφω
ἡρμόσθαι. τὸ μὲν γὰρ δικανικὸν σοφιστικῇ τινι περι-
βολῇ ἐκόσμησε, τὸ δὲ σοφιστικὸν κέντρῳ δικανικῷ
ἐπέρρωσεν. ἡ δὲ ἰδέα τῶν λόγων τοῦ μὲν ἀρχαίου καὶ
πολιτικοῦ ἀποβέβηκεν, ὑπόβακχος γὰρ καὶ διθυραμ-
βώδης, τὰς δ' ἐννοίας ἰδίας τε καὶ παραδόξους ἐκδί-
δωσιν, ὥσπερ "οἱ βακχεῖοι θύρσοι" τὸ μέλι καὶ "τοὺς
ἑσμοὺς τοῦ γάλακτος."

(46) Μεγάλων δ' ἀξιούμενος τῆς Σμύρνης τί οὐκ

---

90 The younger Pliny (*Ep.* 6.6.3) studied with Nicetes and
praises him; Tacitus uses him as an example of how far the Greek
orators of his day fall below the standard of Aeschines and Demosthenes, claiming that the fall in Latin oratory from the standard of Cicero has not been so severe (*Dial.* 15.3).

(45) 19. We will pass over Ariobarzanes of Cilicia and Xenophron of Sicily and Peithagoras who came from Cyrene, who seemed without skill in invention and in expressing their ideas, but were taken seriously by the Greeks of their time due to the lack of first-rate sophists, much as people eat bitter vetch when they lack other food. Let us move on to Nicetes of Smyrna.[90] This man took up the science of speaking when it had been reduced to such straits, and gave it entranceways still more stunning than those he himself built at Symrna, connecting the city to the gates to Ephesus and by their magnitude raising to an equal height his deeds and his words. And this man seemed greater in forensic oratory when he spoke in the courts, but greater in sophistic oratory when he spoke as a sophist, because of the ambidextrous and competitive way that he composed appropriately for each type. He decorated forensic oratory with a certain sophistic amplification, and he strengthened sophistic oratory with a forensic sting. His form of rhetoric departed from the ancient and political kind, since it was imbued with Bacchus and dithyrambic, and produced individual and paradoxical ideas, like the thrysi of Bacchants produce honey and swarms of milk.[91]

(46) Although he was held in great esteem (and what

511

[91] Wright treats "the thyrsi of Bacchants" and "swarms of milk" as examples of Nicetes' phrases, not entirely inappropriately, as Philostratus is here describing Nicetes' work in the Smyrnean's own style. These words are, however, a simile comparing Nicetes' style to the astonishing powers of the Dionysian thyrsus. The phrases are based on Eur. *Bacch.* 710–11.

ἐπ᾽ αὐτῷ βοώσης ὡς ἐπ᾽ ἀνδρὶ θαυμασίῳ καὶ ῥήτορι,
οὐκ ἐθάμιζεν εἰς τὸν δῆμον, ἀλλ᾽ αἰτίαν παρὰ τοῖς
πολλοῖς ἔχων φόβου "φοβοῦμαι," ἔφη, "δῆμον ἐπαί-
ροντα μᾶλλον ἢ λοιδορούμενον." τελώνου δέ ποτε
θρασυναμένου πρὸς αὐτὸν ἐν δικαστηρίῳ καὶ εἰπόντος, "παῦσαι ὑλακτῶν με," μάλα ἀστείως ὁ Νικήτης
"νὴ Δία," ἔφη "ἢν καὶ σὺ παύσῃ δάκνων."

512   (47) Ἡ δὲ ὑπὲρ Ἄλπεις τε καὶ Ῥῆνον ἀποδημία τοῦ
ἀνδρὸς ἐγένετο μὲν ἐκ βασιλείου προστάγματος,
αἰτία δὲ αὐτῆς ἥδε· ἀνὴρ ὕπατος, ᾧ ὄνομα Ῥοῦφος,
τοὺς Σμυρναίους ἐλογίστευε πικρῶς καὶ δυστρόπως.
τούτῳ τι προσκρούσας ὁ Νικήτης "ἔρρωσο," εἶπε, καὶ
οὐκέτι προσῄει δικάζοντι. τὸν μὲν δὴ χρόνον, ὃν μιᾶς
πόλεως ἦρξεν, οὔπω δεινὰ πεπονθέναι ᾤετο, ἐπιτρα-
πεὶς δὲ τὰ Κελτικὰ στρατόπεδα ὀργῆς ἀνεμνήσθη—
αἱ γὰρ εὐπραγίαι τά τε ἄλλα τοὺς ἀνθρώπους
ἐπαίρουσι καὶ τὸ μηκέτι καρτερεῖν, ἃ πρὶν εὖ πράττειν ἀνθρωπίνῳ λογισμῷ ἐκαρτέρουν—καὶ γράφει
πρὸς τὸν αὐτοκράτορα Νέρωνα⁴⁰ πολλὰ ἐπὶ τὸν Νικήτην καὶ σχέτλια, καὶ ὁ αὐτοκράτωρ, "αὐτὸς," εἶπεν
"ἀκροάσῃ ἀπολογουμένου, κἂν ἀδικοῦντα εὕρῃς,
ἐπίθες δίκην." ταυτὶ δ᾽ ἔγραφεν οὐ τὸν Νικήτην ἐκδι-
δούς, ἀλλὰ τὸν Ῥοῦφον εἰς συγγνώμην ἑτοιμάζων, οὐ
γὰρ ἄν ποτε ἄνδρα τοιοῦτον ἐφ᾽ ἑαυτῷ γεγονότα οὔτ᾽

---

⁴⁰ Νέρωνα is Jüttner's correction for the nonsensical ἔρωνα of
one MS (Stefec's Vb) and the Νέρβαν or Νερούαν, that is Nerva,
of others (β).

boast did Smyrna not cry out about him, a man so astonishing and a rhetor?) he did not go often to the public assembly, but when the crowd accused him of being afraid, "I am afraid," he said, "of the people when they exalt me more than when they abuse me." And once when a tax collector was angry with him in court and said, "Stop barking at me," Nicetes replied with great urbanity, "Yes, by Zeus, if you just stop biting."

(47) The man's journey beyond the Alps and the Rhine   512
was made at the command of the Emperor, and the reason was as follows: There was a man of consular rank, whose name was Rufus,[92] who was regulating the finances of the Smyrneans harshly and with malice. When Nicetes came into some conflict with him he said, "Goodbye," and no longer went before him when he was judging cases. During the time when Rufus ruled one city, he did not yet take great offense, but when he had received the command of the armies in Gaul, he recalled his anger, because successes often elevate men in other respects and bring them no longer to tolerate what they used to tolerate, by reference to a normal human standard, before they were doing well. And Rufus wrote to the Emperor Nero many ridiculous things against Nicetes, and the emperor said, "You yourself will hear him make his defense, and if you find him guilty, set the penalty." He wrote this not to abandon Nicetes to his fate, but to prepare Rufus to forgive him. For he thought that Rufus, if the decision were in his

[92] On the likely identity of this Rufus as L. Verginius Rufus, see Fant 1981.

101

ἂν ἀποκτεῖναι ὁ Ῥοῦφος, οὔτ᾽ ἂν ἕτερον ζημιῶσαι οὐδέν, ὡς μὴ φανείη βαρὺς τῷ καθιστάντι αὐτὸν δικα-
στὴν ἐχθροῦ. διὰ μὲν δὴ ταῦτα ἐπὶ Ῥῆνόν τε καὶ
Κελτοὺς ἦλθε, παρελθὼν δ᾽ ἐπὶ τὴν ἀπολογίαν οὕτω
τι κατέπληξε τὸν Ῥοῦφον, ὡς πλείω μὲν ἀφεῖναι ἐπὶ
τῷ Νικήτῃ δάκρυα οὗ διεμέτρησεν αὐτῷ ὕδατος, ἀπο-
πέμψαι δὲ οὐκ ἄτρωτον μόνον, ἀλλὰ καὶ περίβλεπτον
καὶ ἐν τοῖς ζηλωτοῖς Σμυρναίων. τὸν δὲ ἄνδρα τοῦτον
χρόνοις ὕστερον Ἡρακλείδης ὁ Λύκιος σοφιστὴς
διορθούμενος ἐπέγραψε Νικήτην τὸν κεκαθαρμένον,
ἠγνόησε δὲ ἀκροθίνια Πυγμαῖα κολοσσῷ ἐφαρμόζων.

(48) 20. κʹ. Ἰσαῖος δ᾽ ὁ σοφιστὴς ὁ Ἀσσύριος τὸν
μὲν ἐν μειρακίῳ χρόνον ἡδοναῖς ἐδεδώκει, γαστρός τε
513 γὰρ καὶ φιλοποσίας ἥττητο καὶ λεπτὰ ἠμπίσχετο καὶ
θαμὰ ἤρα καὶ ἀπαρακαλύπτως ἐκώμαζεν, ἐς δὲ ἄνδρας ἥκων οὕτω τι μετέβαλεν, ὡς ἕτερος ἐξ ἑτέρου
νομισθῆναι· τὸ μὲν γὰρ φιλόγελων ἐπιπολάζειν αὐτῷ
δοκοῦν ἀφεῖλε καὶ προσώπου καὶ γνώμης, λυρῶν τε
καὶ αὐλῶν κτύποις οὐδ᾽ ἐπὶ σκηνῆς ἔτι παρετύγχανεν,
ἀπέδυ δὲ καὶ τὰ λήδια καὶ τὰς τῶν ἐφεστρίδων βα-
φάς, καὶ τράπεζαν ἐκόλασε καὶ τὸ ἐρᾶν μεθῆκεν,[41]
ὥσπερ τοὺς προτέρους ὀφθαλμοὺς ἀποβαλών· Ἄρ-
δυος γοῦν τοῦ ῥήτορος ἐρομένου αὐτόν, εἰ ἡ δεῖνα

41 μετέθηκεν α

hands, would never put to death such a man nor punish the other at all, so that he would not appear harsh to the one who had appointed him the judge of his enemy. For these reasons, Nicetes came to the Rhine and the Celts, and when he came forward to make his defense, he so powerfully affected Rufus that he shed tears over Nicetes greater than the water measured out for his speech.[93] He sent him away not just unharmed but both admired and among the most enviable of the people of Smyrna. Some years later, the sophist Heracleides of Lycia attempted to correct the speeches of this man and called his work *Nicetes Corrected*, but did not realize that he was attaching pygmy spoils to a colossus.[94]

(48) 20. Isaeus the Assyrian sophist had given the period of his youth over to pleasure, for he was at the mercy 513 of his stomach and love of drinking, and dressed himself in soft clothes and was often in love and openly joined in drunken revels. But when he came to manhood he changed so much that he appeared a different person. He discarded from his face and his thought the frivolity that had seemed to bubble up to the surface in him, and he did not pay attention to the sounds of the lyre and the aulos, even in the theater. And he put off his soft clothes and brightly colored cloaks, reduced the extravagance of his diet, and let go of his love affairs, as if he had thrown away the eyes that he had before. For instance, when the rhetorician Ardus asked him if he thought such-and-such a woman

[93] Speeches in the courts were timed using the water clock (*klepsydra*).   [94] Despite this disparaging comparison, Philostratus gives a largely positive appraisal of Heracleides' abilities below (*VS* 612–13).

αὐτῷ καλὴ φαίνοιτο, μάλα σωφρόνως ὁ Ἰσαῖος,
"πέπαυμαι," εἶπεν, "ὀφθαλμιῶν." ἐρομένου δὲ αὐτὸν
ἑτέρου, τίς ἄριστος τῶν ἰχθύων καὶ τῶν ὀρνίθων ἐς
βρῶσιν, "πέπαυμαι," ἔφη ὁ Ἰσαῖος, "ταῦτα σπουδάζων, ξυνῆκα γὰρ τοὺς Ταντάλου κήπους τρυγῶν,"
ἐνδεικνύμενος δήπου τῷ ἐρομένῳ ταῦτα, ὅτι σκιὰ καὶ
ὀνείρατα αἱ ἡδοναὶ πᾶσαι.

(49) Τῷ δὲ Μιλησίῳ Διονυσίῳ ἀκροατῇ ὄντι τὰς
μελέτας ξὺν ᾠδῇ ποιουμένῳ ἐπιπλήττων ὁ Ἰσαῖος
"μειράκιον," ἔφη, "Ἰωνικόν, ἐγὼ δέ σε ᾄδειν οὐκ ἐπαί-
δευσα." νεανίσκου δὲ Ἰωνικοῦ θαυμάζοντος πρὸς
αὐτὸν τὸ τῷ Νικήτῃ μεγαλοφώνως ἐπὶ τοῦ Ξέρξου
εἰρημένον "ἐκ τῆς βασιλείου νεὼς Αἴγιναν ἀναδησώ-
μεθα," καταγελάσας πλατὺ ὁ Ἰσαῖος, "ἀνόητε," εἶπε,
"καὶ πῶς ἀναχθήσῃ;"

514
(50) Τὰς δὲ μελέτας οὐκ αὐτοσχεδίους ἐποιεῖτο,
ἀλλ' ἐπεσκεμμένας[42] τὸν ἐξ ἕω ἐς μεσημβρίαν καιρόν.
ἰδέαν δ' ἐπήσκησε λόγων οὔτ' ἐπιβεβλημένην, οὔτ'
αὖον, ἀλλ' ἀπέριττον καὶ κατὰ φύσιν καὶ ἀποχρῶσαν
τοῖς πράγμασι. καὶ τὸ βραχέως ἑρμηνεύειν, τοῦτό τε
καὶ πᾶσαν τὴν ὑπόθεσιν συνελεῖν ἐς βραχὺ Ἰσαίου
εὕρημα, ὡς ἐν πλείοσι μὲν ἑτέροις, μάλιστα δὲ ἐν
τοῖσδε ἐδηλώθη· τοὺς μὲν γὰρ Λακεδαιμονίους ἀγωνιζόμενος τοὺς βουλευομένους περὶ τοῦ τείχους ἀπὸ
τῶν Ὁμήρου ἐβραχυλόγησε τοσοῦτον·

[42] ἐπεσκεμμένος Cobet

seemed beautiful to him, Isaeus replied with great restraint. "I have ceased," he said, "to have eye trouble." And when someone else asked him, what the best fish and birds were for eating, Isaeus said, "I have ceased to take these things seriously, because I realized that I was eating the gardens of Tantalus."[95] He showed the one who asked these things, I suppose, that all pleasures are a shadow and dreams.

(49) When Dionysius of Meletus, who had been his student, was delivering his declamation with "the song,"[96] Isaeus rebuked him saying, "Young man from Ionia, I did not teach you to sing." And when an Ionian youth expressed amazement in his presence at the grandiloquent saying of Nicetes about Xerxes, "let us fasten Aegina to the king's ship," Isaeus laughed heartily and said, "You idiot, and how will you put to sea?"

(50) The declamations that he produced were not improvised but deliberated upon from dawn until midday. The style of eloquence at which he worked was neither ornate nor dry, but simple and natural and suited to the subject matter. Moreover concise expression and the capacity briefly to sum up the whole topic was the invention of Isaeus, as can be seen in many passages, but especially in the following example. He was arguing about the Lacedaemonians debating whether they should build a wall, and he employed this brief quotation from Homer:

514

[95] This proverb of fleeting joys, which also appears at *VS* 595 and at *VA* 4.25, refers to the punishment of Tantatlus in Homer (*Od.* 11.588.)   [96] On this practice of a singing delivery, especially at the conclusion of a speech, see the life of Favorinus above (*VS* 492) and ᾠδή in the Rhetorical Glossary.

"ἀσπὶς ἄρ' ἀσπίδ' ἔρειδε, κόρυς κόρυν, ἀνέρα δ'
ἀνήρ·

οὕτω στῆτέ μοι, Λακεδαιμόνιοι, καὶ τετειχίσμεθα."
κατηγορῶν δὲ τοῦ Βυζαντίου Πύθωνος, ὡς δεθέντος
μὲν ἐκ χρησμῶν ἐπὶ προδοσίᾳ, κεκριμένης δὲ τῆς
προδοσίας, ὡς ἀνέζευξεν ὁ Φίλιππος, ξυνέλαβε τὸν
ἀγῶνα τοῦτον ἐς τρεῖς ἐννοίας. ἔστι γὰρ τὰ εἰρημένα
ἐν τρισὶ τούτοις· "ἐλέγξω Πύθωνα προδεδωκότα τῷ
χρήσαντι θεῷ, τῷ δήσαντι δήμῳ, τῷ ἀναζεύξαντι Φιλίππῳ, ὁ μὲν γὰρ οὐκ ἂν ἔχρησεν, εἰ μή τις ἦν, ὁ δὲ
οὐκ ἂν ἔδησεν, εἰ μὴ τοιοῦτος ἦν, ὁ δ' οὐκ ἂν ἀνέζευξεν, εἰ μὴ, δι' ὃν ἦλθεν, οὐχ εὗρεν."

(51) 21. κα'. Ὑπὲρ Σκοπελιανοῦ τοῦ σοφιστοῦ δια-
λέξομαι καθαψάμενος πρότερον τῶν κακίζειν αὐτὸν
πειρωμένων, ἀπαξιοῦσι γὰρ δὴ τὸν ἄνδρα τοῦ τῶν
σοφιστῶν κύκλου, διθυραμβώδη καλοῦντες καὶ ἀκό-
515 λαστον καὶ πεπαχυσμένον. ταυτὶ δὲ περὶ αὐτοῦ
λέγουσιν οἱ λεπτολόγοι καὶ νωθροὶ καὶ μηδὲν ἀπ'
αὐτοσχεδίου γλώττης ἀναπνέοντες· φύσει μὲν γὰρ
ἐπίφθονον χρῆμα ἄνθρωποι.[43] διαβάλλουσι γοῦν τοὺς
μὲν εὐμήκεις οἱ μικροί, τοὺς δὲ εὐειδεῖς οἱ πονηροὶ τὸ
εἶδος, τοὺς δὲ κούφους τε καὶ δρομικοὺς οἱ βραδεῖς
καὶ ἑτερόποδες, τοὺς θαρσαλέους οἱ δειλοὶ καὶ οἱ

---

[43] ἄνθρωπος Jacobs

97 Hom. *Il.* 13.131, 16.215. On the later fortification of Sparta,
cf. Paus. 1.13. This was a famous theme and was inspired by

"Shield pressed against shield, helm against helm,
   man against man.

Thus stand firm, Lacedaemonians, for these are our forti-
fications."[97] And when he was prosecuting Python of Byzantium, who had been imprisoned for treason on the
command of an oracle, and had been tried for treason,
when Philip traveled on, he summarized this case in three
propositions. For what was said is contained in these
three: "I shall find Python guilty of treason because of the
prophecy of the god, the people who imprisoned him, and
Philip who departed. The god would not have prophesied,
if there were not a traitor; the people would not have
imprisoned him, if he were not that kind of man; and
Philip would not have departed, if he had not found the
man he had come to find."

(51) 21. I shall speak now about the sophist Scopelian,
after first dealing with those who attempt to heap abuse
on him. They say that he is unworthy of membership of
the circle of sophists, calling him dithyrambic and undisciplined and thick-witted. Those who say this about him   515
are quibblers and sluggish and do not breathe the inspiration of improvised speech. For humanity is a thing envious
by nature. At any rate the short disparage the tall, ugly
people disparage those who are well formed, and people
who are slow and have an awkward gait disparage those
who are lightly built and good runners, cowards disparage
the brave, the unmusical those who play the lyre, the un-

the saying *Non est Sparta lapidibus circumdata* (Sen. *Suas.* 2.3);
cf. below, *VS* 584, on Aelius Aristides' treatment of this same
theme.

ἄμουσοι τοὺς λυρικούς, τοὺς δ᾽ ἀμφὶ παλαίστραν οἱ
ἀγύμναστοι, καὶ οὐ χρὴ θαυμάζειν, εἰ πεπηδημένοι
τὴν γλῶττάν τινες καὶ βοῦν ἀφωνίας ἐπ᾽ αὐτὴν βε-
βλημένοι καὶ μήτ᾽ ἂν αὐτοί τι ἐνθυμηθέντες μέγα
μήτ᾽ ἂν ἐνθυμηθέντος ἑτέρου ξυμφήσαντες διαπτύοιέν
τε καὶ κακίζοιεν τὸν ἑτοιμότατα δὴ καὶ θαρραλεώτατα
καὶ μεγαλειότατα τῶν ἐφ᾽ ἑαυτοῦ Ἑλλήνων ἑρμηνεύ-
σαντα. ὡς δὲ ἠγνοήκασι τὸν ἄνδρα, ἐγὼ δηλώσω, καὶ
ὁποῖον αὐτῷ καὶ τὸ τοῦ οἴκου σχῆμα.

(52) Ἀρχιερεὺς μὲν γὰρ ἐγένετο τῆς Ἀσίας αὐτός
τε καὶ οἱ πρόγονοι αὐτοῦ παῖς ἐκ πατρὸς πάντες, ὁ δὲ
στέφανος οὗτος πολὺς καὶ ὑπὲρ πολλῶν χρημάτων.
δίδυμός τε ἀποτεχθεὶς ἄμφω μὲν ἤστην ἐν σπαργά-
νοις, πεμπταίων δὲ ὄντων κεραυνῷ μὲν ἐβλήθη ὁ ἕτερος, ὁ δὲ οὐδεμίαν ἐπηρώθη τῶν αἰσθήσεων ξυγκατα-
κείμενος τῷ βληθέντι. καίτοι τὸ τῶν σκηπτῶν πῦρ
οὕτω δριμὺ καὶ θειῶδες, ὡς τῶν ἀγχοῦ τοὺς μὲν ἀποκτείνειν κατ᾽ ἔκπληξιν, τῶν δὲ ἀκοάς τε καὶ ὀφθαλμοὺς σίνεσθαι, τῶν δὲ ἐς τοὺς νοῦς ἀποσκήπτειν.
ἀλλ᾽ οὐδενὶ τούτων ὁ Σκοπελιανὸς ἥλω, διετέλεσε γὰρ
δὴ καὶ ἐς γῆρας βαθὺ ἀκέραιός τε καὶ ἄρτιος. τουτὶ
δὲ ὁπόθεν θαυμάζω, δηλῶσαί σοι βούλομαι· ἐδεί-
πνουν μὲν κατὰ τὴν Λῆμνον ὑπὸ δρυὶ μεγάλῃ θερισταὶ ὀκτὼ περὶ τὸ καλούμενον Κέρας τῆς νήσου, τὸ
δὲ χωρίον τοῦτο λιμήν ἐστιν εἰς κεραίας ἐπιστρέφων
516   λεπτάς, νέφους δὲ τὴν δρῦν περισχόντος καὶ σκηπτοῦ
ἐς αὐτὴν ἐκδοθέντος ἡ μὲν ἐβέβλητο, οἱ θερισταὶ δὲ

athletic those active in the wrestling school. So it is no surprise if some people who stumble in their own speech and have cast the ox of silence on their tongues,[98] and who would never have a great thought of their own nor acknowledge one from anyone else, should spit on him and heap abuse on the man who declaimed most fluently and boldly and magnificently of the Greeks of his age. Since they have failed to understand the man, I will reveal what dignity both he and his household possessed.

(52) He was high priest of Asia himself as were his ancestors before him, all of them, with son succeeding father. And this crown was prestigious and valuable beyond great wealth. He was born a twin, but when they were lying in their swaddling bands, being just five days old, the other was struck by a thunderbolt, but Scopelian was not damaged in any of his senses by the blast. And yet, the fire of the thunderbolt was so fierce and sulfurous that some of those who stood near died from shock, others were damaged in their hearing and vision, and others were struck in their minds. But Scopelian suffered from none of these things. In fact he lived into deep old age, unimpaired and in sound health. And I shall demonstrate why I am amazed at this fact: eight reapers were having lunch on Lemnos under a great oak, near the part of the island called the Horn—this place is a harbor curved in the shape of slender horns—when a cloud covered the oak and a lightning bolt was thrown onto it. The oak was struck and

516

---

[98] A proverb for silence first found in Theognis 651; cf. Aesch. *Ag.* 36; Philostr. *VA* 6.11. Its precise origin is not clear, but it may refer to the weight of the ox, or to coins engraved with an ox and laid on the tongue, e.g., of a victim.

ἐκπλήξεως αὐτοῖς ἐμπεσούσης, ἐφ' οὗπερ ἕκαστος
ἔτυχε πράττων, οὕτως ἀπέθανεν· ὁ μὲν γὰρ κύλικα
ἀναιρούμενος, ὁ δὲ πίνων, ὁ δὲ μάττων, ὁ δὲ ἐσθίων,
ὁ δὲ ἄλλο τι ποιῶν τὰς ψυχὰς ἀφῆκαν ἐπιτεθυμμένοι
καὶ μέλανες, ὥσπερ οἱ χαλκοῖ τῶν ἀνδριάντων περὶ
τὰς ἐμπύρους τῶν πηγῶν.[44] ὁ δὲ οὕτω τι οὐκ ἀθεεὶ
ἐτρέφετο, ὡς διαφυγεῖν μὲν τὸν ἐκ τοῦ σκηπτοῦ θάνατον, ὃν μηδὲ οἱ σκληρότατοι τῶν ἀγροίκων διέφυ-
γον, ἄτρωτος δὲ μεῖναι τὰς αἰσθήσεις καὶ τὸν νοῦν
ἕτοιμος καὶ ὕπνου κρείττων, καὶ γὰρ δὴ καὶ τὸ νω-
θρὸν αὐτοῦ ἀπῆν.

(53) Ἐφοίτησε δὲ τοὺς ῥητορικοὺς τῶν λόγων παρὰ
τὸν Σμυρναῖον Νικήτην μελετήσαντα μὲν ἐπιφανῶς,
πολλῷ δὲ μεῖζον ἐν δικαστηρίοις πνεύσαντα. δεο-
μένων δὲ τῶν Κλαζομενίων τὰς μελέτας αὐτὸν οἴκοι
ποιεῖσθαι καὶ προβήσεσθαι τὰς Κλαζομενὰς ἐπὶ
μέγα ἡγουμένων, εἰ τοιόσδε ἀνὴρ ἐμπαιδεύσοι σφίσι,
τουτὶ μὲν οὐκ ἀμούσως παρῃτήσατο, τὴν ἀηδόνα φήσας ἐν οἰκίσκῳ μὴ ᾄδειν, ὥσπερ δὲ ἄλσος τι τῆς ἑαυτοῦ εὐφωνίας τὴν Σμύρναν ἐσκέψατο καὶ τὴν ἠχὼ τὴν
ἐκεῖ πλείστου ἀξίαν ᾠήθη. πάσης γὰρ τῆς Ἰωνίας
οἷον μουσείου πεπολισμένης ἀρτιωτάτην ἐπέχει τάξιν
ἡ Σμύρνα, καθάπερ ἐν τοῖς ὀργάνοις ἡ μαγάς.

---

[44] Kayser, followed by Wright, unnecessarily adds κεκαπνι-
σμένοι.

---

[99] Echo is a favorite image of Philostratus, suggesting the au-
dible qualities of rhetoric or poetry, the echoing of earlier works

each of the harvesters died just in the action that he happened to be performing, when the shock fell upon them. One was lifting a cup, another drinking, another kneading bread, another eating, another doing something else, and lost their lives and were burned and blackened, like bronze statues at hot springs. But Scopelian was raised so much under the care of the gods that he not only escaped death from the thunderbolt, which even the toughest of the field laborers did not, but he remained uninjured in his senses and keen witted and impervious to sleep, for he never experienced even sluggishness.

(53) He learned rhetoric by attending the school of Nicetes of Smyrna, who was exceptional in declamation, but was much more powerful still in the courts. When the Clazomenians asked him to practice declamation in his home town and believed it would bring great honor to Clazomenae, if such a great man should teach among them, he made his refusal with elegance, saying that the nightingale does not sing in a cage. And he found Smyrna like a sacred grove for his eloquence, and valued very highly the echo there.[99] For while the whole of Ionia is built like a shrine of the Muses, Smyrna has the most perfect arrangement, like the bridge on a musical instrument.[100]

in a later writer, and on this occasion apparently the response to a sophist's work by an appreciative audience. On some of this range of associations, see Philostr. *Her.* 55, and Miles 2005.

[100] Philostratus uses the same simile at *VS* 487, of Dio's ability to mix former styles in creating his own. Here it indicates both the excellence of Smyrna in itself and its importance to the rest of the "instrument" (i.e., Ionia).

(54) Αἱ δὲ αἰτίαι, δι᾽ ἃς ὁ πατὴρ ἐξ ἡμέρου τε καὶ πράου χαλεπὸς αὐτῷ ἐγένετο, λέγονται μὲν ἐπὶ πολλά, καὶ γὰρ ἡ δεῖνα καὶ ἡ δεῖνα καὶ πλείους, ἀλλ᾽ ἐγὼ τὴν ἀληθεστάτην δηλώσω· μετὰ γὰρ τὴν τοῦ Σκοπελιανοῦ μητέρα γυναῖκα ὁ πρεσβύτης ἤγετο ἡμίγαμόν τε καὶ οὐ κατὰ νόμους, ὁ δὲ ὁρῶν ταῦτα ἐνουθέτει καὶ ἀπῆγεν, τουτὶ δὲ τοῖς ἐξώροις ἀηδές. ἡ δ᾽ αὖ ξυνετίθει κατ᾽ αὐτοῦ λόγον, ὡς ἐρῶντος μὲν αὐτῆς, τὴν διαμαρτίαν δὲ μὴ καρτεροῦντος. ξυνελάμβανε δὲ αὐτῇ τῶν διαβολῶν καὶ οἰκέτης τοῦ πρεσβύτου μάγειρος, ᾧ ἐπωνυμία Κύθηρος, ὑποθωπεύων, ὥσπερ ἐν δράματι, τὸν δεσπότην καὶ τοιαυτὶ λέγων· "ὦ δέσποτα, βούλεταί σε ὁ υἱὸς ἤδη τεθνάναι, οὐδὲ τὸν αὐτόματον καὶ μετ᾽ οὐ πολὺ θάνατον ἐνδιδοὺς τῷ σῷ γήρᾳ, ἀλλ᾽ αὐτουργῶν μὲν τὴν ἐπιβουλήν, μισθούμενος δὲ καὶ τὰς ἐμὰς χεῖρας. ἔστι γὰρ αὐτῷ φάρμακα ἀνδροφόνα ἐπὶ σέ, ὧν τὸ καιριώτατον κελεύει με ἐμβαλεῖν εἰς ἕν τι τῶν ὄψων ἐλευθερίαν τε ὁμολογῶν καὶ ἀγροὺς καὶ οἰκίας καὶ χρήματα καὶ πᾶν ὅ τι βουλοίμην ἔχειν τοῦ σοῦ οἴκου· καὶ ταυτὶ μὲν πειθομένῳ εἶναι, ἀπειθοῦντι δὲ μαστίγωσίν τε καὶ στρέβλωσιν καὶ παχείας πέδας καὶ κύφωνα βαρύν." τοιοῖσδε θωπεύμασι περιελθὼν τὸν δεσπότην τελευτῶντος μετ᾽ οὐ πολὺ καὶ πρὸς διαθήκαις ὄντος γράφεται κληρονόμος, υἱός τε προσρηθεὶς καὶ ὀφθαλμοὶ καὶ ψυχὴ πᾶσα. καὶ οὐχὶ ταυτὶ χρὴ θαυμάζειν, ἐπεὶ πρεσβύτην ἐρῶντα ἔθελξεν ἴσως που καὶ παραπαίοντα ὑπὸ ἡλικίας καὶ αὐτοῦ τοῦ ἐρᾶν—καὶ γὰρ δὴ καὶ νέοι ἐρῶντες οὐκ ἔστιν ὅστις

(54) The reasons why his father became harsh toward him after earlier being kind and gentle, are told in many ways—some say one reason, some another and some more than one. But I shall reveal the truest one. After the death of Scopelian's mother, the old man took another woman, half-married and not in accordance with the laws. Seeing this, Scopelian tried to advise and deter him, but this is 517 irritating to those past their season. The woman then put together a story against him, claiming that he was in love with her, but could not bear his lack of success. A slave also joined with her in these slanders, the old man's cook whose nickname was Cytherus, who used to flatter his master, like a slave in a play, and said this: "Master, your son wishes you to die now at once, and does not grant to your old age the death that must come of its own accord and not in a long time. Rather he is preparing the plot himself, and attempting to hire my hands as well. He possesses manslaying drugs to use against you, and commands me to put some of them into one of your dishes at the most opportune time. And he promises me my freedom and land and houses and money and everything that I might want to have from your home. He says these things will be mine if I obey, but if I disobey he promises flogging and torture and thick shackles and a heavy pillory." With such flattery he beguiled his master, and when he was dying not long after and was making a will, the cook was appointed his heir, and was called his son and eyes and his whole soul. And there is no need to be astonished at this, because the one he bewitched was an old man in love and perhaps already impaired by his age as well as by his desire. (What is more even when young men are in love, there is not one

αὐτῶν τὸν ἑαυτοῦ νοῦν ἔχει—ἀλλ' ὅτι καὶ τῆς τοῦ
Σκοπελιανοῦ νεότητος⁴⁵ τε καὶ τῆς ἐν τοῖς δικαστηρίοις ἀκμῆς κρείττων ἔδοξεν, ἀγωνισάμενος μὲν περὶ
τῶν διαθηκῶν πρὸς αὐτόν, ἀντεκτείνας δὲ τῇ ἐκείνου
δεινότητι τὸν αὐτοῦ⁴⁶ πλοῦτον· ἀπαντλῶν γὰρ τῆς οὐσίας καὶ μισθούμενος ὑπερβολαῖς χρημάτων γλώττας ὁμοῦ πάσας καὶ δικαστῶν ψήφους πανταχοῦ τὴν
νικῶσαν ἀπηνέγκατο, ὅθεν ὁ Σκοπελιανὸς τὰ μὲν
Ἀναξαγόρου μηλόβοτα εἶναι, τὰ δὲ αὐτοῦ δουλόβοτα
ἔλεγεν. ἐπιφανὴς δὲ καὶ τὰ πολιτικὰ ὁ Κύθηρος γενόμενος γηράσκων ἤδη καὶ τὴν οὐσίαν ὁρῶν ὑποδιδοῦ-
σαν καταφρονούμενός τε ἱκανῶς καί που καὶ πληγὰς
λαβὼν πρὸς ἀνδρός, ὃν χρήματα ἀπαιτῶν ἐτύγχανεν,
518 ἱκέτης τοῦ Σκοπελιανοῦ γίγνεται μνησικακίαν τε
αὐτῷ παρεῖναι καὶ ὀργὴν ἀπολαβεῖν τε τὸν τοῦ πατρὸς οἶκον ἀνέντα μὲν αὐτῷ μέρος τῆς οἰκίας πολλῆς
οὔσης, ᾧ⁴⁷ μὴ ἀνελευθέρως ἐνδιαιτήσηται, συγχωρή-
σαντα δὲ ἀγροὺς δύο τῶν ἐπὶ θαλάττῃ. καὶ Κυθήρου
οἶκος ἐπωνόμασται νῦν ἔτι τὸ μέρος τῆς οἰκίας, ἐν ᾧ
κατεβίω. ταυτὶ μέν, ὡς μὴ ἀγνοεῖν αὐτά, συνιέναι δὲ
κἀκ τούτων, ὅτι οἱ ἄνθρωποι μὴ θεοῦ μόνον, ἀλλὰ καὶ
ἀλλήλων παίγνια.

⁴⁵ δεινότητος Kayser
⁴⁶ αὐτοῦ (αὐ-) a; ἐκείνου β
⁴⁷ ᾧ Reiske

[101] Anaxagoras, when exiled from Athens, lost his property,

of them who keeps his wits.) But it is astonishing that he seems to have overcome Scopelian's youthful energy and his dominance in the law courts, when he was contending about the will with him, and he countered that man's rhetorical power with his own wealth. Drawing upon the estate and bribing with extravagant sums all tongues equally and the votes of the jury, he won the victory at every point. For this reason Scopelian said that while Anaxagoras' property became a sheep pasture, his own was a slave pasture.[101] And in fact Cytherus became eminent in political life, but when he was growing old and saw that his property was depleted and that he was appropriately treated with contempt, and that he had even been struck by a man from whom he was trying to recover some money, he became a suppliant to Scopelian and begged him to forget the wrong he had done him and let go of his anger, and to take back his father's house, leaving him only a spacious part of the house so that he could live as befitted a free man, and to grant him as well two fields by the sea. And the part of the house in which he lived is called the Home of Cytherus even now. I have told all this so that it may not be unknown, but also so that one may understand from it that human beings are not only playthings of god but of one another.[102]

518

which was then neglected; the story is told by Diogenes Laertius 2.9; cf. Pl. *Hp. mi.* 283a; Philostr. *VA* 1.13.

[102] The idea of human beings as playthings of the gods has Pl. *Leg.* 644d as its *locus classicus*. The saying became a proverb, but is varied here to claim that we are playthings both of the gods and of human beings. Somewhat similarly at *VA* 4.36 (where the Platonic origin is named), it conveys the paradoxical idea of a ruler who is the plaything of his people.

PHILOSTRATUS

(55) Σκοπελιανοῦ δὲ σπουδάζοντος ἐν τῇ Σμύρνῃ ξυμφοιτᾶν μὲν ἐς αὐτὴν Ἰωνάς τε καὶ Λυδοὺς καὶ Κᾶρας καὶ Μαίονας, Αἰολέας τε καὶ τοὺς ἐκ Μυσῶν καὶ Φρυγῶν Ἕλληνας οὔπω μέγα, ἀγχίθυρος γὰρ τοῖς ἔθνεσι τούτοις ἡ Σμύρνα καὶ καιρίως ἔχουσα τῶν γῆς καὶ θαλάττης πυλῶν, ὁ δὲ ἦγε μὲν Καππαδόκας τε καὶ Ἀσσυρίους, ἦγε δὲ Αἰγυπτίους καὶ Φοίνικας, Ἀχαιῶν τε τοὺς εὐδοκιμωτέρους καὶ νεότητα τὴν ἐξ Ἀθηνῶν πᾶσαν. δόξαν μὲν οὖν ἐς τοὺς πολλοὺς παραδεδώκει ῥᾳστώνης τε καὶ ἀμελείας, ἐπειδὴ τὸν πρὸ τῆς μελέτης καιρὸν ξυνῆν ὡς ἐπὶ πολὺ τοῖς τῶν Σμυρναίων τέλεσιν ὑπὲρ τῶν πολιτικῶν. ὁ δὲ ἀπεχρῆτο μὲν καὶ τῇ φύσει λαμπρᾷ τε οὔσῃ καὶ μεγαλογνώμονι καὶ τὸν μεθ' ἡμέραν δὲ καιρὸν ἧττον ἐσπούδαζεν, ἀυπνότατος δ' ἀνθρώπων γενόμενος "ὦ νύξ," ἔλεγε, "σὺ γὰρ δὴ πλεῖστον σοφίας μετέχεις μέρος θεῶν," ξυνεργὸν δὲ αὐτὴν ἐποιεῖτο τῶν ἑαυτοῦ φροντισμάτων. λέγεται γοῦν καὶ ἐς ὄρθρον ἀποτεῖναι σπουδάζων ἀπὸ ἑσπέρας.

Προσέκειτο μὲν οὖν ἅπασι ποιήμασι, τραγῳδίας δὲ καὶ ἐνεφορεῖτο, ἀγωνιζόμενος πρὸς τὴν τοῦ διδασκάλου μεγαλοφωνίαν—ἀπὸ γὰρ τούτου τοῦ μέρους ὁ Νικήτης ἐθαυμάζετο—ὁ δὲ οὕτω τι μεγαλοφωνίας ἐπὶ μεῖζον ἤλασεν, ὡς καὶ Γιγαντίαν ξυνθεῖναι παραδοῦναί τε Ὁμηρίδαις ἀφορμὰς ἐς τὸν λόγον. ὡμίλει

[103] Men. *Misoumen.* 1–2. Scopelian adapted the line by substituting "wisdom" for "love".

116

(55) When Scopelian taught in Smyrna it is no wonder that Ionians, Lydians, Carians and Maeonians, Aeolians and the Greeks from Mysia and Phrygia traveled there to his school, because Smyrna neighbors these peoples and is a convenient gateway by land and sea. But he also attracted Cappadocians and Assyrians, and Egyptians and Phoenicians, the more honored of the Achaeans and all of the youth from Athens. He gave an appearance of nonchalance and negligence to the crowd, since for the most part he spent the time just before his declamation doing public business with the magistrates of Smyrna. But he employed his innate ability, which was brilliant and elevated, and though he did not work much during daylight hours, he was the most sleepless of men and used to say, "Night, you of all the gods possess the greatest share of wisdom,"[103] and he made her the coauthor of his speeches. At any rate, he is said to have continued working from dusk to dawn.

He devoted himself to all kinds of poetry, but especially filled himself with tragedy, contending with the grand style of his teacher, because it was for this aspect of his style that Nicetes was wondered at. And he went so far in this grand style that he even composed a *Gigantia* and provided the Homeridae with subjects for discussion.[104]

---

[104] The details here are not entirely clear, but it appears that Scopelian wrote an epic on the battle of the gods with the giants (*Gigantia*), which proved influential on subsequent, more derivative, poets. This is the reading of both Brodersen and Wright (in translations and notes ad loc.) Olearius translates the lines to mean that Scopelian's epic was performed by Homeric rhapsodes. For further discussion, see Sánchez Hernández 2011.

δὲ σοφιστῶν μὲν μάλιστα Γοργίᾳ τῷ Λεοντίνῳ, ῥη-
519 τόρων δὲ τοῖς λαμπρὸν ἠχοῦσιν. τὸ δὲ ἐπίχαρι φύσει
μᾶλλον εἶχεν ἢ μελέτῃ, προσφυὲς μὲν γὰρ τοῖς Ἰω-
νικοῖς τὸ ἀστεΐζεσθαι, τῷ δ' αὖ καὶ ἐπὶ τῶν λόγων τοῦ
φιλόγελω περιῆν, τὸ γὰρ κατηφὲς δυσξύμβολόν τε
καὶ ἀηδὲς ἡγεῖτο. παρῄει δὲ καὶ ἐς τοὺς δήμους ἀνειμένῳ[48] τῷ προσώπῳ, καὶ πολλῷ πλέον, ὅτε ξὺν ὀργῇ
ἐκκλησιάζοιεν, ἀνιεὶς αὐτοὺς καὶ διαπραΰνων τῇ τοῦ
εἴδους εὐθυμίᾳ. τὸ δ' ἐν τοῖς δικαστηρίοις ἦθος οὔτε
φιλοχρήματος οὔτε φιλολοίδορος· προῖκα μὲν γὰρ
ξυνέταττεν ἑαυτὸν τοῖς ὑπὲρ ψυχῆς κινδυνεύουσι, τοὺς
δὲ λοιδορουμένους ἐν τοῖς λόγοις καὶ θυμοῦ τινα ἐπίδειξιν ᾑρημένους[49] ποιεῖσθαι γραΐδια ἐκάλει μεθύοντα
καὶ λυττῶντα. τὰς δὲ μελέτας μισθοῦ μὲν ἐποιεῖτο, ὁ
δὲ μισθὸς ἦν ἄλλος ἄλλου καὶ ὡς ἕκαστος οἴκου εἶχεν, παρῄει τε ἐς αὐτοὺς οὔθ' ὑπερφρονῶν καὶ σεσο-
βημένος οὔθ' ὥσπερ οἱ δεδιότες, ἀλλ' ὡς εἰκὸς ἦν τὸν
ἀγωνιῶντα μὲν ὑπὲρ τῆς ἑαυτοῦ δόξης, θαρροῦντα δὲ
τῷ μὴ ἂν σφαλῆναι. διελέγετο δὲ ἀπὸ μὲν τοῦ θρόνου
ξὺν ἁβρότητι, ὅτε δὲ ὀρθὸς διαλέγοιτο, ἐπιστροφήν
τε εἶχεν ὁ λόγος καὶ ἔρρωτο. καὶ ἐπεσκοπεῖτο οὐκ
ἔνδον, οὐδ' ἐν τῷ ὁμίλῳ, ἀλλ' ὑπεξιὼν ἐν βραχεῖ τοῦ
καιροῦ διεώρα πάντα. περιῆν δὲ αὐτῷ καὶ εὐφωνίας,
καὶ τὸ φθέγμα ἡδονὴν εἶχε τόν τε μηρὸν θαμὰ ἔπλητ-
τεν ἑαυτόν τε ὑπεγείρων καὶ τοὺς ἀκροωμένους. ἄριστος μὲν οὖν καὶ σχηματίσαι λόγον καὶ ἐπαμφοτέρως

[48] ἀνειμένῳ τε καὶ διακεχυμένῳ MAb

118

Among the sophists he especially kept company with Gorgias of Leontini, and of the orators those with a brilliant tone. His charm was due more to nature than to study— since eloquent wit is innate to Ionians—and even in his speeches there was a love of humor, because he considered it unsociable and unpleasant to be sorrowful. He went even before the people with a relaxed expression, and much more than that, when the public assembly debated angrily, he relaxed and calmed them by the cheerfulness of his appearance. And his character in the law courts was neither greedy nor abusive, since he even worked for free for those who were in danger of their lives, and when men were abusive in their speeches and chose to make a show of anger, he called them drunken, mad old women. He produced speeches for a fee, but the fee was different for different people depending on their wealth. He went before his audience not with arrogance or swaggering, nor like those who are afraid, but as is right for one who is contending for his own glory, and is confident that he will not fail. While he was seated he spoke with charm, but when he stood upright, his speech became more vehement and powerful. He did not contemplate his theme in private, nor in front of his audience, but would withdraw for a short time and think through everything. His voice was extremely beautiful and his pronunciation charming, and he would often slap his thighs, rousing both himself and his listeners. He excelled in language adorned with formal figures and in ambiguity,[105] and was even more

519

---

[105] For these terms, see the Rhetorical Glossary.

---

49 ἡγουμένους ω; ᾑρημένους (or αἱρουμένους) Schröder

εἰπεῖν, θαυμασιώτερος δὲ περὶ τὰς ἀκμαιοτέρας τῶν
ὑποθέσεων καὶ πολλῷ πλέον περὶ τὰς Μηδικάς, ἐν αἷς
520 οἱ Δαρεῖοί τέ εἰσι καὶ οἱ Ξέρξαι· ταύτας γὰρ αὐτός τέ
μοι δοκεῖ ἄριστα σοφιστῶν ἑρμηνεῦσαι παραδοῦναί
τε τοῖς ἐπιγιγνομένοις ἑρμηνεύειν. καὶ γὰρ φρόνημα
ἐν αὐταῖς ὑπεκρίνατο καὶ κουφότητα τὴν ἐν τοῖς βαρβάροις ἤθεσιν. ἐλέγετο καὶ σείεσθαι μᾶλλον ἐν ταύταις, ὥσπερ βακχεύων, καί τινος τῶν ἀμφὶ Πολέμωνα
τυμπανίζειν αὐτὸν φήσαντος λαβόμενος ὁ Σκοπελιανὸς τοῦ σκώμματος, "τυμπανίζω μέν," εἶπεν "ἀλλὰ
τῇ τοῦ Αἴαντος ἀσπίδι."

(56) Βασίλειοι δὲ αὐτοῦ πρεσβεῖαι πολλαὶ μέν, καὶ
γάρ τις καὶ ἀγαθὴ τύχη ξυνηκολούθει πρεσβεύοντι,
ἀρίστη δὲ ἡ ὑπὲρ τῶν ἀμπέλων· οὐ γὰρ ὑπὲρ Σμυρναίων μόνον, ὥσπερ αἱ πλείους, ἀλλ' ὑπὲρ τῆς Ἀσίας
ὁμοῦ πάσης ἐπρεσβεύθη. τὸν δὲ νοῦν τῆς πρεσβείας
ἐγὼ δηλώσω. ἐδόκει τῷ βασιλεῖ μὴ εἶναι τῇ Ἀσίᾳ
ἀμπέλους, ἐπειδὴ ἐν οἴνῳ στασιάζειν ἔδοξαν, ἀλλ'
ἐξῃρῆσθαι μὲν τὰς ἤδη πεφυτευμένας, ἄλλας δὲ μὴ
φυτεύειν ἔτι. ἔδει δὴ πρεσβείας ἀπὸ τοῦ κοινοῦ καὶ
ἀνδρός, ὃς ἔμελλεν ὥσπερ Ὀρφεύς τις ἢ Θάμυρις
ὑπὲρ αὐτῶν θέλξειν. αἱροῦνται τοίνυν Σκοπελιανὸν
πάντες, ὁ δ' οὕτω τι ἐκ περιουσίας ἐκράτει τὴν πρεσβείαν, ὡς μὴ μόνον τὸ ἐξεῖναι φυτεύειν ἐπανελθεῖν

---

106 Homer describes the shield of Ajax at length immediately
before his battle with Hector: it is a shield of seven layers of ox
hide and one layer of bronze (*Il.* 7.219–25). In the combat that

astonishing on more elevated themes, and most of all by far on those concerning the Persian Wars, in which there are characters like Darius and Xerxes. He himself of all sophists seems to have treated these themes the best, and to have passed on to those later the ways to treat them. For in them he acted the arrogance and frivolity in barbarian characters. And it is said that he trembled more in these speeches, as if in Bacchic possession, and when one of Polemo's students said that he beat a loud drum, he took up the joke and said, "I do drum, but on the shield of Ajax."[106]

(56) He went on many embassies to emperors, and while good fortune always attended him when he was an ambassador, the most successful was the one on behalf of the grapevines. This embassy was not on behalf of the Smyrneans only, as were most of them, but was sent equally for the whole of Asia. I will relate the aim of the embassy. The emperor decided that there should not be vines in Asia, since the people seemed to become discordant under the influence of wine. Instead those already planted should be torn out, and no others planted. So a common embassy from the various cities was needed, and required a man who would be able to cast a spell on their behalf like some Orpheus or Thamyris. Therefore they unanimously chose Scopelian, who succeeded at the embassy so far beyond expectations that he returned having

520

follows, Hector's spear pierces through the bronze and six of the seven layers of hide but stops in the last (*Il.* 7.232–47). Ajax's shield is then an image of particular, heroic toughness, which Scopelian uses to ward off, or at least to temper, the Dionysian associations of drumming.

ἔχων, ἀλλὰ καὶ ἐπιτίμια κατὰ τῶν μὴ φυτευόντων. ὡς
δὲ ηὐδοκίμησε τὸν ἀγῶνα τὸν ὑπὲρ τῶν ἀμπέλων, δηλοῖ μὲν καὶ τὰ εἰρημένα, ὁ γὰρ λόγος ἐν τοῖς θαυμα-
σιωτάτοις, δηλοῖ δὲ καὶ τὰ ἐπὶ τῷ λόγῳ, δώρων τε
γὰρ ἐπ᾽ αὐτῷ ἔτυχεν, ἃ νομίζεται παρὰ βασιλεῖ, πολλῶν τε προσρήσεων καὶ ἐπαίνων, νεότης τε αὐτῷ
λαμπρὰ ξυνηκολούθησεν ἐς Ἰωνίαν, σοφίας ἐρῶντες.

521   (57) Ἐπεὶ δὲ Ἀθήνησιν ἐγένετο, ποιεῖται αὐτὸν ξένον ὁ Ἡρώδου τοῦ σοφιστοῦ πατὴρ Ἀττικός, θαυμά-
ζων ἐπὶ ῥητορικῇ μᾶλλον ἢ τὸν Γοργίαν ποτὲ Θετta-
λοί. ὁπόσοι γοῦν τῶν πάλαι ῥητόρων ἑρμαῖ ἦσαν ἐν
τοῖς τῆς οἰκίας δρόμοις, ἐκέλευε τούτους βάλλεσθαι
λίθοις, ὡς διεφθορότας αὐτῷ τὸν υἱόν. μειράκιον μὲν
δὴ ἐτύγχανεν ὢν ὁ Ἡρώδης τότε καὶ ὑπὸ τῷ πατρὶ
ἔτι, τοῦ δὲ αὐτοσχεδιάζειν ἥρα μόνου, οὐ μὴν ἐθάρρει
γε αὐτῷ, οὐδὲ γὰρ τῷ Σκοπελιανῷ ξυγγεγονὼς ἦν ἐς
ἐκεῖνό πω τοῦ χρόνου, οὐδ᾽ ἥτις ἡ τῶν αὐτοσχεδίων
ὁρμὴ γιγνώσκων· ὅθεν ἀσμένῳ οἱ ἐγένετο ἡ ἐπιδημία
τοῦ ἀνδρός. ἐπειδὴ γὰρ λέγοντος ἤκουσε καὶ διατι-
θεμένου τὸν αὐτοσχέδιον, ἐπερρώσθη[50] ὑπ᾽ αὐτοῦ καὶ
ἡτοιμάσθη, καὶ τὸν πατέρα δὲ ᾖσαι διανοηθεὶς ἀπαγ-
γέλλει οἱ μελέτην ἐς τὴν ἰδέαν τοῦ ξένου. ὁ πατὴρ δὲ
ἠγάσθη τε αὐτὸν τῆς μιμήσεως καὶ πεντακόσια[51] ἔδω-

[50] ἐπτερώθη ω
[51] πεντήκοντα Valckenaer

[107] The episode of Domitian's edict against the planting of
vines in Asia, which is told here in order to praise Sopelian's

not only permission to plant, but even penalties against those who did not plant.[107] How great a reputation he won for the contest about the vines is clear from what he said— since the speech is among his most astonishing—and is evident also in the results of the speech, for he acquired the gifts that are customary with an emperor, and many compliments and praise, and a brilliant group of youths followed him to Ionia, in love with his wisdom.

(57) When he was at Athens, Atticus, the father of the sophist Herodes, made him his guest-friend, astonished at   521
his rhetoric more than the Thessalians were once astonished by Gorgias. In fact, he commanded that all of the herms of ancient rhetoricians that were in the porticoes of his house, should be pelted with stones, because they had corrupted his son. Though Herodes was then a mere boy and still under his father's control, he loved only improvised speaking, though he was not yet confident in it, since he had not been the student of Scopelian at that time, nor did he know the vigor that improvisation requires. For these reasons he was delighted by the man's visit. When he heard him speak and compose an improvised speech, he was made strong and ready by him, and with the intention of pleasing his father, he performed a declamation in the style of their guest. His father admired his imitation, and gave him fifty talents, and gave fifteen as well to Sco-

embassy, also appears at *VA* 6.42, where Apollonius is credited with a successful intervention, apparently by means of philosophical gravitas and a witty aphorism. The same paradoxical conclusion (the punishment of those who do not plant vines) appears in both versions.

κεν αὐτῷ τάλαντα, ἔδωκε δὲ καὶ αὐτῷ Σκοπελιανῷ
πεντεκαίδεκα, ὁ δέ, ὅσαπερ ὁ πατήρ, τοσαῦτα ἀπὸ
τῆς ἑαυτοῦ δωρεᾶς προσέδωκεν αὐτῷ, ἔτι καὶ διδάσκαλον ἑαυτοῦ προσειπών. τουτὶ δὲ συνιέντι Ἡρώδου
καὶ τῶν τοῦ Πακτωλοῦ πηγῶν ἥδιον.

(58) Τὴν δὲ εὐτυχίαν, ᾗ περὶ τὰς πρεσβείας ἐχρῆτο,
ξυμβαλεῖν ἐστι καὶ τοῖσδε· ἔδει μὲν γὰρ τοῖς Σμυρναίοις τοῦ πρεσβεύσοντος ὑπὲρ αὐτῶν ἀνδρός, ἡ πρε-
σβεία δὲ ἦν ὑπὲρ τῶν μεγίστων. ὁ μὲν δὴ ἐγήρασκεν
ἤδη καὶ τοῦ ἀποδημεῖν ἐξώρως εἶχεν, ἐχειροτονεῖτο δὲ
ὁ Πολέμων οὔπω πεπρεσβευκὼς πρότερον. εὐξάμενος
οὖν ὑπὲρ τῆς ἀγαθῆς τύχης ἐδεῖτο γενέσθαι οἱ τὴν
τοῦ Σκοπελιανοῦ πειθώ, καὶ περιβαλὼν αὐτὸν ἐπὶ τῆς
ἐκκλησίας

δὸς δὲ μοι ὤμοιιν τὰ σὰ τεύχεα θωρηχθῆναι,
αἴ κ᾽ ἐμὲ σοὶ ἴσκωσι,

μάλα ἀστείως ὁ Πολέμων τὰ τοῦ Πατρόκλου ἐπειπὼν
τῷ ἀνδρί.[52] καὶ Ἀπολλώνιος δὲ ὁ Τυανεὺς ὑπερενεγ-
κὼν σοφίᾳ τὴν ἀνθρωπίνην φύσιν τὸν Σκοπελιανὸν
ἐν θαυμασίοις τάττει.

(59) 22. κβ΄. Διονύσιος δὲ ὁ Μιλήσιος εἴθ᾽, ὡς ἔνιοί
φασι, πατέρων ἐπιφανεστάτων ἐγένετο, εἴθ᾽, ὥς τινες,
αὐτὸ τοῦτο ἐλευθέρων, ἀφείσθω τούτου τοῦ μέρους,
ἐπειδὴ οἰκείᾳ ἀρετῇ ἐλαμπρύνετο, τὸ γὰρ καταφεύγειν

522

---

[52] Cobet's proposal to transpose δὸς δέ—ἴσκωσι and μάλα—
ἀνδρί (also adopted by Stefec) improves the run of the sentence.

plian himself. But Herodes from his own gift gave Scopelian as much as his father had given, and called him his
own teacher. Hearing this from Herodes was sweeter to
him than the springs of Pactolus.[108]

(58) The good fortune that he enjoyed concerning his
embassies is evident in the following story too. The people
of Smyrna needed a man to go as an ambassador on their
behalf, and the embassy was concerned with the most important affairs. Scopelian was an old man, and past the age
for traveling, so Polemo was elected, though he had not
previously served as an ambassador. So when he prayed
for good fortune, he asked that the persuasion of Scopelian be with him, and embracing him in front of the assembly, Polemo said,

> give me your armor to wear on my shoulders,
> so that they might mistake me for you,

very aptly applying the verses of Patroclus to the man.[109]
And Apollonius of Tyana, who surpassed human nature
in his wisdom, ranked Scopelian among those to be admired.[110]

(59) 22. Regarding Dionysius of Miletus whether, as
some say, he was descended from the most distinguished
ancestors or whether, as others say, he was merely of free
birth, let him be free of this question, since he achieved   522
fame by his own excellence. Running away to one's ances-

---

[108] The springs of Pactolus in the Tmolus mountain range in
Lydia were famous for their electrum and alluvial gold (Hdt.
1.93.1, 5.101.2).   [109] Hom. *Il.* 16.40–41.

[110] See *VA* 1.23–24. Penella (1974) is right to see fiction in this
part of the *VA*.

ἐς τοὺς ἄνω ἀποβεβληκότων ἐστὶ τὸν ἐφ᾽ ἑαυτῶν
ἔπαινον. Ἰσαίου δὲ ἀκροατὴς γενόμενος, ἀνδρός, ὡς
ἔφην, κατὰ φύσιν ἑρμηνεύοντος, τουτὶ μὲν ἱκανῶς
ἀπεμάξατο καὶ πρὸς τούτῳ τὴν εὐταξίαν τῶν νοη-
μάτων· καὶ γὰρ δὴ καὶ τοῦτο Ἰσαίου. μελιχρότατος
δὲ περὶ τὰς ἐννοίας γενόμενος οὐκ ἐμέθυε περὶ τὰς
ἡδονάς, ὥσπερ ἔνιοι τῶν σοφιστῶν, ἀλλ᾽ ἐταμιεύετο
λέγων πρὸς τοὺς γνωρίμους, ὅτι χρὴ τοῦ μέλιτος
ἄκρῳ δακτύλῳ, ἀλλὰ μὴ κοίλῃ χειρὶ γεύεσθαι, ὡς ἐν
ἅπασι μὲν τοῖς εἰρημένοις δεδήλωται τῷ Διονυσίῳ,
λογικοῖς τε καὶ νομικοῖς καὶ ἠθικοῖς ἀγῶσι, μάλιστα
δ᾽ ἐν τῷ ἐπὶ Χαιρωνείᾳ θρήνῳ. διεξιὼν γὰρ τὸν Δη-
μοσθένην τὸν μετὰ Χαιρώνειαν προσαγαγόντα[53] τῇ
βουλῇ ἑαυτόν, ἐς τήνδε τὴν μονῳδίαν τοῦ λόγου ἐτε-
λεύτησεν· "ὦ Χαιρώνεια πονηρὸν χωρίον." καὶ πάλιν
"ὦ αὐτομολήσασα πρὸς τοὺς βαρβάρους Βοιωτία.
στενάξατε οἱ κατὰ γῆς ἥρωες, ἐγγὺς Πλαταιῶν νενι-
κήμεθα." καὶ πάλιν ἐν τοῖς κρινομένοις ἐπὶ τῷ μισθο-
φορεῖν Ἀρκάσιν "ἀγορὰ πολέμου πρόκειται καὶ τὰ
τῶν Ἑλλήνων κακὰ τὴν Ἀρκάδων τρέφει," καὶ "ἐπέρ-
χεται πόλεμος αἰτίαν οὐκ ἔχων."

(60) Τοιάδε μὲν ἡ ἐπίπαν ἰδέα τοῦ Διονυσίου, καθ᾽
ἣν τὰ τῆς μελέτης αὐτῷ προὔβαινεν ἐπισκοπουμένῳ
καιρόν, ὅσονπερ ὁ Ἰσαῖος, ὁ δὲ λόγος ὁ περὶ τοῦ

[53] The MSS vary here between προσαγαγόντα and προσά-
γοντα, and M gives before it θρῆνον, which seems to have
intruded from the previous sentence.

tors is typical of those who despair of acclaim in their own right. And he was a student of Isaeus, a man who, as I said earlier, declaimed in a natural style. He took the impression of this style adequately, and in addition to this his capacity for ordering his thoughts. This too, in fact, was characteristic of Isaeus. And though he positively dripped with honey in his ideas, he did not luxuriate in these pleasures, as some sophists do, but he rationed them, and would say to his students that honey must be tasted with a fingertip, not by the handful. This is clear in all of the speeches by Dionysius, whether they are logical, legal or ethical, and most of all in his *Lament for Chaeronea.* When he represented Demosthenes denouncing himself to the council after Chaeronea,[111] he ended the speech with this monody: "O Chaeronea, wicked city!" and again, "O Boeotia, deserter to the barbarians! Groan, you heroes below the earth! We have been conquered near Plataea!" And again in the speech where the Arcadians are on trial for being mercenaries he said: "The marketplace of war lies open and the evils afflicting the Greeks nourish the land of the Arcadians." And "A war comes without a cause."[112]

(60) That is what Dionysius' general style was like, in accordance with which the points of his declamation proceeded. He used to contemplate his theme for about as long as did Isaeus. As to the story told about Dionysius,

523

---

[111] This imaginary situation appears again in the repertoire of Polemo (*VS* 542). It is also mentioned in Syrianus' *Commentary on Hermogenes* (2.165) and in Apsines (9.471).

[112] On the Asianic rhythms in these quotations, see Norden 1923, 1.413. The Arcadians were notorious mercenaries; cf. Xen. *Hell.* 7.23.

Διονυσίου λεγόμενος, ὡς Χαλδαίων τέχναις τοὺς ὁμιλητὰς τὸ μνημονικὸν ἀναπαιδεύοντος πόθεν εἴρηται,
ἐγὼ δηλώσω. τέχναι μνήμης οὔτε εἰσὶν οὔτ᾿ ἂν γέ-
νοιντο, μνήμη μὲν γὰρ δίδωσι τέχνας, αὐτὴ δὲ ἀδί-
δακτος καὶ οὐδεμιᾷ τέχνῃ ἁλωτός, ἔστι γὰρ πλεονέκτημα φύσεως ἢ τῆς ἀθανάτου ψυχῆς μοῖρα. οὐ γὰρ
ἄν ποτε μαθητὰ[54] νομισθείη τὰ ἀνθρώπεια, οὔτ᾿ αὖ[55]
διδακτά, ἃ ἐμάθομεν, εἰ μὴ μνήμη συνεπολιτεύετο ἀνθρώποις, ἣν εἴτε μητέρα χρόνου δεῖ καλεῖν, εἴτε
παῖδα, μὴ διαφερώμεθα πρὸς τοὺς ποιητάς, ἀλλ᾿ ἔστω
ὅ τι βούλονται. πρὸς δὲ τούτοις τίς οὕτως εὐήθης
κατὰ τῆς ἑαυτοῦ δόξης ἐν σοφοῖς γραφόμενος, ὡς
γοητεύων ἐν μειρακίοις διαβάλλειν καὶ ἃ ὀρθῶς ἐπαιδεύθη; πόθεν οὖν τὸ μνημονικὸν τοῖς ἀκρωμένοις;
ἄπληστα τὴν ἡδονὴν ἐδόκει τὰ τοῦ Διονυσίου καὶ
πολλάκις ἐπαναλαμβάνειν αὐτὰ ἠναγκάζετο, ἐπειδὴ
ξυνίει σφῶν χαιρόντων τῇ ἀκροάσει. οἱ δὴ εὐμαθέ-
στεροι τῶν νέων ἐνετυποῦντο αὐτὰ ταῖς γνώμαις καὶ
ἀπήγγελλον ἑτέροις μελέτῃ μᾶλλον ἢ μνήμῃ ξυνειλη-

[54] μαθητά Jacobs; θνητά ω; ἀθάνατα Jahn
[55] οὔτ᾿ αὖ Reiske; οὔτ᾿ ἄν is the reading of the archetype

113 The *Chaldean Oracles* date from the latter part of the
second century, but it is not likely that they had come close
enough to the cultural mainstream that Philostratus' allusion here
is to them. Nor does he refer to Chaldean astrology. Rather all of
these ascriptions to the Chaldeans in Graco-Roman culture make
use of the same mystique associated with this type of barbarian
wisdom.

that he used to educate his students in memory by means of the arts of the Chaldeans,[113] I shall show how it arose. There neither are arts of memory nor could there be, because memory gives us the arts, but cannot itself be taught or captured by any art. Rather it is a gift of nature, or a part of the immortal soul. For human things could not be learned, nor could they be taught (which we have indeed learned), if memory did not dwell in human beings. Let us not argue with the poets whether we should call memory the mother of time or its child, but let it be however they wish.[114] Besides these considerations, what man who was enlisted in the ranks of the sophists, due to his own reputation, would be so foolish as to bring scandal on what had been correctly taught, by using sorcery with young men?[115] So how did strength of memory come to his students? The speeches of Dionysius seemed to give them unlimited delight, and he was compelled to repeat them many times, since he knew that they enjoyed hearing them. So the better students among the youths engraved them on their minds and used to recite them to the others,

---

[114] Philostratus takes a deliberately provocative position in denying the possibility of an art of memory, since such an art was indeed often taught as part of rhetorical training. See most famously the *Rhet. Her.* 3.16–3.24, which begins its discussion by noting the disagreement that Philostratus also raises (i.e., whether memory is entirely natural or a matter of technique), before assuming the opposite of Philostratus' claim. The sophistic art of memory goes back to the poet Simonides.

[115] Somewhat similarly, Philostratus has Apollonius appeal to the implausibility of wise men condoning or using magic in his defense against a charge of *goēteia* before Domitian (*VA* 8.6.7).

φότες, ὅθεν μνημονικοί τε ὠνομάζοντο καὶ τέχνῃ αὐτὸ
524 πεπαιδευμένοι.[56] ἔνθεν ὁρμώμενοί τινες τὰς τοῦ Διονυσίου μελέτας ἐσπερματολογῆσθαί φασιν, ὡς δὴ ἄλλο
ἄλλου ξυνενεγκόντος[57] ἐς αὐτάς, ἐν ᾧ ἐβραχυλόγη-
σεν.

(61) Μεγάλων μὲν οὖν ἠξιοῦτο κἀκ τῶν πόλεων,
ὁπόσαι αὐτὸν ἐπὶ σοφίᾳ ἐθαύμαζον, μεγίστων δὲ ἐκ
βασιλέως. Ἀδριανὸς γὰρ σατράπην μὲν αὐτὸν ἀπέφη-
νεν οὐκ ἀφανῶν ἐθνῶν, κατέλεξε[58] δὲ τοῖς δημοσίᾳ
ἱππεύουσι καὶ τοῖς ἐν τῷ Μουσείῳ σιτουμένοις, τὸ δὲ
Μουσεῖον τράπεζα Αἰγυπτία ξυγκαλοῦσα τοὺς ἐν
πάσῃ τῇ γῇ ἐλλογίμους. πλείστας δὲ ἐπελθὼν πόλεις
καὶ πλείστοις ἐνομιλήσας ἔθνεσιν οὔτε ἐρωτικήν ποτε
αἰτίαν ἔλαβεν οὔτε ἀλαζόνα ὑπὸ τοῦ σωφρονέστατός
τε φαίνεσθαι καὶ ἐφεστηκώς. οἱ δὲ ἀνατιθέντες Διονυσίῳ τὸν Ἀράσπαν τὸν τῆς Πανθείας ἐρῶντα ἀνήκοοι
μὲν τῶν τοῦ Διονυσίου ῥυθμῶν, ἀνήκοοι δὲ τῆς ἄλλης
ἑρμηνείας, ἄπειροι δὲ τῆς τῶν ἐνθυμημάτων τέχνης·
οὐ γὰρ Διονυσίου τὸ φρόντισμα τοῦτο, ἀλλὰ Κέλερος
τοῦ τεχνογράφου, ὁ δὲ Κέλερ βασιλικῶν μὲν ἐπιστο-

---

[56] τέχνην . . . πεποιημένοι a
[57] The MSS vary between ἄλλο ἄλλου and ἄλλου, in place
of which Callistus suggested ἄλλο ἄλλων, to agree with ξυνενεγ-
κόντων. I have adopted Boter's suggestion of the singular
participle ξυνενεγκόντος.   [58] ἐγκατέλεξε Valckenaer

---

[116] That is, procurator. An Ephesian inscription refers to Dionysius as ἐπίτροπον τοῦ Σεβαστοῦ.

because they had grasped them from practice rather than sheer memory. For this reason they acquired a name as memory artists and for having learned that skill by art. It is because of this that some say that the declamations 524 of Dionysius are pieced together, since different people added different things into them, where he himself had been concise.

(61) He was greatly honored by the cities that admired his wisdom, but honored most of all by an emperor. For Hadrian appointed him satrap[116] over a people by no means insignificant, and enrolled him in the equestrian order and among those who dined in the Museum. This is a state table in Egypt, which calls together the most eminent men in all the world. Though he traveled to a great number of cities and lived among a great number of peoples, he never incurred a charge of being lecherous or a charlatan, because he appeared most self-controlled and focused. And those who ascribe to Dionysius *Araspes the Lover of Panthea*[117] have not paid attention to Dionysius' rhythms, nor have they paid attention to the rest of his style of composition. They are, moreover, ignorant of the whole art of rhetorical invention, because this is not the intellectual work of Dionysius, but of Celer, who wrote about rhetoric. But Celer, although he was a good *ab*

[117] Panthea, wife of the Persian king Abradatas, was taken captive by the Elder Cyrus and placed in charge of the Mede Araspes, who fell in love with her; cf. Xen. *Cyr.* 5.1.4. Philostr. *Imag.* 2.9 imagines her appearance on the basis of her moral character (Miles 2018, 91–96). Celer's work, as described here, shows how close declamation could be to historical fiction in the manner of Chariton.

λῶν ἀγαθὸς προστάτης, μελέτῃ δὲ οὐκ ἀποχρῶν, Διονυσίῳ δὲ τὸν ἐκ μειρακίου χρόνον διάφορος.

(62) Μηδ᾽ ἐκεῖνα παρείσθω μοι Ἀρισταίου γε ἠκρο-
αμένῳ αὐτὰ πρεσβυτάτου τῶν κατ᾽ ἐμὲ Ἑλλήνων καὶ
πλεῖστα ὑπὲρ σοφιστῶν εἰδότος· ἐγήρασκε μὲν ὁ Διονύσιος ἐν δόξῃ λαμπρᾷ, παρῄει δ᾽ ἐς ἀκμὴν ὁ Πολέμων οὔπω γιγνωσκόμενος τῷ Διονυσίῳ καὶ ἐπεδήμει
ταῖς Σάρδεσιν ἀγορεύσων⁵⁹ δίκην ἐν τοῖς ἑκατὸν ἀνδράσιν, ὑφ᾽ ὧν ἐδικαιοῦτο ἡ Λυδία. ἑσπέρας οὖν ἐς
525   τὰς Σάρδεις ἥκων ὁ Διονύσιος ἤρετο Δωρίωνα τὸν
κριτικὸν ξένον ἑαυτοῦ· "εἰπέ μοι," ἔφη "ὦ Δωρίων, τί
Πολέμων ἐνταῦθα;" καὶ ὁ Δωρίων, "ἀνὴρ" ἔφη, "πλουσιώτατος τῶν ἐν Λυδίᾳ κινδυνεύων περὶ τῆς οὐσίας
ἄγει συνήγορον τὸν Πολέμωνα ἀπὸ Σμύρνης πείσας
διταλάντῳ μισθῷ, καὶ ἀγωνιεῖται τὴν δίκην αὔριον."
καὶ ὁ Διονύσιος, "οἶον," ἔφη, "ἕρμαιον εἴρηκας, εἰ καὶ
ἀκοῦσαί μοι ἔσται Πολέμωνος οὔπω ἐς πεῖραν αὐτοῦ
ἀφιγμένῳ." "ἔοικεν," εἶπεν ὁ Δωρίων, "στρέφειν σε ὁ
νεανίας ἐς ὄνομα ἤδη προβαίνων μέγα." "καὶ καθεύ-
δειν γε οὐκ ἐᾷ, μὰ τὴν Ἀθηνᾶν," ᾗ δ᾽ ὁ Διονύσιος,
"ἀλλ᾽ ἐς πήδησιν ἄγει τὴν καρδίαν καὶ τὴν γνώμην
ἐνθυμουμένῳ, ὡς πολλοὶ οἱ ἐπαινέται αὐτοῦ, καὶ τοῖς
μὲν δωδεκάκρουνος⁶⁰ δοκεῖ τὸ στόμα, οἱ δὲ καὶ πήχεσι
διαμετροῦσι τὴν γλῶτταν, ὥσπερ τὰς τοῦ Νείλου

---

⁵⁹ Cobet proposed ἀγορεύσων for the MSS᾽ ἀγορεύων.

⁶⁰ δωδεκάκρουνον is the reading of Stefec's β group; δωδεκάκρουνον of the other MSS. Wright compares Cratinus, *Oil
Flask frag.* 7.

epistulis Graecis, did not practice declamation, and had a long-standing disagreement with Dionysius from their youth.

(62) I must not pass over the things that I heard from Aristaeus, who was the oldest of the educated Hellenes in my day and knew the most about sophists. When Dionysius was growing old and enjoyed a glowing reputation, Polemo was coming to his peak, but was not yet personally known to Dionysius. Polemo paid a visit to Sardis in order to plead a case before the Centumviri who had jurisdiction over Lydia. When Dionysius came to Sardis in the evening he asked the critic Dorion, who was his host: "Tell me,   525 Dorion, why is Polemo here?" And Dorion said, "A very wealthy Lydian man is in danger of losing his property, and he brings Polemo here from Smyrna as his advocate, persuading him with a payment of two talents, and Polemo will contend the case tomorrow." And Dionysius said, "What a stroke of luck you've told me about, if it will really be possible for me listen to Polemo, since I have not yet come to experience him." "It seems," said Dorion, "that the young man torments you by coming so quickly to a great reputation." "Indeed he doesn't let me sleep," said Dionysius, "but he makes my heart and mind palpitate, since so many praise him. To some his mouth seems to flow with twelve springs, and others measure his tongue in cubits, like the inundations of the Nile.[118] But you might

---

[118] The adjective "having twelve springs" indicates the volume and variety of his oratory. On the cubits of the Nile's rising, a familiar image in art and text of this period, see also Philostr. *Imag.* 1.5.

ἀναβάσεις. σὺ δ᾽ ἂν ταύτην ἰάσαιό μοι τὴν φροντίδα
εἰπών, τί μὲν πλέον, τί δὲ ἧττον ἐν ἐμοί τε κἀκείνῳ
καθεώρακας." καὶ ὁ Δωρίων μάλα σωφρόνως, "αὐτός,"
εἶπεν, "ὦ Διονύσιε, σεαυτῷ τε κἀκείνῳ δικάσεις ἄμει-
νον· σὺ γὰρ ὑπὸ σοφίας οἷος σαυτόν τε γιγνώσκειν,
ἕτερόν τε μὴ ἀγνοῆσαι."

Ἤκουσεν ὁ Διονύσιος ἀγωνιζομένου τὴν δίκην καὶ
ἀπιὼν τοῦ δικαστηρίου "ἰσχύν," ἔφη, "ὁ ἀθλητὴς ἔχει,
ἀλλ᾽ οὐκ ἐκ παλαίστρας." ταῦτα ὡς ἤκουσεν ὁ Πολέμων, ἦλθε μὲν ἐπὶ θύρας τοῦ Διονυσίου μελέτην αὐτῷ
ἐπαγγέλλων, ἀφικομένου δὲ διαπρεπῶς ἀγωνιζόμενος
526 προσῆλθε τῷ Διονυσίῳ καὶ ἀντερείσας τὸν ὦμον,
ὥσπερ οἱ τῆς σταδιαίας πάλης ἐμβιβάζοντες, μάλα
ἀστείως ἐπετώθασεν εἰπὼν

ἦσάν ποτ᾽, ἦσαν ἄλκιμοι Μιλήσιοι.

(63) Ἀνδρῶν μὲν οὖν ἐπιφανῶν πᾶσα γῆ τάφος,
Διονυσίῳ δὲ σῆμα ἐν τῇ ἐπιφανεστάτῃ Ἐφέσῳ· τέθαπται γὰρ ἐν τῇ ἀγορᾷ κατὰ τὸ κυριώτατον τῆς Ἐφέσου, ἐν ᾗ κατεβίω, παιδεύσας τὸν πρῶτον βίον ἐν
Λέσβῳ.

(64) 23. κγ'. Λολλιανὸς δὲ ὁ Ἐφέσιος προὔστη μὲν
τοῦ Ἀθήνησι θρόνου πρῶτος, προὔστη δὲ καὶ τοῦ
Ἀθηναίων δήμου στρατηγήσας αὐτοῖς τὴν ἐπὶ τῶν

---

119 For this iambic response of Apollo, which became a proverb for the degenerate, cf. Ar. *Plut.* 1002, quoting Anac. fr. 81.

cure this anxiety for me, by saying what strengths and weaknesses you have observed in me and in him." And Dorion answered very diplomatically, "You yourself, Dionysius, will be a better judge of yourself and of him. You have the wisdom to know yourself, and accurately to observe another."

Dionysius listened to Polemo contending the case and as he left the law court he said, "The athlete has strength, but not from the wrestling school." When Polemo heard this he went to Dionysius' door and announced that he would declaim for him. And when Dionysius came and Polemo contended before him magnificently, he approached Dionysius and, leaning on his shoulder like those who are beginning a standing wrestling match, he teased him very wittily, saying,

> Once, oh once they were strong the men of
>   Miletus.[119]

(63) Famous men have the whole earth for their tomb,[120] but Dionysius' tomb was in the most famous part of Ephesus. He was buried in the agora, in the most important place in Ephesus, in which he came to the end of his life, though he had taught for the first part of it on Lesbos.[121]

(64) 23. Lollianus of Ephesus was the first to be appointed to the chair of rhetoric at Athens,[122] and was appointed also to power over the Athenian people, since he

[120] Echoing Pericles' funeral oration in Thuc. 2.43.

[121] On the tomb of Dionysius, see Bowersock 1969, 51–53; and J. Robert and L. Robert 1971, 491–92.

[122] That is, the municipal, as distinct from the imperial chair.

135

ὅπλων. ἡ δὲ ἀρχὴ αὕτη πάλαι μὲν κατέλεγέ τε καὶ
ἐξῆγεν εἰς τὰ πολέμια, νυνὶ δὲ τροφῶν ἐπιμελεῖται καὶ
σίτου ἀγορᾶς. θορύβου δὲ καθεστηκότος παρὰ τὰ ἀρ-
τοπώλια καὶ τῶν Ἀθηναίων βάλλειν αὐτὸν ὡρμη-
κότων Παγκράτης ὁ κύων ὁ μετὰ ταῦτα ἐν Ἰσθμῷ
φιλοσοφήσας παρελθὼν ἐς τοὺς Ἀθηναίους καὶ εἰπών,
"Λολλιανὸς οὐκ ἔστιν ἀρτοπώλης, ἀλλὰ λογοπώλης,"
διέχεεν οὕτω τοὺς Ἀθηναίους, ὡς μεθεῖναι τοὺς λίθους
διὰ χειρῶν αὐτοῖς ὄντας. σίτου δὲ ἐκ Θετταλίας ἐσπε-
πλευκότος καὶ χρημάτων δημοσίᾳ οὐκ ὄντων ἐπέτρε-
ψεν ὁ Λολλιανὸς ἔρανον τοῖς αὐτοῦ γνωρίμοις, καὶ
χρήματα συχνὰ ἠθροίσθη. καὶ τοῦτο μὲν ἀνδρὸς εὐ-
527 μηχάνου δόξει καὶ σοφοῦ τὰ πολιτικά, ἐκεῖνο δὲ δικαίου τε καὶ εὐγνώμονος· τὰ γὰρ χρήματα ταῦτα τοῖς
ξυμβαλομένοις ἀπέδωκεν ἐπανεὶς τὸν μισθὸν τῆς
ἀκροάσεως.

(65) Ἔδοξε δὲ ὁ σοφιστὴς οὗτος τεχνικώτατός
τε καὶ φρονιμώτατος τὸ ἐπιχειρηματικὸν ἐν ἐπινοίᾳ
τεχνικῇ κείμενον ἱκανὸς[61] ἐκπονῆσαι, καὶ ἑρμηνεῦσαι
μὲν ἀποχρῶν, νοῆσαι δέ τε καὶ τὰ νοηθέντα τάξαι
ἀπέριττος. διαφαίνονται δὲ τοῦ λόγου καὶ λαμπρότη-
τες λήγουσαι ταχέως, ὥσπερ τὸ τῆς ἀστραπῆς σέλας.
δηλοῦται δὲ τοῦτο ἐν πᾶσι μέν, μάλιστα δὲ ἐν τοῖσδε·
κατηγορῶν μὲν γὰρ τοῦ Λεπτίνου διὰ τὸν νόμον, ἐπεὶ

[61] ἱκανός Gruter; ἱκανῶς ω

[123] If our Philostratus is the L. Flavius Philostratus who appears in three inscriptions, he himself held this office between

served as hoplite general there. Long ago the duty of this office was to enlist troops and lead them to war, but now it is concerned with the food supply and produce market.[123] Once when there was a riot in the bread-sellers' quarter, and the Athenians were rushing forward to stone Lollianus, Pancrates the Cynic, who later taught philosophy at the Isthmus, came before the Athenians and said, "Lollianus is not a bread merchant, but a word merchant." Saying this he dispersed the crowd, so that they dropped the stones in their hands. And once when a cargo of grain came in from Thessaly, and there was no public money to pay for it, Lollianus had his students contribute, and a great sum of money was collected. This shows that he was a resourceful man and wise in political affairs, but what he did next shows that he was just and considerate. For he gave back the money to those who contributed it, by waiving his lecture fee.

(65) This sophist was considered very skilled in his art and very clever at successfully working out a detailed, technical argument with skillful invention. He was capable at invention, and concise at thinking through arranging his ideas. Flashes of brilliance glow through his words and suddenly cease, like bolts of lightning. This is evident in many places, but especially in the passage that I will now quote: when he was prosecuting Leptines due to his law,[124]

527

200/1 and 210/11. See Bowie 2009, 19–20, for further bibliography.

[124] This fictitious theme is based on Demosthenes, *Leptines* 30, delivered in 355, and assumes that the law of Leptines to abolish exemptions from public services was in force, and that the evils foreboded by Demosthenes had come about; cf. Apsines 232 for the same theme.

μὴ ἐφοίτα τοῖς Ἀθηναίοις ἐκ τοῦ Πόντου σῖτος, ὧδε
ἤκμασε· "κέκλεισται τὸ στόμα τοῦ Πόντου νόμῳ καὶ
τὰς Ἀθηναίων τροφὰς ὀλίγαι κωλύουσι συλλαβαί,
καὶ ταὐτὸν δύναται Λύσανδρος ναυμαχῶν καὶ Λεπτίνης νομοθετῶν·" ἀντιλέγων δὲ τοῖς Ἀθηναίοις ἀπορίᾳ
χρημάτων βουλευομένοις πωλεῖν τὰς νήσους ὧδε
ἔπνευσε· "λῦσον, ὦ Πόσειδον, τὴν ἐπὶ Δήλῳ χάριν,
συγχώρησον αὐτῇ πωλουμένῃ φυγεῖν." ἐσχεδίαζε μὲν
οὖν κατὰ τὸν Ἰσαῖον, οὗ δὴ καὶ ἠκροάσατο, μισθοὺς
δὲ γενναίους ἐπράττετο τὰς ξυνουσίας οὐ μελετηρὰς
μόνον, ἀλλὰ καὶ διδασκαλικὰς παρέχων. εἰκόνες δὲ
αὐτοῦ Ἀθήνησι μία μὲν ἐπ' ἀγορᾶς, ἑτέρα δὲ ἐν τῷ
ἄλσει τῷ μικρῷ, ὃ αὐτὸς λέγεται ἐκφυτεῦσαι.

(66) 24. κδ΄. Οὐδὲ τὸν Βυζάντιον σοφιστὴν παρα-
λείψω Μᾶρκον, ὑπὲρ οὗ κἂν ἐπιπλήξαιμι τοῖς Ἕλλησιν, εἰ τοιόσδε γενόμενος, ὁποῖον δηλώσω, μήπω τυγχάνει τῆς ἑαυτοῦ δόξης. Μάρκῳ τοίνυν ἦν ἀναφορὰ
τοῦ γένους εἰς τὸν ἀρχαῖον Βύζαντα, πατὴρ δὲ ὁμώνυμος ἔχων θαλαττουργοὺς οἰκέτας ἐφ' Ἱερῷ, τὸ δὲ
Ἱερὸν παρὰ τὰς ἐκβολὰς τοῦ Πόντου. διδάσκαλος δὲ
αὐτοῦ Ἰσαῖος ἐγένετο, παρ' οὗ καὶ τὸ κατὰ φύσιν
ἑρμηνεύειν μαθὼν ἐπεκόσμησεν αὐτὸ ὡραισμένῃ

---

[125] Norden (1923, 410) quotes this passage for its "similar
endings."

[126] Delos was once a "floating" island and was made stationary
by Poseidon; cf. Ov. *Met.* 6.191.

because the supply of corn did not reach the Athenians from the Pontus, he came to the following climax: "The mouth of the Pontus has been locked up by law, and a few syllables keep back the food supply of Athens, so that Lysander fighting with his ships and Leptines with his law have the same power."[125] And again when his theme was to oppose the Athenians, when they were planning to sell the islands for lack of money, he declaimed forcefully: "Release, Poseidon, the favor that you granted Delos, allow her, while she is being sold, to flee."[126] He improvised in the style of Isaeus, whose student he had been. He charged handsome fees, not only for classes in declamation but also in the principles of the art. There are two statues of him at Athens, one in the agora, another in the small grove that he himself is said to have planted.

(66) 24. Nor must I pass over the sophist Marcus of Byzantium, for whose sake I rebuke the Greeks, because even though he was as great as I will show him to be, he has not yet achieved the reputation he deserves. Marcus could trace his ancestry back to the ancient Byzas,[127] and Marcus' father, who had the same name, owned slaves who were fishermen at Hieron. (Hieron is near the entrance to the Pontus.)[128] Marcus' teacher was Isaeus, from whom he learned how to treat rhetorical themes naturally, and he adorned this approach with a gentleness infused with

528

[127] The legendary founder of Byzantium, said to have been the son of Poseidon. For the traditions concerning him, see the opening chapters of the *Patria of Constantinople*.

[128] Philostratus describes in the *Imagines* (1.12) a fishing scene including, it seems, this same temple (Hieron) on the Bosporus.

πρᾳότητι. καὶ παράδειγμα ἱκανώτατον τῆς Μάρκου
ἰδέας ὁ Σπαρτιάτης ὁ ξυμβουλεύων τοῖς Λακεδαιμονίοις μὴ δέχεσθαι τοὺς ἀπὸ Σφακτηρίας γυμνοὺς
ἥκοντας. τῆσδε γὰρ τῆς ὑποθέσεως ἤρξατο ὧδε·
"ἀνὴρ Λακεδαιμόνιος μέχρι γήρως φυλάξας τὴν
ἀσπίδα ἡδέως μὲν ἂν τοὺς γυμνοὺς τούτους ἀπέ-
κτεινα." ὅστις δὲ καὶ τὰς διαλέξεις ὅδε ὁ ἀνὴρ ἐγένετο, ξυμβαλεῖν ἐστιν ἐκ τῶνδε· διδάσκων γὰρ περὶ
τῆς τῶν σοφιστῶν τέχνης, ὡς πολλὴ καὶ ποικίλη,
παράδειγμα τοῦ λόγου τὴν ἶριν ἐποιήσατο καὶ ἤρξατο τῆς διαλέξεως ὧδε· "ὁ τὴν ἶριν ἰδών ὡς ἓν
χρῶμα, οὐκ εἶδεν ὡς θαυμάσαι, ὁ δέ ὅσα χρώματα,
μᾶλλον ἐθαύμασεν." οἱ δὲ τὴν διάλεξιν ταύτην Ἀλκι-
νόῳ τῷ Στωικῷ ἀνατιθέντες διαμαρτάνουσι μὲν ἰδέας
λόγου, διαμαρτάνουσι δὲ ἀληθείας, ἀδικώτατοι δ' ἀνθρώπων εἰσὶ προσαφαιρούμενοι τὸν σοφιστὴν καὶ τὰ
οἰκεῖα.

(67) Τὸ δὲ τῶν ὀφρύων ἦθος καὶ ἡ τοῦ προσώπου
σύννοια σοφιστὴν ἐδήλου τὸν Μάρκον, καὶ γὰρ ἐτύγχανεν ἀεί τι ἐπισκοπῶν τῇ γνώμῃ καὶ ἀναπαιδεύων
ἑαυτὸν τοῖς εἰς τὸ σχεδιάζειν ἄγουσι. καὶ τοῦτο ἐδηλοῦτο μὲν τῇ τῶν ὀφθαλμῶν στάσει πεπηγότων τὰ

---

129 The punishment of these men by Sparta is described at
Thuc. 5.534.   130 A *dialexis* (here translated "discourse")
was a relatively informal, reflective discussion, sometimes on light
philosophical topics. Marcus' example was evidently concerned
with *poikilia* (variability) as a sophistic virtue.

beauty. The most characteristic example of the style of
Marcus is the Spartan advising the Lacedaemonians not
to receive those returning without their weapons from
Sphacteria.[129] He began this topic in this way: "As a Spartan man, who up till old age has guarded his shield, I would
slay with pleasure these men who have lost theirs." What
this man was like in discourses[130] may be learned from the
following. When he was teaching about the art of the sophists, how extensive and varied it is, he used as his analogy
the rainbow, and began his discourse like this: "The one
who sees the rainbow as one color, does not see something
to marvel at. But the one who sees how many colors it has,
wonders more."[131] Those who ascribe this discourse to
Alcinous the Stoic[132] fail to observe the style of the speech,
and they fail to observe the truth. They are the most crim-
inal of men, in that they try to rob the sophist even of what
he wrote about his own art.

(67) The expression of his brows and the deep concen-
tration of his face revealed that Marcus was a sophist, for
he was in fact always brooding over something for his
theme and training himself in the methods that prepare
one for improvisation. This was also revealed by the steady
gaze of his eyes, which were usually intent on hidden

[131] Iris (the rainbow) was the daughter of Thaumas, whose
name means "Wonder." The play on the word θαυμάζειν, "to
wonder," seems to echo Pl. *Tht.* 155c–d: "philosophy begins in
wonder." Plato goes on to apply the image of the rainbow (Iris) to
philosophy.   [132] Alcinous the Stoic does not appear to be
mentioned elsewhere. Perhaps Philostratus has confused the
philosophical affiliation of the Platonist Alcinous, who does indeed draw upon Stoicism.

πολλὰ ἐς ἀπορρήτους ἐννοίας, ὡμολογήθη δὲ καὶ ὑπὸ
τοῦ ἀνδρός. ἐρομένου γάρ τινος αὐτὸν τῶν ἐπιτηδείων, ὅπως χθὲς ἐμελέτα, "ἐπ᾽ ἐμαυτοῦ μέν," ἔφη, "λό-
529 γου ἀξίως, ἐπὶ δὲ τῶν γνωρίμων ἧττον." θαυμάσαντος
δὲ τὴν ἀπόκρισιν, "ἐγώ," ἔφη ὁ Μᾶρκος, "καὶ τῇ
σιωπῇ ἐνεργῷ χρῶμαι καὶ γυμνάζουσί με δύο καὶ
τρεῖς ὑποθέσεις ἐπὶ[62] τὴν μίαν, ἣν ἐς τὸ κοινὸν ἀγωνίζομαι." γενειάδος δὲ καὶ κόμης αὐχμηρῶς εἶχεν, ὅθεν
ἀγροικότερος ἀνδρὸς πεπνυμένου ἐδόκει τοῖς πολλοῖς.
τουτὶ δὲ καὶ Πολέμων ὁ σοφιστὴς πρὸς αὐτὸν ἔπαθε·
παρῆλθε μὲν γὰρ ἐς τὴν τοῦ Πολέμωνος διατριβὴν
ὀνομαστὸς ἤδη ὤν, ξυγκαθημένων δὲ τῶν ἐς τὴν
ἀκρόασιν ἀπηντηκότων ἀναγνούς τις αὐτὸν τῶν ἐς τὸ
Βυζάντιον πεπλευκότων διεμήνυσε τῷ πέλας, ὁ δὲ τῷ
πλησίον, καὶ διεδόθη ἐς πάντας, ὅτι ὁ Βυζάντιος εἴη
σοφιστής, ὅθεν τοῦ Πολέμωνος αἰτοῦντος τὰς ὑποθέσεις ἐπεστρέφοντο πάντες ἐς τὸν Μᾶρκον, ἵνα προ-
βάλοι. τοῦ δὲ Πολέμωνος εἰπόντος, "τί ἐς τὸν ἄγροι-
κον ὁρᾶτε; οὐ γὰρ δώσει γε οὗτος ὑπόθεσιν," ὁ
Μᾶρκος ἐπάρας τὴν φωνήν, ὥσπερ εἰώθει, καὶ τραχὺ
βλέψας,[63] "καὶ προβαλοῦμαι,"[64] ἔφη, "καὶ μελετήσομαι." ἔνθεν ἑλὼν ὁ Πολέμων καὶ ξυνιεὶς δωριάζοντος
διελέχθη ἐς τὸν ἄνδρα πολλά τε καὶ θαυμάσια ἐφιεὶς
τῷ καιρῷ, μελετήσας δὲ καὶ μελετῶντος ἀκροασάμενος καὶ ἐθαυμάσθη καὶ ἐθαύμασε.

62 ὑπό VaLVb   63 τραχὺ βλέψας β; ἀνακύψας LVbM
64 The words quoted from Marcus, in the manuscript readings
of this sentence, contain no Doric elements, leaving the

thoughts, and was confirmed indeed by the man himself. When one of his acquaintances asked him how he had declaimed the previous day he said, "by myself, remarkably well, but in front of my students, less so." When the man was astonished at this answer, Marcus said, "I use my silence actively, and work at two or three arguments against the one that I deliver publicly." He wore his beard and hair unkempt, so that he seemed to most people too boorish for an intelligent man. And this is just what happened to the sophist Polemo in relation to Marcus. Marcus went, when he had already made his name, to the school of Polemo. When those who had come to hear the lecture were seated, someone who had sailed to Byzantium recognized him and pointed him out to the person next to him, and that person pointed him out to the one next to him, and it was handed on through all of them that he was the Byzantine sophist. So when Polemo asked them to propose themes, everyone turned to Marcus, so that he would propose one. And Polemo said, "Why are you looking to this rustic man? He won't give you a theme." Marcus rose up his voice, as he always did, and with a fierce gaze said, "I shall both propose a theme and declaim on it myself." Then Polemo understood and recognized that he was merely dressed in a Doric fashion, and Polemo gave a long and astonishing speech improvised for that moment. When he had declaimed and heard the other declaim, he both wondered and was wondered at in turn.

529

---

observation of Marcus' dialect by Polemo in the following sentence unexplained. Various Doric emendations have been proposed (see Stefec *ad loc.*). With Hesseling I have taken δωρι-άζειν to refer to Marcus' rustic and therefore "Doric" appearance rather than dialect.

(68) Μετὰ ταῦτα παρήκων ὁ Μᾶρκος εἰς τὰ Μέ-
γαρα, οἰκισταὶ δὲ οὗτοι Βυζαντίων, ἐστασίαζον μὲν
οἱ Μεγαρεῖς πρὸς τοὺς Ἀθηναίους ἀκμαζούσαις ταῖς
γνώμαις, ὥσπερ ἄρτι τοῦ πινακίου ἐπ᾽ αὐτοὺς γε-
γραμμένου, καὶ οὐκ ἐδέχοντο σφᾶς ἐς τὰ Πύθια τὰ
μικρὰ ἥκοντας. παρελθὼν δὲ ἐς μέσους ὁ Μᾶρκος
οὕτω τι μεθήρμοσε τοὺς Μεγαρέας, ὡς ἀνοῖξαι πεῖσαι
τὰς οἰκίας καὶ δέξασθαι τοὺς Ἀθηναίους ἐπὶ γυναῖκάς
530   τε καὶ παῖδας. ἠγάσθη αὐτὸν καὶ Ἀδριανὸς ὁ αὐτοκράτωρ πρεσβεύοντα ὑπὲρ Βυζαντίων, ἐπιτηδειότατος
τῶν πάλαι βασιλέων γενόμενος ἀρετὰς αὐξῆσαι.

(69) 25. κε΄. Πολέμων δὲ ὁ σοφιστὴς οὔθ᾽, ὡς οἱ
πολλοὶ δοκοῦσι, Σμυρναῖος, οὔθ᾽, ὥς τινες, ἐκ Φρυγῶν, ἀλλ᾽ ἤνεγκεν αὐτὸν Λαοδίκεια ἡ ἐν Καρίᾳ, ποταμῷ πρόσοικος Λύκῳ, μεσογεία μέν, δυνατωτέρα δὲ
τῆς[65] ἐπὶ θαλάττῃ. ἡ μὲν δὴ τοῦ Πολέμωνος οἰκία
πολλοὶ ὕπατοι καὶ ἔτι, ἐρασταὶ δὲ αὐτοῦ πολλαὶ μὲν
πόλεις, διαφερόντως δὲ ἡ Σμύρνα· οὗτοι γὰρ ἐκ μειρακίου κατιδόντες τι ἐν αὐτῷ μέγα πάντας τοὺς οἴκοι
στεφάνους ἐπὶ τὴν τοῦ Πολέμωνος κεφαλὴν συνήνεγ-
καν, αὐτῷ τε ψηφισάμενοι καὶ γένει τὰ οἴκοι ζηλωτά·
προκαθῆσθαι γὰρ τῶν Ἀδριανῶν Ὀλυμπίων ἔδοσαν
τῷ ἀνδρὶ καὶ ἐγγόνοις, καὶ τῆς ἱερᾶς τριήρους ἐπιβα-

[65] Reading Lucarini's conjecture τῆς ἐπὶ θαλάττῃ for τῶν ἐπὶ
θαλάττῃ, which Stefec identifies as an error in the archetype.
While the inland Laodicea is not greater than all the cities on the
sea, Philostratus does assert that it is greater than the other
Laodicea, which is on the sea.

(68) Later, when Marcus went to Megara—and Byzantium was originally a colony of Megara—the Megarians were quarreling with the Athenians with the utmost energy of their minds, as if the famous decree against them had only just been drawn up.[133] And they did not receive the Athenians when they came for the Lesser Pythian Games. When Marcus came among them he exerted such an influence on the Megarians that he persuaded them to open their homes and to receive the Athenians even into the company of their wives and children. The emperor Hadrian also admired him when he came on an embassy for the Byzantines, since of all the emperors of the past he was the one most inclined to promote excellence.

530

(69) 25. The sophist Polemo was not, as most people think, from Smyrna, nor, as others believe, from Phrygia, but Laodicea in Caria produced him, a town that lies on the river Lycus. This is an inland city, but it is more powerful than the Laodicea on the sea. Polemo's family had been the source of many men of consular rank and still is, and many cities were in love with him, but most of all Smyrna. From his youth they saw something great in him and brought together all the garlands they had onto the head of Polemo, and voted all their most coveted honors on him and his family. They bestowed on the man and his descendants the right to preside over the Olympics founded by Hadrian,[134] and to go on board the sacred trireme.

---

[133] This was the decree by which the Megarians were proscribed by the Athenians in the fifth century BC.

[134] These games were held at Smyrna.

531 τεύειν. πέμπεται γάρ τις μηνὶ Ἀνθεστηριῶνι μεταρ-
σία τριήρης ἐς ἀγοράν, ἣν ὁ τοῦ Διονύσου ἱερεύς,
οἷον κυβερνήτης, εὐθύνει πείσματα ἐκ θαλάττης λύ-
ουσαν.

(70) Ἐνσπουδάζων δὲ τῇ Σμύρνῃ τάδε αὐτὴν ὤνη-
σεν· πρῶτον μὲν τὴν πόλιν πολυανθρωποτάτην αὑτῆς
φαίνεσθαι, νεότητος αὐτῇ ἐπιρρεούσης ἐξ ἠπείρων τε
καὶ νήσων οὐκ ἀκολάστου καὶ ξυγκλύδος, ἀλλ' ἐξει-
λεγμένης τε καὶ καθαρᾶς,[66] ἔπειτα ὁμονοοῦσαν καὶ
ἀστασίαστον πολιτεύειν. τὸν γὰρ πρὸ τοῦ χρόνον
ἐστασίαζεν ἡ Σμύρνα καὶ διεστήκεσαν οἱ ἄνω πρὸς
τοὺς ἐπὶ θαλάττῃ. πλείστου δὲ ἄξιος τῇ πόλει καὶ τὰ
πρεσβευτικὰ ἐγένετο φοιτῶν τε παρὰ τοὺς αὐτοκράτο-
ρας καὶ προαγωνιζόμενος τῶν ἠθῶν. Ἀδριανὸν γοῦν
προσκείμενον τοῖς Ἐφεσίοις οὕτω τι μετεποίησε τοῖς
Σμυρναίοις, ὡς ἐν ἡμέρᾳ μιᾷ χιλίας μυριάδας ἐπαν-
τλῆσαι αὐτὸν τῇ πόλει, ἀφ' ὧν τά τε τοῦ σίτου ἐμ-
πόρια ἐξεποιήθη καὶ γυμνάσιον τῶν κατὰ τὴν Ἀσίαν
μεγαλοπρεπέστατον καὶ νεὼς τηλεφανὴς ὁ ἐπὶ τῆς
ἄκρας ἀντικεῖσθαι δοκῶν τῷ Μίμαντι. καὶ μὴν καὶ
τοῖς ἁμαρτανομένοις δημοσίᾳ ἐπιπλήττων καὶ κατὰ
σοφίαν πλεῖστα νουθετῶν ὠφέλει, ὕβριν τε ὁμοίως
ἐξῄρει καὶ ἀγερωχίαν πᾶσαν, τοσούτῳ πλέον, ὅσῳ

---

[66] Reading καθαρᾶς (with the weight of MS evidence) rather
than καθαρᾶς Ἑλλάδος with VaP². No doubt the "purity" of
Polemo's students relates, in Philostratus' view, to their traditional
Hellenic education, but it does not seem that he spelled this out
on this occasion.

146

For in the month of Anthesterion a trireme in full sail is   531
brought in procession into the agora, which the priest of
Dionysus steers like a helmsman, as it comes from the sea,
having cast off its cables.

(70) By opening his school at Smyrna, he benefitted the
city in the following ways. First, he made the city appear
far more populous than before, because the youth flowed
into it from both continents and from the islands. This was
not an undisciplined rabble, but the select and pure youth.
Second, he produced in the city a government that was
like-minded and free from faction. In the time before this
Smyrna was torn by factions, and those on the high ground
were in disagreement with those on the sea. He was also
of very great value to the city both by going on embassies
to the emperors and defending their customs. For instance, he converted Hadrian, who had formerly favored
the Ephesians, so thoroughly to the people of Smyrna
that in a single day he poured upon the city ten million
drachmae. With this money the corn markets were built
and a gymnasium that was the most magnificent in Asia
and a temple that can be seen from far away, which seems
to stand on the headland in challenge to Mimas.[135] And
what is more when the people of Smyrna made mistakes
in public policy, he chastised them and very often
gave them wise advice, and he similarly removed every
kind of insolence and arrogance, which is all the greater
an achievement since it was not in the Ionic character

---

[135] "Windy Mimas" (Hom. *Od.* 3.172) is a headland opposite
Chios. This temple was destroyed by an earthquake and rebuilt
by Marcus Aurelius.

532 μηδὲ τοῦ Ἰωνικοῦ ἀπεθίζειν ἦν.[67] ὠφέλει δὲ κἀκεῖνα
δήπου· τὰς δίκας τὰς πρὸς ἀλλήλους οὐκ ἄλλοσέ πη
ἐκφοιτᾶν εἴα, ἀλλ᾽ οἴκοι ἔπαυε· λέγω δὲ τὰς ὑπὲρ χρημάτων, τὰς γὰρ ἐπὶ μοιχοὺς καὶ ἱεροσύλους καὶ σφα-
γέας, ὧν ἀμελουμένων ἄγη φύεται, οὐκ ἐξάγειν παρεκελεύετο μόνον, ἀλλὰ καὶ ἐξωθεῖν τῆς Σμύρνης,
δικαστοῦ γὰρ δεῖσθαι αὐτὰς ξίφος ἔχοντος.

Καὶ ἡ αἰτία δέ, ἣν ἐκ τῶν πολλῶν εἶχεν, ὡς ὁδοι-
ποροῦντι αὐτῷ πολλὰ μὲν σκευοφόρα ἔποιτο, πολλοὶ
δὲ ἵπποι, πολλοὶ δὲ οἰκέται, πολλὰ δὲ ἔθνη κυνῶν
ἄλλα ἐς ἄλλην θήραν, αὐτὸς δὲ ἐπὶ ζεύγους ἀργυροχαλίνου Φρυγίου τινὸς ἢ Κελτικοῦ πορεύοιτο, εὔκλειαν
τῇ Σμύρνῃ ἔπραττεν· πόλιν γὰρ δὴ λαμπρύνει μὲν
ἀγορὰ καὶ κατασκευὴ μεγαλοπρεπὴς οἰκοδομημάτων,
λαμπρύνει δὲ οἰκία εὖ πράττουσα· οὐ γὰρ μόνον δίδωσι πόλις ἀνδρὶ ὄνομα, ἀλλὰ καὶ αὐτὴ ἄρνυται ἐξ
ἀνδρός. ἐπεσκοπεῖτο δὲ καὶ τὴν Λαοδίκειαν ὁ Πολέμων θαμίζων ἐς τὸν ἑαυτοῦ οἶκον καὶ δημοσίᾳ ὠφελῶν
ὅ τι ἠδύνατο.

(71) Τὰ δὲ ἐκ βασιλέων αὐτῷ τοιαῦτα· Τραιανὸς
μὲν αὐτοκράτωρ ἀτελῆ πορεύεσθαι διὰ γῆς καὶ
θαλάττης, Ἀδριανὸς δὲ καὶ τοῖς ἀπ᾽ αὐτοῦ πᾶσι, κατέλεξε δὲ αὐτὸν καὶ τῷ τοῦ Μουσείου κύκλῳ ἐς τὴν
533 Αἰγυπτίαν σίτησιν, ἐπί τε τῆς Ῥώμης ἀπαιτουμένου
πέντε καὶ εἴκοσι μυριάδας ὑπεραπέδωκε πάντα τὰ

---

[67] There is a lacuna here. Like Wright and Brodersen, I follow
Kayser's suggestion of ἦν.

to change customs. And in fact he benefitted them in the 532
following way: the cases that they brought against one
another he did not allow them to take elsewhere, but he
ended them at home. I mean those cases that concerned
money, because the cases against adulterers and temple
robbers and murderers, which breed pollution when they
are neglected, he not only urged them to take away, but
even to drive away from Smyrna. For he said that they
needed a judge armed with a sword.

The masses found fault with him because when he traveled many baggage animals followed him and many horses
and many slaves, and many breeds of dogs for different
types of hunting, and he himself rode on a Phrygian or
Gallic chariot with silver bridles. But by doing this he contributed to the glory of Smyrna. Just as an agora and magnificently constructed buildings shine a light of fame on a
city, so too does a household that is flourishing. Not only
does a city give renown to a man, but itself acquires it from
a man. Polemo also closely examined the affairs of Laodicea, and often visited his own house there and gave what
assistance he could in public affairs.

(71) The following were the kind of honors that he
received from emperors. The emperor Trajan granted him
the right to travel free of cost by land and sea, and Hadrian
extended this to all his descendants as well, and also enrolled him in the circle of the Museum with the Egyptian
right to free meals. When he was in Rome and he de- 533
manded two hundred and fifty thousand drachmae, the

χρήματα οὔτε εἰπόντος, ὡς δέοιτο, οὔτε προειπών, ὡς
δώσοι. αἰτιωμένης δὲ αὐτὸν τῆς Σμύρνης, ὡς πολλὰ
τῶν ἐπιδοθέντων σφίσιν ἐκ βασιλέως χρημάτων ἐς τὸ
ἑαυτοῦ ἡδὺ καταθέμενον ἔπεμψεν ὁ αὐτοκράτωρ ἐπιστολὴν ὧδε ξυγκειμένην· "Ἀντώνιος Πολέμων τῶν
ἐπιδοθέντων ὑμῖν ὑπ' ἐμοῦ χρημάτων ἐμοὶ τοὺς λογισμοὺς ἔδωκε." ταῦτα δὲ εἰ καὶ συγγνώμην ἐρεῖ τις,
οὐκ ἦν δήπου συγγνώμην αὐτὸν τὴν ἐπὶ τοῖς χρήμασι
μὴ οὐκ εἰς τὸ προὔχον τῆς ἄλλης ἀρετῆς εὕρασθαι.
τὸ δὲ Ἀθήνησιν Ὀλυμπίειον[68] δι' ἑξήκοντα καὶ πεντακοσίων ἐτῶν ἀποτελεσθὲν καθιερώσας ὁ αὐτοκράτωρ,
ὡς χρόνου μέγα ἀγώνισμα, ἐκέλευσε καὶ τὸν Πολέμωνα ἐφυμνῆσαι τῇ θυσίᾳ. ὁ δέ, ὥσπερ εἰώθει, στήσας τοὺς ὀφθαλμοὺς ἐπὶ τὰς ἤδη παρισταμένας ἐννοίας ἐπαφῆκεν ἑαυτὸν τῷ λόγῳ καὶ ἀπὸ τῆς κρηπῖδος
τοῦ νεὼ διελέχθη πολλὰ καὶ θαυμάσια, προοίμιον
ποιούμενος τοῦ λόγου τὸ μὴ ἀθεεὶ τὴν περὶ αὐτοῦ
ὁρμὴν γενέσθαι οἱ.

Διήλλαξε δὲ αὐτῷ καὶ τὸν ἑαυτοῦ παῖδα Ἀντωνῖνον
534 ὁ αὐτοκράτωρ ἐν τῇ τοῦ σκήπτρου παραδόσει θεὸς ἐκ
θνητοῦ γιγνόμενος. τουτὶ δὲ ὁποῖον, ἀνάγκη δηλῶσαι·
ἦρξε μὲν γὰρ πάσης ὁμοῦ Ἀσίας ὁ Ἀντωνῖνος, καὶ

[68] Ὀλυμπίειον Cobet; Ὀλύμπιον ω

[136] The original Olympieion, begun about 530 BC by Peisistratus, was never completed. The existing temple was begun
about 174 BC by Antiochus Epiphanes and was completed by the
emperor Hadrian and dedicated in AD 130.

emperor gave him all of that money, though he had not said that he needed it, nor had the emperor said beforehand that he would give it. When the people of Smyrna accused him of having expended on his own pleasure much of the money that the emperor had given to them, the emperor sent a letter to the following effect: "Antonius Polemo has given to me accounts of the money that was sent by me to you." And if someone should say that this was effectively a pardon, nonetheless he would not have pardoned him if he had not achieved eminence in another kind of virtue. The Temple of Olympian Zeus had been completed after six hundred and fifty years,[136] and when the emperor consecrated it as a marvelous triumph of time, he bade Polemo to give a hymn to accompany the sacrifice.[137] And he fixed his eyes, just as was his habit, on the thoughts that were already taking their place in his mind, and then flung himself into his speech, and delivered a long and astonishing speech from the base of the temple. In his proem to the speech he said that the impetus to give it did not come to him without divine inspiration.

Moreover, the emperor reconciled his own son Antoninus with Polemo, at the time when he handed over his scepter and became a god instead of a mortal.[138] I must relate how this happened. Antoninus ruled over the whole

534

[137] Polemo evidently delivered a prose hymn. This genre, which came into its own during Philostratus' Second Sophistic, is best exemplified in the works of Aelius Aristides (*Or.* 37–46).

[138] That is, Hadrian brought about the reconciliation at the end of his life, shortly before he died and was deified.

κατέλυσεν ἐν τῇ τοῦ Πολέμωνος οἰκίᾳ ὡς ἀρίστη τῶν
κατὰ τὴν Σμύρναν καὶ ἀρίστου ἀνδρός, νύκτωρ δὲ ἐξ
ἀποδημίας ἥκων ὁ Πολέμων ἐβόα ἐπὶ θύραις, ὡς
δεινὰ πάσχοι τῶν ἑαυτοῦ εἰργόμενος, εἶτα συνηνάγ-
κασε τὸν Ἀντωνῖνον εἰς ἑτέραν οἰκίαν μετασκευάσα-
σθαι. ταῦτα ἐγίγνωσκε μὲν ὁ αὐτοκράτωρ, ἠρώτα δ'
ὑπὲρ αὐτῶν οὐδέν, ὡς μὴ ἀναδέροιτο, ἀλλ' ἐνθυμηθεὶς
τὰ μεθ' αὑτὸν καὶ ὅτι πολλάκις καὶ τὰς ἡμέρους ἐκ-
καλοῦνται φύσεις οἱ προσκείμενοί τε καὶ παροξύνον-
τες, ἔδεισε περὶ τῷ Πολέμωνι, ὅθεν ἐν ταῖς ὑπὲρ τῆς
βασιλείας διαθήκαις "καὶ Πολέμων ὁ σοφιστὴς,"
ἔφη, "ξύμβουλος τῆς διανοίας ἐμοὶ ταύτης ἐγένετο,"
τῷ κατὰ χάριν ὡς εὐεργέτῃ πράττειν τὴν συγγνώμην
ἐκ περιουσίας ἑτοιμάζων.

Καὶ ὁ Ἀντωνῖνος ἠστείζετο μὲν πρὸς τὸν Πολέμωνα
περὶ τῶν κατὰ τὴν Σμύρναν ἐνδεικνύμενός που τὸ μὴ
ἐκλελῆσθαι, ταῖς δὲ ἑκάστοτε τιμαῖς ἐπὶ μέγα ἦρεν
ἐγγυώμενός που τὸ μὴ μεμνῆσθαι. ἠστείζετο δὲ τάδε
ἐς τὴν πόλιν ἥκοντος τοῦ Πολέμωνος περιβαλὼν
αὐτὸν Ἀντωνῖνος, "δότε," ἔφη, "Πολέμωνι καταγωγὴν
καὶ μηδεὶς αὐτὸν ἐκβάλῃ." ὑποκριτοῦ δὲ τραγῳδίας
ἀπὸ τῶν κατὰ τὴν Ἀσίαν Ὀλυμπίων, οἷς ἐπεστάτει ὁ
535   Πολέμων, ἐφιέναι φήσαντος, ἐξελαθῆναι γὰρ παρ'
αὐτοῦ κατ' ἀρχὰς τοῦ δράματος, ἤρετο ὁ αὐτοκράτωρ
τὸν ὑποκριτήν, πηνίκα εἴη, ὅτε τῆς σκηνῆς ἠλάθη,
τοῦ δὲ εἰπόντος, ὡς μεσημβρία τυγχάνοι οὖσα, μάλα
ἀστείως ὁ αὐτοκράτωρ, "ἐμὲ δέ," εἶπεν, "ἀμφὶ μέσας
νύκτας ἐξήλασε τῆς οἰκίας, καὶ οὐκ ἐφῆκα."

of Asia, and was lodging in Polemo's house, since it was the most excellent house in Smyrna and belonged to the city's most excellent man. When Polemo came home by night from a journey he shouted on the doorstep that he was outrageously treated in being locked out from his own house, then he forced Antoninus to move to a different house. The emperor learned of these things, but did not inquire into them at all, so that he should not reopen the wound. But when he was considering his succession and reflected that those who are aggressive and irritating often provoke even mild natures, he was afraid for Polemo. Accordingly in his last testament on the affairs of the Empire, he wrote, "Polemo the sophist was my advisor in making these decisions." By doing this he prepared the way for Polemo to find favor as a benefactor and forgiveness in abundance.

In fact Antoninus used to joke with Polemo about what had happened in Smyrna, showing him that he had not forgotten, but by heaping honors upon him on every occasion he seemed to pledge not to remember. This is the sort of joke he would make: when Polemo came to Rome, Antoninus embraced him, and said, "Give Polemo a lodging and don't let anyone throw him out." And once a tragic actor, who had competed at the Olympic games in Asia, over which Polemo presided, declared that he would prosecute him, because Polemo had expelled him at the beginning of the play, the emperor asked the actor when it was that he had been driven from the stage. When the man said that it happened to be midday, the emperor very wittily said, "It was midnight when he drove me out of his house, and I didn't prosecute him." 535

(72) Ἐχέτω μοι καὶ ταῦτα δήλωσιν βασιλέως τε
πρᾴου καὶ ἀνδρὸς ὑπέρφρονος. ὑπέρφρων γὰρ δὴ
οὕτως ὁ Πολέμων, ὡς πόλεσι μὲν ἀπὸ τοῦ προὔχον-
τος, δυνάσταις δὲ ἀπὸ τοῦ μὴ ὑφειμένου, θεοῖς δὲ ἀπὸ
τοῦ ἴσου διαλέγεσθαι. Ἀθηναίοις μὲν γὰρ ἐπιδεικνύμενος αὐτοσχεδίους λόγους, ὅτε καὶ πρῶτον Ἀθήναζε
ἀφίκετο, οὐκ εἰς ἐγκώμια κατέστησεν ἑαυτὸν τοῦ
ἄστεος, τοσούτων ὄντων, ἅ τις ὑπὲρ Ἀθηναίων ἂν
εἴποι, οὐδ' ὑπὲρ τῆς ἑαυτοῦ δόξης ἐμακρηγόρησε, καίτοι καὶ τῆς τοιᾶσδε ἰδέας ὠφελούσης τοὺς σοφιστὰς
ἐν ταῖς ἐπιδείξεσιν, ἀλλ' εὖ γιγνώσκων, ὅτι τὰς Ἀθηναίων φύσεις ἐπικόπτειν χρὴ μᾶλλον ἢ ἐπαίρειν διελέχθη ὧδε· "φασὶν ὑμᾶς, ὦ Ἀθηναῖοι, σοφοὺς εἶναι
ἀκροατὰς λόγων· εἴσομαι." ἀνδρὸς δέ, ὃς ἦρχε μὲν
Βοσπόρου, πᾶσαν δὲ Ἑλληνικὴν παίδευσιν ἥρμοστο,
καθ' ἱστορίαν τῆς Ἰωνίας ἐς τὴν Σμύρναν ἥκοντος οὐ
μόνον οὐκ ἔταξεν ἑαυτὸν ἐν τοῖς θεραπεύουσιν, ἀλλὰ
καὶ δεομένου ξυνεῖναί οἱ θαμὰ ἀνεβάλλετο, ἕως ἠνάγ-
κασε τὸν βασιλέα ἐπὶ θύρας ἀφικέσθαι ἀπάγοντα
μισθοῦ δέκα τάλαντα. ἥκων δὲ ἐς τὸ Πέργαμον, ὅτε
δὴ τὰ ἄρθρα ἐνόσει, κατέδαρθε μὲν ἐν τῷ ἱερῷ, ἐπιστάντος δὲ αὐτῷ τοῦ Ἀσκληπιοῦ καὶ προειπόντος
ἀπέχεσθαι ψυχροῦ ποτοῦ ὁ Πολέμων "βέλτιστε," εἶπεν, "εἰ δὲ βοῦν ἐθεράπευες;"

(73) Τὸ δὲ μεγαλόγνωμον τοῦτο καὶ φρονηματῶδες

(72) Let these anecdotes suffice to show the gentleness of an emperor and the arrogance of a man. In fact Polemo was so arrogant that he spoke with cities as his inferiors, with rulers as not his superiors, and with gods as his equals. For instance, when he gave a demonstration of improvised speeches, when he first went to Athens, he did not set himself to giving encomia of the city, though there are so many things that one could say about the Athenians, nor did he give a speech in praise of his own fame, although this type of theme is beneficial for sophists in their rhetorical displays. Rather, since he well knew that it was necessary to restrain the Athenians' natural character rather than to excite it, he spoke like this: "They say, Athenians, that you are discerning judges of speeches. We will soon know." And once a man who ruled the Bosporus, and who had mastered all of Hellenic culture, came to Smyrna to study Ionia. Not only did Polemo not join those who went to honor him, but when the man invited him to visit many times he kept postponing it, until he forced the king to come to his door, bringing a payment of ten talents.[139] And when he went to Pergamum, when he already suffered from a disease of the joints, he slept in the temple. When Asclepius appeared to him and advised him to abstain from cold drinks Polemo said, "My good man, what if you were treating a cow?"[140]

(73) He drew this arrogance and haughtiness from the

[139] At this date there were kings at the Bosporus under the protectorate of Rome.   [140] These three anecdotes illustrate the formulation with which this section begins, demonstrating Polemo's arrogance toward cities (Athens), rulers (the anonymous Bosporan king), and gods (Asclepius).

ἐκ Τιμοκράτους ἔσπασε τοῦ φιλοσόφου, ξυγγενόμε-
536 νος αὐτῷ ἥκοντι ἐς Ἰωνίαν ἐτῶν τεττάρων. οὐ χεῖρον
δὲ καὶ τὸν Τιμοκράτην δηλῶσαι· ἦν μὲν γὰρ ἐκ τοῦ
Πόντου ὁ ἀνὴρ οὗτος καὶ ἦν αὐτῷ πατρὶς Ἡράκλεια
τὰ Ἑλλήνων ἐπαινοῦντες, ἐφιλοσόφει δὲ κατ' ἀρχὰς
μὲν τοὺς ἰατρικοὺς τῶν λόγων, εἰδὼς εὖ τὰς Ἱππο-
κράτους τε καὶ Δημοκρίτου δόξας, ἐπεὶ δὲ ἤκουσεν
Εὐφράτου τοῦ Τυρίου, πλήρεσιν ἱστίοις ἐς τὴν ἐκείνου φιλοσοφίαν ἀφῆκεν. ἐπιχολώτερος δὲ οὕτω τι ἦν
τοῦ ξυμμέτρου, ὡς ὑπανίστασθαι αὐτῷ διαλεγομένῳ
τήν τε γενειάδα καὶ τὰς ἐν τῇ κεφαλῇ χαίτας, ὥσπερ
τῶν λεόντων ἐν ταῖς ὁρμαῖς. τῆς δὲ γλώττης εὐφόρως
εἶχε καὶ σφοδρῶς καὶ ἑτοίμως, διὸ καὶ τῷ Πολέμωνι
πλείστου ἦν ἄξιος ἀσπαζομένῳ τὴν τοιάνδε ἐπιφορὰν
τοῦ λόγου. διαφορᾶς γοῦν τῷ Τιμοκράτει πρὸς τὸν
Σκοπελιανὸν γενομένης ὡς ἐκδεδωκότα ἑαυτὸν πίττῃ
καὶ παρατιλτρίαις διέστη μὲν ἡ ἐνομιλοῦσα νεότης τῇ
Σμύρνῃ, ὁ δὲ Πολέμων ἀμφοῖν ἀκροώμενος τῶν τοῦ
Τιμοκράτους στασιωτῶν ἐγένετο πατέρα καλῶν αὐτὸν
τῆς ἑαυτοῦ γλώττης. ἀπολογούμενος δὲ αὐτῷ καὶ
ὑπὲρ τῶν πρὸς Φαβωρῖνον λόγων εὐλαβῶς ὑπέστειλε
καὶ ὑφειμένως, ὥσπερ τῶν παίδων οἱ τὰς ἐκ τῶν διδασκάλων πληγάς, εἴ τι ἀτακτήσειαν, δεδιότες.

(74) Τῷ δὲ ὑφειμένῳ τούτῳ καὶ πρὸς τὸν Σκοπελιανὸν ἐχρήσατο χρόνῳ ὕστερον χειροτονηθεὶς μὲν
πρεσβεύειν ὑπὲρ τῶν Σμυρναίων, ὡς ὅπλα δὲ Ἀχίλ-

philosopher Timocrates, with whom he associated when   536
Timocrates came to Ionia for four years.[141] It does not
seem a bad thing to show as well what Timocrates was like.
This man was from Pontus and had Heraclea as his home
city, whose citizens admire Hellenic culture. He directed
his philosophical work at first toward medical studies, and
knew very well the teachings of Hippocrates and Democritus. But as soon as he heard the teaching of Euphrates
of Tyre,[142] he set full sail for that man's philosophy. And
he was irascible beyond measure, so that when he engaged
in discussion his beard and hair stood up on his head, like
a lion springing to attack. His language was fluent, vehement and ready, and it was for this reason that Polemo,
who welcomed the impetuousness of his speech, valued
him very highly. At any rate when a disagreement arose
between Timocrates and Scopelian, because Scopelian
had given himself up to waxing and hair pluckers, the
youth of Smyrna formed opposing camps. Polemo, who
was a student of both men, joined the faction supporting
Timocrates, calling him the father of his eloquence. And
when he was defending himself before Timocrates for the
speeches he made against Favorinus, he cowered timidly
and submissively, like boys do who fear the blows of their
teachers, if they have been disobedient.[143]

(74) And Polemo behaved submissively toward Scopelian as well, at a later time, when he had been voted to go
on an embassy on behalf of the people of Smyrna, and he

[141] Lucian (*Demonax* 3) praises Timocrates of Heraclea.

[142] On Euphrates, see above, *VS* 488 and note.

[143] On the hypermasculinity of Polemo's self-presentation and
on his quarrel with Favorinus, see Gleason 1995.

λεια τὴν ἐκείνου πειθὼ αἰτήσας. Ἡρώδη δὲ τῷ Ἀθηναίῳ πῃ μὲν ἀπὸ τοῦ ὑφειμένου, πῃ δὲ ἀπὸ τοῦ
ὑπεραίροντος ξυνεγένετο. ὅπως δὲ καὶ ταῦτα ἔσχε,
δηλῶσαι βούλομαι· καλὰ γὰρ καὶ μεμνῆσθαι ἄξια.
ἦρα μὲν γὰρ τοῦ αὐτοσχεδιάζειν μᾶλλον ὁ Ἡρώδης
ἢ τοῦ ὑπατός τε καὶ ἐξ ὑπάτων δοκεῖν, τὸν Πολέμωνα
537 δὲ οὔπω γιγνώσκων ἀφῖκτο μὲν ἐς τὴν Σμύρναν ἐπὶ
ξυνουσίᾳ τοῦ ἀνδρὸς κατὰ χρόνους, οὓς τὰς ἐλευ-
θέρας τῶν πόλεων αὐτὸς διωρθοῦτο, περιβαλὼν δὲ καὶ
ὑπερασπασάμενος ὁμοῦ τῷ τὸ στόμα ἀφελεῖν τοῦ
στόματος "πότε," εἶπεν, "ὦ πάτερ, ἀκροασόμεθά σου;"
καὶ ὁ μὲν δὴ ᾤετο ἀναβαλεῖσθαι αὐτὸν τὴν ἀκρόασιν
ὀκνεῖν φήσαντα ἐπ᾽ ἀνδρὸς τοιούτου ἀποκινδυνεύειν,
ὁ δὲ οὐδὲν πλασάμενος "τήμερον," ἔφη, "ἀκροῶ, καὶ
ἴωμεν." τοῦτο ἀκούσας ὁ Ἡρώδης ἐκπλαγῆναι ἔφησε
τὸν ἄνδρα, ὡς καὶ τὴν γλῶτταν αὐτοσχέδιον καὶ τὴν
γνώμην. ταῦτα μὲν οὖν φρόνημα ἐνδείκνυται τοῦ ἀνδρὸς καί, νὴ Δία, σοφίαν, ᾗ ἐς τὴν ἔκπληξιν ἐχρήσατο, ἐκεῖνα δὲ σωφροσύνην τε καὶ κόσμον· ἀφικόμε-
νον γὰρ ἐς τὴν ἐπίδειξιν ἐδέξατο ἐπαίνῳ μακρῷ καὶ
ἐπαξίῳ τῶν Ἡρώδου λόγων τε καὶ ἔργων.

Τὴν δὲ σκηνὴν τοῦ ἀνδρός, ᾗ ἐς τὰς μελέτας ἐχρήσατο, ἔστι μὲν καὶ Ἡρώδου μαθεῖν ἐν μιᾷ τῶν πρὸς
τὸν Βάρβαρον ἐπιστολῶν εἰρημένον, δηλώσω δὲ

144 This incident is described above, in VS 591. Philostratus'
Homeric allusion places Polemo in the position of Patroclus to
Scopelian's Achilles.

145 See further VS 548 below.   146 On "theatrical effects"
(σκήνη), see the Rhetorical Glossary.

begged for that man's persuasiveness as if it were the arms of Achilles.[144] In his relations with Herodes the Athenian Polemo was sometimes submissive and sometimes arrogant. I want to relate how this was, because it is a good story and worth remembering. Herodes loved improvised eloquence more than he loved his status as a consul and one descended from consuls. When he did not yet know Polemo he went to Smyrna to be in the company of the man, during the time when Herodes alone managed the free cities.[145] When he had embraced Polemo and greeted him affectionately along with a kiss on the mouth he said, "When, father, shall I hear you speak?" Herodes thought that he would put off the declamation and say that he feared to risk a bad performance in front of so great a man. But he made no excuses and said, "Hear me today, and let's get going." Herodes said that when he heard this he was amazed at Polemo, at how both his eloquence and the underlying thought was improvised. This story shows Polemo's pride and also, by Zeus, the cleverness that he used to stagger his listeners, but the next part of the story reveals his modesty and sense of the appropriate. When Herodes came to his presentation Polemo received him with a long and worthy speech on the words and deeds of Herodes.

The theatrical effects of the man,[146] which he used in his declamations, can be learned from Herodes in one of his letters, which is called *To Barbarus*,[147] and I too shall

537

---

[147] This is M. Ceionius Civica Barbarus, who was consul in AD 157. The base of a statue voted to him by the city of Athens and erected by Herodes Atticus was found at Athens in 1937. For details see Meritt, Woodhead, and Stamires 1957, 220, number 78.

κἀγὼ ἐκεῖθεν· παρήει μὲν ἐς τὰς ἐπιδείξεις διακεχυμένῳ τῷ προσώπῳ καὶ τεθαρρηκότι, φοράδην δὲ ἐσε-
φοίτα διεφθορότων αὐτῷ ἤδη τῶν ἄρθρων. καὶ τὰς
ὑποθέσεις οὐκ ἐς τὸ κοινὸν ἐπεσκοπεῖτο, ἀλλ᾽ ἐξιὼν
τοῦ ὁμίλου βραχὺν καιρόν. φθέγμα δὲ ἦν αὐτῷ λαμπρὸν καὶ ἐπίτονον καὶ κρότος θαυμάσιος οἷος ἀπεκτύ-
πει τῆς γλώττης. φησὶ δὲ αὐτὸν ὁ Ἡρώδης καὶ ἀνα-
πηδᾶν τοῦ θρόνου περὶ τὰς ἀκμὰς τῶν ὑποθέσεων,
τοσοῦτον αὐτῷ περιεῖναι ὁρμῆς, καὶ ὅτε ἀποτορνεύ-
οιτο περίοδον, τὸ ἐπὶ πᾶσιν αὐτῆς κῶλον σὺν μειδι-
άματι φέρειν, ἐνδεικνύμενον πολὺ τὸ ἀλύπως φράζειν,
καὶ κροαίνειν ἐν τοῖς τῶν ὑποθέσεων χωρίοις οὐδὲν
538   μεῖον τοῦ Ὁμηρικοῦ ἵππου. ἀκροᾶσθαι δὲ αὐτοῦ τὴν
μὲν πρώτην, ὡς οἱ δικάζοντες, τὴν δὲ ἐφεξῆς, ὡς οἱ
ἐρῶντες, τὴν δὲ τρίτην, ὡς οἱ θαυμάζοντες, καὶ γὰρ
δὴ καὶ τριῶν ἡμερῶν ξυγγενέσθαι οἱ. ἀναγράφει καὶ
τὰς ὑποθέσεις ὁ Ἡρώδης, ἐφ᾽ αἷς ξυνεγένετο· ἦν τοίνυν ἡ μὲν πρώτη Δημοσθένης ἐξομνύμενος ταλάντων
πεντήκοντα δωροδοκίαν, ἣν ἦγεν ἐπ᾽ αὐτὸν Δημάδης,
ὡς Ἀλεξάνδρου τοῦτο Ἀθηναίοις ἐκ τῶν Δαρείου λο-
γισμῶν ἐπεσταλκότος, ἡ δὲ ἐφεξῆς τὰ τρόπαια κατ-
έλυε τὰ Ἑλληνικὰ τοῦ Πελοποννησίου πολέμου ἐς
διαλλαγὰς ἥκοντος, ἡ δὲ τρίτη τῶν ὑποθέσεων τοὺς

---

148 Hom. Il. 6.507. It helps Herodes' witticism that the parts
of the speech are choria, suggesting a place or area as well. Polemo stamps as he traverses the space of his speech.

demonstrate it from there. He used to go in to declaim with his face relaxed and confident, and he always arrived in a litter, because his joints were already diseased. And he did not contemplate in public the themes that had been proposed, but would withdraw from the crowd for a little while. And his voice was clear and intense and astonishing in its impact, so greatly did he project the sound of his language. Herodes says that Polemo also used to come to such a pitch of excitement that he would leap up from his chair around the climax of his arguments. Whenever he rounded off a period, he would utter the final clause with a smile, showing how easily he spoke it, and he stamped his foot in key sections of his arguments like the horse in Homer.[148] Herodes says that he listened to him for the first time as one forming a judgment, the next time as one in love, and for the third time as one overcome by astonishment. For indeed he was with him for three days. Moreover Herodes records the themes, on which he heard Polemo declaim. The first was: "Demosthenes swears that he did not take the bribe of fifty talents," which was the charge Demades brought against him, on the grounds that Alexander had informed the Athenians of this, having learned it from the accounts of Darius. And the next was, after the end of the Peloponnesian War, he urged that the trophies of the Greeks should be taken down.[149] The third of his themes was to persuade the Athenians to return to

538

[149] Apsines 219 mentions this theme, and it was also declaimed by Herodes; cf. VS 539. The argument was that there must not be permanent monuments of Greek victories over Greeks.

Ἀθηναίους μετὰ Αἰγὸς ποταμοὺς ἐς τοὺς δήμους ἀνε-
σκεύαζεν· ὑπὲρ οὗ φησιν ὁ Ἡρώδης πέμψαι οἱ πεντεκαίδεκα μυριάδας προσειπὼν αὐτὰς μισθὸν τῆς ἀκροάσεως, μὴ προσεμένου δὲ αὐτὸς μὲν ὑπερῶφθαι
οἴεσθαι, ξυμπίνοντα δὲ αὐτῷ Μουνάτιον τὸν κριτικόν,
ὁ δὲ ἀνὴρ οὗτος ἐκ Τραλλέων, "ὦ Ἡρώδη," φάναι,
"δοκεῖ μοι Πολέμων ὀνειροπολήσας πέντε καὶ εἴκοσι
μυριάδας παρὰ τοῦτ᾽ ἔλαττον ἔχειν ἡγεῖσθαι, παρ᾽ ὃ
μὴ τοσαύτας ἔπεμψας." προσθεῖναί φησιν ὁ Ἡρώδης
τὰς δέκα καὶ τὸν Πολέμωνα προθύμως λαβεῖν, ὥσπερ
539   ἀπολαμβάνοντα. ἔδωκε τῷ Πολέμωνι ὁ Ἡρώδης καὶ
τὸ μὴ παρελθεῖν ἐπ᾽ αὐτῷ ἐς λόγων ἐπίδειξιν, μηδ᾽
ἐπαγωνίσασθαί οἱ, νύκτωρ δὲ ἐξελάσαι τῆς Σμύρνης,
ὡς μὴ βιασθείη· θρασὺ γὰρ καὶ τὸ βιασθῆναι ᾤετο.
διετέλει δὲ καὶ τὸν ἄλλον χρόνον ἐπαινῶν τὸν Πολέμωνα καὶ ὑπερθαυμάζων. Ἀθήνησι μὲν γὰρ διαπρεπῶς ἀγωνισάμενος τὸν περὶ τῶν τροπαίων ἀγῶνα καὶ
θαυμαζόμενος ἐπὶ τῇ φορᾷ τοῦ λόγου "τὴν Πολέμωνος," ἔφη, "μελέτην ἀνάγνωτε, καὶ εἴσεσθε ἄνδρα."
Ὀλυμπίασι δὲ βοησάσης ἐπ᾽ αὐτῷ τῆς Ἑλλάδος "εἷς
ὡς Δημοσθένης," "εἴθε γὰρ," ἔφη, "ὡς ὁ Φρύξ," τὸν
Πολέμωνα ὧδε ἐπονομάζων, ἐπειδὴ τότε ἡ Λαοδίκεια
τῇ Φρυγίᾳ συνετάττετο. Μάρκου δὲ τοῦ αὐτοκράτορος

their demes after the battle of Aegos Potami.[150] Herodes
says that because of this he sent to him 150,000 drachmas,
calling this the fee for his lectures, but because he did not
accept it, Herodes thought that he had been treated with
contempt. But Munatius the critic, who happened to be
drinking with him (and this man was from Tralles) said,
"Herodes, Polemo seems to me to have dreamed of
250,000 and so believes that he is being short changed
because you did not send so large a sum." Herodes says
that he added the 100,000 and that Polemo accepted it
eagerly, as if taking what was his due. Herodes granted
leave to Polemo not to appear after him to give an exhibi-   539
tion of rhetoric, and not to contend against him, and allowed him to go out from Smyrna by night, so that he
would not be forced, because Polemo considered it harsh
to be forced to do anything. And ever afterward he went
on praising Polemo and expressing great admiration for
him. For example when Herodes declaimed brilliantly on
the theme of the contest about the war trophies, and people were astonished by the fluency and vigor of his speech,
he said, "Read the declamation of Polemo, then you will
know a real man." And when at Olympia the crowd of
Greeks cried out about him, "The equal of Demosthenes!"
he said, "I wish I were the equal of the Phrygian." He
referred to Polemo this way, because in those days Laodicea counted as part of Phrygia. And when the emperor

[150] This theme is similar to that of Isocrates mentioned above,
at *VS* 505; it was designed to induce the Athenians to renounce
their empire of the sea.

πρὸς αὐτὸν εἰπόντος "τί σοι δοκεῖ ὁ Πολέμων;" στήσας τοὺς ὀφθαλμοὺς ὁ Ἡρώδης

ἵππων μ᾽

ἔφη

ὠκυπόδων ἀμφὶ κτύπος οὔατα βάλλει,

ἐνδεικνύμενος δὴ τὸ ἐπίκροτον καὶ τὸ ὑψηχὲς τῶν λόγων. ἐρομένου δὲ αὐτὸν καὶ Βαρβάρου τοῦ ὑπάτου,
τίσι καὶ διδασκάλοις ἐχρήσατο, "τῷ δεῖνι μὲν καὶ τῷ
δεῖνι," ἔφη, "παιδευόμενος, Πολέμωνι δὲ ἤδη παιδεύων."

(75) Φησὶν ὁ Πολέμων ἠκροᾶσθαι καὶ Δίωνος, ἀποδημίαν ὑπὲρ τούτου στείλας ἐς τὸ Βιθυνῶν ἔθνος.
ἔλεγε δὲ ὁ Πολέμων τὰ μὲν τῶν καταλογάδην ὤμοις
δεῖν ἐκφέρειν, τὰ δὲ τῶν ποιητῶν ἁμάξαις.

(76) Κἀκεῖνα τῶν Πολέμωνι τιμὴν νεμόντων· ἤριζεν
ἡ Σμύρνα ὑπὲρ τῶν ναῶν καὶ τῶν ἐπ᾽ αὐτοῖς δικαίων,
ξύνδικον πεποιημένη τὸν Πολέμωνα ἐς τέρμα ἤδη τοῦ
βίου ἥκοντα. ἐπεὶ δὲ ἐν ὁρμῇ τῆς ὑπὲρ τῶν δικαίων
ἀποδημίας ἐτελεύτησεν, ἐγένετο μὲν ἐπ᾽ ἄλλοις ξυν-
δίκοις ἡ πόλις, πονηρῶς δὲ αὐτῶν ἐν τῷ βασιλείῳ
δικαστηρίῳ διατιθεμένων τὸν λόγον βλέψας ὁ αὐτοκράτωρ ἐς τοὺς τῶν Σμυρναίων ξυνηγόρους, "οὐ Πολέμων," εἶπεν, "τουτουὶ τοῦ ἀγῶνος ξύνδικος ὑμῖν ἀπε-
δέδεικτο;" "ναί," ἔφασαν, "εἴ γε τὸν σοφιστὴν λέγεις."
καὶ ὁ αὐτοκράτωρ "ἴσως οὖν," ἔφη, "καὶ λόγον τινὰ
ξυνέγραψεν ὑπὲρ τῶν δικαίων, οἷα δὴ ἐπ᾽ ἐμοῦ τε

540

Marcus said to him, "What is your opinion of Polemo?" Herodes fixed his gaze before him and said,

The crash of swift horses strikes my ears.[151]

He indicated in this way how resonant and far-echoing was his eloquence. And when the consul Barbarus asked him what teachers he had, he replied, "This man and that when I was a student, but Polemo when I was a teacher myself."

(75) Polemo says that he also studied with Dio, and that he made an expedition to the Bithynians for this reason. And Polemo used to say that one should bring out prose works by the armload, but those of the poets by the wagon-load.

(76) Let the following anecdotes also convey the honor of Polemo. Smyrna was contending for the sake of its temples and its rights, and it made Polemo one of its representatives, though he was already coming to the end of his life. But when he died on the point of setting out on the embassy, the city was put into the hands of other representatives, and they presented the case very badly in the   540 emperor's court. The emperor gazed at the advocates of the people of Smyrna and said, "Wasn't Polemo appointed as a representative in this case?" "Yes," they said, "if you mean the sophist." "So perhaps," he said, "he wrote down a speech about your rights, giving the points that he

151 Hom. *Il*. 10.535.

ἀγωνιούμενος καὶ ὑπὲρ τηλικούτων." "ἴσως," ἔφασαν,
"ὦ βασιλεῦ, οὐ μὴν ἡμῖν γε εἰδέναι." καὶ ἔδωκεν ἀνα-
βολὰς ὁ αὐτοκράτωρ τῇ δίκῃ, ἔστ' ἂν διακομισθῇ ὁ
λόγος, ἀναγνωσθέντος δὲ ἐν τῷ δικαστηρίῳ κατ'
αὐτὸν ἐψηφίσατο ὁ βασιλεύς, καὶ ἀπῆλθεν ἡ Σμύρνα
τὰ πρωτεῖα νικῶσα καὶ τὸν Πολέμωνα αὐτοῖς ἀναβε-
βιωκέναι φάσκοντες.

(77) Ἐπεὶ δὲ ἀνδρῶν ἐλλογίμων ἀξιομνημόνευτα οὐ
μόνον τὰ μετὰ σπουδῆς λεχθέντα, ἀλλὰ καὶ τὰ ἐν
ταῖς παιδιαῖς, ἀναγράψω καὶ τοὺς ἀστεϊσμοὺς τοῦ
Πολέμωνος, ὡς μηδὲ οὗτοι παραλελειμμένοι φαί-
νοιντο. μειράκιον Ἰωνικὸν ἐτρύφα κατὰ τὴν Σμύρναν
ὑπὲρ τὰ Ἰώνων ἤθη, καὶ ἀπώλλυ αὐτὸ πλοῦτος βα-
θύς, ὅσπερ ἐστὶ πονηρὸς διδάσκαλος τῶν ἀκολάστων
φύσεων. ὄνομα μὲν δὴ τῷ μειρακίῳ Οὐᾶρος, διεφθο-
ρὸς δὲ ὑπὸ κολάκων ἐπεπείκει αὐτὸ ἑαυτό, ὡς καλῶν
τε εἴη ὁ κάλλιστος καὶ μέγας ὑπὲρ τοὺς εὐμήκεις καὶ
τῶν ἀμφὶ παλαίστραν γενναιότατός τε καὶ τεχνικώτατος καὶ μηδ' ἂν τὰς Μούσας ἀναβάλλεσθαι αὐτοῦ
ἥδιον, ὁπότε πρὸς τὸ ᾄδειν τράποιτο. παραπλήσια δὲ
τούτοις καὶ περὶ τῶν σοφιστῶν ᾤετο, παριππεῦσαι
γὰρ ἂν καὶ τὰς ἐκείνων γλώττας, ὁπότε μελετῴη, καὶ
γὰρ δὴ καὶ ἐμελέτα, καὶ οἱ δανειζόμενοι παρ' αὐτοῦ
χρήματα τὸ καὶ μελετῶντος ἀκροάσασθαι προσέγρα-
φον τῷ τόκῳ. ὑπήγετο καὶ ὁ Πολέμων τῷ δασμῷ
541 τούτῳ νέος ὢν ἔτι καὶ οὔπω νοσῶν, δεδάνειστο γὰρ
παρ' αὐτοῦ χρήματα, καὶ ἐπεὶ μὴ ἐθεράπευε μηδὲ ἐς
τὰς ἀκροάσεις ἐφοίτα, χαλεπὸν ἦν τὸ μειράκιον καὶ

intended to argue before me and on such an important matter." "Perhaps, emperor," they replied, "but we do not know." The emperor adjourned the case until the speech could be brought, and when it had been read aloud in court the emperor gave his decision in accordance with it, and Smyrna went away having won victory, and saying that Polemo had come back to life to aid them.

(77) Since it is not only the serious sayings of illustrious men that are worthy of notice, but also the things said in jest, I will record as well the witty sayings of Polemo, so that these too might not seem to have been neglected. There was an Ionian youth who was living in luxury at Smyrna beyond the habits of the Ionians, and was being ruined by his enormous wealth, which is a wicked teacher for undisciplined natures. The youth's name was Varus, and he had been so ruined by flatterers that he believed that he was the most handsome of the handsome, the tallest of the tall, the noblest and most skilled of those at the wrestling school, and that when he turned to singing, the Muses themselves could not strike up a song more beautifully than him. And he had similar thoughts about the sophists, that is, he believed that he could outstrip even their tongues, whenever he declaimed. And what is more he did declaim, and those who had borrowed money from him considered it part of their interest payments to listen to him declaiming. Even Polemo paid this tribute, when he was still young and not yet sick (because he had borrowed money from him), and when Polemo did not go to see him and did not go to his declamations, the youth was angry and threatened to bring a summons against him to recover 541

ἠπείλει τύπους. οἱ δὲ τύποι γράμμα εἰσὶν ἀγορᾶς,
ἐρήμην ἐπαγγέλλον τῷ οὐκ ἀποδιδόντι. αἰτιωμένων
οὖν τὸν Πολέμωνα τῶν οἰκείων, ὡς ἀηδῆ καὶ δύστροπον, εἰ παρὸν αὐτῷ μὴ ἀπαιτεῖσθαι καὶ τὸ μειράκιον
ἐκκαρποῦσθαι παρέχοντα αὐτῷ νεῦμα εὔνουν μὴ ποιεῖ
τοῦτο, ἀλλ' ἐκκαλεῖται αὐτὸ καὶ παροξύνει, τοιαῦτα
ἀκούων ἀπήντησε μὲν ἐπὶ τὴν ἀκρόασιν, ἐπεὶ δὲ ἐς
δείλην ἤδη ὀψίαν τὰ τῆς μελέτης αὐτῷ προὔβαινε καὶ
οὐδεὶς ὅρμος ἐφαίνετο τοῦ λόγου, σολοικισμῶν τε καὶ
βαρβαρισμῶν καὶ ἐναντιώσεων πλέα ἦν πάντα, ἀναπηδήσας ὁ Πολέμων καὶ ὑποσχὼν τὼ χεῖρε, "Οὐᾶρε,"
εἶπε, "φέρε τοὺς τύπους." λῃστὴν δὲ πολλαῖς αἰτίαις
ἑαλωκότα στρεβλοῦντος ἀνθυπάτου καὶ ἀπορεῖν φάσκοντος, τίς γένοιτ' ἂν ἐπ' αὐτῷ τιμωρία τῶν εἰρ-
γασμένων ἀξία, παρατυχὼν ὁ Πολέμων, "κέλευσον,"
ἔφη, "αὐτὸν ἀρχαῖα ἐκμανθάνειν." καίτοι γὰρ πλεῖστα
ἐκμαθὼν ὁ σοφιστὴς οὗτος ὅμως ἐπιπονώτατον ἡγεῖτο
τῶν ἐν ἀσκήσει τὸ ἐκμανθάνειν. ἰδὼν δὲ μονόμαχον
ἱδρῶτι ῥεόμενον καὶ δεδιότα τὸν ὑπὲρ τῆς ψυχῆς
ἀγῶνα, "οὕτως," εἶπεν, "ἀγωνιᾷς, ὡς μελετᾶν μέλλων."
σοφιστῇ δὲ ἐντυχὼν ἀλλᾶντας ὠνουμένῳ καὶ μαινί-
δας καὶ τὰ εὐτελῆ ὄψα, "ὦ λῷστε," εἶπεν, "οὐκ ἔστι τὸ
Δαρείου καὶ Ξέρξου φρόνημα καλῶς ὑποκρίνασθαι
ταῦτα σιτουμένῳ." Τιμοκράτους δὲ τοῦ φιλοσόφου
πρὸς αὐτὸν εἰπόντος, ὡς λάλον χρῆμα ὁ Φαβωρῖνος
γένοιτο, ἀστειότατα ὁ Πολέμων, "καὶ πᾶσα," ἔφη,
"γραῦς," τὸ εὐνουχῶδες αὐτοῦ διασκώπτων. ἀγωνιστοῦ
δὲ τραγῳδίας ἐν τοῖς κατὰ τὴν Σμύρναν Ὀλυμπίοις

the debt. This summons is a writ issued by the law court proclaiming judgment by default against the debtor who fails to pay. When his friends reproached Polemo for being so unpleasant and surly, since it was possible for him to avoid being sued and to enjoy the youth's money, by merely giving an amiable nod of approval, he would not do this but provoked and irritated him. Taking this advice he went to hear him, but when it was already late in the evening and the youth's declamation was still going on, and no place of anchorage for his speech was in sight, and the whole thing was full of solecisms, barbarisms and inconsistencies, Polemo leaped to his feet and stretching out his hands said, "Varus, bring your summons." Once when a proconsul was putting to torture a bandit who had been captured for multiple offenses, and said that he was at a loss what punishment would be fitting for his crimes, Polemo happened to be present and said, "Get him to learn by heart some ancient stuff." Even though this sophist had memorized a great deal, nevertheless he considered learning by heart the most laborious part of the training. And once, when he saw a gladiator dripping with sweat and terrified of the coming life and death contest, he said, "You are in as great an agony as though you were going to declaim." And once when he encountered a sophist who was buying sausages, sprats, and cheap snacks he said, "My dear man, one cannot finely act the pride of Darius and Xerxes while eating like that." When the philosopher Timocrates said to him what a chatty thing Favorinus had become, Polemo wittily replied, "All old women are like that," taking a dig at the fact that he was like a eunuch. And when a tragic actor was performing at the Olympics at Smyrna and ges-

τὸ "ὦ Ζεῦ" ἐς τὴν γῆν δείξαντος, τὸ δὲ "καὶ γᾶ" ἐς τὸν
οὐρανὸν ἀνασχόντος, προκαθήμενος τῶν Ὀλυμπίων ὁ
542 Πολέμων ἐξέωσεν αὐτὸν τῶν ἄθλων εἰπών, "οὗτος τῇ
χειρὶ ἐσολοίκισε." μὴ πλείω ὑπὲρ τούτων, ἀπόχρη
γὰρ καὶ ταῦτα τὸ ἐπίχαρι τοῦ ἀνδρὸς δηλῶσαι.

(78) Ἡ δὲ ἰδέα τῶν Πολέμωνος λόγων θερμὴ καὶ
ἐναγώνιος καὶ τορὸν ἠχοῦσα, ὥσπερ ἡ Ὀλυμπικὴ
σάλπιγξ, ἐπιπρέπει δὲ αὐτῇ καὶ τὸ Δημοσθενικὸν τῆς
γνώμης, καὶ ἡ σεμνολογία οὐχ ὑπτία, λαμπρὰ δὲ καὶ
ἔμπνους, ὥσπερ ἐκ τρίποδος. διαμαρτάνουσι μέντοι
τοῦ ἀνδρὸς οἱ φάσκοντες αὐτὸν τὰς μὲν ἐπιφορὰς
ἄριστα σοφιστῶν μεταχειρίσασθαι, τὰς δὲ ἀπολογίας ἧττον, ἐλέγχει γὰρ τὸν λόγον τοῦτον ὡς οὐκ
ἀληθῆ καὶ ἡ δεῖνα μὲν καὶ ἡ δεῖνα τῶν ὑποθέσεων, ἐν
αἷς ἀπολογεῖται, μάλιστα δὲ ὁ Δημοσθένης ὁ τὰ
πεντήκοντα τάλαντα ἐξομνύμενος. ἀπολογίαν γὰρ
οὕτω χαλεπὴν διαθέμενος ἤρκεσε τῷ λόγῳ ξὺν περι-
βολῇ καὶ τέχνῃ. τὴν αὐτὴν ὁρῶ διαμαρτίαν καὶ περὶ
τοὺς ἡγουμένους αὐτὸν ἐκφέρεσθαι τῶν ἐσχηματισμέ-
νων ὑποθέσεων εἰργόμενον τοῦ δρόμου, καθάπερ ἐν
δυσχωρίᾳ ἵππον, παραιτούμενόν τε αὐτὰς τὰς Ὁμη-
ρείους γνώμας εἰπεῖν

ἐχθρὸς γάρ μοι κεῖνος ὁμῶς Ἀίδαο πύλῃσιν,
ὅς χ' ἕτερον μὲν κεύθῃ ἐνὶ φρεσίν, ἄλλο δὲ εἴπῃ,

---

152 Eur. *Or.* 1496.

153 That is, Polemo's eloquence had an oracular quality like
the utterances of the Pythia at Delphi. The sound and content of
Polemo's language is described by reference to two of the most

tured toward the earth while saying the words, "O Zeus" and reached to the heavens on the line "and earth,"[152] Polemo, who was presiding at the games, expelled him from the contest, and said, "This man commits a solecism 542 with his hand." I will give no more anecdotes than these, since they are enough to show the wit of the man.

(78) The style of Polemo's speeches is fiery and combative and brilliantly echoing, like the Olympic trumpet. The style of thinking of Demosthenes is evident in it and a solemnity that is not dull, but is bright and inspired, as if uttered from the tripod.[153] Those people are wrong who say that while the man wrote invective best of all the sophists, he was less good at defense speeches. Several of the speeches in which he makes defense cases disprove this argument, since it is not true, and especially his speech as Demosthenes swearing not to have received the fifty talents.[154] In treating this difficult defense he showed himself equal to the argument with his expansiveness and artistry. I see the same error in the case of those who believe that he was not able to sustain covert arguments,[155] but that he was forced off the course, like a horse on difficult ground, and that he criticized these themes by quoting the Homeric lines,

> Hateful to me as the gates of Hades is the man
> who hides one thing in his mind but speaks
> another.[156]

important places of Greek religion: Olympia and Delphi. Apollonius of Tyana also speaks "as if from the tripod" (VA 1.17).

[154] For this theme see Apsines 9.535.

[155] See the Rhetorical Glossary on "covert arguments" (ἐσχη-ματίσματα) under σχηματίζειν.

[156] Hom. Il. 9.312.

171

ταῦτα γὰρ ἴσως ἔλεγεν αἰνιττόμενος καὶ παραδηλῶν
τὸ δύστροπον τῶν τοιούτων ὑποθέσεων, ἄριστα δὲ
κἀκεῖνα ἠγωνίσατο, ὡς δηλοῦσιν ὅ τε μοιχὸς ὁ ἐγκε-
καλυμμένος[69] καὶ ὁ Ξενοφῶν ὁ ἀξιῶν ἀποθνήσκειν ἐπὶ
Σωκράτει καὶ ὁ Σόλων ὁ αἰτῶν ἀπαλείφειν τοὺς νόμους λαβόντος τὴν φρουρὰν τοῦ Πεισιστράτου καὶ οἱ
Δημοσθένεις,[70] ὁ μετὰ Χαιρώνειαν προσάγων[71] ἑαυτὸν
543   καὶ ὁ δοκῶν θανάτου ἑαυτῷ τιμᾶσθαι ἐπὶ τοῖς Ἁρπα-
λείοις καὶ ὁ ξυμβουλεύων ἐπὶ τῶν τριήρων φεύγειν
ἐπιόντος μὲν Φιλίππου, νόμον δὲ Αἰσχίνου κεκυρω-
κότος ἀποθνήσκειν τὸν πολέμου μνημονεύσαντα. ἐν
γὰρ ταύταις μάλιστα τῶν ὑπ' αὐτοῦ κατὰ σχῆμα
προηγμένων ἠνία τε ἐμβέβληται τῷ λόγῳ καὶ τὸ
ἐπαμφότερον αἱ διάνοιαι σῴζουσιν.

(79) Ἰατροῖς δὲ θαμὰ ὑποκείμενος λιθιώντων αὐτῷ
τῶν ἄρθρων παρεκελεύετο αὐτοῖς ὀρύττειν καὶ τέμνειν
τὰς Πολέμωνος λιθοτομίας. Ἡρώδῃ δὲ ἐπιστέλλων
ὑπὲρ τῆς νόσου ταύτης ὧδε ἐπέστειλε· "δεῖ ἐσθίειν,
χεῖρας οὐκ ἔχω· δεῖ βαδίζειν, πόδες οὐκ εἰσί μοι· δεῖ
ἀλγεῖν, τότε καὶ πόδες εἰσί μοι καὶ χεῖρες."

[69] Damilas' conjecture ἐκκεκαλυμμένος would make the title
of the speech "The Adulterer Unmasked."

[70] Δημοσθένεις β; θεσμοθέται aP²

[71] Here, as at 522 (where Dionysius of Miletus' treatment of
the same theme is mentioned), I have preferred the MSS reading
προσάγων to Wright's προσαγγέλλων. I have omitted the
unexplained τε of β (obelized by Stefec) immediately before this
word. Lucarini suggests adding τῇ βουλῇ ("before the council")
after it.

Perhaps he used to say this with a double meaning and showing how difficult to treat such themes are. Yet he contended brilliantly at these too, as is evident from his *Veiled Adulterer*, *Xenophon Unwilling to Outlive Socrates*, and *Solon Demanding that his Laws be Rescinded after Peisistratus has Obtained a Bodyguard*.[157] And there are the speeches on Demosthenes: the one where he denounces himself after Chaeronea,[158] the one where he pretends that he ought to be punished with death for the affair of Harpalus, and the one where he advises that the Athenians should flee on their triremes when Philip is coming to attack, although Aeschines has passed a law that anyone mentioning the war will be put to death.[159] In these especially of his speeches on simulated themes he has given free rein to the argument, and the working out of the theme preserves both sides.

(79) When doctors were regularly treating him for hardening of the joints he bade them "to dig and cut in the quarries of Polemo."[160] In a letter to Herodes concerning this illness he wrote: "I must eat, I don't have hands. I must walk. I don't have feet. I must suffer pain. Then indeed I have feet and hands."

543

[157] Solon's efforts to check the tyranny of Peisistratus are described at Arist. [*Ath. Pol.*] 14.2, Plut. *Vit. Solon*, and elsewhere; but this precise incident is not recorded. For the bodyguard see Hdt. 1.59.

[158] See *VS* 522 for the treatment of this same theme by Dionysius of Miletus.

[159] This was perhaps modeled on the famous rhetorical theme in which Themistocles gives similar advice in the Persian War.

[160] The verb used to describe the condition of hardening of the joints, $\lambda\iota\theta\acute{o}\omega$, means literally that they were turning to stone.

(80) Ἐτελεύτα μὲν περὶ τὰ ἓξ καὶ πεντήκοντα ἔτη,
τὸ δὲ μέτρον τῆς ἡλικίας τοῦτο ταῖς μὲν ἄλλαις ἐπι-
στήμαις γήρως ἀρχή, σοφιστικῇ[72] δὲ νεότης ἔτι· γη-
ράσκουσα γὰρ ἤδε ἡ ἐπιστήμη σοφίαν ἀρτύνει.

Τάφος δὲ αὐτοῦ κατὰ τὴν Σμύρναν οὐδείς, εἰ καὶ
πλείους λέγονται. οἱ μὲν γὰρ ἐν τῷ κήπῳ τοῦ τῆς
Ἀρετῆς ἱεροῦ ταφῆναι αὐτόν, οἱ δὲ οὐ πόρρω τούτου
ἐπὶ θαλάττῃ, νεὼς δέ τίς ἐστι βραχὺς καὶ ἄγαλμα ἐν
αὐτῷ Πολέμωνος ἐσταλμένον, ὡς ἐπὶ τῆς τριήρους
ὠργίαζεν, ὑφ᾽ ᾧ κεῖσθαι τὸν ἄνδρα, οἱ δὲ ἐν τῇ τῆς
οἰκίας αὐλῇ ὑπὸ τοῖς χαλκοῖς ἀνδριᾶσιν. ἔστι δὲ οὐδὲν τούτων ἀληθές· εἰ γὰρ ἐτελεύτα κατὰ τὴν Σμύρναν, οὐδενὸς ἂν τῶν θαυμασίων παρ᾽ αὐτοῖς ἱερῶν
ἀπηξιώθη τὸ μὴ οὐκ ἐν αὐτῷ κεῖσθαι. ἀλλ᾽ ἐκεῖνά γε
ἀληθέστερα, κεῖσθαι μὲν αὐτὸν ἐν τῇ Λαοδικείᾳ παρὰ
τὰς Συρίας πύλας, οὗ δὴ καὶ τῶν προγόνων αὐτοῦ
θῆκαι, ταφῆναι δὲ αὐτὸν ζῶντα ἔτι. τουτὶ γὰρ τοῖς
544   φιλτάτοις ἐπισκῆψαι, κείμενόν τε ἐν τῷ σήματι παρα-
κελεύεσθαι τοῖς συγκλείουσι τὸν τάφον, "ἔπειγε,
ἔπειγε,[73] μὴ γὰρ ἴδοι με σιωπῶντα ἥλιος." πρὸς δὲ
τοὺς οἰκείους ὀλοφυρομένους αὐτὸν ἀνεβόησε· "δότε
μοι σῶμα καὶ μελετήσομαι."

(81) Μέχρι Πολέμωνος τὰ Πολέμωνος· οἱ γὰρ ἐπ᾽
αὐτῷ γενόμενοι ξυγγενεῖς μέν, οὐ μὴν οἷοι πρὸς τὴν
ἐκείνου ἀρετὴν ἐξετάζεσθαι, πλὴν ἑνὸς ἀνδρός, περὶ
οὗ μικρὸν ὕστερον λέξω.

---

[72] σοφιστικῇ Lucarini; σοφιστῇ ω

(80) He died at around fifty six, but though this age limit is for the other learned professions the beginning of old age, for the sophistic art it still counts as youthfulness. For as this art grows old it seasons its wisdom.

He has no tomb in Smyrna, though several there are said to be his. Some say that he was buried in the garden of the temple of Virtue. Others say that it was not far from there, near the sea. There is a small temple there and a statue in it of Polemo, dressed as he was when he celebrated Dionysus' rites on the trireme,[161] and they say that the man lies under this. Others again say that he lies in the courtyard of his house, under the bronze statues. None of these is true. For if he had died at Smyrna, he would not have been deemed unworthy to lie in any of the astonishing temples in that city. But another version in fact is truer: that he lies at Laodicea near the Syrian gates, where too are the sepulchers of his ancestors, and he was buried while still alive. He had commanded his closest friends to do this, and as he lay in the tomb he urged on those were closing it up, saying, "Hurry, hurry! Do not let the sun see me silent." And when his friends lamented over him he cried out, "Give me a body and I shall declaim!"

(81) With Polemo ended the house of Polemo. His descendants, though they were his kin, could not be compared with his excellence, except for one man, about whom I shall speak a little later.[162]

---

[161] See VS 530 above for Polemo's involvement in this rite in Smyrna.   [162] This is Polemo's great-grandson, Hermocrates, whose *bios* Philostratus gives below at VS 608.

---

73 ἔπειγε, ἔπειγε Cobet; ἔπαγε, ἔπαγε ω

(82) 26. κϛ'. Μηδὲ Σεκούνδου τοῦ Ἀθηναίου ἀμνημονῶμεν, ὃν ἐκάλουν ἐπίουρόν τινες ὡς τέκτονος παῖδα. Σεκοῦνδος τοίνυν ὁ σοφιστὴς γνῶναι μὲν περιττός, ἑρμηνεῦσαι δὲ ἀπέριττος, Ἡρώδην δὲ ἐκπαιδεύσας ἐς διαφορὰν αὐτῷ ἀφίκετο παιδεύοντι ἤδη, ὅθεν ὁ Ἡρώδης διετώθαζεν αὐτὸν ἐκεῖνο ἐπιλέγων·

καὶ κεραμεὺς κεραμεῖ κοτέει καὶ ῥήτορι τέκτων,

ἀλλ' ἀποθανόντι καὶ λόγον ἐπεφθέγξατο καὶ δάκρυα ἐπέδωκε καίτοι γηραιῷ τελευτήσαντι.

545

(83) Μνήμης δὲ ἄξια τοῦ ἀνδρὸς τούτου καὶ πλείω μέν, μάλιστα δὲ ἥδε ἡ ὑπόθεσις· "ὁ ἄρξας στάσεως ἀποθνησκέτω καὶ ὁ παύσας στάσιν ἐχέτω δωρεάν· ὁ αὐτὸς καὶ ἄρξας καὶ παύσας αἰτεῖ τὴν δωρεάν." τήνδε τὴν ὑπόθεσιν ὧδε ἐβραχυλόγησεν· "οὐκοῦν," ἔφη, "τί πρότερον; τὸ κινῆσαι στάσιν. τί δεύτερον; τὸ παῦσαι. δοὺς οὖν τὴν ἐφ' οἷς ἠδίκεις τιμωρίαν, τὴν ἐφ' οἷς εὖ πεποίηκας δωρεάν, εἰ δύνασαι, λάβε." τοιόσδε μὲν ὁ ἀνὴρ οὗτος, τέθαπται δὲ πρὸς τῇ Ἐλευσῖνι ἐν δεξιᾷ τῆς Μεγαράδε ὁδοῦ.

(82) 26. Let us not forget Secundus the Athenian, whom some used to call Wooden Peg because he was the son of a carpenter. Secundus the sophist was richly inventive of themes but straightforward in his interpretation of them. Though he trained Herodes he fell into a disagreement with him when Herodes was already himself a teacher, so that Herodes teased him, saying:

> The potter envies the potter, and the carpenter the rhetorician.[163]

But when Secundus died he gave a eulogy and wept, although he had died an old man.

(83) Several of the man's compositions are worthy of memory, but especially the theme, "Suppose that the one who began a revolt is to be put to death, and suppose that the one who ended one is to receive a reward. The same man, who both began and ended a revolt, asks for the reward." Secundus summed up the argument as follows: "And so," he said, "which of the two came first? Inciting revolt. Which second? Ending it. Therefore first pay the penalty for your crime, then for the good that you did, take the reward if you are able." That is what this man was like, and he is buried near Eleusis, to the right of the road to Megara.

545

---

[163] Hes. *Op.* 25. Herodes changed the word τέκτονι (carpenter) to ῥήτορι (orator), the orator being himself.

PHILOSTRATUS

Β΄

(1) 1. α΄. Περὶ δὲ Ἡρώδου τοῦ Ἀθηναίου τάδε χρὴ εἰδέναι· ὁ σοφιστὴς Ἡρώδης ἐτέλει μὲν ἐκ πατέρων ἐς τοὺς δισυπάτους, ἀνέφερε δὲ ἐς τὰ τῶν Αἰακιδῶν, οὓς ξυμμάχους ποτὲ ἡ Ἑλλὰς ἐπὶ τὸν Πέρσην ἐποιεῖτο, ἀπηξίου δὲ οὐδὲ τὸν Μιλτιάδην οὐδὲ τὸν Κίμωνα, ὡς ἄνδρε ἀρίστω καὶ πολλοῦ ἀξίω Ἀθηναίοις τε καὶ τοῖς ἄλλοις Ἕλλησι περὶ τὰ Μηδικά· ὁ μὲν γὰρ ἦρξε τροπαίων Μηδικῶν, ὁ δὲ ἀπῄτησε δίκας τοὺς βαρβάρους, ὧν μετὰ ταῦτα ὕβρισαν.

(2) Ἄριστα δὲ ἀνθρώπων πλούτῳ ἐχρήσατο. τουτὶ δὲ μὴ τῶν εὐμεταχειρίστων ἡγώμεθα, ἀλλὰ τῶν παγχαλέπων τε καὶ δυσκόλων· οἱ γὰρ πλούτῳ μεθύοντες ὕβριν τοῖς ἀνθρώποις ἐπαντλοῦσιν, προσδιαβάλλουσι δὲ ὡς καὶ τυφλὸν τὸν Πλοῦτον, ὃς εἰ καὶ τὸν ἄλλον χρόνον ἐδόκει τυφλός, ἀλλ᾽ ἐπὶ Ἡρώδου γε ἀνέβλεψεν· ἔβλεψε μὲν γὰρ ἐς φίλους, ἔβλεψε δὲ ἐς πόλεις, ἔβλεψε δ᾽ ἐς ἔθνη, πάντων περιωπὴν ἔχοντος τοῦ ἀνδρὸς καὶ θησαυρίζοντος τὸν πλοῦτον ἐν ταῖς

---

1 Hdt. 8.64.2 describes the invocation by the Athenians of the Aeacids Ajax and Telamon, which Philostratus also recalls at *Her.* 53.15.

2 They were descended from Aeacus. Philostratus seems to

178

BOOK II

(1) 1. Concerning Herodes the Athenian one must know the following points. The sophist Herodes on his father's side belonged to a family that twice held consulships, and also dated back to the Aeacids,[1] whom Greece once made   546
allies against the Persians. Nor was he ashamed of Miltiades and Cimon,[2] since they were excellent men and did great service to the Athenians and the rest of the Greeks during the war with the Medes. While Miltiades was the   547
first to triumph over the Medes, Cimon punished the barbarians for their insolent acts afterward.[3]

(2) He employed his wealth the best of all men. And let us not consider this a very easy thing, but full of difficulties and troublesome. Those who are drunk with wealth tend to let loose a flood of insults on their fellow men, and they bring the slander on Plutus that he is blind.[4] Even if at all other times he seemed blind, in the case of Herodes he recovered his sight. For he had eyes for his friends, had eyes for the cities, had eyes for the nations, since Herodes kept watch over them all and stored his wealth in the

reprove Plato, who disparaged them at *Grg.* 515. Direct or indirect sniping at Plato and Platonic attitudes to sophists is common in Philostratus.

[3] In 466 Cimon defeated the Persians by sea and land, and, later, expelled them from the Thracian Chersonese.

[4] Plutus was the god of wealth. That wealth or fortune were blind was an ancient commonplace.

τῶν μετεχόντων αὐτοῦ γνώμαις. ἔλεγε γὰρ δή, ὡς
προσήκοι τὸν ὀρθῶς πλούτῳ χρώμενον τοῖς μὲν δεομένοις ἐπαρκεῖν, ἵνα μὴ δέωνται, τοῖς δὲ μὴ δεομένοις,
ἵνα μὴ δεηθῶσιν, ἐκάλει τε τὸν μὲν ἀσύμβολον
πλοῦτον καὶ φειδοῖ κεκολασμένον νεκρὸν πλοῦτον,
τοὺς δὲ θησαυρούς, ἐς οὓς ἀποτίθενται τὰ χρήματα
ἔνιοι, πλούτου δεσμωτήρια, τοὺς δὲ καὶ θύειν ἀξιοῦν-
τας ἀποθέτοις χρήμασιν Ἀλωάδας ἐπωνόμαζε θύον-
τας Ἄρει μετὰ τὸ δῆσαι αὐτόν.

(3) Πηγαὶ δὲ αὐτῷ τοῦ πλούτου πολλαὶ μὲν κἀκ
πολλῶν οἴκων, μέγισται δὲ ἥ τε πατρῴα καὶ ἡ μη-
τρόθεν. ὁ μὲν γὰρ πάππος αὐτοῦ Ἵππαρχος ἐδημεύθη
τὴν οὐσίαν ἐπὶ τυραννικαῖς αἰτίαις, ἃς Ἀθηναῖοι μὲν
οὐκ ἐπῆγον, ὁ δὲ αὐτοκράτωρ οὐκ ἠγνόησεν, Ἀττικὸν
δὲ τὸν ἐκείνου μὲν παῖδα, Ἡρώδου δὲ πατέρα οὐ πε-
ριεῖδεν ἡ Τύχη πένητα ἐκ πλουσίου γενόμενον, ἀλλ'
ἀνέδειξεν αὐτῷ θησαυροῦ χρῆμα ἀμύθητον ἐν μιᾷ
τῶν οἰκιῶν, ἃς πρὸς τῷ θεάτρῳ ἐκέκτητο, οὗ διὰ
548 μέγεθος εὐλαβὴς μᾶλλον ἢ περιχαρὴς γενόμενος
ἔγραψε πρὸς τὸν αὐτοκράτορα ἐπιστολὴν ὧδε ξυγκει-
μένην· "θησαυρόν, ὦ βασιλεῦ, ἐπὶ τῆς ἐμαυτοῦ οἰκίας
εὕρηκα. τί οὖν περὶ αὐτοῦ κελεύεις;" καὶ ὁ αὐτοκράτωρ, Νέρβας δὲ ἦρχε τότε, "χρῶ," ἔφη, "οἷς εὗρες."
τοῦ δὲ Ἀττικοῦ ἐπὶ τῆς αὐτῆς εὐλαβείας μείναντος καὶ
γράψαντος ὑπὲρ ἑαυτὸν εἶναι τὰ τοῦ θησαυροῦ μέτρα

minds of those who shared them with him. Indeed he used to say that one who used wealth rightly ought to give to the needy so that they would not be in need, to those who were not needy, so that they would not become so. And he used to call wealth that did not circulate and was tied up by thrift "dead wealth," and the treasure chambers into which some people put it "prisons of wealth," and he named those who even think it right to make sacrifice to their hoarded money Aloadae, because they sacrifice to Ares after imprisoning him.[5]

(3) The springs of his wealth were many and flowed from many families, but the greatest were his father's and his mother's. His grandfather Hipparchus had his property confiscated on a charge of conspiring for tyranny, which the Athenians did not prosecute, but of which the emperor was not ignorant.[6] Fortune, however, did not overlook Atticus, that man's son and the father of Herodes, though he had become poor after being rich earlier, but revealed to him an unspeakably enormous treasure in one of the houses that he possessed near the theater. Because of its great size, he was cautious rather than joyful and wrote the 548 emperor a letter as follows: "I have found, emperor, a treasure in my own house. What do you command concerning it?" And the emperor—Nerva was ruling then—said, "Use what you have found." But Atticus was still cautious and wrote again, saying that the sum of the treasure was beyond his station. "Then misuse your windfall," the em-

5 Hom. *Il.* 5.385. Otus and Ephialtes, the Aloadae, imprisoned Ares for thirteen months; he was released by Hermes.

6 Suet. *Vesp.* 13 refers to the trial of Hipparchus as an example of the emperor's tolerance of the views of others.

"καὶ παραχρῶ," ἔφη, "τῷ ἑρμαίῳ, σὸν γάρ ἐστιν."
ἐντεῦθεν μέγας μὲν ὁ Ἀττικός, μείζων δὲ Ἡρώδης·
πρὸς γὰρ τῷ πατρῴῳ πλούτῳ καὶ ὁ μητρῷος αὐτῷ
πλοῦτος οὐ παρὰ πολὺ τούτου ἐπερρύη.

(4) Μεγαλοψυχία δὲ λαμπρὰ καὶ περὶ τὸν Ἀττικὸν
τοῦτον· ἦρχε μὲν γὰρ τῶν κατὰ τὴν Ἀσίαν ἐλευθέρων
πόλεων ὁ Ἡρώδης, ἰδὼν δὲ τὴν Τρῳάδα βαλανείων τε
πονήρως ἔχουσαν καὶ γεῶδες ὕδωρ ἐκ φρεάτων ἀνι-
μῶντας ὀμβρίων τε ὑδάτων θήκας ὀρύττοντας ἐπέ-
στειλεν Ἀδριανῷ τῷ αὐτοκράτορι μὴ περιιδεῖν πόλιν
ἀρχαίαν καὶ εὐθάλαττον αὐχμῷ φθαρεῖσαν, ἀλλ᾽ ἐπι-
δοῦναί σφισι τριακοσίας μυριάδας ἐς ὕδωρ, ὧν πολ-
λαπλασίας ἤδη καὶ κώμαις ἐπιδεδώκοι. ἐπῄνεσεν ὁ
αὐτοκράτωρ τὰ ἐπεσταλμένα ὡς πρὸς τρόπου ἑαυτῷ
ὄντα καὶ τὸν Ἡρώδην αὐτὸν ἐπέταξε τῷ ὕδατι. ἐπεὶ
δὲ ἐς ἑπτακοσίας μυριάδας ἡ δαπάνη προὔβαινεν ἐπέ-
στελλόν τε τῷ αὐτοκράτορι οἱ τὴν Ἀσίαν ἐπιτροπεύον-
τες, ὡς δεινὸν πεντακοσίων πόλεων φόρον ἐς μιᾶς
πόλεως δαπανᾶσθαι κρήνην, ἐμέμψατο πρὸς τὸν Ἀττικὸν ὁ αὐτοκράτωρ ταῦτα, καὶ ὁ Ἀττικὸς μεγαλοφρο-
νέστατα ἀνθρώπων "ὦ βασιλεῦ," εἶπεν, "ὑπὲρ μικρῶν
μὴ παροξύνου· τὸ γὰρ ὑπὲρ τὰς τριακοσίας μυριάδας
ἀναλωθὲν ἐγὼ μὲν τῷ υἱῷ ἐπιδίδωμι, ὁ δὲ υἱὸς τῇ
549 πόλει."[1] καὶ αἱ διαθῆκαι δέ, ἐν αἷς τῷ Ἀθηναίων δήμῳ
κατέλιπε καθ᾽ ἕκαστον ἔτος μνᾶν καθ᾽ ἕνα, μεγαλο-

[1] Cobet adds ἐπιδώσει; MSS Va and L have ἐπιδίδωσι, which
is omitted by the other MSS.

peror wrote, "because it is yours." From this Atticus became powerful and Herodes still more powerful, because in addition to his father's wealth his mother's wealth, which was not much less, flowed to him too.

(4) The ardent ambition of this Atticus was manifest. For instance when Herodes was governing the free cities in Asia, and he saw that Troy[7] was badly supplied with baths and the inhabitants drew muddy water from their wells and dug trenches for rain water, he wrote to the emperor Hadrian, asking him not to overlook a city ancient and well-sited on the sea, when it was suffering from drought, but to give them three million drachmae for the water supply, since he had already given to mere villages many times that sum. The emperor approved the contents of the letter since they were in line with his own thinking, and he appointed Herodes himself to take charge of the water supply. But when the expenditure had extended to seven million drachmae, the governors of Asia kept writing to the emperor, complaining that it was a scandal that the tribute received from five hundred cities should be used to pay for the fountain of just one. The emperor complained of this to Atticus and Atticus, the most ardently ambitious of men, said, "Emperor, do not allow yourself to be worked up over such a small sum. The amount in excess of the three million I present to my son, and he will present to the city." And then there is his will, 549 in which he left to the Athenian people one mina per person per year, which proclaims the ardent ambition of

[7] This is the later city known as Alexandria Troas.

φροσύνην κατηγοροῦσι τοῦ ἀνδρός, ᾗ καὶ ἐς τὰ ἄλλα
ἐχρῆτο, ἑκατὸν μὲν βοῦς τῇ θεῷ θύων ἐν ἡμέρᾳ μιᾷ
πολλάκις, ἑστιῶν δὲ τῇ θυσίᾳ τὸν Ἀθηναίων δῆμον
κατὰ φυλὰς καὶ γένη, ὁπότε δὲ ἥκοι Διονύσια καὶ
κατίοι ἐς Ἀκαδημίαν τὸ τοῦ Διονύσου ἕδος, ἐν Κεραμεικῷ ποτίζων ἀστοὺς ὁμοίως καὶ ξένους κατακειμέ-
νους ἐπὶ στιβάδων κιττοῦ.

(5) Ἐπεὶ δὲ τῶν τοῦ Ἀττικοῦ διαθηκῶν ἐπεμνήσθην,
ἀνάγκη καὶ τὰς αἰτίας ἀναγράψαι, δι' ἃς προσέκρου-
σεν Ἡρώδης Ἀθηναίοις. εἶχον μὲν γὰρ αἱ διαθῆκαι,
ὡς εἶπον, ἔγραψε δὲ αὐτὰς ξυμβουλίᾳ τῶν ἀμφ' ἑαυτὸν ἀπελευθέρων, οἳ χαλεπὴν ὁρῶντες τὴν Ἡρώδου
φύσιν ἀπελευθέροις τε καὶ δούλοις ἀποστροφὴν ἐποιοῦντο τοῦ Ἀθηναίων δήμου,[2] ὡς τῆς δωρεᾶς αὐτοὶ
αἴτιοι. καὶ ὁποῖα μὲν τῶν ἀπελευθέρων τὰ πρὸς τὸν
Ἡρώδην, δηλούτω ἡ κατηγορία, ἣν πεποίηται σφῶν
πᾶν κέντρον ἡρμένος τῆς ἑαυτοῦ γλώττης. ἀναγνω-
σθεισῶν δὲ τῶν διαθηκῶν ξυνέβησαν οἱ Ἀθηναῖοι
πρὸς τὸν Ἡρώδην πέντε μνᾶς αὐτὸν ἐσάπαξ ἑκάστῳ
καταβαλόντα πρίασθαι παρ' αὐτῶν τὸ μὴ ἀεὶ διδόναι.
ἀλλ' ἐπεὶ προσῄεσαν μὲν ταῖς τραπέζαις ὑπὲρ τῶν
ὡμολογημένων, ἐπανεγιγνώσκετο δὲ αὐτοῖς ξυμβό-
λαια πατέρων τε καὶ πάππων ὡς ὀφειλόντων τοῖς
Ἡρώδου γονεῦσιν ἀντιλογισμοῖς τε ὑπήγοντο καὶ οἱ
μὲν μικρὰ ἠριθμοῦντο, οἱ δὲ οὐδέν, οἱ δὲ συνείχοντο
ἐπ' ἀγορᾶς ὡς ἀποδώσοντες. ταῦτα παρώξυνε τοὺς

2 τὸν Ἀθηναίων δῆμον Valckenaer

the man. And he practiced it in other ways also. He often used to sacrifice to the goddess a hundred oxen in a single day, and entertain at the sacrificial feast the whole population of Athens by tribes and families. And whenever the Dionysia came around and the sacred image of Dionysus paraded to the Academy,[8] he would supply wine to drink for citizens and strangers alike in the Cerameicus, as they lay on couches of ivy leaves.

(5) Since I have mentioned the will of Atticus, I must also record the reasons why Herodes offended the Athenians. The terms of the will were as I have said, and he wrote them in consultation with his freedmen. Because they saw that Herodes was by nature harsh toward freedmen and slaves, they made the will a means of escape among the Athenian people, since they would themselves be held responsible for the bequest. What sort of complaints the freedmen had against Herodes can be learned from the invective that he composed against them, using every barb of his tongue. When the will had been read, the Athenians came to an agreement with Herodes, that he could pay them each five minas once rather than making the regular payment. But when they went to the banks for the sum agreed upon, they had to listen to the contracts made by their fathers and grandfathers, showing that they were in debt to the parents of Herodes, and they were held liable to counterpayments. Some received only a small sum, others nothing, and others again were detained at the agora as debtors who must pay. This treatment exasper-

---

[8] Cf. Paus. 1.38.8. The image of Dionysus of Eleutherae was taken in procession once a year to the god's small temple near the Academy.

Ἀθηναίους ὡς ἡρπασμένους τὴν δωρεάν, καὶ οὐκ
ἐπαύσαντο μισοῦντες, οὐδὲ ὁπότε τὰ μέγιστα εὐεργε-
τεῖν ᾤετο. τὸ οὖν στάδιον δικαίως³ ἔφασαν ἐπωνομά-
σθαι Παναθηναϊκόν, κατεσκευάσθαι γὰρ αὐτὸ ἐξ ὧν
ἀπεστεροῦντο Ἀθηναῖοι πάντες.

(6) Καὶ μὴν καὶ ἐλειτούργησεν Ἀθηναίοις τήν τε
ἐπώνυμον καὶ τὴν τῶν Πανελληνίων· στεφανωθεὶς δὲ
καὶ τὴν τῶν Παναθηναίων "καὶ ὑμᾶς," εἶπεν, "ὦ Ἀθη-
550 ναῖοι, καὶ τῶν Ἑλλήνων τοὺς ἥξοντας καὶ τῶν ἀθλη-
τῶν τοὺς ἀγωνιουμένους ὑποδέξομαι σταδίῳ λίθου
λευκοῦ." καὶ εἰπὼν ταῦτα τὸ στάδιον τὸ ὑπὲρ τὸν
Ἰλισσὸν εἴσω τεττάρων ἐτῶν ἀπετέλεσεν ἔργον ξυνθεὶς ὑπὲρ πάντα τὰ θαύματα· οὐδὲν γὰρ θέατρον
αὐτῷ ἁμιλλᾶται. κἀκεῖνα περὶ τῶν Παναθηναίων τούτων ἤκουον· πέπλον μὲν ἀνῆφθαι τῆς νεὼς ἡδίω γραφῆς ξὺν οὐρίῳ τῷ κόλπῳ, δραμεῖν δὲ τὴν ναῦν οὐχ
ὑποζυγίων ἀγόντων, ἀλλ' ὑπογείοις μηχαναῖς ἐπολι-
σθαίνουσαν, ἐκ Κεραμεικοῦ δὲ ἄρασαν χιλίᾳ κώπῃ
ἀφεῖναι ἐπὶ τὸ Ἐλευσίνιον καὶ περιβαλοῦσαν αὐτὸ
παραμεῖψαι τὸ Πελασγικὸν κομιζομένην τε παρὰ τὸ
Πύθιον ἐλθεῖν οἷ νῦν ὥρμισται. τὸ δὲ ἐπὶ θάτερα τοῦ
σταδίου νεὼς ἐπέχει Τύχης καὶ ἄγαλμα ἐλεφάντινον

³ Stefec adds δικαίως; Kayser proposed εὖ after ἔφασαν. An
adverb of this kind is clearly needed to convey the aptness of the
name to the Athenians' deprivation.

⁹ The eponymous Archon at Athens gave his name to the year.

ated the Athenians, who felt that they had been robbed of the bequest, and they did not stop hating Herodes, even when he believed that he was performing the greatest public services. So they said that the Panathenaic stadium was rightly named, since he built it with the money of which all the Athenians had been deprived.

(6) Furthermore he held the office of eponymous archon at Athens[9] and the curatorship of the Panathenaic festival. And when he was crowned with the charge of the Panathenaic festival he said, "I shall welcome you, Athenians, and those Hellenes who will attend and the athletes who will compete, in a stadium of pure, white marble." Just as he said, he completed within four years the stadium on the far side of the Ilissus, and so constructed a monument beyond all wonders, for there is no theater that can rival it. I have also heard the following about this Panathenaic festival. The peplos of Athena that was hung on the ship was more beautiful than can be described and billowed in the wind, and the ship moved, not with animals pulling it, but glided forward on a subterranean mechanism. Setting sail at the Cerameicus with a thousand rowers, it arrived at the Eleusinium, and after circling it, passed by the Pelasgicum. Accompanied in this way it came to the Pythium, where it is now moored.[10] On the other side of the stadium stands a temple of Fortune with

550

[10] The Panathenaea were held every year and in each fourth year there was a great Panathenaea, which is evidently what is celebrated here so lavishly by Herodes. In a great Panathenaea both the athletic events and the procession were on a grander scale. In both greater and lesser festivals, the procession brought a robe (*peplos*) to Athena.

187

ὡς κυβερνώσης πάντας. μετεκόσμησε δὲ καὶ τοὺς
Ἀθηναίων ἐφήβους ἐς τὸ νῦν σχῆμα, χλαμύδας πρῶτος ἀμφιέσας λευκάς· τέως γὰρ δὴ μελαίνας ἐνημμένοι τὰς ἐκκλησίας περιεκάθηντο καὶ τὰς πομπὰς
ἔπεμπον πενθούντων δημοσίᾳ τῶν Ἀθηναίων τὸν κή-
ρυκα τὸν Κοπρέα, ὃν αὐτοὶ ἀπέκτειναν τοὺς Ἡρακλεί-
δας τοῦ βωμοῦ ἀποσπῶντα.

551   Ἀνέθηκε δὲ Ἡρώδης Ἀθηναίοις καὶ τὸ ἐπὶ Ῥηγίλλῃ
θέατρον κέδρου ξυνθεὶς τὸν ὄροφον· ἡ δὲ ὕλη καὶ ἐν
ἀγαλματοποιίαις σπουδαία· δύο μὲν δὴ ταῦτα Ἀθήνησιν, οἷα οὐχ ἑτέρωθι τῆς ὑπὸ Ῥωμαίοις, ἀξιούσθω δὲ
λόγου καὶ τὸ ὑπωρόφιον θέατρον, ὃ ἐδείματο Κοριν-
θίοις, παρὰ πολὺ μὲν τοῦ Ἀθήνησιν, ἐν ὀλίγοις δὲ τῶν
παρ’ ἄλλοις ἐπαινουμένων, καὶ τὰ Ἰσθμοῖ ἀγάλματα
ὅ τε τοῦ Ἰσθμίου κολοσσὸς καὶ ὁ τῆς Ἀμφιτρίτης καὶ
τὰ ἄλλα, ὧν τὸ ἱερὸν ἐνέπλησεν, οὐδὲ τὸν τοῦ Μελι-
κέρτου παρελθὼν δελφῖνα. ἀνέθηκε δὲ καὶ τῷ Πυθίῳ
τὸ Πυθοῖ στάδιον καὶ τῷ Διὶ τὸ ἐν Ὀλυμπίᾳ ὕδωρ,
Θετταλοῖς τε καὶ τοῖς περὶ τὸν Μηλιέα κόλπον Ἕλλησι τὰς ἐν Θερμοπύλαις κολυμβήθρας τοῖς νοσοῦσι
παιωνίους. ᾤκισε δὲ καὶ τὸ ἐν τῇ Ἠπείρῳ Ὠρικὸν

---

11 Hom. *Il.* 15.639 describes the death of Copreus' son at the
hands of Hector and refers there to the father's relative worthless-
ness. Apollod. *Bibl.* 2.5 relates that Copreus relayed Eurystheus'
messages to Heracles, as the king of Tiryns was too afraid to see
Heracles himself.   12 This is the Odeum that still stands on
the slope of the Athenian acropolis. On the death of Regilla and
Herodes' grief, see below, VS 555–57.

an ivory statue, to show that she steers all people. And he changed the dress of the Athenian ephebes to its current form, being the first to put white cloaks on them. Previously they had worn black ones when they sat in the assembly and marched in processions, because the Athenians publicly mourned the herald Copreus,[11] whom they themselves had killed when he was dragging the children of Heracles from the altar.

Herodes also dedicated to the Athenians the theater in memory of Regilla,[12] building its ceiling from cedar wood. And this material is considered costly even for making statues. These two monuments are at Athens, and nothing like them exists elsewhere in the Roman Empire. But I must also mention the roofed theater that he built for the Corinthians, which is much inferior to the one for the Athenians, but ranks among the few most lauded monuments among other peoples. And then there are the statues at the Isthmus: the colossus of the Isthmian god[13] and that of Amphitrite, and the other offerings with which he filled the temple. Nor must I omit the dolphin of Melicertes.[14] And he dedicated to the Pythian god the stadium at Pytho and to Zeus the aqueduct at Olympia, and to the Thessalians and the Greeks around the Melean gulf he gave the baths at Thermopylae that cure the sick. He colonized Oricum in Epirus, which had fallen into decay,

[13] Poseidon, in whose honor the Isthmian Games were held, though these were said to have been founded as funeral games for Melicertes.

[14] Paus. 1.44.11. The corpse of Melicertes, or Palaemon, who was drowned by his mother, Ino Leucothea, was carried by dolphins to the shore near Corinth.

ὑποδεδωκὸς ἤδη καὶ τὸ ἐν τῇ Ἰταλίᾳ Κανύσιον
ἡμερώσας ὕδατι μάλα τούτου δεόμενον· ὤνησε δὲ καὶ
τὰς ἐν Εὐβοίᾳ καὶ Πελοποννήσῳ καὶ Βοιωτίᾳ πόλεις
ἄλλο ἄλλην. καὶ τοσοῦτος ὢν ἐν μεγαλουργίᾳ μέγα
οὐδὲν εἰργάσθαι ᾤετο, ἐπεὶ μὴ τὸν Ἰσθμὸν ἔτεμε,
λαμπρὸν ἡγούμενος ἤπειρον ἀποτεμεῖν καὶ πελάγη
ξυνάψαι διττὰ καὶ περίπλουν ἑξακισχιλίων ἐς εἴκοσι
σταδίων θαλάττης ξυνελεῖν μήκη.[4] καὶ τούτου ἤρα
μέν, οὐκ ἐθάρρει δὲ αὐτὸ αἰτεῖν ἐκ βασιλέως, μὴ δια-
βληθείη διανοίας δοκῶν ἅπτεσθαι, ᾗ μηδὲ Νέρων
ἤρκεσεν. ἐξελάλησε δὲ αὐτὸ ὧδε· ὡς γὰρ ἐγὼ Κτησι-
552 δήμου τοῦ Ἀθηναίου ἤκουον, ἤλαυνε μὲν τὴν ἐπὶ
Κορίνθου ὁ Ἡρώδης ξυγκαθημένου τοῦ Κτησιδήμου,
γενόμενος δὲ κατὰ τὸν Ἰσθμόν, "Πόσειδον," εἶπε,
"βούλομαι μέν, ξυγχωρήσει δὲ οὐδείς." θαυμάσας οὖν
ὁ Κτησίδημος τὸ εἰρημένον ἤρετο τὴν αἰτίαν τοῦ λόγου. καὶ ὁ Ἡρώδης, "ἐγώ," ἔφη, "πολὺν ἤδη χρόνον
ἀγωνίζομαι σημεῖον ὑπολιπέσθαι τοῖς μετ᾽ ἐμὲ ἀνθρώποις διανοίας δηλούσης ἄνδρα καὶ οὔπω δοκῶ μοι
τῆς δόξης ταύτης τυγχάνειν." ὁ μὲν δὴ Κτησίδημος

[4] The last part of this sentence, especially the numerals, has
suffered considerable confusion in the MSS. See Stefec's *apparatus criticus* for details. I have followed, with some hesitation,
the conjecture of Westermann, who amends the version reported
in the β family.

and Canusium in Italy, and made life civilized there by providing a water supply, since the town lacked one. And he endowed the cities in Euboea and the Peloponnese and Boeotia with various gifts. Being so ardently ambitious as he was,[15] he believed that he had achieved nothing since he had not cut the Isthmus. He believed that it would be a truly brilliant achievement to cut away the mainland and to join two seas and to contract the voyage of six thousand into twenty stades of sea. He longed to do this, but was not brave enough to ask permission from the emperor, in case he was accused of planning something which not even Nero had achieved.[16] Yet he let this plan out in conversation: I heard from Ctesidemus of Athens that Herodes drove to Corinth with Ctesidemus sitting beside him, and when they were at the Isthmus Herodes said, "Poseidon, I wish to do it, but no one will allow me." Ctesidemus was astonished at what he had said and asked the cause for his words. And Herodes said, "I have already been striving for a long time to leave behind some monument for the people of the future of a plan that will reveal a real man, and I do not yet believe that I have achieved this reputation."

552

[15] Herodes is said here to have the same quality that characterized his father, μεγαλουργία. This is literally a drive to perform great works, for which it is impossible to find an equally succinct English equivalent. I have used "ardently ambitious."

[16] Nero had earlier attempted to cut the Isthmus of Corinth (in AD 67). Philostratus has Apollonius prophesy the failure of this project at VA 4.24, and it appears as the situation in which the brief dialogue Nero takes place, while the philosopher Musonius Rufus is engaged in digging the attempted channel through the Isthmus.

ἐπαίνους διῄει τῶν τε λόγων αὐτοῦ καὶ τῶν ἔργων
ὡς οὐκ ἐχόντων ὑπερβολὴν ἑτέρῳ, ὁ δὲ Ἡρώδης
"φθαρτά," ἔφη, "λέγεις ταῦτα· καὶ γάρ ἐστι χρόνῳ
ἁλωτά, καὶ τοὺς λόγους ἡμῶν τοιχωρυχοῦσιν ἕτεροι
ὁ μὲν τὸ μεμφόμενος, ὁ δὲ τό, ἡ δὲ τοῦ Ἰσθμοῦ τομὴ
ἔργον ἀθάνατον καὶ ἀπιστούμενον τῇ φύσει."[5]

(7) Δοκεῖ γάρ μοι τὸ ῥῆξαι τὸν Ἰσθμὸν Ποσειδῶνος
δεῖσθαι ἢ ἀνδρός. ὃν ἐκάλουν οἱ πολλοὶ Ἡρώδου
Ἡρακλέα, νεανίας οὗτος ἦν ἐν ὑπήνῃ πρώτῃ Κελτῷ
μεγάλῳ ἴσος καὶ ἐς ὀκτὼ πόδας τὸ μέγεθος. διαγρά-
φει δὲ αὐτὸν ὁ Ἡρώδης ἐν μιᾷ τῶν πρὸς τὸν Ἰουλιανὸν ἐπιστολῶν· κομᾶν τε ξυμμέτρως καὶ τῶν ὀφρύων
λασίως ἔχειν, ἃς καὶ ξυμβάλλειν ἀλλήλαις οἷον μίαν,
χαροπήν τε ἀκτῖνα ἐκ τῶν ὀμμάτων ἐκδίδοσθαι παρ-
εχομένην τι ὁρμῆς ἦθος καὶ γρυπὸν εἶναι καὶ εὐτρα-
φῶς ἔχοντα τοῦ αὐχένος· τουτὶ δὲ ἐκ πόνων ἥκειν
αὐτῷ μᾶλλον ἢ σίτου. εἶναι δὲ αὐτῷ καὶ στέρνα εὐ-
παγῆ καὶ ξὺν ὥρᾳ κατεσκληκότα, καὶ κνήμην μικρὸν
ἐς τὰ ἔξω κυρτουμένην καὶ παρέχουσαν τῇ βάσει τὸ
553 εὖ βεβηκέναι. ἐνῆφθαι δὲ αὐτὸν καὶ δορὰς λύκων, ῥα-
πτὸν ἔσθημα, ἄθλους τε ποιεῖσθαι τοὺς ἀγρίους τῶν
συῶν καὶ τοὺς θῶας καὶ τοὺς λύκους καὶ τῶν ταύρων
τοὺς ὑβρίζοντας, καὶ ὠτειλὰς δὲ δεικνύναι τούτων τῶν

[5] There is an abrupt transition here from the cutting of the
Isthmus to the story of Herodes' Heracles. Editions of the text
have broken the paragraph after ἄνδρος since Olearius until
Stefec, who allows the sentence to run on. Nesselrath proposes a
lacuna after ἤ.

Ctesidemus went through a catalog of praise of his speeches and his deeds, which no one could claim to surpass, but Herodes said, "Perishable are all these things you mention. They will be captured by time, and other people will plunder my speeches, one finding fault with one thing, another with something else. But the cutting of the Isthmus is an immortal work and beyond the belief of nature."

(7) To break through the Isthmus seems to me require Poseidon or a man, whom most people used to call Herodes' Heracles. He was a youth in early manhood,[17] as tall as a big Celt and in fact eight feet in height. Herodes describes him in one of his letters to Julianus: his hair grew evenly and his eyebrows were bushy and grew together as if they were one. His eyes had a piercing gaze that showed his impetuous character. His nose was aquiline and he had a solidly built neck, which he had from work rather than diet. His chest was well built and slim with youthful beauty, and his calves curved a little to the outside and were conducive to a good gait.[18] He was dressed in the   553
skins of wolves, stitched together as a garment, and he used to contend against wild boars, jackals, wolves, and raging bulls, and showed the scars from these contests.

[17] Hom. *Od.* 10.279, πρῶτον ὑπηνήτῃ, τοῦ περ χαριεστάτη ἥβη. Lucian, *Demonax* 1, calls him Sostratus. On Agathion, see Whitmarsh 2001, 105–8; Côté 2011.

[18] These details are chosen for their positive connotations in contemporary physiognomics, as can be seen by comparison with Polemo's *Physiognomica*. They also fit well with Polemo's ideal Hellenic type. See Miles 2018, 131–32.

ἀγώνων. γενέσθαι δὲ τὸν Ἡρακλέα τοῦτον οἱ μὲν γη-
γενῆ φασιν ἐν τῷ Βοιωτίῳ Δηλίῳ,[6] Ἡρώδης δὲ ἀκοῦσαι λέγοντός φησιν, ὡς μήτηρ μὲν αὐτῷ γένοιτο
γυνὴ βουκόλος[7] οὕτω τι ἐρρωμένη, ὡς βουκτονεῖν,[8]
πατὴρ δὲ Μαραθών, οὗ τὸ ἐν Μαραθῶνι ἄγαλμα· ἔστι
δὲ ἥρως γεωργός. ἤρετό τε τὸν Ἡρακλέα τοῦτον ὁ
Ἡρώδης, εἰ καὶ ἀθάνατος εἴη, ὁ δὲ "θνητοῦ," ἔφη,
"μακροημερώτερος." ἤρετο αὐτὸν καὶ ὅ τι σιτοῖτο, ὁ
δὲ "γαλακτοφαγῶ," ἔφη, "τὸ πλέον τοῦ χρόνου καί με
βόσκουσιν αἶγές τε καὶ ποῖμναι τῶν τε βοῶν καὶ τῶν
ἵππων αἱ τοκάδες, ἐκδίδοται δέ τι καὶ θηλῆς ὄνων
γάλα εὔποτόν τε καὶ κοῦφον· ἐπειδὰν δὲ ἀλφίτοις
προσβάλω, δέκα σιτοῦμαι χοίνικας, καὶ ξυμφέρουσί
μοι τὸν ἔρανον τοῦτον γεωργοὶ Μαραθώνιοί τε καὶ
Βοιώτιοι, οἵ με καὶ Ἀγαθίωνα ἐπονομάζουσιν, ἐπειδὴ
καὶ εὐξύμβολος αὐτοῖς φαίνομαι." "τὴν δὲ δὴ γλῶτταν," ἔφη ὁ Ἡρώδης, "πῶς ἐπαιδεύθης καὶ ὑπὸ τίνων;
οὐ γάρ μοι τῶν ἀπαιδεύτων φαίνῃ." καὶ ὁ Ἀγαθίων,
"ἡ μεσόγεια," ἔφη, "τῆς Ἀττικῆς ἀγαθὸν διδασκαλεῖον ἀνδρὶ βουλομένῳ καθαρῶς[9] διαλέγεσθαι. οἱ μὲν
γὰρ ἐν τῷ ἄστει Ἀθηναῖοι μισθοῦ δεχόμενοι Θρᾴκια
καὶ Ποντικὰ μειράκια κἀξ ἄλλων ἐθνῶν βαρβάρων

---

[6] Δηλίῳ is the reading of the α group. The β group gives the
reading δήμῳ, as have editions and translations prior to Stefec. A
reference to a place makes better sense here than one to a people,
as the point of the story describing Agathion as earthborn is that
he did not have parents or a people but was, so to speak, a first-
generation autochthon.

Some say that he was earthborn and came from Delium in Boeotia, but Herodes says that he heard him say that his mother was a woman cowherd, who was so strong that she could slay oxen, and his father was Marathon, whose statue stands at Marathon.[19] And he is a farmer hero.[20] Herodes asked this Heracles if he was immortal, and he said, "I am longer in my days than a mortal." He asked him what he ate, and he said, "I live on milk most of the time and goats and herds of cows and brood mares feed me, and the she-ass also provides a milk that is good to drink and light. Whenever I come across barley meal, I eat ten quarts, and the farmers of Marathon and Boeotia supply me with this feast. They call me Agathion, because they think that I am a good omen." "Your language," Herodes said, "how were you taught to speak like that and by whom? You do not seem to me to be uneducated." And Agathon said, "The inland of Attica is a good school for a man who wishes to learn to converse. The Athenians in the city take in for pay Thracian and Pontic youths and those who throng in from

19 On the hero Marathon: Pausanias 1.32.4–5.
20 The farmer hero as a type seems to have appealed to Philostratus. See also Protesilaus' agricultural activities in the *Heroicus* (8–16).

---

7 βουκόλος was deleted by Kayser in his third edition.
8 I have preferred Jacobs' conjecture βουκτονεῖν, on grounds of sense and of the ease of the corruption, over βουκολεῖν, the reading of the archetype, as has Stefec.
9 I follow Stefec in adding καθαρῶς, a conjecture of Schröder, who proposed either this or ἀττικῶς or πεπαιδευμένως.

ξυνερρυηκότα παραφθείρονται παρ' αὐτῶν τὴν φωνὴν
μᾶλλον ἢ ξυμβάλλονταί τι αὐτοῖς ἐς εὐγλωττίαν· ἡ
μεσόγεια δὲ ἄμικτος βαρβάροις οὖσα ὑγιαίνει αὐτοῖς
ἡ φωνὴ καὶ ἡ γλῶττα τὴν ἄκραν Ἀτθίδα ἀποψάλλει."
"πανηγύρει δέ," ἦ δ' ὁ Ἡρώδης, "παρέτυχες;" καὶ ὁ
Ἀγαθίων, "τῇ γε Πυθοῖ," ἔφη, "οὐκ ἐπιμιγνὺς τῷ
ὁμίλῳ, ἀλλ' ἐκ περιωπῆς τοῦ Παρνασοῦ ἀκούων τῶν
τῆς μουσικῆς ἀγωνιστῶν, ὅτε Παμμένης ἐπὶ τραγῳ-
554 δίᾳ ἐθαυμάσθη, καί μοι ἔδοξαν οἱ σοφοὶ Ἕλληνες οὐ
χρηστὸν πρᾶγμα ἐργάζεσθαι τὰ τῶν Πελοπιδῶν καὶ
τὰ τῶν Λαβδακιδῶν κακὰ ξὺν ἡδονῇ ἀκούοντες· ξύμ-
βουλοι γὰρ σχετλίων ἔργων μῦθοι μὴ ἀπιστούμενοι."
φιλοσοφοῦντα δὲ αὐτὸν ἰδὼν ὁ Ἡρώδης ἤρετο καὶ
περὶ τῆς γυμνικῆς ἀγωνίας ὅπως γιγνώσκοι, καὶ ὅς,
"ἐκείνων," ἔφη, "καταγελῶ μᾶλλον ὁρῶν τοὺς ἀνθρώπους διαγωνιζομένους ἀλλήλοις παγκράτιον καὶ πυγ-
μὴν καὶ δρόμον καὶ πάλην καὶ στεφανουμένους ὑπὲρ
τούτου. στεφανούσθω δὲ ὁ μὲν δρομικὸς ἀθλητὴς
ἔλαφον παρελθὼν ἢ ἵππον, ὁ δὲ τὰ βαρύτερα ἀσκῶν
ταύρῳ συμπλακεὶς ἢ ἄρκτῳ, ὃ ἐγὼ ὁσημέραι πράττω
μέγαν ἆθλον ἀφῃρημένης μοι τῆς τύχης, ἐπεὶ μηκέτι
βόσκει λέοντας Ἀκαρνανία." Ἀγασθεὶς οὖν ὁ Ἡρώδης ἐδεῖτο αὐτοῦ ξυσσιτῆσαί οἱ. καὶ ὁ Ἀγαθίων,
"αὔριον," ἔφη, "ἀφίξομαί σοι κατὰ μεσημβρίαν ἐς τὸ

---

21 See below, VS 624, where the Italian Aelian is said to write
as purely as those from inland Attica.

other barbarian peoples and they are corrupted by them in their speech more than they do them any good in eloquence. But because the inland is unmixed with barbarians its dialect is healthy and its language sounds the height of Attic."[21] "Have you ever been to a festival?" Herodes asked. And Agathion said, "Yes, at Pytho. I did not mix with the crowd, but from the summit of Parnassus I listened to those contending in music, when they marveled at Pammenes in tragedy.[22] And these wise Greeks did not seem to me to do a useful thing, when they listened with pleasure to the evils of the houses of Pelops and Labdacus. For myths are councilors of wicked deeds when they are not disbelieved." Herodes perceived that he was philosophically inclined and asked him his opinion of the gymnastic contests, and he said, "I laugh at them, when I see men struggling against one another at pancration and boxing and running and wrestling, and being garlanded as victors for these things. Let the athlete who is a runner be declared the victor when he outruns a deer or horse, and let the one training for a heavier contest be the victor for wrestling with a bull or bear. I do these things every day, since fate has robbed me of a great contest, because Acarnania no longer breeds lions." Herodes was amazed at this and asked Agathion to dine with him. And Agathion said, "Tomorrow, I shall come to you at midday at the temple

554

---

[22] This Pammenes does not appear to be otherwise attested. There was, however, an eminent family of Marathon who used the names Pammenes and Zenon regularly (Geagan 1992). This family appears to have fallen from elite status around the time of Augustus, so it is possible that the allusion to a member may imply that Agathion was indeed "longer of days than a mortal."

τοῦ Κανώβου ἱερόν, ἔστω δέ σοι κρατὴρ ὁ μέγιστος
τῶν ἐν τῷ ἱερῷ γάλακτος πλέως, ὃ μὴ γυνὴ ἤμελξε."
καὶ ἀφίκετο μὲν ἐς τὴν ὑστεραίαν, καθ᾿ ὃν ὡμολόγησε
καιρόν, τὴν δὲ ῥῖνα ἐρείσας ἐς τὸν κρατῆρα, "οὐ κα-
θαρόν," ἔφη, "τὸ γάλα· προσβάλλει γάρ με χεὶρ γυναικός." καὶ εἰπὼν ταῦτα ἀπῆλθε μὴ ἐπισπασάμενος
τοῦ γάλακτος. ἀπιστήσας[10] οὖν ὁ Ἡρώδης τῷ περὶ
τῆς γυναικὸς λόγῳ ἔπεμψεν ἐς τὰ αἰπόλια τοὺς ἐπι-
σκεψομένους τἀληθές, καὶ μαθὼν αὐτὸ οὕτως ἔχον,
ξυνῆκεν ὡς δαιμονία φύσις εἴη περὶ τὸν ἄνδρα.

(8) Οἱ δὲ ποιούμενοι κατηγορίαν τῶν Ἡρώδου χειρῶν ὡς ἐπενεχθεισῶν Ἀντωνίνῳ ἐν τῇ Ἴδῃ τῷ ὄρει
κατὰ χρόνους, οὓς ὁ μὲν τῶν ἐλευθέρων πόλεων, ὁ δὲ
555 πασῶν τῶν κατὰ τὴν Ἀσίαν ἦρχον, ἠγνοηκέναι μοι
δοκοῦσι τὸν Δημοστράτου πρὸς τὸν Ἡρώδην ἀγῶνα,
ἐν ᾧ πλεῖστα διαβάλλων αὐτὸν οὐδαμοῦ τῆς παροινίας ταύτης ἐπεμνήσθη, ὅτι μηδὲ ἐγένετο. ὠθισμὸς
μὲν γάρ τις αὐτοῖς ξυνέπεσεν, ὡς ἐν δυσχωρίᾳ καὶ
στενοῖς, αἱ δὲ χεῖρες οὐδὲν παρηνόμησαν, ὥστε οὐκ
ἂν παρῆκεν ὁ Δημόστρατος διελθεῖν αὐτὰ ἐν τῇ πρὸς
τὸν Ἡρώδην δίκῃ πικρῶς οὕτω καθαψάμενος τοῦ ἀνδρός, ὡς διαβάλλειν αὐτοῦ καὶ τὰ ἐπαινούμενα.

(9) Ἦλθεν ἐπὶ τὸν Ἡρώδην καὶ φόνου δίκη ὧδε
ξυντεθεῖσα· κύειν μὲν αὐτῷ τὴν γυναῖκα Ῥήγιλλαν

[10] ἀπιστήσας Morel; ἐπιστήσας ω

[23] Canobus, or Canopus, was the helmsman of Menelaus, who

of Canobus,[23] and bring me the largest crater in the temple full of milk, which has not been milked by a woman." He did come the next day, at the agreed time, and putting his nose into the crater he said, "This milk is not pure. The smell of a woman's hand assaults my senses." Saying this he went away without tasting the milk. Herodes disbelieved what he had said about the woman and sent men to the goat pastures to find out the truth. When learned that it was true, he knew that there was a daemonic nature to the man.

(8) Those who accuse Herodes of lifting his hand against Antoninus[24] on Mount Ida at the time when Herodes governed the free cities and Antoninus governed all the cities in Asia, seem to me to be ignorant of the action brought by Demostratus against Herodes, in which he accuses him of very many things but made no mention of this insolent action, because it never happened. There was some shoving between them, as happens on a rough place and narrow road, but they did not break the law by coming to blows. And Demostratus would not have passed this by in his case against Herodes, since he attacked the man so bitterly that he censured him even for the things that are regularly praised.

(9) A charge of murder was also brought against Herodes, and it was made up in this way. His wife Regilla

555

died in Egypt, and a city was named after him at the mouth of the Nile. His cult was often confused with that of Serapis, who had long been worshiped at Athens, and it is possible that the latter's temple is meant here (Paus. 1.34).

[24] Later, the emperor Antoninus Pius; for his quarrel with Polemo about the same time, see *VS* 534.

ὄγδοόν που μῆνα, τὸν δὲ Ἡρώδην οὐχ ὑπὲρ μεγάλων
Ἀλκιμέδοντι ἀπελευθέρῳ προστάξαι τυπτῆσαι αὐτήν,
πληγεῖσαν δὲ ἐς τὴν γαστέρα τὴν γυναῖκα ἀποθανεῖν
ἐν ὠμῷ τῷ τόκῳ. ἐπὶ τούτοις ὡς ἀληθέσι γράφεται
αὐτὸν φόνου Βραδούας ὁ τῆς Ῥηγίλλης ἀδελφὸς εὐδοκιμώτατος ὢν ἐν ὑπάτοις καὶ τὸ ξύμβολον τῆς εὐγενείας περιηρτημένος τῷ ὑποδήματι, τοῦτο δέ ἐστιν
ἐπισφύριον ἐλεφάντινον μηνοειδές, καὶ παρελθὼν ἐς
τὸ Ῥωμαίων βουλευτήριον πιθανὸν μὲν οὐδὲν διῄει
περὶ τῆς αἰτίας, ἣν ἐπῆγεν, ἑαυτοῦ δὲ ἔπαινον ἐμα-
κρηγόρει περὶ τοῦ γένους, ὅθεν ἐπικόπτων αὐτὸν ὁ
Ἡρώδης, "σύ," ἔφη, "τὴν εὐγένειαν ἐν τοῖς ἀστρα-
γάλοις ἔχεις." μεγαλαυχουμένου δὲ τοῦ κατηγόρου
καὶ ἐπ' εὐεργεσίᾳ μιᾶς τῶν ἐν Ἰταλίᾳ πόλεων μάλα
556 γενναίως ὁ Ἡρώδης, "κἀγώ," ἔφη, "πολλὰ τοιαῦτα
περὶ ἐμαυτοῦ διῄειν ἄν, εἰ ἐν ἁπάσῃ τῇ γῇ ἐκρι-
νόμην." ξυνήρατο δὲ αὐτῷ τῆς ἀπολογίας πρῶτον μὲν
τὸ μηδὲν προστάξαι τοιοῦτον ἐπὶ τὴν Ῥήγιλλαν,
ἔπειτα τὸ ὑπερπενθῆσαι ἀποθανοῦσαν· διεβάλλετο
μὲν γὰρ καὶ ταῦτα ὡς πλάσμα, ἀλλ' ὅμως τἀληθὲς
ἴσχυεν· οὐ γάρ ποτε οὔτ' ἂν θέατρον αὐτῇ ἀναθεῖναι
τοιοῦτον, οὔτ' ἂν δευτέραν κλήρωσιν τῆς ὑπάτου ἀρχῆς ἐπ' αὐτῇ ἀναβαλέσθαι μὴ καθαρῶς ἔχοντα τῆς
αἰτίας, οὔτ' ἂν τὸν κόσμον αὐτῆς ἐς τὸ ἐν Ἐλευσῖνι
ἱερὸν ἀναθεῖναι φέροντα φόνῳ μεμιασμένον· τουτὶ
γὰρ τιμωροὺς τοῦ φόνου ποιοῦντος ἦν τὰς θεὰς μᾶλλον ἢ ξυγγνώμονας. ὁ δὲ καὶ τὸ σχῆμα τῆς οἰκίας ἐπ'

was eight months pregnant, and Herodes instructed his freedman Alcimedon to beat her for something trivial. The woman was hit in the stomach and died in premature labor. On these grounds, as though true, Regilla's brother Braduas brought a suit against him for murder. He was a most distinguished man among those of consular rank and he wore the symbol of his high birth, the crescent-shaped ivory buckle, on his sandals.[25] When he came before the Roman tribunal he made no persuasive points concerning the charge, but spoke at great length in praise of himself concerning his ancestry. So Herodes cut down his boastfulness and said, "You wear your pedigree on your ankles." And when the accuser boasted of his benefactions to one of the cities of Italy, Herodes said with great nobility, "I too could recount many such things about myself, wherever in all the world I were being tried." Two things assisted Herodes in his defense: firstly, that he had given no such order against Regilla, and secondly his overwhelming grief at her death. Even this was slandered as a pretense, but the truth was strong. He would never have dedicated such a theater to her memory, nor postponed the second casting of lots for his consulship if he had not been innocent of the charge, nor would he have dedicated her clothing at the temple at Eleusis if he had been polluted with murder. If he had done such a thing, it would have made the goddesses into avengers rather than have won their forgiveness. He changed the appearance of his household

556

[25] Roman patricians and senators wore a half moon as a badge on their shoes; cf. Juv. 7.191. In one of Herodes' inscriptions commemorating Regilla, their son's inheritance of "starry sandals" is mentioned. See on this commemoration, Gleason 2010.

αὐτῇ ὑπήλλαξε μελαίνων τὰ τῶν οἴκων ἄνθη παραπε-
τάσμασι καὶ χρώμασι καὶ λίθῳ Λεσβίῳ—κατηφὴς δὲ
ὁ λίθος καὶ μέλας—ὑπὲρ ὧν λέγεται καὶ Λούκιος
ἀνὴρ σοφὸς ἐς ξυμβουλίαν τῷ Ἡρώδῃ καθιστάμενος,
ὡς οὐκ ἔπειθε μεταβαλεῖν, αὐτὸν διασκῶψαι.

(10) Ἄξιον δὲ μηδὲ τοῦτο παρελθεῖν λόγου παρὰ
τοῖς σπουδαίοις ἀξιούμενον. ἦν μὲν γὰρ ἐν τοῖς φα-
νεροῖς σπουδαῖος ὁ ἀνὴρ οὗτος, Μουσωνίῳ δὲ τῷ
Τυρρηνῷ¹¹ προσφιλοσοφήσας εὐσκόπως εἶχε τῶν
ἀποκρίσεων καὶ τὸ ἐπίχαρι ξὺν καιρῷ ἐπετήδευεν,
557 ἐπιτηδειότατος δὲ ὢν τῷ Ἡρώδῃ παρῆν αὐτῷ πονήρως διατιθεμένῳ τὸ πένθος καὶ ἐνουθέτει τοιαῦτα
λέγων· "ὦ Ἡρώδη, πᾶν τὸ ἀποχρῶν μεσότητι ὥρι-
σται, καὶ ὑπὲρ τούτου πολλὰ μὲν ἤκουσα Μουσωνίου
διαλεγομένου, πολλὰ δὲ αὐτὸς διείλεγμαι, καὶ σοῦ δὲ
ἠκροώμην ἐν Ὀλυμπίᾳ ἐπαινοῦντος αὐτὸ πρὸς τοὺς
Ἕλληνας, ὅτε δὴ καὶ τοὺς ποταμοὺς ἐκέλευες μέσους
τῆς ὄχθης ῥεῖν. ἀλλὰ νῦν ποῦ ταῦτα; σεαυτοῦ γὰρ
ἐκπεσὼν ἄξια τοῦ πενθεῖσθαι πράττεις περὶ τῇ δόξῃ
κινδυνεύων," καὶ πλείω ἔτερα. ὡς δὲ οὐκ ἔπειθεν,
ἀπῄει δυσχεράνας. ἰδὼν δὲ παῖδας ἐν κρήνῃ τινὶ τῶν
κατὰ τὴν οἰκίαν ῥαφανῖδας πλύνοντας ἤρετο αὐτούς,

---

¹¹ Stefec is surely right to correct this word to Τυρρηνῷ; Τυρίῳ is a corruption going back to the archetype.

---

²⁶ This is the famous philosopher, Musonius Rufus, who also
appears in Philostratus' VA (4.35, 4.46, 5.19, and 7.16). Though

in mourning for her, blackening all the bright things in the house with hangings and dyes and marble from Lesbos— for this is a gloomy and black stone. They say that Lucius, a wise man, tried to give Herodes advice about this, and as he could not persuade him to change, he ridiculed him for it.

(10) This incident too must not be omitted from my narrative, for it has been thought worth of discussion by serious authors. Lucius was a serious figure among eminent philosophers, and because he had practiced philosophy with Musonius of Etruria[26] his responses were likely to hit the mark and he practiced a quick, timely wit. Lucius was a very close associate of Herodes and was with him 557 when he was most deeply affected by his grief, and he advised him like this: "Herodes, what is sufficient is defined on every occasion by moderation, and I have heard Musonius in his conversations say much on behalf of this principle, and I myself have discussed it at length, and I have heard you praise it at Olympia before the Greeks, when you even urged the rivers to flow moderately between their banks. But what has become of all this now? You have fallen from yourself and do things worthy of regret, and you are endangering your reputation." And he said more of this sort. But when he did not persuade him, he went away in anger. He saw some slaves at a well washing radishes for those in the household and he asked them

he wrote nothing, his teachings were recorded by a student or students, possibly by Lucius himself. Extracts survive in Stobaeus. He also features as a character in the *Nero* that survives among the works of Lucian but that is almost certainly by our Philostratus.

ὅτου εἴη τὸ δεῖπνον, οἱ δὲ ἔφασαν Ἡρώδῃ εὐτρεπίζειν
αὐτό. καὶ ὁ Λούκιος, "ἀδικεῖ," ἔφη, "Ῥήγιλλαν Ἡρώδης λευκὰς ῥαφανῖδας σιτούμενος ἐν μελαίνῃ οἰκίᾳ."
ταῦτα ὡς ἤκουσεν ἐσαγγελθέντα ὁ Ἡρώδης ἀφεῖλε
τὴν ἀχλὺν τῆς οἰκίας, ὡς μὴ ἄθυρμα γένοιτο ἀνδρῶν
σπουδαίων.

(11) Λουκίου τούτου κἀκεῖνο θαυμάσιον. ἐσπούδαζε
μὲν ὁ αὐτοκράτωρ Μᾶρκος περὶ Σέξτον τὸν ἐκ Βοιω-
τίας φιλόσοφον, θαμίζων αὐτῷ καὶ φοιτῶν ἐπὶ θύρας,
ἄρτι δὲ ἥκων ἐς τὴν Ῥώμην ὁ Λούκιος ἤρετο τὸν
αὐτοκράτορα προϊόντα, ποῖ βαδίζοι καὶ ἐφ᾿ ὅ τι, καὶ
ὁ Μᾶρκος, "καλὸν," ἔφη, "καὶ γηράσκοντι τὸ μανθά-
νειν· εἶμι δὴ πρὸς Σέξτον τὸν φιλόσοφον μαθησόμε-
νος, ἃ οὔπω οἶδα." καὶ ὁ Λούκιος ἐξάρας τὴν χεῖρα ἐς
τὸν οὐρανὸν, "ὦ Ζεῦ," ἔφη, "ὁ Ῥωμαίων βασιλεὺς γηράσκων ἤδη δέλτον ἐξαψάμενος ἐς διδασκάλου φοιτᾷ,
ὁ δὲ ἐμὸς βασιλεὺς Ἀλέξανδρος δύο καὶ τριάκοντα
ἐτῶν ἀπέθανεν." ἀπόχρη καὶ τὰ εἰρημένα δεῖξαι τὴν
ἰδέαν, ἣν ἐφιλοσόφει Λούκιος· ἱκανὰ γάρ που ταῦτα
δηλῶσαι τὸν ἄνδρα, καθάπερ τὸν ἀνθοσμίαν τὸ
γεῦμα.

(12) Τὸ μὲν δὴ ἐπὶ Ῥηγίλλῃ πένθος ὧδε ἐσβέσθη·
τὸ δὲ ἐπὶ Παναθηναΐδι τῇ θυγατρὶ Ἀθηναῖοι ἐπράυ-
ναν, ἐν ἄστει τε αὐτὴν θάψαντες καὶ ψηφισάμενοι τὴν
ἡμέραν, ἐφ᾿ ἧς ἀπέθανεν, ἐξαιρεῖν τοῦ ἔτους. ἀποθα-
νούσης δὲ αὐτῷ καὶ τῆς ἄλλης θυγατρός, ἣν Ἐλπι-
νίκην ὠνόμαζεν, ἔκειτο μὲν ἐν τῷ δαπέδῳ τὴν γῆν
παίων καὶ βοῶν, "τί σοι, θύγατερ, καθαγίσω; τί σοι

558

204

whose dinner they were to be, and they said they were preparing them for Herodes. And Lucius said, "Herodes dishonors Regilla by eating white radishes in a black house." When Herodes heard this reported inside he cleared away the dark mist from his house, so that he would not be a laughingstock for serious men.

(11) The following is another astonishing saying of this Lucius. The emperor Marcus took a keen interest in Sextus, the philosopher from Boeotia, and used to attend his classes and visit his home. Lucius had just arrived in Rome and he asked the emperor, who was on his way out, where he was going and for what reason. And Marcus said, "It is a good thing for one growing old still to be learning. So I am going to Sextus the philosopher, to learn from him, what I do not yet know." And Lucius raised up his hands to the heavens and said, "O Zeus, the king of the Romans grows old but he hangs a tablet around his neck and goes to school, while my king, Alexander, died at thirty two." What I have quoted is enough to show the style in which Lucius practiced philosophy. For these examples are enough to reveal the man, just as a sip reveals the bouquet of wine.

(12) So his grief for Regilla was quenched in this way, but the Athenians mitigated his grief for his daughter Panathenais by burying her in the city and voting that the 558 day on which she had died should be taken out of the year. When his other daughter died, whom he called Elpinice, he lay on the floor beating the earth and crying aloud, "What offerings, daughter, should I consecrate to you? What should I bury with you?" Sextus the philosopher,

ξυνθάψω;" παρατυχὼν δὲ αὐτῷ Σέξτος ὁ φιλόσοφος,
"μεγάλα," ἔφη, "τῇ θυγατρὶ δώσεις ἐγκρατῶς αὐτὴν
πενθήσας."

(13) Ἐπένθει δὲ ταῖς ὑπερβολαῖς ταύταις τὰς θυ-
γατέρας, ἐπειδὴ Ἀττικὸν τὸν υἱὸν ἐν ὀργῇ εἶχε. διεβέβλητο δὲ πρὸς αὐτὸν ὡς ἠλιθιώδη καὶ δυσγράμματον
καὶ παχὺν τὴν μνήμην· τὰ γοῦν πρῶτα γράμματα
παραλαβεῖν μὴ δυνηθέντος ἦλθεν ἐς ἐπίνοιαν τῷ
Ἡρώδῃ ξυντρέφειν αὐτῷ τέτταρας παῖδας καὶ εἴκοσιν
ἰσήλικας ὠνομασμένους ἀπὸ τῶν γραμμάτων, ἵνα ἐν
τοῖς τῶν παίδων ὀνόμασι τὰ γράμματα ἐξ ἀνάγκης
αὐτῷ μελετῷτο. ἑώρα δὲ αὐτὸν καὶ μεθυστικὸν καὶ
ἀνοήτως ἐρῶντα, ὅθεν ζῶν μὲν ἐπεχρησμῴδει τῇ ἑαυτοῦ οὐσίᾳ ἐκεῖνο τὸ ἔπος·

εἷς δ᾽ ἔτι που μωρὸς καταλείπεται εὐρέι οἴκῳ,

τελευτῶν δὲ τὰ μὲν μητρῷα ἀπέδωκεν, εἰς ἑτέρους δὲ
κληρονόμους τὸν ἑαυτοῦ οἶκον μετέστησεν. ἀλλ᾽ Ἀθηναίοις ἀπάνθρωπα ἐδόκει ταῦτα οὐκ ἐνθυμουμένοις
τὸν Ἀχιλλέα καὶ τὸν Πολυδεύκην καὶ τὸν Μέμνονα,
οὓς ἴσα γνησίοις ἐπένθησε τροφίμους ὄντας, ἐπειδὴ
καλοὶ μάλιστα κἀγαθοὶ ἦσαν γενναῖοί τε καὶ φιλομα-
θεῖς καὶ τῇ παρ᾽ αὐτῷ τροφῇ πρέποντες. εἰκόνας γοῦν
559 ἀνετίθει σφῶν θηρώντων τε καὶ τεθηρακότων καὶ θη-
ρασόντων τὰς μὲν ἐν δρυμοῖς, τὰς δὲ ἐπ᾽ ἀγροῖς, τὰς
δὲ πρὸς πηγαῖς, τὰς δὲ ὑπὸ σκιαῖς πλατάνων, οὐκ

who happened to be present, said, "You will give your daughter a great gift if you control your grief for her."

(13) He mourned his daughters with these extravagant gestures because he was angry at his son Atticus. Atticus had been slandered to him as senseless, bad at his letters and dull in his memory. At any rate when it came to Herodes' notice that he was not able to learn his alphabet, it occurred to Herodes to raise twenty four boys of the same age and to name each one after a letter of the alphabet, so that in saying the names of the boys he would practice by necessity the letters of the alphabet. He saw that his son was a problem drinker and senseless in his love affairs, so that while he was still alive he made the following prophecy over his own property:

One fool, I suppose, is still left in the wide house.[27]

And when he died, he left the wealth from his mother's side to his son, but left his own house to other heirs. But this seemed inhuman to the Athenians, who did not take into consideration Achilles and Polydeuces and Memnon, whom he mourned equally to his own legitimate children, since they were highly honorable youths, noble-minded and dedicated to study, a credit to their upbringing with him. At any rate he set up statues of them hunting and having hunted and about to hunt, some in the thickets, some in the fields, some by springs, others in the shade of plane trees, not hidden away, but inscribed with curses on

559

---

[27] The original of this verse, often parodied by the sophists, and several times by Dionysius of Halicarnassus, is Hom. *Od.* 4.498: εἷς δ᾽ ἔτι που ζωὸς κατερύκεται εὐρέι πόντῳ (One man, I believe, is still detained on the wide sea).

ἀφανῶς, ἀλλὰ ξὺν ἀραῖς τοῦ περικόψοντος ἢ κινήσον-
τος, οὓς οὐκ ἂν ἐπὶ τοσοῦτον ἦρεν, εἰ μὴ ἐπαίνων
ἀξίους ἐγίγνωσκε. Κυντιλίων δέ, ὁπότε ἦρχον τῆς
Ἑλλάδος, αἰτιωμένων αὐτὸν ἐπὶ ταῖς τῶν μειρακίων
τούτων εἰκόσιν ὡς περιτταῖς, "τί δὲ ὑμῖν," ἔφη, "διενή-
νοχεν, εἰ ἐγὼ τοῖς ἐμοῖς ἐμπαίζω λιθαρίοις;"

(14) Ἦρξε δὲ αὐτῷ τῆς πρὸς τοὺς Κυντιλίους διαφορᾶς, ὡς μὲν οἱ πολλοί φασι, Πυθικὴ πανήγυρις,
ἐπειδὴ ἑτεροδόξως τῆς μουσικῆς ἠκροῶντο, ὡς δὲ
ἔνιοι, τὰ παιχθέντα περὶ αὐτῶν Ἡρώδῃ πρὸς Μάρκον·
ὁρῶν γὰρ αὐτοὺς Τρῶας μέν, μεγάλων δὲ ἀξιουμένους
παρὰ τοῦ βασιλέως, "ἐγώ," ἔφη, "καὶ τὸν Δία μέμφο-
μαι τὸν Ὁμηρικόν, ὅτι τοὺς Τρῶας φιλεῖ." ἡ δὲ ἀλη-
θεστέρα αἰτία ἥδε· τὼ ἄνδρε τούτω, ὁπότε ἄμφω τῆς
Ἑλλάδος ἠρχέτην, καλέσαντες ἐς τὴν ἐκκλησίαν
Ἀθηναῖοι φωνὰς ἀφῆκαν τυραννουμένων πρὸς τὸν
Ἡρώδην ἀποσημαίνοντες καὶ δεόμενοι ἐπὶ πᾶσιν ἐς
τὰ βασιλέως ὦτα παραπεμφθῆναι τὰ εἰρημένα. τῶν
δὲ Κυντιλίων παθόντων τι πρὸς τὸν δῆμον καὶ ξὺν
ὁρμῇ ἀναπεμψάντων, ἃ ἤκουσαν, ἐπιβουλεύεσθαι
παρ' αὐτῶν ὁ Ἡρώδης ἔφασκεν ὡς ἀναθολούντων ἐπ'
αὐτὸν τοὺς Ἀθηναίους. μετ' ἐκείνην γὰρ τὴν ἐκκλησίαν Δημόστρατοι ἀνέφυσαν καὶ Πραξαγόραι καὶ
Μαμερτῖνοι καὶ ἕτεροι πλείους ἐς τὸ ἀντίξοον τῷ
Ἡρώδῃ πολιτεύοντες.

---

[28] As special legates, ca. 174.

[29] A related episode concerning Herodes' grief is recounted

anyone who should pull them down or move them. He would not have exalted them like this, if he had not known that they were worthy of his praises. And when the Quintilii, during their governing of Greece,[28] censured him for the statues of these youths, on the grounds that they were an extravagance, he said, "What difference does it make to you if I play with my marbles?"[29]

(14) The quarrel with the Quintilii began,[30] so most people say, with the Pythian festival, when they had different opinions of the musical contest, but some say that it began with the jokes about the Quintilii that Herodes made to Marcus. When Herodes saw that they were Trojans, and had been deemed worthy of great honors by the emperor he said, "I find fault as well with Homer's Zeus, because he loves the Trojans." But there is more truth in the following account. When these two men were governing Greece together, the Athenians invited them to the assembly and let loose speeches to the effect that they were oppressed by a tyrant, namely Herodes, and asked finally that what they had said be conveyed to the ears of the emperor. Because the Quintilii sympathized with the people and rapidly sent on word of what they had heard, Herodes alleged that they were plotting against him, by stirring up the Athenians against him. Certainly after that assembly men like Demostratus and Praxagoras and Mamertinus and many others like them sprang up, taking political positions hostile to Herodes.

by Aulus Gellius (*NA* 19.12), though there the grief is said to be for a singular boy. In that passage Herodes tells a fable rejecting the Stoic ideal of freedom from emotion (ἀπάθεια).

[30] These brothers are mentioned at Cass. Dio 72.33.

560   Γραψάμενος δὲ αὐτοὺς ὁ Ἡρώδης ὡς ἐπισυνιστάν-
τας αὐτῷ τὸν δῆμον ἦγεν ἐπὶ τὴν ἡγεμονίαν, οἱ δὲ
ὑπεξῆλθον ἀφανῶς πρὸς τὸν αὐτοκράτορα Μᾶρκον,
θαρροῦντες τῇ τε φύσει τοῦ βασιλέως δημοτικωτέρᾳ
οὔσῃ καὶ τῷ καιρῷ· ὧν γὰρ ὑπώπτευσε Λούκιον κοινωνὸν αὐτῷ τῆς ἀρχῆς γενόμενον, οὐδὲ τὸν Ἡρώδην
ἠφίει τοῦ μὴ οὐ ξυμμετέχειν αὐτῷ. ὁ μὲν δὴ αὐτοκράτωρ ἐκάθητο ἐς τὰ Παιόνια ἔθνη ὁρμητηρίῳ τῷ
Σιρμίῳ χρώμενος, κατέλυον δὲ οἱ μὲν ἀμφὶ τὸν Δημόστρατον περὶ τὰ βασίλεια, παρέχοντος αὐτοῖς ἀγορὰν
τοῦ Μάρκου καὶ θαμὰ ἐρωτῶντος, εἴ του δέοιντο.
φιλανθρώπως δὲ πρὸς αὐτοὺς ἔχειν αὐτός τε ἑαυτὸν
ἐπεπείκει καὶ τῇ γυναικὶ ἐπέπειστο καὶ τῷ θυγατρίῳ
ψελλιζομένῳ ἔτι· τοῦτο γὰρ μάλιστα ξὺν πολλοῖς θωπεύμασι περιπῖπτον τοῖς γόνασι τοῦ πατρὸς ἐδεῖτο
σῶσαί οἱ τοὺς Ἀθηναίους. ὁ δὲ Ἡρώδης ἐν προαστείῳ
ἐσκήνου, ἐν ᾧ πύργοι ἐξῳκοδόμηντο καὶ ἡμιπύργια,
καὶ δὴ ξυναπεδήμουν αὐτῷ καὶ δίδυμοι κόραι πρὸς
ἀκμῇ γάμων θαυμαζόμεναι ἐπὶ τῷ εἴδει, ἃς ἐκνηπιώ-
σας ὁ Ἡρώδης οἰνοχόους ἑαυτῷ καὶ ὀψοποιοὺς ἐπε-
ποίητο θυγάτρια ἐπονομάζων καὶ ὧδε ἀσπαζόμενος—
Ἀλκιμέδοντος μὲν δὴ αὗται θυγατέρες, ὁ δὲ Ἀλκιμέδων
ἀπελεύθερος τοῦ Ἡρώδου—καθευδούσας δὲ αὐτὰς ἐν
ἑνὶ τῶν πύργων, ὃς ἦν ἐχυρώτατος, σκηπτὸς ἐμπεσὼν
νύκτωρ ἀπέκτεινεν.

---

31 Lucius Verus, the emperor's son-in-law and colleague; cf.
Cass. Dio 71.1–2.

Herodes brought a charge against them, that they were   560
inciting the people against him, and tried to bring them to
the proconsular court. But they went away secretly to the
emperor Marcus, taking heart from the character of the
emperor, which tended to be democratic, and from their
timing. This was when the emperor suspected Lucius,[31]
who shared imperial rule with him, of plotting against
him, and had not acquitted Herodes of being in the conspiracy against him. The emperor had made his headquar-
ters among the tribes of Paeonia, with Sirmium[32] as his
base, and Demostratus and his associates lodged near the
emperor's quarters. Marcus offered them supplies and often asked if they needed anything. Not only was he himself
convinced that he should behave with this benevolence
toward them, but he listened as well to his wife and his
little daughter, who was still too young to speak clearly.
The little girl especially used to fall on her father's knees
and ask him, with many endearments, to save the Athenians for her. But Herodes lodged in a suburb in which
towers had been built and half-towers, and there had traveled with him from home twin girls, who were just at the
age of marriage and were astonishing in their beauty.
Herodes had raised them from infancy and appointed
them his cupbearers and cooks, and he used to call them
his little daughters and embraced them as though they
were. These girls were in fact the daughters of Alcimedon,
who was a freedman of Herodes. While they were sleeping
in one of the towers, which was strongly built, a thunderbolt fell upon it during the night and killed them.

[32] Sremska Mitrovica, in modern-day Serbia.

211

Ὑπὸ τούτου δὴ τοῦ πάθους ἔκφρων ὁ Ἡρώδης
ἐγένετο καὶ παρῆλθεν ἐς τὸ βασίλειον δικαστήριον
561 οὔτε ἔννους καὶ θανάτου ἐρῶν. παρελθὼν γὰρ καθ-
ίστατο ἐς διαβολὰς τοῦ αὐτοκράτορος οὐδὲ σχηματί-
σας τὸν λόγον, ὡς εἰκὸς ἦν ἄνδρα γεγυμνασμένον
τῆς τοιᾶσδε ἰδέας μεταχειρίσασθαι τὴν ἑαυτοῦ χολήν, ἀλλ᾽ ἀπηγκωνισμένῃ τῇ γλώττῃ καὶ γυμνῇ δια-
τείνετο λέγων, "ταῦτά μοι ἡ Λουκίου ξενία, ὃν σύ μοι
ἔπεμψας· ὅθεν δικάζεις, γυναικί με καὶ τριετεῖ παιδίῳ
καταχαριζόμενος." Βασσαίου δὲ τοῦ πεπιστευμένου
τὸ ξίφος θάνατον αὐτῷ[12] φήσαντος ὁ Ἡρώδης, "ὦ λῷστε," ἔφη, "γέρων ὀλίγα φοβεῖται."

Ὁ μὲν οὖν Ἡρώδης ἀπῆλθε τοῦ δικαστηρίου εἰπὼν
τοῦτο καὶ μετέωρον καταλείψας πολὺ τοῦ ὕδατος,
ἡμεῖς δὲ τῶν ἐπιδήλως τῷ Μάρκῳ φιλοσοφηθέντων
καὶ τὰ περὶ τὴν δίκην ταύτην ἡγώμεθα· οὐ γὰρ ξυνή-
γαγε τὰς ὀφρῦς, οὐδὲ ἔτρεψε τὸ ὄμμα, ὃ κἂν διαιτη-
τής τις ἔπαθεν, ἀλλ᾽ ἐπιστρέψας ἑαυτὸν ἐς τοὺς Ἀθηναίους, "ἀπολογεῖσθε," ἔφη, "ὦ Ἀθηναῖοι, εἰ καὶ μὴ
ξυγχωρεῖ Ἡρώδης." καὶ ἀκούων ἀπολογουμένων ἐπὶ
πολλοῖς μὲν ἀφανῶς ἤλγησεν, ἀναγιγνωσκομένης δὲ
αὐτῷ καὶ Ἀθηναίων ἐκκλησίας, ἐν ᾗ ἐφαίνοντο καθα-

---

[12] θανατᾶν αὐτόν Cobet

[33] That is, the occasion called for a speech of "covert allusion";
see the Rhetorical Glossary, under σχηματίζειν.

Herodes was driven out of his mind by this grief and went before the emperor's tribunal when he was irrational and in love with death. When he came forward to speak 561 he launched into invective against the emperor and did not even bother to shape his speech into rhetorical figures,[33] though one would expect a man who had been trained in such a style of speaking would manage his own anger. But with an aggressive and unadorned tongue he persisted in the attack: "This is what I get for showing hospitality to Lucius, whom you sent to me. On these grounds you judge me, to please a woman and a three-year-old child." When Bassaeus, the praetorian prefect, said this would be the death of him, Herodes said, "My good fellow, an old man fears few things."

So Herodes went away from the court when he had said this and left a lot of water in the water clock. Let us consider Marcus' conduct in this trial among the most outstanding examples of his philosophical practice. For he did not draw together his eyebrows, nor did he alter the expression of his eyes,[34] which might happen even to a mere magistrate, but turning to the Athenians he said, "Make your defense, Athenians, even if Herodes does not give you leave." When he listened to them making their defense, he was pained at many points, though without showing it. But when the decree of the Athenian assembly was read out, in which they openly attacked Herodes for

[34] Philostratus once more notes physiognomic details, this time as indicators of Marcus' emotional control. The eye and eyebrows figure prominently in Polemo's *Physiognomica*. Marcus' *Meditations* are a record of his striving to achieve the calm that Philostratus describes.

213

πτόμενοι τοῦ Ἡρώδου, ὡς τοὺς ἄρχοντας τῆς Ἑλλάδος ὑποποιουμένου πολλῷ τῷ μέλιτι καί που καὶ βε-
βοηκότες, "ὦ πικροῦ μέλιτος," καὶ πάλιν, "μακάριοι
οἱ ἐν τῷ λοιμῷ ἀποθνήσκοντες," οὕτως ἐσείσθη τὴν
καρδίαν ὑφ' ὧν ἤκουσεν, ὡς ἐς δάκρυα φανερὰ ὑπ-
αχθῆναι. τῆς δὲ τῶν Ἀθηναίων ἀπολογίας ἐχούσης
κατηγορίαν τοῦ τε Ἡρώδου καὶ τῶν ἀπελευθέρων τὴν
ὀργὴν ὁ Μᾶρκος ἐς τοὺς ἀπελευθέρους ἔτρεψε κολάσει χρησάμενος ὡς οἷόν τε ἐπιεικεῖ, οὕτω γὰρ αὐτὸς
χαρακτηρίζει τὴν ἑαυτοῦ κρίσιν, μόνῳ δὲ Ἀλκιμέδοντι τὴν τιμωρίαν ἐπανῆκεν ἀποχρῶσαν οἱ εἶναί φήσας τὴν ἐπὶ τοῖς τέκνοις συμφοράν. ταῦτα μὲν δὴ ὧδε
ἐφιλοσοφεῖτο τῷ Μάρκῳ.

562   (15) Ἐπιγράφουσι δὲ ἔνιοι καὶ φυγὴν οὐ φυγόντι
καὶ φασιν αὐτὸν οἰκῆσαι τὸ ἐν τῇ Ἠπείρῳ Ὠρικόν, ὃ
καὶ πολίσαι αὐτόν, ὡς εἴη δίαιτα τῷ σώματι ἐπιτηδεία. ὁ δὲ Ἡρώδης ᾤκησε μὲν τὸ χωρίον τοῦτο νοσήσας ἐν αὐτῷ καὶ θύσας ἐκβατήρια τῆς νόσου, φυγεῖν
δὲ οὔτε προσετάχθη οὔτε ἔτλη. καὶ μάρτυρα τοῦ λόγου τούτου ποιήσομαι τὸν θεσπέσιον Μᾶρκον· μετὰ
γὰρ τὰ ἐν τῇ Παιονίᾳ διῃτᾶτο μὲν ὁ Ἡρώδης ἐν τῇ
Ἀττικῇ περὶ τοὺς φιλτάτους ἑαυτῷ δήμους Μαραθῶνα
καὶ Κηφισιὰν ἐξηρτημένης αὐτοῦ τῆς πανταχόθεν
νεότητος, οἳ κατ' ἔρωτα τῶν ἐκείνου λόγων ἐφοίτων
Ἀθήναζε, πεῖραν δὲ ποιούμενος, μὴ χαλεπὸς αὐτῷ εἴη
διὰ τὰ ἐν τῷ δικαστηρίῳ πέμπει πρὸς αὐτὸν ἐπιστολὴν οὐκ ἀπολογίαν ἔχουσαν, ἀλλ' ἔγκλημα· θαυμάζειν γὰρ ἔφη, τοῦ χάριν οὐκέτι αὐτῷ ἐπιστέλλοι

trying to corrupt those governing Greece with his honeyed
eloquence, and when they exclaimed, "alas, what bitter
honey," and again, "happy are those who died in the
plague," he was so shaken to the heart by what he heard,
that he was openly moved to tears. But since the Athenian
defense contained a condemnation not only of Herodes
but also of his freedmen, Marcus turned his anger against
the freedmen, though employing a punishment "as mild
as possible," which was in fact the phrase he used to describe his own judgment. Only in the case of Alcimedon
did he remit the punishment, saying that the loss of his
children was enough. So Marcus handled these things in
a truly philosophical manner.

(15) Some place on record an exile of Herodes, who 562
was never exiled at all, and they say that he lived at Oricum
in Epirus, and that he in fact founded the city, so that it
would offer a way of life suited to his constitution. Herodes
did indeed live in this place, fell ill there and sacrificed in
thanks for growing well again, but he was not condemned
to exile nor did he suffer this penalty. And as a witness of
the truth of this statement I will employ the divine Marcus. After the events in Paeonia, Herodes lived in Attica
around the demes that he loved best, Marathon and Ce-
phisia. Youths from all places hung upon him, who flocked
to Athens out of a desire for his eloquence. In order to test
whether the emperor was angry with him for what had
happened in the court, he sent a letter, which did not
contain an apology but a complaint. He said that he was
astonished and at a loss as to why the emperor had not yet

PHILOSTRATUS

καίτοι τὸν πρὸ τοῦ χρόνον θαμὰ οὕτω γράφων, ὡς καὶ
τρεῖς γραμματοφόρους ἀφικέσθαι ποτὲ παρ' αὐτὸν ἐν
ἡμέρᾳ μιᾷ κατὰ πόδας ἀλλήλων. καὶ ὁ αὐτοκράτωρ
διὰ πλειόνων μὲν καὶ ὑπὲρ πλειόνων, θαυμάσιον δὲ
ἦθος ἐγκαταμίξας τοῖς γράμμασιν ἐπέστειλε πρὸς
τὸν Ἡρώδην, ὧν ἐγὼ τὰ ξυντείνοντα ἐς τὸν παρόντα
μοι λόγον ἐξελὼν τῆς ἐπιστολῆς δηλώσω. τὸ μὲν
δὴ προοίμιον τῶν ἐπεσταλμένων, "χαῖρέ μοι, φίλε
Ἡρώδη." διαλεχθεὶς δὲ ὑπὲρ τῶν τοῦ πολέμου χειμα-
δίων, ἐν οἷς ἦν τότε, καὶ τὴν γυναῖκα ὀλοφυράμενος
ἄρτι αὐτῷ τεθνεῶσαν εἰπών τέ τι καὶ περὶ τῆς τοῦ
σώματος ἀσθενείας ἐφεξῆς γράφει, "σοὶ δὲ ὑγιαίνειν
τε εὔχομαι καὶ περὶ ἐμοῦ ὡς εὔνου σοι διανοεῖσθαι,
μηδὲ ἡγεῖσθαι ἀδικεῖσθαι, εἰ καταφωράσας τινὰς τῶν
σῶν πλημμελοῦντας κολάσει ἐπ' αὐτοὺς ἐχρησάμην
ὡς οἷόν τε ἐπιεικεῖ. διὰ μὲν δὴ ταῦτα μή μοι ὀργίζου·
εἰ δέ τι λελύπηκά σε ἢ λυπῶ, ἀπαίτησον παρ' ἐμοῦ
δίκας ἐν τῷ ἱερῷ τῆς ἐν ἄστει Ἀθηνᾶς ἐν μυστηρίοις.
ηὐξάμην γάρ, ὁπότε ὁ πόλεμος μάλιστα ἐφλέγμαινε,
καὶ μυηθῆναι, εἴη δὲ καὶ σοῦ μυσταγωγοῦντος." τοιάδε ἡ ἀπολογία τοῦ Μάρκου καὶ οὕτω φιλάνθρωπος
καὶ ἐρρωμένη. τίς ἂν οὖν ποτε ἢ ὂν φυγῇ περιέβαλεν
οὕτω προσεῖπεν ἢ τὸν ἄξιον οὕτω προσειρῆσθαι φεύγειν ἔταξεν;

563

---

35 Cf. Philostratus' comment on character (ἦθος) in the letters
of Aeschines (VS 510). The instructions on letter writing by Philostratus of Lemnos (often wrongly titled *Dialexis* 1 and ascribed
to our Philostratus) suggest that infusing a letter with ἦθος is the

216

written to him, although previously he had written to him so often that three letter carriers once came to him in a single day, treading in one another's footsteps. And the emperor wrote to Herodes at great length and on many subjects, infusing the letter with an astonishing sense of character.[35] I shall extract from the letter all that relates to my present narrative, and publish it. "I greet you, my friend, Herodes." Then after discussing the military winter quarters, where he was at the time, and mourning for his wife, of whom he had recently been bereaved by death,[36] and after some remarks on his own ill health, he writes next: "I pray that you are well and that you think of me as well disposed to you. And do not think that you are treated unjustly if, after I detected the offenses of some in your household, I punished them with a penalty as mild as possible. So do not be angry with me for these things. But if I have caused you pain, or I continue to cause you pain, demand reparation from me in the temple of Athena in the city at the time of the Mysteries. For I made a vow, when the war began to blaze highest, that I too would be initiated. May it happen with you as my initiator." This was the nature of Marcus' defense of his actions, so compassionate and firm. So who would have spoken like this to one whom he had condemned to exile, or imposed exile on one whom he thought worthy of this kind of address?

563

goal of good epistolary style. The same point is made in [Demetr.] *Eloc.* 227 and appears to have been standard rhetorical wisdom. Cf. also the life of Antipater of Hierapolis (*VS* 607), whose work as *ab epistulis Graecis* is described as essentially mimicking the emperor's character in imperial correspondence.

[36] The empress Faustina died suddenly at the foot of Mount Taurus, about AD 175.

PHILOSTRATUS

(16) Ἔστι δὲ τις λόγος, ὡς νεώτερα μὲν ὁ τὴν ἑῴαν
ἐπιτροπεύων Κάσσιος ἐπὶ τὸν Μᾶρκον βουλεύοι, ὁ δὲ
Ἡρώδης ἐπιπλήξειεν αὐτῷ δι᾽ ἐπιστολῆς ὧδε ξυγκει-
μένης, "Ἡρώδης Κασσίῳ· ἐμάνης." τήνδε τὴν ἐπιστολὴν μὴ μόνον ἐπίπληξιν ἡγώμεθα, ἀλλὰ καὶ ῥώμην
ἀνδρὸς ὑπὲρ τοῦ βασιλέως τιθεμένου τὰ τῆς γνώμης
ὅπλα.

(17) Ὁ δὲ λόγος, ὃν διῆλθε πρὸς τὸν Ἡρώδην ὁ
Δημόστρατος, ἐν θαυμασίοις δοκεῖ. ἰδέα δὲ αὐτοῦ ἡ
μὲν τοῦ ἤθους μία (τὸ γὰρ ἐμβριθὲς ἐκ προοιμίων ἐς
τέλος διῆκε τοῦ λόγου), αἱ δὲ τῆς ἑρμηνείας ἰδέαι
πολλαὶ καὶ ἀνόμοιαι μὲν ἀλλήλαις, λόγου δὲ ἄξιαι.
ἔστω που καὶ τὸ δι᾽ Ἡρώδην παρὰ τοῖς βασκάνοις
εὐδοκιμεῖν τὸν λόγον, ἐπειδὴ ἀνὴρ τοιοῦτος ἐν αὐτῷ
κακῶς ἤκουσεν. ἀλλ᾽ ὅπως γε καὶ πρὸς τὰς λοιδορίας
ἔρρωτο, δηλώσει καὶ τὰ πρὸς τὸν κύνα Πρωτέα λεχθέντα ποτὲ ὑπ᾽ αὐτοῦ Ἀθήνησιν. ἦν μὲν γὰρ τῶν
οὕτω θαρραλέως φιλοσοφούντων ὁ Πρωτεὺς οὗτος, ὡς
καὶ ἐς πῦρ ἑαυτὸν ἐν Ὀλυμπίᾳ ῥῖψαι, ἐπηκολούθει δὲ
τῷ Ἡρώδῃ κακῶς ἀγορεύων αὐτὸν ἡμιβαρβάρῳ
γλώττῃ· ἐπιστραφεὶς οὖν ὁ Ἡρώδης, "ἔστω," ἔφη,
"κακῶς με ἀγορεύεις. πρὸς τί καὶ οὕτως;" ἐπικειμένου
δὲ τοῦ Πρωτέως ταῖς λοιδορίαις "γεγηράκαμεν," ἔφη,
564 "σὺ μὲν κακῶς με ἀγορεύων, ἐγὼ δὲ ἀκούων," ἐνδεικνύμενος δήπου τὸ ἀκούειν μέν, καταγελᾶν δὲ ὑπὸ τοῦ

37 For the revolt of Cassius, see Cass. Dio 72.22.

(16) There is a story that when Cassius the governor of the eastern provinces was plotting rebellion against Marcus,[37] Herodes rebuked him in a letter which read, "Herodes to Cassius. You've gone mad." We must consider this letter not only a sharp rebuke, but an indication of the strength of a man taking up the arms of the intellect for his emperor.

(17) The speech that Demostratus delivered against Herodes seems to me to rank among the most astonishing ones. The style of its character is unified (for the gravitas of its opening continued to the end of the speech.) But the formal modes of expression are many and differ from one another, and are worthy of discussion. I grant that the speech has become famous among the malicious, partly on account of Herodes, because it attacked a man so eminent. But his strength in response to insults is clear from what he said once at Athens to Proteus the Cynic.[38] This Proteus was one of those who was are so audacious in the practice of philosophy that he even threw himself into fire at Olympia, and he used to follow Herodes about insulting him in semibarbarous language. So Herodes turned to him and said, "You speak ill of me, so be it. But why in such bad Greek?" And when Proteus persisted in his abuse, Herodes said, "We have grown old, you in speaking ill of me, and I in listening to it." He implied in this way that though he had heard, he laughed at him scornfully, be-   564

[38] Lucian in his *Peregrinus* gives a full account of the self-immolation, of which Lucian himself was a witness, of Peregrinus Proteus, the Cynic philosopher. This took place in AD 165. Aulus Gellius, however, who heard Peregrinus' teaching just outside Athens, gives a more positive portrait (*NA* 12.11).

πεπεῖσθαι τὰς ψευδεῖς λοιδορίας μὴ περαιτέρω ἀκοῆς
ἥκειν.

(18) Ἑρμηνεύσω καὶ τὴν γλῶτταν τοῦ ἀνδρὸς ἐς
χαρακτῆρα ἰὼν τοῦ λόγου· ὡς μὲν δὴ Πολέμωνα καὶ
Φαβωρῖνον καὶ Σκοπελιανὸν ἐν διδασκάλοις ἑαυτοῦ
ἦγε καὶ ὡς Σεκούνδῳ τῷ Ἀθηναίῳ ἐφοίτησεν, εἰρημένον μοι ἤδη, τοὺς δὲ κριτικοὺς τῶν λόγων Θεαγένει
τε τῷ Κνιδίῳ καὶ Μουνατίῳ τῷ ἐκ Τραλλέων συνεγέ-
νετο καὶ Ταύρῳ τῷ Τυρίῳ ἐπὶ ταῖς Πλάτωνος δόξαις.
ἡ δὲ ἁρμονία τοῦ λόγου ἱκανῶς κεκολασμένη καὶ ἡ
δεινότης ὑφέρπουσα μᾶλλον ἢ ἐγκειμένη κρότος τε
σὺν ἀφελείᾳ καὶ κριτιάζουσα ἠχὼ καὶ ἔννοιαι οἷαι μὴ
ἑτέρῳ ἐνθυμηθῆναι κωμική τε εὐγλωττία οὐκ ἐπεί-
σακτος, ἀλλ' ἐκ τῶν πραγμάτων, καὶ ἡδὺς ὁ λόγος
καὶ πολυσχημάτιστος καὶ εὐσχήμων καὶ σοφῶς ἐξ-
αλλάττων τὸ πνεῦμά τε οὐ σφοδρόν, ἀλλὰ λεῖον καὶ
καθεστηκὸς καὶ ἡ ἐπίπαν ἰδέα τοῦ λόγου χρυσοῦ
ψῆγμα ποταμῷ ἀργυροδίνῃ ὑπαύγαζον. προσέκειτο
μὲν γὰρ πᾶσι τοῖς παλαιοῖς, τῷ δὲ Κριτίᾳ καὶ προσ-
ετετήκει καὶ παρήγαγεν αὐτὸν ἐς ἤθη Ἑλλήνων τέως
ἀμελούμενον καὶ περιορώμενον. βοώσης δὲ ἐπ' αὐτῷ

39 The phrase here echoes, but varies, Aeschines, *On the False
Embassy* 149: τὸ γὰρ ψευδὲς ὄνειδος οὐ περαιτέρω τῆς ἀκοῆς
ἀφικνεῖται.   40 Theagenes of Cnidus is otherwise unknown.
Munatius of Tralles may be the same Munatius who was a com-
mentator on Theocritus, and whose name appears eight times in
the Theocritean scholia.

41 This is presumably Calvenus Taurus, the Platonic philoso-

cause he believed that false insults go no deeper than the hearing.[39]

(18) I shall also describe the eloquence of Herodes, by proceeding to the main characteristics of his speech. I have said already, how Herodes counted Polemo and Favorinus and Scopelian among his teachers and how he went to the classes of Secundus the Athenian. For the critical branch of oratory he studied with Theagenes of Cnidus and Munatius of Tralles,[40] and for the doctrines of Plato with Taurus of Tyre.[41] The harmony of his speech was sufficiently disciplined and its strength crept up on a listener rather than attacking. His fullness of tone was combined with simplicity, and his resonant sound was in the manner of Critias. His ideas would not occur to someone else, and his eloquent wit was not dragged in, but arose from the subjects themselves. His diction was pleasing and most abounding in figures, and gracefully constructed. He judiciously varied the breath and did not employ it vehemently, but smoothly and steadily.[42] His style in general was flecks of gold flashing below a river of whirling silver. While he devoted himself to all the ancients, from Critias he was inseparable, and he brought him back to the knowledge of the Greeks, since until then he had been disregarded and overlooked. When all Greece

pher, though it is unclear why Philostratus names him "of Tyre" rather than "of Berytus." This philosopher makes many appearances in the work of Aulus Gellius (*NA* 1.9, 1.26, 2.2, 7.10, 7.13, 8.6, 9.5, 10.19, 12.5, 17.8, 18.10, 19.6, 20.4), who knew both him and Herodes.

[42] The description of Herodes' style is dense with technical terms of rhetoric. For these see the Rhetorical Glossary.

τῆς Ἑλλάδος καὶ καλούσης αὐτὸν ἕνα τῶν δέκα οὐχ
ἡττήθη τοῦ ἐπαίνου μεγάλου δοκοῦντος, ἀλλ' ἀστει-
565 ότατα πρὸς τοὺς ἐπαινέσαντας, "Ἀνδοκίδου μέν," ἔφη,
"βελτίων εἰμί." εὐμαθέστατος δὲ ἀνθρώπων γενόμενος
οὐδὲ τοῦ πονεῖν ἠμέλησεν, ἀλλὰ καὶ παρὰ πότον
ἐσπούδαζε καὶ νύκτωρ ἐν τοῖς διαλείμμασι τῶν ὕπνων,
ὅθεν ἐκάλουν αὐτὸν σιτευτὸν ῥήτορα οἱ ὀλίγωροί τε
καὶ λεπτοί. ἄλλος μὲν οὖν ἄλλο ἀγαθὸς καὶ ἄλλος ἐν
ἄλλῳ βελτίων ἑτέρου· (ὁ μὲν γὰρ σχεδιάσαι θαυμάσιος, ὁ δὲ ἐκπονῆσαι λόγον), ὁ δὲ τὰ ξύμπαντα ἄριστος τῶν σοφιστῶν, καὶ τὸ παθητικὸν οὐκ ἐκ τῆς
τραγῳδίας μόνον, ἀλλὰ κἀκ τῶν ἀνθρωπίνων συνελέ-
ξατο.

Ἐπιστολαὶ δὲ πλεῖσται Ἡρώδου καὶ διαλέξεις καὶ
ἐφημερίδες ἐγχειρίδιά τε καίρια τὴν ἀρχαίαν πο-
λυμάθειαν ἐν βραχεῖ ἀπηνθισμένα. οἱ δὲ προφέροντες
αὐτῷ νέῳ ἔτι τὸ λόγου τινὸς ἐν Παιονίᾳ ἐκπεσεῖν ἐπὶ
τοῦ αὐτοκράτορος ἠγνοηκέναι μοι δοκοῦσιν, ὅτι καὶ
Δημοσθένης ἐπὶ Φιλίππου λέγων ταὐτὸν ἔπαθε· κἀκεῖνος μὲν ἥκων Ἀθήναζε τιμὰς προσῄει καὶ στεφάνους ἀπολωλυίας Ἀθηναίοις Ἀμφιπόλεως, Ἡρώδης
δέ, ἐπεὶ τοῦτο ἔπαθεν, ἐπὶ τὸν Ἴστρον ἦλθεν ὡς ῥίψων
ἑαυτόν· τοσοῦτον γὰρ αὐτῷ περιῆν τοῦ ἐν λόγοις
βούλεσθαι ὀνομαστῷ εἶναι, ὡς θανάτου τιμᾶσθαι τὸ
σφαλῆναι.

---

[43] That is, one of the ten canonical Attic orators.

cried out Herodes' name and called him one of the Ten,[43] he was not abashed by praise that seemed so great, but he wittily said to those who praised him, "I'm better than Andocides, at least." He was the quickest at learning of all men but did not neglect hard work. Even when having drinks he used to study and he studied at night in intervals of waking; because of this, lazy and superficial people called him the Stuffed Orator. Different people excel in different ways, and one person is better than another in some respect. (One is good at improvisation, another at working to develop a speech.) But Herodes was the best of the sophists at all these things, and to move the emotions of his listeners he drew not only on tragedy but also on human life.

There are extant by Herodes very many letters, discourses and diaries, handbooks for our times that bring together in a small space the flowers of ancient learning. Those who criticize him for the fact that when he was still young he broke down during a speech in Pannonia in front of the emperor seem to me to be unaware that the same thing happened to Demosthenes when he was speaking in front of Philip. And Demosthenes returned to Athens and demanded honors and crowns, even though Amphipolis had been lost to the Athenians,[44] but Herodes, when this had happened to him, rushed to the river Danube to throw himself in. Herodes put so much weight on wanting to become famous for eloquence that he believed the penalty for failure to be death.

[44] Philip had taken Amphipolis in 357, eleven years before this embassy, and the failure of Demosthenes had nothing to do with its retention by him.

PHILOSTRATUS

(19) Ἐτελεύτα μὲν οὖν ἀμφὶ τὰ ἓξ καὶ ἑβδομήκοντα
ξυντακὴς γενόμενος. ἀποθανόντος δὲ αὐτοῦ ἐν τῷ Μαραθῶνι καὶ ἐπισκήψαντος τοῖς ἀπελευθέροις ἐκεῖ θάπτειν, Ἀθηναῖοι ταῖς τῶν ἐφήβων χερσὶν ἁρπάσαντες
ἐς ἄστυ ἤνεγκαν προαπαντῶντες τῷ λέχει πᾶσα ἡλι-
566 κία δακρύοις ἅμα καὶ ἀνευφημοῦντες, ὅσα παῖδες
χρηστοῦ πατρὸς χηρεύσαντες, καὶ ἔθαψαν ἐν τῷ Παν-
αθηναικῷ ἐπιγράψαντες αὐτῷ βραχὺ καὶ πολὺ ἐπί-
γραμμα τόδε·

Ἀττικοῦ Ἡρώδης Μαραθώνιος, οὗ τάδε πάντα
κεῖται τῷδε τάφῳ, πάντοθεν εὐδόκιμος.

τοσαῦτα περὶ Ἡρώδου τοῦ Ἀθηναίου, τὰ μὲν εἰρημένα, τὰ δὲ ἠγνοημένα ἑτέροις.

(20) 2. β′. Ἐπὶ τὸν σοφιστὴν Θεόδοτον καλεῖ με ὁ
λόγος. οὗτος προὔστη μὲν τοῦ Ἀθηναίων δήμου κατὰ
χρόνους, οὓς προσέκρουον Ἡρώδῃ Ἀθηναῖοι, καὶ ἐς
ἀπέχθειαν φανερὰν οὐδεμίαν τῷ ἀνδρὶ ἀφίκετο, ἀλλ'
ἀφανῶς αὐτὸν ὑπεκάθητο δεινὸς ὢν χρῆσθαι τοῖς
πράγμασι, καὶ γὰρ δὴ καὶ τῶν ἀγοραίων εἷς οὗτος·
τοῖς γοῦν ἀμφὶ τὸν Δημόστρατον οὕτω ξυνεκέκρατο,
ὡς καὶ ξυνάρασθαί σφισι τῶν λόγων, οὓς ἐξεπόνουν
πρὸς τὸν Ἡρώδην. προέστη δὲ καὶ τῆς Ἀθηναίων

---

45 This was the magnificent stadium that Herodes himself had
constructed while curator of the Panathenaea. See above, VS
549–50. On the death and burial of Herodes, see Rife 2008.

(19) He died at the age of about seventy six of a wasting sickness. Though he died at Marathon and gave instructions to his freedmen to bury him there, the Athenians carried him off by the hands of the youths, and brought him to the city. Every age went out to meet the bier with tears and auspicious cries, like children bereft of a good 566 father. And they buried him in the Panathenaic stadium,[45] and inscribed over him this brief and apt epitaph:

> Here lies all that remains of Herodes son of Atticus,
>   of Marathon, in this tomb. But his fame is
>   everywhere.

That is all I have to say about Herodes the Athenian. Some of it had already been said, but some was previously unknown.

(20) 2. My story calls me to the sophist Theodotus.[46] This man was archon of the Athenian people at the time when they were in conflict with Herodes, and though he never came into open enmity with the man, he secretly plotted against him, since he was clever at using events to his advantage. What is more he was one of those embroiled in the business of the agora. At any rate he became so thoroughly mixed up with Demostratus and his associates, that he collaborated with them on the speeches that they were carefully preparing against Herodes. He was also the first appointed to the chair of rhetoric to teach the

---

[46] Despite Philostratus' lukewarm praise, which is no doubt due to the fact that Theodotus turned against his former teacher Herodes, he clearly had a prominent career as a sophist and holder of public office. See Bowersock 1969, 97; and Avotins 1975, 315–16.

νεότητος πρῶτος ἐπὶ ταῖς ἐκ βασιλέως μυρίαις. καὶ
οὐ τοῦτό πω λόγου ἄξιον, οὐ γὰρ πάντες οἱ ἐπιβα-
τεύοντες τοῦ θρόνου τούτου λόγου ἄξιοι, ἀλλ᾿ ὅτι τοὺς
μὲν Πλατωνείους καὶ τοὺς ἀπὸ τῆς Στοᾶς καὶ τοῦ
Περιπάτου καὶ αὐτὸν Ἐπίκουρον προσέταξεν ὁ Μᾶρκος τῷ Ἡρώδῃ κρῖναι, τὸν δὲ ἄνδρα τοῦτον ἀπὸ τῆς
567   περὶ αὐτὸν δόξης αὐτὸς ἐπέκρινε τοῖς νέοις ἀγωνι-
στὴν τῶν πολιτικῶν προσειπὼν λόγων καὶ ῥητορικῆς
ὄφελος. ὁ δ᾿ ἀνὴρ οὗτος Λολλιανοῦ μὲν ἀκροατής,
Ἡρώδου δὲ οὐκ ἀνήκοος. ἐβίω μὲν οὖν ὑπὲρ τὰ πεντήκοντα δυοῖν ἐτοῖν κατασχὼν τὸν θρόνον, τὴν δὲ
ἰδέαν τῶν λόγων ἀποχρῶν καὶ τοῖς δικανικοῖς καὶ
τοῖς ὑπερσοφιστεύουσιν.

(21) 3. γ΄. Ὀνομαστὸς ἐν σοφισταῖς καὶ Ἀριστοκλῆς ὁ ἐκ τοῦ Περγάμου, ὑπὲρ οὗ δηλώσω, ὁπόσα
τῶν πρεσβυτέρων ἤκουον· ἐτέλει μὲν γὰρ ἐς ὑπάτους
ὁ ἀνὴρ οὗτος, τὸν δὲ ἐκ παίδων ἐς ἥβην χρόνον τοὺς
ἀπὸ τοῦ Περιπάτου φιλοσοφήσας λόγους ἐς τοὺς σοφιστὰς μετερρύη θαμίζων ἐν τῇ Ῥώμῃ τῷ Ἡρώδῃ
διατιθεμένῳ σχεδίους λόγους. ὃν δὲ ἐφιλοσόφει χρόνον αὐχμηρὸς δοκῶν καὶ τραχὺς τὸ εἶδος καὶ δυσπι-
νὴς τὴν ἐσθῆτα, ἥβρυνε καὶ τὸν αὐχμὸν ἀπετρίψατο,
ἡδονάς τε, ὁπόσαι λυρῶν τε καὶ αὐλῶν καὶ εὐφωνίας
εἰσί, πάσας ἐσηγάγετο ἐπὶ τὴν δίαιταν, ὥσπερ ἐπὶ
θύρας αὐτῷ ἡκούσας· τὸν γὰρ πρὸ τοῦ χρόνον οὕτω
κεκολασμένος ἀτάκτως ἐς τὰ θέατρα ἐφοίτα καὶ ἐπὶ
τὴν τούτων ἠχώ. εὐδοκιμοῦντι δὲ αὐτῷ κατὰ τὸ Πέργαμον κἀξηρτημένῳ πᾶν τὸ ἐκείνῃ Ἑλληνικὸν ἐξε-

youth of the Athenians, for a salary of ten thousand from the emperor. This in itself is not worth mentioning, since not everyone who ascends to this chair is worth talking about, but Marcus appointed Herodes to judge the chairs for Platonic philosophy, for Stoicism, for the Peripatetics, and even Epicureanism, but the emperor himself chose Theodotus to educate the young, and called him a champion of political oratory and an ornament to rhetoric. This man was a student of Lollianus, and had attended the lectures of Herodes. He lived past fifty and held the chair for two years. The style of his speeches in forensic and in purely sophistic oratory was sufficiently good.

567

(21) 3. Aristocles of Pergamum also won a name among the sophists, and I will relate about him all that I have heard from my elders. This man belonged to a family of consular rank, and though from childhood to early manhood he dedicated himself to Peripatetic philosophy, he went over entirely to the sophists, and frequented at Rome Herodes' classes on improvised speeches. During the time that he practiced philosophy he seemed squalid and rough in his appearance and shabby in his dress, but now he became fastidious and discarded his squalor and admitted into his habits all the pleasures of the lyre and the aulos and singing, as if they had come to his door.[47] Though previously he had lived with such strict discipline, he now frequented without restraint the theaters and their noise. When he was famous at Pergamum and all those of Greek

[47] An echo of Pl. *Phdr.* 233e.

λαύνων ὁ Ἡρώδης ἐς Πέργαμον ἔπεμψε τοὺς ἑαυτοῦ
568 ὁμιλητὰς πάντας καὶ τὸν Ἀριστοκλέα ᾕρεν, ὥσπερ
τις Ἀθηνᾶς ψῆφος. ἡ δὲ ἰδέα τοῦ λόγου διαυγὴς μὲν
καὶ ἀττικίζουσα, διαλέγεσθαι δὲ ἐπιτηδεία μᾶλλον ἢ
ἀγωνίζεσθαι, χολή τε γὰρ ἄπεστι τοῦ λόγου καὶ ὁρ-
μαὶ πρὸς βραχύ, αὐτή τε ἡ ἀττίκισις, εἰ παρὰ τὴν τοῦ
Ἡρώδου γλῶτταν βασανίζοιτο, λεπτολογεῖσθαι δόξει
μᾶλλον ἢ κρότου τε καὶ ἠχοῦς ξυγκεῖσθαι. ἐτελεύτα
δὲ ὁ Ἀριστοκλῆς μεσαιπόλιος, ἄρτι προσβαίνων τῷ
γηράσκειν.

(22) 4. δ΄. Ἀντίοχον δὲ τὸν σοφιστὴν αἱ Κιλίκων
Αἰγαὶ ἤνεγκαν οὕτω τι εὐπατρίδην, ὡς νῦν ἔτι τὸ ἀπ᾽
αὐτοῦ γένος ὑπάτους εἶναι. αἰτίαν δὲ ἔχων δειλίας,
ἐπεὶ μὴ παρήει ἐς τὸν δῆμον, μηδὲ ἐς τὸ κοινὸν ἐπο-
λίτευεν, "οὐχ ὑμᾶς," εἶπεν, "ἀλλ᾽ ἐμαυτὸν δέδοικα,"
εἰδώς που τὴν ἑαυτοῦ χολὴν ἄκρατόν τε καὶ οὐ καθ-
εκτὴν οὖσαν. ἀλλ᾽ ὅμως ὠφέλει τοὺς ἀστοὺς ἀπὸ τῆς
οὐσίας, ὅ τι εἴη δυνατός,[13] σῖτόν τε ἐπιδιδούς, ὁπότε
τούτου δεομένους αἴσθοιτο, καὶ χρήματα ἐς τὰ πεπο-
νηκότα τῶν ἔργων. τὰς δὲ πλείους τῶν νυκτῶν ἐς τὸ
τοῦ Ἀσκληπιοῦ ἱερὸν ἀπεκάθευδεν ὑπέρ τε ὀνειράτων

[13] εἴη δυνατός; α ἠδύνατο β

---

[48] The vote of Athena given in the trial of Orestes in Aesch.
Eum. became a proverb.
[49] The Greek epithet is from Hom. *Il.* 13.361.
[50] This phrase has been mistranslated since Olearius as saying
that Aristocles died at the beginning of old age. The dative with

education there hung on his words, Herodes came to visit the city and sent all his own students to Aristocles, and so elevated him, as though Athena herself had cast her vote.[48]   568
His style of eloquence was translucent and Atticizing, but it was more suited to formal discourse than to forensic contests, because there was no anger in his speech nor brief, impulsive outbreaks. His Atticism itself, if one should test it against the language of Herodes, will seem oversubtle and lacking in rhythm and resonance. Aristocles died when his hair was streaked with gray,[49] well advanced into old age.[50]

(22) 4. Cilician Aegae produced the sophist Antiochus, who was of such a distinguished family that even now his descendants are made consuls. When he was accused of cowardice, because he did not go before the people, nor contribute to public affairs, he said, "It is not you but myself that I fear." No doubt he knew that his temper was powerful and could not be restrained. Nevertheless he benefited his fellow citizens with his wealth as much as he could, by giving them food whenever he perceived that they needed it, and also by giving them money for dilapidated buildings.[51] He used to sleep very many nights in the temple of Asclepius, both for dreams and for the com-

---

προσβαίνων (unlike the accusative) indicates going right up to or into something (e.g., Pl. *Phdr.* 227d). The chronology that can be reconstructed for Aristocles' life confirms his longevity: see Bowie 1982, 48–49.

[51] Though the sophistic literature of this period often speaks of the decay of Greek towns, the archaeological record paints a different picture. See Alcock 1996.

ὑπέρ τε ξυνουσίας, ὁπόση ἐγρηγορότων τε καὶ διαλε-
γομένων ἀλλήλοις· διελέγετο γὰρ αὐτῷ καὶ ἐγρη-
γορότι ὁ θεὸς καλὸν ἀγώνισμα ποιούμενος τῆς ἑαυτοῦ
τέχνης τὸ τὰς νόσους τοῦ Ἀντιόχου ἐρύκειν.

(23) Ἀκροατὴς ὁ Ἀντίοχος ἐν παισὶ μὲν Δαρδάνου
τοῦ Ἀσσυρίου, προϊὼν δὲ ἐς τὰ μειράκια Διονυσίου
τοῦ Μιλησίου κατέχοντος ἤδη τὴν Ἐφεσίων. διελέγετο μὲν οὖν οὐκ ἐπιτηδείως—φρονιμώτατος δ᾽ ἀνθρώπων γενόμενος διέβαλλεν αὐτὸ ὡς μειρακιῶδες,
ἵνα ὑπερεωρακὼς αὐτοῦ μᾶλλον ἢ ἀπολειπόμενος
φαίνοιτο—τὰ δὲ ἀμφὶ μελέτην ἦν[14] ἐλλογιμώτατος·
ἀσφαλὴς μὲν γὰρ ἐν ταῖς κατὰ σχῆμα προηγμέναις
τῶν ὑποθέσεων, σφοδρὸς δὲ ἐν ταῖς κατηγορίαις καὶ
ἐπιφοραῖς, εὐπρεπὴς δὲ τὰς ἀπολογίας καὶ τῷ ἠθικῷ
ἰσχύων, καὶ καθάπαξ τὴν ἰδέαν τοῦ λόγου δικανικῆς
μὲν σοφιστικώτερος, σοφιστικῆς δὲ δικανικώτερος.
καὶ τὰ πάθη ἄριστα σοφιστῶν μετεχειρίσατο· οὐ γὰρ
μονῳδίας ἀπεμήκυνεν οὐδὲ θρήνους ὑποκειμένους,
ἀλλ᾽ ἐβραχυλόγει αὐτὰ ξὺν διανοίαις λόγου κρείττο-
σιν, ὡς ἔκ τε τῶν ἄλλων ὑποθέσεων δηλοῦται καὶ
μάλιστα ἐκ τῶνδε· κόρη βιασθεῖσα θάνατον ᾕρηται
τοῦ βιασαμένου· μετὰ ταῦτα γέγονε παιδίον ἐκ τῆς
βίας καὶ διαμιλλῶνται οἱ πάπποι, παρ᾽ ὁποτέρῳ τρέ-
φοιτο ἄν. ἀγωνιζόμενος οὖν ὑπὲρ τοῦ πρὸς πατρὸς

[14] ἦν Stefec

[52] The most vivid record of dream incubation in the temples

pany of those who are awake and speaking with each other there. Indeed the god used to converse with him even when he was awake, and considered it a triumph of his art to ward off diseases from Antiochus.[52]

(23) As a child Antiochus was a student of Dardanus the Assyrian, and as he came into young manhood he studied with Dionysius of Miletus,[53] who was already living in Ephesus. He was not even adequate at formal discourse, but since he was the shrewdest of men he used to heap abuse on the practice as juvenile, so that he would seem 569 to despise it rather than not to be good enough. But in declamation he was very famous, because he was unfailing in simulated arguments, was vehement in accusations and invective, brilliant in defense speeches and strong in the use of character, and in a word, his style was more sophistic than forensic oratory, and more forensic than sophistic. He handled the emotions the best of all sophists. This because he did not draw out long monodies nor common laments, but expressed them briefly, with ideas better than I can describe, as is made clear by his other cases, but especially by the following. A girl who has been raped chooses death as the penalty for the rapist.[54] Later a child is born from the rape and the grandfathers dispute over which one of them will raise the child. So Antiochus was arguing the case of the paternal grandfather and said,

of Asclepius is Aelius Aristides' *Sacred Discourses*. See also the appearance of Asclepius to Apollonius of Tyana (*VA* 1.8).

[53] See the account of his life, above, *VS* 522–26.

[54] That is, she had the alternative of marrying him; for a dilemma arising out of a similar case, cf. Hermog. Περὶ στάσεων 3.15.

πάππου, "ἀπόδος," ἔφη, "τὸ παιδίον, ἀπόδος ἤδη, πρὶν
γεύσηται μητρῴου γάλακτος." ἡ δὲ ἑτέρα ὑπόθεσις
τοιαύτη· τύραννον καταθέμενον τὴν ἀρχὴν ἐπὶ τῷ
ἐκλελῆσθαι ἀπέκτεινέ τις εὐνοῦχος ὑπ᾽ αὐτοῦ γεγονὼς
καὶ ἀπολογεῖται ὑπὲρ τοῦ φόνου. ἐνταῦθα τὸ μάλιστα
ἐρρωμένον τῆς κατηγορίας τὸν περὶ τῶν σπονδῶν λόγον ἀπεώσατο περίνοιαν ἐγκαταμίξας τῷ πάθει· "τίσι
γὰρ," ἔφη, "ταῦτα ὡμολόγησε; παισὶ γυναίοις μειρακίοις πρεσβύταις ἀνδράσιν· ἐγὼ δὲ ὄνομα ἐν ταῖς
συνθήκαις οὐκ ἔχω." ἄριστα δὲ καὶ ὑπὲρ τῶν Κρητῶν
ἀπολελόγηται τῶν κρινομένων ἐπὶ τῷ τοῦ Διὸς σήματι
φυσιολογίᾳ τε καὶ θεολογίᾳ πάσῃ ἐναγωνισάμενος
λαμπρῶς. τὰς μὲν οὖν μελέτας αὐτοσχεδίους ἐποιεῖτο,
570 ἔμελε δὲ αὐτῷ καὶ φροντισμάτων, ὡς ἕτερά τε δηλοῖ
τῶν ἐκείνου καὶ μάλιστα ἡ ἱστορία, ἐπίδειξιν γὰρ ἐν
αὐτῇ πεποίηται λέξεώς τε καὶ θεωρίας,[15] ἐσποιῶν
ἑαυτῷ[16] καὶ τὸ φιλοκαλεῖν. περὶ τῆς τελευτῆς τοῦ ἀνδρός, οἱ μὲν ἑβδομηκοντούτην τεθνάναι αὐτόν, οἱ δὲ
οὔπω, καὶ οἱ μὲν οἴκοι, οἱ δὲ ἑτέρωθι.

(24) 5. ε΄. Ἀλεξάνδρῳ δέ, ὃν Πηλοπλάτωνα οἱ πολλοὶ ἐπωνόμαζον, πατρὶς μὲν ἦν Σελεύκεια πόλις οὐκ
ἀφανὴς ἐν Κιλικίᾳ, πατὴρ δὲ ὁμώνυμος καὶ τοὺς ἀγο-
ραίους λόγους ἱκανώτατος, μήτηρ περιττὴ τὸ εἶδος,

[15] θεωρίας ³Kayser; ἱστορίας ω
[16] ἑαυτῷ Stefec; ἑαυτόν Kayser; ἐς αυτόν ω

55 This is the only reference to a declamation on the topic of

232

"Give it up. Give the child up now, before it tastes its mother's milk." The other theme was as follows. A tyrant gave up his power on condition of immunity for himself. A eunuch, who was made a eunuch by the tyrant, killed him, and makes his defense for the murder. In this case Antiochus forcefully repelled the strongest point made by the prosecution concerning the agreement with the tyrant, and threw in an ingenious argument that he mixed with eunuch's own suffering: "With whom," he said, "was this agreement made? With children, women, boys, old men, men. I do not find my name in that contract." Most brilliantly of all he made a defense of the Cretans standing trial in the matter of the tomb of Zeus,[55] when he made brilliant use of natural philosophy and all that is taught concerning the gods. He delivered improvised declamations, but he also worked at written compositions, as others of his work make clear but especially his *History*. In this he gave a demonstration of language and of thought, and adopted as his own the love of the beautiful. Regarding the death of the man, some say that he died at seventy, others that he was not so old. Some say he died at home, others elsewhere.

570

(24) 5. Alexander, whom the masses called Clay Plato, was from the city of Seleucia, a famous city in Cilicia. His father had the same name, and was very talented in forensic oratory, and his mother was extraordinarily beautiful,

the Cretan tomb of Zeus. On the long polemics concerning this Cretan belief, see Kokolakis (1995), who is very likely correct in seeing Philostratus' brief description of Antiochus' defense as implying an allegorical interpretation, drawing on both physical and metaphysical allegories.

PHILOSTRATUS

ὡς αἱ γραφαὶ ἑρμηνεύουσι, καὶ προσφερὴς τῇ τοῦ
Εὐμήλου Ἑλένῃ· Εὐμήλῳ γάρ τις Ἑλένη γέγραπται
οἵα ἀνάθεμα εἶναι τῆς Ῥωμαίων ἀγορᾶς. ἐρασθῆναι
τῆς γυναικὸς ταύτης καὶ ἑτέρους μέν, ἐπιδήλως δὲ
Ἀπολλώνιόν φασι τὸν Τυανέα, καὶ τοὺς μὲν ἄλλους
ἀπαξιῶσαι, τῷ δὲ Ἀπολλωνίῳ ξυγγενέσθαι δι᾽ ἔρωτα
εὐπαιδίας, ἐπειδὴ θειότερος ἀνθρώπων. τοῦτο μὲν δὴ
ὁπόσοις τρόποις ἀπίθανον, εἴρηται σαφῶς ἐν τοῖς ἐς
Ἀπολλώνιον. θεοειδὴς δὲ ὁ Ἀλέξανδρος καὶ περίβλε-
πτος ξὺν ὥρᾳ, γενειάς τε γὰρ ἦν αὐτῷ βοστρυχώδης
καὶ καθειμένη τὸ μέτριον ὄμμα τε ἁβρὸν καὶ μέγα καὶ
ῥὶς ξύμμετρος καὶ ὀδόντες λευκότατοι δάκτυλοί τε
εὐμήκεις καὶ τῇ τοῦ λόγου ἡνίᾳ ἐπιπρέποντες. ἦν δὲ
αὐτῷ καὶ πλοῦτος δαπανώμενος ἐς ἡδονὰς οὐ μεμ-
πτάς.

(25) Ἐς δὲ ἄνδρας ἥκων ἐπρέσβευε μὲν ὑπὲρ τῆς
Σελευκείας παρὰ τὸν πρῶτον Ἀντωνῖνον, διαβολαὶ δὲ
ἐπ᾽ αὐτὸν ἐφοίτησαν, ὡς νεότητα ἐπιποιοῦντα τῷ εἴδει. ἧττον δὲ αὐτῷ προσέχειν δοκοῦντος τοῦ βασιλέως ἐπάρας τὴν φωνὴν ὁ Ἀλέξανδρος, "πρόσεχέ μοι,"
ἔφη, "Καῖσαρ." καὶ ὁ αὐτοκράτωρ παροξυνθεὶς πρὸς
αὐτὸν ὡς θρασυτέρᾳ τῇ ἐπιστροφῇ χρησάμενον,
"προσέχω," ἔφη, "καὶ ξυνίημί σου· σὺ γὰρ ὁ τὴν
κόμην ἀσκῶν καὶ τοὺς ὀδόντας λαμπρύνων καὶ τοὺς
ὄνυχας ξέων καὶ τοῦ μύρου ἀεὶ πνέων."

(26) Τὸ μὲν δὴ πλεῖστον τοῦ βίου τῇ τε Ἀντιοχείᾳ
ἐνεσπούδαζε καὶ τῇ Ῥώμῃ καὶ τοῖς Ταρσοῖς καὶ νὴ

234

as her portraits represent her, and in fact resembled the Helen of Eumelus. For a Helen was painted by Eumelus to be dedicated in the Roman Forum. They say that, among others who fell in love with this woman, Apollonius of Tyana loved her especially, and that she rejected the others, but gave herself to Apollonius out of a desire for noble offspring, since he was more divine than ordinary humans. In my work on Apollonius I have stated clearly for how many reasons this is implausible.[56] But Alexander did have a godlike appearance and was conspicuous for his beauty. His beard was curly and of moderate length, his eyes were large and graceful, his nose straight, his teeth very white, and his fingers long and slender and well suited to holding the reins of eloquence. He had a large fortune too, which he spent on pleasures that were beyond reproach.

(25) When he came to manhood he went on an embassy for Seleucia to the first Antoninus, and slanders circulated against him, that he cosmetically enhanced his youthful beauty. When the emperor appeared to be paying insufficient attention to him, Alexander raised his voice and said, "Pay attention to me, Caesar." The emperor was irritated at him for using such a bold form of address and said, "I am paying attention and I know you well. You are the one who takes trouble over his hair, and whitens his teeth, and polishes and his nails, and always smells of myrrh."

571

(26) For most of his life he practiced his art at Antioch, Rome, Tarsus and even, by Zeus, in the whole of Egypt,

56 *VA* 1.13, 6.42.

Δία Αἰγύπτῳ πάσῃ, ἀφίκετο γὰρ καὶ ἐς τὰ τῶν
Γυμνῶν ἤθη. αἱ δὲ Ἀθήνησι διατριβαὶ τοῦ ἀνδρὸς
ὀλίγαι μέν, οὐκ ἄξιαι δὲ ἀγνοεῖσθαι. ἐβάδιζε μὲν γὰρ
ἐς τὰ Παιονικὰ ἔθνη κατακληθεὶς[17] ὑπὸ Μάρκου βασιλέως ἐκεῖ στρατεύοντος καὶ δεδωκότος αὐτῷ τὸ ἐπιστέλλειν Ἕλλησιν· ἀφικόμενος δὲ ἐς τὰς Ἀθήνας
ὁδοῦ δὲ μῆκος τοῦτο οὐ μέτριον τῷ ἐκ τῆς ἑῴας ἐλαύ-
νοντι), "ἐνταῦθα," ἔφη, "γόνυ κάμψωμεν." καὶ εἰπὼν
τοῦτο ἐπήγγειλε τοῖς Ἀθηναίοις αὐτοσχεδίους λόγους
ἐρῶσιν αὐτοῦ τῆς ἀκροάσεως. ἀκούων δὲ τὸν Ἡρώδην
ἐν Μαραθῶνι διαιτώμενον καὶ τὴν νεότητα ἐπακολου-
θοῦσαν αὐτῷ πᾶσαν γράφει πρὸς αὐτὸν ἐπιστολὴν
αἰτῶν τοὺς Ἕλληνας, καὶ ὁ Ἡρώδης, "ἀφίξομαι,"
ἔφη, "μετὰ τῶν Ἑλλήνων καὶ αὐτός." ξυνελέγοντο μὲν
δὴ ἐς τὸ ἐν τῷ Κεραμεικῷ θέατρον, ὃ δὴ ἐπωνόμασται
Ἀγριππεῖον, προϊούσης δὲ ἤδη τῆς ἡμέρας καὶ τοῦ
Ἡρώδου βραδύνοντος ἤσχαλλον οἱ Ἀθηναῖοι ὡς
ἐκλυομένης τῆς ἀκροάσεως καὶ τέχνην αὐτὸ ᾤοντο,
572   ὅθεν ἀνάγκη τῷ Ἀλεξάνδρῳ ἐγένετο παρελθεῖν ἐπὶ
τὴν διάλεξιν καὶ πρὶν ἥκειν τὸν Ἡρώδην. ἡ μὲν δὴ
διάλεξις ἔπαινοι ἦσαν τοῦ ἄστεος καὶ ἀπολογία πρὸς
τοὺς Ἀθηναίους ὑπὲρ τοῦ μήπω πρότερον παρ' αὐτοὺς

---

[17] μετακληθεὶς ²Kayser

---

[57] For the Naked Ones, or Gymnosophists, see the life of
Eudoxus of Cnidus above at VS 484, with note.

[58] For this phrase, cf. Aesch. PV 32; in tragedy, as here, it
means "sit" or "rest," but not "kneel."

for he traveled even to the home of the Naked Ones.[57] He spent little time at Athens, but the time he was there was worthy to be remembered. He went to the dwellings of the Pannonians when the emperor Marcus compelled him, at the time when he was conducting the war there, and he gave to Alexander the role of *ab epistulis Graecis*. And when he came to Athens (and the length of the journey is considerable for one traveling from the east) he said, "Here let us bend the knee."[58] He said this, then announced to the Athenians that he would give improvised declamations, since they desired to hear him. But when he heard that Herodes was living at Marathon, and that all of the youth had followed him, he wrote a letter to Herodes, asking him to send his Hellenes. And Herodes said, "I shall come myself and bring my Hellenes with me." So they were gathered in the theater at the Cerameicus, which has been called the Theater of Agrippa,[59] and as the day was passing and Herodes was late, the Athenians complained that they were being deprived of the performance and they believed that the delay was a trick. So Alexander was forced to begin his introductory speech[60] before Herodes arrived. This introductory speech was in praise of the city and a defense of the fact that he had not earlier

572

[59] For this theater, see below, VS 580. On the remains and history of this building, see Thompson (1950, 141), who notes that by the time of the anecdote, which Philostratus records, the auditorium had been reduced in size to be suitable for declamations rather than for the musical performances given in the building before the construction of the Odeum of Herodes.

[60] This was his *dialexis*, on which see the Rhetorical Glossary.

ἀφῖχθαι. εἶχε δὲ τὸ ἀποχρῶν μῆκος· Παναθηναϊκοῦ
γὰρ λόγου ἐπιτομὴ ἕκαστο. εὐσταλὴς δὲ οὕτω τοῖς
Ἀθηναίοις ἔδοξεν, ὡς καὶ βόμβον διελθεῖν αὐτῶν ἔτι
σιωπῶντος ἐπαινεσάντων αὐτοῦ τὸ εὔσχημον. ἡ μὲν
δὴ νενικηκυῖα ὑπόθεσις ὁ τοὺς Σκύθας ἐπανάγων ἐς
τὴν προτέραν πλάνην, ἐπειδὴ πόλιν οἰκοῦντες νοσοῦσι, καιρὸν δ᾽ ἐπισχὼν βραχὺν ἀνεπήδησε τοῦ
θρόνου φαιδρῷ τῷ προσώπῳ, καθάπερ εὐαγγέλια
ἐπάγων τοῖς ἀκροωμένοις ὧν εἰπεῖν ἔχοι.

Προϊόντος δὲ αὐτῷ τοῦ λόγου ἐπέστη ὁ Ἡρώδης
Ἀρκάδι πίλῳ τὴν κεφαλὴν σκιάζων, ὡς ἐν ὥρᾳ θέρους
εἰώθει Ἀθήνησιν, ἴσως δέ που καὶ ἐνδεικνύμενος αὐτῷ
τὸ ἐκ τῆς ὁδοῦ ἥκειν. καὶ ὁ Ἀλέξανδρος ἔνθεν ἑλὼν
διελέχθη μὲν ἐς τὴν παρουσίαν τοῦ ἀνδρὸς ὑποσέμνῳ
τῇ λέξει καὶ ἠχούσῃ, ἐπ᾽ αὐτῷ δὲ ἔθετο, εἴτε βούλοιτο
τῆς ἤδη σπουδαζομένης ὑποθέσεως ἀκροᾶσθαι, εἴτε
ἑτέραν αὐτὸς δοῦναι. τοῦ δὲ Ἡρώδου ἄνω βλέψαντος
ἐς τοὺς ἀκροωμένους καὶ εἰπόντος, ὡς ποιήσοι, ὅπερ
ἂν ἐκείνοις δόξῃ, πάντες ξυνεπένευσαν ἐς τὴν τῶν
Σκυθῶν ἀκρόασιν· καὶ γὰρ δὴ καὶ λαμπρῶς διῄει τὸν
ἀγῶνα, ὡς δηλοῖ τὰ εἰρημένα. θαυμασίαν δὲ ἰσχὺν
ἐνεδείξατο καὶ ἐν τοῖσδε· τὰς γὰρ διανοίας τὰς πρὶν
ἥκειν τὸν Ἡρώδην λαμπρῶς αὐτῷ εἰρημένας μετεχειρίσατο ἐπιστάντος οὕτω τι ἑτέρᾳ λέξει καὶ ἑτέροις
ῥυθμοῖς, ὡς τοῖς δεύτερον ἀκροωμένοις μὴ διλογεῖν
δόξαι. τὸ γοῦν εὐδοκιμώτατον τῶν πρὶν ἐπιστῆναι τὸν

---

61 A favorite theme was the comparison of nomadic with city

come before them. And it had sufficient length, for it
seemed like a condensation of a Panathenaic oration. He
seemed to the Athenians so perfectly dressed that a low
buzz went through them while he was still silent, as they
praised his perfect elegance. The theme that they chose
was this: "The speaker recalls the Scythians to their earlier
wandering, since they are ill due to living in a city."[61] He
held back for a little while, then sprang from his seat with
a radiant expression, like one who brings good news to
those listening to what he has to tell them.

As his speech continued, Herodes arrived, shading his
head with an Arcadian hat, as he used to do in the summer
season at Athens, and perhaps to show to Alexander that
he had arrived from a journey. Then Alexander, adapting
his speech to the man's presence, put the question to
him, in impressive and sonorous language, of whether he
wished to listen to the theme that he was already discussing or to propose another himself. Herodes glanced up to
the audience and said that he should do whatever seemed
best to them, and they all agreed that they would hear *The
Scythians*. For indeed Alexander was brilliantly making
his case, as is clear from what I have said, but he showed
his astonishing strength also in the follow ways. The ideas
that he had spoken so brilliantly before Herodes' arrival
he reworked when he had arrived, in such different expression and different rhythms, that he would not seem to
repeat himself for those listening a second time.[62] The
phrase that was best received, of all those he spoke before

life, with the Scythians embodying the former; cf. below, VS 575,
620; Apsines 228, 247.   [62] See VS 619, where Hippodromus
similarly improvises anew on the theme that he has just treated.

Ἡρώδην εἰρημένων "ἑστὼς καὶ τὸ ὕδωρ νοσεῖ," μετὰ
573 ταῦτα ἐπιστάντος ἑτέρᾳ δυνάμει μεταλαβὼν, "καὶ
ὑδάτων," εἶπεν, "ἡδίω τὰ πλανώμενα." κἀκεῖνα τῶν
Ἀλεξάνδρου Σκυθῶν· "καὶ πηγνυμένου μὲν Ἴστρου
πρὸς μεσημβρίαν ἤλαυνεν, λυομένου δὲ ἐχώρουν
πρὸς ἄρκτον ἀκέραιος τὸ σῶμα καὶ οὐχ ὥσπερ νυνὶ
κείμενος. τί γὰρ ἂν πάθοι δεινὸν ἄνθρωπος ταῖς
ὥραις ἑπόμενος;" ἐπὶ τελευτῇ δὲ τοῦ λόγου διαβάλλων
τὴν πόλιν ὡς πνιγηρὸν οἰκητήριον τὸ ἐπὶ πᾶσιν ὧδε
ἀνεφθέγξατο· "ἀλλ᾽ ἀναπέτασον τὰς πύλας, ἀναπνεῦ-
σαι θέλω." προσδραμὼν δὲ τῷ Ἡρώδῃ καὶ περισχὼν
αὐτόν, "ἀντεφεστίασόν με," ἔφη, καὶ ὁ Ἡρώδης, "τί
δὲ οὐ μέλλω," εἶπε, "λαμπρῶς οὕτως ἑστιάσαντα;"
διαλυθείσης δὲ τῆς ἀκροάσεως καλέσας ὁ Ἡρώδης
τῶν ἑαυτοῦ γνωρίμων τοὺς ἐν ἐπιδόσει ἠρώτα, ποῖός
τις αὐτοῖς ὁ σοφιστὴς φαίνοιτο, Σκέπτου δὲ τοῦ ἀπὸ
τῆς Κορίνθου τὸν μὲν πηλὸν εὑρηκέναι φήσαντος, τὸν
δὲ Πλάτωνα ζητεῖν, ἐπικόπτων αὐτὸν ὁ Ἡρώδης,
"τουτὶ," ἔφη, "πρὸς μηδένα εἴπῃς ἕτερον· σεαυτὸν γὰρ
διαβαλεῖς ὡς ἀμαθῶς κρίναντα, ἐμοὶ δὲ ἕπου μᾶλλον
ἡγουμένῳ αὐτὸν Σκοπελιανὸν νήφοντα."

Ταυτὶ δὲ ὁ Ἡρώδης ἐχαρακτήριζε καθεωρακὼς τὸν
ἄνδρα κεκραμένην ἑρμηνείαν ἐφαρμόττοντα τῇ περὶ
τὰς σοφιστικὰς ἐννοίας τόλμῃ. ἐπιδεικνύμενος δὲ τῷ
Ἀλεξάνδρῳ τήν τε ἠχὼ τῆς διαλέξεως προσῆρεν,
ἐπειδὴ ἐγίγνωσκε τούτῳ καὶ μάλιστα χαίροντα αὐτὸν
τῷ τόνῳ, ῥυθμούς τε ποικιλωτέρους αὐλοῦ καὶ λύρας
ἐσηγάγετο ἐς τὸν λόγον, ἐπειδὴ πολὺς αὐτῷ καὶ περὶ

Herodes' arrival was, "When it stands still, even water sickens." After his arrival he gave it a different force saying, "Sweeter are the wandering waters." Here are some more quotations from *The Scythians* of Alexander. "When the Danube froze I would travel south, but when it thawed I would go north, pure in my body and not, as now, lying ill. For what harm can come to a man who follows the seasons?" And at the end of the speech he denounced the city as a stifling dwelling, and in concluding he cried out, "Fling open the gates, I want to breathe." Then he ran up to Herodes and embraced him and said, "Be my host in turn," and Herodes said, "How could I not, when you have so brilliantly hosted me?" When the audience had dispersed, Herodes called together the more advanced of his students and asked how the sophist seemed to them. When Sceptus of Corinth said that he had found the clay but was still looking for the Plato, Herodes cut him short and said, "Don't say this to anyone else, or you will bring scorn on yourself as one who has made an ignorant judgment. Follow me instead in believing him to be a sober Scopelian."[63]

Herodes characterized him in this way because he had observed that the man had a well tempered interpretation of his theme, harmoniously joined with boldness in the use of sophistic ideas. And when he himself declaimed before Alexander he increased the sonic impact of his oratory, because he knew that Alexander was especially graceful in maintaining elevation of style. And he introduced into his speech rhythms more varied than the aulos and the lyre, since he considered Alexander most skillful in elaborate

573

[63] For Scopelian's style, see above, *VS* 518, 519.

574 τὰς ἐξαλλαγὰς ἔδοξεν. ἡ δὲ σπουδασθεῖσα ὑπόθεσις
οἱ ἐν Σικελίᾳ ἡττηθέντες[18] ἦσαν αἰτοῦντες τοὺς ἀπα-
νισταμένους ἐκεῖθεν Ἀθηναίους τὸ ὑπ᾽ αὐτῶν ἀποθνήσκειν. ἐπὶ ταύτης τῆς ὑποθέσεως τὸ θρυλούμενον
ἐκεῖνο ἱκέτευσεν ἐπιτέγξας τοὺς ὀφθαλμοὺς δακρύοις,
"ναὶ Νικία, ναὶ πάτερ, οὕτως Ἀθήνας ἴδοις," ἐφ᾽ ᾧ τὸν
Ἀλέξανδρόν φασιν ἀναβοῆσαι· "ὦ Ἡρώδη, τεμάχιά
σου ἐσμὲν οἱ σοφισταὶ πάντες," καὶ τὸν Ἡρώδην
ὑπερησθέντα τῷ ἐπαίνῳ καὶ τῆς ἑαυτοῦ φύσεως γενόμενον δοῦναί οἱ δέκα μὲν σκευοφόρα, δέκα δὲ ἵππους,
δέκα δὲ οἰνοχόους, δέκα δὲ σημείων γραφέας, τάλαντα δὲ εἴκοσι χρυσοῦ, πλεῖστον δὲ ἄργυρον, δύο δὲ
ἐκ Κολλυτοῦ παιδία ψελλιζόμενα, ἐπειδὴ ἤκουεν αὐτὸν χαίροντα νέαις φωναῖς. τοιαῦτα μὲν οὖν αὐτῷ τὰ
Ἀθήνησιν.

(27) Ἐπεὶ δὲ καὶ ἑτέρων σοφιστῶν ἀπομνημο-
νεύματα παρεθέμην, δηλούσθω καὶ ὁ Ἀλέξανδρος ἐκ
πλειόνων, οὐδὲ γὰρ ἐς πλῆρές πω τῆς ἑαυτοῦ δόξης
ἀφῖκται παρὰ τοῖς Ἕλλησιν. ὡς μὲν δὴ σεμνῶς τε
καὶ ξὺν ἡδονῇ διελέγετο, δηλοῦσι τῶν διαλέξεων αἵδε·
"Μαρσύας ἦρα Ὀλύμπου καὶ Ὄλυμπος τοῦ αὐλεῖν,"
καὶ πάλιν, "Ἀραβία γῆ δένδρα πολλά, πεδία κατά-
σκια, γυμνὸν οὐδέν, φυτὰ ἡ γῆ, τὰ ἄνθη. οὐδὲ φύλλον
Ἀράβιον ἐκβαλεῖς, οὐδὲ κάρφος ἀπορρίψεις οὐδὲν

---

[18] ἡττηθέντες has better authority in the MSS than τρωθέν-
τες, which was printed by Kayser.

variations. The theme elected by the audience[64] was, "The   574
defeated in Sicily implore the Athenians who are retreat-
ing from there to kill them with their own hands."[65] In this
theme, eyes wet with tears, he spoke in supplication the
much quoted line "Yes, Nicias! Yes, father! So may you
see Athens once more!" At that, they say, Alexander cried
out aloud, "Herodes, we sophists are all merely slices of
you."[66] Herodes was overjoyed at this praise, and following
his own innate generosity he gave to him ten pack animals,
ten horses, ten cupbearers, ten shorthand writers, twenty
talents of gold, a very great quantity of silver, and two
lisping children from the deme of Collytus, because he
had heard that Alexander enjoyed hearing childish voices.
This then is what happened to Alexander at Athens.

(27) Now since I have set before my readers certain
memorable sayings of the other sophists, I must reveal
Alexander's character by quoting several of his, because
he has not yet achieved his due recognition among the
Greeks. These extracts from his discourses show how he
spoke with a mixture of dignity and delight. "Marsyas was
in love with Olympus, but Olympus with playing the aulos." And also, "Arabia is a land of abundant woods, shaded
plains. There is no barren patch, but only plants, earth,
flowers. You would cast away no leaf from Arabia, nor

[64] This is the technical term to describe the theme voted for
by the audience when several had been proposed. On its further
meaning, see the Rhetorical Glossary.   [65] This theme is
based on the narrative in Thuc. 7.75, which does not, however,
state that the defeated soldiers asked to be killed.

[66] An echo of the famous saying of Aeschylus that his plays
were slices ($\tau\epsilon\mu\acute{a}\chi\eta$) from Homer's splendid feasts.

ἐκεῖ φυέν, τοσοῦτον ἡ γῆ περὶ τοὺς ἱδρῶτας εὐτυχεῖ."
καὶ πάλιν "ἀνὴρ πένης ἀπ' Ἰωνίας, ἡ δὲ Ἰωνία Ἕλληνές εἰσιν οἰκήσαντες ἐν τῇ βαρβάρων." τὴν δὲ
ἰδέαν ταύτην διατωθάζων ὁ Ἀντίοχος καὶ διαπτύων
αὐτὸν ὡς τρυφῶντα ἐς τὴν τῶν ὀνομάτων ὥραν, παρελθὼν ἐς τὴν Ἀντιόχειαν διελέχθη ὧδε· "Ἰωνίαι Λυ-
δίαι Μαρσύαι μωρίαι, δότε προβλήματα."

575   Τὰ δὲ ἐν τῇ μελέτῃ πλεονεκτήματα δεδήλωται μὲν
καὶ ἐπὶ τούτων, δηλούσθω δὲ καὶ ἐπ' ἄλλων ὑποθέ-
σεων· διεξιὼν μὲν γὰρ τὸν Περικλέα τὸν κελεύοντα
ἔχεσθαι τοῦ πολέμου καὶ μετὰ τὸν χρησμόν, ἐν ᾧ καὶ
καλούμενος καὶ ἄκλητος ὁ Πύθιος ἔφη τοῖς Λακεδαιμονίοις συμμαχήσειν, ὧδε ἀπήντησε τῷ χρησμῷ·
"ἀλλ' ὑπισχνεῖται, φησι, τοῖς Λακεδαιμονίοις ὁ Πύθιος βοηθήσειν· ψεύδεται· οὕτως αὐτοῖς καὶ Τεγέαν
ἐπηγγείλατο." διεξιὼν δὲ τὸν ξυμβουλεύοντα τῷ Δα-
ρείῳ ζεῦξαι τὸν Ἴστρον· "ὑπορρείτω σοι ὁ Σκυθῶν
Ἴστρος, κἂν εὔρους τὴν στρατιὰν διαγάγῃ, τίμησον
αὐτὸν ἐξ αὐτοῦ πιών." τὸν δὲ Ἀρτάβαζον ἀγωνιζόμενος τὸν ἀπαγορεύοντα τῷ Ξέρξῃ μὴ τὸ δεύτερον
στρατεύειν ἐπὶ τὴν Ἑλλάδα ὧδε ἐβραχυλόγησε· "τὰ

---

67 Quoted by Norden (1923, 411) to illustrate the excessive
use of rhythm in prose.
68 This is presumably Antiochus of Aegae, whose life appears
immediately before Alexander's (568–70).
69 The point lies in the magniloquent use of the plural and the
hackneyed allusions.   70 Thuc. 1.118 speaks of this oracle,
but not in connection with Pericles.

throw aside a stem or stalk that grew there, so richly is the earth favored in all it exudes."[67] And again, "I am a poor man from Ionia. But Ionia is made up of Greeks who colonized the land of the barbarians." Antiochus[68] made fun of this style, and despised him as precious in his indulgence in pretty words. So when Antiochus went to Antioch and declaimed there he began, "Ionias, Lydias, Marsyases, foolishnesses, propose me themes."[69]

In these quotations I have shown Alexander's great talents in declamation, but let me also show it in other themes. For instance, when his theme was "Pericles urges that they should continue the war, even after the oracle in which the Pythian god said that, whether summoned to their aid or not, he would be the ally of the Lacedaemonians," he opposed the oracle with these words: "But the Pythian god, you say, promises to aid the Lacedaemonians.[70] He lies. In the same way he promised them Tegea."[71] And again, when representing the man advising Darius to build a bridge over the Danube:[72] "Let the Danube of the Scythians flow beneath you, and if it flows kindly to lead across your army, honor it by drinking from it." And again when he was contending in the character of Artabazus, attempting to dissuade Xerxes from mounting a second invasion of Greece,[73] he used the following suc-

575

71 Hdt. 1.66 describes the misleading oracle that refused the Spartans the conquest of Arcadia, but promised that they should take Tegea; they were defeated and captured by the Tegeans.

72 Hdt. 4.89 may have inspired this theme, where the Ionian allies of Darius bridge the Danube.

73 See Hdt. 7.10 for the speech that this declamatory theme sets out to rewrite.

μὲν δὴ Περσῶν τε καὶ Μήδων τοιαῦτά σοι, βασιλεῦ,
κατὰ χώραν μένοντι, τὰ δὲ Ἑλλήνων γῇ λεπτὴ θά-
λαττα στενὴ καὶ ἄνδρες ἀπονενοημένοι καὶ θεοὶ βά-
σκανοι." τοὺς δὲ ἐν τοῖς πεδίοις νοσοῦντας ἐς τὰ ὄρη
ἀνοικίζεσθαι πείθων ὧδε ἐφυσιολόγησε· "δοκεῖ δέ μοι
καὶ ὁ τοῦ παντὸς δημιουργὸς τὰ μὲν πεδία, ὥσπερ
ἀτιμοτέρας ὕλης, ῥῖψαι κάτω, ἐπαίρειν δὲ τὰ ὄρη,
ὥσπερ ἀξιώματα. ταῦτα πρῶτα μὲν ἥλιος ἀσπάζεται,
τελευταῖα δὲ ἀπολείπει. τίς οὐκ ἀγαπήσει τόπον μα-
κροτέρας ἔχοντα τὰς ἡμέρας;"

(28) Διδάσκαλοι τῷ Ἀλεξάνδρῳ ἐγένοντο Φαβω-
ρῖνός τε καὶ Διονύσιος· ἀλλὰ Διονυσίου μὲν ἡμιμα-
θὴς ἀπῆλθε μεταπεμφθεὶς ὑπὸ τοῦ πατρὸς νοσοῦντος,
ὅτε δὴ καὶ ἐτελεύτα, Φαβωρίνου δὲ γνησιώτατα
ἠκροάσατο, παρ' οὗ μάλιστα καὶ τὴν ἰδέαν[19] τοῦ λόγου ἔσπασε. τελευτῆσαι τὸν Ἀλέξανδρον οἱ μὲν ἐν
Κελτοῖς φασιν ἔτι ἐπιστέλλοντα, οἱ δ' ἐν Ἰταλίᾳ πε-
παυμένον τοῦ ἐπιστέλλειν, καὶ οἱ μὲν ἑξηκοντούτην,
οἱ δὲ καὶ οὔπω, καὶ οἱ μὲν ἐπὶ υἱῷ, οἱ δ' ἐπὶ θυγατρί,
ὑπὲρ ὧν οὐδὲν εὗρον λόγου ἄξιον.

(29) 6. ϛ'. Ἀξιούσθω λόγου καὶ Οὖαρος ὁ ἐκ τῆς
Πέργης. Οὐάρῳ πατὴρ μὲν Καλλικλῆς ἐγένετο ἀνὴρ
ἐν τοῖς δυνατωτάτοις τῶν Περγαίων, διδάσκαλος δὲ
Κοδρατίων ὁ ὕπατος ἀποσχεδιάζων τὰς θετικὰς ὑποθέσεις καὶ τὸν Φαβωρίνου τρόπον σοφιστεύων. πε-
λαργὸν δὲ τὸν Οὖαρον οἱ πολλοὶ ἐπωνόμαζον διὰ τὸ

19 ἰδέαν β; ὥραν α

246

cinct formulation: "The condition of the Persians and the Medes, my king, will be as I have said, if you remain in our land. But the soil of the Greeks is poor, their sea is narrow, their men desperate and their gods jealous." And when he was making the case that those who were ill on the plains should move to the mountains, he spoke on nature as follows: "It seems to me that the Demiurge of all things hurled down the plains, since they were of less honorable matter, and lifted up the mountains, as worthy of honor. These are the first things the sun embraces, and the last it leaves. Who will not love a place that holds longer days?" 576

(28) Alexander's teachers were Favorinus and Dionysius. But he left Dionysius when he was only half-educated, as he was called home due to his father's illness. Then when his father died, he became the genuine disciple of Favorinus, from whom especially he drew the style of his oratory. Some say that Alexander died among the Celts, still in the role of *ab epistulis*. Others say that he died in Italy, after he had ceased from this role. Some say that he left a son, others a daughter, but about these I could find nothing worth mentioning.

(29) 6. We must consider worthy of mention Varus who came from Perge. Varus' father was Callicles, a man who was among the most powerful of those in Perge, and his teacher was Quadratus,[74] the consular, who used to improvise on themes positing an abstract argument, and declaimed as a sophist in the manner of Favorinus. Most people nicknamed Varus The Stork, because of the fiery

---

[74] This may be the Quadratus who was proconsul of Asia in AD 165 and who is mentioned by Aristides as a rhetor (*Or.* 50.63), characteristically (for Aristides) avoiding the word sophist.

πυρσὸν τῆς ῥινὸς καὶ ῥαμφῶδες· καὶ τοῦτο μὲν ὡς
οὐκ ἀπὸ δόξης ἠστείζοντο, ἔξεστι συμβαλεῖν ταῖς
εἰκόσιν, αἳ ἀνάκεινται ἐν τῷ τῆς Περγαίας ἱερῷ. ὁ δὲ
χαρακτὴρ τοῦ λόγου τοιοῦτος· "ἐφ᾽ Ἑλλήσποντον ἐλθὼν ἵππον αἰτεῖς; ἐπ᾽ Ἄθω δὲ ἐλθὼν πλεῦσαι θέλεις;
οὐκ οἶδας, ἄνθρωπε, τὰς ὁδούς; ἀλλ᾽ Ἑλλησπόντῳ
577 γῆν ὀλίγην ἐπιβαλὼν ταύτην οἴει σοι μενεῖν, τῶν
ὀρῶν μὴ μενόντων;" ἐλέγετο δὲ ἀπαγγέλλειν ταῦτα
λαμπρᾷ τῇ φωνῇ καὶ ἠσκημένῃ. ἐτελεύτα μὲν οὖν
οἴκοι οὔπω γηράσκων καὶ ἐπὶ παισί, τὸ δὲ ἀπ᾽ αὐτοῦ
γένος εὐδόκιμοι πάντες ἐν τῇ Πέργῃ.

(30) 7. ζ᾽. Ἑρμογένης δέ, ὃν Ταρσοὶ ἤνεγκαν, πεντεκαίδεκα ἔτη γεγονὼς ἐφ᾽ οὕτω μέγα προὔβη τῆς τῶν
σοφιστῶν δόξης, ὡς καὶ Μάρκῳ βασιλεῖ παρασχεῖν
ἔρωτα ἀκροάσεως· ἐβάδισε γοῦν ἐπὶ τὴν ἀκρόασιν
αὐτοῦ ὁ Μάρκος καὶ ἤσθη μὲν διαλεγομένου, ἐθαύμαζε
δὲ σχεδιάζοντος, δωρεὰς δὲ λαμπρὰς ἔδωκεν. ἐς δὲ
ἄνδρας ἥκων ἀφῃρέθη τὴν ἕξιν ὑπ᾽ οὐδεμιᾶς φανερᾶς
νόσου, ὅθεν ἀστεισμοῦ λόγον παρέδωκε τοῖς βασκάνοις, ἔφασαν γὰρ τοὺς λόγους ἀτεχνῶς καθ᾽ Ὅμηρον
πτερόεντας εἶναι, ἀποβεβληκέναι γὰρ αὐτοὺς τὸν Ἑρ-
μογένην καθάπερ πτερά. καὶ Ἀντίοχος ὁ σοφιστὴς
ἀποσκώπτων ποτὲ ἐς αὐτόν, "οὗτος," ἔφη, "Ἑρμο-
578 γένης, ὁ ἐν παισὶ μὲν γέρων, ἐν δὲ γέρουσι παῖς." ἡ
δὲ ἰδέα τοῦ λόγου, ἣν ἐπετήδευε, τοιάδε τις ἦν· ἐπὶ

---

75 That is, in the temple of Artemis at Perge: cf. Strabo 14.4.2.

248

color and beaked shape of his nose. And this witticism did indeed suit his appearance, as can be observed from the images of him that are dedicated in the temple of the goddess[75] of Perge. The following is characteristic of his eloquence: "When you arrive at the Hellespont do you ask for a horse? Arriving at Athos do you wish to sail? Do you not know the ways, man? You throw this little soil onto the Hellespont and think that it will remain for you, though mountains do not remain."[76] It is said that he used to declaim these things in a brilliant and well disciplined voice. He died at home when he was not yet an old man, leaving children, and his descendants are all highly esteemed in Perge.

577

(30) 7. Hermogenes, whom Tarsus produced, by the time he was fifteen had come to such esteem among sophists that even the emperor Marcus longed to hear him. At any rate Marcus traveled to hear him declaim and took pleasure in his formal discourse, but was especially astonished by his improvisation, and gave him lavish gifts. But when Hermogenes came to manhood, he lost his skill through no obvious illness, which provided jealous people with a topic for a witticism. They said that his words truly were "winged" in Homer's phrase, and that Hermogenes had molted them like feathers. And Antiochus the sophist mocked him once saying, "Hermogenes who was an old man among the boys, is a boy among the old men."[77] The style that he practiced was like this: when delivering a

578

---

[76] This type of antithesis, very common in sophistic rhetoric, is ridiculed by Lucian, *Rhetorum Praeceptor* 18. Dio used a similar antithesis about Xerxes (Dio Chrys. *Or.* 3.310).

[77] A parody of Pind. *Nem.* 3.72.

γὰρ τοῦ Μάρκου διαλεγόμενος, "ἰδοὺ ἥκω σοι," ἔφη,
"βασιλεῦ, ῥήτωρ παιδαγωγοῦ δεόμενος, ῥήτωρ ἡλικίαν περιμένων," καὶ πλείω ἕτερα διελέχθη καὶ ὧδε
βωμόλοχα. ἐτελεύτα μὲν οὖν ἐν βαθεῖ γήρᾳ, εἷς δὲ
τῶν πολλῶν νομιζόμενος, κατεφρονήθη γὰρ ἀπολι-
πούσης αὐτὸν τῆς τέχνης.

(31) 8. η´. Φίλαγρος δὲ ὁ Κίλιξ Λολλιανοῦ μὲν
ἀκροατὴς ἐγένετο, σοφιστῶν δὲ θερμότατος καὶ ἐπι-
χολώτατος· λέγεται γὰρ δὴ νυστάζοντά ποτε ἀκροατὴν καὶ ἐπὶ κόρρης πλῆξαι· καὶ ὁρμῇ δὲ λαμπρᾷ ἐκ
μειρακίου χρησάμενος οὐκ ἀπελείφθη αὐτῆς οὐδ᾽
ὁπότε ἐγήρασκεν, ἀλλ᾽ οὕτω τι ἐπέδωκεν, ὡς καὶ
σχῆμα τοῦ διδασκάλου νομισθῆναι. πλείστοις δὲ ἐπι-
μίξας ἔθνεσι καὶ δοκῶν ἄριστα μεταχειρίζεσθαι τὰς
ὑποθέσεις οὐ μετεχειρίσατο Ἀθήνησιν εὖ τὴν αὐτοῦ
χολήν, ἀλλ᾽ εἰς ἀπέχθειαν Ἡρώδῃ κατέστησεν ἑαυτόν, καθάπερ ὑπὲρ τούτου ἀφιγμένος. ἐβάδιζε μὲν
γὰρ δείλης ἐν Κεραμεικῷ μετὰ τεττάρων, οἷοι Ἀθήνησιν οἱ τοὺς σοφιστὰς θηρεύοντες, ἰδὼν δὲ νεανίαν ἐκ
δεξιᾶς ἀναστρέφοντα μετὰ πλειόνων σκώπτεσθαί τι
ὑπ᾽ αὐτοῦ δόξας, "ἀλλ᾽ ἦ σύ," ἔφη, "τίς;" "Ἀμφικλῆς

78 It is striking that Philostratus makes no mention of the technical works that Hermogenes wrote on rhetoric, especially his *Peri Ideôn* (*On Styles*), which discusses with great sophistication rhetorical concepts on which Philostratus himself draws in his discussion of the sophists. It is possible that Philostratus did not know these works, or that he deemed their writing irrelevant to a discussion of Hermogenes' rhetorical practice.

speech in the presence of Marcus he said, "Look, emperor, at an orator who still needs an attendant to take him to school, an orator still waiting to come of age." And he said many similar things and equally ridiculous. He died in extreme old age, but was counted as one of the rank and file, for he was a figure of scorn when his art deserted him.[78]

(31) 8. Philagrus of Cilicia[79] was a student of Lollianus,[80] and was the most excitable and irascible of the sophists. For instance when someone in the audience fell asleep he slapped him across the face. He had brilliant impetus when he was a youth, and did not lose it even when he was old, but rather increased in power to such an extent that he was an image of his teacher.[81] He mixed with many peoples and had a very fine reputation for handling themes, but did not handle well his own anger when at Athens, but put himself into conflict with Herodes as though he had come there for that purpose. He was walking in the evening in the Cerameicus with four men of the sort who hunt out the sophists at Athens, and he saw a young man on his right with several others who kept turning around, and Philagrus believed that he was saying something mocking about him. "Who are you then?" he

---

[79] See Jones (1972) for the probable identification of Philagrus as the target of Lucian's *Lexiphanes*. Artemidorus (4.1) reports a dream that Philagrus had of "the sophist Varus" that predicted the end of Philagrus' own career.

[80] On Lollianus see above, *VS* 526–27.

[81] Philostratus also remarks at length on the "flashes of brilliance" (*VS* 527) in Lollianus' style.

ἐγώ," ἔφη, "εἰ δὴ τὸν Χαλκιδέα ἀκούεις." "ἀπέχου τοίνυν," ἔφη, "τῶν ἐμῶν ἀκροάσεων, οὐ γάρ μοι δοκεῖς
ὑγιαίνειν." τοῦ δὲ ἐρομένου, "τίς δὲ ὢν ταῦτα κηρύτ-
τεις;" δεινὰ πάσχειν ἦ δ' ὁ Φίλαγρος, εἰ ἀγνοεῖταί
ποι. ἐκφύλου δὲ αὐτὸν ῥήματος ὡς ἐν ὀργῇ διαφυγόν-
τος λαβόμενος ὁ Ἀμφικλῆς, καὶ γὰρ δὴ καὶ ἐτύγχανε
τῶν Ἡρώδου γνωρίμων τὴν πρώτην φερόμενος, "παρὰ
τίνι τῶν ἐλλογίμων," ἔφη, "τοῦτο εἴρηται;" καὶ ὅς,
"παρὰ Φιλάγρῳ."

579   Αὕτη μὲν δὴ ἡ παροινία ἐς τὰ τοιαῦτα προὔβη, τῆς
δὲ ὑστεραίας μαθὼν τὸν Ἡρώδην ἐν προαστίῳ διαιτώμενον γράφει πρὸς αὐτὸν ἐπιστολὴν καθαπτόμενος
τοῦ ἀνδρὸς ὡς ἀμελοῦντος τοῦ τῶν ἀκροατῶν κόσμου.
καὶ ὁ Ἡρώδης, "δοκεῖς μοι," ἔφη, "οὐ καλῶς προοι-
μιάζεσθαι," ἐπιπλήττων αὐτῷ ὡς μὴ κτωμένῳ ἀκροατῶν εὔνοιαν, ἣν προοίμιον ἡγεῖσθαι χρὴ τῶν ἐπιδείξεων. ὁ δὲ ὥσπερ οὐ ξυνιεὶς τοῦ αἰνίγματος, ἢ ξυνιεὶς
μέν, ἐν γέλωτι δὲ τὴν τοῦ Ἡρώδου γνώμην βελτίστην
οὖσαν τιθέμενος ἐψεύσθη τῆς ἐπιδείξεως παρελθὼν ἐς
ἀκροατὰς οὐκ εὔνους. ὡς γὰρ τῶν πρεσβυτέρων
ἤκουον, προσέκρουσε μὲν ἡ διάλεξις νεαροηχὴς δό-
ξασα καὶ διεσπασμένη[20] τὰς ἐννοίας, ἔδοξε δὲ καὶ
μειρακιώδης· γυναικὸς γὰρ θρῆνος ἐγκατεμέμικτο

---

[20] διεσπασμένη, though it is the reading only of Ab (a MS of
the 15th century) is a likely correction of the ἐσπασμένη, which
appears (as Stefec notes) to be the reading of the archetype.

asked. "I am Amphicles," he said, "if you have heard of a man from Calchis of that name." "Keep away from my lectures in that case," he said, "because you don't seem to me to be in your right mind." And the other asked, "And who are you who makes this proclamation?" Philagrus said that was an outrageous insult, if he were not recognized anywhere. A foreign word escaped him,[82] since he was angry, and Amphicles, who happened to be the most distinguished student of Herodes, seized upon it and said, "In which illustrious author is that word spoken?" And he said, "In Philagrus."

This exchange of insults unfolded like this, but on the next day, when he learned that Herodes was living in his suburban villa, he wrote a letter to him, accusing him of failing to teach his students proper behavior. And Herodes said, "You seem to me not to be handling your prooemium very well." In this way he criticized Philagrus for not winning the goodwill of his listeners, which one must consider the purpose of the proem of a declamation. But Philagrus, as though he did not understand this riddle, or as if he understood it but thought Herodes' advice was ridiculous, though it was in fact very good, was disappointed in his public declamation, because he came before an audience that was not well disposed to him. As I have heard from my elders, his introductory speech grated on them as it seemed to have a fashionable sound and to drag in incompatible ideas. It seemed, in short, juvenile. For mixed in

579

---

[82] The avoidance of terms not found in classical texts was a prominent feature of Atticizing rhetoric. If Lucian's *Lexiphanes* is indeed an attack on Philagrus, it emphasizes and exaggerates precisely this tendency to neologism.

τοῖς Ἀθηναίων ἐγκωμίοις τεθνώσης αὐτῷ ἐν Ἰωνίᾳ.
τὴν δὲ μελέτην οὕτως ἐπεβουλεύθη· ἠγώνιστό τις
αὐτῷ κατὰ τὴν Ἀσίαν ὑπόθεσις οἱ παραιτούμενοι τὴν
τῶν ἀκλήτων συμμαχίαν. ταύτης ἐκδεδομένης ἤδη
τῆς ὑποθέσεως μνήμην ξυνελέξατο, καὶ γὰρ δὴ καὶ
εὐδοκιμηκὼς ἐπ' αὐτῇ ἐτύγχανε· λόγου δὲ ἥκοντος ἐς
τοὺς ἀμφὶ τὸν Ἡρώδην, ὡς ὁ Φίλαγρος τὰς μὲν
πρῶτον ὁριζομένας ὑποθέσεις αὐτοσχεδιάζοι, τὰς δὲ
καὶ δεύτερον οὐκέτι, ἀλλ' ἕωλα μελετῴη καὶ ἑαυτῷ
προειρημένα, προὔβαλον μὲν αὐτῷ τοὺς ἀκλήτους
τούτους, δοκοῦντι δὲ ἀποσχεδιάζειν ἀντανεγιγνώ-
σκετο ἡ μελέτη. θορύβου δὲ πολλοῦ καὶ γέλωτος τὴν
ἀκρόασιν κατασχόντος βοῶν ὁ Φίλαγρος καὶ κεκρα-
γώς, ὡς δεινὰ πάσχοι τῶν ἑαυτοῦ εἰργόμενος, οὐ διέ-
φυγε τὴν ἤδη πεπιστευμένην αἰτίαν. ταῦτα μὲν οὖν ἐν
τῷ Ἀγριππείῳ ἐπράχθη, διαλιπὼν δὲ ἡμέρας ὡς τέτ-
580 ταρας παρῆλθεν ἐς τὸ τῶν τεχνιτῶν βουλευτήριον, ὃ
δὴ ᾠκοδόμηται παρὰ τὰς τοῦ Κεραμεικοῦ πύλας οὐ
πόρρω τῶν ἱππέων. εὐδοκιμώτατα δὲ ἀγωνιζόμενος

---

83 That is, Philagrus was delivering his μελετή, a formal declamation, rather than the shorter and less formal διάλεξις, with
which he had initially caused offense.

84 This theme is possibly derived from Thuc. 8.86, where Alcibiades declines the aid of the Argives. A short quotation from it
appears below at VS 580.

85 These are the Artists (τεχνῖται) of Dionysus, an association
of actors, musicians, and other theatrical workers with roots in the
Hellenistic era. Their capacity to promote their members' inter-

with the praise of the Athenians was a lament for his wife who had died in Ionia. So when he gave the full declamation,[83] a plot was brought against him: He had presented in Asia a theme "They reject as allies the uninvited."[84] This piece had already been published and he had committed it to memory, for in fact he happened to be famous for this theme. Word had come to the circle of Herodes that Philagrus would improvise the first theme that was chosen, but after that he would not, but would declaim stale speeches that he had given before. They proposed to him the theme of "The Uninvited," and when he pretended to improvise they read the declamation along with him. A great uproar and laughter took hold of the audience, and Philagrus was shouting and screaming that he had been treated outrageously by being deprived of what was his own, but he did not acquit himself of a charge that was already well proven. These things happened in the theater of Agrippa, but about four days later he went into the council chamber of the Theatrical Artists,[85] that is, the building that stands near the gates of the Cerameicus, not far from the equestrian statues.[86] He was winning univer- 580

ests can be inferred from Philostratus' comments in the *bios* of Euodianus of Smyrna (*VS* 596) on the difficulty of governing them. Aulus Gellius (*NA* 20.4) reports that the philosopher Taurus instructed one of his students who was involved with theater that he should daily contemplate a *problema* of Aristotle concerning the Craftsmen's bad moral character ([*Pr.*] 30.10).

[86] Diog. Laert. 7.182 mentions equestrian statues in the Cerameicus, and these appear to have been a commemoration of the Athenian cavalry, but the details of Philostratus' allusion do not appear to be clear.

τὸν Ἀριστογείτονα τὸν ἀξιοῦντα κατηγορεῖν τοῦ μὲν
Δημοσθένους Μηδισμοῦ, τοῦ δὲ Αἰσχίνου Φιλιππι-
σμοῦ, ὑπὲρ ὧν καὶ γεγραμμένοι ἀλλήλους ἐτύγχανον,
ἐσβέσθη τὸ φθέγμα ὑπὸ τῆς χολῆς ἐπισκοτοῦντος
φύσει τοῖς ἐπιχόλοις τὴν ῥώμην[21] τοῦ φωνητικοῦ
πνεύματος. χρόνῳ μὲν οὖν ὕστερον ἐπεβάτευσε τοῦ
κατὰ τὴν Ῥώμην θρόνου, Ἀθήνησι δὲ ἀπηνέχθη τῆς
ἑαυτοῦ δόξης δι᾽ ἃς εἴρηκα αἰτίας.

(32) Χαρακτὴρ τῶν τοῦ Φιλάγρου λόγων ὁ μὲν ἐν
ταῖς διαλέξεσι τοιοῦτος· "εἶτα οἴει ἥλιον ἑσπέρῳ φθο-
νεῖν ἢ μέλειν αὐτῷ, εἴ τίς ἐστιν ἀστὴρ ἄλλος ἐν
οὐρανῷ; οὐχ οὕτως ἔχει τὰ τοῦ μεγάλου τούτου πυ-
ρός. ἐμοὶ μὲν γὰρ δοκεῖ καὶ ποιητικῶς ἑκάστῳ διανέ-
μειν, σοὶ μὲν ἄρκτον δίδωμι, λέγοντα, σοὶ δὲ μεσημβρίαν,[22] σοὶ δὲ ἑσπέραν, πάντες δὲ ἐν νυκτί, πάντες,
ὅταν ἐγὼ μὴ βλέπωμαι·

Ἥλιος δ᾽ ἀνόρουσε λιπὼν περικαλλέα λίμνην,

καὶ ἀστέρες οὐδαμοῦ." τίνες δὲ καὶ οἱ τῆς μελέτης
αὐτῷ ῥυθμοὶ ἦσαν, δηλώσει τὰ πρὸς τοὺς ἀκλήτους
εἰρημένα, καὶ γὰρ χαίρειν αὐτοῖς ἐλέγετο· "φίλε, τή-
μερόν σε τεθέαμαι καὶ τήμερον ἐν ὅπλοις καὶ μετὰ

---

[21] ῥώμην Reiske; φωνήν ω   [22] Cobet wished to insert
σοὶ δὲ ἑῴαν for the symmetry of the phrase.

---

[87] This clearly fictitious theme, which appears as well in Mar-
cellinus 4.472 Walz, reflects several sophistic preoccupations.

256

sal approval in the role of Aristogeiton demanding the
right to denounce Demosthenes for collaboration with
the Medes and Aeschines for collaboration with Philip—
accusations that they had in fact brought against each
other[87]—but his voice was extinguished by his anger. In
the case of people very prone to outbursts of anger, the
breath throws into shadow the strength of the voice. So
though it's true that later he ascended to the chair of rhetoric at Rome, nevertheless at Athens, for the reasons that
I have said, he was deprived of his due recognition.

(32) The characteristic style of Philagrus' in his introductory speeches was like this: "Do you think then that the
sun is jealous of the Evening Star, or that he cares if some
other star is in the sky? That is not the nature of this great
fire. For it seems to me that he distributes like the poet[88]
to each one saying: 'To you I give the North, to you the
South, to you the evening, but all of you, truly all of you
are in night when I am not seen:

The sun rose, leaving the beautiful sea,[89]

and the stars are nowhere.'" What the rhythms of his declamations were like can be seen from what he said in "The
Uninvited," and indeed he is said to have delighted in
those rhythms. "My friend, today I have seen you, and

---

[88] An allusion to Hom. *Il.* 15.189–93, where Poseidon describes the partition of the universe among Zeus, Hades, and
himself. The adverb ποιητικῶς is ambiguous and may mean that
the sun carries out this work of definition like a poet or may draw
attention to the allusion to Homer, who is often simply "the poet."

[89] Hom. *Od.* 3.1. The speech is quoted by Norden (1923, 413)
as an example of the metrical rhythms of Sophistic prose.

ξίφους μοι λαλεῖς," καὶ, "τὴν ἀπὸ τῆς ἐκκλησίας
μόνην οἶδα φιλίαν. ἄπιτε οὖν, ἄνδρες φίλοι, τοῦτο
γὰρ ὑμῖν τηροῦμεν τοὔνομα, κἂν δεηθῶμέν ποτε συμ-
μάχων, ἐφ᾽ ὑμᾶς πέμψομεν, εἴ ποτε δήπου."²³

(33) Μέγεθος μὲν οὖν ὁ Φίλαγρος μετρίου μείων,
τὴν δὲ ὀφρὺν πικρὸς καὶ τὸ ὄμμα ἕτοιμος καὶ ἐς ὀρ-
581 γὴν ἐκκληθῆναι πρόθυμος, καὶ τὸ ἐν αὐτῷ δύστροπον
οὐδ᾽ αὐτὸς ἠγνόει. ἐρομένου γοῦν αὐτὸν ἑνὸς τῶν
ἑταίρων, τί παθὼν παιδοτροφίᾳ οὐ χαίροι, "ὅτι," ἔφη,
"οὐδὲ ἐμαυτῷ χαίρω." ἀποθανεῖν δὲ αὐτὸν οἱ μὲν ἐν
τῇ θαλάττῃ, οἱ δὲ ἐν Ἰταλίᾳ περὶ πρῶτον γῆρας.

(34) 9. θ΄. Ἀριστείδην δὲ τὸν εἴτε Εὐδαίμονος εἴτε
Εὐδαίμονα Ἀδριανοὶ μὲν ἤνεγκαν, οἱ δὲ Ἀδριανοὶ
πόλις οὐ μεγάλη ἐν Μυσοῖς, Ἀθῆναι δὲ ἤσκησαν
κατὰ τὴν Ἡρώδου ἀκμὴν καὶ τὸ ἐν τῇ Ἀσίᾳ Πέργαμον κατὰ τὴν Ἀριστοκλέους γλῶτταν. νοσώδης δὲ ἐκ
μειρακίου γενόμενος οὐκ ἠμέλησε τοῦ πονεῖν. τὴν μὲν
οὖν ἰδέαν τῆς νόσου καὶ ὅτι τὰ νεῦρα αὐτῷ ἐπεφρίκει,
ἐν Ἱεροῖς βιβλίοις αὐτὸς φράζει, τὰ δὲ βιβλία ταῦτα
ἐφημερίδων ἐπέχει τινὰ αὐτῷ λόγον, αἱ δὲ ἐφημερίδες
ἀγαθαὶ διδάσκαλοι τοῦ περὶ παντὸς εὖ διαλέγεσθαι.
582 ἐπὶ δὲ τὸ σχεδιάζειν μὴ ἑπομένης αὐτῷ τῆς φύσεως

²³ Stefec prints but obelizes the reading of the archetype, εἴ-
πατε δέ που. I have tentatively adopted the conjecture of Jacobs,
as did Wright and Brodersen.

⁹⁰ This appears to be merely a pun, playing on the name of
Aristides' father (Fortunate).

today in arms and holding a sword you speak to me." And, "The only friendship I know comes from the assembly of the people. So go, friends, for we reserve this name for you, and if ever we need allies, we shall send for you, if ever indeed."

(33) In height Philagrus was below average. He had a sharp expression in his eyebrow, alertness in his gaze and was easily roused to anger, and he himself was not ignorant 581 of his ill temper. For instance when one of his friends asked him what had happened to him that he did not enjoy raising his children he said, "Because I do not even enjoy myself." Some say that he died at sea, others in Italy at the beginning of old age.

(34) 9. Aristides, whether he was the son of Eudaemon or whether we should call him *eudaemon* himself,[90] was born at Hadriani, a town of no great size among the Mysians. But it was Athens that trained him when Herodes was at the peak of his powers, and Pergamum in Asia, when Aristocles taught eloquence there. Though he had poor health from his youth, he did not fail to work hard. He himself describes in his *Sacred Discourses* the nature of his illness and relates that he suffered from a nervous disorder.[91] These books served the purpose of a diary, and diaries are excellent teachers of speaking well on any subject.[92] His natural talent did not tend toward improvisa- 582

[91] Quoting Aristid. *Or.* 48.6 (396.5 Keil).

[92] Synesius (*On Dreams* 155a–d) develops the idea that writing about dreams is an excellent rhetorical practice and contrasts with (as he sees it) the pointless practice of declaiming in historical or fictional character, which Philostratus places at the center of his Second Sophistic (VS 481).

ἀκριβείας ἐπεμελήθη καὶ πρὸς τοὺς παλαιοὺς ἔβλεψεν ἱκανῶς τε τῷ γονίμῳ ἴσχυσε κουφολογίαν ἐξελὼν
τοῦ λόγου. ἀποδημίαι δὲ Ἀριστείδου οὐ πολλαί (οὔτε
γὰρ ἐς χάριν τῶν πολλῶν διελέγετο οὔτε ἐκράτει χολῆς ἐπὶ τοὺς μὴ ξὺν ἐπαίνῳ ἀκροωμένους,) ἃ δέ γε
ἐπῆλθεν ἔθνη, Ἰταλοί τέ εἰσι καὶ Ἑλλὰς καὶ ἡ πρὸς
τῷ Δέλτα κατῳκημένη Αἴγυπτος, οἳ χαλκοῦν ἔστησαν
αὐτὸν ἐπὶ τῆς κατὰ τὴν Σμύρναν ἀγορᾶς.

(35) Οἰκιστὴν δὲ καλεῖν²⁴ καὶ τὸν Ἀριστείδην τῆς
Σμύρνης οὐκ ἀλαζὼν ἔπαινος, ἀλλὰ δικαιότατός τε
καὶ ἀληθέστατος· τὴν γὰρ πόλιν ταύτην ἀφανισθεῖ-
σαν ὑπὸ σεισμῶν τε καὶ χασμάτων οὕτω τι ὠλο-
φύρατο πρὸς τὸν Μᾶρκον, ὡς τῇ μὲν ἄλλῃ μονῳδίᾳ
θαμὰ ἐπιστενάξαι τὸν βασιλέα, ἐπὶ δὲ τῷ "ζέφυροι
ἐρήμην καταπνέουσι" καὶ δάκρυα τῷ βιβλίῳ ἐπιστά-
ξαι ξυνοικίαν τε τῇ πόλει ἐκ τῶν τοῦ Ἀριστείδου ἐν-
δοσίμων νεῦσαι. ἐτύγχανε δὲ καὶ ξυγγεγονὼς ἤδη τῷ
Μάρκῳ ὁ Ἀριστείδης ἐν Ἰωνίᾳ· ὡς γὰρ τοῦ Ἐφεσίου
Δαμιανοῦ ἤκουον, ἐπεδήμει μὲν ὁ αὐτοκράτωρ ἤδη τῇ
Σμύρνῃ τρίτην ἡμέραν, τὸν δὲ Ἀριστείδην οὔπω γιγνώσκων ἤρετο τοὺς Κυντιλίους, μὴ ἐν τῷ τῶν ἀσπα-
ζομένων ὁμίλῳ παρεωραμένος αὐτῷ ὁ ἀνὴρ εἴη, οἱ δὲ
οὐδὲ αὐτοὶ ἔφασαν ἑωρακέναι αὐτόν, οὐ γὰρ ἂν παρεῖναι τὸ μὴ οὐ ξυστῆσαι, καὶ ἀφίκοντο τῆς ὑστεραίας
τὸν Ἀριστείδην ἄμφω δορυφοροῦντες. προσειπὼν δὲ
αὐτὸν ὁ αὐτοκράτωρ, "διὰ τί σε," ἔφη, "βραδέως εἴδο-

²⁴ καλεῖν Jacobs; λέγειν χ

tion, but he worked diligently for accuracy and looked to the ancients. He was sufficiently powerful in his natural ability, and excised empty verbiage from his speech. Aristides did not travel widely, because he did not speak for the sake of pleasing the crowd, nor could he master his anger against those in an audience who did not praise him. The countries that he did visit were Italy, Greece and the part of Egypt near the Delta, the people of which set up a bronze statue of him in the agora of Smyrna.

(35) To call Aristides the founder of Smyrna is no pretentious boast, but is very just and very true. This is because when the city had been blotted out by earthquakes and chasms he lamented the city so powerfully to Marcus that Marcus groaned often during other parts of the monody, but at the words "winds blow down through the desolation" he shed tears on the book, and agreed to rebuild the city, in tune with Aristides' request.[93] And Aristides happened to meet Marcus once before in Ionia. As I have heard from Damianus of Ephesus, the emperor had already been visiting Smyrna for three days, and as he had not yet made the acquaintance of Aristides, he asked the Quintilii[94] whether he had somehow overlooked the man in the crowd of people greeting him, and they said that they too had not seen him, or else they would not have failed to present him. The next day, both of the Quintilii came, escorting Aristides as his guards. When the emperor addressed him, he asked, "Why have we had to wait

[93] This is *Or*. 19.3 (13.9 Keil). The surviving text is presented as a letter, suggesting that Aristides performed the letter as a speech before the emperor.

[94] See above, *VS* 559.

PHILOSTRATUS

μεν;" καὶ ὁ Ἀριστείδης, "θεώρημα," ἔφη, "ὦ βασιλεῦ,
ἠσχόλει, γνώμη δὲ θεωροῦσά τι μὴ ἀποκρεμαννύσθω
οὗ ζητεῖ." ὑπερησθεὶς δὲ ὁ αὐτοκράτωρ τῷ ἤθει τἀν-
δρὸς ὡς ἁπλοικωτάτῳ τε καὶ σχολικωτάτῳ, "πότε,"
583 ἔφη, "ἀκροάσομαί σου;" καὶ ὁ Ἀριστείδης "τήμερον,"
εἶπεν, "πρόβαλε καὶ αὔριον ἀκροῶ· οὐ γὰρ ἐσμὲν τῶν
ἐμούντων, ἀλλὰ τῶν ἀκριβούντων. ἐξέστω δέ, ὦ βασιλεῦ, καὶ τοὺς γνωρίμους παρεῖναι τῇ ἀκροάσει."
"ἐξέστω," ἦ δ' ὁ Μᾶρκος, "δημοτικὸν γάρ." εἰπόντος
δὲ τοῦ Ἀριστείδου, "δεδόσθω δὲ αὐτοῖς ἐμβοᾶν καὶ
κροτεῖν, ὦ βασιλεῦ, ὁπόσον δύνανται," μειδιάσας ὁ
αὐτοκράτωρ, "τοῦτο," ἔφη, "ἐπὶ σοὶ κεῖται." οὐκ
ἔγραψα τὴν μελετηθεῖσαν ὑπόθεσιν, ἐπειδὴ ἄλλοι ἄλλην φασίν, ἐκεῖνό γε μὴν πρὸς πάντων ὁμολογεῖται,
τὸν Ἀριστείδην ἀρίστῃ φορᾷ ἐπὶ τοῦ Μάρκου χρῆσα-
σθαι πόρρωθεν τῇ Σμύρνῃ ἑτοιμαζούσης τῆς τύχης
τὸ δι' ἀνδρὸς τοιούτου δὴ ἀνοικισθῆναι. καὶ οὔ φημι
ταῦτα, ὡς οὐχὶ καὶ τοῦ βασιλέως ἀνοικίσαντος ἂν
ἀπολωλυῖαν πόλιν, ἣν οὖσαν ἐθαύμασεν, ἀλλ' ὅτι αἱ
βασίλειοί τε καὶ θεσπέσιοι φύσεις, ἣν προσεγείρῃ
αὐτὰς ξυμβουλία καὶ λόγος, ἀναλάμπουσι μᾶλλον
καὶ πρὸς τὸ ποιεῖν εὖ ξὺν ὁρμῇ φέρονται.

(36) Δαμιανοῦ κἀκεῖνα ἤκουον, τὸν σοφιστὴν τοῦτον διαβάλλειν μὲν τοὺς αὐτοσχεδίους ἐν ταῖς διαλέξεσι, θαυμάζειν δὲ οὕτω τὸ σχεδιάζειν, ὡς καὶ ἰδίᾳ

so long to see you?" And Aristides said, "Emperor, a subject that I was contemplating kept me busy, and when the mind is absorbed in contemplation it should not be dislodged from what it seeks." The emperor took great pleasure in the man's character, because it was so straightforward and dedicated to study. "When," he asked, "will I hear you speak?" And Aristides said, "Propose a theme today and you will hear it tomorrow. I am not one of those speakers who vomits out words, but who speaks with exactness.[95] And allow, emperor, that my students may be in the audience." "Let it be permitted," said the emperor, "for that is democratic." And when Aristides said, "Allow them also, emperor, to shout and applaud as much as they can." The emperor smiled and said, "That is in your hands." I have not recorded the theme that he declaimed, since different people say different things, but what is agreed by everyone is that Aristides spoke in the presence of Marcus with such noble force that fate was preparing, from a great distance, that Smyrna would be rebuilt through the efforts of a man like this. And I do not mean by this that the emperor would not have rebuilt the city that he had marveled at while it still stood, but that natures that are royal and divine, if good advice and eloquence spur them on, shine out more brightly and are carried on to good actions with great impetus.

583

(36) I have also heard from Damianus that this sophist used to heap abuse in his introductory speeches on speakers who improvised. Nevertheless he marveled at impro-

---

[95] This saying was later echoed by other sophists; cf. Eunap. 488; Synesius, *Dio* 56c; Aristides perhaps echoed Cic. *Epist. ad Div.* 12.2: *omnibus est visus vomero suo more, non dicere.*

ἐκπονεῖν αὐτὸ ἐν δωματίῳ ἑαυτὸν καθειργνύντα, ἐξ-
επόνει δὲ κῶλον ἐκ κώλου καὶ νόημα ἐκ νοήματος
ἐπανακυκλῶν. τουτὶ δὲ ἡγώμεθα μασωμένου μᾶλλον
ἢ ἐσθίοντος, αὐτοσχέδιος γὰρ γλώττης εὐροούσης
ἀγώνισμα. κατηγοροῦσι δὲ τοῦ Ἀριστείδου τινὲς ὡς
εὐτελὲς εἰπόντος προοίμιον ἐπὶ τῶν μισθοφόρων τῶν
ἀπαιτουμένων τὴν γῆν, ἄρξασθαι γὰρ δὴ αὐτὸν τῆς
ὑποθέσεως ταύτης ὧδε· "οὐ παύσονται οὗτοι οἱ ἄνθρωποι παρέχοντες ἡμῖν πράγματα." λαμβάνονται δέ
τινες καὶ ἀκμῆς τοῦ ἀνδρὸς ἐπὶ τοῦ παραιτουμένου
584   τὸν τειχισμὸν τῆς Λακεδαίμονος, εἴρηται δὲ ὧδε· "μὴ
γὰρ δὴ ἐν τείχει ἐπιπτήξαιμεν ὀρτύγων ἀναψάμενοι[25]
φύσιν." λαμβάνονται καὶ παροιμίας ὡς ταπεινῶς
προσερριμμένης· ἐπιδιαβάλλων γὰρ τὸν Ἀλέξανδρον
ὡς πατρῴζοντα τὴν ἐν τοῖς πράγμασι δεινότητα τοῦ
πατρὸς ἔφη τὸ παιδίον εἶναι. οἱ αὐτοὶ κατηγοροῦσι
καὶ σκώμματος, ἐπειδὴ τοὺς Ἀριμασποὺς τοὺς μονομ-
μάτους ἔφη ξυγγενεῖς εἶναι τοῦ Φιλίππου, ὥσπερ τοῦ
Δημοσθένους ἀπολελογημένου τοῖς Ἕλλησιν ὑπὲρ
τοῦ τραγικοῦ πιθήκου καὶ τοῦ ἀρουραίου Οἰνομάου.
ἀλλὰ μὴ ἐκ τούτων τὸν Ἀριστείδην, δηλούτω δὲ αὐτὸν

---

[25] ἐναψάμενοι Cobet

---

[96] A scholiast on Hermogenes explains that lands had been
assigned instead of pay to certain mercenaries; after they had
founded a city, they were ordered to take their pay and give up
their land.

visation so much that he used to he used to work at it in
private, shutting himself up in a room. He used to labor at
it by unfolding clause from clause and thought from
thought. But let us regard this as chewing rather than eating, because improvisation is the crowning achievement
of a fluent tongue. Some accuse Aristides of making an
introduction that was too obvious when he spoke on the
theme "The mercenaries are asked to give back their
land,"[96] because he began like this: "These people will
never stop making trouble for us." Some criticize the climax of the man's speech in the role of the Spartan entreat-
ing against the fortification of Lacedaemon,[97] and it was   584
expressed like this: "Let us never huddle within walls,
taking on the nature of quails." They seized as well on a
proverbial expression of his, on the grounds that it was
expressed in a common way. For he was heaping abuse on
Alexander as merely imitating his father's power in political affairs, and said that "he was his father's son." These
same people also criticize a joke of his, when he said that
the one-eyed Arimaspi were Philip's relatives,[98] though
Demosthenes defended himself before the Greeks for the
sake of "the tragic ape" and "the rustic Oenomaus."[99] We
should not, however, judge Aristides from these lines, but
let his style be observed in the speech "Isocrates leads the

[97] For this theme see above, VS 514.

[98] Philip had lost an eye at the siege of Methone in 352 BC.
The fabulous Arimaspi are described at Hdt. 4.27.

[99] Dem. De cor. 242. "Tragic ape" was a proverbial phrase for
an arrogant person; Oenomaus was the hero of a lost play of
Sophocles. Both of these expressions were sneering references to
the career of Aeschines as a traveling actor.

ὅ τε Ἰσοκράτης ὁ τοὺς Ἀθηναίους ἐξάγων τῆς θαλάττης καὶ ὁ ἐπιτιμῶν τῷ Καλλιξείνῳ ἐπὶ τῷ μὴ θάπτειν
τοὺς δέκα καὶ οἱ βουλευόμενοι περὶ τῶν ἐν Σικελίᾳ
καὶ ὁ μὴ λαβὼν Αἰσχίνης παρὰ τοῦ Κερσοβλέπτου
585 τὸν σῖτον καὶ οἱ παραιτούμενοι τὰς σπονδὰς μετὰ τὸ
κτεῖναι τὰ γένη, ἐν ᾗ μάλιστα ὑποθέσεων ἀναδιδά-
σκει ἡμᾶς, πῶς ἄν τις ἀσφαλῶς κεκινδυνευμένας τε
καὶ τραγικὰς ἐννοίας μεταχειρίσαιτο. καὶ πλείους
ἑτέρας ὑποθέσεις οἶδα εὐπαιδευσίαν ἐνδεικνυμένας
τοῦ ἀνδρὸς τούτου καὶ ἰσχὺν καὶ ἦθος, ἀφ' ὧν μᾶλλον
αὐτὸν θεωρητέον, ἢ εἴ που καὶ παρέπτυσέ τι ἐς φιλοτιμίαν ἐκπεσών. καὶ τεχνικώτατος δὲ σοφιστῶν ὁ
Ἀριστείδης ἐγένετο καὶ πολὺς ἐν θεωρήμασιν, ὅθεν
καὶ τοῦ σχεδιάζειν ἀπηνέχθη· τὸ γὰρ κατὰ θεωρίαν
βούλεσθαι προάγειν πάντα ἀσχολεῖ τὴν γνώμην καὶ
ἀπαλλάττει τοῦ ἑτοίμου.

Ἀποθανεῖν δὲ τὸν Ἀριστείδην οἱ μὲν οἴκοι γράφου-
σιν, οἱ δὲ ἐν Ἰωνίᾳ ἔτη βιώσαντα οἱ μὲν ἑξήκοντά
φασιν, οἱ δὲ ἀγχοῦ τῶν ἑβδομήκοντα.

(37) 10. ιʹ. Ἀδριανὸν δὲ τὸν Φοίνικα Τύρος μὲν

---

100 This theme is based on Isocrates, *On the Peace* 64.

101 This favorite theme is based on a fictitious situation in
which Callixenus advises the Athenians not to bury the generals
who were executed after the battle of Arginusae. It is quoted by
Hermogenes and Syrianus.

102 This theme is quoted by Hermogenes.

103 Presumably, this is imagined as taking place during the
period of the Thracian king Cersobleptes' alliance with the Athe-

Athenians away from the sea,"[100] and "The speaker pours criticism on Callixenus for not granting burial to the Ten,"[101] and "Those deliberating on events in Sicily,"[102] and "Aeschines, when he had not received the corn from Cersobleptes,"[103] and "They reject the treaty after the murder of their offspring." In this especially of all themes he teaches us how one may handle risky and tragic themes without making any error. I know many other themes that demonstrate this man's erudition, and his forcefulness and characterization, and it is from these that we should examine him, rather than where he spat something out carelessly and fell into striving after effect. Aristides was the most skilled of the sophists in his art and great in contemplation of a theme, for which reason he refrained from improvisation. This is because the desire to produce everything after proper contemplation keeps the mind occupied and deprives it of alertness.

585

Some write that Aristides died at home, others that he died in Ionia. Some say he lived sixty years, others that he was nearly seventy.

(37) 10. Tyre produced Hadrian the Phoenician,[104] but

---

nians (Diod. Sic. 16.34.4). It is possible that the theme derives, as Wright observed, from Polyaenus 7.32, though the details are far from clear.

[104] A brief, possibly incomplete declamation by Hadrian survives, which calls for the burning of a woman who has just burned a witch (on the grounds that she too is a witch): see Hinck 1873, 44–45. Hadrian attended the anatomy lectures of Galen in Rome (Gal. 14.627; 629 Kuhn). Jones (1972) has argued that he is the target of Lucian's *Pseudologistes*.

ἤνεγκεν, Ἀθῆναι δὲ ἤσκησαν. ὡς γὰρ τῶν ἐμαυτοῦ
διδασκάλων ἤκουον, ἀφίκετο μὲν ἐς αὐτὰς κατὰ Ἡρώδην, φύσεως δὲ ἰσχὺν σοφιστικωτάτην ἐνδεικνύμενος
καὶ οὐκ ἄδηλος ὢν ὡς ἐπὶ μέγα ἥξοι· ἐφοίτησε μὲν
γὰρ τῷ Ἡρώδῃ ὀκτὼ καὶ δέκα ἴσως γεγονὼς ἔτη καὶ
ταχέως ἀξιωθείς, ὧν Σκέπτος τε καὶ Ἀμφικλῆς ἠξι-
οῦντο, ἐνεγράφη καὶ τῇ τοῦ Κλεψυδρίου ἀκροάσει. τὸ
δὲ Κλεψύδριον ὧδε εἶχε· τῶν τοῦ Ἡρώδου ἀκροατῶν
δέκα οἱ ἀρετῆς ἀξιούμενοι ἐπεσιτίζοντο τῇ ἐς πάντας
ἀκροάσει κλεψύδραν ξυμμεμετρημένην ἐς ἑκατὸν ἔπη,
ἃ διῄει ἀποτάδην ὁ Ἡρώδης παρῃτημένος τὸν ἐκ
τῶν ἀκροατῶν ἔπαινον καὶ μόνου γεγονὼς τοῦ λέγειν.
586 παραδεδωκότος δὲ αὐτοῦ τοῖς γνωρίμοις τὸ μηδὲ τὸν
τοῦ πότου καιρὸν ἀνιέναι, ἀλλὰ κἀκεῖ τι ἐπισπουδά-
ζειν τῷ οἴνῳ ξυνέπινε μὲν ὁ Ἀδριανὸς τοῖς ἀπὸ τῆς
κλεψύδρας ὡς κοινωνὸς μεγάλου ἀπορρήτου, λόγου
δὲ αὐτοῖς περὶ τῆς ἑκάστου τῶν σοφιστῶν ἰδέας προ-
βαίνοντος παρελθὼν ἐς μέσους ὁ Ἀδριανός, "ἐγὼ,"
ἔφη, "ὑπογράψω τοὺς χαρακτῆρας οὐ κομματίων ἀπο-
μνημονεύων ἢ νοιδίων ἢ κώλων ἢ ῥυθμῶν, ἀλλ' ἐς
μίμησιν ἐμαυτὸν καθιστὰς καὶ τὰς ἁπάντων ἰδέας
ἀποσχεδιάζων ξὺν εὐροίᾳ καὶ ἐφιεὶς τῇ γλώττῃ."
παραλιπόντος δὲ αὐτοῦ τὸν Ἡρώδην ὁ μὲν Ἀμφικλῆς
ἤρετο τοῦ χάριν τὸν διδάσκαλον αὐτῶν παρέλθοι
αὐτός τε ἐρῶν τῆς ἰδέας ἐκείνους τε ἰδὼν ἐρῶντας,

Athens trained him. As I heard from my own teachers, he came to Athens in the time of Herodes, where he demonstrated great force of talent as a sophist and it was not hard to see that he would come to something great. He began to attend the classes of Herodes when he was about eighteen and was soon considered worthy of the same honor as Sceptus and Amphicles,[105] and was even enrolled in the audience of the Clepsydrion.[106] And the Clepsydrion was conducted as follows. Of the students of Herodes the ten most worthy of a prize for excellence used to dine together, after the lecture that was open to everyone, for a period limited by a water clock timed to last through a hundred verses. Herodes used to expound these verses at great length, and forbade applause from his listeners, and was entirely intent on what he was saying. Because Herodes used to instruct his students not to waste even the time appropriate for drinking, but even then to study something worthwhile, Hadrian used to drink with those who belonged to the water clock as if he were sharing with them in a mystery rite. Once when conversation turned to the style of each of the sophists, Hadrian came forward and said, "I shall sketch their types of style, not by quoting from memory brief phrases or witty sayings or clauses or rhythms, but undertaking myself to imitate them and to improvise the styles of all of them with fluency and giving free rein to my tongue." But because he left out Herodes, Amphicles asked, why he passed over their teacher, since he himself loved Herodes' style and could see that they

586

---

[105] On Sceptus in the circle of Herodes, see above, *VS* 573.

[106] "A lecture timed by the water clock" (*klepsydra*). See above, *VS* 594.

"ὅτι," ἔφη, "οὗτοι μὲν οἷοι καὶ μεθύοντι παραδοῦναι
μίμησιν, Ἡρώδην δὲ τὸν βασιλέα τῶν λόγων ἀγαπη-
τὸν ἦν ἄοινός τε καὶ νήφων ὑποκρίνωμαι." ταῦτα
ἀπαγγελθέντα τῷ Ἡρώδῃ διέχεεν αὐτὸν ἥττω καὶ ἄλλως ὄντα εὐδοξίας. ἐπήγγειλε δὲ τῷ Ἡρώδῃ καὶ
ἀκρόασιν σχεδίου λόγου νεάζων ἔτι, καὶ ὁ Ἡρώδης
οὐχ, ὡς διαβάλλουσί τινες, βασκαίνων τε καὶ τωθά-
ζων, ἀλλ᾿ ἀπὸ τοῦ διακειμένου τε καὶ ἵλεω ἀκροασάμενος ἐπέρρωσε τὸν νεανίαν εἰπὼν ἐπὶ πᾶσι, "κολοσ-
σοῦ ταῦτα μεγάλα σπαράγματ᾿ ἂν εἴη," ἅμα μὲν
διορθούμενος αὐτὸν ὡς ὑφ᾿ ἡλικίας διεσπασμένον τε
καὶ μὴ ξυγκείμενον, ἅμα δὲ ἐπαινῶν ὡς μεγαλόφωνόν
τε καὶ μεγαλογνώμονα. καὶ λόγον τῷ Ἡρώδῃ ἀποθανόντι ἐπεφθέγξατο ἐπάξιον τοῦ ἀνδρός, ὡς ἐς
δάκρυα ἐκκληθῆναι τοὺς Ἀθηναίους ἐν τῇ τοῦ λόγου
ἀκροάσει.

(38) Μεστὸς δὲ οὕτω παρρησίας ἐπὶ τὸν θρόνον
παρῆλθε τὸν Ἀθήνησιν, ὡς προοίμιόν οἱ γενέσθαι τῆς
πρὸς αὐτοὺς διαλέξεως μὴ τὴν ἐκείνων σοφίαν, ἀλλὰ
τὴν ἑαυτοῦ· ἤρξατο γὰρ δὴ ὧδε· "πάλιν ἐκ Φοινίκης
γράμματα." τὸ μὲν δὴ προοίμιον τοῦτο ὑπερπνέοντος
ἦν τοὺς Ἀθηναίους καὶ διδόντος τι αὐτοῖς ἀγαθὸν
μᾶλλον ἢ λαμβάνοντος· μεγαλοπρεπέστατα δὲ τοῦ
Ἀθήνησι θρόνου ἐπεμελήθη, ἐσθῆτα μὲν πλείστου
ἀξίαν ἀμπεχόμενος, ἐξηρτημένος δὲ τὰς θαυμασιω-

587

[107] This plays on the double sense of "letters" (i.e., literature

loved it too. "Because," Hadrian said, "these sophists make it possible even for one who is drunk to imitate them, but as for Herodes, the king of eloquence, I would be delighted if I could act as him even when I have had no wine and am sober." When this was reported to Herodes it melted his heart, because he was always overcome by praise. And when he was still a mere youth Hadrian invited Herodes to listen to an improvised speech, and Herodes did listen, not as some slanderously say, with jealousy and mocking him, but rather he listened with his usual calm and kindly bearing, and he encouraged the young man, saying in conclusion, "These may well be great fragments of a colossus." So while Herodes corrected his fragmentary and ill composed style as an error of youth, he praised him at the same time for his greatness of expression and of thought. When Herodes died, Hadrian delivered a funerary oration fully worthy of the man, so that the Athenians were moved to tears as they listened to the speech.

(38) He was so outspoken that when he ascended to the chair of rhetoric at Athens, the proem of his introductory speech was dedicated not to the wisdom of the Athenians but to his own. He began like this: "Once more, letters have come from Phoenicia."[107] This proem was that of one who breathed on a higher plane than the Athenians and was giving them some benefit rather than receiving anything. He fulfilled the duties of the chair at Athens with the greatest ostentation: he wore the most expensive clothes, decorated himself with the most astonishing jew- 587

and the alphabet itself) and the tradition that writing had come to Greece with Cadmus the Phoenician.

τέρας τῶν λίθων καὶ κατιὼν δὲ ἐπὶ τὰς σπουδὰς ἐπ᾽
ἀργυροχαλίνου ὀχήματος, ἐπεὶ δὲ σπουδάσειε, ζηλω-
τὸς αὖ ἐπανιὼν ξὺν πομπῇ τοῦ πανταχόθεν Ἑλληνικοῦ. ἤδη[26] γὰρ ἐθεράπευον αὐτὸν ὥσπερ τὰ γένη τῆς
Ἐλευσῖνος ἱεροφάντην λαμπρῶς ἱερουργοῦντα. ὑπ-
εποιεῖτο δὲ αὐτοὺς καὶ παιδιαῖς καὶ πότοις καὶ θήραις
καὶ κοινωνίᾳ πανηγύρεων Ἑλληνικῶν, ἄλλα ἄλλῳ
ξυννεάζων, ὅθεν διέκειντο πρὸς αὐτὸν ὡς πρὸς πατέρα
παῖδες ἡδύν τε καὶ πρᾷον καὶ ξυνδιαφέροντα αὐτοῖς
τὸ Ἑλληνικὸν σκίρτημα. ἐγώ τοι καὶ δακρύοντας
αὐτῶν ἐνίους οἶδα, ὁπότε ἐς μνήμην τοῦ ἀνδρὸς
τούτου καθίσταιντο, καὶ τοὺς μὲν τὸ φθέγμα ὑποκο-
ριζομένους, τοὺς δὲ τὸ βάδισμα, τοὺς δὲ τὸ εὔσχημον
τῆς στολῆς.

(39) Ἐπαχθεῖσαν δὲ αὐτῷ καὶ φονικὴν αἰτίαν ὧδε
ἀπέφυγεν· ἦν Ἀθήνησιν ἀνθρώπιον οὐκ ἀγύμναστον
τοῦ περὶ τοὺς σοφιστὰς δρόμου· τούτῳ ἀμφορέα μέν
τις οἴνου προσάγων ἢ ὄψα ἢ ἐσθῆτα ἢ ἀργύριον εὐ-
μεταχειρίστῳ ἐχρῆτο καθάπερ οἱ τὰ πεινῶντα τῶν
θρεμμάτων τῷ θαλλῷ ἄγοντες, εἰ δὲ ἀμελοῖτο, φιλο-
λοιδόρως εἶχε καὶ ὑλάκτει. τῷ μὲν οὖν Ἀδριανῷ προσ-
εκεκρούκει διὰ τὴν εὐχέρειαν τοῦ ἤθους, Χρῆστον δὲ
τὸν ἐκ Βυζαντίου σοφιστὴν ἐθεράπευε, καὶ ὁ μὲν
Ἀδριανὸς ἐκαρτέρει τὰ ἐξ αὐτοῦ πάντα, δήγματα

588

---

[26] ἤδη Jahn; οἴδε ω

els, and he went to his lectures in a carriage with silver bridles. When he had finished speaking, he would go home a figure of envy, accompanied by the Hellenes from everywhere. In fact they revered him as the tribes of Eleusis revere the hierophant when he is magnificently performing the rites. And he used to win them over with games and drinking parties and hunts, and by taking part with them in the Hellenic festivals, sharing different youthful pursuits with each one, so that they related to him as if to a father, who is kind and gentle, and keeps up with them in vigorous, Hellenic dancing. I know some of them who weep even now when they remember this man, and some who try to imitate his voice, some his walk, some the stylishness of his dress.

(39) When a charge of murder was brought against him, he escaped it in the following way. There was a little man in Athens who had some experience of the curriculum of the sophists. One could keep him happy by bringing him a jar of wine or some food or clothing or silver, just as people lead hungry animals by waving branches.[108] But if he was neglected, he became abusive and started barking. He had clashed with Hadrian because of the looseness of his character, but he used to flatter Chrestus the sophist from Byzantium. Hadrian patiently endured everything

588

---

[108] An echo of Pl. *Phd.* 230d. Socrates says that Phaedrus has enticed him into the country by the promise of hearing a discourse, just as men wave branches to entice hungry animals to follow them. The *Phaedrus* was a popular dialogue among nonspecialist readers of Plato in the Roman era and appears, for instance, as an important point of intertextual reference in the opening chapters of Philostratus' *Heroicus*. See Hodkinson 2011.

κόρεων τὰς ἐκ τῶν τοιούτων λοιδορίας καλῶν, οἱ γνώριμοι δὲ οὐκ ἐνεγκόντες παρεκελεύσαντο τοῖς ἑαυτῶν
οἰκέταις παίειν αὐτόν, καὶ ἀνοιδησάντων αὐτῷ τῶν
σπλάγχνων ἐν ἡμέρᾳ τριακοστῇ ἀπέθανε παρασχών
τινα καὶ αὐτὸς τῷ θανάτῳ λόγον, ἐπειδὴ ἀκράτου νοσῶν ἔσπασεν. οἱ δὲ προσήκοντες τῷ τεθνεῶτι γράφονται τὸν σοφιστὴν φόνου παρὰ τῷ τῆς Ἑλλάδος ἄρ-
χοντι ὡς ἕνα Ἀθηναίων, ἐπειδὴ φυλή τε ἦν αὐτῷ καὶ
δῆμος Ἀθήνησιν, ὁ δὲ ἀπέγνω τὴν αἰτίαν ὡς μήτε
ταῖς ἑαυτοῦ χερσὶ μήτε ταῖς τῶν ἑαυτοῦ δούλων τετυ-
πτηκότος τὸν τεθνάναι λεγόμενον. ξυνήρατο δὲ αὐτῷ
τῆς ἀπολογίας πρῶτα μὲν τὸ Ἑλληνικὸν τίνας οὐχὶ
ἀφιέντες ὑπὲρ αὐτοῦ φωνὰς δακρύοις ἅμα, ἔπειτα ἡ
ἐπὶ τῷ οἴνῳ τοῦ ἰατροῦ μαρτυρία.

(40) Κατὰ δὲ τοὺς χρόνους, οὓς ὁ αὐτοκράτωρ Μᾶρκος Ἀθήναζε ὑπὲρ μυστηρίων ἐστάλη, ἐκράτει μὲν
ἤδη τοῦ τῶν σοφιστῶν θρόνου ὁ ἀνὴρ οὗτος, ἐν μέρει
δὲ ὁ Μᾶρκος τῆς τῶν Ἀθηνῶν ἱστορίας ἔθετο μηδὲ
τὴν ἐκείνου σοφίαν ἀγνοῆσαι· καὶ γὰρ δὴ καὶ ἐπέτα-
ξεν αὐτὸν τοῖς νέοις οὐκ ἀκροάσει βασανίσας, ἀλλὰ
ξυνθέμενος τῇ περὶ αὐτοῦ φήμῃ. Σεουήρου δὲ ἀνδρὸς
ὑπάτου διαβάλλοντος αὐτὸν ὡς τὰς σοφιστικὰς ὑποθέσεις ἐκβακχεύοντα διὰ τὸ ἐρρῶσθαι πρὸς τοὺς
ἀγῶνας, ἔλεγχον τούτου ποιούμενος ὁ Μᾶρκος προὔ-
βαλε μὲν αὐτῷ τὸν Ὑπερείδην τὸν ἐς μόνας ἐπιστρέ-

---

109 An echo of Dem. *De cor.* 195.
110 See above, VS 563.

from him, and used to refer to insults from that kind of man as flea bites. But his students took offense and commanded their own slaves to beat him, and the man developed a swelling of the intestines and died after thirty days. He contributed something to his own death, because he drank unmixed wine during his illness. The relatives of the dead man brought a case for murder against the sophist, before the proconsul of all of Greece, on the grounds that Hadrian was an Athenian, since both his tribe and his deme were at Athens. Hadrian, however, denied the charge on the grounds that neither by his own hands nor by those of his own slaves had the man been struck who was said to have died. His defense was assisted, firstly by the crowd of Hellenes who omitted no possible argument,[109] weeping as they spoke, and secondly by the evidence of the doctor about the wine.

(40) At the time when the emperor Marcus traveled to Athens to be initiated in the mysteries,[110] this man was already ruling over the chair of rhetoric, and one of the things that Marcus wanted to inquire into in Athens was that man's skill. For he had appointed him to educate the youth without having put him to the test by hearing him, but by depending on the reputation surrounding him. One Severus, a man of consular rank,[111] was slandering him, saying that he raved like a bacchant in his sophistic themes because of his strength in forensic oratory. Marcus put this to the test by setting him the theme "Hypereides, when

111 This was probably Claudius Severus, the teacher of Marcus Aurelius, who was consul for the second time in 173. For an inscription in which Hadrian honors Severus in elegiacs, cf. Groag 1879.

589 φοντα τὰς Δημοσθένους γνώμας, ὅτε δὴ ἐν Ἐλατείᾳ
Φίλιππος ἦν· ὁ δὲ οὕτως τὸν ἀγῶνα εὐηνίως διέθετο,
ὡς μηδὲ τοῦ Πολέμωνος ῥοίζου λείπεσθαι δόξαι. ἀγασθεὶς δὲ αὐτὸν ὁ αὐτοκράτωρ ἐπὶ μέγα ἦρε δωρεαῖς
τε καὶ δώροις· καλῶ δὲ δωρεὰς μὲν τάς τε σιτήσεις
καὶ τὰς προεδρίας καὶ τὰς ἀτελείας καὶ τὸ ἱερᾶσθαι
καὶ ὅσα ἄλλα λαμπρύνει ἄνδρας, δῶρα δὲ χρυσὸν
ἄργυρον ἵππους ἀνδράποδα καὶ ὅσα ἑρμηνεύει πλοῦτον, ὧν αὐτόν τε ἐνέπλησε καὶ γένος τὸ ἐκείνου πάντας.

(41) Κατασχὼν δὲ καὶ τὸν ἄνω θρόνον οὕτως τὴν
Ῥώμην πρὸς αὐτὸν[27] ἐπέστρεψεν, ὡς καὶ τοῖς ἀξυ-
νέτοις γλώττης Ἑλλάδος ἔρωτα παρασχεῖν ἀκροάσεως. ἠκροῶντο δὲ ὥσπερ εὐστομούσης ἀηδόνος, τὴν
εὐγλωττίαν ἐκπεπληγμένοι καὶ τὸ σχῆμα καὶ τὸ εὔ-
στροφον τοῦ φθέγματος καὶ τοὺς πεζῇ τε καὶ ξὺν ᾠδῇ
ῥυθμούς. ὁπότε οὖν σπουδάζοιεν περὶ τὰς ἐγκυκλίους
θέας, ὀρχηστῶν δὲ αὗται τὸ ἐπίπαν, φανέντος ἂν περὶ
τὴν σκηνὴν τοῦ τῆς ἀκροάσεως ἀγγέλου ἐξανίσταντο
μὲν οἱ ἀπὸ τῆς συγκλήτου βουλῆς, ἐξανίσταντο δὲ
τῶν δημοσίᾳ ἱππευόντων οὐχ οἱ τὰ Ἑλλήνων σπου-

[27] There is some confusion in this phrase in the MSS, though
it does not substantially affect the meaning. I have adopted the
suggestion of Stefec.

[112] A similar theme is mentioned by Apsines 219; it has no
historical basis. Cf. Dem. *De cor.* 169–79.

Philip is at Elateia, listens to the advice only of Demosthenes."[112] Hadrian handled the argument on such a skillful   589
rein that he seemed to equal the rushing force of Polemo.
The emperor was amazed by him, and elevated him greatly
with grants and gifts. And by grants I mean the right to
dine at the expense of the state, a seat of honor, exemption
from taxes, priestly offices, and everything that shines a
light on men. By gifts I mean gold, silver, horses, slaves
and everything that reveals wealth, with which he lavishly
endowed Hadrian and all of his family.

(41) When he attained the higher chair,[113] he so successfully drew the attention of Rome to himself, that he
inspired a desire to hear him even in those who were ignorant of the Greek language. They listened to him like
a sweet-voiced nightingale,[114] overwhelmed by his eloquence and appearance and the flexibility of his voice and
rhythms of his prose passages and in song.[115] So whenever
they were intent on common spectacles—and these were
for the most part dance performances—if a messenger
appeared around the stage and announced that Hadrian
was going to declaim, even the members of the senate
would get up and leave, and those of the equestrian order
would get up too, and not only those who studied Greek

---

[113] This phrase always means the chair at Rome.

[114] An echo of Soph. *OC* 18. The association of the nightingale
with the Attic landscape (cf. Philostr. *Her.* 5.4) suggests the Attic
nature of Hadrian's eloquence.   [115] This is the $\dot{\omega}\delta\dot{\eta}$ (song).
Philostratus' description of the style and effect of Favorinus is
very similar (*VS* 491–92). He too was able to make an impression
even on those who did not speak Greek, in large part because of
this sung component of his performance.

δάζοντες μόνον, ἀλλὰ καὶ ὁπόσοι τὴν ἑτέραν γλῶτταν
ἐπαιδεύοντο ἐν τῇ Ῥώμῃ καὶ δρόμῳ ἐχώρουν ἐς τὸ
Ἀθήναιον ὁρμῆς μεστοὶ καὶ τοὺς βάδην πορευομέ-
νους κακίζοντες.

(42) Νοσοῦντι δὲ αὐτῷ κατὰ τὴν Ῥώμην, ὅτε δὴ
590 καὶ ἐτελεύτα, ἐψηφίσατο μὲν τὰς ἐπιστολὰς ὁ Κόμμο-
δος ξὺν ἀπολογίᾳ τοῦ μὴ καὶ θᾶττον, ὁ δὲ ἐπιθειάσας
μὲν ταῖς Μούσαις, ὥσπερ εἰώθει, προσκυνήσας δὲ τὰς
βασιλείους δέλτους τὴν ψυχὴν πρὸς αὐταῖς ἀφῆκεν
ἐνταφίῳ τῇ τιμῇ χρησάμενος· ἐτελεύτα δὲ ἀμφὶ τὰ
ὀγδοήκοντα ἔτη, οὕτω τι εὐδόκιμος, ὡς καὶ πολλοῖς
γόης δόξαι. ὅτι μὲν οὖν ἀνὴρ οὐκ ἄν ποτε πεπαιδευμένος ἐς γοήτων ὑπαχθείη τέχνας, ἱκανῶς ἐν τοῖς
ὑπὲρ Διονυσίου λόγοις εἴρηκα· ὁ δέ, οἶμαι, τερατευό-
μενος ἐν ταῖς ὑποθέσεσι περὶ τὰ τῶν μάγων ἤθη τὴν
ἐπωνυμίαν ταύτην παρ' αὐτοῖς ἔσπασε. διαβάλλουσι
δὲ αὐτὸν ὡς καὶ ἀναιδῆ τὸ ἦθος· πέμψαι μὲν γὰρ
αὐτῷ τινα τῶν γνωρίμων ἰχθῦς διακειμένους ἐπὶ δί-
σκου ἀργυροῦ πεποικιλμένου χρυσῷ, τὸν δὲ ὑπερησθέντα τῷ δίσκῳ μήτε ἀποδοῦναι καὶ ἀποκρίνασθαι
τῷ πέμψαντι, "εὖγε, ὅτι καὶ τοὺς ἰχθῦς." τουτὶ δὲ δια-

---

116 This is, of course, Latin. There is more than a hint of con-
descension in Philostratus' reference to the "other language."

117 The Athenaeum at Rome was a school founded by the
emperor Hadrian.

118 See above, VS 523–24. In Dionysius' case the suspicion of
magic was aroused due to his astonishing memory, whereas in the
case of Hadrian it appears due rather to the extraordinary force

culture, but even those who were being educated in the other language in Rome.[116] And they went at a run to the Athenaeum,[117] full of enthusiasm and shouting abuse at those who went at a walking pace.

(42) When he was ill at Rome, and was in fact dying, Commodus appointed him *ab epistulis Graecis*, with apologies for not doing so sooner. Then Hadrian invoked the Muses, as he was accustomed, and prostrated himself before the emperor's message, and exhaled his dying breath on it, so making the honor his shroud. He died at around eighty, held in such high esteem that to many he seemed a magician. But I have already said in my account of Dionysius[118] that an educated man would never allow himself to be misled into the arts of magicians. But he, I think, because he told astonishing tales in his orations about the customs of the *magi*[119] brought on himself a name for this with his hearers. They slander him too by saying that he was disrespectful in character. For instance when one of his students sent him some fish on a silver plate artfully decorated with gold, he was delighted with the plate and did not give it back and acknowledging the present to the sender he said, "It was kind of you to send the fish as well."

590

of his rhetorical performances, especially on topics concerning the *magi*.

119 Though the suspicion reported here is that Hadrian was a sorcerer/magician (γόης), the source of it is due rather to his declamations about μάγοι. Though μάγος can be synonymous with γόης, it can also retain its original sense of a Persian priest. See, for instance, Apollonius' visit to them at *VA* 1.25. The only surviving speech by Hadrian presents the case against a witch who has burned another witch out of professional jealousy.

τριβῆς μὲν ἕνεκα παῖξαι λέγεται πρός τινα τῶν ἑαυτοῦ γνωρίμων, ὃν ἤκουε μικροπρεπῶς τῷ πλούτῳ
χρώμενον, τὸν δὲ ἄργυρον ἀποδοῦναι σωφρονίσας
τὸν ἀκροατὴν τῷ ἀστεϊσμῷ.

(43) Ὁ δὲ σοφιστὴς οὗτος πολὺς μὲν περὶ τὰς ἐννοίας καὶ λαμπρὸς καὶ τὰς διασκευὰς τῶν ὑποθέσεων
ποικιλώτατος ἐκ τῆς τραγῳδίας τοῦτο ᾑρηκώς, οὐ μὴν
τεταγμένος γε οὐδὲ τῇ τέχνῃ ἑπόμενος, τὴν δὲ παρα-
σκευὴν τῆς λέξεως ἀπὸ τῶν ἀρχαίων σοφιστῶν περιεβάλλετο ἤχῳ προάγων[28] μᾶλλον ἢ κρότῳ. πολλαχοῦ
δὲ τῆς μεγαλοφωνίας ἐξέπεσεν ἀταμιεύτως τῇ τραγῳδίᾳ χρησάμενος.

(44) 11. ιαʹ. Τὸν δὲ Βυζάντιον σοφιστὴν Χρῆστον
ἀδικεῖ ἡ Ἑλλὰς ἀμελοῦντες ἀνδρός, ὃς ἄριστα μὲν
591 Ἑλλήνων ὑπὸ Ἡρώδου ἐπαιδεύθη, πολλοὺς δὲ ἐπαίδευσε καὶ θαυμασίους ἄνδρας, ὧν ἐγένετο Ἱππόδρο-
μός τε ὁ σοφιστὴς καὶ Φιλίσκος καὶ Ἰσαγόρας ὁ τῆς
τραγῳδίας ποιητὴς ῥήτορές τε εὐδόκιμοι Νικομήδης
ὁ ἐκ τοῦ Περγάμου καὶ Ἀκύλας ὁ ἐκ τῆς ἑῴου Γαλατίας καὶ Ἀρισταίνετος ὁ Βυζάντιος καὶ τῶν ἐλλογίμως
φιλοσοφησάντων Κάλλαισχρός τε ὁ Ἀθηναῖος καὶ ὁ
ἐπὶ βωμῷ Σῶσπις καὶ πλείους ἕτεροι λόγου ἄξιοι.
παιδεύοντι δὲ αὐτῷ κατὰ τοὺς Ἀδριανοῦ τοῦ σοφιστοῦ
καιροὺς ἑκατὸν ἔμμισθοι ἀκροαταὶ ἦσαν καὶ ἄριστοι

---

[28] προάγων Schmid; προσάγων ω

---

[120] In the case of both Chrestus and Marcus of Byzantium (see
VS 527–31), the only two sophists of Byzantine origin in the text,

But he is said to have done this as an instructive joke to one of his students, whom he had heard was using his wealth stingily, but that he gave back the silver when he had taught his student a lesson with this witticism.

(43) This sophist was rich in ideas and brilliant and showed the greatest variety in his handling of his themes, taking this skill from his study of tragedy. He did not in fact employ conventional arrangement nor follow the rules of the art, but he clothed his style with diction drawn from the ancient sophists, speaking with sonorousness rather than effects of sound. But he sometimes fell short of grandeur of style, because he employed tragedy too liberally.

(44) 11. The Greeks do an injustice to the Byzantine sophist Chrestus[120] when they neglect the man, who was the best educated by Herodes of all the Hellenes, and who educated in turn many astonishing men. Among these were Hippodromus the sophist and Philiscus and Isagoras the tragic poet, and eminent rhetoricians, namely Nicomedes of Pergamum and Aquila from eastern Galatia and Aristaenetus of Byzantium, and among those who practiced philosophy most brilliantly there was Callaeschrus the Athenian and Sospis who was a priest at the altar,[121] and many others worthy of mention. He taught in the time of the sophist Hadrian, and had a hundred fee-paying students, the best of whom were those I men-

591

Philostratus complains that the sophist's reputation was neglected, as Bowersock observed, perhaps in the aftermath of Septimius Severus' siege of the city: Bowersock 1969, 19–20.

[121] He was priest at the sacrifices, perhaps at the public games.

τούτων, οὓς εἶπον. Ἀδριανοῦ δὲ καθιδρυθέντος ἐς τὴν
Ῥώμην ἐψηφίζοντο μὲν οἱ Ἀθηναῖοι πρεσβεύσασθαι
ὑπὲρ Χρήστου τὸν Ἀθήνησιν αὐτῷ θρόνον ἐκ βασιλέως αἰτοῦντες, ὁ δὲ παρελθὼν ἐς αὐτοὺς ἐκκλησιάζον-
τας διέλυσε τὴν πρέσβευσιν ἄλλα τε διαλεχθεὶς ἀξιό-
λογα καὶ ἐπὶ πᾶσιν εἰπών, "οὐχ αἱ μύριαι τὸν ἄνδρα."

(45) Οἴνου δὲ ἡττώμενος παροινίας ἐκράτει καὶ εὐ-
χερείας καὶ ἀγερωχίας, ἣν ὁ οἶνος ἐπὶ τὰς γνώμας
τῶν ἀνθρώπων ἄγει· τοσοῦτον δὲ αὐτῷ περιῆν τοῦ
νήφειν, ὡς καὶ ἐς ἀλεκτρυόνων ᾠδὰς προβάντος τοῦ
πότου σπουδῆς αὐτὸν ἅπτεσθαι, πρὶν ὕπνου σπάσαι.
διεβέβλητο δὲ μάλιστα πρὸς τοὺς ἀλαζόνας τῶν νέων
καίτοι χρησιμωτέρους τῶν ἄλλων ὄντας ἐς τὰς ξυμ-
592 βολὰς τοῦ μισθοῦ. Διογένη γοῦν τὸν Ἀμαστριανὸν
ὁρῶν τετυφωμένον ἐκ μειρακίου καὶ περινοοῦντα μὲν
σατραπείας, περινοοῦντα δὲ αὐλὰς καὶ τὸ ἀγχοῦ βασιλέων ἑστήξειν, λέγοντα δέ, ὡς ὁ δεῖνα Αἰγύπτιος
προειρήκοι αὐτῷ ταῦτα, †ὁ <. . .> μηδὲ τὰ ἑαυτοῦ
σιωπῶν.†[29]

(46) Τὴν δὲ ἰδέαν τῶν λόγων πεποίκιλται μὲν ἐκ
τῶν Ἡρώδου πλεονεκτημάτων, λείπεται δὲ αὐτῶν τοῦ
ἑτοίμου, καθάπερ ἐν ζωγραφίᾳ ἡ ἄνευ χρωμάτων
ἐσκιαγραφημένη μίμησις· προὔβη δὲ ἂν καὶ ἐς τὸ
ἴσον τῆς ἀρετῆς, εἰ μὴ πεντηκοντούτης ἀπέθανεν.

[29] I have followed Stefec's prudent choice in obelizing; see his
edition for the conjectures of Reiske and Morel.

tioned. After Hadrian took the chair at Rome, the Athenians voted to send an embassy on behalf of Chrestus asking for him from the emperor the chair at Athens.[122] But he came before them when they were holding the assembly and broke up the embassy. And he said many other things worth remembering and in concluding said, "The ten thousand drachmas do not make the man."[123]

(45) He was addicted to wine, but kept under control the drunken insolence and recklessness and arrogance that wine puts into people's minds. So great was his ability to keep sober, that even when his drinking went on till the roosters crowed, he would begin his study before he had snatched any sleep. He was especially obnoxious to pretentious youths, even though they are much more profitable than the rest for the payment of fees. For instance he saw that Diogenes of Amastris was puffed up with pride from his youth and always thinking about satrapies, thinking about courts and being close to emperors, and what is more he said that a certain Egyptian had foretold all this to him, he . . . did not keep silence about his own story.

592

(46) He achieved a varied style of speaking, drawing upon the excellent qualities of Herodes, but he fell short of them, just as in painting a likeness falls short that is merely done in outline without colors.[124] But he would have reached an equal level of excellence, if he had not died at fifty.

[122] On the timing of this embassy on Chrestus' behalf, see Avotins 1975, 320–21.   [123] This was the salary of the chair.
[124] Possibly a distant echo of Pl. *Plt.* 277c. Philostratus has Apollonius discuss the possibilities and limitations of representations with and without color at *VA* 2.22.4.

PHILOSTRATUS

(47) 12. ιβ′. Πολυδεύκη δὲ τὸν Ναυκρατίτην οὐκ οἶδα, εἴτε ἀπαίδευτον δεῖ καλεῖν εἴτε πεπαιδευμένον, εἴθ᾽, ὅπερ εὔηθες δόξει, καὶ ἀπαίδευτον καὶ πεπαιδευμένον· ἐνθυμουμένῳ γὰρ αὐτοῦ τὰ ὀνόματα ἱκανῶς ἐγεγύμναστο τὴν γλῶτταν τῆς ἀττικιζούσης λέξεως, διορῶντι δὲ τὸ ἐν ταῖς μελέταις εἶδος οὐδὲν βέλτιον ἑτέρου ἡττίκισε. τάδε οὖν χρὴ περὶ αὐτοῦ εἰδέναι· Πολυδεύκης τὰ μὲν κριτικὰ ἱκανῶς ἤσκητο, πατρὶ ξυγγενόμενος τοὺς κριτικοὺς λόγους εἰδότι, τοῖς δὲ σοφιστικοῖς τόλμῃ μᾶλλον ἢ τέχνῃ ξυνέβαλε θαρρήσας τῇ φύσει, καὶ γὰρ δὴ καὶ ἄριστα ἐπεφύκει. Ἀδριανοῦ δὲ ἀκροατὴς γενόμενος ἴσον ἀφέστηκεν αὐτοῦ καὶ τῶν πλεονεκτημάτων καὶ τῶν ἐλαττωμάτων, ἥκιστα μὲν γὰρ πίπτει, ἥκιστα δὲ αἴρεται, πλὴν ἀλλ᾽ εἰσί τινες ἡδονῶν λιβάδες διακεκραμέναι τοῦ λόγου. ἰδέα δὲ αὐτοῦ διαλεγομένου μὲν ὧδε· "ὁ Πρωτεὺς ὁ Φάριος, τὸ θαῦμα τὸ Ὁμηρικόν, πολλαὶ μὲν αὐτοῦ καὶ πολυειδεῖς αἱ μορφαί, καὶ γὰρ ἐς ὕδωρ αἴρεται καὶ ἐς πῦρ ἅπτεται καὶ ἐς λέοντα θυμοῦται καὶ ἐς σῦν ὁρμᾷ καὶ ἐς δράκοντα χωρεῖ καὶ ἐς πάρδαλιν ἄττει καὶ δένδρον ἦν γένηται, κομᾷ." μελετῶντος δὲ αὐτοῦ χαρακτῆρα ποιώμεθα τοὺς νησιώτας τοὺς τὰ γένη πιπράσκοντας ἐς τὴν ἀπαγωγὴν τῶν φόρων, ἐπειδὴ βούλονται καὶ

593

---

[125] Naucratis produced several noted sophists in the second half of the second century, as Bowersock observed, "for reasons that are obscure" (1969, 20). In addition to Polydeuces: Ptolemy (VS 596), Apollonius (VS 599), Proclus (VS 603). All left Naucratis to pursue their careers elsewhere.

284

(47) 12. I do not know about Polydeuces of Naucratis,[125] whether one should call him uneducated or educated, or whether, ridiculous as it seems, he was both uneducated and educated. When one considers his individual words, it is clear that he had been sufficiently trained at speaking in Atticizing discourse, but when one examines closely the structure in his declamations, he Atticizes no better than the average. The following facts are what one ought to know about him. Polydeuces was sufficiently well trained in criticism, because he studied with his father, who was an expert in critical discourse. But he took part in sophistic activity employing audacity more than training, taking courage from his natural ability, and in fact he was highly talented. He was a student of Hadrian, and stood midway between his strengths and weaknesses, because he very rarely fell short, but very rarely soared, except that there are some rivulets of pleasure running through his speech. His style of speaking was as follows: "Proteus of Pharos, that marvel of Homer,[126] becomes 593 many and multiform shapes, for he rises up into water, kindles into fire, rages into a lion, surges into a boar, crawls into a serpent, leaps into a leopard, and as a tree, when he becomes one, lets down his leaves." So that we can demonstrate his characteristic style in declamation, let me

[126] Hom. *Od.* 4.439–70. It is probable that Polydeuces used Proteus as a paradigm of sophistic versatility (*poikilia*). The sea god is certainly used this way in two orations of Himerius (*Or.* 31.73–75, 68.63ff.). He is also, in a somewhat different way, the mythic paradigm of Apollonius of Tyana (*VA* 1.4). See Miles 2016.

PHILOSTRATUS

ἄριστα εἰρῆσθαι τήνδε τὴν ὑπόθεσιν, ἧς τὸ ἐπὶ πᾶσιν
ὧδε εἴρηται· "παῖς ἠπειρώτης ἀπὸ Βαβυλῶνος πατρὶ
νησιώτῃ γράφει· δουλεύω βασιλεῖ δῶρον ἐκ σατρά-
που δοθείς, οὔτε δὲ ἵππον ἀναβαίνω Μηδικὸν οὔτε
τόξον λαμβάνω Περσικόν, ἀλλ᾿ οὐδὲ ἐπὶ πόλεμον ἢ
θήραν, ὡς ἀνήρ, ἐξέρχομαι, ἐν γυναικωνίτιδι δὲ κάθη-
μαι καὶ τὰς βασιλέως θεραπεύω παλλακάς, καὶ βασιλεὺς οὐκ ὀργίζεται, εὐνοῦχος γάρ εἰμι. εὐδοκιμῶ δὲ
παρ᾿ αὐταῖς θάλατταν Ἑλληνικὴν διηγούμενος καὶ τὰ
τῶν Ἑλλήνων μυθολογῶν καλά, πῶς Ἠλεῖοι πανηγυ-
ρίζουσι, πῶς Δελφοὶ θεσπίζουσι, τίς ὁ παρ᾿ Ἀθηναίοις Ἐλέου βωμός. ἀλλὰ καὶ σύ, πάτερ, μοι γράφε,
πότε παρὰ Λακεδαιμονίοις Ὑακίνθια καὶ παρὰ Κοριν-
θίοις Ἴσθμια καὶ παρὰ Δελφοῖς Πύθια καὶ εἰ νικῶσιν
Ἀθηναῖοι ναυμαχοῦντες. ἔρρωσο καὶ τὸν ἀδελφόν μοι
προσαγόρευσον, εἰ μήπω πέπραται." ταῦτα μὲν δὴ
ὁποῖα τοῦ ἀνδρὸς τούτου σκοπεῖν ἔξεστι τοῖς ἀδεκά-
στως ἀκροωμένοις. ἀδεκάστους δὲ ἀκροατὰς καλῶ
τοὺς μήτε εὔνους μήτε δύσνους. ἐλέγετο δὲ ταῦτα καὶ
μελιχρᾷ τῇ φωνῇ ἀπαγγέλλειν, ᾗ καὶ βασιλέα Κόμ-
μοδον θέλξας τὸν Ἀθήνησι θρόνον παρ᾿ αὐτοῦ εὕρατο.
ἐβίω μὲν οὖν ἐς ὀκτὼ καὶ πεντήκοντα ἔτη, ἐτελεύτα δὲ
ἐπὶ παιδὶ γνησίῳ μέν, ἀπαιδεύτῳ δέ.

(48) 13. ιγ΄. Καισάρεια δὲ ἡ Καππαδοκῶν ὄρει Ἀρ-

---

[127] The figure of the eunuch appealed to rhetoricians as well
as to the writers of the ancient novels. Philostratus also develops

quote the theme, "The islanders sell their children to pay their taxes": "A child now in Asia writes from Babylon to his father who is an islander: I am a slave for the king, since I was given as a gift by a satrap. I do not mount a Median horse nor take up a Persian bow, nor do I go out to war or to hunt like a man, but I sit in the women's quarters and serve the king's concubines, and the king is not angry, because I am a eunuch. And I win a fine reputation with them by telling them of the sea of Greece and recounting tales of the fine deeds of the Greeks—how the Eleans hold their festival, how the Delphians provide oracles, what is the altar of pity among the Athenians. But please, father, write to tell me when the Lacedaemonians celebrate the Hyacinthia, when the Corinthians celebrate the Isthmian games and when do the Delphians celebrate the Pythian games, and are the Athenians victorious in their naval battles? Farewell, and greet my brother for me, if he has not yet been sold."[127] So from this one speech impartial listeners can see what the man was like. I call impartial those listeners who are prejudiced neither for nor against. He is said to have declaimed these things in a mellifluous voice, with which he bewitched even the emperor Commodus so that he won from him the chair at Athens. He lived to the age of fifty-eight, and died leaving a son who was legitimate but uneducated.

(48) 13. Caesarea in Cappadocia, near mount Argaeus,

an incident involving a eunuch at some length in the *VA* (1.33–37). The prospect of losing Hellenic culture when transported to a foreign land is also contemplated at *VA* 1.23–24, on which see Penella 1974.

γαίῳ πρόσοικος Παυσανίου τοῦ σοφιστοῦ οἶκος. ὁ δὲ
594 Παυσανίας ἐπαιδεύθη μὲν ὑπὸ Ἡρώδου καὶ τῶν τοῦ
Κλεψυδρίου μετεχόντων εἷς ἐγένετο, οὓς ἐκάλουν οἱ
πολλοὶ διψῶντας, ἐς πολλὰ δὲ ἀναφέρων τῶν Ἡρώδου
πλεονεκτημάτων καὶ μάλιστα τὸ αὐτοσχεδιάζειν· ἀπ-
ήγγελλε δὲ αὐτὰ παχείᾳ τῇ γλώττῃ καὶ ὡς Καππα-
δόκαις ξύνηθες, ξυγκρούων μὲν τὰ σύμφωνα τῶν
στοιχείων, συστέλλων δὲ τὰ μηχυνόμενα καὶ μη-
χύνων τὰ βραχέα, ὅθεν ἐκάλουν αὐτὸν οἱ πολλοὶ μά-
γειρον πολυτελῆ ὄψα πονήρως ἀρτύοντα. ἡ δὲ ἰδέα
τῆς μελέτης³⁰ ὑπτιωτέρα, ἔρρωται δὲ ὅμως καὶ οὐχ
ἁμαρτάνει τοῦ ἀρχαίου, ὡς ὑπάρχει ταῖς μελέταις
ξυμβαλεῖν· πολλαὶ γὰρ τοῦ Παυσανίου κατὰ τὴν Ῥώμην, οὗ δὴ καταβιοὺς ἀπέθανε γηράσκων ἤδη †καὶ
μετέχων δὲ καὶ τοῦ Ἀθήνησιν†³¹ ὅτε δὴ καὶ ἀπιὼν
ἐκεῖθεν ἐπὶ πᾶσιν, οἷς πρὸς τοὺς Ἀθηναίους διεξῆλθε,
καιριώτατα τὸ τοῦ Εὐριπίδου ἐπεφθέγξατο,

Θησεῦ, πάλιν με στρέψον, ὡς ἴδω πόλιν.

³⁰ τῆς μελέτης is the addition of Schröder.
³¹ Something has clearly gone wrong with the text here.
Reiske proposed a lacuna after Ἀθήνησιν; Kayser suggested τοῦ
θρόνου μετέχων καὶ μετεῖχε δὲ καὶ τοῦ Ἀθήνησιν. Something
like this must have stood here, as the end of Philostratus' account
relates Pausanias' words when vacating the Athenian chair.

¹²⁸ There is no certain identification of this sophist with the
travel writer Pausanias or the lexicographer, who was the author
of an Atticizing lexicon. If this Pausanias were the latter figure,
this *bios* would continue the theme of sophists who were also

was the home of Pausanias the sophist.[128] Pausanias was   594
educated by Herodes and was one of those who belonged
to the Clepsydrion, whom common people used to call
"the thirsty ones."[129] He largely carried on the strengths
of Herodes' style, especially in improvisation. But he declaimed these things with a thick accent, as is typical for
Cappadocians.[130] He used to clash together the sounds of
his syllables, and shortened the long syllables and lengthened the short ones, so that most people called him a cook
who spoiled expensive foods with bad preparation. His
style in declamation was somewhat sluggish, but nevertheless had force, and he did not fall short of the ancient tone,
as one may see from his extant declamations. There are
many of these that Pausanias gave at Rome, where he grew
old and died, having also held the chair at Athens. And
when he was vacating the chair, he concluded the speech
that he gave to the Athenians by quoting very aptly the line
from Euripides:

> Turn me around, Theseus, so that I may see the
>   city.[131]

lexicographers from the life of Polydeuces immediately before it,
though in neither case is this aspect of the sophist's work discussed.

[129] For the Clepsydrion, see above, *VS* 585–86. By giving the
nickname "thirsty ones" (διψῶντες) to the members of the *klepsy-
dria*, these "common people" (οἱ πολλοί) seem to suggest that
Herodes' inner circle was merely a pretentious drinking party.

[130] Lucian, *Epigram* 43, says that it would be easier to find
white crows and flying tortoises than a Cappadocian who was a
reputable orator. For the bad accent of the Cappadocians, cf. *VA*
1.7.   [131] Eur. *HF* 1406. Pausanias substituted "city" for the
"children" of the original.

(49) 14. ιδ΄. Ἀθηνόδωρος δὲ ὁ σοφιστὴς τὸ μὲν ἐς
πατέρας ἧκον ἐπιφανέστατος ἦν τῶν κατὰ τὴν Αἶνον,
τὸ δὲ ἐς διδασκάλους καὶ παίδευσιν φανερώτατος τοῦ
Ἑλληνικοῦ. Ἀριστοκλέους μὲν γὰρ ἤκουσε παῖς ἔτι,
Χρήστου δὲ ἤδη ξυνιείς, ὅθεν ἀπ᾽ ἀμφοῖν ἐκράθη τὴν
γλῶτταν ἀττικίζων τε κἀκ περιβολῆς ἑρμηνεύων. παιδεύων δὲ Ἀθήνῃσι κατὰ χρόνους, οὓς καὶ Πολυδεύκης
ἐπαίδευσεν, ἐπέσκωπτεν αὐτὸν ταῖς διαλέξεσιν ὡς
595 μειρακιώδη λέγων, "οἱ Ταντάλου κῆποι," δοκεῖν ἐμοὶ
τὸ κοῦφον τοῦ λόγου καὶ ἐπιπόλαιον φαντασίᾳ προσ-
εικάζων οὔσῃ τε καὶ οὐκ οὔσῃ. ἐμβριθὴς δὲ καὶ τὸ
ἦθος γενόμενος ἐτελεύτα ἡβῶν ἔτι, ἀφαιρεθεὶς ὑπὸ
τῆς τύχης τὸ καὶ πρόσω ἐλάσαι δόξης.

(50) 15. ιε΄. Λαμπρὸν ἐν σοφισταῖς καὶ Πτολεμαῖος
ὁ Ναυκρατίτης ἤχησεν. ἦν μὲν γὰρ τῶν μετεχόντων
τοῦ ἱεροῦ τοῦ περὶ Ναύκρατιν ὀλίγοις Ναυκρατιτῶν
ὑπάρχον, Ἡρώδου δὲ ἀκροατὴς μέν, οὐ μὴν ζηλωτὴς
ἐγένετο, ἀλλ᾽ ἐς τὸν Πολέμωνα μᾶλλον ὑπηνέχθη· τὸν
γὰρ ῥοῖζον τοῦ λόγου καὶ τὸ πνεῦμα καὶ τὸ ἐκ περιβολῆς φράζειν ἐκ τῆς Πολέμωνος σκηνῆς ἐσηγάγετο.
λέγεται δὲ καὶ αὐτοσχεδιάσαι ξὺν εὐροίᾳ ἀμηχάνῳ,
δικῶν τε καὶ δικαστηρίων παρέτραγεν, οὐ μὴν ὡς
ὄνομα ἐντεῦθεν ἄρασθαι. Μαραθῶνα δὲ αὐτὸν ἐπωνό-

---

132 A town in Thrace, first mentioned in Homer as the home
of Peros (*Il.* 4.519–20).

133 This proverb for the unsubstantial is based on the description of the vanishing fruits that mocked Tantalus (Hom. *Od.*

(49) 14. Athenodorus the sophist was in respect of his ancestors the most eminent of the citizens of Aenus,[132] but in respect of his teachers and education he was the most notable of all the Greeks. He was a student of Aristocles when he was still a boy, and of Chrestus when he had developed his intelligence. Consequently from both of them he blended his eloquence, and he Atticized and interpreted his themes with full development. He taught at Athens in the time when Polydeuces also taught there, and he used to ridicule Polydeuces as juvenile in his introductory speeches, calling his work "the gardens of Tantalus." By this he seems to me to have compared his light and superficial style to an illusion that both is and is not.[133] He was certainly a man of dignified character, but he died while still young, having been prevented by fate from pressing on to still greater fame.

595

(50) 15. The voice of Ptolemy of Naucratis[134] rang out brightly among sophists. He was allowed to participate in the temple at Naucratis, which is granted to few of the people of that city. He was a student of Herodes, but not an emulator of him, but rather came under the influence of Polemo. For he brought in the rushing flow of words, the inspired force, and his way of embellishing a speech from the theater of Polemo. He is also said to have improvised with an irresistible fluency, but he merely nibbled at legal cases and the courts, and not enough to make a name at it. They used to call him Marathon. Some say that this

11.598). Apollonius likens the Lamia's illusory banquet to the gardens of Tantalus at *VA* 4.25.4.

[134] On the prominent sophists who came from Naucratis, see above, note 125, on Polydeuces of Nacuratis, *VS* 593.

μαζον, ὡς μέν τινες, ἐπειδὴ τῷ Μαραθῶνι δήμῳ ἐνεγράφη Ἀθήνησιν, ὡς δὲ ἐνίων ἤκουον, ἐπειδὴ ἐν ταῖς
Ἀττικαῖς τῶν ὑποθέσεων τῶν Μαραθῶνι προκινδυνευ-
σάντων θαμὰ ἐμνημόνευε.

(51) Κατηγοροῦσι δὲ τοῦ Πτολεμαίου τινὲς ὡς μὴ
διορῶντος τὰς ὑποθέσεις, μηδὲ ὅπη ξυνεστᾶσί τε καὶ
μή, τεκμήριον τόδε τιθέμενοι τῆς κατηγορίας ταύτης·
τοὺς Μεσσηνίους οἱ Θηβαῖοι γράφονται τὴν τῶν
596 ἀχαριστησάντων, ἐπεὶ τοὺς φεύγοντας αὐτῶν μὴ ἐδέ-
ξαντο, ὅτε καὶ Θῆβαι ὑπὸ Ἀλεξάνδρου ἥλωσαν.
ταύτην γὰρ ἐπιφανῶς αὐτῷ εἰρημένην τὴν ὑπόθεσιν
καὶ σοφῶς, ὡς οἷόν τε, συκοφαντοῦσι λέγοντες, ὡς εἰ
μὲν ζῶντος Ἀλεξάνδρου κρίνονται, τίς οὕτω θρασύς,
ὡς καταψηφίσασθαι Μεσσηνίων· εἰ δὲ τεθνεῶτος, τίς
οὕτω πρᾷος, ὡς ἀπογνῶναι τὴν αἰτίαν; οὐ γὰρ ξυνιᾶ-
σιν οἱ ταῦτα διαβάλλοντες, ὡς ἡ τῶν Μεσσηνίων
ἀπολογία κατὰ ξυγγνώμην ἵσταται τὸν Ἀλέξανδρον
προϊσχομένων καὶ τὸν ἐκείνου φόβον, οὗ μηδὲ ἡ ἄλλη
Ἑλλὰς ἀπείρως εἶχε. ταῦτά μοι ἀπολελογήσθω ὑπὲρ
τοῦ ἀνδρὸς παραιτουμένῳ αὐτὸν ἀδίκου καὶ πεπα-
νουργημένης αἰτίας· καὶ γὰρ δὴ καὶ εὐδοκιμώτατος
σοφιστῶν οὗτος. πλεῖστα δὲ ἐπελθὼν ἔθνη καὶ πλεί-
σταις ἐνομιλήσας πόλεσιν οὐδαμοῦ διέβαλε τὸ ἑαυτοῦ κλέος, οὐδὲ ἥττων ἢ προσεδοκήθη ἔδοξεν, ἀλλ᾽
ὥσπερ ἐπὶ λαμπροῦ ὀχήματος τῆς φήμης πορευόμε-
νος διῄει τὰ ἄστη. ἐτελεύτα δὲ γηραιὸς ἐν Αἰγύπτῳ
τοὺς ὀφθαλμοὺς οὐκ ἀφαιρεθεὶς μὲν ὑπὸ τοῦ τῆς κε-
φαλῆς ῥεύματος, ἐπικοπεὶς δέ.

was because he was enrolled in the deme Marathon at Athens, but I hear from others that it was because in Attic themes he made frequent reference to those who risked their lives at Marathon.

(51) Some used to accuse Ptolemy of failing to define his themes and of not understanding where they were consistent and where they were not. As evidence for this they quote the following: "The Thebans bring a case against the Messenians for ingratitude, because they did not take in the Theban exiles, when Thebes was captured by Alexander." Though he spoke on this theme brilliantly and as skillfully as possible, they made an unfair case against it, saying that if the case was being judged while Alexander was alive, who would be so bold as to give a judgment against the Messenians? If it was when he had died, who would be so lenient as to acquit them of the charge? Those who criticize him in this way do not understand that the defense of the Messenians is framed as a plea for forgiveness, claiming as their excuse Alexander and the fear of him, which the rest of Greece also experienced. Let this be my defense of the man against anyone who brings an unjust and scurrilous accusation against him. Moreover this man had the finest reputation of all sophists. He visited very many peoples and kept company with those in very many cities, but brought no shame to his repute. Nor did he ever fall below their expectations of him, but rather traveled through the cities as if on a shining chariot of fame. He died in Egypt as an old man, when he had not quite lost his sight from a catarrh of the head, but had been impaired in it.

596

(52) 16. ιϛ'. Εὐοδιανὸν δὲ τὸν Σμυρναῖον τὸ μὲν γένος ἐς Νικήτην τὸν σοφιστὴν ἀνῆγεν, αἱ δὲ οἴκοι τιμαὶ ἐς τοὺς ἀρχιερέας τε καὶ στεφανουμένους τὴν ἐπὶ τῶν ὅπλων, τὰ δὲ τῆς φωνῆς ἆθλα ἐς τὴν Ῥώμην καὶ τὸν ἐκείνῃ θρόνον. ἐπιταχθεὶς δὲ καὶ τοῖς ἀμφὶ τὸν Διόνυσον τεχνίταις (τὸ δὲ ἔθνος τοῦτο ἀγέρωχοι καὶ χαλεποὶ[32] ἀρχθῆναι,) ἐπιτηδειότατος τὴν ἀρχὴν ἔδοξε καὶ κρείττων ἢ λαβεῖν αἰτίαν. υἱοῦ δὲ αὐτῷ τε- λευτήσαντος ἐν τῇ Ῥώμῃ οὐδὲν θῆλυ οὐδὲ ἀγεννὲς ἀνεφθέγξατο, ἀλλ', "ὦ τέκνον," τρὶς ἀνακαλέσας ἔθα-
597   ψεν. ἀποθνήσκοντι δὲ αὐτῷ κατὰ τὴν Ῥώμην παρῆ- σαν μὲν οἱ ἐπιτήδειοι πάντες, βουλὴν δὲ αὐτῶν ποιουμένων ὑπὲρ τοῦ σώματος, εἴτε χρὴ καταθάπτειν αὐτόθι, εἴτε ταριχεύσαντας πορθμεύειν ἐς τὴν Σμύρ- ναν ἀναβοήσας ὁ Εὐοδιανός, "οὐ καταλείπω," ἔφη, "τὸν υἱὸν μόνον." ὧδε μὲν δὴ σοφῶς ἐπέσκηψε τὸ τῷ παιδὶ ξυνταφῆναι. ἀκροατὴς δὲ Ἀριστοκλέους γενόμε- νος πανηγυρικῆς ἰδέας ἥψατο ἐν στρυφνῷ κρατῆρι ξυγκεράσας οἷον νᾶμα πότιμον. εἰσὶ δὲ οἵ φασι καὶ Πολέμωνος ἠκροᾶσθαι αὐτόν.

[32] χαλεποί a; λεπτοί β

(52) 16. Euodianus of Smyrna[135] ranked by birth as a descendant of the sophist Nicetes, and the honors of his house ranked him among the high priests and generals in charge of supplies, and the victories of his oratory brought him to Rome and to the chair of rhetoric there. He was also appointed to oversee the craftsmen of Dionysus[136] (and this class of men is arrogant and difficult to govern), but he proved himself very capable and beyond reproach. When his son died in Rome, he spoke no womanish or ignoble word, but called out three times, "O child," and buried him. When he himself was dying at Rome his 597 friends gathered around him and were debating about his body, deciding whether they should bury him there, or whether to embalm his body and ship it to Smyrna, and Euodianus cried out, "I will not leave my son alone." In this way he wisely urged them to bury him along with his son. Because he had been a student of Aristocles, he practiced the panegyric style, but he mixed, as it were, drinkable water in a bitter vessel.[137] Some say that he was also a student of Polemo.

[135] Euodianus' ancestor Nicetes of Smyrna is commemorated above (VS 511–12) as the one who revived the sophistic art after the long gap between Aeschines, as its supposed founder, and what we might call the Second Sophistic proper. Euodianus' eminence adds to that of his illustrious ancestor, while Euodianus' own standing is enhanced by the genealogical connection.

[136] See above, VS 579 with note 85.

[137] This is a commonplace in sophistic prose and the Christian Fathers. Three Platonic passages seem to be echoed: *Phdr.* 235c, *Tim.* 75e, but especially *Phdr.* 243d, ἐπιθυμῶ ποτίμῳ λόγῳ οἷον ἁλμυρὰν ἀκοὴν ἀποκλύσασθαι; cf. Lib. *Or.* 13.67 Foerster; Himer. *Ecl.* 10.76.

(53) 17. ιζ'. Ῥοῦφον δὲ τὸν ἐκ τῆς Περίνθου σοφιστὴν μὴ ἀπὸ τῆς οὐσίας, μηδὲ εἰ πολλοὶ ὕπατοι τὸ
ἐκείνου γένος, μηδὲ εἰ τῆς τῶν Πανελληνίων Ἀθήνησιν εὐκλεῶς ἦρξε, ταυτὶ γὰρ εἰ καὶ πλείω λέγοιτο,
οὔπω τῇ σοφίᾳ τοῦ ἀνδρὸς παραβεβλῆσθαι ἄξια,
ἀλλ' ἡ γλῶττα δηλούτω αὐτὸν καὶ ἡ ξύνεσις, ᾗ περὶ
τὰς ἐσχηματισμένας μάλιστα τῶν ὑποθέσεων ἐχρήσατο. τὴν δὲ ἰδέαν ταύτην ἐθαυμάσθη πρῶτον μέν,
ὅτι χαλεπὴ ἑρμηνεῦσαι, δεῖ γὰρ ἐν ταῖς κατὰ σχῆμα
ξυγκειμέναις τῶν ὑποθέσεων τοῖς μὲν λεγομένοις
ἡνίας, τοῖς δὲ σιωπωμένοις κέντρου, ἔπειτα, οἶμαι, καὶ
διὰ τὴν ἑαυτοῦ φύσιν, ἐγκειμένως[33] γὰρ τοῦ ἤθους καὶ
ἀπανούργως ἔχων ὑπεκρίνετο εὖ καὶ ἃ μὴ ἐπεφύκει.
598 πλουσιώτατος δὲ τῶν κατὰ τὸν Ἑλλήσποντον καὶ
Προποντίδα γενόμενος καὶ δόξης αὐτῷ ἐπὶ τῷ σχεδιάζειν πολλῆς μὲν ὑπαρχούσης Ἀθήνησι, πολλῆς δὲ
ἐν Ἰωνίᾳ τε καὶ Ἰταλίᾳ, οὐδαμοῦ κατέστησεν ἑαυτὸν
ἐς ἀπέχθειαν ἢ πόλεως ἢ ἀνδρός, ἀλλὰ πραότητος ἦν
χρηματιστής. ἐλέγετο δὲ καὶ γυμναστικῇ κρατύνειν
τὸ σῶμα ἀναγκοφαγῶν ἀεὶ καὶ διαπονῶν αὐτὸ παρα-
πλησίως τοῖς ἀγωνιζομένοις. ἀκροατὴς δὲ Ἡρώδου

---

[33] ἐκκειμένως is the conjecture of Morel for the MSS' ἐγκειμένως.

---

138 Under the name of Rufus there survives a very brief di-
dactic text, which aims to add a historical *genos* to the more usual
three *genera causarum*. Philostratus' *bios* makes no reference to
this work, just as it omits the written accomplishments of Aris-

(53) 17. The sophist Rufus of Perinthus[138] will not feature for his wealth, even though many consuls came from his family, nor because he presided over the Panhellenic festival at Athens with great distinction, because even though many more such things could be mentioned, they are not enough to compare with the man's wisdom. But let his tongue show what he was like and his understanding, which he especially used in arguments concealing the speaker's intentions.[139] He was wondered at for this style firstly because it is a difficult one to perform, because in themes that are composed as covert arguments it is necessary to keep a tight rein on what is actually said, but to apply the spur to what one leaves unsaid. Moreover, I think, he was admired taking his natural disposition into account, because although he was open and without guile in his own character, he acted well parts that were not of the same nature. Although he became the richest man in the Hellespont and Propontis, and although he had a great reputation at Athens for his improvisation, as well as in Ionia and Italy, he never came into enmity with a city or a man, but was a trader on kindness. He is said to have strengthened his body by athletics, always eating only what he needed and training himself as competing athletes do. As a boy he was a student of Herodes, but as a

598

tocles of Pergamum (*VS* 567–68) and Hermogenes (*VS* 577–78). See Gaines (1986), who argues that this work aimed at revision of existing handbooks rather than completeness (with further bibliography).

139 See the Rhetorical Glossary *s.v.* σχηματίζειν, and above, *VS* 542, 561.

μὲν ἐν παισίν, Ἀριστοκλέους δὲ ἐν μειρακίοις γενόμενος, καὶ μεγάλων ὑπ᾿ αὐτοῦ ἀξιωθεὶς ἐλαμπρύνετο τῷ
Ἡρώδῃ μᾶλλον, δεσπότην τε αὐτὸν ἀποκαλῶν καὶ
Ἑλλήνων γλῶτταν καὶ λόγων βασιλέα καὶ πολλὰ
τοιαῦτα. ἐτελεύτα δὲ οἴκοι ἓν καὶ ἑξήκοντα ἔτη γενόμενος καὶ ἐπὶ παισίν, ὑπὲρ ὧν μέγα οὐδὲν ἔχω εἰπεῖν,
πλήν γε δὴ ὅτι ἀπ᾿ ἐκείνου.

(54) 18. ιη΄. Ὀνόμαρχος ὁ ἐκ τῆς Ἄνδρου σοφιστὴς
οὐκ ἐθαυμάζετο μέν, οὐ μεμπτὸς δὲ ἐφαίνετο. ἐπαίδευσε μὲν γὰρ κατὰ χρόνους, οὓς Ἀδριανός τε καὶ
Χρῆστος Ἀθήνησι, πρόσοικος δὲ ὢν τῆς Ἀσίας τῆς
Ἰωνικῆς ἰδέας οἷον ὀφθαλμίας ἔσπασε, σπουδαζομένης μάλιστα τῇ Ἐφέσῳ, ὅθεν ἐδόκει τισὶν οὐδ᾿
ἠκροᾶσθαι Ἡρώδου καταψευδομένοις τοῦ ἀνδρός· τὰ
μὲν γὰρ τῆς ἑρμηνείας παρέφθορεν ἔσθ᾿ ὅπη δι᾿ ἣν
εἴρηκα αἰτίαν, αἱ δὲ ἐπιβολαὶ τῶν νοημάτων Ἡρώ-
δειοί τε καὶ ἀπορρήτως γλυκεῖαι. ἔξεστι δὲ αὐτὸν θεωρεῖν ἐπὶ τοῦ τῆς εἰκόνος ἐρῶντος, εἰ μὴ μειρακιεύε-
σθαι δόξω. εἴρηται δὲ ὧδε· ὦ κάλλος ἔμψυχον ἐν
ἀψύχῳ σώματι, τίς ἄρα σε δαιμόνων ἐδημιούργησε;
Πειθώ τις ἢ Χάρις ἢ αὐτὸς ὁ Ἔρως, ὁ τοῦ κάλλους
πατήρ; ὡς πάντα σοι πρόσεστιν ἐν ἀληθείᾳ—προσώπου στάσις χρόας ἄνθος βλέμματος κέντρον μει-
δίαμα κεχαρισμένον παρειῶν ἔρευθος ἀκοῆς ἴχνος.
ἔχεις δὲ καὶ φωνὴν μέλλουσαν[34] ἀεί. τάχα τι καὶ λαλεῖς, ἀλλ᾿ ἐμοῦ μὴ παρόντος, ἀνέραστε καὶ βάσκανε,

599

---

[34] Van Wulfften Palthe μελιτοῦσσαν; μέλλουσαν ω

young man of Aristocles, and he was esteemed very highly by him. But he prided himself more on Herodes, calling him his master, and the tongue of the Greeks, and the king of words, and many other such things. He died at home aged sixty one, leaving sons of whom I have nothing great to report, except that they were his.

(54) 18. The sophist Onomarchus of Andros[140] was not astonishing, but he was clearly not contemptible. He taught at the time that Hadrian and Chrestus taught at Athens, and living near Asia he contracted the Ionic style of oratory, which was practiced especially at Ephesus, as one might contract ophthalmia. Because of this he seemed never to have studied with Herodes, or at least it seemed so to those who told lies about the man. He corrupted his interpretation of themes for the reason I have stated, but his apprehension of ideas was true to Herodes and inexpressibly sweet. It is possible to consider what he was like in his speech on a man in love with a statue, if I do not seem juvenile to mention it: "Beauty ensouled in a soulless image, which demon crafted you? Was it some Persuasion or a Grace or Eros himself, the father of beauty? Truly all beauties are in you: the expression of your face, the bloom of color in your skin, the sting in your glance, smile full of charm, the blush in your cheeks, the impression of listening. And you have indeed a voice forever about to speak. Perhaps you will speak, but only when I am not here,

599

---

140 Onomarchus has left no trace beyond this passage and seems to be included in part because of his connection to Herodes (as Eshleman suggests: 2012, 132.)

πρὸς πιστὸν ἐραστὴν ἄπιστε. οὐδενός μοι μετέδωκας
ῥήματος· τοιγαροῦν τὴν φρικωδεστάτην ἄπασιν ἀεὶ
τοῖς καλοῖς ἀρὰν ἐπὶ σοὶ θήσομαι· εὔχομαί σοι γη-
ρᾶσαι."

Τελευτῆσαι δὲ αὐτὸν οἱ μὲν Ἀθήνησι, οἱ δὲ οἴκοι,
μεσαιπόλιόν τε καὶ παριόντα ἐς γῆρας, γενέσθαι δὲ
ἀγροικότερον τὸ εἶδος καὶ κατὰ τὸν Μάρκου τοῦ Βυζαντίου αὐχμόν.

(55) 19. ιθ'. Ἀπολλώνιος δὲ ὁ Ναυκρατίτης Ἡρα-
κλείδῃ μὲν ἐναντία ἐπαίδευσε τὸν Ἀθήνησι θρόνον
κατειληφότι, λόγου δὲ ἐπεμελήθη πολιτικοῦ καὶ εὖ
κεκολασμένου, ἧττον δὲ ἀγωνιζομένου, περιβολὴ γὰρ
ἄπεστιν αὐτοῦ καὶ πνεῦμα. ὄντι δὲ αὐτῷ κακῷ τὰ ἐρω-
τικὰ γίγνεται παῖς ἐξ ἀδίκων γάμων Ῥουφῖνος ὁ ἐπ᾽
αὐτῷ σοφιστεύσας οὐδὲν γόνιμον, οὐδὲ ἐκ καρδίας,
ἀλλὰ τῶν ἐκείνου κομματίων καὶ νοιδίων ἐχόμενος,
ἐφ᾽ ᾧ καὶ λαβὼν αἰτίαν ἐξ ἀνδρὸς σοφοῦ, "οἱ νόμοι,"
ἔφη, "διδόασί μοι χρῆσθαι τοῖς πατρῴοις," καὶ ὅς,
"διδόασι μέν," εἶπεν, "ἀλλὰ τοῖς κατὰ νόμους γεγο-
νόσι." καθάπτονται δὲ αὐτοῦ τινες καὶ τὸ σταλῆναι ἐς
600 Μακεδονίαν μισθωτὸν οἰκίας οὐδὲ εὖ πραττούσης.
ἀλλ᾽ ἀφείσθω τῶν τοιούτων· εὕροιμεν γὰρ ἂν καὶ τῶν
πολὺ σοφῶν ἐνίους πολλὰ καὶ ἀνελεύθερα ὑπὲρ χρημάτων πράξαντας, οὐ μὴν τόν γε Ἀπολλώνιον τοῦτον·
κοινήν τε γὰρ παρέσχε τὴν οὐσίαν τῶν Ἑλλήνων τοῖς

---

141 Despite the mixed assessment that Philostratus gives of
Onomarchus, this is the longest quotation in the text. Philostratus

loveless and begrudging one, faithless to a faithful lover. To me you have not granted a word. Well then I place on you the curse that most makes you beautiful people shudder: I pray that you grow old."[141]

Some say he died at Athens, others at home, when he was beginning to go gray and was on the verge of old age. And they say that he was rather rustic in appearance, and unkempt like Marcus of Byzantium.

(55) 19. Apollonius of Naucratis[142] taught in rivalry with Heracleides when he held the chair at Athens. He worked at a type of political oratory that was well disciplined, but not suited to actual controversy, because it was lacking in expansiveness and vital force.[143] Due to his poor moral character in love, he had a son, Rufinus, from an extramarital affair, who carried on in sophistry after him, but not legitimately, nor from the heart, but employing his father's phrases and little ideas. When he was criticized for this by a learned man he said, "The laws allow me to use my patrimony." "They allow it," the other said, "for those who are born within the law." Some find fault with him for going to Macedonia on the pay of a family who were not even in good circumstances. But let us acquit him of such accusations. We could even find some of the very wisest who did for money many things unworthy of a free man, but not this Apollonius. He put his fortune at the disposal

600

also tells a story of a man in love with the Cnidian Aphrodite (one of a number of such stories in Greek imperial literature), at *VA* 6.40.   [142] On the prominent sophists who came from Naucratis, see above, note 125 on Polydeuces, *VS* 593.

[143] These qualities are περιβολή and πνεῦμα, on which see the Rhetorical Glossary.

δεομένοις, καὶ οὐ βαρὺς ἦν ὑπὲρ μισθοῦ ξυμβῆναι.
ἐτελεύτα δὲ ἑβδομηκοντούτης Ἀθήνησιν ἔχων ἐντά-
φιον τὴν ἐξ ἁπάντων Ἀθηναίων εὔνοιαν. Ἀδριανοῦ
μὲν καὶ Χρήστου τῶν σοφιστῶν ἀκροατὴς ἐγένετο,
ἀμφοῖν δὲ ἀφέστηκεν, ὅσον οἱ μηδὲ ἀκούσαντες.
ἐφεώρα δὲ τὰς ὑποθέσεις ὑπεξιὼν μὲν τοῦ κοινοῦ, καιρὸν δὲ πλείω τοῦ ξυμμέτρου.

(56) 20. κ'. Ὁ δὲ Ἀπολλώνιος ὁ Ἀθηναῖος ὀνόματος
μὲν ἠξιώθη καθ' Ἕλληνας ὡς ἱκανὸς τὰ δικανικὰ καὶ
τὰ ἀμφὶ μελέτην οὐ μεμπτός, ἐπαίδευσε δὲ Ἀθήνησι
καθ' Ἡρακλείδην τε καὶ τὸν ὁμώνυμον τοῦ πολιτικοῦ
θρόνου προεστὼς ἐπὶ ταλάντῳ. διαπρεπὴς δὲ καὶ τὰ
πολιτικὰ γενόμενος ἔν τε πρεσβείαις ὑπὲρ τῶν μεγίστων ἐπρέσβευσεν ἔν τε λειτουργίαις, ἃς μεγίστας
Ἀθηναῖοι νομίζουσι, τήν τε ἐπώνυμον καὶ τὴν ἐπὶ τῶν
ὅπλων ἐπετράπη καὶ τὰς ἐξ ἀνακτόρου φωνὰς ἤδη
601 γηράσκων, Ἡρακλείδου καὶ Λογίμου καὶ Γλαύκου
καὶ τῶν τοιούτων ἱεροφαντῶν εὐφωνίᾳ μὲν ἀποδέων,
σεμνότητι δὲ καὶ μεγαλοπρεπείᾳ καὶ κόσμῳ παρὰ
πολλοὺς δοκῶν τῶν ἄνω.

(57) Πρεσβεύων δὲ παρὰ Σουῆρον ἐν Ῥώμῃ τὸν
αὐτοκράτορα ἀπεδύσατο πρὸς Ἡρακλείδην τὸν σοφιστὴν τὸν ὑπὲρ μελέτης ἀγῶνα, καὶ ἀπῆλθεν ὁ μὲν τὴν

144 That is, Apollonius of Naucratis, the subject of the preced-
ing bios.
145 As Avotins observed, this municipal (πολιτικός) chair,
which paid 24,000 sesterces, cannot be the same as the one es-

of those of the Greeks who were in need, nor was he hard to deal with concerning fees. He died at Athens aged seventy, and for his shroud he had the goodwill of all the Athenians. He was a student of the sophists Hadrian and Chrestus, but he differed as much from both as did those who never studied with them. He used to retire from public view to think about themes, and spent an inordinate length of time on this.

(56) 20. Apollonius of Athens won a name for himself among the Greeks since he was capable in legal oratory and not contemptible in declamation. He taught at Athens in the time of Heracleides and his own namesake,[144] and held the chair of political oratory[145] at a salary of one talent. Since he was distinguished in political affairs, he acted as an ambassador in embassies on the most important issues. He also acted in the public offices that the Athenians consider the highest, taking on the role of eponymous archon and food controller, and when he was already an old man he spoke the sacred words from the shrine.[146] In beauty of enunciation he fell short of Heracleides and Logimus and Glaucus and other hierophants of that kind, but in dignity and magnificence and attire he appeared superior to many of his predecessors.

601

(57) When he went on an embassy to the emperor Severus at Rome, he entered into a competitive rivalry in declamation with the sophist Heracleides. Heracleides

tablished by Marcus Aurelius, which paid 40,000: Avotins 1975, 314.

[146] That is, Apollonius acted as hierophant at the Eleusinian Mysteries of Demeter. The hierophants in this period were often sophists, whose training was evidently well suited to the role.

ἀτέλειαν ἀφαιρεθείς, ὁ δὲ Ἀπολλώνοις δῶρα ἔχων.
διαδόντος δὲ τοῦ Ἡρακλείδου λόγον οὐκ ἀληθῆ ὑπὲρ
τοῦ Ἀπολλωνίου, ὡς αὐτίκα δὴ βαδιουμένου ἐς Λιβύην, ἡνίκα Λεπτίνης[35] ἦν ὁ αὐτοκράτωρ ἐκεῖ καὶ τὰς
ἐξ ἁπάσης γῆς ἀρετὰς συνῆγε, καὶ πρὸς αὐτὸν εἰπόντος, "ὥρα σοι ἀναγιγνώσκειν τὸν πρὸς Λεπτίνην."
"σοὶ μὲν οὖν," ἦ δ' ὁ Ἀπολλώνιος, "καὶ γὰρ δὴ καὶ
ὑπὲρ τῆς ἀτελείας γέγραπται."

(58) Βαλβῖδα μὲν δὴ τοῦ λόγου ὁ Ἀπολλώνιος ἐκ
τῆς Ἀδριανοῦ ἰδέας βέβληται ἅτε δὴ καὶ ἀκροατὴς
γενόμενος, παραλλάττει δὲ ὅμως ἐς ῥυθμοὺς ἐμ-
μέτρους τε καὶ ἀναπαίοντας, οὓς εἰ φυλάξαιτο, σεμνο-
πρεπὴς τὴν ἀπαγγελίαν ἂν ἐδόκει[36] καὶ βεβηκώς.
τουτὶ δέ ἐστιν εὑρεῖν καὶ ἐπ' ἄλλων μὲν ὑποθέσεων,
μάλιστα δὲ ἐπὶ τοῦ Καλλίου, ὃς ἀπαγορεύει τοῖς
Ἀθηναίοις πυρὶ μὴ θάπτειν· ὑψηλὴν ἆρον, ἄνθρωπε,
602 τὴν δᾷδα. τί βιάζῃ καὶ κατάγεις κάτω καὶ βασανίζεις
τὸ πῦρ; οὐράνιόν ἐστιν, αἰθέριόν ἐστιν, πρὸς τὸ ξυγ-
γενὲς ἔρχεται. τοῦτο τὸ πῦρ οὐ κατάγει νεκρούς, ἀλλ'
ἀνάγει θεούς. ἰὼ Προμηθεῦ δᾳδοῦχε καὶ πυρφόρε, οἷά
σου τὸ δῶρον ὑβρίζεται· νεκροῖς ἀναισθήτοις ἀνα-
μίγνυται. ἐπάρηξον βοήθησον κλέψον, εἰ δυνατόν,

35 Λεπτίνης is the addition of Valesius, making clearer the
pun of Apollonius.
36 ἂν ἐδόκει Reiske; δοκεῖ ω

147 As Bowersock observed, the ease with which emperors
removed sophist's exemptions illustrates "the insecurity and im-
permanence of such grants" (1969, 40–41).

went away stripped of his exemptions,[147] but Apollonius departed with gifts. When Heracleides put out a false rumor about Apollonius, that he was about to depart to Libya, since the emperor, who was from Leptis Magna, was there, and was drawing talent from the whole world, Heracleides said to him, "this is a good time for you to read *Against Leptines*." But Apollonius replied, "for you too, since it was written about exemption."[148]

(58) Apollonius took the starting point of his eloquence from the style of Hadrian, since he had indeed been his student, but he departed from that into rhythms belonging to verse and especially anapestic rhythms. If he had guarded against this, he would have shown great dignity of style and stateliness. One can find this in others of his themes, but especially in his "Callias," who tries to persuade the Athenians not to burn the dead: "Lift the torch high, man. Why do you do violence to it and bring it low and torment the fire? It belongs to the sky, it belongs to the ether, it moves to that which is its kin. This fire does not lead down the dead, but leads up gods. Ah Prometheus, torchbearer and fire-bringer, look how they insult your gift. It is mingled with corpses without sensation. Rescue it, help it, steal the fire, if you can, back from this place."[149]

602

---

[148] Heracleides' joke plays on the double meaning of Λεπτίνης as "person from Leptis Magna" and as a man's name. Septimius Severus was from Leptis, but the speech to which Heracleides refers, Demosthenes' *Against Leptines*, secured the repeal of Leptines' law banning exemptions. Heracleides, in other words, seems to have set himself up for Apollonius' joke.

[149] Quoted by Norden (1923, 414) for its dochmiac rhythm, which was one of the marks of Asianism.

κἀκεῖθεν τὸ πῦρ." παρεθέμην δὲ ταῦτα οὐ παραιτού-
μενος αὐτὸν τῶν ἀκολάστων ῥυθμῶν, ἀλλὰ διδάσκων,
ὅτι μηδὲ τοὺς σωφρονεστέρους ῥυθμοὺς ἠγνόει.

Ἐτελεύτα μὲν οὖν ἀμφὶ τὰ πέντε καὶ ἑβδομήκοντα
ἔτη πολὺς καὶ ἐν τῷ Ἀθηναίων δήμῳ πνεύσας, ἐτάφη
δὲ ἐν τῷ προαστίῳ τῆς Ἐλευσινάδε λεωφόρου. ὄνομα
τῷ προαστίῳ Ἱερὰ συκῆ, τὰ δὲ Ἐλευσινόθεν ἱερά,
ἐπειδὰν ἐς ἄστυ ἄγωσιν, ἐκεῖ ἀναπαύουσιν.

(59) 21. κα'. Ἀναγράφω καὶ Πρόκλον τὸν Ναυκρατίτην εἰδὼς εὖ τὸν ἄνδρα, καὶ γὰρ δὴ καὶ τῶν ἐμῶν
διδασκάλων εἷς οὗτος. Πρόκλος τοίνυν ἦν μὲν τῶν
603   οὐκ ἀφανῶν κατ' Αἴγυπτον, στασιάζουσαν δὲ ἰδὼν
τὴν Ναύκρατιν καὶ παρὰ τὰ ἤθη πολιτεύοντας τὴν
Ἀθήνησιν ἡσυχίαν ἠσπάσατο καὶ ὑπεκπλεύσας ἐκεῖ
ἔζη πολλὰ μὲν ἀγαγὼν χρήματα, πολλοὺς δὲ οἰκέτας
καὶ τὴν ἄλλην κατασκευὴν μεγαλοπρεπῶς κεκοσμη-
μένην. εὖ δὲ ἀκούων Ἀθήνησι καὶ τὸν ἐν μειρακίῳ
χρόνον, ηὐδοκίμησε πολλῷ μᾶλλον ἀνὴρ γενόμενος,
πρῶτον μὲν ἐπὶ τῇ τοῦ βίου αἱρέσει, ἔπειτα, οἶμαι, καὶ
ἐπὶ εὐεργετήματι γενομένῳ μὲν περὶ ἕνα Ἀθηναῖον,
δήλωσιν δὲ παρασχομένῳ χρηστοῦ ἤθους· ἐς γὰρ τὸν
Πειραιᾶ ἐσπλεύσας ἤρετό τινα τῶν αὐτόθεν, εἰ ὁ
δεῖνα καλῶς Ἀθήνησι ζῇ καὶ εὖ πράττει, ἠρώτα δὲ
ταῦτα ὑπὲρ τοῦ ξένου, ᾧ προσέμιξεν Ἀθήνησι νέος

---

150 This appears to be the place mentioned by Pausanias, who
says that here Phytalus received the goddess Demeter and was
given the fig (Paus. 1.37). He quotes Phytalus' epitaph. Athenaeus

I have not quoted these lines to excuse him for his lack of discipline in rhythms, but to show that he also was not ignorant of the more self-controlled rhythms.

He died aged about seventy five, having spoken powerfully among the Athenian people. And he was buried in the suburbs near the main road to Eleusis. The name of the suburb is Sacred Fig Trees,[150] and when they carry sacred objects in procession to the city, it is there that they rest.

(59) 21. I will also record Proclus of Naucratis,[151] since I knew the man well. What is more, he was one of my teachers. Proclus, then, was a person of some eminence in Egypt, but because he saw that Naucratis was troubled by political discord and governed contrary to its traditional character, he embraced the quiet at Athens, and sailed away and lived there, bringing a great deal of money, many slaves, and the other requirements of a household, all splendidly ornate. And he had a good reputation at Athens even during the period of his youth, but was much more highly esteemed when he became a man, firstly because of his choice of way of life, secondly, I believe, because of a benefaction. Though this concerned just one Athenian, it demonstrated a kind nature. When he arrived by ship at the Piraeus, he asked someone there about a certain man, whether he was living at Athens and was doing well. He asked this about a friend and host, whose company he had kept at Athens when he was young, when he had been

says that "the Athenians name 'Sacred Fig' the place where [the fig] was first discovered" (Ath. 74d).

[151] On the prominent sophists who came from Naucratis, see above, note 125 on Polydeuces, *VS* 593.

ὤν, ὅτε δὴ καὶ Ἀδριανῷ ἐφοίτα. μαθὼν δὲ αὐτὸν εἶναί
τε καὶ ζῆν, ἐκπεσεῖσθαι δὲ αὐτίκα τῆς οἰκίας διακη-
ρυττομένης ἐπ᾽ ἀγορᾶς πρὸς δραχμὰς μυρίας, ἃς ἐπ᾽
αὐτῇ ἐδεδάνειστο, ἔπεμψεν αὐτῷ τὰς μυρίας μηδὲ
ἀνελθών πω ἐς τὸ ἄστυ εἰπὼν, "ἐλευθέρωσον τὴν
οἰκίαν, ἵνα μή σε κατηφῆ ἴδω." ταῦτα μὴ πλουσίου
μόνον ἡγώμεθα, ἀλλὰ καὶ πλούτῳ καλῶς χρωμένου
πεπαιδευμένου τε ἱκανῶς καὶ τὰ φιλικὰ ἀκριβοῦντος.

(60) Ἐκτήσατο δὲ καὶ οἰκίας τέτταρας, δύο μὲν ἐν
ἄστει, μίαν δὲ ἐν Πειραιεῖ καὶ ἄλλην Ἐλευσῖνι. ἐφοίτα
δὲ αὐτῷ καὶ ἀπ᾽ Αἰγύπτου λιβανωτὸς ἐλέφας μύρον
βίβλος βιβλία καὶ πᾶσα ἡ τοιάδε ἀγορά, καὶ ἀποδι-
δόμενος αὐτὰ τοῖς διατιθεμένοις τὰ τοιαῦτα οὐδαμοῦ
φιλοχρήματος ἔδοξεν οὐδὲ ἀνελεύθερος οὐδὲ ἐραστὴς
τοῦ πλείονος οὐδὲ ἐπικέρδειαν μαστεύων ἢ τόκους,
ἀλλ᾽ αὐτὸ ἀγαπῶν τὸ ἀρχαῖον. υἱῷ τε ἀσώτῳ περὶ
ἀλεκτρυόνων τροφὴν περί τε ὀρτύγων κυνῶν τε καὶ
κυνιδίων καὶ ἵππων ξυννεάζων μᾶλλον ἢ ἐπιπλήττων
καὶ παρὰ τοῖς πολλοῖς ἔχων αἰτίαν, "θᾶττον," ἔφη,
"μεταβαλεῖ τὸ μετὰ γερόντων παίζειν ἢ μετὰ ἡλίκων."
ἀποθανόντος δὲ αὐτῷ τοῦ παιδὸς καὶ τῆς γυναικὸς ἐπὶ
παλλακῇ ἐγένετο διὰ τὸ καὶ γηράσκοντας ὀφθαλμοὺς
604 ὑπάγεσθαι,[37] θηλυτάτη δὲ αὐτῇ γενομένῃ πᾶσαν ἐφιεὶς ἡνίαν οὐκ ἀγαθὸς ἔδοξε προστάτης τοῦ οἴκου.

---

[37] ὑπάγεσθαι Jahn; ἐπάγεσθαι ω

studying under Hadrian. Proclus learned that the man was alive and living there, but that he was just being evicted from his home, which was advertised for sale in the agora for ten thousand drachmas, for which value he had mort-gaged it. So Proclus sent him the ten thousand, when he had not yet gone up to the city, saying, "Free your home, so that I do not see you downcast." Let us not consider this the act only of a rich man, but of one who knew how to use wealth well, and was amply cultured, and had an exact understanding of matters of friendship.

(60) He bought four houses, two in the city, one in the Piraeus and another in Eleusis. And there used to come to him from Egypt frankincense, ivory, myrrh, papyrus, books and all such merchandise, and he sold them on to those who traded in such things. But he never appeared avaricious nor unworthy of a free man nor a lover of profit, and did not strive after profit or interest, but was content with the principal itself. He had a son who was spendthrift in his raising of fighting cocks, and concerning quails, dogs and puppies and horses. But he joined with him in these youthful pursuits rather than taking him to task for them and when he drew blame from many people for it he said, "He will sooner grow tired of playing with old men than with those his own age." When his son died and his wife, he took up with a mistress, because even eyes that are growing old can be captivated.[152] Since she had all of the womanly qualities he gave her the reins of his affairs and showed himself a poor manager of his own household.

604

[152] The close connection of love and sight is a commonplace in Greek literature, which Philostratus employs frequently in his *Letters*.

(61) Τὰ δὲ τῆς μελέτης πάτρια τῷ ἀνδρὶ τούτῳ διέκειτο ὧδε· ἑκατὸν δραχμὰς ἅπαξ καταβαλόντι ἐξῆν ἀκροᾶσθαι τὸν ἀεὶ χρόνον. ἦν δὲ αὐτῷ καὶ θήκη βιβλίων ἐπὶ τῆς οἰκίας, ὧν μετῆν τοῖς ξυλλεγομένοις ἐς τὸ πλήρωμα τῆς ἀκροάσεως. ὡς δὲ μὴ συρίττοιμεν ἀλλήλους μηδὲ σκώπτοιμεν, ἃ ἐν ταῖς τῶν σοφιστῶν ξυνουσίαις φιλεῖ γίγνεσθαι, ἀθρόοι ἐσεκαλούμεθα καὶ ἐκαθήμεθα ἐσκληθέντες, οἱ μὲν παῖδες καὶ οἱ παιδαγωγοὶ μέσοι, τὰ μειράκια δὲ αὐτοί. τὸ μὲν οὖν διαλεχθῆναι αὐτὸν ἐν σπανίοις ἔκειτο, ὅτε δὲ ὁρμήσειεν ἐς διάλεξιν, ἱππιάζοντί τε ἐῴκει καὶ γοργιάζοντι. ἡ μελέτη δὲ τῆς προτεραίας προεωραμένη ἐσεκυκλεῖτο. τὸ δὲ μνημονικὸν ἐνενηκοντούτης ἤδη γηράσκων καὶ ὑπὲρ τὸν Σιμωνίδην ἔρρωτο, καὶ ἑρμήνευε μὲν κατὰ φύσιν, Ἀδριάνειοι δὲ ἦσαν αἱ ἐπιβολαὶ τῶν νοημάτων.

(62) 22. κβ΄. Φοῖνιξ δὲ ὁ Θετταλὸς οὐδὲ θαυμάσαι ἄξιος, οὐδὲ αὖ διαβαλεῖν πάντα. ἦν μὲν γὰρ τῶν Φιλάγρῳ πεφοιτηκότων, γνῶναι δὲ ἀμείνων ἢ ἑρμηνεῦσαι τάξιν τε γὰρ τὸ νοηθὲν εἶχε καὶ οὐθὲν ἔξω καιροῦ ἐνοεῖτο, ἡ δὲ ἑρμηνεία διεσπάσθαι τε ἐδόκει καὶ ῥυθ-

---

153 That is, the attendants who brought the boys to the school.

154 That is, a *dialexis*, on which see the Rhetorical Glossary.

155 Simonides was the standard example of excellence in memory. Philostratus also remarks at VS 523 on the memory of Dionysius of Miletus, emphasizing that this was a gift of nature rather than something acquired by training.

310

(61) This man laid down the following traditions for participation in his school: it was possible for someone to pay a hundred drachmas once and listen at all times. He had a library of books at his home, which was open for those chosen as his students, to supplement his lectures. So that we would not hiss at or mock each other, which often happens in the schools of the sophists, we were called in all together and sat as we were called: boys first and their pedagogues[153] in the middle, and the youths by themselves. It was a rare thing for him to give a preliminary speech,[154] but when he did launch into one he seemed like Hippias or Gorgias. He used to think through his declamations the previous day before wheeling them out to an audience. Even as an old man of ninety he had powers of memory beyond Simonides.[155] He interpreted his themes through natural talent, but his apprehension of ideas was that of Hadrian.

(62) 22. Phoenix the Thessalian[156] was not worthy of astonishment nor altogether worthy of reproach. He was one of those who studied under Philagrus, but he was better at inventing than interpreting themes. His ideas were in good order and there was nothing in his thinking out of place, but his interpretation of themes seemed broken up

---

[156] A base found at Delphi once bore a statue of Phoenix, dedicated by his students. See Puech 2002, 384–85, with further bibliography. Another Delphic inscription records the dedication of a statue by Phoenix and his brother Phylax to their father, the sophist Titus Flavius Alexander (Puech 2002, 44–45). Initially, the dedication named only Phylax (on whom see below, VS 605 with note), and Phoenix's name was added later.

311

μοῦ ἀφέστηκεν. ἐδόκει δὲ ἐπιτηδειότερος γεγονέναι
τοῖς ἀρχομένοις τῶν νέων ἢ τοῖς ἕξιν τινὰ ἤδη κεκτη-
μένοις· τὰ γὰρ πράγματα γυμνὰ ἐξέκειτο καὶ οὐ περι-
ήμπισχεν αὐτὰ ἡ λέξις. ἑβδομηκοντούτης δὲ ἀπο-
θανὼν Ἀθήνησιν ἐτάφη οὐκ ἀφανῶς, κεῖται γὰρ πρὸς
τοῖς ἐκ τῶν πολέμων ἐν δεξιᾷ τῆς Ἀκαδημίανδε καθόδου.

605   (63) 23. κγ΄. Ἄγει με ὁ λόγος ἐπ᾽ ἄνδρα ἐλλογιμώτατον Δαμιανὸν τὸν ἐκ τῆς Ἐφέσου, ὅθεν ἐξηρήσθων
Σωτῆροί τε καὶ Σῶσοι καὶ Νίκανδροι καὶ Φαῖδροι
Κῦροί τε καὶ Φύλακες· ἀθύρματα γὰρ τῶν Ἑλλήνων
οὗτοι μᾶλλον προσρηθεῖεν ἂν ἢ σοφισταὶ λόγου
ἄξιοι. Δαμιανῷ τοίνυν ἐλλογιμώτατον μὲν καὶ τὸ ἄνω
γένος καὶ πλείστου ἄξιον τῇ Ἐφέσῳ, εὐδοκιμώτατοι
δὲ καὶ οἱ ἀπ᾽ αὐτοῦ φύντες, ξυγκλήτου γὰρ βουλῆς
ἀξιοῦνται πάντες ἐπ᾽ εὐδοξίᾳ θαυμαζόμενοι καὶ ὑπερ-
οψίᾳ χρημάτων, αὐτός τε πλούτῳ ποικίλῳ καὶ πολυ-
πρεπεῖ κατεσκευασμένος ἐπήρκει μὲν καὶ τοῖς δεομένοις τῶν Ἐφεσίων, πλεῖστα δὲ ὠφέλει τὸ κοινόν,
χρήματά τε ἐπιδιδοὺς καὶ τὰ ὑποδεδωκότα τῶν δημοσίων ἔργων ἀνακτώμενος. ξυνῆψε δὲ καὶ τὸ ἱερὸν τῇ

---

[157] Soter was an Athenian by birth, though he was educated at Ephesus. We have the inscription found there, in which he is made to boast that the Ephesians twice honored him with the title of "leading sophist"; this was probably set up by the eleven pupils whose names precede the inscription: Keil 1953.

[158] This is very likely Titus Flavius Phylax, a sophist who was

and stepped out of rhythm. He had a reputation for being
a better teacher for youths who were beginners than for
those who already had acquired some skill, because his
subject matter appeared in its bare form and his diction
failed to clothe it. He died at Athens aged seventy and
received no obscure burial, for he lies near the graves of
those who died in the wars, on the right of the road that
leads to the Academy.

(63) 23. My account leads me to a most illustrious man,   605
Damianus of Ephesus, so let me omit from it men like
Soter,[157] Sosus, Nicander, Phaedrus, Cyrus and Phylax.[158]
There were the toys of the Greeks rather than sophists
worthy of mention. Damianus then was descended from
the most illustrious ancestors, who were highly esteemed
at Ephesus, and his offspring likewise were held in high
repute because they were descended from him, and they
were all honored with seats in the Senate and were objects
of astonishment for their fine reputation and their disdain
for money. He himself was equipped with varied and magnificent wealth, and he maintained on the one hand those
in need in Ephesus, and on the other greatly assisted the
state, by donating large sums of money and repairing any
public buildings that were falling into disrepair.[159] Moreover he connected the temple[160] to Ephesus, extending to

honored with a statue at Olympia, the inscription from which can
be found, along with further bibliography, in Puech 2002, 385–86.
If this is so, he was the brother of Phoenix (to whom Philostratus
gives a short *bios* above, at VS 604) and the son of the Alexander
to whom both brothers dedicated a statue at Delphi.

[159] On the contributions of Damianus to public buildings in
Ephseus, see Bowersock 1969, 27–28.   [160] Of Artemis.

313

Ἐφέσῳ κατατείνας ἐς αὐτὸ τὴν διὰ τῶν Μαγνητικῶν
κάθοδον· ἔστι δὲ αὕτη στοὰ ἐπὶ ἑξ[38] στάδια λίθου
πᾶσα, νοῦς δὲ τοῦ οἰκοδομήματος μὴ ἀπεῖναι τοῦ ἱεροῦ τοὺς θεραπεύσοντας,[39] ὁπότε ὕοι. τοῦτο μὲν δὴ
τοὔργον ἀπὸ πολλῶν χρημάτων ἀποτελεσθὲν ἐπέγρα-
ψεν ἀπὸ τῆς ἑαυτοῦ γυναικός, τὸ δὲ ἐν τῷ ἱερῷ ἑστι-
ατήριον αὐτὸς ἀνέθηκε μεγέθει τε ἐξάρας ὑπὲρ πάνθ᾽
ὁμοῦ τὰ παρ᾽ ἑτέροις καὶ λόγου κρείττω περιβαλὼν
κόσμον· ὡράισται γὰρ Φρυγίῳ λίθῳ, οἷος οὔπω
ἐτμήθη. πλούτῳ δὲ χρῆσθαι καλῶς ἐκ μειρακίου ἤρξατο. Ἀριστείδου γὰρ δὴ καὶ Ἀδριανοῦ κατειληφότοιν
τοῦ μὲν τὴν Σμύρναν, τοῦ δὲ τὴν Ἔφεσον, ἠκροάσατο ἀμφοῖν ἐπὶ μυρίαις, εἰπὼν πολλῷ ἥδιον ἐς τοιαῦτα δαπανᾶν παιδικὰ ἢ ἐς καλούς τε καὶ καλάς,
ὥσπερ ἔνιοι. καὶ ὁπόσα ὑπὲρ τῶν ἀνδρῶν τούτων ἀνα-
γέγραφα Δαμιανοῦ μαθὼν εἴρηκα εὖ τὰ ἀμφοῖν εἰδότος. πλούτου δὲ ἐπίδειξιν τῷ ἀνδρὶ τούτῳ κἀκεῖνα
606 εἶχε· πρῶτον μὲν ἡ γῆ πᾶσα, ὁπόσην ἐκέκτητο, ἐκπε-
φυτευμένη δένδρεσι καρπίμοις τε καὶ εὐσκίοις, ἐν δὲ
τοῖς ἐπὶ θαλάττῃ καὶ νῆσοι χειροποίητοι καὶ λιμένων
προχώσεις βεβαιοῦσαι τοὺς ὅρμους καταιρούσαις τε
καὶ ἀφιείσαις ὁλκάσιν, οἰκίαι τε ἐν προαστίοις αἱ μὲν
κατεσκευασμέναι τὸν ἐν ἄστει τρόπον, αἱ δὲ ἀντρώ-

[38] ἑξ add. Engelmann
[39] θεραπεύσοντας Richards; θεραπεύοντας ω

it the way down through the Magnesian gates. This work
is a stoa six stades in length made entirely of stone, and
the intention behind the building is that those going to
worship there do not stay away from the temple when it
rains. When this work was completed at great expense he
dedicated it to his wife,[161] but he offered in his own name
the banqueting hall within the temple, which he raised up
to be greater in magnitude than those in all other places
combined, and decorated with an ornateness beyond
words. For it is decorated with Phrygian stone, which had
never before been quarried. Even as a youth he began to
use his wealth well. When Aristides and Hadrian held
sway, the former at Smyrna, the latter at Ephesus, he paid
tens of thousands to hear them both, saying that it was
much more pleasant to spend money on loves of that kind
than on beautiful boys and girls, as some people did. And
in fact everything that I have written about these men, I
have said on the authority of Damianus, who knew well
the lives of both men. The following was a further demonstration of his wealth. Firstly, all of the land that he had   606
acquired, was planted with trees that bear fruit and give
shade. On the lands that were by the sea he built artificial
islands and moles for harbors, which provided safe anchorage for cargo ships when they put in or set sail. Of his
houses in the suburbs, some were built in the style of city
houses, but others like caves. Then there was the character

[161] Vedia, the wife of Damianus, was the daughter of P. Vedius
Antoninus, who was himself a wealthy benefactor of Ephesus.
The children of Damianus and Vedia, as Bowersock notes, included three consuls and two wives of consuls: Bowersock, 1969,
28.

δεις, ἔπειτα αὐτοῦ τοῦ ἀνδρὸς τὸ ἐν τῇ ἀγορᾷ ἦθος
οὐ πᾶν ἀσπαζομένου κέρδος οὐδὲ ἐπαινοῦντος τὸ ἐξ
ἅπαντος λαμβάνειν, ἀλλ' οὓς αἴσθοιτο ἀποροῦντας
προῖκα τούτοις τὴν ἑαυτοῦ φωνὴν διδόντος. παραπλήσιον δὲ ἦν κἀν τοῖς σοφιστικοῖς τῶν λόγων· οὓς γὰρ
αἴσθοιτο ἀποροῦντας ἐξ ὑπερορίων ἐθνῶν ἥκοντας,
ἠφίει τούτοις τὸν μισθὸν τῆς ἀκροάσεως, μὴ λάθοιεν
δαπανώμενοι.

(64) Ἦν δὲ δικανικοῦ μὲν σοφιστικώτερος, σοφιστικοῦ δὲ δικανικώτερος. προϊὼν δ' ἐς γῆρας μεθῆκεν
ἄμφω τὰς σπουδὰς τὸ σῶμα καταλυθεὶς μᾶλλον ἢ
τὴν γνώμην. τοῖς γοῦν κατὰ κλέος αὐτοῦ φοιτῶσιν ἐς
τὴν Ἔφεσον παρέχων ἑαυτὸν ἀνέθηκε κἀμοί τινα ξυνουσίαν πρώτην τε καὶ δευτέραν καὶ τρίτην, καὶ εἶδον
ἄνδρα παραπλήσιον τῷ Σοφοκλείῳ ἵππῳ· νωθρὸς γὰρ
ὑφ' ἡλικίας δοκῶν νεάζουσαν ὁρμὴν ἐν ταῖς σπουδαῖς
ἀνεκτᾶτο. ἐτελεύτα δὲ οἴκοι ἔτη βιοὺς ἑβδομήκοντα
καὶ ἐτάφη ἐν προαστίῳ τινὶ τῶν ἑαυτοῦ, ᾧ μάλιστα
ἐνεβίωσεν.

(65) 24. κδ'. Ἀντιπάτρῳ δὲ τῷ σοφιστῇ πατρὶς μὲν
ἦν Ἱεράπολις, καταλεκτέα δ' αὕτη ταῖς κατὰ τὴν
Ἀσίαν εὖ πραττούσαις, πατὴρ δὲ Ζευξίδημος τῶν
ἐπιφανεστάτων ἐκείνῃ, Ἀδριανῷ δὲ καὶ Πολυδεύκει
φοιτήσας ἀπὸ τοῦ Πολυδεύκους μᾶλλον ἥρμοσται,
τὰς ὁρμὰς τῶν νοημάτων ἐκλύων τοῖς τῆς ἑρμηνείας

of the man himself in his dealings in the agora, where he did not embrace every chance of making a profit nor did he approve of taking whatever one can from everyone, but rather when he perceived that people were in difficulties, he would offer to speak for them without payment. It was the same with his sophistic lectures: if he perceived that one of those coming from distant peoples was in financial difficulty, he waived the lecture fee for them, so that they did not spend too much without realizing.

(64) He was more sophistic in style than a forensic orator but more forensic than a sophist.[162] When he came into old age, he gave away both pursuits, from weakness of body rather than of mind. This was clear from the fact that when people came to Ephesus because of his fame he made himself available, and he granted me a first interview, then a second and a third, and I saw that the man was like the horse in Sophocles:[163] though he was sluggish from age he seemed to regain the impetus of youth in our discussions. He died at home aged seventy, and was buried in one of his suburban villas, in which he had lived the most.

(65) 24. Antipater the sophist's birthplace was Hierapolis, and this must be included among the flourishing cities in Asia. His father was Zeuxidemus, who was one of the most eminent men there, and although Antipater attended the classes of Hadrian and Polydeuces, he took his inspiration more from Polydeuces, and he undid the impulse of his ideas with the rhythms of his interpretation. 607

---

[162] See above, *VS* 511 and 569, where the same is said of Nicetes and Antiochus.

[163] Alluding to, rather than quoting, Soph. *El.* 25.

ῥυθμοῖς. ἀκροασάμενος δὲ καὶ Ζήνωνος τοῦ Ἀθηναίου
τὸ περὶ τὴν τέχνην ἀκριβὲς ἐκείνου ἔμαθεν. αὐτοσχέδιος δὲ ὢν οὐδὲ φροντισμάτων ἠμέλει, ἀλλ᾽ Ὀλυμπι-
κούς τε ἡμῖν διῄει καὶ Παναθηναικοὺς καὶ ἐς ἱστορίαν
ἔβαλε τὰ Σεουήρου τοῦ βασιλέως ἔργα, ἐφ᾽ οὗ μάλιστα ταῖς βασιλείοις ἐπιστολαῖς ἐπιταχθεὶς λαμπρόν
τι ἐν αὐταῖς ἤχησεν. ἐμοὶ μὲν γὰρ δὴ ἀποπεφάνθω
μελετῆσαι μὲν καὶ ξυγγράψαι τοῦ ἀνδρὸς τούτου
πολλοὺς βέλτιον, ἐπιστεῖλαι δὲ μηδένα ἄμεινον, ἀλλ᾽
ὥσπερ τραγῳδίας λαμπρὸν ὑποκριτὴν τοῦ δράματος
εὖ ξυνιέντα ἐπάξια τοῦ βασιλείου προσώπου φθέγξα-
σθαι. σαφήνειάν τε γὰρ τὰ λεγόμενα εἶχε καὶ γνώμης
μέγεθος καὶ τὴν ἑρμηνείαν ἐκ τῶν παρόντων καὶ ξὺν
ἡδονῇ τὸ ἀξύνδετον, ὃ δὴ μάλιστα ἐπιστολὴν λαμπρύνει.

(66) Ὑπάτοις δὲ ἐγγραφεὶς ἦρξε μὲν τοῦ τῶν Βιθυνῶν ἔθνους, δόξας δὲ ἑτοιμότερον χρῆσθαι τῷ ξίφει
τὴν ἀρχὴν παρελύθη. βίου μὲν δὴ ὀκτὼ καὶ ἑξήκοντα
ἔτη τῷ Ἀντιπάτρῳ ἐγένετο καὶ ἐτάφη οἴκοι, λέγεται δὲ
ἀποθανεῖν καρτερίᾳ μᾶλλον ἢ νόσῳ. διδάσκαλος μὲν
γὰρ τῶν Σεουήρου παίδων ἐνομίσθη καὶ θεῶν διδάσκαλον ἐκαλοῦμεν αὐτὸν ἐν τοῖς ἐπαίνοις τῆς ἀκροάσεως, ἀποθανόντος δὲ τοῦ νεωτέρου σφῶν ἐπ᾽ αἰτίᾳ,

[164] The office of *ab epistulis* was held by many sophists from
the Greek east in the second and third centuries AD. Though
these were not the most prominent of the sophists, the office was
an important one and involved close proximity to the emperor.

He was also a student of Zeno of Athens, and from him he learned exactness in his art. Although he practiced improvisation, he did not neglect premeditated works, but he went through Olympic and Panathenaic orations for us, and cast into historical form the deeds of the emperor Severus, over whose imperial correspondence he was put in charge,[164] and he showed in these letters a brilliant style. Let me make clear that many people declaimed and wrote history better than this man, but no one wrote better letters, but he was like a brilliant actor of tragic drama, who understands well how it is appropriate to speak in the role of a king. For everything that he said had clarity and greatness of thought and the style depended on circumstances, and he used asyndeton to pleasurable effect, which especially enhances the brilliance of a letter.[165]

(66) When he was promoted to consular rank, he governed the people of Bithynia, but when he turned out to be too ready with the sword he was relieved of the office. Antipater had sixty eight years of life and was buried at home, but he is said to have died more by his steadfastness than by illness. He was appointed as the teacher of Severus' children and we used to call him "teacher of gods" when we praised his lecturing. But when the younger of them[166] was put to death on the charge that he was plotting against

See on the evidence for sophists in this role, Bowersock 1969, 50–58.

[165] On character (*ēthos*) in letter writing, see above, note 35. Antipater's epistolary skill extended beyond instilling his own character to the impersonation of the emperor.

[166] Geta; he was assassinated by Caracalla in AD 212.

ὡς τῷ ἀδελφῷ ἐπιβουλεύοι, γράφει πρὸς τὸν πρε-
σβύτερον ἐπιστολὴν μονῳδίαν ἐπέχουσαν καὶ θρῆνον, ὡς εἷς μὲν αὐτῷ ὀφθαλμὸς ἐκ δυοῖν, χεὶρ δὲ μία,
καὶ οὓς ἐπαίδευσεν ὅπλα ὑπὲρ ἀλλήλων αἴρεσθαι,
τούτους ἀκούοι κατ' ἀλλήλων ἠρμένους. ὑφ' ὧν παρο-
ξυνθῆναι τὸν βασιλέα μὴ ἀπιστῶμεν· καὶ γὰρ ἂν καὶ
ἰδιώτην ταῦτα παρώξυνε βουλόμενόν γε τὸ δοκεῖν
ἐπιβεβουλεῦσθαι μὴ ἀπιστεῖσθαι.

608   (67) 25. κέ. Πολὺς ἐν σοφιστῶν κύκλῳ καὶ Ἑρμοκράτης ὁ Φωκαεὺς ᾄδεται φύσεως ἰσχὺν δηλώσας
παρὰ πάντας, οὓς ἑρμηνεύω· οὐδενὶ γὰρ θαυμασίῳ
σοφιστῇ ξυγγενόμενος, ἀλλὰ Ῥουφίνου τοῦ Σμυρ-
ναίου ἀκηκοὼς τὰ σοφιστικὰ τολμῶντος μᾶλλον ἢ
609 κατορθοῦντος ἑρμηνεῦσαι ποικιλώτατα Ἑλλήνων καὶ
ἔγνω καὶ ἔταξεν, οὐ τὰς μὲν τῶν ὑποθέσεων, τὰς δὲ
οὐχί, ἅπαξ δὲ πάσας τὰς μελετωμένας· καὶ γὰρ δὴ
καὶ τὰς ἐσχηματισμένας εὖ διέθετο ἀμφιβολίας τε
πλείστας ἐπινοήσας καὶ τὸ σημαινόμενον ἐγκαταμίξας τῷ ὑφειμένῳ.

(68) Πάππος μὲν δὴ αὐτῷ ἐγένετο Ἄτταλος ὁ Πολέμωνος τοῦ σοφιστοῦ παῖς, πατὴρ δὲ Ῥουφινιανὸς ὁ
ἐκ Φωκαίας, ἀνὴρ ὕπατος Καλλιστὼ γήμας τὴν Ἀτ-
610 τάλου. τελευτήσαντος δὲ αὐτῷ τοῦ πατρὸς ἐς διαφορὰν κατέστη πρὸς τὴν ἑαυτοῦ μητέρα οὕτω τι ἀπα-
ραίτητον, ὡς μηδὲ δάκρυον ἐπ' αὐτῷ τὴν Καλλιστὼ
ἀφεῖναι ἐν μειρακίῳ ἀποθανόντι, ὅτε δὴ καὶ τοῖς πο-

his brother, Antipater wrote to the elder brother a letter containing a monody and a lament, that he now had one eye instead of two, and one hand, and that those whom he had taught to take up arms for one another, he now heard had taken them up against one another. Let us be quite sure that the emperor would have been enraged by this, because it would have enraged even a private citizen who wished no one to disbelieve in an apparent plot against him.

(67) 25. Hermocrates the Phocian became a legend in   608
the circle of sophists, showing a strength of talent beyond all others whom I describe. He was not a student of any astonishing sophist, but rather learned from Rufinus of Smyrna, who was more noted for daring in sophistic matters than correctness of interpretation, but Hermocrates   609
surpassed by far all the Greeks in variety of invention and arrangement, not of some kinds of themes and not others, but of all the kinds on which he declaimed. Moreover he arranged covert arguments[167] well and devised very many ambiguous expressions and mixed his intended meaning with veiled suggestions.

(68) His grandfather was Attalus the son of the sophist Polemo,[168] and his father was Rufinianus of Phocaea, a man of consular rank who married Callisto the daughter of Attalus. When his father died he quarreled with his own   610
mother so irrevocably that Callisto did not even shed a tear for him when he died in his youth, though it seems pitiable

---

[167] See $\sigma\chi\eta\mu\alpha\tau\dot\iota\zeta\epsilon\iota\nu$ in the Rhetorical Glossary.

[168] At VS 544 Philostratus foreshadows that he will speak of the only worthy descendant of Polemo, though without at that point naming Hermocrates.

PHILOSTRATUS

λεμιωτάτοις ἐλεεινὰ τὰ τῆς ἡλικίας φαίνεται. καὶ τοῦτο οὑτωσὶ μὲν ἀκούσαντι κακίᾳ τοῦ μειρακίου προσκείσεται μᾶλλον, εἰ μηδὲ μήτηρ ἐπ᾽ αὐτῷ τι ἔπαθεν, λογιζομένῳ δὲ τὴν αἰτίαν καὶ ὅτι τὴν μητέρα ἀπέστερξεν ἐπὶ δούλου ἔρωτι, ὁ μὲν ξυμβαίνων τοῖς νόμοις φαίνοιτο ἄν, οἳ δεδώκασι τὸ ἐπὶ ταῖς τοιαῖσδε αἰτίαις καὶ ἀποκτείνειν, ἡ δὲ ἀξία μισεῖσθαι καὶ τοῖς οὐ προσήκουσιν ὑπὲρ ὧν ἑαυτήν τε καὶ τὸν υἱὸν ᾔσχυνεν.

(69) Ὥσπερ δὲ ταύτην ὁ Ἑρμοκράτης διαφεύγει τὴν αἰτίαν, οὕτως ἐκείνην οὐκ ἂν διαφύγοι· τὸν γὰρ πατρῷον οἶκον βαθὺν αὐτῷ παραδοθέντα κατεδαπάνησεν οὐκ ἐς ἱπποτροφίας οὐδὲ ἐς λειτουργίας, ἀφ᾽ ὧν καὶ ὄνομά ἐστιν ἄρασθαι, ἀλλ᾽ ἐς ἄκρατον καὶ ἑταίρους οἵους παρασχεῖν καὶ κωμῳδίᾳ λόγον, οἷον παρέσχον λόγον οἱ Καλλίαν ποτὲ τὸν Ἱππονίκου κολακεύσαντες.

(70) Ἀντιπάτρου δὲ παρεληλυθότος ἐς τὰς βασιλείους ἐπιστολὰς ἤδη ἀσπαζομένου τε ἁρμόσαι οἱ τὴν ἑαυτοῦ θυγατέρα πονήρως ἔχουσαν τοῦ εἴδους οὐκ ἐπήδησε πρὸς τὴν ἐκείνου εὐπραγίαν, ἀλλὰ καὶ τῆς προμνηστρίας ἀναγούσης ἐς τὴν τοῦ Ἀντιπάτρου ἰσχύν, ἣν εἶχε τότε, οὐκ ἄν ποτε ἔφη δουλεῦσαι προικὶ μακρᾷ καὶ πενθεροῦ τύφῳ. ἐξωθούντων δὲ αὐτὸν τῶν ξυγγενῶν ἐς τὸν γάμον καὶ Διὸς Κόρινθον

611

---

[169] Eupolis' lost comedy, the *Flatterers*, was performed at the Dionysia in 421, defeating Aristophanes' *Peace*. It condemned

322

even for one's worst enemies to die at that age. To one who hears only this, it will seem to be due to the youth's evil character, if his mother felt nothing for him, but to one who thinks about the cause of it, namely that he ceased to love his mother due to her passion for a slave, it is obvious that he conformed to the laws, which allow him to put a woman to death for reasons of that sort. But she deserves hatred even from those who are not related to her, for the disgrace that she brought on herself and her son.

(69) So while Hermocrates escapes from this charge, there is another that he would not escape. He inherited a substantial household from his father, but squandered it not on raising horses nor on public benefactions, from which activities at least one elevates one's reputation, but on strong liquor and companions of the sort that provide a plot for a comedy, just as the flatterers around Callias, son of Hipponicus, once did.[169]

(70) When Antipater had taken on the role of imperial secretary,[170] he wished to give in marriage to Hermocrates his daughter who was terribly ugly. Yet Hermocrates did not jump at the chance to share Antipater's prosperity, but when the woman who was arranging the match drew his attention to the power that Antipater then held, he said that he would never be the slave of a large dowry and the swollen pride of a father-in-law. Even when his relatives tried to push him into the marriage and considered Antip-

611

Callias for squandering his fortune on his pleasures. Philostratus ignores here the other indulgence on which Callias is said to have squandered his wealth: sophists. See Pl. *Prt.* 314c–16b.

[170] That is, the role of *ab epistulis Graecis*, in which Philostratus praises Antipater's brilliance above (*VS* 607).

PHILOSTRATUS

ἡγουμένων τὸν Ἀντίπατρον οὐ πρότερον εἶξεν ἢ Σε-
ουῆρον αὐτοκράτορα μεταπέμψαντα αὐτὸν ἐς τὴν
ἑῴαν δοῦναί οἱ τὴν κόρην, ὅτε δὴ καὶ τῶν ἐπιτηδείων
ἐρομένου τινὸς αὐτόν, πότε ἄγοι τὰ ἀνακαλυπτήρια,
ἀστειότατα ὁ Ἑρμοκράτης, "ἐγκαλυπτήρια μὲν οὖν,"
ἔφη, "τοιαύτην λαμβάνων." καὶ διέλυσε μετ᾽ οὐ πολὺ
τὸν γάμον ὁρῶν οὔτε ἰδεῖν ἡδεῖαν οὔτε ἐπιτηδείαν τὸ
ἦθος.

(71) Καὶ ἀκροατὴς δὲ τοῦ Ἑρμοκράτους ὁ αὐτοκράτωρ γενόμενος ἠγάσθη αὐτὸν ἴσα τῷ πάππῳ δω-
ρεάς τε αἰτεῖν ἀνῆκε· καὶ ὁ Ἑρμοκράτης "στεφάνους
μὲν," ἔφη, "καὶ ἀτελείας καὶ σιτήσεις καὶ πορφύραν
καὶ τὸ ἱερᾶσθαι ὁ πάππος ἡμῖν τοῖς ἀπ᾽ αὐτοῦ παρέδωκε, καὶ τί ἂν αἰτοίην παρὰ σοῦ τήμερον, ἃ ἐκ τοσούτου ἔχω; ἐπεὶ δὲ ἐστί μοι προστεταγμένον ὑπὸ τοῦ
κατὰ τὸ Πέργαμον Ἀσκληπιοῦ πέρδικα σιτεῖσθαι λι-
βανωτῷ θυμιώμενον, τὸ δὲ ἄρωμα τοῦτο οὕτω τι σπά-
νιον καθ᾽ ἡμᾶς νῦν, ὡς ψαιστὸν καὶ δάφνης φύλλα
τοῖς θεοῖς θυμιᾶσθαι, δέομαι λιβανωτοῦ ταλάντων
πεντήκοντα, ἵνα θεραπεύοιμι μὲν τοὺς θεούς, θεραπευ-
οίμην δὲ αὐτός." ἔδωκε τὸν λιβανωτὸν ξὺν ἐπαίνῳ ὁ
αὐτοκράτωρ ἐρυθριᾶν εἰπών, ἐπειδὴ μικρὰ ᾐτήθη.

(72) Ξυνελάμβανε δὲ τῷ Ἑρμοκράτει τῶν ἐπιδείξεων πρῶτον μὲν τὸ τοῦ πάππου κλέος· ἡ γὰρ φύσις

---

171 This popular proverb was used in two ways: of empty
boasting, because the Corinthians boasted that their eponymous

324

ater to be "Corinthus, son of Zeus,"[171] he did not give way until the emperor Severus summoned him to the east and gave him the girl in marriage. Then when one of his friends asked him when he was going to celebrate the unveiling of the bride, Hermocrates very wittily replied, "Rather the veiling, when I'm taking a bride like that." And he dissolved the marriage not long after the wedding, when he saw that she was neither pleasant to look at nor companionable in her character.

(71) When the emperor joined the audience of Hermocrates he was amazed by him as much as by his great-grandfather,[172] and gave him the privilege of asking for gifts. But Hermocrates said, "Crowns and immunities and meals at public expense and consular purple and priesthoods my great-grandfather gave to us who are descended from him, so why should I ask from you today, what I have possessed for so long? Since, however, I have been instructed by Asclepius at Pergamum to eat partridge stuffed with frankincense, and this incense is now so scarce in our country that we are burning barley and laurel leaves to the gods, I ask for fifty talents of frankincense, so that I may treat the gods properly, and get proper treatment myself." The emperor gave him the frankincense with his praise, saying that he blushed, since he had been asked for so small a gift.

(72) Hermocrates was assisted in his declamations firstly by the reputation of his great-grandfather, because

hero was Corinthus, son of Zeus, and to express aimless iteration, as in Pind. *Nem.* 8.105. Here it merely implies exaggerated respect for Antipater.

172 Polemo, see *VS* 610.

ἡ ἀνθρωπεία τὰς ἀρετὰς ἀσπάζεται μᾶλλον τὰς ἐκ
πατέρων ἐς παῖδας διαδοθείσας, ὅθεν εὐκλεέστερος
μὲν Ὀλυμπιονίκης ὁ ἐξ Ὀλυμπιονικῶν οἴκου, γενναι-
612 ότερος δὲ στρατιώτης ὁ μὴ ἀστρατεύτων ἡδίους τε
τῶν ἐπιτηδεύσεων αἱ πατέρων τε καὶ προγόνων οἴκου,
καὶ τέχναι βελτίους αἱ κληρονομούμεναι· ξυνελάμβανε δὲ αὐτῷ καὶ ἡ ὥρα ἡ περὶ τῷ εἴδει· καὶ γὰρ
ἐπίχαρις καὶ ἀγαλματίας οἷα ἔφηβοι, καὶ τὸ θάρσος
δὲ τοῦ μειρακίου τὸ ἐν τοῖς πλήθεσιν ἔκπληξιν ἐς
τοὺς πολλοὺς ἔφερεν, ἣν ἐκπλήττονται ἄνθρωποι τοὺς
τὰ μεγάλα μὴ ξὺν ἀγωνίᾳ πράττοντας. ἐδίδου τι καὶ
ἡ εὔροια καὶ ὁ τῆς γλώττης κρότος καὶ τὸ ἐν στιγμῇ
τοῦ καιροῦ ξυνορᾶν τὰς ὑποθέσεις καὶ τὰ ἀναγιγνω-
σκόμενά τε καὶ λεγόμενα παλαιότερα ὄντα ἢ νέῳ γε
ἐνθυμηθῆναι καὶ ἑρμηνεῦσαι. αἱ μὲν δὴ μελέται τοῦ
Ἑρμοκράτους ὀκτώ που ἴσως ἢ δέκα καί τις λόγος οὐ
μακρός, ὃν ἐν Φωκαίᾳ διῆλθεν ἐπὶ τῷ Πανιωνίῳ κρατῆρι. ἐμοὶ δὲ ἀποπεφάνθω μὴ ἄν τινα ὑπερφωνῆσαι
τὴν μειρακίου τούτου γλῶτταν, εἰ μὴ ἀφῃρέθη τὸ
παρελθεῖν ἐς ἄνδρας φθόνῳ ἁλούς. ἐτελεύτα δὲ κατ᾽
ἐνίους μὲν ὀκτὼ καὶ εἴκοσι γεγονώς, ὡς δὲ ἔνιοι, πέντε
καὶ εἴκοσι, καὶ ἐδέξατο αὐτὸν ἡ πατρῷα γῆ καὶ αἱ
πατρῷαι θῆκαι.

(73) 26. κϛ᾽. Ἀνὴρ ἐλλογιμώτατος καὶ Ἡρακλείδης
ὁ Λύκιος καὶ τὰ οἴκοι μέν, ἐπειδὴ πατέρων τε ἀγαθῶν

---

173 For this festival at Smyrna and for the ceremony of the
Panionian mixing bowl from which the assembled Ionians drank
as a sign of their friendship, see VA 4.5–6.

human nature embraces more readily virtues that are
passed down from fathers to sons. For this reason an
Olympic victor is more famous if he comes from a house
of Olympic victors, and a soldier is more honorable who   612
comes from a military family, and there is more pleasure
in pursuits shared with one's fathers and the ancestors of
one's house, and arts are better when inherited. He was
also aided by the youthful beauty of his appearance, for he
both possessed great charm and was like a statue of a
youth. And the young man's courage when he appeared
among crowds astonished most people, since people are
astonished by those who do great things without strain.
His fluency and the striking rhythm of his speech contributed to his success, as did the way that he could comprehend themes in a moment of time, and the fact that what
he read and spoke seemed more mature than a mere youth
could think through and deliver. There are about eight or
ten surviving declamations of Hermocrates and a sort of
short speech that he delivered in Phocaea over the Panionian mixing bowl.[173] But let me put on record my opinion
that no one would have surpassed the eloquence of this
youth, if he had not been prevented from coming to manhood, taken away by Envy. He died, some say at twenty
eight, or as others say, twenty five, and the earth of his
fathers, and the sepulchers of his fathers, received him.

(73) 26. Another most illustrious man was Heracleides
the Lycian,[174] in the first place because of his house, since

173 Puech rightly concludes that the epitaph inscribed on behalf of a Heracleides of Lycia for his wife belongs not to Philostratus' sophist but to "un homonyme beaucoup plus modeste":
Puech 2022, 293.

613 ἔφυ καὶ ἀρχιερεὺς Λυκίων ἐγένετο (τὴν δὲ λειτουργη-
σίαν οὖσαν οὐ μεγάλου ἔθνους Ῥωμαῖοι μεγάλων
ἀξιοῦσιν ὑπὲρ ξυμμαχίας, οἶμαι, παλαιᾶς,) ἐλλογι-
μώτερος δὲ ὁ Ἡρακλείδης τὰ σοφιστικά· ἀποχρῶν
μὲν γὰρ ξυνεῖναι, ἀποχρῶν δὲ ἑρμηνεῦσαι, καὶ τοὺς
ἀγῶνας ἀπέριττος καὶ τὰς πανηγυρικὰς ἐννοίας οὐχ
ὑπερβακχεύων.

(74) Ἐκπεσὼν δὲ τοῦ θρόνου τοῦ Ἀθήνησι ξυστάν-
των ἐπ' αὐτὸν τῶν Ἀπολλωνίου τοῦ Ναυκρατίτου
ἑταίρων, ὧν πρῶτος καὶ μέσος καὶ τελευταῖος ὁ Μαρ-
κιανὸς ὁ ἐκ Δολίχης ἐγένετο, ἐπὶ τὴν Σμύρναν ἐτρά-
πετο θύουσαν μάλιστα δὴ πόλεων ταῖς τῶν σοφιστῶν
Μούσαις. νεότητα μὲν οὖν Ἰωνικήν τε καὶ Λύδιον καὶ
τὴν ἐκ Φρυγῶν καὶ Καρίας ξυνδραμεῖν ἐς Ἰωνίαν
κατὰ ξυνουσίαν τοῦ ἀνδρὸς οὔπω μέγα, ἐπειδὴ ἀγχίθυρος ἁπάσαις ἡ Σμύρνα· ὁ δὲ ἦγε μὲν καὶ τὸ ἐκ
τῆς Εὐρώπης Ἑλληνικόν, ἦγε δὲ τοὺς ἐκ τῆς ἑῴας
νέους, πολλοὺς δὲ ἦγεν Αἰγυπτίων οὐκ ἀνηκόους
αὐτοῦ ὄντας, ἐπειδὴ Πτολεμαίῳ τῷ Ναυκρατίτῃ κατὰ
Αἴγυπτον περὶ σοφίας ἤρισεν, ἐνέπλησε δὲ τὴν Σμύρναν ὁμίλου λαμπροῦ, ὤνησε δὲ καὶ πλείω ἕτερα, ἃ
ἐγὼ δηλώσω· πόλις ἐς ξένους πολλοὺς ἐπεστραμμένη
ἄλλως τε καὶ σοφίας ἐρῶντας σωφρόνως μὲν βουλεύ-
σει, σωφρόνως δὲ ἐκκλησιάσει φυλαττομένη δήπου
τὸ ἐν πολλοῖς τε καὶ σπουδαίοις κακὴ ἁλίσκεσθαι,

---

175 Smyrna had, of course, long been a center of sophistic

he came from good forefathers and became high priest of
the Lycians (though this is not an office over a very large   613
people, the Romans regard it highly because, I suppose,
of their ancient alliance with the Lycians). Secondly, Heracleides was more famous because of his sophistic work: he
was capable in understanding themes, capable too in interpreting them, and he was straightforward in legal arguments and did not indulge in Bacchic excesses in his thinking in panegyrics.

(74) When he had been thrown out of the chair of
rhetoric at Athens, due to a conspiracy against him by the
companions of Apollonius of Naucratis, in which Marcia-
nus of Doliche was the beginning, middle and end, he
turned to Smyrna,[175] since it of all cities sacrificed to the
Muses of the sophists. It is not in itself a great achievement
that the youth of Ionia and Lydia, and that of the Phry-
gians and Carians, flocked into Ionia to study with him,
since Smyrna neighbors all of them. But he also drew
there the Hellenic youth from Europe, drew there the
youths of the east, and drew there many Egyptians, who
had already heard him, because in Egypt he had competed
in wisdom with Ptolemaeus of Naucratis. He filled Smyrna
with a brilliant crowd, and benefitted the city in very many
other respects, as I will show. A city that is visited by many
foreigners, both generally and especially if they are lovers
of wisdom, will make its counsels prudently, and will
hold its assemblies prudently, guarding, I suppose, against
being caught in evil conduct by the many, serious-minded
people in it, and it will take care of its temples and

excellence, due in part to the reputations of Nicetes of Smyrna
and Scopelian, and later of Aelius Aristides.

ἱερῶν τε ἐπιμελήσεται καὶ γυμνασίων καὶ κρηνῶν καὶ
στοῶν, ἵνα ἀποχρῶσα τῷ ὁμίλῳ φαίνοιτο. εἰ δὲ καὶ
ναύκληρος ἡ πόλις εἴη, καθάπερ ἡ Σμύρνα, πολλὰ
καὶ ἄφθονα αὐτοῖς ἡ θάλασσα δώσει. ξυνήρατο δὲ τῇ
Σμύρνῃ καὶ τοῦ εἴδους ἐλαίου κρήνην ἐπισκευάσας ἐν
τῷ τοῦ Ἀσκληπιοῦ γυμνασίῳ χρυσῆν τοῦ ὀρόφου, καὶ
τὴν στεφανηφόρον ἀρχὴν παρ' αὐτοῖς ἦρξεν, ἀφ' ἧς
τοῖς ἐνιαυτοῖς τίθενται Σμυρναῖοι τὰ ὀνόματα.

614   (75) Ἐπὶ Σεουήρου δὲ τοῦ αὐτοκράτορός φασιν
αὐτὸν σχεδίου λόγου ἐκπεσεῖν αὐλὴν καὶ δορυφόρους
δείσαντα. τουτὶ δὲ ἀγοραῖος μέν τις παθὼν κἂν αἰτίαν
λάβοι, τὸ γὰρ τῶν ἀγοραίων ἔθνος ἰταμοὶ καὶ θρα-
σεῖς· σοφιστὴς δὲ ξυσπουδάζων μειρακίοις τὸ πολὺ
τῆς ἡμέρας πῶς ἂν ἀντίσχοι ἐκπλήξει; ἐκκρούει γὰρ
σχεδίου λόγου καὶ ἀκροατὴς σεμνῷ προσώπῳ καὶ
βραδὺς ἔπαινος καὶ τὸ μὴ κροτεῖσθαι ξυνήθως, εἰ δὲ
καὶ φθόνου ὑποκαθημένου ἑαυτὸν αἴσθοιτο, ὥσπερ ὁ
Ἡρακλείδης τὸν τοῦ Ἀντιπάτρου τότε ὑφεωρᾶτο, ἧττον μὲν ἐνθυμηθήσεται, ἧττον δὲ εὐροήσει· αἱ γὰρ
τοιαίδε ὑποψίαι γνώμης ἀχλὺς καὶ δεσμὰ γλώττης.

(76) Ἱερὰς δὲ λέγεται κέδρους ἐκτεμὼν δημευθῆναι
τὸ πολὺ τῆς οὐσίας, ὅτε δὴ καὶ ἀπιόντι αὐτῷ τοῦ δικαστηρίου ἐπηκολούθουν μὲν οἱ γνώριμοι παραμυ-
θούμενοί τε καὶ ἀνέχοντες τὸν ἄνδρα· ἑνὸς δὲ αὐτῶν
εἰπόντος, "ἀλλ' οὐ μελέτην ἀφαιρήσεταί τις, ὦ Ἡρα-
κλείδη, οὐδὲ τὸ ἐπ' αὐτῇ κλέος," καὶ ἐπιρραψῳδήσαν-
τος αὐτῷ τὸ "εἷς δή που λοιπὸς κατερύκεται εὐρεῖ"—

gymnasia and fountains and porticoes, so that it appears sufficient for the crowd of visitors. And if a city also has mastery at sea, as Smyrna does, the sea will give it many, ungrudging gifts. He also enhanced the beauty of Smyrna with the fountain of olive oil, roofed over with gold, which he built in the gymnasium of Asclepius. And he held among them the office of the one who wears the crown, from which the people of Smyrna give names to the years.

(75) They say that in the presence of the emperor Severus he broke down in an improvised speech, because he was afraid of the court and bodyguards. If this were to happen to a forensic orator, it would indeed be worthy of criticism, because the tribe of forensic orators are bold and self-confident. But since a sophist spends his time in study with youths for most of the day, how should he resist being overcome by panic? A single listener with a stern expression interferes with an improvised speech, as does praise that is too slow, and applause that is not of the accustomed kind. And if a sophist is aware of malice lying in wait against him, as Heracleides was aware of that of Antipater at that time, he will think of ideas less readily, and he will not speak so fluently, because suspicions of this kind are a darkness on thought and a restraint on the tongue.

(76) It is said that he was fined a great part of his estate for cutting down sacred cedars, and when he was going out from the court his students followed him, consoling and sustaining the man. And one of them said, "No one will ever take away your ability to declaim, Heracleides, nor your fame for it." And he recited to him the line, "One man is still detained on the wide . . ." "imperial trea-

614

"φίσκῳ," ἔφη, ἀστειότατα δὴ ἐπιπαίξας τοῖς ἑαυτοῦ κακοῖς.

(77) Δοκεῖ δὲ μάλιστα σοφιστῶν οὗτος τὴν ἐπιστήμην πόνῳ κατακτήσασθαι μὴ ξυγχωρούσης αὐτῷ τῆς φύσεως, καὶ ἔστιν αὐτῷ φρόντισμα οὐκ ἀηδές, βιβλίον ξύμμετρον, ὃ ἐπιγέγραπται Πόνου ἐγκώμιον. 615 τὸ δὲ βιβλίον τοῦτο πρόχειρον⁴⁰ ἔχων ἐνέτυχε Πτολεμαίῳ τῷ σοφιστῇ κατὰ Ναύκρατιν. ὁ δὲ ἤρετο αὐτόν, ὅ τι σπουδάζοι· τοῦ δὲ εἰπόντος, ὅτι πόνου εἴη ἐγκώμιον, λαβὼν ὁ Πτολεμαῖος τὸ βιβλίον καὶ ἀπαλείψας τὸ πῖ "ὥρα σοι," ἔφη, "ἀναγιγνώσκειν τὸ ὄνομα τοῦ ἐγκωμίου." καὶ αἱ διαλέξεις δέ, ἃς Ἀπολλώνιος ὁ Ναυκρατίτης κατ' αὐτοῦ διελέγετο, ὡς νωθροῦ καθάπτονται καὶ μοχθοῦντος.

(78) Ἡρακλείδου διδάσκαλοι Ἡρώδης μὲν τῶν οὐκ ἀληθῶς πεπιστευμένων, Ἀδριανὸς δὲ καὶ Χρῆστος ἐν γνησίοις, καὶ Ἀριστοκλέους δὲ ἠκροᾶσθαι αὐτὸν μὴ ἀπιστῶμεν. λέγεται δὲ καὶ γαστρὶ κοίλῃ χρήσασθαι καὶ πλεῖστα ὀψοφαγῆσαι, καὶ ἡ πολυφαγία αὕτη ἐς οὐδὲν αὐτῷ ἀποσκῆψαι. ἐτελεύτα γοῦν ὑπὲρ τὰ ὀγδοήκοντα ἔτη ἄρτιος τὸ σῶμα καὶ τάφος μὲν αὐτῷ Λυκία λέγεται, ἐτελεύτα δὲ ἐπὶ θυγατρὶ καὶ ἀπελευθέροις οὐ σπουδαίοις, ὑφ' ὧν καὶ τὴν Ῥητορικὴν ἐκληρονο-

⁴⁰ πρόχειρον Schmid; πρὸ χειρῶν ω

176 For this quotation (Hom. *Od.* 4.498), which was popular because it was easily parodied, see VS 558; here the pupil means

sury,"[176] Heracleides said, very wittily joking about his own misfortunes.

(77) This man of all the sophists seems to have acquired his skill by hard work, since his nature did not grant it to him. And there is a work of his that has a certain charm, a book of moderate size, which is entitled *In Praise of Work*. He had this book at hand once when he happened to meet the sophist Ptolemy in Naucratis. And Ptolemy asked him what he was studying. And when he said that it was an encomium of work, Ptolemy took the book and crossed out the P[177] and said, "Now it's appropriate for you to read the name of your encomium." In fact the preliminary speeches that Apollonius of Naucratis made against him find fault with him for being sluggish and plodding.

615

(78) As for the teachers of Heracleides, for Herodes there is no real evidence, but Hadrian and Chrestus are among those who were genuinely his teachers. Let us believe as well that he was a student of Aristocles. He is said to have had a hollow belly and to have eaten a great deal of rich food, but this gluttony did him no harm. Rather he died aged more than eighty, sound in body. Lycia is said to be his place of burial, and he died leaving behind a daughter and some freedmen, who were none too honest, to whom he bequeathed Rhetoric. And Rhetoric was a

---

that Heracleides and his fame survive, but the sophist by his allusion to the confiscation of his property to the emperor alters the sense of the verb to mean "is checked by" and changes the last word from "sea" to "imperial treasury."

177 By dropping the first letter, "work," πόνος, is altered to ὄνος, "ass."

μήθη· ἡ δὲ Ῥητορικὴ γήδιον δεκατάλαντον ἦν αὐτῷ
κατὰ τὴν Σμύρναν ἐωνημένον ἐκ τῶν ἀκροάσεων.

(79) 27. κζ'. Μὴ δὲ δεύτερα τῶν προειρημένων σοφιστῶν μηδὲ Ἱππόδρομόν τις ἡγείσθω τὸν Θετταλόν,
τῶν μὲν γὰρ βελτίων φαίνεται, τῶν δὲ οὐκ οἶδα ὅ τι
λείπεται. Ἱπποδρόμῳ τοίνυν πατρὶς μὲν ἦν Λάρισσα
πόλις εὖ πράττουσα ἐν Θετταλοῖς, πατὴρ δὲ Ὀλυμ-
πιόδωρος παρελθὼν ἱπποτροφίᾳ Θετταλοὺς πάντας.

(80) Μεγάλου δὲ ἐν Θετταλίᾳ δοκοῦντος τοῦ καὶ
ἅπαξ προστῆναι τῶν Πυθίων ὁ Ἱππόδρομος προέστη
616 δὶς τῶν Πυθικῶν ἄθλων, πλούτῳ τε ὑπερήνεγκε τοὺς
ἄνω καὶ κόσμῳ τῷ περὶ τὸν ἀγῶνα καὶ μεγέθει
γνώμης καὶ δικαιότητι βραβευούσῃ τὸ εὐθύ. τὸ γοῦν
περὶ τὸν τῆς τραγῳδίας ὑποκριτὴν ὑπ' αὐτοῦ πραχθὲν
οὐδὲ ὑπερβολὴν ἑτέρῳ καταλέλοιπε δικαιότητός τε
καὶ γνώμης· Κλήμης γὰρ ὁ Βυζάντιος τραγῳδίας
ὑποκριτὴς ἦν μὲν οἷος οὔπω τις τὴν τέχνην, νικῶν δὲ
κατὰ τοὺς χρόνους, οὓς τὸ Βυζάντιον ἐπολιορκεῖτο,
ἀπῄει ἁμαρτάνων τῆς νίκης, ὡς μὴ δοκοίη δι' ἑνὸς
ἀνδρὸς κηρύττεσθαι πόλις ὅπλα ἐπὶ Ῥωμαίους ἠρ-
μένη. ἄριστα δὲ αὐτὸν ἀγωνισάμενον κἂν τοῖς Ἀμφι-
κτυονικοῖς ἄθλοις οἱ μὲν Ἀμφικτύονες ἀπεψηφίζοντο
τῆς νίκης δέει τῆς προειρημένης αἰτίας, ἀναπηδήσας

---

178 Another Olympiodorus, probably the grandson of Hippodromus, appears in an inscription on a statue base found at Lou-
tra Aidespou in 1962. See Puech (2002, 308–12) for the inscription and its relation to Hippodromus, as well as further discussion
of the chronology of Hippodromus' life.

little farm worth ten talents that he had bought near Smyrna with the proceeds of his teaching.

(79) 27. Let no one consider Hippodromus of Thessaly second to any of the sophists about whom I have spoken, because he is clearly better than some, and I do not think that he falls behind the rest. Now the birthplace of Hippodromus was Larissa, a flourishing city in Thessaly, and his father was Olympiodorus, who surpassed all other Thessalians as a breeder of horses.[178]

(80) Though in Thessaly it seemed a great achievement to have presided once at the Pythia, Hippodromus presided twice over the Pythian games, and he outdid his predecessors in wealth and in the elegance with which he ordered the games, and in the magnanimity and fairness that he showed as a judge. For example, his actions as judge of the competition for tragic actors left no scope for another to outdo him in fairness and good judgment. Clemens of Byzantium was a tragic actor like no other to this day, but since he was winning his victories at the time when Byzantium was being besieged,[179] he went away robbed of his victories, so that it would not appear that a city that had taken up arms against the Romans was proclaimed victor in the person of one of its men. So after he had performed brilliantly in the Amphictyonic games, the Amphictyons were about to vote against giving him the victory because they were afraid for the reason I have just

616

[179] Byzantium was the last stronghold of the followers of Niger, who contended with Septimius Severus for the principate. On the eventual fall of Byzantium after prolonged siege in AD 195, see Hdn. 3.6.9; Cass. Dio 74.12.1–14.6.

δὲ ξὺν ὁρμῇ ὁ Ἱππόδρομος, "οὗτοι μὲν," εἶπεν, "ἐρρώ-
σθων ἐπιορκοῦντές τε καὶ παραγιγνώσκοντες τοῦ δικαίου, ἐγὼ δὲ Κλήμεντι τὴν νικῶσαν δίδωμι." ἐφέντος
δὲ θατέρου τῶν ὑποκριτῶν ἐπὶ τὸν βασιλέα, ηὐδοκίμησε πάλιν ἡ τοῦ Ἱπποδρόμου ψῆφος· καὶ γὰρ δὴ
καὶ ἐπὶ τῆς Ῥώμης ἐνίκα ὁ Βυζάντιος.

(81) Τοιοῦτος δὲ ὢν ἐς τὰ πλήθη θαυμασίᾳ πρᾳότητι
ἐπὶ τὰς ἐπιδείξεις ἐχρῆτο· παραλαβὼν γὰρ τὴν τέχνην φίλαυτόν τε καὶ ἀλαζόνα οὔτε ἐς ἔπαινον ἑαυτοῦ
κατέστη ποτὲ καὶ ἐπέκοπτε τὰς ὑπερβολὰς τῶν
ἐπαίνων· βοώντων γοῦν ποτε ἐπ᾽ αὐτῷ τῶν Ἑλλήνων
πολλὰ καὶ εὔφημα καί που καὶ τῷ Πολέμωνι ὁμοιούν-
των αὐτόν, "τί μ᾽ ἀθανάτοισιν εἴσκεις;" ἔφη, οὔτε τὸν
Πολέμωνα ἀφελόμενος τὸ νομίζεσθαι θεῖον ἄνδρα
617 οὔτε ἑαυτῷ διδοὺς τὸ τοιούτῳ ὁμοιοῦσθαι. Πρόκλου δὲ
τοῦ Ναυκρατίτου πομπείαν οὐ πρεσβυτικὴν ξυνθέν-
τος ἐπὶ πάντας τοὺς παιδεύοντας Ἀθήνῃσι καὶ τὸν
Ἱππόδρομον ἐγκαταλέξαντος τῷ λοιδορησμῷ τούτῳ
ἡμεῖς μὲν ᾠόμεθα λόγου ἀκροάσεσθαι πρὸς τὴν τῶν
εἰρημένων ἠχὼ ξυγκειμένου, ὁ δὲ οὐδὲν εἰπὼν φλαῦρον
ἔπαινον εὐφημίας διεξῆλθεν, ἀρξάμενος ἀπὸ τοῦ
ταὼ⁴¹ ὡς ἀναπτεροῦντος αὐτὸν τοῦ ἐπαίνου. ὧδε μὲν
δὴ διέκειτο πρὸς τοὺς ἑαυτοῦ πρεσβυτέρους καὶ

⁴¹ Cobet omits the unnecessary τοῦ ὄρνιθος after τοῦ ταώ.

---

¹⁸⁰ Hom. *Od.* 16.187.
¹⁸¹ For the ascription of a divine (θεῖος) character to Polemo,

explained. But Hippodromus leaped to his feet and said, "These men can go away breaking their oaths and making a wrong and unjust decision, but I grant the victory to Clemens." When another of the actors appealed to the emperor, the vote of Hippodromus won wide approval. Moreover the Byzantine was again victorious at Rome.

(81) Though he was as firm as this in the face of crowds, he employed an astonishing gentleness in his declamations. Even though he had taken up an art that is prone to egotism and arrogance, he never lapsed into praise of himself and he cut short any excessive praise from others. For example once when the Greeks were shouting his praises and even comparing him to Polemo, he said, "Why do you compare me to the immortals?"[180] By this response he neither took from Polemo his reputation as a divine man nor did he agree to being likened to someone like him.[181] And when Proclus of Naucratis composed a crude satire, unbefitting for an old man, on all those who were teaching at Athens and included Hippodromus in this abuse, we thought that we would hear from him a speech in reply, echoing the tone of what Proclus had said. But he said nothing small-minded and gave instead a praise of speaking well of others, beginning from the example of the peacock, who spreads his feathers in response to praise.[182] This then was how he behaved toward those older than

617

cf. *VS* 533, where his speech at Olympia is also said to have had a divine inspiration.

[182] The peacock enjoyed some popularity as an animal analogy in sophistic rhetoric. See, for instance, Dio Chrys. *Or.* 12.2–5, where the peacock is an image of the splendid orator (by contrast with Dio, the dowdy, philosophical owl).

χρόνῳ πολλῷ τε καὶ οὐ πολλῷ προειληφότας· ὡς δὲ
καὶ πρὸς τοὺς ἰσήλικας εἶχεν, ὑπάρχει μαθεῖν ἐκ
τῶνδε. νεανίας ἀπ᾽ Ἰωνίας ἥκων Ἀθήναζε διῄει ἐπαίνους τοῦ Ἡρακλείδου πέρα ἀχθηδόνος· ἰδὼν οὖν αὐτὸν ὁ Ἱππόδρομος ἐν τῇ ἀκροάσει, "ὁ νεανίας οὗτος,"
ἔφη, "ἐρᾷ τοῦ ἑαυτοῦ διδασκάλου· καλὸν οὖν ξυλλαβεῖν αὐτῷ τῶν παιδικῶν. καὶ γὰρ ἂν καὶ ξὺν ἑρμαίῳ
ἀπέλθοι μαθὼν ἐγκωμιάζειν." καὶ εἰπὼν ταῦτα ἔπαινον τοῦ Ἡρακλείδου διῆλθεν, οἷος ἐπ᾽ αὐτῷ οὔπω
εἴρηται. τὰ δὲ ἐπὶ Διοδότῳ τῷ Καππαδόκῃ δάκρυα καὶ
τὸ ἐσθῆτα μέλαιναν ἐπ᾽ αὐτῷ ἐνδῦναι φύσιν μὲν παρ-
εσχημένῳ μελέτῃ ἐπιτηδείαν, ἐν⁴² ἐφήβῳ δὲ ἀποθανόντι πατέρα τοῦ Ἑλληνικοῦ ἐκήρυξε τὸν Ἱππόδρομον καὶ περιωπὴν ἔχοντα τοῦ καὶ μεθ᾽ ἑαυτὸν γενέσθαι
τινὰς ἀριπρεπεῖς ἄνδρας. τουτὶ δὲ μάλιστα ἐν Ὀλυμπίᾳ ἐδήλωσε· Φιλοστράτῳ γὰρ τῷ Λημνίῳ γνωρίμῳ
μὲν ἑαυτοῦ ὄντι, δύο δὲ καὶ εἴκοσιν ἔτη γεγονότι
ἀναρριπτοῦντί τινα αὐτοσχέδιον πλεῖστα μὲν ἐνέδωκε
τῇ τέχνῃ τῶν ἐπαίνων, ὧν τε εἰπεῖν ἔδει καὶ μή, ἀξι-
ούσης δὲ καὶ τὸν Ἱππόδρομον τῆς Ἑλλάδος αὐτίκα
παριέναι, "οὐκ ἐπαποδύσομαι," ἔφη, "τοῖς ἐμαυτοῦ
σπλάγχνοις." καὶ εἰπὼν ταῦτα ἀνεβάλετο τὴν ἀκρόασιν ἐπὶ τὴν τῆς θυσίας ἡμέραν. ταῦτα μὲν οὖν ἐχέτω
μοι δήλωσιν ἀνδρὸς πεπαιδευμένου, φιλανθρώπου τε
καὶ πράου τὸ ἦθος.

⁴² ἐν Cobet adds. Wright compared ἐν μειρακίῳ ἀποθανόντι
(at VS 610).

338

him, whether by many years or a few. How he engaged with those of his own age, one can learn from the following examples. A youth came from Ionia to Athens who used to go through praises of Heracleides beyond what anyone could stand. Seeing him in his lecture, Hippodromus said, "This young man is in love with his teacher. It's a fine thing to help him in his passion. It would be a windfall for him if he goes away knowing how to give an encomium." Saying this he gave a speech in praise of Heracleides, the likes of which had never been spoken about him before. And the fact that he shed tears for Diodotus the Cappadocian and wore black clothing in mourning for him, because he had shown great natural talent for declamation, but had died in his youth, proclaimed Hippodromus the father of the Hellenic students, and one who was concerned that after him there should be very distinguished men. He made this especially evident at Olympia. For when Philostratus of Lemnos,[183] his own pupil, aged twenty two, was about to take a chance giving an improvised speech, he gave him a great deal of advice on the technique of encomia, specifying what one ought and ought not to say. And when all Greece asked for Hippodromus to come forward he said, "I will not strip for a contest against my own flesh and blood." Saying this, he postponed his lecture until the day of the sacrifice.[184] So let these examples show that he was a man who was truly educated, being both humane and gentle in his character.

183 The biographer's son-in-law, on whom see VS 628.
184 The last day of the festival.

618   (82) Τὸν δὲ Ἀθήνησι τῶν σοφιστῶν θρόνον κατασχὼν ἐτῶν που τεττάρων ἀπηνέχθη αὑτοῦ ὑπὸ τῆς
γυναικὸς καὶ τοῦ πλούτου· ἐκείνη γὰρ ἐνεργοτάτη γυναικῶν ἐγένετο καὶ φύλαξ ἀγαθὴ χρημάτων, ἀμφοῖν
τε ἀπόντων ἡ οὐσία ὑπεδίδου. τοῦ γε μὴν ἐσφοιτᾶν[43]
τὰς τῶν Ἑλλήνων πανηγύρεις οὐκ ἠμέλει, ἀλλ᾽ ἐθάμιζεν ἐς αὐτὰς ἐπιδείξεων ἕνεκα καὶ τοῦ μὴ ἀγνοεῖσθαι.
βελτίων δὲ κἀκεῖνα ἐφαίνετο ὑπὸ τοῦ καὶ μετὰ τὸ πε-
παῦσθαι τοῦ παιδεύειν ἀεὶ σπουδάζειν. Ἱππόδρομος
μὲν γὰρ δὴ πλεῖστα μὲν ἐξέμαθεν Ἑλλήνων τῶν γε
μετὰ τὸν Καππαδόκην Ἀλέξανδρον μνήμης εὐτυχη-
σάντων, πλεῖστα δὲ ἀνέγνω μετά γε Ἀμμώνιον τὸν
ἀπὸ τοῦ Περιπάτου· ἐκείνου γὰρ πολυγραμματώτερον
ἄνδρα οὔπω ἔγνων. μελέτης δὲ ὁ Ἱππόδρομος οὔτε ἐν
ἀγρῷ διαιτώμενος ἠμέλει οὔτε ὁδοιπορῶν οὔτε ἐν
θαλάττῃ,[44] ἀλλὰ καὶ κρεῖττον ὄλβου κτῆμα ἐκάλει αὐτὴν ἐκ τῶν Εὐριπίδου τε ὕμνων καὶ Ἀμφίονος.

(83) Ἀγροικότερός τε ὢν τὸ εἶδος ὅμως ἀμήχανον
εὐγένειαν ἐπεδήλου τοῖς ὄμμασι γοργόν τε καὶ φαι-
δρὸν βλέπων. τουτὶ δὲ καὶ Μεγιστίας ὁ Σμυρναῖος ἐν
αὑτῷ καθεωρακέναι φησὶν οὐ τὰ δεύτερα τῶν φυσι-
ογνωμονούντων νομισθείς· ἀφίκετο μὲν γὰρ ἐς τὴν
Σμύρναν μετὰ τὸν Ἡρακλείδην ὁ Ἱππόδρομος οὔπω
πρὸ τούτου ἥκων, ἀποβὰς δὲ τῆς νεὼς ἀπῄει ἐς ἀγοράν, εἴ τῳ ἐντύχοι πεπαιδευμένῳ τὰ ἐγχώρια. ἱερὸν δὲ

───────────

[43] ἐσφοιτᾶν is the reading of Vb and of the β family and is
certainly *lectio difficilior*. Stefec deletes ἐς after (ἐσ)φοιτᾶν.

(82) He held the chair of rhetoric at Athens for about 618 four years, but was taken from it by his wife and wealth. For she was the most active of all women and a good guardian of money, but with both of them absent, the property was deteriorating. Still he did not neglect to attend the festivals of the Greeks, but frequented them for the declamations and so that he would not be forgotten. He appeared on these occasions better than ever, because he continued constantly studying even when he ceased teaching. For Hippodromus memorized the most of any of the Greeks who were endowed with good memory, after Alexander the Cappadocian, and he read the most after Ammonius the Peripatetic, for I have never encountered a better read man than him. Moreover Hippodromus never neglected his study of declamation even when he was in the country or on a journey or at sea, but he called it a possession greater than wealth, quoting from the hymns of Euripides and Amphion.[185]

(83) He was rather unkempt in appearance but still showed an irresistible nobility in his eyes, since he had a gaze that was both keen and cheerful. Megistias of Smyrna also says that he perceived this in him, and he was a man considered second to none in physiognomics. For Hippodromus came to Smyrna after the death of Heracleides, never having come there before, and he disembarked from the ship and went to the agora, hoping to find someone educated in the local style. When he saw a temple and

---

[185] Eur. *Antiop.* fr.191 Kannicht.

---

44 θαλάττῃ is Jahn's correction for the MSS' θετταλίᾳ.

κατιδὼν καὶ παιδαγωγοὺς προσκαθημένους ἀκολού-
θους τε παῖδας ἄχθη βιβλίων ἐν πήραις ἀνημμένους
ξυνῆκεν, ὅτι παιδεύοι τις ἔνδον τῶν ἐπιφανῶν, καὶ
εἴσω παρῄει καὶ προσειπὼν τὸν Μεγιστίαν ἐκάθητο
ἐρωτῶν οὐδέν. ὁ μὲν δὴ Μεγιστίας ᾤετο ὑπὲρ μαθητῶν αὐτὸν διαλέξεσθαί οἱ, πατέρα ἴσως ἢ τροφέα παί-
619 δων ὄντα, καὶ ἤρετο, ὑπὲρ ὅτου ἥκοι· ὁ δὲ, "πεύσῃ,"
ἔφη, "ἐπειδὰν αὐτοὶ γενώμεθα." διακωδωνίσας οὖν ὁ
Μεγιστίας τὰ μειράκια, "λέγε," ἔφη, "ὅ τι βούλει." καὶ
ὁ Ἱππόδρομος, "ἀντιδῶμεν ἀλλήλοις τὴν ἐσθῆτα," εἶ-
πεν· ἦν δὲ ἄρα τῷ μὲν Ἱπποδρόμῳ χλαμύς, τῷ δὲ αὖ
δημηγορικὸν ἱμάτιον. "καὶ τίνα σοι νοῦν ἔχει τοῦτο;"
ἦ δ' ὁ Μεγιστίας. "ἐπίδειξιν," ἔφη, "σοι μελέτης ποιή-
σασθαι βούλομαι." δαιμονᾶν μὲν οὖν αὐτὸν ᾠήθη
ταῦτα ἐπαγγείλαντα καὶ τὴν γνώμην ἐλαύνεσθαι, τὰς
δὲ βολὰς ἀνασκοπῶν τῶν ὀμμάτων καὶ ὁρῶν αὐτὸν
ἔννουν καὶ καθεστηκότα ἀντέδωκε τὴν ἐσθῆτα ὑπόθεσίν τε αἰτήσαντι προύβαλε τὸν μάγον τὸν ἀποθνήσκειν ἀξιοῦντα, ἐπειδὴ μὴ ἐδυνήθη ἀποκτεῖναι μάγον
μοιχόν. ὡς δὲ ἱζήσας ἐπὶ τοῦ θρόνου καὶ μικρὸν ἐπισχὼν ἀνεπήδησε, μᾶλλον εἰσῄει τὸν Μεγιστίαν ὁ τῆς
μανίας λόγος καὶ τὰ πλεονεκτήματα ἐμβροντησίαν
ᾤετο, ἀρξαμένου δὲ τῆς ὑποθέσεως καὶ εἰπόντος,
"ἀλλ' ἐμαυτόν γε δύναμαι," ἐξέπεσεν ἑαυτοῦ ὑπὸ θαύματος καὶ προσδραμὼν αὐτῷ ἱκέτευε μαθεῖν, ὅστις
εἴη. "εἰμὶ μέν," ἔφη, "Ἱππόδρομος ὁ Θετταλός, ἥκω δέ
σοι ἐγγυμνασόμενος, ἵν' ἐκμάθοιμι δι' ἑνὸς ἀνδρὸς

paedagogoi sitting by it, and slaves following, heavily laden with books in satchels, he understood that someone eminent was teaching inside. So he entered, greeted Megistias and sat down, without asking anything. So Megistias thought that he was there to speak with him about one of the students, and that he was a father perhaps, or a guardian of one of the boys, and he asked him why he had come. "You will found out," he said, "when we are alone." When 619 Megistias had finished examining the young men, he said, "Tell me what you want." And Hippodromus said, "Let us exchange clothes with one another." Hippodromus was in a traveling cloak, but Megistias in a gown suited to public speaking. "Tell me what you mean by that?" Megistias asked. "I wish to make a display of declamation for you," Hippodromus said. When he said this Megistias thought that he was affected by a demon and that his mind was deranged, but when he observed the keenness of his eyes and saw that he was in his right mind and steady, he exchanged clothes with him. And when Hippodromus asked for a theme, he proposed "The magician who wants to die, because he was unable to kill another magician, who is an adulterer." When he had sat on the lecturer's chair and paused for a moment, Hippodromus leaped to his feet, and the explanation that he was mad occurred more forcibly to Megistias, and he thought these embellishments were signs that he was thunderstruck. But when he began the theme and came to the words, "but at least I can kill myself," Megistias was beside himself with astonishment and ran up to him and begged to learn who he was. "I," he said, "am Hippodromus the Thessalian, and I have come to practice on you,[186] so that I can learn from one man as

---

[186] Perhaps an echo of Pl. *Phdr.* 228e.

οὕτω πεπαιδευμένου τὸ ἦθος τῆς Ἰωνικῆς ἀκροάσεως.
ἀλλ᾽ ὅρα με δι᾽ ὅλης τῆς ὑποθέσεως." περὶ τέρμα δὲ
τοῦ λόγου δρόμος ὑπὸ τῶν κατὰ τὴν Σμύρναν πεπαιδευμένων ἐπὶ τὰς τοῦ Μεγιστίου θύρας ἐγένετο, τα-
χείας τῆς φήμης διαδοθείσης ἐς πάντας ἐπιχωριάζειν
αὐτοῖς τὸν Ἱππόδρομον, ὁ δὲ ἀναλαβὼν τὴν ὑπόθεσιν
ἑτέρᾳ δυνάμει μετεχειρίσατο τὰς ἤδη εἰρημένας ἐννοίας, παρελθών τε ἐς τὸ κοινὸν τῶν Σμυρναίων ἀνὴρ
ἔδοξε θαυμάσιος καὶ οἷος ἐν τοῖς πρὸ αὐτοῦ γράφε-
σθαι.

620   (84) Ἦν δὲ αὐτῷ τὰ μὲν τῆς διαλέξεως Πλάτωνος
ἀνημμένα καὶ Δίωνος, τὰ δὲ τῆς μελέτης κατὰ τὰ Πολέμωνος ἐρρωμένα καί που καὶ ποτιμώτερα, τὰ δὲ τῆς
εὐροίας οἷα τοῖς ἀλύπως ἀναγιγνώσκουσι τὰ σφόδρα
αὐτοῖς καθωμιλημένα. Νικαγόρου δὲ τοῦ σοφιστοῦ
μητέρα σοφιστῶν τὴν τραγῳδίαν προσειπόντος διορθούμενος ὁ Ἱππόδρομος τὸν λόγον "ἐγὼ δέ," ἔφη,
"πατέρα Ὅμηρον." ἐσπούδαζε δὲ καὶ ἀπὸ Ἀρχιλόχου
καλῶν τὸν μὲν Ὅμηρον φωνὴν σοφιστῶν, τὸν δὲ Ἀρ-
χίλοχον πνεῦμα. μελέται μὲν δὴ τοῦ ἀνδρὸς τούτου
τριάκοντα ἴσως, ἄριστοι δὲ αὐτῶν οἱ Καταναῖοι καὶ
οἱ Σκύθαι καὶ ὁ Δημάδης ὁ μὴ ξυγχωρῶν ἀφίστα-
σθαι Ἀλεξάνδρου ἐν Ἰνδοῖς ὄντος. ᾄδονται δὲ αὐτοῦ
καὶ λυρικοὶ νόμοι, καὶ γὰρ δὴ καὶ τῆς νομικῆς λύρας
ἥπτετο. ἐτελεύτα δὲ ἀμφὶ τὰ ἑβδομήκοντα καὶ οἴκοι

---

[187] For a similar feat of virtuosity, see the life of Alexander
above, VS 572.

[188] This theme was inspired by the eruption of Etna in 425

proficient as you are the Ionian character in declamation.
But watch me through the whole theme." Around the end
of the speech, a crowd of educated people from throughout Smyrna came running to the doors of Megistias, because a rumor had quickly gone around to everyone that
Hippodromus was visiting their city. And he took up the
same theme, employing a different possible approach,
and before the crowd of the Smyrneans he went through
the same ideas that he had already expressed,[187] and he
seemed an astonishing man and worthy to be enlisted
among those who had gone before.

(84) His approach to introductory speeches was dependent on Plato and Dio, and his declamations had the
power of Polemo but were somewhat sweeter. In fluency
he was like someone easily reading aloud a very familiar
text. When the sophist Nicagoras said that tragedy was the
mother of sophists, Hippodromus corrected his words and
said, "I say that their father is Homer." He was a keen
student too of Archilochus and called Homer the voice of
sophists, but Archilochus their breath. There are extant
perhaps thirty declamations by this man, and the best of
them are "The Citizens of Catana,"[188] "The Scythians,"[189]
and "Demades argues against revolting against Alexander
while he is in India."[190] His lyric songs are also sung, because he was skillful as well in composing songs for the
lyre. He died at home aged about seventy, and left behind

620

BC, mentioned in Thuc. 3.116. From other references to this
theme in Hermogenes. it seems that the citizens of Catana are
supposed to debate whether they shall migrate.

[189] On this theme see above, VS 572.

[190] Demades is supposed to oppose the advice of Demosthenes.

καὶ ἐπὶ υἱῷ ἀγροῦ μὲν προστῆναι καὶ οἰκίας ἱκανῷ,
παραπλῆγι δὲ καὶ ἔκφρονι τά τε τῶν σοφιστῶν οὐ
πεπαιδευμένῳ.

(85) 28. κη΄. Οἱ τὸν Λαοδικέα Οὖαρον λόγου ἀξιοῦν-
τες αὐτοὶ μὴ ἀξιούσθων λόγου· καὶ γὰρ εὐτελὴς καὶ
διακεχηνὼς καὶ εὐήθης καὶ ἣν εἶχεν εὐφωνίαν αἰ-
σχύνων καμπαῖς ἀσμάτων, αἷς κἂν ὑπορχήσαιτό τις
τῶν ἀσελγεστέρων· οὗ διδάσκαλον ἢ ἀκροατὴν τί ἂν
λέγοιμι, τί δ' ἂν γράφοιμι,[45] εὖ γιγνώσκων, ὅτι μήτ'
ἂν τοιαῦτα διδάξειέ τις καὶ τοῖς μεμαθηκόσιν ὄνειδος
τὸ τοιούτων ἠκροᾶσθαι;

(86) 29. κθ΄. Κυρίνῳ δὲ τῷ σοφιστῇ πατρὶς μὲν
Νικομήδεια ἐγένετο, γένος δὲ οὔτε εὐδόκιμον οὔτ' αὖ
καταβεβλημένον, φύσις ἀγαθὴ παραλαβεῖν μαθήματα καὶ παραδοῦναι βελτίων· οὐ γὰρ μνήμην μόνον,
ἀλλὰ καὶ σαφήνειαν ἦσκει. κομματίας ὁ σοφιστὴς
οὗτος καὶ περὶ μὲν τὰ θετικὰ τῶν χωρίων οὐ πολύς,
ἐρρωμένος μὴν καὶ σφοδρὸς καὶ κατασεῖσαι δεινὸς
ἀκροατοῦ ὦτα, καὶ γὰρ δὴ καὶ ἀπεσχεδίαζεν· προσ-
φυέστερος δὲ ταῖς κατηγορίαις δοκῶν ἐπιστεύθη ἐκ
βασιλέως τὴν τοῦ ταμιείου γλῶτταν, καὶ παρελθὼν ἐς

621

[45] Following Stefec I have adopted λέγοιμι and γράφοιμι,
the reading of the majority of MSS, rather than γράφοιμι and
φράζοιμι of Va (and for the latter word, a marginal note in L).

191 There seems to be no further evidence on Varus of Laodicea, other than Philostratus' recollection of him here in order to
banish him into oblivion.

a son who was capable enough to manage the farm and household, but was mad and stupid and not educated in sophistic matters.

(85) 28. Those who deem Varus of Laodicea[191] worth mentioning should themselves be deemed unworthy of mention. He was trivial and slack-jawed and simple-minded, and what he possessed by way of a pleasing voice he made shameful with twistings of song, to which some immoral person might dance. Why would I speak of any teacher or student of his, and why would I write of them, though I know perfectly well, because no one would teach such things and it would be disgraceful for students to admit that they had listened to such teaching?

(86) 29. The birthplace of Quirinus the sophist was Nicomedia, and his family was neither distinguished nor altogether fallen into obscurity. He had a fine natural talent for receiving learning and was even better at passing it on, because he trained not only in memory but also in clarity. This sophist was a speaker of short clauses and did not speak very fully on abstract themes, but he was indeed powerful and vigorous and skilled at shaking the ears of his listener. Moreover he used to improvise his speeches, but since he appeared more suited by his nature to prosecution speeches, he was appointed by the emperor as *advocatus fisci*.[192] And though he took on this position of

621

---

192 Though the post of *ab epistulis Graecis* was more common for sophists, that of *advocatus fisci* was also suitable for the more "legally minded" (as Bowersock observed). In addition to Quirinus and later Heliodorus serving in this role at Rome (see below, VS 626), Zeuxidemus, apparently the father of Antipater of Hierapolis, was provincial *advocatus* in Asia. See Bowersock 1969, 22 and 57.

τὸ δυνηθῆναί τι οὔτε βαρὺς οὔτε ἀλαζὼν ἔδοξεν,
ἀλλὰ πρᾷός τε καὶ ἑαυτῷ ὅμοιος, οὔτε ἐρασιχρήμα-
τος, ἀλλ᾽ ὥσπερ τὸν Ἀριστείδην Ἀθηναῖοι ᾄδουσι
μετὰ τὴν ἐπίταξιν τῶν φόρων κατὰ τὰς νήσους ἐπανελθεῖν σφισιν ἐν τῷ προτέρῳ τρίβωνι, οὕτω καὶ ὁ
Κυρῖνος ἀφίκετο ἐς τὰ ἑαυτοῦ ἤθη πενίᾳ σεμνυνόμε-
νος. αἰτιωμένων δὲ αὐτὸν τῶν κατὰ τὴν Ἀσίαν ἐνδεικ-
τῶν, ὡς πρᾳότερον περὶ τὰς κατηγορίας ἢ αὐτοὶ
διδάσκουσι, "καὶ μὴν καὶ πολλῷ βέλτιον," εἶπεν,
"ὑμᾶς λαβεῖν τὴν ἐμὴν πρᾳότητα ἢ ἐμὲ τὴν ὑμετέραν
ὠμότητα." ἐνδειξάντων δὲ αὐτῶν καὶ πόλιν οὐ μεγάλην ἐπὶ πολλαῖς μυριάσιν ἐκράτει μὲν ὁ Κυρῖνος
τὴν δίκην ἄκων μάλα, προσιόντες δὲ αὐτῷ οἱ ἐνδεί-
κται, "αὕτη σε," ἔφασαν, "ἡ δίκη ἀρεῖ μέγαν παρελ-
θοῦσα ἐς τὰ τοῦ βασιλέως ὦτα." καὶ ὁ Κυρῖνος, "οὐκ
ἐμοὶ πρέπον," ἔφη, "ἀλλ᾽ ὑμῖν ἐπὶ τῷ πόλιν ἀοίκητον
εἰργάσθαι τιμᾶσθαι." ἐπὶ δὲ υἱῷ τελευτήσαντι παρα-
μυθουμένων αὐτὸν τῶν προσηκόντων, "πότε," εἶπεν,
"ἀνὴρ ἢ νῦν δόξω;" Ἀδριανοῦ δὲ ἀκροατὴς γενόμενος
οὐ πᾶσιν ὡμολόγει τοῖς ἐκείνου, ἀλλ᾽ ἔστιν ἃ καὶ δι-
έγραφεν οὐκ ὀρθῶς εἰρημένα.[46] τέρμα δὲ αὐτῷ τοῦ
βίου ἔτος ἑβδομηκοστὸν καὶ τὸ σῆμα οἴκοι.

(87) 30. λ′. Φιλίσκος δὲ ὁ Θετταλὸς Ἱπποδρόμῳ μὲν

[46] Lucarini suggests ὡς before οὐκ ὀρθῶς εἰρημένα.

193 The base of a statue dedicated to Philiscus at Delphi survives with an inscription in elegiac couplets. This records both the

considerable power, he did not show himself to be too severe or arrogant, but gentle and as he had been earlier, nor did he become avaricious, but just as the Athenians tell the legend of Aristides—how after he had arranged the tribute payments throughout the islands he returned to them in the same worn coat—so too Quirinus came back to his people dignified by poverty. When the informers from throughout Asia found fault with him for being more gentle concerning their prosecutions than suited the evidence that they themselves had given he said, "It would be much better for you to take on my gentleness than for me to take on your brutality." When they cited a city of no great size for tens of thousands of drachmas, Quirinus won the case, but very unwillingly. And the informants came and said to him, "This case will greatly boost your reputation when it comes to the ears of the emperor." And Quirinus said, "It does not suit me but you to be honored for laying waste a city." And when his relatives tried to console him for the death of his son he said, "When if not now will I show myself a man?" Though he was a student of Hadrian he did not follow him in all respects, but there are some passages that he expunged because they were not properly expressed. The end of his life came when he was seventy and his tomb is in his home city.

(87) 30. Philiscus the Thessalian[193] was related to Hip-

dedication of the statue to Philiscus "great in wisdom" (τὸν μέγαν ἐν σοφίῃ) by "men from among the Hellenes" ([ἄν]δρες ἀφ' Ἑλλήνων) and the fact that "scepter-bearing kings" (i.e., Septimius Severus and Caracalla) had granted him "the power of judgment in the cities of Thessaly, which resounds with the sound of horses." See Puech 2002, 376–77.

συνῆπται γένος, τοῦ δὲ Ἀθήνησι θρόνου προύστη
622 ἐτῶν ἑπτὰ τὴν ἀτέλειαν τὴν ἐπ' αὐτῷ ἀφαιρεθείς,
τουτὶ δὲ ὅπως συνέβη, δηλῶσαι ἀνάγκη· Ἐορδαῖοι
Μακεδόνες ἀνειπόντες ἐς⁴⁷ τὰς οἰκείας λειτουργίας τὸν
Φιλίσκον, ὡς δὴ ὑπάρχον αὐτοῖς ἐπὶ πάντας τοὺς ἀπὸ
μητέρων ‹. . .› †ἔφεσιν†⁴⁸ οὗτος νῦν τῆς δίκης γενομένης ἐπὶ τὸν αὐτοκράτορα, Ἀντωνῖνος δὲ ἦν ὁ τῆς
φιλοσόφου παῖς Ἰουλίας, ἐστάλη ἐς τὴν Ῥώμην ὡς
τὰ ἑαυτοῦ εὖ⁴⁹ θησόμενος, καὶ προσρυεὶς τοῖς περὶ τὴν
Ἰουλίαν γεωμέτραις τε καὶ φιλοσόφοις εὕρετο παρ'
αὐτῆς διὰ τοῦ βασιλέως τὸν Ἀθήνησι θρόνον. ὁ δ'
ὥσπερ οἱ θεοὶ Ὁμήρῳ πεποίηνται οὐ πάντα ἑκόντες
ἀνθρώποις⁵⁰ διδόντες, ἀλλ' ἔστιν ἃ καὶ ἄκοντες, οὕτω
δὴ ἠγρίαινε καὶ χαλεπὸς ἦν ὡς περιδραμόντι· ὡς δὲ
ἤκουσεν εἶναί τινα αὐτῷ καὶ δίκην, ἧς αὐτὸς ἀκροατὴς ἔσοιτο, κελεύει τὸν ἐπιτεταγμένον ταῖς δίκαις
προειπεῖν οἷ τὸ μὴ δι' ἑτέρων, δι' ἑαυτοῦ δὲ ἀγωνίσασθαι. ἐπεὶ δὲ παρῆλθεν εἰς τὸ δικαστήριον, προσ-
623 έκρουσε μὲν τὸ βάδισμα, προσέκρουσε δὲ ἡ στάσις,
καὶ τὴν στολὴν οὐκ εὐσχήμων ἔδοξε καὶ τὴν φωνὴν
μιξόθηλυς καὶ τὴν γλῶτταν ὕπτιος καὶ βλέπων
ἑτέρωσέ ποι μᾶλλον ἢ ἐς τὰ νοούμενα· ἐκ τούτων ἀπο-

---

⁴⁷ ἀνειπόντες ἐς is Kayser's conjecture to fill an evident
lacuna. Something of this sort must have been lost here. For other
options proposed, see Stefec's note *ad loc.*

⁴⁸ This phrase is clearly corrupt and lacunose, apparently
from ὡς to ἔφεσιν (the last word of which Stefec retains but
obelizes.) The text constructed by Kayser and adopted by Wright

podromus, and he held the chair at Athens for seven years, 622
though he lost the immunity that went with it. And I must
relate how this happened. The Heordaean Macedonians
had called upon Philiscus to perform public services in
their region, as was their right in the case of all who were
Heordaeans on the maternal side. Since he did not do this,
they referred the matter to the courts. Now when the case
came before the emperor—and this was Antoninus,[194] the
son of the philosopher Julia—Philiscus made his way to
Rome to protect his own interests. And he insinuated himself into the group of geometers and philosophers around
Julia, and obtained from her, with the emperor's consent,
the chair at Athens. But the emperor, like the gods in Homer who grant favors to human beings, but sometimes
against their will, continued to be angry and was harshly
disposed toward him, believing that Philiscus had managed to get around him. So when he heard that there was
to be a case involving Philiscus, and that he himself would
judge it, he ordered the official in charge of lawsuits to
instruct Philiscus not to make his case through other
speakers, but in person. And when he came into the court
room, he gave offense with his walk, he gave offense with 623
his stance, and he seemed wrongly dressed for the occasion and effeminate in his voice and lazy in his speech, and
as though he were looking anywhere rather than to the

---

[194] Better known as Caracalla.

---

gives a plausible sense, but I am not confident that it is close to
what Philostratus wrote.   [49] εὖ Valckenaer

[50] ἀνθρώποις is Valckenaer's conjecture for the MSS' ἀλλήλοις.

στραφεὶς ὁ αὐτοκράτωρ ἐς τὸν Φιλίσκον ἐπεστόμιζεν
αὐτὸν καὶ παρὰ πάντα τὸν λόγον διείρων ἑαυτὸν τοῦ
ὕδατος καὶ ἐρωτήσεις ἐν αὐτῷ στενὰς ποιούμενος, ὡς
δὲ οὐ πρὸς τὰ ἐρωτώμενα αἱ ἀποκρίσεις ἐγένοντο Φιλίσκου, "τὸν μὲν ἄνδρα," ἔφη, "δείκνυσιν ἡ κόμη, τὸν
δὲ ῥήτορα ἡ φωνή," καὶ μετὰ πολλὰς τοιαύτας ἐπικο-
πὰς ἐπήγαγεν ἑαυτὸν τοῖς Ἑορδαίοις. εἰπόντος δὲ τοῦ
Φιλίσκου, "σύ μοι λειτουργιῶν ἀτέλειαν δέδωκας
δοὺς τὸν Ἀθήνησι θρόνον," ἀναβοήσας ὁ αὐτοκράτωρ,
"οὔτε σύ," εἶπεν, "ἀτελὴς οὔτε ἄλλος οὐδεὶς τῶν παι-
δευόντων· οὐ γὰρ ἄν ποτε διὰ μικρὰ καὶ δύστηνα λογάρια τὰς πόλεις ἀφελοίμην τῶν λειτουργησόντων."
ἀλλ᾽ ὅμως καὶ μετὰ ταῦτα Φιλοστράτῳ τῷ Λημνίῳ
λειτουργιῶν ἀτέλειαν ἐπὶ μελέτῃ ἐψηφίσατο τέτταρα
καὶ εἴκοσιν ἔτη γεγονότι. αἱ μὲν δὴ προφάσεις, δι᾽ ἃς
ὁ Φιλίσκος ἀφῃρέθη τὸ εἶναι ἀτελής, αἵδε ἐγένοντο·
μὴ ἀφαιρείσθω δ᾽ αὐτὸν τὰ περὶ τῷ βλέμματι καὶ τῷ
φθέγματι καὶ τῷ σχήματι ἐλαττώματα τὸ μὴ οὐ
κράτιστα ῥητόρων ἑλληνίσαι τε καὶ συνθεῖναι. ἡ δὲ
ἰδέα τοῦ λόγου λάλος μᾶλλον ἢ ἐναγώνιος, διεφαί-
νετο δὲ αὐτῆς καὶ καθαρὰ ὀνόματα καὶ καινοπρεπὴς
ἦχος. ἐτελεύτα μὲν οὖν ἐπὶ θυγατρὶ καὶ υἱῷ οὐδενὸς
ἀξίῳ, μέτρον δὲ αὐτῷ τοῦ βίου ἔτη ἑπτὰ καὶ ἑξήκοντα.
κεκτημένος δὲ Ἀθήνησι χωρίον οὐκ ἀηδὲς οὐκ ἐν
αὑτῷ ἐτάφη, ἀλλ᾽ ἐν τῇ Ἀκαδημίᾳ, οὗ τίθησι τὸν

topic in hand. All of these things made the emperor hostile to Philiscus, so he kept silencing him, interjecting with his own remarks in the other's time and asking abrupt questions throughout the whole speech. And since Philiscus' replies did not address the questions, he said, "The hair reveals the type of man, and the voice the type of speaker," and after cutting him off like this many times, he took the side of the Heordaeans. And when Philiscus said, "It is you who gave me exemption from public services by giving me the chair at Athens," the emperor shouted loudly, "Neither you nor any other teacher is exempt. I would never deprive the cities of men who should perform public services for the sake of a few miserable speeches."[195] Nevertheless, even after this, he did give immunity from public services to Philostratus of Lemnos for his declamation, when he was aged twenty four. So these were the reasons for which Philiscus was deprived of his immunity. But do not let the shortcomings of his gaze and voice and dress deprive him of his dominant position among speakers, both for his use of Greek and his composition. The style of his speech was conversational rather than forensic, and it was illuminated by lexical purity and novelty of sound. He died leaving a daughter and a worthless son, and the measure of his life was sixty seven years. Though he possessed a little property at Athens, which was quite pleasant, he was not buried there, but in the Academy, where

[195] Philostratus has Caracalla echo Demosthenes, *On the False Embassy* 255.

ἀγῶνα ἐπὶ τοῖς ἐκ τῶν πολέμων θαπτομένοις ὁ πο-
λέμαρχος.

624   (88) 31. λα´. Αἰλιανὸς δὲ Ῥωμαῖος μὲν ἦν, ἤττίκιζε
δέ, ὥσπερ οἱ ἐν τῇ μεσογείᾳ Ἀθηναῖοι. ἐπαίνου μοι
δοκεῖ ἄξιος ὁ ἀνὴρ οὗτος, πρῶτον μέν, ἐπειδὴ καθα-
ρὰν φωνὴν ἐξεπόνησε πόλιν οἰκῶν ἑτέρᾳ φωνῇ χρω-
μένην, ἔπειθ᾽ ὅτι προσρηθεὶς σοφιστὴς ὑπὸ τῶν χα-
ριζομένων τὰ τοιαῦτα οὐκ ἐπίστευσεν, οὐδὲ ἐκολάκευσε
τὴν ἑαυτοῦ γνώμην, οὐδὲ ἐπήρθη ὑπὸ τοῦ ὀνόματος
οὕτω μεγάλου ὄντος, ἀλλ᾽ ἑαυτὸν εὖ διασκεψάμενος
ὡς μελέτῃ οὐκ ἐπιτήδειον τῷ συγγράφειν ἐπέθετο καὶ
ἐθαυμάσθη ἐκ τούτου. ἡ μὲν ἐπίπαν ἰδέα τοῦ ἀνδρὸς
ἀφέλεια προσβάλλουσά τι τῆς Νικοστράτου ὥρας, ἡ
δὲ ἐνίοτε πρὸς Δίωνα ὁρᾷ καὶ τὸν ἐκείνου τόνον.

625   (89) Ἐντυχὼν δέ ποτε αὐτῷ Φιλόστρατος ὁ Λήμνιος βιβλίον ἔτι πρόχειρον ἔχοντι καὶ ἀναγιγνώ-
σκοντι αὐτὸ σὺν ὀργῇ καὶ ἐπιτάσει τοῦ φθέγματος
ἤρετο αὐτόν, ὅ τι σπουδάζοι, καὶ ὅς, "ἐκπεπόνηταί
μοι," ἔφη, "κατηγορία τοῦ Γύννιδος, καλῶ γὰρ οὕτω

---

196 These were ceremonies in honor of the famous dead of
classical times and were held yearly. This type of speech is called
a polemarchic oration. Fictitious polemarchic declamations were
a favorite exercise of the sophists.

197 For the purity of speech in the interior of Attica, see VS
553. See Schmidt's analysis of Aelian's Attic, which reveals that he
is indeed much more regular in his adherence to classical Attic
than is Philostratus. Schmid's entire third volume (1893) is dedicated to Aelian.

the polemarch holds the contest for those buried there
who died in the wars.[196]

(88) 31. Aelian was a Roman, but he wrote Attic Greek   624
like the Athenians in the interior of Attica.[197] He seems to
me deserving of praise, firstly, since he labored to achieve
purity of speech, even though he lived in a city that employed another language; and secondly because, although
he was given the name of sophist by those who give such
a title, he did not trust to it, nor did he flatter his own
intelligence nor was he puffed up by the name, great
though it is. Rather, after carefully examining his own
abilities, he saw that he was not suited to declamation and
dedicated himself to writing, and he was admired for this
work. The overall style of the man was a restrained simplicity, achieving something of the beauty of Nicostratus,
but at other times he looked to Dio and the tension of his
style.[198]

(89) Philostratus of Lemnos met him once, holding a   625
book in his hand and reading from it with anger and vehemence of voice, and he asked Aelian what he was studying.
And he said, "I have composed an indictment of Gynnis,[199]
for that is what I call the tyrant who has just been put to

[198] A deliberate and restrained simplicity is indeed characteristic of the surviving works of Aelian, for instance in his *On the
Nature of Animals*. It may be an accident of survival that instances
of tension (τόνος) in the manner of Dio are more difficult to find.

[199] The "womanish man" is a slur applied to Elagabalus, who
was put to death in 222. This diatribe is lost. Aelian also applies
this relatively rare word to a stereotypical adulterer at *VH* 12.12.

τὸν ἄρτι καθῃρημένον τύραννον, ἐπειδὴ ἀσελγείᾳ
πάσῃ τὰ Ῥωμαίων ᾔσχυνε." καὶ ὁ Φιλόστρατος, "ἐγώ
σέ," εἶπεν, "ἐθαύμαζον ἄν, εἰ ζῶντος κατηγόρησας."
εἶναι γὰρ δὴ τὸ μὲν ζῶντα τύραννον ἐπικόπτειν ἀνδρός, τὸ δὲ ἐπεμβαίνειν κειμένῳ παντός.

(90) Ἔφασκε δὲ ὁ ἀνὴρ οὗτος μηδ᾽ ἀποδεδημηκέναι
ποι τῆς γῆς ὑπὲρ τὴν Ἰταλῶν χώραν, μηδὲ ἐμβῆναι
ναῦν, μηδὲ γνῶναι θάλασσαν, ὅθεν καὶ λόγου πλείονος κατὰ τὴν Ῥώμην ἠξιοῦτο ὡς τιμῶν τὰ ἤθη. Παυσανίου μὲν οὖν ἀκροατὴς ἐγένετο, ἐθαύμαζε δὲ τὸν
Ἡρώδην ὡς ποικιλώτατον ῥητόρων. ἐβίω δὲ ὑπὲρ τὰ
ἑξήκοντα ἔτη καὶ ἐτελεύτα οὐκ ἐπὶ παισί· παιδοποιίαν
γὰρ παρῃτήσατο τῷ μὴ γῆμαί ποτε. τοῦτο δὲ εἴτε
εὔδαιμον εἴτε ἄθλιον οὐ τοῦ παρόντος καιροῦ φιλοσο-
φῆσαι.

(91) 32. λβ΄. Ἐπεὶ δὲ ἡ τύχη κράτιστον ἐπὶ πάντα
τἀνθρώπεια, μηδὲ Ἡλιόδωρος ἀπαξιούσθω σοφιστῶν
κύκλου παράδοξον ἀγώνισμα τύχης γενόμενος. ἐχειρο-
τονήθη μὲν γὰρ ὁ ἀνὴρ οὗτος πρόδικος τῆς ἑαυτοῦ
πατρίδος ἐς τὰ Κελτικὰ ἔθνη ξὺν ἑτέρῳ, νοσοῦντος δὲ
θατέρου καὶ λεγομένου τοῦ βασιλέως διαγράφειν
πολλὰς τῶν δικῶν διέδραμεν ὁ Ἡλιόδωρος ἐς τὸ
στρατόπεδον δείσας περὶ τῇ δίκῃ, εἰσκαλούμενος δὲ
θᾶττον ἢ ᾤετο ἐς τὸν νοσοῦντα ἀνεβάλλετο· ὑβριστὴς
δὲ ὢν ὁ τὰς δίκας εἰσκαλῶν οὐ συνεχώρει ταῦτα,
ἀλλὰ παρήγαγεν αὐτὸν εἰς τὰ δικαστήρια ἄκοντά τε
καὶ τοῦ γενείου ἕλκων. ὡς δὲ εἴσω παρῆλθε καὶ θαρ-
ραλέον μὲν ἐς τὸν βασιλέα εἶδεν, καιρὸν δὲ ᾔτησεν

626

356

death, since with every kind of immorality he brought disgrace to the whole Roman Empire." And Philostratus said, "I would admire you, if you had indicted him while he was alive." For he said that it took a real man to attack a living tyrant, but that anyone could trample on one who had fallen.

(90) This man used to say that he had never traveled anywhere in the world outside of Italy, and that he had never boarded a ship, nor known the sea, and because of this he was honored all the more in Rome because he honored their way of life. He was a student of Pausanias, but he admired Herodes as the most versatile of speakers. He lived over sixty years and died leaving no children, but this is not the moment to discuss whether this is fortunate or a cause of suffering.

(91) 32. Since Fortune is the strongest force in all human affairs, let Heliodorus not be considered unworthy of the circle of sophists, because he was one of Fortune's paradoxical victories. This man was elected as advocate of his own country among the Celtic peoples along with a colleague. When the other man was ill and the emperor[200] was canceling many of the suits, Heliodorus hastened to the military camp, fearing for his own suit. He was summoned into court more quickly than he expected, and he asked to postpone it until the sick man could be present. Because the official who called the cases was a bully, he would not allow this, but led him into the court though he was unwilling, and even dragged him by the beard. But when he came into the court Heliodorus actually gazed boldly at the emperor, and asked for his allotted time on

626

[200] Caracalla.

ὕδατος, αὐτὴν δὲ τὴν παραίτησιν ἐντρεχῶς διέθετο
εἰπών, "καινόν σοι δόξει, μέγιστε αὐτοκράτορ, ἑαυτόν
τις παραγραφόμενος, μόνος ἀγωνίσασθαι τὴν δίκην
ἐντολὰς οὐκ ἔχων," ἀναπηδήσας ὁ αὐτοκράτωρ ἄνδρα
τε, "οἷον οὔπω ἔγνωκα, τῶν ἐμαυτοῦ καιρῶν εὕρημα,"
καὶ τὰ τοιαῦτα ἐκάλει τὸν Ἡλιόδωρον ἀνασείων τὴν
χεῖρα καὶ τὸν κόλπον τῆς χλαμύδος. κατ᾽ ἀρχὰς μὲν
οὖν ἐνέπεσέ τις καὶ ἡμῖν ὁρμὴ γέλωτος οἰομένοις ὅτι
διαπτύοι αὐτόν, ἐπεὶ δὲ ἱππεύειν αὐτῷ τε δημοσίᾳ
ἔδωκε καὶ παισίν, ὁπόσους ἔχοι, ἐθαυμάζετο ἡ τύχη
ὡς τὴν ἑαυτῆς ἰσχὺν ἐνδεικνυμένη διὰ τῶν οὕτω
παραλόγων, καὶ πολλῷ πλέον τοῦτο ἐκ τῶν ἐφεξῆς
ἐδηλοῦτο. ὡς γὰρ ξυνῆκεν ὁ Ἀράβιος, ὅτι κατὰ
δαίμονα ἀγαθὸν τὰ πράγματα αὐτῷ προὔβαινεν, ἀπεχρήσατο τῇ φορᾷ τοῦ βασιλέως, καθάπερ τῶν ναυ-
κλήρων οἱ τὰ ἱστία πλήρη ἀνασείοντες ἐν ταῖς εὐ-
πλοίαις καί, "ὦ βασιλεῦ," ἔφη, "ἀνάθες μοι καιρὸν εἰς
ἐπίδειξιν μελέτης," καὶ ὁ βασιλεύς, "ἀκροῶμαι," εἶπε,
"καὶ λέγε ἐς τόδε· ὁ Δημοσθένης ἐπὶ τοῦ Φιλίππου
ἐκπεσὼν καὶ δειλίας φεύγων." μελετῶντι δὲ οὐ μόνον
ἑαυτὸν εὔνουν παρεῖχεν, ἀλλ᾽ ἡτοίμαζε καὶ τὸν ἐξ ἄλλων ἔπαινον φοβερὸν βλέπων ἐς τοὺς μὴ ξὺν ἐπαίνῳ
ἀκούοντας. καὶ μὴν καὶ προὐστήσατο αὐτὸν τῆς με-
γίστης τῶν κατὰ τὴν Ῥώμην συνηγοριῶν ὡς ἐπιτη-
δειότερον δικαστηρίοις καὶ δίκαις. ἀποθανόντος δὲ

---

201 A sign of approval; cf. Eunap. 484 for the same gesture.
202 For this theme, based on Aeschines, *On the False Embassy*
34, cf. Maximus Planudes 5.309 Walz.

the water clock, and then fluently delivered his protest, saying, "It will seem a strange thing to you, great emperor, that a man should nullify his own suit by pleading it alone, when he does not have your order to do so." And the emperor leaped to his feet and called him "a man whose like I have never known, and a new discovery of my times," and other such things. And he lifted up Heliodorus' hand and shook back the fold of his traveling cloak.[201] So at first an urge to laugh came over us, because we thought that the emperor was mocking him, but when he granted the public honor of equestrian rank to him and his children, as many as he should have, we were amazed by Fortune, who showed her great force through events so unexpected, and this appeared even more clearly through what happened next. For when the Arab understood that events were turning out for him through some favorable daemon, he made the most of the emperor's good mood, like a captain who raises full sails in good weather, and he said, "My emperor, appoint me a time for a demonstration of declamation." And the emperor said, "I will hear you now. And speak on this theme: Demosthenes, when he has failed before Philip, defends himself against accusations of cowardice."[202] And the emperor not only gave him a sympathetic audience when he declaimed, but also secured the praise of others present, by gazing terrifyingly at those who listened without applauding. Moreover he placed Heliodorus in charge of the most important body of public advocates,[203] since he was particularly suited to the courts and legal cases. But when the emperor died,

[203] See VS 621 above, where Quirinus is similarly made *advocatus fisci*, and note 192, on the suitability of this office for sophists.

τοῦ βασιλέως προσετάχθη μέν τις αὐτῷ νῆσος, λαβὼν δὲ ἐν τῇ νήσῳ φονικὴν αἰτίαν ἀνεπέμφθη ἐς τὴν
Ῥώμην ὡς ἀπολογησόμενος τοῖς τῶν στρατοπέδων
627 ἡγεμόσι, δόξαντι δὲ αὐτῷ καθαρῷ εἶναι τῆς αἰτίας
ἐπανείθη καὶ ἡ νῆσος. καὶ γηράσκει ἐν τῇ Ῥώμῃ
μήτε σπουδαζόμενος μήτε ἀμελούμενος.

(92) 33. λγ΄. Ἀσπάσιον δὲ τὸν σοφιστὴν Ῥάβεννα
μὲν ἤνεγκεν (ἡ δὲ Ῥάβεννα Ἰταλοί,) Δημητριανὸς δὲ
ὁ πατὴρ ἐπαίδευσεν εὖ γιγνώσκων τοὺς κριτικοὺς τῶν
λόγων. πολυμαθὴς δὲ ὁ Ἀσπάσιος καὶ πολυήκοος καὶ
τὸ μὲν καινοπρεπὲς ἐπαινῶν, εἰς ἀπειροκαλίαν δὲ οὐδαμοῦ ἐκπίπτων ὑπὸ τοῦ ἐν καιρῷ χρῆσθαι οἷς γιγνώσκοι. τουτὶ δέ που καὶ ἐν μουσικῇ κράτιστον· οἱ
γὰρ καιροὶ τῶν τόνων λύρᾳ τε φωνὴν ἔδωκαν καὶ
αὐλῷ καὶ μελῳδίαν ἐπαίδευσαν. ἐπιμεληθεὶς δὲ τοῦ
δοκίμως τε καὶ σὺν ἀφελείᾳ ἑρμηνεύειν πνεύματός τε
καὶ περιβολῆς ἠμέλησε, τὸ σχεδιάζειν τε ἐκ φύσεως
οὐκ ἔχων πόνῳ παρεστήσατο.

(93) Ἦλθε δὲ καὶ ἐπὶ πολλὰ τῆς γῆς μέρη βασιλεῖ
τε ξυνὼν Ἀλεξάνδρῳ †καὶ ξυνεῖναι†.[51] προὔστη δὲ καὶ
τοῦ κατὰ τὴν Ῥώμην θρόνου νεάζων μὲν εὐδοκιμώτατος, γηράσκων δὲ ξὺν αἰτίᾳ τοῦ μὴ ἑτέρῳ ἀποστῆναι
βούλεσθαι. ἡ δὲ πρὸς τὸν Λήμνιον Φιλόστρατον τῷ

---

[51] The MSS are corrupt at this point, and the correct reading
is likely impossible to recover. I have printed the corrupt text, as
the only honest option, and obelized the unintelligible καὶ ξυνεῖναι with Stefec.

Heliodorus was deported to a certain island, and on the
island he was charged with murder and sent to Rome to
make his defense before the military prefects. Since he
proved himself innocent of the charge, he was also released from his exile on the island. He is growing old in
Rome, neither admired nor neglected.

(92) 33. Ravenna produced the sophist Aspasius (Ravenna is in Italy), and his father Demetrianus, who was an
expert in criticism, educated him. Aspasius was a student
of many subjects and studied with many teachers, and he
used to praise the new, but never fell into bad taste, because he had a sense of the appropriate moment in arranging his ideas. And this of course is the most important
thing in music too, for it is the correct timing of the notes
that have given voice to the lyre and aulos and taught
melody.[204] Though he took great care with appropriate-
ness and with simplicity of expression, he neglected vigor
and amplification. He had no natural talent for improvisation, but he mastered it with great effort.

(93) He visited many parts of the world both in company with the emperor Alexander and . . . And he held the
chair at Rome, with great distinction while he was young,
but as he grew older people found fault with him for not
stepping aside to allow it to another. His disagreement
with Philostratus of Lemnos began at Rome, but became

[204] Rhetorical performance and music were frequently compared, not least by Philostratus himself.

Ἀσπασίῳ διαφορὰ ἤρξατο μὲν ἀπὸ τῆς Ῥώμης, ἐπέδωκε δὲ ἐν Ἰωνίᾳ ὑπὸ Κασσιανοῦ τε καὶ Αὐρηλίου
τῶν σοφιστῶν αὐξηθεῖσα. ἦν δὲ αὐτοῖν ὁ μὲν Αὐρή-
λιος οἷος καὶ ἐν καπηλείοις μελετᾶν πρὸς τὸν ἐκεῖ
οἶνον, ὁ δ᾿ οἷος θρασύνεσθαι μὲν ἐπὶ τὸν Ἀθήνησι
θρόνον διὰ καιρούς, οἷς ἀπεχρήσατο, παιδεῦσαι δὲ
μηδένα, πλὴν Πίγρητος τοῦ Λυδοῦ. περὶ μὲν οὖν τοῦ
τρόπου τῆς διαφορᾶς εἴρηταί μοι καὶ τί ἂν αὖθις ἑρ-
μηνεύοιμι τὰ ἀποχρώντως δεδηλωμένα; τὸ δὲ εἶναί τι
628   χρηστὸν καὶ παρ᾿ ἐχθροῦ εὑρέσθαι ἐν πολλοῖς μὲν
τῶν ἀνθρωπίνων διεφάνη, μάλιστα δὲ ἐπὶ τῶν ἀνδρῶν
τούτων· διενεχθέντε γὰρ ὁ μὲν Ἀσπάσιος προσεποίη-
σεν αὑτῷ τὸ σχεδιάζειν ξὺν εὐροίᾳ, ἐπειδὴ ὁ Φιλόστρατος καὶ τούτου τοῦ μέρους ἐλλογίμως εἶχεν, ὁ δ᾿
αὖ τὸν ἑαυτοῦ λόγον τέως ὑλομανοῦντα πρὸς τὴν
ἀκρίβειαν τὴν ἐκείνου ἐκόλασεν.

(94) Ἡ δὲ ξυγγεγραμμένη ἐπιστολὴ τῷ Φιλοστράτῳ περὶ τοῦ πῶς χρὴ ἐπιστέλλειν πρὸς τὸν
Ἀσπάσιον τείνει, ἐπειδὴ παρελθὼν ἐς βασιλείους ἐπιστολὰς τὰς μὲν ἀγωνιστικώτερον τοῦ δέοντος ἐπέ-
στελλε, τὰς δὲ οὐ σαφῶς, ὧν οὐδέτερον βασιλεῖ πρέ-
πον· αὐτοκράτωρ γὰρ δὴ ὁπότε ἐπιστέλλοι, οὐ δεῖ

---

205 There is some uncertainty as to the name of Cassianus'
only student, either Periges (the manuscript reading) or Pigres,
proposed as an emendation by Reiske, and adopted by Stefec.
The point in any case is evidently that the student was as undis-
tinguished as his teacher.

more serious in Ionia, encouraged by the sophists Cassianus and Aurelius. Of these two men, Aurelius was the sort of person who declaims in wineshops while the drinking is going on, and Cassianus was arrogant enough to aspire to the chair at Athens when opportunities arose, though he had taught no one except Pigres the Lydian.[205] Concerning the nature of their disagreement I have already spoken, so why rehearse again what is already sufficiently clear? The saying that even from an enemy one 628 may learn something useful has often been apparent in human affairs, but never more so than in the case of these men. While the pair were feuding Aspasius mastered improvisation with fluency, since Philostratus was already eminent in this branch of eloquence, and Philostratus in turn disciplined his speech, which had begun to run riot, in reaction to the other's precision.

(94) The letter written by Philostratus concerning how one should write letters is directed at Aspasius,[206] because when he was appointed imperial secretary he wrote some letters in a style more controversial than is necessary, and others unclearly, neither of which is appropriate for an emperor. Rather whenever an emperor writes he should not use enthymemes nor dialectical proofs, but express

206 This is almost certainly the work that survives in the Philostratean corpus, but which since Kayser has been misclassified as *Dialexis* 1. The correct identification was already made by Olearius (1709, 914). For a translation and text, see Rusten and König 2014.

ἐνθυμημάτων οὐδ' ἐπιχειρημάτων, ἀλλὰ δόξης, οὐδ'
αὖ ἀσαφείας, ἐπειδὴ νόμους φθέγγεται, σαφήνεια δὲ
ἑρμηνεὺς νόμου.

(95) Παυσανίου μὲν οὖν μαθητὴς ὁ Ἀσπάσιος, Ἱπποδρόμου δὲ οὐκ ἀνήκοος, ἐπαίδευε δὲ κατὰ τὴν Ῥώμην ἱκανῶς γηράσκων, ὁπότε μοι ταῦτα ἐγράφετο.

(96) Τοσαῦτα περὶ Ἀσπασίου. περὶ δὲ Φιλοστράτου
τοῦ Λημνίου καὶ τίς μὲν ἐν δικαστηρίοις ὁ ἀνὴρ
οὗτος, τίς δὲ ἐν δημηγορίαις, τίς δὲ ἐν συγγράμμασι,
τίς δὲ ἐν μελέταις, ὅσος δὲ ἐν σχεδίῳ λόγῳ, καὶ περὶ
Νικαγόρου τοῦ Ἀθηναίου, ὃς καὶ τοῦ Ἐλευσινίου ἱεροῦ κήρυξ ἐστέφθη, καὶ Ἀψίνης ὁ Φοῖνιξ ἐφ' ὅσον
προὔβη μνήμης τε καὶ ἀκριβείας, οὐκ ἐμὲ δεῖ γράφειν, καὶ γὰρ ἂν καὶ ἀπιστηθείην ὡς χαρισάμενος,
ἐπειδὴ φιλία μοι πρὸς αὐτοὺς ἦν.

only his opinion, nor again should he be unclear, since his utterances are laws, and clarity is the interpreter of law.[207]

(95) Aspasius was a student of Pausanias, and a sometime student of Hippodromus, and he was teaching at Rome, though he was really very elderly, when I wrote this.

(96) So much for Aspasius. But regarding Philostratus of Lemnos, what sort of man he is in the law courts, what he is like in public speeches, what he is like in written treatises, what he is like in declamations, and how great he is in improvised speech, it is not for me to write. Nor is it for me to write about Nicagoras the Athenian,[208] who was crowned as herald of the temple at Eleusis, nor about Apsines the Phoenician,[209] despite all his achievements in memory and accuracy. I would be disbelieved for favoring them, since friendship binds me to them.

[207] On the ideal rhetorical approach for a sophist who is appointed *ab epistulis Graecis*, see above, VS 607.

[208] An inscription from Eleusis on the base of a statue honoring Nicagoras as herald ($\kappa\hat{\eta}\rho\nu\xi$) also records that he held a chair of rhetoric. On this inscription, the question of which chair was meant, and the complex family of Nicagoras, see Puech 2002, 357–60. For various works ascribed to Nicagoras, see *Suda* N 373.

[209] An inscription from a statue base in Athens honors Annia, the wife of Apsines. For further genealogical details and bibliography, see Puech 2002, 124–26.

EUNAPIUS

To my teachers of ancient Greek

INTRODUCTION

In his *Lives of Philosophers and Sophists*, Eunapius of Sardes (ca. AD 345–415) offers twenty-nine biographical sketches of third- and fourth-century AD intellectuals active in philosophy, rhetoric, and medicine. Eunapius announces that he will produce lives of "distinguished men" but also includes the life of a remarkable woman (Sosipatra, *VPS* 6.53–93).[1] He reveals that he has relied on both oral and written sources and has also witnessed some of the persons and events he describes. The date of the work cannot be established with precision. (Eunapius is generally vague about dating events.)[2] Woods (2009, 366) has dated the work to AD 399 without giving a clear reason. Goulet (2014, 1:96) is more cautious and opts for "after 396" or even later. The most important historical details for setting an approximate date (*terminus post quem*) are the destruction of the Serapis temple in AD 391 (*VPS* 6.107–9) and of the Eleusis temple by Alaric during his invasion of 395 (*VPS* 7.31), as well as mention of the em-

---

[1] Section numbers follow Goulet; see below, under "History and Constitution of the Text."

[2] Cf. Treadgold (2007, 88n54) on Eunapius' *Chronicle*: "He prided himself on his disregard for dates, even though he apparently wrote in more or less chronological order" (with ref. to Fr. 66.2 Blockley).

peror Theodosius I (r. AD 379–†395) and Theophilus, the patriarch of Alexandria (r. 385–412), so that a date in the range of 396 to 405 seems plausible. Eunapius does not mention Theodosius' death in Milan in 395, so he may not have known about it.

About Eunapius' life we know only a few essentials, mostly based on his own narrative. These self-references assist in pinpointing what he saw as important moments in his upbringing and allow for a rough chronology. He was taught by Chrysanthius from an early age (*VPS* 6.6) and left Sardes for Athens at the age of sixteen (*VPS* 10.2), where he attached himself to Prohaeresius. He mentions that he intended to go to Egypt "five years later" but that his parents recalled him back to Lydia (*VPS* 10.87).[3] His education included rhetoric and religio-philosophical theory and practice, for which he acknowledges his teachers Prohaeresius and Chrysanthius, whose lives take up considerable space and for whom his praise is the most personal. His claim of having medical experience (*VPS* 23.56, οὐδὲ γὰρ ἄπειρος τῆς ἰατρικῆς) is not attributed to a particular teacher, although he clearly admired Oribasius (about whom more below).

We know of two major works by Eunapius:

1. His *Historical Chronicle* (ἱστορία χρονική) covers the period from ca. AD 270 to 400. It survives only in fragments (collected in Blockley 1981) and was a sequel to Dexippus' history of the first two centuries AD. It covers a lot of ground, but the patriarch Photius considered it primarily a panegyrical tribute to Emperor Julian (*Hist.*

[3] For his age when initiated at twenty (*VPS* 6.5–6), see Banchich 1987; 1996; and Goulet 2014, 2:15.

fr. 1 Blockley). In the *Lives*, Eunapius himself refers to them as "writings concerning the times of Julian" (*VPS* 7.5, 7.35, 16.9, 21.4), or as "general writings of history" (*VPS* 6.113, ἐν τοῖς καθολικοῖς συγγράμμασιν), or the "detailed accounts of Julian's time" (*VPS* 7.53, ἐν τοῖς διεξοδικοῖς τοῖς κατὰ Ἰουλιανὸν).[4] Most of these references seem to suggest that the work antedates the *Lives*, though comments where he uses the future tense (*VPS* 8.14, γραφήσεται; *VPS* 10.17, λελέξεται), promising further elaboration in his historical work, do not fit such a dating. These may be due to revisions or interpolations. Barnes (1978; cf. Blockley 1981, 24–25) has dated the *History* to ca. 380.

2. The present work, *Lives of Philosophers and Sophists* (βίοι φιλοσόφων καὶ σοφιστῶν), covers the period from Plotinus (ca. AD 250) up to Chrysanthius (ca. 380). Starting with Plotinus and Porphyry, and then focusing on Iamblichus and his students, as well as several sophists (i.e., orators and teachers of rhetoric), it furnishes brief and selective biographical accounts of these Hellenic intellectuals down to Eunapius' own time. A third category refers to a group of physicians with rhetorical skills. (The label "iatrosophists" for these men is not Eunapius' own.)[5] The teacher-student connections constitute an important structural device, with Iamblichus, Julian the sophist, and Zeno functioning as the figureheads of the three distinct groups. Eunapius considers himself a member of all three and a close friend of Julian's physician, Oribasius, who

[4] Wright misleadingly translated some of these mentions as *Life* of Julian (1921, 439, 447).

[5] Cf. Damasc. ap. Suid. s.v. Γέσιος; Goulet 2014, 1:247–48.

dedicated a medical work to him.[6] Alternative descriptions for the work occur at various moments, such as "the significant actions of distinguished men" (*VPS* 1.2), "the lives of men who were trained in every kind of learning" (*VPS* 6.18), as a "list of wise men" (*VPS* 6.54), and as "a record of noteworthy men" (*VPS* 12.2).

At the start of *VPS*, Eunapius sets up his own narrative in terms of genre and sources: he mentions known biographical works on philosophers authored by Xenophon (ca. 430–354 BC), Sotion (fl. 200–170 BC), Plutarch (AD 46–119), Lucian (ca. AD 125–180), Philostratus (ca. AD 170–250), and Porphyry (ca. AD 234–305), implicitly indicating what kind of philosophical lives he might have known, read, and aligned himself with, but also to what extent they already covered the material Eunapius plans to record.[7] That he does not name all his sources is clear: his life of Libanius suggests he may have had access to the strongly autobiographical *Oration* 1 of the famous orator, but we also find minor discrepancies and omissions. A striking absence among the earlier works mentioned is that of Diogenes Laertius, whose *Lives of Eminent Philosophers* (dated to ca. AD 200–225) would seem a perfect model for the kind of work Eunapius is undertaking. The work may not have been available to him. In many other cases he also relies on eyewitnesses or his own recollections.

Despite Eunapius' praise for Xenophon "the philoso-

---

[6] Oribasius' *Ad Eunapium*, a synopsis of a major compilation in nine medical books, the *Collectiones*. See Goulet 2014, 1:251–55.

[7] On genres in antiquity, see Rosenmeyer 2006. On Eunapius' sources, see also Penella 1990, 23–32.

pher"[8] (*VPS* 1.1), he immediately indicates how his own approach will deviate from that of his predecessor: rather than pay attention to deeds of great *and* lesser importance (ἔργα and πάρεργα), he will focus only on the great deeds (ἔργα) of the distinguished figures he has selected. The early pages also contain echoes of Herodotus in terms of approach and different sources (cf. Hdt. 1.1, 2.99, 2.142). From the overall pattern of the *Lives*, it seems that Eunapius aimed to describe his protagonists by their place of birth (e.g., *VPS* 1.1–3), character (e.g., *VPS* 8.1, 23.20), teachers, talent for philosophical inquiry, rhetorical skills, students, any superhuman abilities (where present), and in many cases, their deaths, especially at an advanced age, often with the euphemism "departed this life/the human realm." But there is great variety in detail and emphasis besides such common elements, while there is limited (and often implicit) reference to philosophical matters.

The *Lives* weave three significant thematic strands throughout the narrative. First, the biographical accounts all have a personal or intellectual connection to the author (either directly or indirectly), placing him at the center of the three groups he discusses. Second, the lives are very selective in content, which is why the label "biography" does not apply without qualifications. In Greek the word *bios* usually refers to "way of life,"[9] and from the start Eunapius emphasizes that the work is focused on the virtues of excellent (pagan) individuals. This strong ethical focus, highlighting moral qualities and behavior, is reaffirmed several times. And third, Eunapius is so eager to ascribe supernatural qualities to several of the individuals,

[8] For Xenophon as "philosopher," cf. Quint. *Inst.* 10.1.75.
[9] Verhasselt 2016.

that one suspects a special agenda. He identifies a small subset of male individuals and one female as being "god-like," "divine," "divinely inspired," or as having "a divine nature." At the same time, the work incorporates subtle and less subtle allusions to the rise of Christianity and the impact it had on Hellenic paganism, adding a polemical tenor to the narrative. As a devout adherent of the tradi-tional religion, Eunapius was deeply disappointed over Julian's failure to reinstate Hellenic religious practices. Julian had set this reversal in motion, but after his prema-ture death in AD 363 it was quickly annulled by his suc-cessors (Constans, Constantius), a trend consummated by Theodosius in the 390s. Eunapius' anger over Christian practices and encroachment upon traditional religious sites bubbles up at regular intervals (e.g., *VPS* 6.5, 6.40, 6.107–16, 7.5, 23.17, 23.36).

As to the special skills and abilities of his subjects, he frequently mentions their "charm" in oratory ($\chi\acute{\alpha}\rho\iota\varsigma$, $\grave{\alpha}\phi\rho o\delta\acute{\iota}\tau\eta$) or the "guile" on their lips (*VPS* 6.39, $\alpha\grave{\iota}\mu\acute{\upsilon}\lambda\iota o\nu$). For a select few, he will claim a "divine quality" (often using $\theta\epsilon\hat{\iota}o\varsigma$ in superlative form, e.g., *VPS* 6.5), a mark for someone special, that is, closer to god (cf., e.g., Pl. *Tht.* 176c). Being declared "divine," however, does not make these figures immortal. In only three cases does he use the adjective $\theta\epsilon\sigma\pi\acute{\epsilon}\sigma\iota o\varsigma$, namely for Plutarch (*VPS* 2.1), Por-phyry (*VPS* 3.1), and Julian (*VPS* 7.47). Such signs of re-ligious sensibility, if taken seriously, underscore the fact that in this period the boundaries between philosophy and religion remained blurred.[10]

---

[10] See also Goulet (2014, 1:367–76) on how one might trans-late the problematic term $\theta\epsilon\iota\alpha\sigma\mu\acute{o}\varsigma$.

Eunapius' style of exposition can be best described as a blend of historical and panegyrical tendencies. Although not completely devoid of literary adeptness, his accounts use techniques one would expect of a historian, but many *bioi* contain elements that defy belief and evoke the suspicion that his adoration for his subjects got the better of him (see esp. *VPS* 2.11), resulting in profiles with exaggerated claims about their abilities. This style suggests that in this work Eunapius exhibits the historian's reflexes as well as a devotee's partialities. Another peculiarity of the narration is his *illeism*, the habit of referring to himself mostly in the third person as "he who wrote this" or "the author" (*VPS* 9.4, ὁ ταῦτα γράφων, ὁ συγγραφεύς). More generally, his literary style (especially his vocabulary and frame of reference) is heavily influenced by the "classical writings." His connection to Platonism emerges from the many echoes of Plato and Plotinus; to illustrate this feature I have especially added more references in the notes to the works of both. Among Eunapius' stylistic peculiarities we find regular parallel pairs of similar words (viz., isodynama; cf. Goulet 2014, 1:434), polysyndeton, Homeric allusions, similes and quotations, litotes (or double negation) used for what we would call "understatement" (e.g., οὐκ ἀμύητοι, "not uninitiated," at *VPS* 6.67; οὐδὲ γὰρ ἄπειρος, "not without experience," at *VPS* 23.56), and colorful adjectives.[11] Last but not least, his comments at times have a sarcastic tone to them, for instance, when he shows his delight over Ablabius (the name translates as "unharmed") getting his comeuppance (*VPS* 6.31), or when he makes scathing remarks about the Christians, for

[11] A fuller analysis of his style in Goulet 2014, vol. 1, chap. 15.

example, "these 'great warriors' and 'honorable men' . . . had stretched out their hands unstained by blood but not free from greed" (*VPS* 6.111–15).

Socrates plays a prominent role in several lives as a philosophical exemplar. Eunapius clearly admires him as a model of the wise man, while he also voices bitter complaints about Socrates' unjust treatment by the Athenians (*VPS* 6.10–12). Eunapius draws implicit and explicit parallels with several among the most venerated individuals: with Iamblichus (*VPS* 5.13), when he suddenly stops during a conversation and "became preoccupied, as though his voice were cut off, and for some moments he fixed his eyes steadily on the ground";[12] with Sopater, who is unjustly put to death with "a charge more idiotic than that brought against Socrates" (*VPS* 6.25); with Sosipatra, who, speaking to Eustathius about their marriage, stops speaking when it comes to her own fate and exclaims, "But my god prevents me" (*VPS* 6.78), or during an inspired discussion of the descent of the soul "became silent, as though her voice had been cut off" (*VPS* 6.91); with Prohaeresius, who defies the cold of winter with ease (*VPS* 10.73, though Socrates is not named); or with Chrysanthius, who is described as speaking to tradespeople and women in the market (*VPS* 8.7) and as "the Platonic Socrates . . . come to life again" (*VPS* 23.20);[13] or with "Hellespontius of Galatia, an unusually gifted man in every way," who desired to find out "whether he could meet anyone who knew more than himself" (*VPS* 23.46–47).[14]

In the few instances where we can compare certain

---

[12] Cf. Plut. *De genio Socr.* 580; Pl. *Symp.* 174d, 175b.

[13] Cf. Becker 2013, 538–39.

[14] Compare Socrates after his oracle (Pl. *Ap.* 21b–22a).

details with other extant sources on the persons and events in *VPS* (e.g., Porphyry's *Life of Plotinus* or Libanius' "autobiography" in his *Oration* 1), discrepancies appear that have raised questions about Eunapius' reliability. Wright (1921, 356n3; cf. Goulet 2014, 1:4, 1:9) commented that "Eunapius *quotes incorrectly* the account of this incident given by Porphyry himself in his *Life of Plotinus* 11.113" (emphasis added). But such a comment seems to impose modern criteria of historicity and assumes that Eunapius had the texts available as we know them today. Penella (1990, 26–29) also points to such discrepancies, allowing for some of these cases to be genuine errors. While memory lapses or errors are plausible explanations for such mishaps, other reasons may have contributed to such discrepancies. Because the well-educated in that era had undergone intensive training that promoted memorization, a faulty memory may not always be the best explanation. Eunapius himself testifies at *VPS* 6.75 that he, and many about whom he writes (cf. *VPS* 6.100, 7.7, 8.1, 10.6, 16.16), knew lots of works by heart, often indicated with the idiomatic expression ἀπὸ στόματος ἔχειν, for having things committed to memory so well that they flow "off the tongue" with ease.[15] The supposed mistakes may require a different explanation.[16]

Eunapius has long stood in the shadow of Philostratus, and similarities with Philostratus regarding their subject matter have obscured essential differences in their agendas and style.[17] Nineteenth- and twentieth-century schol-

[15] Cf. Pl. *Tht*. 142d; Xen. *Mem*. 3.6.9; Ar. *Lys*. 855.

[16] For a suggestion, see Baltussen 2020.

[17] A study as recent as Eshleman 2012 does not even mention him once.

arship tended to focus less on questions of authorial motivation or the religious impulse present in the text.[18] Several stages of interpretation emphasized either rhetoric (Wright) or biography ("collective biography," Cox Miller, Becker), or history (Penella), and more often than not scholars would approach Eunapius' *Lives* as a derivative of Philostratus' *Lives of the Sophists*. Wright seems to have viewed Eunapius solely through the lens of Philostratus' achievement and the history of rhetoric. The original Loeb edition had only one title ("Lives of Sophists") for *both* Philostratus and Eunapius. The scholarly view clearly was that "Eunapius tries to write like Philostratus," as one of the Loeb reviewers put it (*Classical Review* 38 [1924]: 75–76). Given that the philosophers take up a slightly larger part of the text than the sophists, the title should reflect this by retaining the version in the Laurentianus (at f. 218r).[19]

Even though Philostratus' influence cannot be denied, the *VPS* has multiple factors driving the narrative. Paying attention to the religious and polemical threads underlying many comments in the *Lives* may provide a richer understanding of the author's motivation and the work's purpose. The underlying reasons Eunapius himself gives combine personal devotion to his teachers (see *VPS* 23.1) with a broader attempt to rehabilitate the Hellenic cul-

[18] Penella (1990) offers a historical commentary on the lives. Treadgold (2007, 81) places Eunapius among the "New Classical Historians" of the early Byzantine period.

[19] By this time σοφιστής had the neutral sense of "orator" or "professor of rhetoric," rather than Plato's concept that sophists practiced false and devious reasoning.

tural icons against the rise of Christianity and its representatives.[20]

TRANSLATION

This translation is a thoroughly revised version of Wright's Loeb from 1921. While her translation was an excellent piece of scholarship in many respects, it is by now in need of revision to update the language and to benefit from the scholarship of the past century. My translation strives to present a new rendering into faithful yet readable English, aiming for fidelity while avoiding literalness. I have benefitted from Goulet's introduction, translation, and notes (Ed. Budé, 2014, vols. 1–2) as well as from Becker's German translation and extensive commentary (2013), and on occasion from D'Jeranian's French translation (2009). I managed to gain access to Civiletti (2007) only at a very late stage of preparation.

The main principles of translation are as follows. My revision has led to innumerable, substantial changes, leaving Wright's version intact when it could not be improved upon (as LCL policy allows). In particular, I have (1) modernized the English where applicable; (2) replaced Christianizing language with more neutral terms for this pagan (and anti-Christian) author (e.g., removed words like "sainted," "converted," etc.); (3) corrected translations I considered flawed due to inconsistency, misinterpretation, or overinterpretation; (4) rectified omissions (words not translated) and updated references, for instance, where new editions or other relevant scholarship have been pub-

[20] For a detailed argument, see Baltussen 2020; 2021.

lished over the past one hundred years. Occasionally, I have retained Eunapius' idiosyncratic syntax and style (also debated in antiquity; cf. Photius, *Cod.* 77, on the historical *Chronicle*), so long as it would not lead to an awkward translation. Wright tended to smooth over a number of peculiarities, obscuring Eunapius' style and voice.

HISTORY AND CONSTITUTION
OF THE TEXT

The survival and transmission of the *VPS* depend on a few manuscripts, of which the Laurentianus Mediceus Plut. 86.7 (Florence) is the most important. The date of the manuscript is still disputed and placed between the tenth and the fifteenth century, but in all likelihood it belongs to the earlier part of that range.[21] The online version of the manuscript is labeled "saec. XI." It contains a considerable number of corrupt passages and not all problems can be resolved satisfactorily.

As is standard with Loeb volumes, this edition provides only basic textual notes intended to flag uncertainties that bear on translation or interpretation and not an *apparatus criticus*; for full details about the witnesses, I refer interested readers to the critical edition of Goulet. When further examination of the manuscript was necessary, I consulted the Laurentianus in the online digitized version of the Bibliotheca Medicea. I have also reviewed the Greek text and corrected misprints and misreadings, while adjusting the punctuation where appropriate; readings or

---

[21] See Goulet (2014, 1:441–42) for various views.

emendations that had become part of the vulgate text have not been noted.

For ease of cross-reference to other modern editions, the text in this volume uses Goulet's numbering for sections (while changing Roman numerals to in-text Arabic numerals) and subsections (marginal Arabic numerals), with added marginal tags for corresponding pages in Boissonade 1822 (as in Wright) and Giangrande 1956 (e.g., 458B and 12G, respectively).

SIGLA

Manuscripts[22]

A   Laurentianus Mediceus Plut. 86.7 (saec. XI)

D   Parisinus, bibl. nat. gr. 1405 (saec. XVI), fols. 124–70

---

[22] For a full list, see Goulet 2014, 2:v–viii.

REFERENCES

SCHOLARS

Ba	Baltussen (current editor)
Be	Becker 2013
Boiss	Boissonade, J.-F. 1822
Civil	Civilletti 2007 (and *ap.* Goulet)
Cob	Cobet, G. C., *Mnemos*, n.s. 8 (1880): 8–20
Gi	Giangrande, ed. 1956
Go	Goulet 2014
Kays	Kayser 1844, 1849, 1870/71
Vollenbr	Vollenbrecht *ap.* Goulet
Wr	W. C. Wright, Loeb 1921
Wytt	Wyttenbach *ap.* Goulet

EDITIONS

Blockley	Blockley, R. "Eunapius, *Fragments*." In R. C. Blockley, *The Fragmentary Classicising Historians of the Later Roman Empire: Eunapius, Olympiodorus, Priscus and Malchus*, with text, translation and notes. 1–150. Liverpool: Cairns, 1981.
Boissonade	Boissonade, J.-F. *Eunapii Sardiani Vitas sophistarum et fragmenta historiarum.* Amstelodami, 1822.

————. *Eunapii Vitae Sophistarum.*
Paris: Didot, 1849, 1878. (The editions
include works of Callistratus, Philostratus, and Himerius.)

Commelinus   Commelinus, Hieronymus. ΕΥΝΑΠΙΟΥ
ΤΟΥ ΣΑΡΔΙΑΝΟΥ ΒΙΟΙ ΦΙΛΟΣΟ-
ΦΩΝ ΚΑΙ ΣΟΦΙΣΤΩΝ. Eunapius
Sardianus. De Vitis Philosophorum et
Sophistarum. Heidelberg, 1596. Re-
print, 1616.

Giangrande   Giangrande, I. *Eunapii Vitae Sophistarum.* Rome: Istituto Poligrafico dello
Stato, 1956.

Goulet   Goulet, R. *Eunape de Sardes: Vies de
philosophes et de sophistes.* 2 vols.
Paris: Éditions Budé, 2014.

Hornanus   Hornanus, H. J. *The lyves of philosophers
and oratours: written in Greeke, by
Eunapius, of the cittie of Sardeis in
Lydia. Brought into light, translated
into Latine,* [. . .] *By the great learned
man Hadrianus Iunius Hornanus.
1568. And now set foorth in English.* . . . Antwerp, 1568.

Norman   Norman, A. F. *Libanius' Autobiography
(Oration 1).* The Greek Text edited
with introduction, translation, and
notes. London–New York–Toronto:
Oxford University Press, 1956.

Wyttenbach   Wyttenbach, H. *Epistola critica . . . acce-
dunt animadversiones ad Eunapium et
Aristaenetum.* Göttingen, 1769.

GENERAL BIBLIOGRAPHY

Baltussen, H. "Eunapius' *Lives of Philosophers and Sophists*: Was He Constructing 'pagan saints' in the Age of Christianity?" In *Eastern Christianity and Late Antique Philosophy*, edited by E. Anagnostou-Laoutides and K. Parry, 239–60. Leiden: E. J. Brill, 2020.

———. "Polemic, Personality, and the Iamblichean Circle in Eunapius' *Lives of Philosophers and Sophists (VPS).*" In *Polemics, Rivalry and Networking in Greco-Roman Antiquity*, edited by P. d'Hoine, G. Roskam, S. Schorn, and J. Verheyden, 151–76. Leuven: Brepols, 2021.

Banchich, T. M. "On Goulet's Chronology of Eunapius' Life and Work." *Journal of Hellenic Studies* 107 (1987): 164–67.

———. "Eunapius in Athens." *Phoenix* 50.3–4 (1996): 304–11.

Barnes, T. D. *The Sources of the Historia Augusta*. Brussels: Collection Latomus, 1978.

Becker, M. *Eunapios aus Sardes. Biographien über Philosophen und Sophisten*. Einleitung, Übersetzung, Kommentar. Stuttgart: F. Steiner Verlag, 2013.

Civiletti, M. *Eunapio di Sardi, Vite di filosofi e sofisti*. Testo greco a fronte. Introduzione, traduzione, note e apparati a cura di—. Milano: I edizione Bompiani, 2007.

Cox Miller, P. "Strategies of Representation in Collective Biography. Constructing the Subject as Holy." In *Greek Biography and Panegyric in Late Antiquity*, edited by T. Hägg, P. Rousseau, and C. Høgel, 209–54. Berkeley: University of California Press, 2000.

Cribiore, R. *Libanius the Sophist. Rhetoric, Reality and Religion in the Fourth Century*. Ithaca and London: Cornell University Press, 2013.

D'Jeranian, O. *Eunape de Sardes. Vies de Philosophes et de Sophistes*. Texte traduit, annoté et présenté par—. Paris: Éditions Manucius, 2009.

Eshleman, K. *The Social World of Intellectuals in the Roman Empire: Sophists, Philosophers, and Christians*. Cambridge: Cambridge University Press, 2012.

Goulet, R. *Eunape de Sardes. Vies de Philosophes et de Sophistes* (Tomes I–II). Paris: Ed. Budé, 2014.

Penella, R. "Eunapius, Vitae Phil. XXIII 3.15 (Giangrande)." *Rheinisches Museum* 129 (1986): 363.

———. *Greek Philosophers and Sophists in the Fourth Century AD*. Leeds: F. Cairns, 1990.

Rosenmeyer, T. A. "Ancient Literary Genres: A Mirage?" In *Ancient Literary Criticism*, edited by A. Laird, 421–39. Oxford, 2006.

Treadgold, W. *The Early Byzantine Historians*. Basingstoke–New York: Palgrave MacMillan, 2007.

Verhasselt, G. "What Were Works Περὶ βίων?" *Philologus* 160.1 (2016): 59–83.

Woods, D. "Late Antique Historiography: A Brief History of Time." In *A Companion to Late Antiquity*, edited by P. Rousseau, 357–71. Chichester–Malden–Boston: Wiley-Blackwell, 2009.

ΕΥΝΑΠΙΟΥ
ΒΙΟΙ ΦΙΛΟΣΟΦΩΝ
ΚΑΙ ΣΟΦΙΣΤΩΝ

1. Ξενοφῶν ὁ φιλόσοφος, ἀνὴρ μόνος ἐξ ἁπάντων φιλοσόφων ἐν λόγοις τε καὶ ἔργοις φιλοσοφίαν κοσμή-
453B σας | (τὰ μὲν ἐς λόγους ἔστι τε ἐν γράμμασι καὶ τὴν
ἠθικὴν ἀρετὴν γράφει, τὰ δὲ ἐν πράξεσί τε ἦν ἄριστος, ἀλλὰ καὶ ἐγέννα στρατηγοὺς τοῖς ὑποδείγμα-
2 σιν· ὁ γοῦν μέγας Ἀλέξανδρος οὐκ ἂν ἐγένετο μέγας,
εἰ μὴ Ξενοφῶν ἦν), καὶ τὰ πάρεργά φησι δεῖν τῶν
σπουδαίων ἀνδρῶν ἀναγράφειν. ἐμοὶ δὲ οὐκ εἰς τὰ
πάρεργα τῶν σπουδαίων ὁ λόγος φέρει τὴν γραφήν,
ἀλλ᾽ εἰς τὰ ἔργα. εἰ γὰρ τὸ παίγνιον τῆς ἀρετῆς ἄξιον
λόγου, ἀσεβοῖτο ἂν πάντως τὸ σπουδαζόμενον σιω-
3 πώμενον. διαλεχθήσεται δὲ ὁ λόγος τοῖς ἐντυγχάνειν
βουλομένοις, οὔτε περὶ πάντων ἀσφαλῶς (οὐ γὰρ
πάντα ἀκριβῶς ἦν ἀναλέγεσθαι), οὔτε ἀποκρίνων
ἀλλήλων φιλοσόφους ἀρίστους καὶ ῥήτορας, ἀλλὰ
4 παρατιθεὶς ἑκάστῳ τὸ ἐπιτήδευμα. ὅτι δὲ ἄριστος ἦν

---

[1] Cf. Hdt. *Hist.* 3.72.
[2] He wrote about the lives of Cyrus and Agesilaus.

EUNAPIUS
LIVES OF PHILOSOPHERS
AND SOPHISTS

1. Xenophon the philosopher, a man who alone among all philosophers adorned philosophy with words and deeds[1]—as to words, he survives in his literary works and writes about moral excellence, but in his deeds he was also outstanding, engendering leaders of armies by the examples he provided;[2] for instance, the great Alexander would not 2 be great if it were not for Xenophon[3]—he says that one must also detail the lesser activities of distinguished men. My account, however, does not aim to record the lesser activities of distinguished men, but only their significant actions.[4] For if it is worthwhile to record the playful side of excellence, it would be absolutely impious for her seriousness to remain unexpressed. The account will be ex- 3 pounded for those who wish to read it, not with complete certainty in all respects—for it was not possible to collect all the evidence with accuracy—nor by distinguishing very good philosophers and orators from each other but by setting out for each one their way of life. That each person 4

[3] Alexander may have used the *Anabasis* on his Persian campaign (Arr. 1.12.3–4).

[4] Cf. Hdt. 1.1, 1.5; Plut. *Alex.* 1; Philostr. *VS* 540.

εἰς ἄκρον ὁ γραφόμενος ὑπὸ τοῦ λόγου, τῷ βουλομένῳ ταῦτα δικάζειν ἐκ τῶν ὑποκειμένων σημείων
καταλιμπάνει (βούλεται μὲν γάρ) ὁ ταῦτα γράφων.
5   καὶ ὑπομνήμασιν | ἀκριβέσιν ἐντετύχηκε, δι᾽ ὧν, ἢ
2G διαμαρτάνων τῆς ἀληθείας, ἐφ᾽ ἑτέρους ἀναφέροι τὸ
ἁμάρτημα, ὥσπερ ἀγαθός τις μαθητὴς κακῶν τετυ-
χηκὼς διδασκάλων, ἢ κατηγορῶν[1] ἀλήθειαν ἔχοι καὶ
τοὺς ἡγουμένους ἀξίους θαύματος, καὶ τό γε ἴδιον
ἔργον αὐτοῦ καθαρὸν εἴη καὶ ἀμώμητον, ἀκολουθή-
6   σαντος οἷς ἀκολουθεῖν προσῆκεν. ἐπεὶ δὲ ὀλίγοι τε ἢ
παντελῶς ἐλάχιστοί τινες ἦσαν οἱ περὶ τούτων γράφοντες, ἵνα τοῦτο εἴπῃ τις μόνον, οὔτε τὰ ὑπὸ τῶν
πρότερον γραφέντα λήσεται τοὺς ἐντυγχάνοντας,
οὔτε τὰ ἐξ ἀκοῆς ἐς τόνδε καθήκοντα τὸν χρόνον, ἀλλ᾽
ἀμφοτέροις ἀποδοθήσεται τὸ πρέπον, τῶν μὲν γεγραμμένων κινηθῆναι μηδέν, τὰ δὲ ἐκ τῆς ἀκοῆς ὑπὸ
τοῦ χρόνου κατασειόμενα καὶ μεταβάλλοντα διαπῆ-
ξαι καὶ στηρίξαι τῇ γραφῇ πρὸς τὸ στάσιμον καὶ
μονιμώτερον.[2] |

454B   2. Τὴν φιλόσοφον ἱστορίαν καὶ τοὺς τῶν φιλοσόφων ἀνδρῶν βίους Πορφύριος καὶ Σωτίων ἀνελέ-
ξαντο. ἀλλ᾽ ὁ μὲν Πορφύριος (οὕτω συμβάν) εἰς
2   Πλάτωνα ἐτελεύτα καὶ τοὺς ἐκείνου χρόνους· Σωτίων
δὲ καὶ καταβὰς φαίνεται, καίτοι γε ὁ Πορφύριος ἦν

---

[1] κατηγορῶν Kays Go: κατηγοριῶν A
[2] Here A (f. 218r) has Πλωτῖνος Πορφύριος Ἰάμβλιχος.

described by the account was the best in the highest degree, the author leaves to the person who wants to judge (for that is what he wants) on the basis of the evidence provided.[5] He has also read detailed records, and on account of these, if he strays utterly from the truth, he may refer his error back to others, like a diligent pupil who has fallen in with incompetent teachers; or, if he makes truthful claims, he may both have guides worthy of admiration and his own work at least may be untainted and blameless, because he followed those in whose steps it was appropriate to follow. Because few, or hardly anyone, have written on these matters, to make just this one point, neither that which has been composed by earlier authors will be concealed from my readers, nor what has come down by oral tradition to the present day, but the proper treatment will be used for both [kinds of] sources, I mean, that nothing from what was written has been altered, while what depends on the spoken word, which is liable to become disorganized and changeable by the lapse of time, has now been fixed and tied down into a stable and more permanent form through writing.

2. Porphyry and Sotion compiled the history of philosophy and the lives of philosophers.[6] But as it happens Porphyry ends his account with Plato and his times. Sotion, on the other hand, though he lived before Porphyry,

---

[5] A similar principle in Plut. *Per.* 2.4.

[6] Porphyry (ca. AD 234–305) wrote both lives and a history (Theod. *Cur. Aff. Gr.* 2.95 = Porph fr. 195T Smith). Sotion (fl. 200–170 BC) wrote only *Successions* (*Diadochai*) of philosophers. On the absence of Diogenes Laertius here, see Eunapius Introduction.

νεώτερος. τῆς δὲ ἐν τῷ μέσῳ φορᾶς φιλοσόφων τε
ἀνδρῶν καὶ σοφιστῶν ἀδιηγήτου γενομένης κατὰ τὸ
μέγεθος καὶ τὸ ποικίλον τῆς ἀρετῆς, Φιλόστρατος μὲν
ὁ Λήμνιος τοὺς τῶν ἀρίστων σοφιστῶν ἐξ ἐπιδρομῆς
μετὰ χάριτος παρέπτυσε βίους, φιλοσόφων δὲ οὐδεὶς
3   ἀκριβῶς ἀνέγραψεν· ἐν οἷς Ἀμμώνιός τε ἦν ὁ ἐξ Αἰ-
3G γύπτου, | Πλουτάρχου τοῦ θειοτάτου γεγονὼς διδά-
σκαλος, Πλούταρχός τε αὐτός, ἡ φιλοσοφίας ἁπάσης
ἀφροδίτη καὶ λύρα, Εὐφράτης τε ὁ ἐξ Αἰγύπτου καὶ
Δίων ὁ ἐκ Βιθυνίας ὃν ἐπεκάλουν Χρυσόστομον,
Ἀπολλώνιός τε ὁ ἐκ Τυάνων, οὐκέτι φιλόσοφος, ἀλλ'
4   ἦν τι θεῶν τι καὶ ἀνθρώπου μέσον. τὴν γὰρ Πυθα-
γόρειον φιλοσοφίαν ζηλώσας, πολὺ τὸ θειότερον καὶ
ἐνεργὸν κατ' αὐτὴν ἐπεδείξατο. ἀλλὰ τὸ μὲν ἐς τοῦτον
ὁ Λήμνιος ἐπετέλεσε Φιλόστρατος, βίον ἐπιγράψας
Ἀπολλωνίου τὰ βιβλία, δέον Ἐπιδημίαν ἐς ἀνθρώ-
5   πους θεοῦ καλεῖν. Καρνεάδης δὲ ἦν κατὰ τούτους τοὺς
χρόνους, καὶ τῶν κατὰ κυνισμὸν οὐκ ἀφανής, εἴ τινα
καὶ κυνισμοῦ χρὴ λόγον ποιεῖσθαι, παρ' οἷς ἦν Μουσώνιος καὶ Δημήτριος καὶ Μένιππος καὶ ἕτεροί γέ
6   τινες πλείους· οὗτοι δὲ ἦσαν ἐπιφανέστεροι. τούτων
δὲ σαφεῖς μὲν καὶ ἀκριβεῖς οὐκ ἦν ἀνευρεῖν τοὺς
βίους, ἅτε μηδενὸς συγγεγραφότος, ὅσα γε ἡμᾶς εἰ-

---

7 Cf. Philostr. VS 9.7.
8 Plutarch of Chaeronea (AD 45–120).
9 For Euphrates see Philostr. VS 488, 536; Plin. Ep. 1.10.
10 Cf. Philostr. VA 1.1: Empedocles "no more a mortal."

clearly carried on his narrative to later times as well. But since the crop of philosophers and sophists who came between Sotion and Porphyry was not described in proper appreciation of the importance and wide-ranging nature of their excellence, Philostratus of Lemnos in an offhand and agreeable style sketched the lives of the most distinguished sophists;[7] but no one has recorded accurately the lives of the philosophers [for this period]. Among these latter were Ammonius of Egypt, who was the teacher of the divinely inspired Plutarch,[8] and Plutarch himself, the loveliness and lyre of all philosophy; Euphrates[9] of Egypt and Dio of Bithynia (whom they nicknamed Chrysostomos, the "Golden-mouthed") and Apollonius of Tyana, who was no longer a [mortal] philosopher:[10] rather he is something in-between gods and a human. For he was a devotee of the Pythagorean doctrine, and he did much to put on display the more divine and effectual character of that philosophy. But Philostratus of Lemnos wrote a complete account on him, and entitled his books *Life of Apollonius*, though he should have called it *Visit of a god among mortals*. Carneades[11] also lived about this time, a not insignificant figure among the Cynics, if there is a need to take any account of the Cynic school as well, among whom were Musonius, Demetrius, and Menippus,[12] and plenty of others besides; but these were the more celebrated ones. Clear and accurate accounts of their lives it was impossible to discover, since, so far as I know, no one

3

4

5

6

[11] Unknown (not the first-century BC Platonist of that name).
[12] Not Musonius the Stoic (ca. AD 25–100). Demetrius (1st c. AD), a friend of the Stoic Seneca; the Cynic Menippus of Gadara (3rd c. BC) invented Menippean satire.

δέναι· ἱκανοὶ δὲ αὐτῶν ἦσάν τε καί εἰσι βίοι τὰ γράμματα, τοσαύτης ἀνάμεστα παιδείας καὶ θεωρίας ‹ὅση
τείνει καὶ φέρει› ἔς τὴν³ ἠθικὴν ἀρετὴν καὶ ὅση πρὸς
τὴν τῶν ὄντων διήρατο καὶ ἀνέβλεψε φύσιν, τὴν
ἄγνοιαν τῶν δυναμένων ἀκολουθεῖν, ὡς ἀχλύν τινα,

7   σκεδάσασα. αὐτίκα οὖν ὁ θεσπέσιος Πλούταρχος τόν
τε ἑαυτοῦ βίον ἀναγράφει τοῖς βιβλίοις ἐνδιεσπαρ-
μένως καὶ τὸν τοῦ διδασκάλου, καὶ ὅτι γε Ἀμμώνιος
Ἀθήνησιν ἐτελεύτα, οὐ βίον προσειπών. καίτοι γε τὸ
κάλλιστον αὐτοῦ τῶν συγγραμμάτων εἰσὶν οἱ καλού-
μενοι παράλληλοι βίοι τῶν ἀρίστων κατὰ ἔργα καὶ

8   πράξεις ἀνδρῶν· ἀλλὰ | τὸν ἴδιον καὶ τοῦ διδασκάλου
4G καθ᾽ ἕκαστον τῶν βιβλίων ἐγκατέσπειρεν, ὥστε, εἴ τις
ὀξυδορκοίη περὶ ταῦτα, ἀνιχνεύων⁴ κατὰ τὸ προσπί-
πτον καὶ φαινόμενον, καὶ σωφρόνως τὰ κατὰ μέρος
ἀναλέγοιτο, δύνασθαι τὰ πλεῖστα τῶν βεβιωμένων

9   αὐτοῖς εἰδέναι. Λουκιανὸς δὲ ὁ ἐκ Σαμοσάτων, ἀνὴρ
σπουδαῖος ἐς τὸ γελασθῆναι, Δημώνακτος φιλοσόφου κατ᾽ ἐκείνους τοὺς χρόνους βίον ἀνέγραψεν, ἐν
ἐκείνῳ τε τῷ βιβλίῳ καὶ ἄλλοις ἐλαχίστοις δι᾽ ὅλου
σπουδάσας.

10   Καὶ ταῦτά γε εἰς μνήμην ἐγὼ τίθεμαι, τοῦτο συνορῶν, ὅτι τὰ μὲν ἔλαθεν ἴσως ἡμᾶς, τὰ δὲ οὐκ ἔλαθεν.

11   ἐκείνου δὲ καίπερ πολλὴν ποιούμενος φροντίδα καὶ
σπουδήν, τοῦ συνεχῆ καὶ περιγεγραμμένην εἰς ἀκρί-

---

³ ὅση ‹τείνει καὶ φέρει› ἔς τὴν Go: ὅση ἔς τε Α
⁴ ἀνιχνεύων Go: ἀνιχνεύοι Wr

has written them. But their own writings were, and still are, sufficient records of their lives, which are filled with such erudition and thorough research to the extent that it pertains to and conveys the moral excellence, and also to the extent that it raises up and considers the nature of things, and dispersing "like a mist"[13] the ignorance of those who are able to follow. Thus, for example, the in- 7 spired Plutarch records, in statements scattered here and there in his books, both his own life and that of his teacher; and he says that Ammonius[14] died at Athens, without re- counting his life. Yet the most successful of his writings is the one entitled *Parallel Lives* of men highly celebrated for their activities and achievements. But his own life and 8 that of his teacher he has disseminated throughout every one of his books, so that, if one should keep a sharp look- out for these references, tracking them as they occur and appear, and collect each and every one of them with care, one would be able to know most of their lives' experiences. Lucian of Samosata, a man in serious pursuit of a laugh, 9 wrote a life of Demonax, a philosopher of his own time, and in that book and a very small number of others he was serious throughout.

These things, then, I call to mind, knowing that some 10 things have perhaps escaped me, but other things have not. And even though I expended much thought and effort 11 on that point, that is, on undertaking a continuous and

13 Cf. Hom. *Il.* 5.696, 16.344.
14 Plut. fr. 184 Sandbach.

βειαν ἱστορίαν τινὰ λαβεῖν τοῦ φιλοσόφου καὶ ῥητο-
455Β ρικοῦ βίου τῶν ἀρίστων ἀνδρῶν, | εἶτα οὐ τυγχάνων
τῆς ἐπιθυμίας, ταὐτόν τι τοῖς ἐρῶσιν ἐμμανῶς καὶ
12 περιφλέκτως ἔπαθον. καὶ γὰρ ἐκεῖνοι, τὴν μὲν ἐρω-
μένην αὐτὴν ὁρῶντες καὶ τὸ περίψυκτον ἐν τῷ φαινο-
μένῳ κάλλος, κάτω νεύουσιν, ὃ ζητοῦσιν ἰδεῖν ἐξ-
13 ασθενοῦντες καὶ περιλαμπόμενοι· ἐὰν δὲ πέδιλον
αὐτῆς ἢ πλόκιον ἢ ἐλλόβιον ἴδωσιν, ἐκείνοις κατα-
θαρσοῦντες, τὴν ψυχήν τε τῇ ὄψει προσαφιᾶσι καὶ
κατατήκονται πρὸς τῷ θεάματι, τὰ σύμβολα τοῦ κάλλους μᾶλλον ἢ τὸ κάλλος ὁρᾶν ἀνεχόμενοι καὶ στέρ-
14 γοντες. κἀγὼ πρὸς ταύτην ἐξώρμησα τὴν γραφήν,
ὅσα ἢ κατὰ ἀκοήν, ἢ κατὰ ἀνάγνωσιν, ἢ κατὰ ἱστορίαν τῶν κατ’ ἐμαυτὸν ἀνθρώπων ⟨κατέμαθον⟩[5] μὴ
5G παρελθεῖν σιωπῇ καὶ βασκάνως, | ἀλλ’, εἰς ὅσον οἷόν
τε ἦν, ἀληθείας πρόθυρα καὶ πύλας προσκυνήσαντα,
παραδοῦναι τοῖς μετὰ ταῦτα ἢ βουλομένοις ἀκούειν ἢ
δυναμένοις ἀκολουθεῖν πρὸς τὸ κάλλιστον.
15   Ἔσχε μὲν οὖν διακοπήν τινα καὶ ῥῆξιν ὁ χρόνος
διὰ τὰς κοινὰς συμφοράς· τρίτη δὲ ἀνδρῶν ἐγένετο
φορά (ἡ μὲν γὰρ δευτέρα μετὰ τὴν Πλάτωνος πᾶσιν
ἐμφανὴς ἀνακεκήρυκται) [ὅτι][6] κατὰ τοὺς Κλαυδίου
καὶ Νέρωνος· τοὺς γὰρ ἀθλίους καὶ ἐνιαυσίους οὐ
χρὴ γράφειν –οὗτοι δ’ ἦσαν οἱ περὶ Γάλβαν, Βιτέλ-
16 λιον, Ὄθωνα· [Οὐεσπασιανὸς δὲ ὁ ἐπὶ τούτοις καὶ
Τίτος][7] καὶ ὅσοι μετὰ τούτους ἦρξαν– ἵνα μὴ τοῦτο

----

[5] inser. Go   [6] del. Go   [7] del. Go

394

well-defined account of the philosophical and rhetorical
life of the most respectable men, if I fell short of my ambition, I have had the same experience as those who are
madly and feverishly in love. For they, seeing their be-   12
loved and the chilling beauty of their appearance, bow
their heads, too weak to look at what they desire, and totally dazzled. But if they see her sandal or necklace or   13
earring, they take heart from these and pour their souls
into the sight and melt at the vision, being able to see and
love the markers of beauty more easily than beauty itself.
In a similar fashion I have set out to write this narrative in 14
such a way as not to omit in silence and through envy
anything that I learned from spoken reports, or by reading, or by inquiry from anyone of my own time, but, as far
as I was able, I paid my respects to the antechamber and
gates of truth[15] and have handed it down to future gen-
erations who may either wish to hear it or have the power
to follow onto the highest Good.

Now, the period in question experienced disruption   15
and discontinuity, because of the adversity afflicting the
state. Nonetheless, a third crop of men began with the
days of Claudius and Nero—for the second that came next
after Plato has been made very clear to all. There is no
need to talk about those unlucky emperors who lasted for
a year only—I mean Galba, Vitellius, Otho [Vespasian   16
came after these and Titus][16] and those who ruled after

15 Cf. Procl. *Plat. Theol.* 64: the path to wisdom is like entering a building where Truth and Beauty reside.

16 A gloss to the next clause.

σπουδάζειν δόξωμεν, πλὴν ἐπιτρέχοντί γε καὶ συν-
ελόντι εἰπεῖν, τὸ τῶν ἀρίστων φιλοσόφων γένος καὶ
17 εἰς Σεβῆρον διέτεινεν. ἀλλὰ εὐτυχές γε ὑπάρχει τοῖς
βασιλεῦσι κατὰ τὴν συγγραφήν, ὅτι τὸ κατ' ἀρετὴν
ὑπερέχον ἀριθμεῖται τῷ κατὰ τὴν τύχην. νεμεσάτω δὲ
μηδὲ εἷς, εἴ γε καὶ ἡμεῖς οὕτως ἀναγράφοντες τοὺς
χρόνους, ἀφ' ὧν γε ἦν δυνατὸν συντεκμηριώσασθαι
ἢ παραλαβεῖν τὴν προσήκουσαν ἀρχήν, ἀπὸ τούτων
εἰς τὸν λόγον ἐπιβησόμεθα.

3. Πλωτῖνος ἦν ἐξ Αἰγύπτου φιλόσοφος. τὸ ἐξ
Αἰγύπτου νῦν γράφων, καὶ τὴν πατρίδα προσθήσω.
2 Λυκὼ ταύτην ὀνομάζουσι· καίτοι γε ὁ θεσπέσιος
φιλόσοφος Πορφύριος τοῦτο οὐκ ἀνέγραψε, μαθητής
τε αὐτοῦ γεγενῆσθαι λέγων, καὶ συνεσχολακέναι
⟨αὐτῷ⟩[8] τὸν βίον ἅπαντα ἢ τὸν πλεῖστον τούτου. |
3 Πλωτίνου θερμοὶ βωμοὶ νῦν, καὶ | τὰ βιβλία οὐ μόνον
6G τοῖς πεπαιδευμένοις διὰ χειρὸς ὑπὲρ τοὺς Πλατωνι-
κοὺς λόγους, ἀλλ' καὶ τὸ πολὺ πλῆθος, ἐάν τι παρα-
4 κούσῃ δογμάτων, ἐς αὐτὰ κάμπτεται. τὸν βίον αὐτοῦ
πάντα Πορφύριος ἐξήνεγκεν, ὡς οὐδένα οἷόν τε ἦν
5 πλέον εἰσφέρειν· ἀλλ' καὶ πολλὰ τῶν βιβλίων
[. . . . .][9] ἑρμηνεύσας αὐτοῦ φαίνεται. αὐτοῦ δὲ Πορφυρίου βίον ἀνέγραψεν οὐδὲ εἷς, ὅσα γε [εἰς][10] ἡμᾶς
εἰδέναι· ἀναλεγομένῳ δὲ ἐκ τῶν δοθέντων κατὰ τὴν
ἀνάγνωσιν σημείων τοιαῦτα ὑπῆρχε τὰ περὶ αὐτόν.

[8] add. Go   [9] ras. quinque litter. A
[10] del. Hemst Go: καὶ Wytt Wr

396

these men—and no one must suppose that I pay serious attention to them, except mention cursorily and in brief the tribe of the best philosophers continued even into the reign of Severus. And surely it is good fortune for emperors in a historical narrative that a highpoint of virtue is counted according to the fortune [of an emperor].[17] Therefore let no one reject as unseemly if I also record in this way the historical times for which it was possible for me to find supporting evidence, or obtain an appropriate beginning; on the basis of these foundations I shall embark on my narrative. 17

3. Plotinus was a philosopher of Egyptian birth. Describing him just now as a man from Egypt, I will add his place of birth as well: they call it Lyco. Yet the inspired philosopher Porphyry did not place this on record, though he said that he was his pupil and studied with him during the whole of his life, or the greater part of it. Altars in honor of Plotinus are still warm, and not only are his books in the hands of educated men, more so than the Platonic writings, but even great numbers of the common people, though they misunderstand his doctrines, are nevertheless swayed by them. Porphyry set forth his whole life so fully that no one could produce more evidence. Moreover, he is known to have interpreted many of his books [. . .]. But, so far as I know, no one has written a life of Porphyry himself. However, from what I have gathered in my reading of the evidence that has been handed down, I have learned the following facts concerning him. 2 3 4 5

---

[17] That is, dating the lives of philosophers by reigns of emperors.

4. Πορφυρίῳ Τύρος μὲν ἦν πατρίς, ἡ πρώτη τῶν ἀρχαίων Φοινίκων πόλις, καὶ πατέρες δὲ οὐκ ἄσημοι.

2 τυχὼν δὲ τῆς προσηκούσης παιδείας, ἀνά τε ἔδραμε τοσοῦτον καὶ ἐπέδωκεν, ὡς—Λογγίνου μὲν ἦν ἀκροα-

456B τής—| καὶ ἐκόσμει τὸν διδάσκαλον ἐντὸς ὀλίγου χρό-

3 νου. Λογγῖνος δὲ κατὰ τὸν χρόνον ἐκεῖνον βιβλιο-θήκη τις ἦν ἔμψυχος καὶ περιπατοῦν μουσεῖον, καὶ κρίνειν γε τοὺς παλαιοὺς ἐπετέτραπτο, καθάπερ πρὸ ἐκείνου πολλοί τινες ἕτεροι, καὶ ὁ ἐκ Καρίας Διονύ-

4 σιος πάντων ἀριδηλότερος. Μάλχος δὲ κατὰ τὴν Σύρων πόλιν ὁ Πορφύριος ἐκαλεῖτο τὰ πρῶτα (τοῦτο δὲ δύναται βασιλέα λέγειν)· Πορφύριον δε αὐτὸν ὠνόμασε Λογγῖνος, ἐς τὸ βασιλικὸν τῆς ἐσθῆτος παράσημον τὴν προσηγορίαν ἀποτρέψας. παρ᾽ ἐκείνῳ δὴ τὴν ἄκραν ἐπαιδεύετο παιδείαν, γραμματικῆς τε εἰς ἄκρον ἁπάσης, ὥσπερ ἐκεῖνος, ἀφικόμενος καὶ ῥη-τορικῆς, πλὴν ὅσον οὐκ ἐπ᾽ ἐκείνην ἔνευσε, φιλοσο-

5 φίας γε πᾶν εἶδος ἐκματτόμενος. ἦν γὰρ ὁ Λογγῖνος μακρῷ τῶν τότε ἀνδρῶν τὰ πάντα ἄριστος, καὶ τῶν βιβλίων τε αὐτοῦ πολὺ πλῆθος φέρεται, καὶ τὸ φερό-μενον θαυμάζεται. καὶ εἴ τις κατέγνω τινὸς τῶν πα-

7G λαιῶν, | οὐ τὸ δοξασθὲν ἐκράτει πρότερον, ἀλλ᾽ ἡ

6 Λογγίνου πάντως ἐκράτει κρίσις. οὕτω δὲ ἀχθεὶς τὴν πρώτην παιδείαν καὶ ὑπὸ πάντων ἀποβλεπόμενος, τὴν μεγίστην Ῥώμην ἰδεῖν ἐπιθυμήσας, ἵνα κατάσχῃ διὰ σοφίας τὴν πόλιν, ἐπειδὴ τάχιστα εἰς αὐτὴν ἀφίκετο καὶ τῷ μεγίστῳ Πλωτίνῳ συνῆλθεν εἰς ὁμι-λίαν, πάντων ἐπελάθετο τῶν ἄλλων, καὶ προσέθετο

4. Porphyry's birthplace was Tyre, the principal city of the ancient Phoenicians, and his ancestors were men of some distinction. Receiving an education befitting his status, he advanced so rapidly and was such a dedicated student, that, as a student of Longinus, he was a credit to his teacher in a very short time. At that time Longinus was a kind of living and breathing library and a Mouseion on two legs; and what is more, he had been given the role of critic of the ancient authors, like many others before him, such as the most famous of them all, Dionysius of Caria.[18] Porphyry's name in the Syrian town was originally Malchus (this word means "king"), but Longinus gave him the name "Porphyrios," making it refer to the color of imperial attire.[19] While with Longinus, he attained to the highest level of erudition, and like him advanced to a perfect knowledge of grammar and rhetoric, except that he was not drawn to these subjects by nature, since every type of philosophy had made its strong mark on him. For Longinus was in all areas by far the most distinguished of men at this time, and a great number of his books are in circulation and they are much admired. Whenever any critic condemned some ancient author, the opinion did not win at first but Longinus' judgment would hold sway completely. After Porphyry had thus undergone his early education and was looked up to by all, he longed to see the great city of Rome, so that he might captivate the city with wisdom. But as soon as he arrived there and began to meet regularly with that great man Plotinus, he forgot all else

[18] Dionysius of Halicarnassus (fl. 20 BC), who wrote a history of Rome from its origin to the First Punic War.

[19] That is, purple (cf. Porph *Plot.* 17).

7 φέρων ἑαυτὸ ἐκείνῳ. ἀκορέστως δὲ τῆς παιδείας ἐμ-
φορούμενος καὶ τῶν πηγαίων ἐκείνων καὶ τεθειασμέ-
νων λόγων, χρόνον μέν τινα εἰς τὴν ἀκρόασιν ἤρκεσεν, ὡς αὐτός φησιν, εἶτα ὑπὸ τοῦ μεγέθους τῶν
λόγων νικώμενος, τό τε σῶμα ⟨ἔχειν⟩[11] καὶ τὸ ἄνθρωπος εἶναι ἐμίσησε, καὶ διαπλεύσας εἰς Σικελίαν τὸν
πορθμὸν καὶ τὴν Χάρυβδιν, ᾗπερ Ὀδυσσεὺς ἀνα-
πλεῦσαι λέγεται, πόλιν μὲν οὔτε ἰδεῖν ὑπέμεινεν, οὔτε
ἀνθρώπων ἀκοῦσαι φωνῆς (οὕτω τὸ λυπούμενον αὐτῶν[12] καὶ ἡδόμενον ἀπέθετο), συντείνας δὲ ἐπὶ Λιλύ-
βαιον ἑαυτὸν (τὸ δέ ἐστι τῶν τριῶν ἀκρωτηρίων τῆς
Σικελίας τὸ πρὸς Λιβύην ἀνατεῖνον καὶ ὁρῶν), ἔκειτο
καταστένων καὶ ἀποκαρτερῶν, τροφήν τε οὐ προσιέ-
8 μενος, καὶ ἀνθρώπων ἀλεείνων πάτον. οὐδ᾽ ἀλαοσκο-
πιὴν ὁ μέγας εἶχε Πλωτῖνος ἐπὶ τούτοις, ἀλλὰ κατὰ
πόδας ἑπόμενος, ⟨καὶ ἀνιχνεύων⟩[13] ἢ τὸν ἀποπεφευ-
8G γότα νεανίσκον | ἀναζητῶν, ἐπιτυγχάνει κειμένῳ, καὶ
λόγων τε πρὸς αὐτὸν εὐπόρησε τὴν ψυχὴν ἀνακα-
λουμένων ἄρτι ἐξίπτασθαι τοῦ σώματος μέλλουσαν,
9 καὶ τὸ σῶμα ἔρρωσεν ἐς κατοχὴν τῆς ψυχῆς. καὶ ὁ
μὲν ἔμπνους τε ἦν καὶ διανίστατο, ὁ δὲ τοὺς ῥηθέντας
λόγους εἰς βιβλίον κατέθετο τῶν γεγραμμένων.

Τῶν δὲ φιλοσόφων τὰ ἀπόρρητα καλυπτόντων
ἀσαφείᾳ, καθάπερ τῶν ποιητῶν τοῖς μύθοις, ὁ Πορφύριος, τὸ φάρμακον τῆς σαφηνείας ἐπαινέσας καὶ

[11] add. Go   [12] αὐτῶν Gi: αὐτω A: αὐτῷ Wr
[13] add. Gi et Go pro lacuna [12 litt.]

and devoted himself completely to him. And filling himself 7
up with his teachings and his original and divinely inspired
discourses with an insatiable appetite, for some time he
was content to be his student, as he himself says.[20] But
then, overcome by the enormity of those teachings, he
came to hate having a body and being human, and sailed
to Sicily across the straits and Charybdis, along the route
where Odysseus is said to have sailed;[21] and he could not
endure either to see a city or to hear the human voice (thus
he kept himself away from both pain and pleasure [of
these]), continuing on to Lilybaeum—one of Sicily's three
promontories that stretches out and looks toward Libya.
There he lay groaning and starving himself to death, refus-
ing to take nourishment and "avoiding the path of men."[22]
The great Plotinus "kept no vain watch"[23] on these things, 8
but followed in his footsteps, [and tracking him] or searching the young man who had fled, found him lying there;
then he found an abundance of words that recalled to life
his soul, as it was just about to flee from the body, and he
reinvigorated his body so that it might hold onto his soul.
So Porphyry for his part was revived again and arose, Plo- 9
tinus on the other hand recorded the arguments he had
used in a book among his writings.[24]

While philosophers shield their secret teachings by obscuring it, in the way that poets conceal theirs in myths,[25]
Porphyry praised the salutary effect of clarity, and since

20 *Plot.* 18.8–20.   21 Hom. *Od.* 12.426–46; cf. Thuc. 4.24.
22 Hom. *Il.* 6.202.
23 Hom. *Il.* 10.515 (said of Apollo), 13.10 (of Poseidon).
24 Not extant (but cf. *Enn.* 3.2.5–6 on adversity).
25 Cf. Julian. *Or.* 5.170, 7.217c.

διαπείρας γευσάμενος, ὑπόμνημα γράψας εἰς φῶς

10 ἤγαγεν. αὐτὸς μὲν οὖν ἐπὶ τὴν Ῥώμην ἐπανῆλθε καὶ
τῆς περὶ λόγους εἴχετο σπουδῆς, ὥστε παρῄει καὶ εἰς
τὸ δημόσιον κατ᾿ ἐπίδειξιν· τὸ δὲ Πορφυρίου κλέος εἰς
Πλωτῖνον πᾶσα μὲν ἀγορά, πᾶσα δὲ πληθὺς ἀνέφε-
ρεν. ὁ μὲν γὰρ Πλωτῖνος τῷ τε τῆς ψυχῆς οὐρανίῳ
καὶ τῷ λοξῷ καὶ αἰνιγματώδει τῶν λόγων, βαρὺς

11 ἐδόκει καὶ δυσήκοος· | ὁ δὲ Πορφύριος, ὥσπερ Ἑρ-
457B μαϊκή τις σειρὰ καὶ πρὸς ἀνθρώπους ἐπινεύουσα, διὰ
ποικίλης παιδείας πάντα εἰς τὸ εὔγνωστον καὶ καθαρὸν ἐξήγγελλεν. αὐτὸς μὲν οὖν φησι (νέος δὲ ὢν
ἴσως ταῦτα ἔγραφεν, ὡς ἔοικεν), ἐπιτυχεῖν χρηστηρίῳ

12 μηδενὶ τῶν δημοσίων· ἐν δὲ αὐτῷ τῷ βιβλίῳ κατα-
9G γράφει, καὶ μετὰ ταῦτα ἄλλα πραγματεύεται | πολλά,
ὅπως χρὴ τούτων ποιεῖσθαι τὴν ἐπιμέλειαν. φησὶ δὲ
καὶ δαιμόνιόν τινα φύσιν ἀπὸ λουτροῦ τινὸς ἐκδιῶξαι
καὶ ἐκβαλεῖν· Καυσάθαν τοῦτον ἔλεγον οἱ ἐπιχώριοι.

13 Συμφοιτηταὶ μὲν οὖν, ὡς αὐτὸς ἀναγράφει, κρά-
τιστοί τινες ὑπῆρχον, Ὠριγένης τε καὶ Ἀμέριος καὶ
Ἀκυλῖνος, καὶ συγγράμματά γε αὐτῶν περισῴζεται,
λόγος δὲ αὐτῶν οὐδὲ εἷς· πολὺ γὰρ τὸ ἀκύθηρον,
εἰ καὶ τὰ δόγματα ἔχει καλῶς, καὶ ἐπιτρέχει τοῖς λό-

14 γοις. ἀλλ᾿ ὅ γε Πορφύριος ἐπαινεῖ τοὺς ἄνδρας τῆς
δεινότητος, πᾶσαν μὲν αὐτὸς ἀνατρέχων χάριν, μόνος
δὲ ἀναδεικνὺς καὶ ἀνακηρύττων τὸν διδάσκαλον, οὐ-

---

26 Hom. *Il.* 8.19. Platonist symbol of succession (Marinus, *Procl.* 26.53).

he had had a taste of it from experience, he wrote a dissertation on it, and published it. Now Porphyry returned 10 to Rome and resumed his interest in discourses, so that he even appeared in public to hold speeches for display; and every gathering, every crowd attributed the credit of Porphyry's renown to Plotinus. For Plotinus, because of the celestial quality of his soul and the oblique and enigmatic character of his discourses, came across as overly serious and not easy to understand. But Porphyry, like a chain of 11 Hermes let down to mortals,[26] expounded all subjects by way of his wide-ranging erudition in such a manner that they were easy to comprehend and clear. He himself says (but perhaps he wrote this while he was still young, or so it seems), that he did not chance upon any oracle of the popular kind. In the same book he described (and after 12 these expounded many others) how men ought to pay attention to these oracles. And he says too that he harried and expelled some sort of demon from a certain bath; the inhabitants called this demon Kausatha.[27]

As he himself records, he had for fellow students some 13 highly skilled men, Origen[28] and Amerius and Aquilinus,[29] whose writings are preserved, though there is not one account of them; for, although their doctrines are admirable, their discourses are marked by a pervasive lack of charm. Nevertheless, Porphyry praises these men for their exper- 14 tise, even if he himself can produce all varieties of stylistic charm, and he alone advertises and celebrates his teacher,

---

[27] Meaning of the name unclear (see Becker 2013, 200).

[28] Not the famous Christian teacher (d. 254 CE).

[29] Porphyry (*Plot*. 16) calls him a Christian Gnostic who led others astray by his doctrines.

δὲν παιδείας εἶδος παραλελοιπώς. ἔστι γοῦν ἀπορῆ-
σαι καθ᾽ ἑαυτὸν καὶ θαυμάσαι, τί πλεῖόν ἐστι τῶν
ἐσπουδασμένων· πότερον τὰ εἰς ὕλην ῥητορικὴν τείνοντα, ἢ τὰ εἰς γραμματικὴν ἀκρίβειαν φέροντα, ἢ
ὅσα τῶν ἀριθμῶν ἤρτηται, ἢ ὅσα νεύει πρὸς γεω-
15   μετρίαν, ἢ ὅσα πρὸς μουσικὴν ῥέπει. τὰ δὲ εἰς φιλοσοφίαν, οὐδὲ τὸ περὶ λόγους καταληπτόν, οὔτε τὸ
ἠθικὸν ἐφικτὸν λόγῳ· τὸ δὲ φυσικὸν καὶ θεουργὸν
τελεταῖς ἀφείσθω καὶ μυστηρίοις· οὕτω παντομιγὲς
πρὸς ἅπασαν ἀρετὴν ὁ ἀνὴρ αὐτὸς χρῆμά τι γέγονεν.
16   καὶ τὸ κάλλος αὐτοῦ τῶν λόγων ἄν τις μᾶλλον ⟨ἐπαι-
10G νέσειε⟩[14] ἢ τὰ δόγματα, | ὁ πλέον εἰς αὐτὰ ἀπιδὼν ἢ
17   τὴν δύναμιν τοῦ λόγου. γάμοις τε ὁμιλήσας φαίνεται,
καὶ πρὸς Μάρκελλάν γε αὐτοῦ γυναῖκα γενομένην
βιβλίον φέρεται, ἥν φησιν ἀγαγέσθαι καὶ ταῦτα οὖσαν πέντε μητέρα τέκνων, οὐχ ἵνα παῖδας ἐξ αὐτῆς
ποιήσηται, ἀλλ᾽ ἵνα οἱ γεγονότες παιδείας τύχωσιν·
ἐκ φίλου γὰρ ἦν αὐτοῦ τῇ γυναικὶ τὰ τέκνα προϋπάρ-
18   ξαντα. φαίνεται δὲ ἀφικόμενος εἰς γῆρας βαθύ· πολλὰς γοῦν τοῖς ἤδη προπεπραγματευμένοις βιβλίοις
θεωρίας ἐναντίας κατέλιπε, περὶ ὧν οὐκ ἔστιν ἕτερόν
τι δοξάζειν, ἢ ὅτι προϊὼν ἕτερα ἐδόξασεν. ἐν Ῥώμῃ
δὲ λέγεται μεταλλαχέναι τὸν βίον.

[14] inser. Go

---

30 Lacuna and corrupt text (cf. Goulet ad loc.).

inasmuch as there was no branch of learning that he neglected. We may well be puzzled on his behalf and wonder
which one of the subjects he studied most intensely: was
it the one that concerns the subject matter of rhetoric, or
that which strives for accuracy in grammar, or that which
depends on numbers, or inclines to geometry, or is directed toward music? With regard to philosophy, one can   15
grasp neither his genius for reasoned arguments nor that
for moral philosophy by way of reason. As for natural philosophy and the art of divination, let us leave those to sacred rites and secret rituals. So multifarious in view of
every kind of excellence, the man himself was a marvel.
The beauty of the style of his discourse [one might praise] 16
more than his doctrines, . . . , if one paid closer attention
to these than to the force of his oratory.[30] We know that   17
he entered the married state, and there is even a book of
his addressed to Marcella,[31] who had become his wife; he
says that he married her, although she was already the
mother of five[32] children, and this was not that he might
have children by her, but that those she had might be
educated; for the father of his wife's children had been a
friend of his. It is apparent that he reached an advanced   18
old age. For he did leave behind many speculations that
are in conflict with the books that he had previously published; with regard to which we can only suppose that he
changed his opinions as he grew older. He is said to have
departed this life in Rome.

[31] His *Epist. ad Marcellam* is extant but missing the ending;
for text and translation, see K. O'Brien Wicker (SBL, 1987).

[32] See Penella (1990, 29–30) on this number (she had seven
children).

19 Κατὰ τούτους ἦσαν τοὺς χρόνους καὶ τῶν ῥητορικῶν οἱ ἐν Ἀθήνῃσι προεστῶτες Παῦλός τε καὶ Ἀν-
δρόμαχος ἐκ Συρίας. τοὺς δὲ χρόνους ἐς Γαλλίηνόν
τε καὶ Κλαύδιον ἀκμάζειν συνέβαινεν, Τάκιτόν τε καὶ
Αὐρηλιανὸν καὶ Πρόβον, καθ᾽ οὓς ἦν καὶ Δέξιππος
ὁ τὴν χρονικὴν ἱστορίαν συγγράψας, ἀνὴρ ἁπάσης
παιδείας τε καὶ δυνάμεως λογικῆς ἀνάπλεως.

5. Ἰάμβλιχος· Μετὰ τούτους ὀνομαστότατος ἐπιγί-
νεται φιλόσοφος, Ἰάμβλιχος, ὃς ἦν καὶ κατὰ γένος
μὲν ἐπιφανὴς καὶ τῶν ἁβρῶν καὶ τῶν εὐδαιμόνων·
πατρὶς δὲ ἦν αὐτῷ Χαλκίς· κατὰ τὴν Κοίλην Συρίαν

2 προσαγορευομένην ἐστὶν ἡ πόλις. οὗτος Ἀνατολίῳ
τῶν κατὰ Πορφύριον τὰ δεύτερα φερομένων συγγενόμενος, πολύ γε ἐπέδωκε καὶ εἰς ἄκρον φιλοσοφίας
458B ἤκμασεν·¹⁵ | εἶτα μετ᾽ Ἀνατόλιον | Πορφυρίῳ προσθεὶς
11G ἑαυτόν, οὐκ ἔστιν ὅ τι καὶ Πορφυρίου διήνεγκεν, πλὴν

3 ὅσον κατὰ τὴν συνθήκην καὶ δύναμιν τοῦ λόγου. οὔτε
γὰρ εἰς ἀφροδίτην αὐτοῦ καὶ χάριν τὰ λεγόμενα βέ-
βαπται, οὔτε ἔχει λευκότητά τινα καὶ τῷ καθαρῷ καλ-
λωπίζεται· οὐ μὴν οὐδὲ ἀσαφῆ παντελῶς τυγχάνει,
οὐδὲ κατὰ τὴν λέξιν ἡμαρτημένα, ἀλλ᾽ ὥσπερ ἔλεγε
περὶ Ξενοκράτους ὁ Πλάτων, ταῖς Ἑρμαϊκαῖς οὐ τέθυ-

4 ται Χάρισιν. οὔκουν κατέχει τὸν ἀκροατὴν καὶ γοη-
τεύει πρὸς τὴν ἀνάγνωσιν, ἀλλ᾽ ἀποστρέφειν καὶ
ἀποκναίειν τὴν ἀκοὴν ἔοικεν. δικαιοσύνην δὲ ἀσκή-
σας, εὐηκοΐας ἔτυχε θεῶν τοσαύτης, ὥστε πλῆθος μὲν

15 ἤλασεν Cob: ἤκμασεν Boiss Gi Go

At this time there were also among the orators in Ath-   19
ens the distinguished Paulus and the Syrian Androma-
chus. As to his life time, Porphyry happened to be at his
prime up to Gallienus and to Claudius, Tacitus, Aurelian,
and Probus. In those days there lived also Dexippus,[33] who
composed his historical chronicle, a man brimming with
erudition and rhetorical power.

5. Iamblichus. After these men comes a highly celebrated philosopher, Iamblichus, who was both of illustrious ancestry and son of refined and prosperous parents.
His birthplace was Chalcis, a city in the region called
Koilê.[34] As a pupil of Anatolius, who was successor to Por-   2
phyry, he made much progress and attained to the highest
distinction in philosophy. And after Anatolius he attached
himself to Porphyry, and in no respect was he inferior to
Porphyry except in the composition and force of his language. For his utterances are neither dipped in attractive   3
charm and grace, nor are they lucid or embellished with
the purity [of Attic]. Nevertheless, they are not altogether
obscure, nor do they have faults of diction, but as Plato
used to say of Xenocrates, "he has not sacrificed to the
Graces" of Hermes.[35] Therefore he does not captivate the   4
listener nor enchant them to read, but seems to repel him
and irritate the ears. But because he practiced moral rec-
titude, he gained an easy access to the ears of the gods, so
much so that he had a multitude of students, and those

---

[33] A famous general who wrote a history. See Eunapius Introduction.   [34] Coele Syria. The district between the Lebanon
and Anti-Lebanon mountain ranges was called "Syria in the
Hollow."   [35] Cf. Diog. Laert. 4.6; Plut. *Con. praec.* 141f. On
Hermes cf. 10.51.

ἦσαν οἱ ὁμιλοῦντες, πανταχόθεν δὲ ἐφοίτων οἱ παιδείας ἐπιθυμοῦντες· ἦν δὲ ἐν αὐτοῖς τὸ κάλλιστον
5 δύσκριτον. Σώπατρος γὰρ ἦν ὁ ἐκ Συρίας, ἀνὴρ εἰπεῖν τε καὶ γράψαι δεινότατος, Αἰδέσιός τε καὶ Εὐστάθιος ἐκ Καππαδοκίας, ἐκ δὲ τῆς Ἑλλάδος Θεόδω-
ρός τε καὶ Εὐφράσιος, οἱ κατ᾽ ἀρετὴν ὑπερέχοντες,
ἄλλοι τε πλῆθος, οὐ πολὺ λειπόμενοι κατὰ τὴν ἐν
λόγοις δύναμιν, ὥστε θαυμαστὸν ἦν ὅτι πᾶσι ἐπήρ-
6 κει· καὶ γὰρ ἦν πρὸς ἅπαντας ἄφθονος. ὀλίγα μὲν οὖν
χωρὶς τῶν ἑταίρων καὶ ὁμιλητῶν ἔπραττεν ἐφ᾽ ἑαυτοῦ,
τὸ θεῖον σεβαζόμενος· τὰ δὲ πλεῖστα τοῖς ἑταίροις
συνῆν, τὴν μὲν δίαιταν ὢν εὔκολος καὶ ἀρχαῖος, τῇ
δὲ παρὰ πότον ὁμιλίᾳ τοὺς παρόντας καθηδύνων καὶ
7 διαπιμπλὰς ὥσπερ νέκταρος. οἱ δέ, ἀλήκτως ἔχοντες
καὶ ἀκορέστως τῆς ἀπολαύσεως, ἠνώχλουν αὐτῷ συνεχῶς καὶ προστησάμενοί γε τοὺς ἀξίους λόγου πρὸς
αὐτὸν ἔφασκον· "τί δῆτα μόνος, ὦ διδάσκαλε θειότατε,
καθ᾽ ἑαυτόν τινα πράττεις, οὐ μεταδιδοὺς τῆς τελεω-
8 τέρας σοφίας ἡμῖν; καίτοι γε ἐκφέρεται πρὸς ἡμᾶς
12G λόγος ὑπὸ | τῶν σῶν ἀνδραπόδων ὡς εὐχόμενος τοῖς
θεοῖς μετεωρίζῃ μὲν ἀπὸ τῆς γῆς πλέον ἢ δέκα πήχεις
εἰκάζεσθαι· τὸ σῶμα δέ σοι καὶ ἡ ἐσθὴς εἰς χρυσοει-
δές τι κάλλος ἀμείβεται, παυομένῳ δὲ τῆς εὐχῆς

---

36 The elder Sopater put to death by Constantine (see below,
VPS 6.7–17); his son Sopater corresponded with Libanius and was
a friend of Emperor Julian.

who desired an education flocked to him from all directions. But it is hard to decide the most eminent aspect
among them. Sopater[36] the Syrian was among them, a man 5
most eloquent both in his speeches and writings, and
Aedesius and Eustathius from Cappadocia, while from
Greece came Theodorus[37] and Euphrasius, men of superlative virtue, and a crowd of other men not inferior in their
powers of oratory, so that it seemed a marvel that Iamblichus was sufficient for them all; and indeed he was equally
generous to all of them. Occasionally, however, he did 6
perform certain rites on his own, apart from his friends
and students, when he worshipped the divine. But for the
most part he kept company with his pupils and in his mode
of life he was pleased with little and of an ancient simplicity. As they drank their wine he used to delight those present with his conversation and filled them as if with nectar.
And because of their insatiable and never-ending desire 7
for this pleasure, they never gave him any peace, and
choosing the most eloquent to speak for them, they would
put it to him: "O most divine master, why do you do these
rituals alone for your own benefit, instead of sharing with
us your more perfect wisdom?[38] And further a rumor has 8
reached us through your slaves that when you pray to the
gods you soar aloft from the earth more than ten cubits to
all appearance;[39] that your body and your garments change
to a beautiful golden hue; and presently when your prayer

[37] Theodorus of Asine, who wrote a commentary on Plato's
Timaeus (cf. Julian. *Ep. ad Prisc.* 2).

[38] For theurgic virtues, "more perfect" may mean teaching at
a higher level than before (e.g., political or cathartic virtues).

[39] Cf. Philostr. *VA* 3.15.

EUNAPIUS

σῶμά τε γίνεται τῷ πρὶν εὔχεσθαι ὅμοιον, καὶ κατελθὼν ἐπὶ τῆς γῆς τὴν πρὸς ἡμᾶς ποιῇ συνουσίαν."

9 οὔ τι μάλα γελασείων, ἐγέλασεν ἐπὶ τούτοις τοῖς λό-
10 γοις Ἰάμβλιχος. ἀλλ᾽ εἰπὼν πρὸς αὐτούς, ὡς "ὁ μὲν
ἀπατήσας ὑμᾶς¹⁶ οὐκ ἦν ἄχαρις, ταῦτα δὲ οὐχ οὕτως
ἔχει· τοῦ λοιποῦ δὲ οὐδὲν χωρὶς ὑμῶν πεπράξεται"
11 τοιαῦτα ἐπεδείξατο· εἰς δὲ τὸν ταῦτα γράφοντα ἦλθε
παρὰ τοῦ διδασκάλου Χρυσανθίου τοῦ ἐκ Σάρδεων.
ἐκεῖνος δὲ ἦν Αἰδεσίου μαθητής, Αἰδέσιος δὲ ἀνὰ τοὺς
πρώτους τοῦ Ἰαμβλίχου καὶ τῶν ταῦτα πρὸς αὐτὸν
εἰρηκότων.

12 Ἔλεγεν οὖν ἐπιδείξεις αὐτοῦ μεγάλας τῆς θειότη-
τος γεγενῆσθαι τάσδε. ἥλιος μὲν ἐφέρετο πρὸς τοῦ
Λέοντος ὅρια, ἡνίκα συνανατέλλει τῷ καλουμένῳ
Κυνί, καὶ θυσίας καιρὸς ἦν· ἡ δὲ εὐτρέπιστο ἔν τινι
13 τῶν ἐκείνου προαστείων. ὡς δὲ τὰ πάντα εἶχε καλῶς
καὶ ἐπὶ τὴν πόλιν ὑπέστρεφον, βάδην καὶ σχολαίως
προϊόντες· καὶ γὰρ διάλεξις ἦν αὐτοῖς περὶ θεῶν τῇ
θυσίᾳ πρέπουσα· τὸν νοῦν ἐπιστήσας ὁ Ἰάμβλιχος
μεταξὺ διαλεγόμενος, ὥσπερ ἀποκοπεὶς τὴν φωνήν, |
459B καὶ τὰ ὄμματα εἰς τὴν γῆν ἀτρεμίζοντα χρόνον τινὰ
ἐρείσας, ἀνά τε ἔβλεψεν εἰς τοὺς ἑταίρους, καὶ πρὸς
αὐτοὺς ἐξεβόησεν· "ἄλλην ὁδὸν πορευώμεθα· νεκρὸς
14 γὰρ ἐντεῦθεν ἔναγχος παρακεκόμισται." ὁ μὲν οὖν

¹⁶ ἡμᾶς A Gi: ὑμᾶς Junius Go

⁴⁰ An echo of Pl. *Phd.* 64b.

is ended your body becomes as it was before you prayed, and then you come down to earth and associate with us." While not at all inclined to laughter, Iamblichus laughed 9 at these remarks.[40] But in response he said to them: "The 10 person who deluded you in this way is not without a sense of humor; but the facts are otherwise. In future, however, you shall be present at all that goes on." And he displayed to them rites of a similar nature; the report of it reached 11 the author of this work from his teacher Chrysanthius of Sardis. He was a pupil of Aedesius, and Aedesius was one of the leading students of Iamblichus, and one of those who spoke to him.

He[41] said that there occurred the following sure mani- 12 festations of his divine nature. The sun was traveling to- ward the limits of the [constellation of the] Lion at the time when it rises along with the star called the Dog.[42] It was the proper time for sacrifice, and this had been prepared in one of the suburban villas belonging to Iamblichus. When the rites had been duly performed 13 and they were returning to the city, walking slowly and at their leisure—for their conversation was about the gods as was in keeping with the sacrifice—Iamblichus, even while conversing suddenly became preoccupied, as though his voice were cut off, and for some moments he fixed his eyes steadily on the ground and then looked up at his friends and called to them in a loud voice: "Let us go by another road, for a dead body has recently been carried along this way." After saying this he turned 14

[41] Aedesius or Chrysanthius (*via* Aidesius).
[42] Sun at the edge of Leo (star sign), rising at the same time as Sirius (the Dog Star), suggesting August–September.

ταῦτα εἰπών, ἄλλην ἐβάδιζε ἥτις ἐφαίνετο καθαρω-
τέρα, καὶ σὺν αὐτῷ τινὲς ὑπέστρεφον, ὅσοις τὸ κατα-
13G λιπεῖν | τὸν διδάσκαλον αἰσχύνης ἄξιον ἔδοξεν· οἱ δὲ
πλείους καὶ φιλονεικότεροι τῶν ἑταίρων, ἐν οἷς καὶ ὁ
Αἰδέσιος ἦν, ἔμειναν αὐτοῦ, τὸ πρᾶγμα ἐπὶ τερατείαν
φέροντες καὶ τὸν ἔλεγχον ὥσπερ κύνες ἀνιχνεύοντες.
15 καὶ μετὰ μικρὸν ἐπανῄεσαν οἱ θάψαντες τὸν τετελευ-
τηκότα· οἱ δὲ οὐδὲ οὕτως ἀπέστησαν, ἀλλ᾽ ἠρώτησαν
εἰ ταύτην εἶεν παρεληλυθότες τὴν ὁδόν· οἱ δέ, "ἀναγκαῖον ἦν·" ἔφασαν· "ἄλλην γὰρ οὐκ ἔχειν."

16 Ἔτι δὲ τούτου θειωδέστερον συνεμαρτύρουν, ὡς
ἐνοχλοῖ ἡ μὲν ⟨τῶν ὁμιλητῶν πληθὺς⟩[17] αὐτῷ πολλάκις, μικρὸν τοῦτο εἶναι φάσκοντες καὶ ὀσφρήσεως
ἴσως που πλεονέκτημα, βούλεσθαι δὲ διάπειραν λαβεῖν ἑτέρου μείζονος· ὁ δὲ πρὸς αὐτούς· "ἀλλ᾽ οὐκ ἐπ᾽
17 ἐμοί γε τοῦτο," ἔλεγεν, "ἀλλ᾽ ὅταν καιρὸς ᾖ." μετὰ δὲ
χρόνον τινὰ δόξαν αὐτοῖς ἐπὶ τὰ Γάδαρα (θερμὰ δέ
ἐστι λουτρὰ τῆς Συρίας, τῶν γε μετὰ τὴν Ῥωμαϊκὴν
ἐν Βαΐαις δεύτερα, ἐκείνοις δὲ οὐκ ἔστιν ἕτερα παρα-
βαλέσθαι), πορεύονται δὲ εἰς τὰ Γάδαρα κατὰ τὴν
ὥραν τοῦ ἔτους. ὁ μὲν ἐτύγχανε λούμενος, οἱ δὲ καὶ
συνελοῦντο καὶ περὶ τῶν αὐτῶν ἐνέκειντο. μειδιάσας
δὲ ὁ Ἰάμβλιχος, "ἀλλ᾽ οὐκ εὐσεβὲς μέν," ἔφη, "ταῦτα
18 ἐπιδείκνυσθαι, ὑμῶν δὲ ἕνεκα πεπράξεται." Καὶ τῶν
θερμῶν κρηνῶν δύο, τὰς μὲν μικροτέρας, τῶν δὲ ἄλλων χαριεστέρας, ἐκέλευσεν ἐκπυνθάνεσθαι τοὺς ὁμι-

---

[17] ⟨τῶν ὁμιλητῶν πληθὺς⟩ add. Gi Go (cf. below, VPS 5.22)

into another road that seemed to be less impure,[43] and some of them turned aside with him, who thought it was shameful to desert their teacher. But the greater number and the more obstinate of his students, among whom was Aedesius, stayed where they were, ascribing the deed to a portent and scenting like hounds[44] for the disproof. And 15 very soon those who had buried the dead man came back. But even so the students did not desist but inquired whether they had passed along this road. "We had to," they replied, "for there was no other road."

But they testified to a still more awe-inspiring incident. 16 When the group kept pestering Iamblichus and saying that this [amazing deed] was insignificant, and perhaps due to a superior sense of smell, and that they wished to experience [by way of a trial] an even greater sign [of his powers], his reply to them was: "that does not rest with me, but whenever the appointed hour arises." Sometime after, 17 they decided to go to Gadara; it is a place with warm baths in Syria, inferior only to the Roman one at Baiae,[45] with which no other baths can be compared. So they set out for Gadara in the summer season. Now he happened to be bathing and the others were bathing with him, and they were pressing him over the same matters, whereupon Iamblichus smiled and said: "It is irreverent to the gods to put such things on display, but for your sakes it shall be done." There were two hot springs, smaller than the oth- 18 ers but prettier, and he bade his students to ask the locals

[43] A Pythagorean notion. Iamblichus wrote a *Life of Pythagoras*.

[44] Cf. Philostr. *VS* 1.12.

[45] The famous sea resort near Naples (Italy).

λητὰς παρὰ τῶν ἐπιχωρίων ὅπως ἐκ παλαιοῦ προσω-
14G νομάζοντο. οἱ δὲ τὸ προσταχθὲν | ἐπιτελέσαντες,
"ἀλλ' οὐκ ἔστι γε πρόφασις," εἶπον, "ἀλλ' αὕτη μὲν
Ἔρως καλεῖται, τῇ παρακειμένῃ δὲ Ἀντέρως ὄνομα."
19 ὁ δὲ εὐθὺς ἐπιψαύσας τοῦ ὕδατος (ἐτύγχανε δὲ καὶ ἐπὶ
τῆς κρηπῖδος κατὰ τὴν ὑπέρκλυσιν καθήμενος), καὶ
βραχέα τινὰ προσειπών, ἐξεκάλεσεν ἀπὸ τῆς κρήνης
20 κάτωθεν παιδίον. λευκὸν ἦν τὸ παιδίον καὶ μετρίως
εὐμέγεθες, καὶ χρυσοειδεῖς αὐτῷ κόμαι καὶ τὰ μετά-
φρενα καὶ τὰ στέρνα περιέστιλβον, καὶ ὅλον ἐῴκει
λουομένῳ τε καὶ λελουμένῳ. καταπλαγέντων δὲ τῶν
ἑταίρων, "ἐπὶ τὴν ἐχομένην," εἶπε, "κρήνην ἴωμεν,"
21 καὶ ἡγεῖτο ἀπιών, καὶ σύννους ἦν. εἶτα κἀκεῖ τὰ αὐτὰ
δράσας, ἐξεκάλεσεν ἕτερον Ἔρωτα τῷ προτέρῳ παραπλήσιον ἅπαντα, πλὴν ὅσον αἱ κόμαι μελάντεραί τε
καὶ ἡλιῶσαι κατεκέχυντο. καὶ περιεπλέκετό γε ἀμφότερα αὐτῷ τὰ παιδία καί, καθάπερ γνησίου τινὸς πατρὸς ἐμφύντα, περιείχετο. ὁ δὲ ἐκεῖνά τε ταῖς οἰκείαις
ἀπέδωκε λήξεσι καί, σεβαζομένων τῶν ἑταίρων, ἐξῄει
22 λουσάμενος. οὐδὲν μετὰ τοῦτο ἐζήτησεν ἡ τῶν ὁμιλητῶν πληθύς, ἀλλὰ ἀπὸ τῶν φανέντων δειγμάτων,
ὥσπερ ὑπ' ἀρρήκτου ῥυτῆρος, εἵλκοντο καὶ πᾶσιν
ἐπίστευον.

Ἐλέγετο δὲ καὶ παραδοξότερα καὶ τερατωδέστερα,
ἐγὼ δὲ τούτων ἀνέγραφον οὐδέν, σφαλερόν τι καὶ |
460B θεομισὲς πρᾶγμα ἡγούμενος εἰς συγγραφὴν στάσιμον καὶ πεπηγυῖαν ἐπεισάγειν ἀκοὴν διεφθαρμένην

414

of the place by what names they used to be called in former times. When they had completed the task he had
given them, they reported: "There is no particular reason
for it, but this spring is called Eros, and the name of the
one next to it is Anteros."[46] Immediately he touched the   19
water with his hand—he happened to be sitting on the
ledge of the spring where the overflow runs off—and uttering a brief summons he called forth a boy from the
depth of the spring. The boy was white-skinned and of   20
medium height, his golden locks provided a glow to his
back and chest, and he completely resembled someone
who was bathing or had just bathed. His students were
overwhelmed with amazement, but Iamblichus said, "Let
us go to the next spring," and he rose and led the way, with
a thoughtful air. Then he did the same thing again on that   21
spot and summoned another Eros resembling the first in
all respects, except that his hair was darker and fell loose
while gleaming in the sunlight. Both the boys embraced
Iamblichus and clung to him as though he were their real
father. He restored them to their proper places and went
away after having bathed, while his pupils were filled with
a deep sense of reverence. After this the crowd of his   22
students sought no further evidence, but believed everything from the clear perceptual evidence that had been
revealed to them and hung on to him as though by an
unbreakable chain.

Even more unusual and portentous things were related
of him, but I wrote down none of these, since I thought it
a hazardous and sacrilegious thing to introduce an unreli-
able and fluid oral tradition into a stable and well-founded

46 For the fable of Eros and Anteros, cf. Them. *Or*. 304d.

23 καὶ ῥέουσαν. ἀλλὰ καὶ ταῦτα γράφω δεδοικὼς ἀκοὴν
οὖσαν, πλὴν ὅσα γε ἕπομαι ἀνδράσιν οἳ τοῖς ἄλλοις
ἀπιστοῦντες πρὸς τὴν τοῦ φανέντος αἴσθησιν συν-
εκάμφθησαν. οὐδεὶς δὲ αὐτοῦ τῶν ἑταίρων ἀνέγραψεν,
24 ὅσα γε ἡμᾶς εἰδέναι· τοῦτο | δὲ εἶπον μετρίως, Αἰδε-
15G σίου φήσαντος μήτε αὐτὸν γεγραφέναι, μήτε ἄλλον
τινὰ τετολμηκέναι.

25 Κατὰ τοὺς Ἰαμβλίχου καιροὺς ἦν καὶ ὁ διαλεκτι-
κώτατος Ἀλύπιος, ὃς ἔτυχε μὲν σώματος μικροτά-
του—καὶ τὸ σῶμα πυγμαῖον παρέβαινεν ἐλάχιστον—
ἐκινδύνευε δὲ καὶ τὸ φαινόμενον σῶμα ψυχὴ καὶ νοῦς
26 εἶναι· οὕτω τὸ φθειρόμενον οὐκ ἐπέδωκεν εἰς μέγεθος,
δαπανηθὲν εἰς τὸ θεοειδέστερον. ὥσπερ οὖν ὁ μέγας
Πλάτων φησὶ τὰ θεῖα σώματα τὸ ἀνάπαλιν ἔχειν
ἐγκείμενα ταῖς ψυχαῖς, οὕτως ἄν τις εἴποι κἀκεῖνον
ἐμβεβηκέναι τῇ ψυχῇ καὶ συνέχεσθαι καὶ κρατεῖσθαι
27 ᾗ[18] παρά του κρείττονος. ζηλωτὰς μὲν οὖν εἶχε πολλοὺς ὁ Ἀλύπιος, ἀλλ' ἡ παίδευσις ἦν μέχρι συνουσ-
σίας μόνης, βιβλίον δὲ προέφερεν οὐδὲ εἷς· ὥστε
μάλα ἀσμένως πρὸς τὸν Ἰάμβλιχον ἀπέτρεχον, ὡς ἐκ
πηγῆς ὑπερβλυζούσης, οὐ μενούσης καθ' ἑαυτήν, ἐμ-
φορησόμενοι καὶ πιούμενοι. κατὰ δὲ τὸ κλέος ἀμφοῖν
αὐξόμενον ἄνω καὶ συνέτυχόν ποτε ἀλλήλοις ἢ συνή-

---

18 ἤ A: del. Wytt Wr: ᾗ Boiss Go

47 Seems to contradict his claim in VPS 1.6 (in identical wording).

written narrative.[47] Even these [portents] I record, although I fear that they are hearsay, except for the ones where I follow the lead of men who, though they distrusted other [signs], were brought around to the manifest reality of the event. Yet no one of his followers recorded 23
it, as far as I know. And this I say with good reason, since 24
Aedesius himself asserted that he had not written about it, nor had anyone else ventured to do so.

During Iamblichus' lifetime the outstanding dialecti- 25
cian Alypius lived as well, who was of very small stature and his body was not much larger than that of a dwarf, but even the body as it appeared was practically all soul and intelligence; to such a degree did the perishable matter in 26
him fail to increase his height, since it was absorbed into his diviner nature. Therefore, just as the great Plato says[48] that divine bodies [unlike human bodies] dwell within souls, so one might also say of him that he had migrated into a soul, and that he was confined and overpowered, as if by some supernatural force. Now Alypius had many 27
keen followers, but his teaching was limited to conversations, and no one ever cited a book by him. Consequently, they very eagerly betook themselves to Iamblichus, to drink and fill themselves up, as though from a spring that bubbles over[49] and does not stay within its limits.[50] Now as the renown of both men increased and kept pace, they encountered one another by chance (or crossed paths as

[48] Perhaps a reference to Pl. *Tim.* 36, where the world-soul is said to envelop the body of the universe.

[49] Cf. Philostr. *VA* 3.14; 25.

[50] Like the inexhaustible source of the Good in Plotinus (e.g., *Enn.* 3.8.10); cf. note 20.

ν</u>τησαν ὥσπερ ἀστέρες, καὶ περιεκαθέσθη γε αὐτοὺς
28 θέατρον οἷον εἰκάσαι μεγάλου μουσείου. Ἰαμβλίχου
δὲ τὸ ἐπερωτηθῆναι μᾶλλον ὑπομείναντος ἢ τὸ ἐπε-
ρωτᾶν, ὁ Ἀλύπιος παρὰ πᾶσαν ὑπόνοιαν ἀφεὶς ἅπασαν φιλόσοφον ἐρώτησιν, τοῦ δὲ θεάτρου γενόμενος,
"Εἰπέ μοι, φιλόσοφε," πρὸς αὐτὸν ἔφη, "ὁ πλούσιος ἢ
ἄδικος ἢ ἀδίκου κληρονόμος, ναὶ ἢ οὔ; τούτων γὰρ
μέσον οὐδέν." ὁ δὲ τὴν πληγὴν τοῦ λόγου μισήσας,
"ἀλλ' οὐχ οὗτός γε," ἔφη, "θαυμασιώτερε[19] πάντων
16G ἀνδρῶν, ὁ τρόπος τῆς ἡμετέρας | διαλέξεως, εἴ τῷ τι
περιττόν ἐστι κατὰ τὰ ἐκτός, ἀλλ' εἴ τι πλεονάζει
κατὰ τὴν οἰκείαν ἀρετὴν φιλοσόφῳ καὶ πρέπουσαν."
29 ταῦτα εἰπὼν ἀπεχώρησε καί, διαναστάντος, οὐκ ἦν ὁ
σύλλογος. ἀπελθὼν δὲ καὶ γενόμενος ἐφ' ἑαυτοῦ, καὶ
τὴν ὀξύτητα θαυμάσας, πολλάκις τε ἰδίᾳ συνέτυχεν
αὐτῷ, καὶ οὕτως ὑπερηγάσθη τὸν ἄνδρα τῆς ἀκριβείας καὶ συνέσεως, ὥστε καὶ ἀπελθόντος βίον συν-
30 έγραψε. καὶ ἐνέτυχεν ὁ ταῦτα γράφων τοῖς γεγραμμέ-
νοις· τὰ γεγραμμένα δὲ ὑπὸ τῆς συνθήκης ἐμελαίνετο
καὶ νέφος αὐτοῖς ἐπέτρεχε βαθύ (οὔ τι δι' ἀσάφειαν
τῶν γενομένων, ἀλλὰ διδασκαλικὸν εἶχε τῶν Ἀλυπίου
λόγον μακρόν τινα), καὶ διαλέξεων οὐ προσῆν μνήμη
31 λόγον ἐχουσῶν. ἀποδημίας τε εἰς τὴν Ῥώμην ἔφραζε
τὸ βιβλίον, αἷς οὔτε αἰτία προσῆν οὔτε τὸ τῆς ψυχῆς
συνεφαίνετο μέγεθος. ἀλλ' ὅτι μὲν εἵποντο πολλοὶ
τεθηπότες τὸν ἄνδρα παραδηλοῦται· ὅ τι δὲ εἶπεν ἢ

---

[19] θαυμασιώτερε A Gi Go (q.v.): θαυμασιώτατε Junius Wr

happens with shooting stars), and around them in a circle sat an audience as though in some great seat of the Muses. Now Iamblichus was waiting to have questions put to him rather than to ask them, but Alypius, contrary to all expectation, relinquished all questioning about philosophy and seeking to make an effect with his audience[51] said to Iamblichus: "Tell me, philosopher, is a rich man either unjust or the heir of the unjust, yes or no? For there is no middle course." Disliking the catch in the question, Iamblichus replied, "This, most admired among all men, is not our method of conversation, [to ask] whether someone possesses more external things than other men, but rather whether he has abundance in accordance with the virtue that is peculiar and appropriate to a philosopher." Having spoken thus he went away, and after he had risen the meeting ended. But once he had left and collected his thoughts, he admired the acuteness of the question, and often met with Alypius privately, and he was so profoundly impressed by the subtlety and intelligence of the man, that, when Alypius had died, he even wrote an account of his life. In fact, the author of the present book once read the work: the writings were obscured by its composition and a thick cloud lay over it, though not because of any lack of clarity of the events, for he had as his guide a long account on things relevant to Alypius, and there was no mention of discussions that contained an argument. The book told of journeys to Rome for which no reason was given, and it did not make manifest the greatness of his soul on those occasions. He intimates that Alypius had many admiring followers, but it is not made clear that he

28

29

30

31

51 Perhaps an echo of Pl. *Symp.* 194b.

32 ἔπραξεν ἀξιόλογον, οὐκ ἐπιφαίνεται· ἀλλ' ἔοικεν ὁ
θαυμάσιος Ἰάμβλιχος ταὐτὸν πεπονθέναι τοῖς γρα-
φικοῖς, οἳ τοὺς ἐν ὥρᾳ γράφοντες, ὅταν χαρίσασθαί
τι παρ' ἑαυτῶν εἰς τὴν γραφὴν βουληθῶσι· τὸ πᾶν
εἶδος τῆς ὁμοιώσεως διαφθείρουσιν, ὥστε ἅμα τε τοῦ
461B | παραδείγματος ἡμαρτηκέναι καὶ τοῦ κάλλους. οὕτω
33 κἀκεῖνος ἐπαινέσαι προελόμενος διὰ τὴν ἀλήθειαν, τὸ
μὲν μέγεθος ἐμφαίνει τῶν καθ' ἑαυτὸν ἐν τοῖς δικαστηρίοις κολάσεων καὶ ἀτυχημάτων, αἰτίας δὲ ἐπὶ
τούτοις ἢ προφάσεις οὔτε πεφυκὼς ἐξηγεῖσθαι πο-
λιτικῶς οὔτε προελόμενος, τὸν πάντα χαρακτῆρα
συνέχεε τοῦ βίου, μόλις τοῦτο καταλιπὼν τοῖς ὀξυ-
δορκοῦσι ξυλλαβεῖν, ὅτι τὸν ἄνδρα ἐθαύμαζε καὶ διαφερόντως αὐτοῦ τήν τε παρὰ τὰ δεινὰ καρτερίαν καὶ
17G τὸ ἀνέκπληκτον, τήν | τε ἐν τοῖς λόγοις ὀξύτητα καὶ
τό<λ>μην κατεσεβάζετο.[20] Ἐξ Ἀλεξανδρείας δὲ οὗτος
ἦν. καὶ τὰ μὲν εἰς Ἀλύπιον ταῦτα. καὶ ἐτελεύτα γε ἐν
Ἀλεξανδρείᾳ γηραιός, Ἰάμβλιχός τε ἐπ' αὐτῷ, πολλὰς ῥίζας τε καὶ πηγὰς φιλοσοφίας ἀφείς. ταύτης ὁ
ταῦτα γράφων τῆς φορᾶς εὐτύχησεν. ἄλλοι μὲν γὰρ
ἀλλαχοῦ τῶν εἰρημένων ὁμιλητῶν διεκρίθησαν εἰς
ἅπασαν τὴν Ῥωμαϊκὴν ἐπικράτειαν· Αἰδέσιος δὲ κατ-
έλαβε τὸ Μύσιον Πέργαμον.

6. Αἰδέσιος. Ἐκδέχεται δὲ τὴν Ἰαμβλίχου διατριβὴν καὶ ὁμιλίαν ἐς τοὺς ἑταίρους Αἰδέσιος ὁ ἐκ Καπ-

[20] τό<λ>μην κατεσεβάζετο Go: τομὴν κατεσκευαζετο A

420

either did or said anything remarkable.[52] The admirable   32
Iamblichus, it seems, had the same thing happen to him
as painters who are painting youths in their bloom and
wish to add to the painting some charisma of their own
invention, whereby they destroy the whole appearance of
the likeness, so that they fail to achieve either a resem-
blance or the beauty at which they aim.[53] So it was with   33
Iamblichus when he chose to praise by telling the truth—
for though he clearly shows how severe were the punish-
ments and sufferings in the law courts [for Alypius], yet
the causes of these things and their purposes he neither
had talent to expound like one versed in politics, nor the
intention—he muddled up the whole character of the
man's life, and he hardly even left it for the most keen-
sighted to grasp that he admired the man, and above all
his fortitude and constancy amid dangers, and revered
the keenness and daring of his style in his discourses.
He was by birth an Alexandrian. Regarding Alypius this is   34
all I have to say. He died an old man, in Alexandria, and
Iamblichus after him, having generated many "roots and
springs" for philosophy. The author of this narrative had
the good fortune to benefit by the crop that arose from
here. In fact, others of his students who have been mentioned were scattered in all directions over the whole Roman Empire, but Aedesius chose to settle at Pergamon in
Mysia.

    6. Aedesius. The person who took over the school of
Iamblichus and his circle of students was Aedesius from

[52] Cf. *VPS* 1.1 on the importance of words and deeds.
[53] For biography as painting, cf. Plut. *Alex*. 1.2–3; Eunap.
Hist. fr. 50.

παδοκίας. ἦν δὲ τῶν εὖ γεγονότων εἰς ἄκρον, πλοῦτος
δὲ οὐχ ὑπῆν τῷ γένει πολύς, καὶ ὅ γε πατὴρ αὐτὸν
ἐκπέμψας ἐπὶ παιδείαν χρηματιστικὴν ἐκ Καππαδοκίας ἐπὶ τὴν Ἑλλάδα, εἶτα ἐκδεχόμενος ὡς θησαυρὸν
ἐπὶ τῷ παιδὶ εὑρήσων, ἐπειδή ποτε, ἐπανελθόντος,
φιλοσοφοῦντα ᾔσθετο, τῆς οἰκίας ὡς ἀχρεῖον ἀπή-
2 λαυνε. καὶ ἐκδιώκων "τί γάρ," ἔφη, "φιλοσοφία ὠφε-
λεῖ;" ὁ δὲ ὑποστραφεὶς "οὐ μικρά, πάτερ," ἔφη, "πα-
3 τέρα καὶ διώκοντα προσκυνεῖν." καὶ τοῦτο ἀκούσας ὁ
πατὴρ ἀνά τε ἐκαλέσατο τὸν παῖδα καὶ τὸ ἦθος
ἐθαύμασε. καὶ ὅλον ἐπιδοὺς ἑαυτὸν ἀνέθηκε φέρων ἐς
τὴν ἔτι λειπομένην παιδείαν. καὶ ὁ μὲν τὸν παῖδα
προπέμψας εὔθυμος ἦν καὶ περιέχαιρεν, ὡς θεοῦ γεγονὼς μᾶλλον ἢ ἀνθρώπου πατήρ.

4 Ὁ δὲ τοὺς ἄλλους ἅπαντας παραδραμών, ὅσοι τῶν
τότε ἦσαν εὐκλεέστεροι καὶ ὧν ἐτύγχανεν ἀκηκοώς,
καὶ πείρᾳ τὴν σοφίαν συλλεξάμενος, ἐπὶ τὸν ἐρικυδέ-
στατον Ἰάμβλιχον [οὐ] μακρὰν[21] ὁδὸν ἐκ Καππαδοκίας εἰς Συρίαν συνέτεινε καὶ διήνυεν. ὡς δὲ εἶδέ
18G τε τὸν ἄνδρα καὶ ἤκουσε λέγοντος, | ἐξεκρέματο τῶν
5 λόγων καὶ τῆς ἀκροάσεως οὐκ ἐνεπίμπλατο· ἐς ὃ τελευτῶν Αἰδέσιός τε ἐγένετο καὶ μικρὸν ἀποδέων Ἰαμβλίχου, πλὴν ὅσα γε εἰς θειασμὸν Ἰαμβλίχου φέρει.
τούτων γὰρ οὐδὲν εἴχομεν ἀναγράφειν, ὅτι τὸ μὲν
ἐπέκρυπτεν ἴσως Αἰδέσιος αὐτὸς διὰ τοὺς χρόνους
(Κωνσταντῖνος γὰρ ἐβασίλευε, τά τε τῶν ἱερῶν ἐπι-

---

[21] οὐ del. Cob 1878: οὐ μικρὰν Go in app.

Cappadocia. He came from the highest echelons of society, even though his family did not have great wealth, and therefore his father sent him away from Cappadocia to Greece to get an education that would earn him money, thinking that he would find a treasure in his son. But on his son's return, when he found out that he was engaged in doing philosophy, he drove him out of the house as useless.[54] And as he chased him out, he asked: "Why, what 2 benefit does wisdom bring us?" Whereupon his son turned around and replied: "It is no small thing, father, to show respect for your father, even when he is chasing you away." When his father heard this, he called his son back and 3 expressed admiration for his virtuous character. And Aedesius devoted himself entirely to finishing his interrupted education. Moreover, his father cheerfully encouraged his son to go, and was overjoyed as though he had become the father of a god rather than of a mere man.

When Aedesius had outstripped all the more notable 4 men of his time, and all whose student he had been, and by experience had gathered wisdom, he made the effort to complete a long journey from Cappadocia to Syria, to see the highly renowned Iamblichus. And when he saw the man and heard him speak, he hung on his words and never could have enough of hearing him, until finally Aedesius 5 himself became famous and hardly inferior to Iamblichus, except when it concerned the latter's divinely inspired power. On this point I had nothing to write, perhaps, on the one hand, because Aedesius himself kept it secret owing to the times (for Constantine was emperor and was

[54] Perhaps an echo of Ael. *VH* 9.33.

423

φανέστατα καταστρέφων καὶ τὰ τῶν χριστιανῶν ἀνε-
γείρων οἰκήματα), τὰ δὲ ἴσως καὶ τὸ τῶν ὁμιλητῶν
ἄριστον πρὸς μυστηριώδη τινὰ σιωπὴν καὶ ἱεροφαν-
6 τικὴν ἐχεμυθίαν ἐπιρρεπὲς ἦν καὶ συνεκέκλιτο. ὁ γοῦν
ταῦτα γράφων ἐκ παιδὸς ἀκροατὴς Χρυσανθίου γενόμενος, μόλις εἰς εἰκοστὸν ἔτος ἠξιοῦτο τῶν ἀληθε-
στέρων, οὕτω μέγα τι χρῆμα εἰς ἡμᾶς τῆς Ἰαμβλίχου
φιλοσοφίας διετάθη καὶ συμπαρέτεινε τῷ χρόνῳ.

7 Ἰαμβλίχου δὲ καταλιπόντος τὸ ἀνθρώπειον, ἄλλοι
462B μὲν ἀλλαχῆ διεσπάρησαν, | καὶ οὐδεὶς ἦν ἔξω φήμης
καὶ ἄγνωστος. Σώπατρος δὲ ὁ πάντων δεινότερος, διά
τε φύσεως ὕψος καὶ ψυχῆς μέγεθος οὐκ ἐνεγκὼν τοῖς
ἄλλοις ἀνθρώποις ὁμιλεῖν, ἐπὶ τὰς βασιλικὰς αὐλὰς
ἔδραμεν ὀξύς, ὡς τὴν Κωνσταντίνου πρόφασίν τε καὶ
8 φορὰν τυραννήσων καὶ μεταστήσων τῷ λόγῳ. καὶ ἐς
τοσοῦτόν γε ἐξίκετο σοφίας καὶ δυνάμεως, ὡς ὁ μὲν
βασιλεὺς ἑαλώκει τε ὑπ' αὐτῷ καὶ δημοσίᾳ σύνεδρον
εἶχεν, εἰς τὸν δεξιὸν καθίζων τόπον, ὃ καὶ ἀκοῦσαι
9 καὶ ἰδεῖν ἄπιστον. οἱ δὲ παραδυναστεύοντες ῥηγνύμε-
νοι τῷ φθόνῳ πρὸς βασιλείαν ἄρτι φιλοσοφεῖν μετα-
μανθάνουσαν, τὸν Κερκώπων ἐπετήρουν καιρόν, οὐ
τὸν Ἡρακλέα καθεύδοντα μόνον, ἀλλὰ καὶ τὴν ἄλο-
19G γον ἐγρηγορυῖαν Τύχην, | καὶ συλλόγους τε λα-

---

55 Iamblichus died in the reign of Constantine the Great, and
probably before AD 333; Eunapius wrote about sixty years later.
56 At VPS 5.5 Sopater was first on the list of Iamblichus' students.

pulling down the most celebrated temples and construct- ing buildings for the Christians); but perhaps on the other hand, it was because all his most distinguished students leaned toward and inclined to a silence appropriate to the mysteries, and a reserve worthy of a hierophant. At any 6 rate, the present author, though he became a pupil of Chrysanthius from boyhood, was deemed worthy of the deeper truths as a student barely in his twentieth year, so wondrous a thing was the philosophy of Iamblichus, ex- tending its influence and reaching down from that time even to our own day.[55]

When Iamblichus had departed from the human race, 7 his students were dispersed in different directions, and not one of them was without fame and high repute. Sopa- ter,[56] the most eloquent of all, on account of his lofty na- ture and greatness of soul, could not bear to associate with ordinary men and went in haste to the imperial court, hoping to dominate and convert by his arguments the pur- pose and tendencies of Constantine. And he attained to 8 such a level of wisdom and competence that the emperor was captivated by him and publicly made him a council member, giving him a seat at his right hand, a thing unbe- lievable to hear and see. Those closely involved in ruling 9 were bursting with envy against a court that had recently turned to the study of philosophy. They lay in wait for their opportunity, like the Cercopes,[57] [to catch] not only a sleeping Heracles, but also irrational, unsleeping Fortune, and they held clandestine meetings and there was not any

[57] Two brothers, turned into monkeys, who were caught trying to steal from a sleeping Heracles.

θραίους ἐποιοῦντο καὶ οὐκ ἔστι καθ᾽ ὅ τι μέρος τῆς
10 κακοδαίμονος ἐπιβουλῆς ἠμέλουν. ὥσπερ οὖν [ὃ]²² ἐπὶ
τοῦ παλαιοῦ καὶ μεγάλου Σωκράτους ἁπάντων Ἀθηναίων (εἰ καὶ δῆμος ἦσαν) οὐκ ἄν τις ἐτόλμησε κατηγορίαν καὶ γραφὴν ⟨εἰς⟩²³ ὅν γε ᾤοντο πάντες Ἀθηναῖοι περιπατοῦν ἄγαλμα σοφίας τυγχάνειν, εἰ μὴ
μέθῃ καὶ παραφροσύνῃ καὶ τὸν τῶν Διονυσίων τῆς
ἑορτῆς καὶ παννυχίδος ἀνειμένον, ὑπὸ γέλωτος καὶ
ὀλιγωρίας καὶ τῶν εὐκόλων καὶ σφαλερῶν παθῶν ἐπὶ
τοῖς ἀνθρώποις ἐξευρημένων, πρῶτος Ἀριστοφάνης
ἐπὶ διεφθαρμέναις ψυχαῖς τὸν γέλωτα ἐπεισαγαγὼν
καὶ τὰ ἀπὸ²⁴ τῆς σκηνῆς κινήσας ὑπορχήματα, τότε
θέατρον ἀνέπεισεν, ἐπὶ τοσαύτῃ σοφίᾳ ψυλλῶν πη-
δήματα καταμωκώμενος καὶ νεφελῶν διαγράφων εἴδη
καὶ σχήματα καὶ τἄλλα ὅσα κωμῳδία ληρεῖν εἴωθεν
11 εἰς γέλωτος κίνησιν. ὡς δὲ εἶδον ἐγκεκλικὸς πρὸς τὴν
ἡδονὴν τὸ θέατρον, κατηγορίας ἥψαντό τινες καὶ τὴν
ἀσεβῆ γραφὴν εἰς ἐκεῖνον ἐτόλμησαν, καὶ δῆμος
12 ὅλος ἐπ᾽ ἀνδρὸς ἠτύχει φόνῳ. ἔστι γὰρ ἐκ τῶν χρόνων
λογιζομένῳ συλλαβεῖν ὅτι, Σωκράτους ἀπελθόντος
βιαίως, οὐδὲν ἔτι λαμπρὸν Ἀθηναίοις ἐπράχθη, ἀλλ᾽
ἥ τε πόλις ὑπέδωκε, καὶ διὰ τὴν πόλιν τὰ τῆς Ἑλλά-
13 δος ἅπαντα συνδιεφθάρη· οὕτω καὶ τότε συνορᾶν
ἐξῆν τὸ κατὰ Σώπατρον ἐπιβούλευμα. ἡ μὲν γὰρ
Κωνσταντίνου πόλις, τὸ ἀρχαῖον Βυζάντιον, κατὰ μὲν

22 del. Go (suspic. loc. corr.)   23 add. Go
24 ἀπὸ Boiss Go   ἐπὶ A

426

part of their wickedly-inspired plot that they neglected. Just as in the time of the revered Socrates from long ago, 10 when no one of all the Athenians, even though they were a sovereign people,[58] would have ventured to bring an accusation and indictment [against someone] whom at any rate all the Athenians thought of as a walking effigy of wisdom, had it not been that in the drunkenness, insanity, and license of the Dionysia and the night-long festivities, when laughter as well as disparagement and careless and dangerous emotions are discovered among men, Aristophanes was the first to introduce ridicule into their already corrupted souls;[59] and by moving dances to the *orchestra,* he made the audience see things his way, mocking with regard to such great wisdom the jumps of fleas[60] and types and shapes of clouds, and all those other foolish moves to which comedy resorts in order to get a laugh going. When 11 they saw that the audience in the theater was inclined to such indulgence, certain men set up an accusation and had the effrontery to bring the impious indictment against him; and the whole populace suffered misfortune due to the killing of one man. For if one calculates from these 12 times, it is possible to grasp that after Socrates' violent death nothing brilliant was ever again achieved by the Athenians, but the city gradually decayed and because of her decay the whole of Greece was ruined along with her. So, too, at that time it was possible to comprehend the plot 13 against Sopater. For the city of Constantine (ancient By-

58 For this sense of δῆμος, cf. Hdt. 3.82; Arist. [*Ath. Pol.*] 8.4.
59 Close to the version of Pl. *Ap.*
60 Cf. Ar. *Nub.* 144–52, 263–74.

τοὺς παλαιοὺς χρόνους Ἀθηναίοις παρεῖχε τὴν σιτο-
14 πομπίαν, καὶ περιττὸν ἦν τὸ ἐκεῖθεν ἀγώγιμον· ἐν δὲ
τοῖς καθ᾽ ἡμᾶς καιροῖς, οὐδὲ τὸ ἀπ᾽ Αἰγύπτου πλῆθος
20G | τῶν ὁλκάδων, οὐδὲ τὸ ἐξ Ἀσίας ἁπάσης, Συρίας τε
καὶ Φοινίκης καὶ τῶν ἄλλων ἐθνῶν συμφερόμενον
πλῆθος σίτου, κατὰ ἐπαγωγὴν φόρου, ἐμπλῆσαι καὶ
κορέσαι τὸν μεθύοντα δύναται δῆμον, ὃν Κωνσταντῖνος, τὰς ἄλλας χηρώσας πόλεις ἀνθρώπων, εἰς τὸ
Βυζάντιον μετέστησε, καὶ πρὸς τοὺς ἐν τοῖς θεάτροις
κρότους παραβλυζόντων κραιπάλης ἀνθρώπων ἑαυτῷ
συνεστήσατο, σφαλλομένων ἀνθρώπων ἀγαπήσας
ἐγκώμια καὶ μνήμην ὀνόματος, τῶν μόλις ὑπὸ εὐη-
15 θείας φθεγγομένων τοὔνομα· συμβέβηκε δὲ καὶ τῇ
θέσει τὸ Βυζάντιον[25] μηδὲ εἰς πλοῦν ἁρμόζειν τῶν
καταφερομένων πλοίων, ἂν μὴ καταπνεύσῃ νότος
ἀκραὴς καὶ ἄμικτος. καὶ τότε δὴ τοῦ πολλάκις συμ-
463B βαίνοντος κατὰ τὴν ὡρῶν φύσιν συμβάντος, | ὅ τε
δῆμος ὑπὸ λιμοῦ παρεθέντες συνῄεσαν ἐς τὸ θέατρον
καὶ σπάνις ἦν τοῦ μεθύοντος ἐπαίνου καὶ τὸν βασι-
16 λέα κατεῖχεν ἀθυμία. καὶ οἱ πάλαι βασκαίνοντες,
εὑρηκέναι καιρὸν ἡγούμενοι κάλλιστον, "ἀλλὰ Σώπα-
τρός γε," ἔφασαν, "ὁ παρὰ σοῦ τιμώμενος κατέδησε
τοὺς ἀνέμους δι᾽ ὑπερβολὴν σοφίας, ἣν καὶ αὐτὸς
ἐπαινεῖς, καὶ δι᾽ ἣν ἔτι τοῖς βασιλείοις ἐγκάθηται
17 θρόνοις." καὶ ὁ Κωνσταντῖνος ταῦτα ἀκούσας καὶ
συμπεισθείς, κατακοπῆναι κελεύει τὸν ἄνδρα, καὶ ἐγίνετο διὰ τοὺς βασκαίνοντας ταῦτα θᾶττον ἢ ἐλέγετο.

25 τὸ Βυζάντιον Go: τοῦ Βυζαντίου A Gi

zantium) in distant times used to provide the corn supply
to the Athenians, and the quantity imported was enormous. But in our times neither the enormous number of   14
merchant vessels from Egypt nor that from all Asia that is
contributed from Syria and Phoenicia and the other nations, nor the huge quantity of corn as the payment of
tribute, can be enough to satisfy the drunken mob that
Constantine transferred to Byzantium by emptying the
other cities, and established near him because he loved to
be applauded in the theaters by men so drunk that they
could not hold their liquor. For he desired to be praised
by the fickle populace and that his name should be on their
lips, though so simpleminded were they that they could
hardly pronounce his name. Moreover, due to its position,   15
Byzantium happens to be not suited for the arrival of ships
that approach there, except when a strong wind is blowing
straight from the southwest. At that time, then, what often
used to happen according to the nature of the seasons did
happen there, and the citizens, worn out by hunger, were
assembled in the theater, and there was a scarcity of the
drunken applause, and despondency would take hold of
the Emperor. Then those who had long been envious   16
thought that they had found a most opportune moment,
and said: "It is Sopater, respected by you, who has fettered
the winds[61] by that excessive cleverness that even you
yourself praise, and on account of which he already sits on
the Imperial throne." When Constantine heard this, he   17
was won over and ordered the man's head to be cut off;
and due to those disparagers this took place quicker than
he uttered the command.

[61] Cf. Hom. *Od.* 10.20 (Aeolus). It implies the use of magic.

18   Ὁ δὲ τῶν κακῶν ἁπάντων αἴτιος ἦν Ἀβλάβιος,
ἔπαρχος μὲν τῆς βασιλικῆς αὐλῆς, ὑπὸ Σωπάτρου δὲ
παρευδοκιμούμενος ἀπήγχετο. ἐμοὶ δέ, ὥσπερ προ-
είρηται, πεπαιδευμένων ἀνδρῶν εἰς πᾶσαν παιδείαν
ἀναγράφοντι βίους, τὰ εἰς τὴν ἐμὴν ἀκοὴν σωζόμενα,
δύσφορον οὐδὲν εἰ καὶ τῶν εἰς αὐτοὺς ἐξημαρτηκότων
19   βραχέα τινὰ ἐπιδράμοιμι. | Ἀβλαβίῳ τῷ τὸν φόνον
21G   ἐργασαμένῳ γένος ἦν ἀδοξότατον καὶ τὰ ἐκ πατέρων
τοῦ μετρίου καὶ φαύλου ταπεινότερα. καὶ λόγος τε
ὑπὲρ αὐτοῦ τοιοῦτος διασώζεται καὶ οὐδεὶς τοῖς λεγομένοις ἀντέλεγεν. τῶν ἐξ Αἰγύπτου τις περὶ τὸ καλούμενον μάθημα συντεταμένων παρελθὼν εἰς τὴν πόλιν
(ἱκανοὶ δέ εἰσιν Αἰγύπτιοι καὶ δημοσίᾳ μετ᾽ ὀλιγω-
20   ρίας ἐν ταῖς ἀποδημίαις ἀσχημονεῖν· εἰκὸς δὲ αὐτοὺς
καὶ οἴκοθεν οὕτω παιδεύεσθαι), παρελθὼν δὲ ὅμως,
εἰς τὸ πολυτελέστερον ὠθεῖται τῶν καπηλείων καὶ ξη-
ρός τε εἶναι, πολλὴν ἀνύσας ὁδόν, ἔφασκεν καὶ ὑπὸ
δίψους αὐτίκα μάλα ἀποπεπνίξεσθαι, καὶ γλυκὺν ἠρτυμένον ἐγχεῖν ἐκέλευσε τὸν οἶνον καὶ προέκειτο τὸ
21   ἀργύριον. ἡ δὲ προεστῶσα τοῦ καπηλείου τὸ κέρδος
ὁρῶσα πρὸς τὴν ὑπηρεσίαν παρεσκευάζετο καὶ διε-
τρόχαζεν. ἡ δὲ ἐτύγχανεν μὲν ἱκανὴ καὶ μαιώσασθαι
γυναῖκας ἐπὶ τῷ λοχεύεσθαι. ⟨καὶ⟩ προθεμένης αὐτῆς
τὴν κύλικα τῷ Αἰγυπτίῳ καὶ τὸν ἠρτυμένον οἶνον
καταχεομένης, προσδραμοῦσά τις ἐκ γειτόνων "ἀλλὰ
κινδυνεύει σοι" εἶπε λέγουσα πρὸς τὸ οὖς "ἐπὶ ταῖς

The person responsible for all the wicked acts was   18
Ablabius, for, though he was praetorian prefect, he felt
stifled by Sopater, who received more consideration than
himself. And since I am, as I have already said, recording
the lives of men who were trained in every kind of learning—so much, that is, as is preserved and has come to my
ears—it will not be out of place if I also treat in summary
fashion those who have done wrong to them. Ablabius who   19
brought about the murder [of Sopater] came from a family entirely lacking a good name, and on his father's side of
rather obscure and common stock. A story about him survives, and no one has contradicted the reports. One of the
people from Egypt, belonging to those devoted to the
study called astrology,[62] who was visiting the City[63]—and
when they are on their travels Egyptians are capable of
behaving even in public with a lack of decorum, so that   20
they are probably brought up that way at home)—as I say,
he came on a visit, pushed his way into one of the more
expensive wineshops, loudly declared that he was parched
after finishing a long journey, even said that he would
choke on the spot with thirst, and ordered them to prepare
and pour some wine for him, sweet and spiced, and the
money for it was produced. The hostess of the wineshop,   21
recognizing a profit, made ready to serve him and began
bustling about. But she also happened to be good at assist-
ing women who were about to give birth. And when she
had just set the goblet before the Egyptian and was in the
act of pouring out the wine that she had prepared, one of
her neighbors ran in and whispered in her ear: "Your

62 *Mathêma*, "the science of drawing horoscopes."
63 Rome.

ὠδῖσιν ἡ φίλη καὶ συγγενής," καὶ γὰρ οὕτως εἶχεν,
22 "εἰ μὴ θᾶττον ἀφίκοιο." καὶ ἡ μὲν ταῦτα ἀκούσασα
καὶ καταλιποῦσα τὸν Αἰγύπτιον, πρὶν τὸ θερμὸν ὕδωρ
ἐπιβαλεῖν, κεχηνότα, κἀκείνην ἀπολύσασα τῶν ὠδί-
νων καὶ συντελέσασά γε ὅσα ἐπὶ ταῖς λοχείαις γίνεται, παρῆν αὐτίκα, διακαθήρασα τὰς χεῖρας, πρὸς
23 τὸν ξένον. ὡς δὲ ἀγανακτοῦντα κατέλαβε καὶ | τῷ
22G θυμῷ περιζέοντα, τὴν αἰτίαν ἀπήγγειλεν ἡ γυνὴ τῆς
βραδυτῆτος. ὡς δὲ ἤκουσεν ὁ βέλτιστος Αἰγύπτιος
καὶ πρὸς τὴν ὥραν εἶδεν ὀξέως μᾶλλον ἐδίψησεν ἐξει-
πεῖν τὸ παρὰ τῶν θεῶν ἐπελθὸν ἢ τὸ τοῦ σώματος
24 θεραπεῦσαι πάθος, καὶ μέγα φθεγξάμενος· "ἀλλ᾽
ἄπιθί γε, ὦ γύναι· φράζε τῇ τεκούσῃ ὅτι μικροῦ βασιλέα τέτοκεν." καὶ τοῦτο δηλώσας, ἑαυτόν τε ἐπλήρω-
σεν ἀφθόνως τῆς κύλικος καὶ τὸ ὄνομα ὅστις εἴη κατ-
25 έλιπε τῇ γυναικὶ εἰδέναι. καὶ ὁ τεχθεὶς ἦν Ἀβλάβιος
καὶ τοσοῦτον ἐγένετο παίγνιον τῆς εἰς ἅπαντα νεω-
τεριζούσης Τύχης, ὥστε οὕτω πλείονα ἐδύνατο τοῦ
464B βασιλεύοντος, | ὥστε καὶ Σώπατρον ἀπέκτεινεν, αἰτίαν
ἐπενεγκὼν τῆς Σωκρατικῆς εὐηθεστέραν, ὥσπερ ἀτά-
26 κτῳ δήμῳ τῷ τότε βασιλεύοντι χρώμενος. Κωνσταντῖνος μὲν οὖν ὡς²⁶ Ἀβλάβιον τιμῶν ἐκολάζετο καὶ
ὅπως γε ἐτελεύτα ἐν τοῖς περὶ ἐκείνου γέγραπται,
Ἀβλαβίῳ δὲ τὸν παῖδα κατέλιπε Κωνστάντιον, συμ-
βασιλεύσαντα μὲν αὐτῷ, διαδεξάμενον δὲ τὴν ἀρχὴν
τοῦ πατρὸς σὺν Κωνσταντίνῳ καὶ Κώνσταντι τοῖς

²⁶ ὡς Go: καὶ A

friend and kinswoman" (as was in fact the case) "is facing the risk of a difficult childbirth, unless you come quickly." The moment she heard this she abandoned the Egyptian—the man's jaw dropped wide open—before she had even poured in the warm water. When she had relieved the woman in her labor and done all that is usual in childbirth situations, she washed her hands and came back at once to the stranger. When she found him greatly vexed and seething with rage,[64] the woman explained the reason for the delay. When he had heard this and quickly noted the time, the excellent Egyptian immediately felt a greater thirst to utter the message that had come to him from the gods than to tend to his physical needs; and he loudly proclaimed: "So go, madam, and tell the mother that she has nearly given birth to an emperor." After this revelation he drank his fill of the cup without holding a grudge; and he left the [boy's] name for the woman to know who he would be. The one just born was Ablabius,[65] and he proved to be so much the puppet of Fortune who overturns everything, that he became so much more powerful than the emperor that he even put Sopater to death, after bringing against him a charge more idiotic than that brought against Socrates, because he [used] the emperor as though the latter were an unruly mob. Constantine, however, was punished because he honored Ablabius, and how he died I have described in my account of him. He entrusted to Ablabius his son Constantius, who had been his co-regent in the Empire and succeeded to the rule of his father together with his brothers Constantine and Constans. And

22

23

24

25

26

---

64 Cf. Pl. *Phdr.* 251c.   65 The name ("invulnerable," "harmless") will prove to be ironic (cf. *VPS* 6.31 below).

ἀδελφοῖς. ἐν δὲ τοῖς κατὰ τὸν θειότατον Ἰουλιανὸν
27 ἀκριβέστερον ταῦτα εἴρηται. διαδεξάμενος δὲ ὁ Κωνστάντιος τὴν βασιλείαν καὶ κληρωθεὶς ὅσα γε ἐκλη-
ρώθη, ταῦτα δὲ ἦν τὰ ἐξ Ἰλλυριῶν εἰς τὴν ἑῴαν καθήκοντα, τὸν μὲν Ἀβλάβιον αὐτίκα παραλύει τῆς
28 ἀρχῆς, ἄλλο δὲ περὶ αὐτὸν ἑταιρικὸν συνέστησε. καὶ
ὁ μὲν Ἀβλάβιος τὰ περὶ Βιθυνίαν χωρία πάλαι παρ-
εσκευασμένος, βασιλικάς τε καταφυγὰς καὶ ῥᾳθυ-
μίας ἔχοντα, διέτριβεν ἐν ἀφθόνοις, πάντων ἀνθρώ-
29 πων θαυμαζόντων ὅτι βασιλεύειν οὐ βούλεται. ὁ δὲ
Κωνστάντιος ἐγγύθεν ἐκ τῆς τοῦ πατρὸς πόλεως ξι-
23G φηφόρους τινὰς | ἐπ' αὐτὸν ἐκπέμψας οὐκ ὀλίγους,
τοῖς μὲν πρώτοις ἐκέλευσεν ἀποδιδόναι γράμματα.
καὶ προσεκύνησάν γε αὐτόν, ὥσπερ νομίζουσι Ῥωμαῖοι βασιλέα προσκυνεῖν, οἱ τὰ γράμματα ἐγχειρί-
ζοντες· καὶ ὃς μάλα σοβαρῶς δεξάμενος τὰ γράμματα καὶ παντὸς ἀπολυθεὶς φόβου, τήν τε ἁλουργίδα
τοὺς ἐλθόντας ἀπῄτει, βαρύτερος ἤδη γινόμενος, καὶ
30 φοβερὸν ἦν τοῖς ὁρωμένοις. οἱ δὲ ἔφασαν πρὸς αὐτόν,
αὐτοὶ μὲν τὰ γράμματα κομίζειν, πρὸ θυρῶν δὲ εἶναι
31 τοὺς ταῦτα πεπιστευμένους. καὶ ὁ μὲν ἐκείνους ἐκάλει
μέγα φρονῶν καὶ τῇ γνώμῃ διῃρμένος· οἱ δὲ συγχω-
ρηθέντες εἰσελθεῖν πλῆθός τε ἦσαν καὶ ξιφηφόροι
πάντες, καὶ ἀντὶ τῆς ἁλουργίδος ἐπῆγον αὐτῷ τὸν
"πορφύρεον θάνατον," κρεουργηδὸν ὥσπερ τι τῶν ἐν

---

66 A separate life or in his *History*.
67 Cf. Ar. *Eq.* 967.

434

in my account[66] of the godlike Julian I have related these matters more thoroughly. When Constantius had suc- 27 ceeded to the throne and had been allotted his proper portion of the Empire, that is to say, the countries that extend from Illyricum to the East, he at once relieved Ablabius of his authority, and established a different set of favorites around himself. Since Ablabius had long before- 28 hand made ready his estate in Bithynia, which provided him with a regal retreat and place of relaxation, he spent his time in luxury; meanwhile, everybody marveled that he did not aspire to be emperor. Then Constantius, from 29 his father's city nearby, dispatched some swordsmen in considerable numbers against him, and to the leaders he gave orders that they should hand him a letter. Those who delivered the letter into his hands actually prostrated themselves before him, as Romans are accustomed to do when saluting the emperor; and he, after receiving the document in a pompous manner and now completely freed from anxiety, demanded the purple robe[67] from those who had come, his expression already having be- come more stern, and he was a frightening sight for the onlookers. They replied that their task had been to bring 30 the letter, but that those entrusted with that task were at the door. Thereupon he summoned them inside with an 31 arrogant air and by his reckless judgment. But those who were then admitted were a large number and all carried swords; and instead of the purple robe they brought down upon him "purple death,"[68] and hacked him to pieces like

---

[68] Hom. *Il.* 5.83, the verse that Julian is said to have quoted when he was invested with the purple as Caesar, because he dis- trusted the intentions of Constantius (Amm. Marcell. 15.8).

ταῖς εὐωχίαις ζῷον κατακόψαντες. καὶ ταύτην ἔτισε
Σωπάτρῳ δίκην ὁ πάντα εὐδαίμων Ἀβλάβιος.

32   Τούτων δὴ οὕτω κεχωρηκότων καὶ τῆς προνοίας
οὐκ ἀφιείσης τὸ ἀνθρώπινον, ὁ τῶν περιλειφθέντων
ἐνδοξότατος Αἰδέσιος κατελείπετο. καταφυγὼν δὲ ἐπί
τινα μαντείαν δι᾽ εὐχῆς ᾗπερ ἐπίστευε μάλιστα (αὕτη
δὲ ἦν δι᾽ ὀνείρατος), ὁ μὲν θεὸς ἐφίστατο πρὸς τὴν
33   εὐχήν καὶ ἔχρησεν ἐν ἑξαμέτρῳ τόνῳ τάδε· (ὁ δέ ἀνα-
καλύψας ἄρτι τὰ βλέφαρα καὶ περίφοβος ὢν ἔτι, τὸν
μὲν νοῦν ἐμέμνητο τῶν εἰρημένων, τὸ δὲ ὑπερφυὲς καὶ
οὐρανόμηκες τῶν ἐπῶν περιέφευγεν αὐτὸν καὶ διω-
λίσθαινε. τόν τε οὖν παῖδα καλεῖ, τὴν ὄψιν καὶ τὸ
πρόσωπον ἀποσμῆσαι τῷ ὕδατι βουλόμενος, καὶ ὁ
24G   θεράπων | πρὸς αὐτὸν ἔλεγεν, "ἀλλ᾽ ἡ ἀριστερά γε
34   χεὶρ ἔξωθεν κατάπλεως ἐστι γραμμάτων." καὶ ὃς εἶδεν
καὶ τὸ πρᾶγμα θεῖον εἶναι συνεφρόνησε, καὶ προσκυνήσας τὴν ἑαυτοῦ χεῖρα καὶ τὰ γεγραμμένα, εὗρε τὸν
35   χρησμὸν ἐπὶ τῆς χειρὸς γεγραμμένον. ἔστι δὲ οὗτος·)

δοιῶν Μοιράων ἐπὶ νήμασι νήματα κεῖται
εἵνεκα σῆς βιοτῆς. εἰ μὲν πτολίεθρ᾽ ἀγαπάζοις
ἄστεά τ᾽ αὖ φωτῶν, καί σοι κλέος ἄφθιτον ἔσται,
ἀνδρῶν ποιμαίνοντι νέων θεοείκελον ὁρμήν. |
465B   ἢν δ᾽ αὖ ποιμαίνῃς μήλων νομὸν ἠδ᾽ ἔτι ταύρων,
δὴ πότε σαυτὸν ἔελπε συνήμονα καὶ μακάρεσσιν
ἔμμεναι ἀθανάτοισι. λίνον δέ τοι ὧδε νένευκεν.

---

69 The response follows below (it may have been transposed).
70 Common after a vision: Ar. *Ran.*137f.; Aesch. *Pers.* 201.

those who cut up an animal at a public feast. In this way Ablabius the "all-fortunate" paid the penalty for Sopater.

When these events had happened in this way (showing 32 providence had not deserted humanity), there remained Aedesius, the most renowned of those that survived. Once when he took refuge at an oracle by means of a prayer, in which he particularly placed trust (this came in a dream), the god stood over him in answer to his prayer and gave him the following oracular response in hexameter verse. . . .[69] (And just after he had opened his eyes, while 33 still terrified, he remembered the meaning of what had been said, though the supernatural and exalted nature of the words began to escape and fade from his mind. So, wanting to wipe clean his eyes and face with water,[70] he called a slave boy, and the slave said to him: "Look, the back of your left arm is covered with writing." He looked, 34 and realized that the thing was a divine portent, and after reverently acknowledging his arm and the letters, he discovered the oracle that had been written on his arm). This 35 is the text:

On the warp of the two Fates' spinning sit
the threads to your life. If you should be content with
the cities and
towns of mortals, your fame shall be never-ending,
shepherding the godlike impulse of youths.
But if instead you will be a shepherd of sheep and
bulls,
then hope that you yourself will one day even be the
associate of the blessed
immortals. The thread of life is thus inclined for you.

36 καὶ ὁ μὲν χρησμὸς ταῦτα εἶχεν· ὁ δὲ ἑπόμενος, ὥσπερ
ἕπεσθαι χρή, πρὸς τὸν κρείττονα ὁδὸν συνηπείγετο
καὶ χωρίδιον τέ τι περιεσκόπει καὶ πρὸς αἰπολίου τινὸς ἢ βοτῆρος ἑαυτὸν ἐνέτεινε βίον· τοὺς δὲ λόγων
δεομένους ἢ παιδείας διὰ τὸ προκατακεχυμένον κλέος
οὐκ ἐλάνθανεν, ἀλλ᾽ ἀνιχνεύοντες αὐτὸν περιεστήκε-
σαν, ὥσπερ κύνες ὠρυόμενοι περὶ τὰ πρόθυρα, καὶ
διασπάσασθαι[27] ἀπειλοῦντες, εἰ τοσαύτην καὶ τηλι-
καύτην σοφίαν ἐπὶ τὰ ὄρη καὶ τοὺς κρημνοὺς καὶ τὰ
δένδρα τρέποι, καθάπερ οὐδὲ ἄνθρωπος γεγονὼς οὐδὲ
37 εἰδὼς τὸ ἀνθρώπινον. τοιούτοις δὲ λόγοις τε καὶ ἔργοις ἐκβιασθεὶς εἰς τὴν κοινὴν ὁμιλίαν, ἐπέδωκεν ἑαυτὸν φέρων τῇ χείρονι τῶν ὁδῶν καὶ τὴν μὲν Καππα-
δοκίαν ἐξέλιπεν, Εὐσταθίῳ παραδοὺς ἐπιμελεῖσθαι
25G τῶν ἐκείνῃ (καὶ κατὰ | γένος οὐκ ἀφεστήκεσαν). αὐτὸς
38 δὲ εἰς τὴν Ἀσίαν διαβάς, ὅλης Ἀσίας προτεινούσης
αὐτῷ χεῖρας, ἐν τῷ παλαιῷ Περγάμῳ καθιδρύθη, καὶ
παρ᾽ ἐκεῖνον μὲν Ἕλληνές τε ἐφοίτων καὶ οἱ πρόσχω-
ροι, καὶ ἡ δόξα τῶν ἄστρων ἔψαυεν.

39 Περὶ δὲ Εὐσταθίου καὶ ἀσεβές ἐστι παραλιπεῖν τὰ
ἐς ἀλήθειαν φέροντα· παρὰ πάντων γὰρ συνωμολογεῖτο τὸν ἄνδρα τοῦτον ὀφθῆναι καὶ εἶναι κάλλιστον
καὶ εἰς πεῖραν λόγων ἐλθεῖν δεινότατον, τό τε ἐπὶ τῇ
γλώσσῃ καὶ τοῖς χείλεσιν αἱμύλιον οὐκ ἔξω γοητείας
ἐδόκει. καὶ τὸ μείλιχον καὶ ἥμερον ἐπὶ τοῖς λεγομένοις ἐπήνθει καὶ συνεξεχεῖτο τοσοῦτον ὥστε οἱ τῆς

---

[27] διασπάσεσθαι Cob (Go: fort. recte)

This was the content of the oracular response. Obeying it, 36
as was his duty, he set out with all speed in pursuit of the
better path and looked around for a small estate and devoted his energies to the life of a goatherd or herdsman.
But he could not remain hidden from those who longed
for training in eloquence or for learning, because of his
widespread previous renown. They tracked him down and
surrounded him like hounds baying near his front door
and threatening to tear him in pieces, if he should devote
so much wisdom and of such quality to mountains and
rocks and trees, as though he were not born a human
or with knowledge of human life. Compelled by such 37
speeches and actions of this sort to return to a life in the
community, he now applied his talents to the less attractive of the two paths and left Cappadocia, handing over to
Eustathius the charge of his property there—they were in
fact not far apart in familial kinship. He himself traveled 38
into the province of Asia, since all Asia was holding out her
arms in welcome. He settled in ancient Pergamon, and
both Greeks and neighboring people used to resort to him
as a teacher, and his fame continued to rise up to the stars.

With regard to Eustathius, it would be impious to leave 39
out what bears on the truth. For everyone agreed that this
man was both observed to be a very fine person and most
skilled in undertaking the testing of speeches, while the
seductive guile that sat on his tongue and lips seemed to
be nothing less than wizardry. His mildness and amiability
so flourished in what he said and flowed out with his words
so much so that those who heard his voice and speeches

439

φωνῆς ἀκούσαντες καὶ τῶν λόγων, παραδόντες αὑτούς
καθάπερ οἱ τοῦ λωτοῦ γευσάμενοι, τῆς φωνῆς ἐξεκρέ-
40 μαντο καὶ τῶν λόγων. οὕτω δὴ πολύ τι τῶν μουσικῶν
οὐκ ἀπεῖχε Σειρήνων, ὥστε ὁ βασιλεὺς αὐτὸν μετ-
εκάλεσε,[28] καίτοι γε τοῖς τῶν χριστιανῶν ἐνεχόμενος
βιβλίοις, ἐπειδὴ θόρυβος αὐτὸν κατεῖχε καὶ παρὰ τοῦ
Περσῶν βασιλέως ἀνάγκη τις ἐπέκειτο, καὶ τὴν Ἀντιόχειαν ἤδη περιειργασμένου καὶ συντοξεύοντος, ὅς
γε τὴν ἄκραν τὴν ὑπερκειμένην τοῦ θεάτρου καταλαβὼν ἀδοκήτως καὶ ἐξαπιναίως, τὸ πολὺ πλῆθος
41 τῶν θεωμένων συνετόξευσε καὶ διέφθειρε. τούτων δὲ
ὅμῶς[29] κατεχόντων, οὕτως πάντες ἦσαν ᾑρημένοι καὶ
κατακεκηλημένοι, ὥστε μὴ κατοκνῆσαί τινα Ἕλληνα
ἄνθρωπον ἐς τὰ ὦτα τοῦ βασιλέως παραβαλεῖν· καίτοι γε εἰώθεσαν πρότερον οἱ βασιλεύοντες τοὺς κατὰ
26G στρατιὰν ἐπαινουμένους ἐπὶ τὰς πρεσβείας | χειροτο-
νεῖν, ἤτοι γε στρατοπεδάρχας ἢ ὅσοι γε μετ' ἐκείνους
42 ἐς τὸ ἄρχειν ἐξῃρημένοι· τότε καὶ ἀνάγκης τυραννού-
σης, ὁ φρονιμώτατος ἁπάντων περιεσκοπεῖτο καὶ
συνωμολογεῖτο Εὐστάθιος. μετεκλήθη τε οὖν ἐκ τοῦ
βασιλέως καὶ αὐτίκα παρῆν, καὶ τοσαύτη τις ἐπῆν
ἀφροδίτη τοῖς χείλεσιν ὥστε οἱ συμβουλεύσαντες
τὴν πρεσβείαν δι' Εὐσταθίου πεμφθῆναι ἀξιωμάτων
τε ἔτυχον παρὰ τῷ βασιλεῖ μειζόνων καὶ πρὸς τὴν

28 Vollebr Gi (cf. 6. 62): μετεπέμψατο αὐτὸν Go
29 ὁμῶς Wr Ba: ὅμως A Boiss Gi Go

surrendered themselves like men who had tasted the lo-
tus, and they hung on his voice and speeches. So closely   40
in fact did he resemble the musical Sirens, that the emperor, even though he was engrossed in the books of the
Christians, sent for him at the time when he was alarmed
by the state of affairs, and was under pressure by impend-
ing danger from the king of the Persians, who had already
laid siege to Antioch and raided it with his archers.[71] For
unexpectedly and without forewarning he seized the highest point of the theater, and with his arrows shot and killed
a considerable number of the crowd of spectators. In the   41
same way as these were held prisoner, all men were held
captive and under a spell [by Eustathius] in such a way,
that they did not hesitate to commend a Hellene to the
ears of the emperor; and yet previously emperors had
been accustomed to appoint[72] for embassies men who had
won distinction in the army, or military prefects, or their
adjutants selected for the office. But at that time of impos-   42
ing necessity, the well-considered and widely agreed view
was that Eustathius was the most judicious of all men.
Accordingly, he was summoned by the emperor, and came
forthwith, and so compelling was the attractiveness of his
conversation[73] that those who had advised that the embassy with Eustathius in charge should be dispatched won
greater consideration than before from the emperor, and

[71] Constantius sent Eustathius on this embassy, but this incident at Antioch occurred much earlier, in the reign of Gallienus,
about AD 258; cf. Amm. Marcell. 23.5.

[72] Pl. *Leg.* 763e.   [73] Lit., "charm on his lips," Eupolis' famous saying about the oratory of Pericles (*Dêmoi* fr. 102 Storey);
cf. Julian. *Or.* 33a, 426b.

EUNAPIUS

43   εὔνοιαν αὐτῶν ὁ βασιλεὺς ἐπεκλίνετο. τούτων μὲν οὖν
τινες αὐτῷ καὶ ἐθελονταὶ συνεξώρμησαν ἐπὶ τὴν πρε-
466B σβείαν, | μείζονα διάπειραν θέλοντες λαβεῖν, εἰ καὶ
πρὸς τοὺς βαρβάρους ἔχοι τὸ αὐτὸ θελκτήριον ὁ ἄν-
44   θρωπος. ὡς δὲ εἰς τὴν τῶν Περσῶν ἀφίκοντο χώραν,
καίτοι γε τυραννικὸς καὶ ἄγριός τις Σαπώρης εἶναι
πρὸς τοὺς ἐσιόντας, ἤν τε ἀληθῶς, ἐξηγγέλλετο, ἀλλ᾽
ὅμως ἐπεὶ πρόσοδος Εὐσταθίῳ κατὰ τὴν κοινὴν πρεσβείαν ἐγένετο πρὸς τὸν βασιλέα, τήν τε ὑπεροψίαν
τὴν ἐν τοῖς ὄμμασι καὶ τὸ μείλιχον ἐθαύμασε, καίτοι
γε πολλὰ ἐς κατάπληξιν τοῦ ἀνδρὸς μηχανησάμενος.
45   καὶ ὡς ἡμέρως καὶ ἀλύπως διαλεγομένου τῆς φωνῆς
ἤκουσε καὶ τῶν ἐπιτρεχουσῶν κοσμίως καὶ εὐκόλως
ἀποδείξεων, ἐξελθεῖν μὲν αὐτὸν κελεύει, καὶ ὃς ἐξῄει
λόγῳ συνῃρηκὼς τύραννον· ὁ δὲ ἐπὶ τράπεζάν τε
εὐθὺς διὰ τῶν θαλαμηπόλων εἰσεκάλει, καί, πρὸς
τοῦτο ὑπακούσαντος (ἐῴκει γὰρ εὖ πεφυκέναι πρὸς
46   ἀρετῆς ῥοπήν), ἀπήντησεν ἐπὶ τὴν θοίνην. καὶ ὁμοτράπεζος ἐγένετο καὶ κατεκράτει τῷ λόγῳ τοσοῦτον
ὥστε μικροῦ τινος ἐδέησε τὸν Περσῶν βασιλέα τήν
27G τε ὀρθὴν μεταβαλεῖν τιάραν καὶ | τοὺς περιπορφύρους
καὶ λιθοκολλήτους ἀπολῦσαι κόσμους καὶ τὸ τριβώνιον Εὐσταθίου μεταμφιάσασθαι, τοσαύτην τῆς
τύχης ἐποιήσατο καταδρομὴν καὶ τῶν περὶ σῶμα κό-
σμων, καὶ εἰς τοσοῦτο κακοδαιμονίας τοὺς φιλοσω-
47   μάτους ἀνήγαγεν. ἀλλὰ τοῦτο μὲν ἐκώλυσαν οἱ παρα-

he felt more favorably inclined toward them. Moreover, 43
some of these men set out of their own accord on the
embassy, because they wished to employ a still greater
test, whether that man [i.e., Eustathius] in his encounter
with the barbarians should prove to possess the same persuasive charm. When they arrived in Persia, the word was 44
that Sapor was tyrannical and savage toward those who
approached him, and this turned out to be true; nevertheless, when Eustathius, within the context of the joint embassy, gained access to the king, the latter admired the
expression in his eyes, simultaneously proudly indifferent
and kindhearted, in spite of the many preparations that
the king had devised to impress the man. And when he 45
heard the gentle and inoffensive manner of his voice,
when he heard him run over his rational arguments in an
orderly and calm fashion, he told him to leave the room;
and Eustathius went out, leaving the tyrant captivated by
his eloquence. But straightaway he sent a message by his
household officials to invite him back in to join him at the
meal; and when he obeyed the summons, since the king
seemed to him to have a natural bent for virtue, Eustathius
joined him at the banquet. Thus he became his companion 46
at table, and by his eloquence won such influence over him
that the king of Persia came very close to renouncing the
upright tiara, laying aside his purple and bejeweled clothing, and adopting instead the philosopher's cloak of Eustathius; so successfully did the latter denounce the life of
luxury and the pomp and vanity of the flesh, to such an
ill-starred mood did he seem to bring down those who
loved their bodies.[74] But this was prevented by certain 47

[74] Cf. Plotinus, *Plot*. 1.1; Porphyry, above, *VPS* 4.7; and Iambl.
Myst. 3.21, 3.30 (on soul and evil spirits).

τυχόντες τῶν μάγων, γόητα εἶναι τελείως τὸν ἄνδρα
φάσκοντες, καὶ τὸν βασιλέα συμπείσαντες ἀποκρίνα-
48 σθαι τῷ βασιλεῖ Ῥωμαίων· τί δήποτε ἄνδρας εὐ-
τυχοῦντες τοσούτους, εἶτα πέμπουσιν ἀνδραπόδων
πλουτούντων οὐδὲν διαφέροντας; τὰ δὲ κατὰ τὴν πρεσβείαν ἅπαντα ἦν παρ' ἐλπίδας.

49 Περὶ τούτου γε τοῦ ἀνδρὸς καὶ τοιοῦτόν τι ἐς τὴν
ἐμὴν ἱστορίαν συνέπεσεν, ὡς ἅπασα μὲν ἡ Ἑλλὰς
ἰδεῖν αὐτὸν ηὔχοντο καὶ ᾔτουν τοὺς θεοὺς τὴν ἐπιδη-
50 μίαν· καὶ αἵ γε μαντεῖαι τοῖς περὶ ταῦτα δεινοῖς ἐς
τοῦτο συνέβαινον. ὡς δὲ διημάρτανον, οὐ γὰρ ἐπεδήμει, πρεσβείαν παρ' αὐτὸν στέλλουσιν οἱ Ἕλληνες,
τοὺς ἄκρους ἐπὶ σοφίᾳ κατὰ τὴν πρεσβείαν προελό-
μενοι. νοῦς δὲ ἦν αὐτοῖς διαλέγεσθαι πρὸς τὸν μέγαν
51 Εὐστάθιον· τί δήποτε ἐπὶ τοῖσδε τοῖς σημείοις τὸ ἔργον οὐκ ἀπήντησεν; ὁ δὲ ἀκούσας καὶ τοὺς ὀνομα-
στοὺς ἐπ' ἐκείνοις καὶ πολυυμνήτους ἀναθεωρῶν καὶ
διακρίνων ἐβασάνιζε, καὶ συνηρώτα τό τε μέγεθος
καὶ τὴν χροιὰν καὶ τὸ σχῆμα τῶν σημείων, εἶτα μειδιάσας συνήθως πρὸς αὐτούς, ὡς ἤκουσε τὰ ὄντα
(ψεῦδος γὰρ οὐ μόνον ἔξω θείου χοροῦ, ἀλλὰ καὶ λόγου ἵσταται), "ἀλλὰ ταῦτά γε," εἶπε, "τὴν ἐμὴν τήνδε
52 ἐπιδημίαν οὐκ ἐμαντεύετο." | καὶ πού τι καὶ παρὰ τὸ
28G ἀνθρώπειον κατά γε ἐμὴν ἐφθέγξατο κρίσιν· ἀπεκρίνατο γὰρ ὡς "μικρότερα ἦν καὶ βραδύτερα τῶν ἐμῶν
καλῶν τὰ φανθέντα σημεῖα."

---

75 Persian priests (cf. Hdt. 7.37) who interpreted dreams.

Magi[75] who happened to be at the court and kept asserting
that the man was a magician through and through; and   48
they persuaded the king to reply to the Roman emperor
by asking him why, when blessed with so many distinguished men, they [i.e., the Romans] sent individuals no
better than slaves who enriched themselves? And the entire outcome of the embassy was contrary to people's expectations.[76]

Concerning this man, similar information also came my   49
way for my inquiry, namely, that the whole of Greece
prayed to see him and implored the gods that he might
visit them. And at any rate the oracles amounted to the   50
same thing to those who were skilled in these matters. But
when they proved to be mistaken, for he did not visit
Greece, the Greeks sent an embassy to him and chose for
this embassy their most famous wise men. Their intention
was to discuss with the renowned Eustathius [the ques-
tion] "Why did the event not accord with these portents?"   51
Having listened to them, he then scrutinized carefully the
men who were well-known and highly acclaimed experts
in this science, and separating them, asked about the size
and the color and the shape of the signs. Then he smiled
at them in his usual manner, on hearing the true facts (for
falsehood is not only alien to the divine choir,[77] but also to
rationality), and said: "these omens did not foretell this
visit from me." Then he said something that in my judg-   52
ment was beyond the human realm, for this was his reply:
"The omens that were revealed were too insignificant and
too slow for my good qualities."

[76] Cf. Amm. Marcell. 17.5 (embassy to Ctesiphon in 358).
[77] An echo of Pl. *Phdr.* 247a and rhetorical commonplace.

53 Οὕτως Εὐστάθιος ὁ τοσοῦτος Σωσιπάτρα συνῴκη-
σεν, ἢ τὸν ἄνδρα τὸν ἑαυτῆς δι᾽ ὑπεροχὴν σοφίας
54 εὐτελῆ τινὰ καὶ μικρὸν ἀπέδειξεν. περὶ ταύτης δὲ ἐν
ἀνδρῶν σοφῶν καταλόγοις καὶ διὰ μακροτέρων εἰπεῖν
ἁρμόζει, τοσοῦτον κλέος τῆς γυναικὸς ἐξεφοίτησεν.
καὶ ἦν γὰρ ἐκ τῆς περὶ Ἔφεσον Ἀσίας, ὅσην Κάϋ-
467B στρος ποταμὸς ἐπιὼν καὶ διαρρέων | τὴν ἐπωνυμίαν
ἀφ᾽ ἑαυτοῦ τῷ πεδίῳ δίδωσι. πατέρων δὲ ἦν καὶ γένους εὐδαίμονός τε καὶ ὀλβίου· παιδίον δὲ ἔτι νήπιον
οὖσα, ἅπαντα ἐποίει ὀλβιώτερα, τοσοῦτό τι κάλλους
55 καὶ αἰδοῦς τὴν ἡλικίαν κατέλαμπεν. καὶ ἡ μὲν εἰς πεν-
ταετῆ συνετέλει χρόνον· ἐν δὲ τούτῳ πρεσβῦται δύο
τινές (ἄμφω μὲν τὴν ἀκμὴν παρήλλαττον, ὁ δὲ ἕτερος
ἦν ἀφηλικέστερος) πήρας βαθείας ἔχοντες καὶ δέρ-
ματα ἐπὶ τῶν νώτων ἐνημμένοι, πρός τι χωρίον συνω-
θοῦνται τῶν γονέων τῆς Σωσιπάτρας καὶ τὸν ἐπιτρο-
πεύοντα συμπείθουσιν (ῥᾴδιον δὲ ἦν αὐτοῖς τοῦτο
56 ποιεῖν) ἀμπελίων ἐπιμέλειαν αὐτοῖς πιστεῦσαι. ὡς δὲ
ὁ καρπὸς ἀπήντησε ὑπὲρ τὴν ἐλπίδα (καὶ ὁ δεσπότης
παρῆν καὶ τὸ παιδίον ἡ Σωσιπάτρα συμπαρῆν), τὸ
μὲν θαῦμα ἄπειρον ἦν καὶ πρὸς ὑπόνοιαν ἔφερε θει-
57 ασμοῦ τινός· ὁ δὲ τοῦ χωρίου δεσπότης ὁμοτραπέζους
αὐτοὺς ἐποιήσατο καὶ πολλῆς ἐπιμελείας ἠξίου, τοῖς
συγγεωργοῦσι τὸ χωρίον καταμεμφόμενος ὅτι μὴ τὰ
58 αὐτὰ πράττοιεν. οἱ δὲ πρεσβῦται ξενίας τε Ἑλληνι-
κῆς καὶ τραπέζης τυχόντες, τοῦ δὲ παιδίου τῆς Σωσιπάτρας τῷ τε περιττῶς καλῷ καὶ λαμυρῷ δηχθέντες
29G καὶ ἁλόντες, "ἀλλ᾽ ἡμεῖς γε," | ἔφασαν, "τὰ μὲν ἄλλα

Thus it came to pass that Eustathius, man of such stat-   53
ure, married Sosipatra, who by her surpassing wisdom
made her own husband seem inferior and insignificant. So   54
far and wide did the fame of this woman travel, that it is
fitting for me to speak of her at greater length, even in a
list of wise men. She was born in Asia, near Ephesus, in
that district that the river Cayster traverses and flows
through, and hence gives its name to the plain. She came
of a prosperous family, blessed with wealth, and while she
was still a small child, she seemed to bring a blessing on
everything, such levels of beauty and modesty illuminated
her infant years. She had just reached the age of five, when   55
two old men (both were past the prime of life, but one was
rather older than the other), carrying large pouches and
wearing garments of animal skins on their backs,[78] made
their way to a country estate belonging to Sosipatra's parents, and persuaded the caretaker, as they had no trouble
doing so, to entrust to them the care of the vines. When a   56
harvest beyond all expectation was the result—the master
of the house was there, as was the little girl Sosipatra—the
amazement was boundless and led them to suspect some
divine intervention. The master of the estate invited them   57
to his table and gave them his full attention, while he reproached the other laborers on the estate for not obtaining
the same results. The old men, on receiving Hellenic hos-   58
pitality and a place at table, were smitten[79] and captivated
by the exceeding beauty and charisma of the little girl
Sosipatra, and they said: "as for us, we keep our other

[78] Cf. Hom. *Od.* 13.434–38.
[79] Pl. *Resp.* 474d; Eur. *Hipp.* 1303.

κρύφια καὶ ἀπόρρητα πρὸς ἑαυτοὺς ἔχομεν, καὶ τὰ
ταυτησὶ τῆς ἐπαινουμένης εὐνοίας[30] ἐστὶ γέλως καὶ
παίγνιόν τι μετ᾽ ὀλιγωρίας τῶν παρ᾽ ἡμῖν πλεονεκτη-
59 μάτων. εἰ δέ τι βούλει σοι τῆς τραπέζης ταύτης καὶ
τῶν ξενίων δοθῆναι παρ᾽ ἡμῶν οὐκ ἐν χρήμασιν οὐδὲ
ἐν ἐπικήροις καὶ διεφθαρμέναις χάρισιν, ἀλλ᾽ ὅσον
ὑπὲρ σέ τέ ἐστι καὶ τὸν σὸν βίον, δῶρον οὐρανόμηκες
καὶ τῶν ἀστέρων ἐφικνούμενον, ἄφες παρ᾽ ἡμῖν τὴν
Σωσιπάτραν ταύτην τροφεῦσι καὶ πατράσιν ἀληθε-
στέροις καὶ εἴς γε πέμπτον ἔτος μηδὲ νόσ‹ον›[31] περὶ
τῇ παιδίσκῃ φοβηθῇς, μηδὲ θάνατον, ἀλλ᾽ ἥσυχος
60 ἔσο καὶ ἔμπεδος. μελέτω δέ σοι μὴ πατῆσαι τὸ χωρίον μέχρις ἂν τὸ πέμπτον ἔτος, περιτελλομένων τῶν
ἡλιακῶν κύκλων, ἐξίκηται. καὶ πλοῦτός τέ σοι αὐτόμα-
τος ἀπὸ τοῦ χωρίου φύσεται καὶ ἀναθηλήσει, καὶ ἡ
θυγάτηρ οὐ κατὰ γυναῖκα καὶ ἄνθρωπον ἔσται ‹οὐ›
μόνον,[32] ἀλλὰ καὶ αὐτὸς ὑπολήψῃ τι περὶ τῆς παιδί-
σκης πλέον. εἰ μὲν οὖν ἀγαθὸν ἔχεις θυμόν, ὑπτίαις
χερσὶ δέξαι τὰ λεγόμενα· εἰ δέ τινας ὑπονοίας ἀνακι-
61 νεῖς, οὐδὲν ἡμῖν εἴρηται." πρὸς ταῦτα τὴν γλῶτταν
ἐνδακὼν καὶ πτήξας ὁ πατὴρ τὸ παιδίον ἐγχειρίζει
καὶ παραδίδωσι, καί, τὸν οἰκονόμον μετακαλέσας,
"χορήγει," πρὸς αὐτὸν εἶπεν, "ὅσα οἱ πρεσβῦται
62 βούλονται, καὶ πολυπραγμόνει μηδέν." ταῦτα εἶπεν·
οὔπω δὲ ἕως ὑπέφαινεν καὶ ἐξῄει καθάπερ φεύγων καὶ
τὴν θυγατέρα καὶ τὸ χωρίον. |

448

powers to ourselves, hidden and unrevealed, and the [acts
of] goodwill that you praised are laughable and a trifle that
does not do justice to our extraordinary abilities. But if you   59
want from us a fitting return for this meal and hospitality,
not in money or perishable and corruptible favors, but one
far above you and your way of life, a gift the fame of which
shall reach the skies and touch the stars, hand over this
child Sosipatra to us who are more truly her parents and
fathers, and until the fifth year from now fear neither disease for the little girl nor death, but remain calm and
steadfast. But take care not to set your feet on this soil till   60
the fifth year comes with the annual revolutions of the
sun.[80] And of its own accord wealth shall spring up for you
and shall blossom forth from the soil. Moreover, not only
will your daughter not be like a woman or a human being,
but you yourself also will come to believe in a higher calling regarding the child. Now if you have a good feeling
about this, accept our words with outspread hands; but if
you have any suspicions, forget we said anything." Hearing   61
this the father bit his tongue, and humble and awestruck
led the child by the hand and entrusted her to them. Then
he summoned his steward and said to him: "Supply the old
men with all that they need and let them be." Thus he   62
spoke, and before the light of dawn began to appear he
departed as though fleeing from his daughter and his estate.

[80] Cf. Hom. *Il.* 2.551.

30 εὐνοίας A Go: εὐοινίας Boiss Gi   31 μηδενός . . . μὴ A:
μὴδὲ νόσ‹ον› . . . μὴδὲ Go   32 ‹οὐ› addidi

63
30G
64

468B

65

66

67

68

Οἱ δὲ παραλαβόντες τὸ παιδίον (εἴτε ἥρωες, εἴτε
δαίμονες, εἴτε τι θειότερον ἦσαν γένος), τίσι μὲν συν-
ετέλουν αὐτὴν μυστηρίοις ἐγίνωσκεν οὐδὲ εἷς καὶ
πρὸς τί τὴν παῖδα ἐξεθείαζον ἀφανὲς ἦν καὶ τοῖς πάνυ
βουλομένοις εἰδέναι. ὁ δὲ χρόνος ἤδη προσῄει, καὶ τά
τε ἄλλα πάντα συνέτρεχε προσόδων πέρι τοῦ χωρίου,
καὶ ὁ πατὴρ τῆς παιδὸς παρῆν εἰς τὸν ἀγρόν, | καὶ
οὔτε τὸ μέγεθος ἐπέγνω τῆς παιδός, τό τε κάλλος ἑτε-
ροῖον αὐτῷ κατεφαίνετο· τὸν δὲ πατέρα σχεδόν τι καὶ
ἠγνόει. ὁ δὲ καὶ προσεκύνησεν αὐτήν, οὕτως ἄλλην
τινὰ ὁρᾶν ἔδοξεν. ὡς δὲ οἵ τε διδάσκαλοι παρῆσαν
καὶ ἡ τράπεζα προὔκειτο, οἱ μὲν ἔφασαν· "ἐρώτα ὅ τι
βούλει τὴν παρθένον." ἡ δὲ ὑπέλαβεν· "ἀλλὰ ἐρώτη-
σόν γε, πάτερ, τί σοι πέπρακται κατὰ τὴν ὁδόν." τοῦ
δὲ εἰπεῖν ἐπιτρέψαντος (διὰ δὲ εὐδαιμονίαν ἐπὶ τετρα-
κύκλου ὀχήματος ἐφέρετο· συμβαίνει δὲ πολλὰ ἐπὶ
τοῖς τοιούτοις ὀχήμασι πάθη), πάντα οὕτως ἐξήγγει-
λεν φωνάς τε καὶ ἀπειλὰς καὶ φόβους, ὥσπερ αὐτὴ
συνηνιοχοῦσα· καὶ εἰς τοσόνδε προῄει θαύματος ὁ
πατήρ ὥστε οὐκ ἐθαύμαζεν, ἀλλὰ κατεπλήττετο καὶ
θεὸν εἶναι τὴν παῖδα ἐπέπειστο. προσπεσὼν δὲ τοῖς
ἀνδράσιν, ἱκέτευεν εἰπεῖν οἵτινες εἶεν· οἱ δὲ μόλις καὶ
βραδέως (δόξαν δὲ ἴσως οὕτω καὶ θεῷ) παρέφηναν
εἶναι τῆς Χαλδαϊκῆς καλουμένης σοφίας οὐκ ἀμύητοι, καὶ τοῦτο δι᾽ αἰνίγματος καὶ κάτω νεύοντες. ὡς δὲ
ὁ τῆς Σωσιπάτρας πατὴρ προσπεσὼν τοῖς γόνασιν

81 For the verb, cf. Plut. *Rom.* 28, *Sert.* 11; Julian. *Gal.* 155d.

Then those men took charge of the child—whether 63
they were heroes or demigods or of some species still more
divine—but no one knew into what mysteries they initiated her, and it was not apparent to what end they made
the girl divine,[81] not even to those who were most eager
to learn. And soon came the appointed time, and all the 64
other matters regarding the revenues of the estate coin-
cided with it. The girl's father came to the farm and did
not recognize[82] the girl's height and her beauty itself
seemed to have changed; and she too hardly knew her
father. He even greeted her reverently, such a different 65
woman did he seem to behold. When her teachers were
present and the table was set, they said: "Ask the maiden
whatever you please." But she interposed: "father, ask me 66
what happened to you on your journey." And he left it to
her to speak. On account of his prosperity he traveled in
a four-wheeled carriage, and with this sort of carriage
many accidents are liable to happen. But she related every
event, not only what had been said, but his very perils and
fears, as though she had been on the carriage with him.
Her father came to be so full of amazement that he did 67
not merely show admiration, but was awestruck, and he
was convinced that his daughter was a divine being. Then
he fell on his knees before those men and implored them
to say who they were. And they, slowly and reluctantly
(perhaps this was also the wish of god) revealed to him that
they were not uninitiated in the wisdom called Chaldean,
and even this they told with a sense of mystery and keeping their heads turned down. And when Sosipatra's father, 68
having fallen on his knees, supplicated them, adjuring

[82] Cf. Hom. *Od.* 24.217.

EUNAPIUS

ἱκέτευεν, δεσπότας εἶναι τοῦ χωρίου παρακαλῶν καὶ
τὴν παῖδα ἔχειν ὑφ᾽ ἑαυτοῖς καὶ μυεῖν εἰς τὸ τελεώτε-
ρον, οἱ μὲν ἐπινεύσαντες ὅτι οὕτω ποιήσουσιν, οὐκέτι
ἐφθέγξαντο· ὁ δὲ ὥσπερ ἔχων ὑπόσχεσίν τινα ἢ
χρησμόν, ἐθάρσει καθ᾽ ἑαυτόν καὶ πρὸς τὸ χρῆμα |
ἠπόρει· καὶ ὑπερεπῄνει γε τὸν Ὅμηρον κατὰ ψυχὴν
ὡς ὑπερφυές τι χρῆμα καὶ δαιμόνιον τοῦτο ἀνυμνή-
σαντα·

καί τε θεοὶ ξείνοισιν ἐοικότες ἀλλοδαποῖσι,
παντοῖοι τελέθοντες, ἐπιστρωφῶσι πόληας.

καὶ γὰρ αὐτὸς ᾤετο ξένοις μὲν ἀνδράσι, θεοῖς δὲ συντετυχηκέναι. καὶ ὁ μὲν τοῦ πράγματος ἐμπιμπλάμε-
νος ὕπνῳ κατείχετο, οἱ δὲ ἀποχωρήσαντες τοῦ δεί-
πνου καὶ τὴν παῖδα παραλαβόντες, τήν τε στολὴν τῆς
ἐσθῆτος ἐν ᾗ τετέλεστο μάλα φιλοφρόνως αὐτῇ καὶ
συνεσπουδασμένως παρέδοσαν, καὶ ἄλλα τινὰ προσ-
θέντες ὄργανα καὶ τὴν κοιτίδα τῇ Σωσιπάτρᾳ κατα-
σημήνασθαι κελεύσαντες, προσεμβαλόντες τινα βι-
βλίδια. καὶ ἡ μὲν ὑπερεγάννυτο τοὺς ἄνδρας τοῦ
πατρὸς οὐκ ἔλαττον. ὡς δὲ ἕως ὑπέφαινε καὶ ἀνεῴ-
γνυντο θύραι καὶ πρὸς ἔργα ἐχώρουν ἄνθρωποι, κἀκεῖνοι τοῖς ἄλλοις συνεξέβησαν κατὰ τὸ εἰωθός. ἡ μὲν
παῖς παρὰ τὸν πατέρα ἔδραμεν εὐαγγέλια φέρουσα
καὶ τὴν κοιτίδα τῶν τις θεραπευτήρων ἐκόμιζεν· ὁ δὲ
πλοῦτόν τε ὃν εἶχε ἐς τὸ παρατυχόν ⟨συναγαγὼν⟩[33]

31G
69

70

71

72

[33] add. Go (fort. recte)

452

them to take charge of the estate and to keep his daughter under their influence and initiate her into even more sacred things, they nodded their assent to this, but without saying a word. Then he took courage as though he had received some sacred promise or oracle, but with regards to the occurrence he was at a loss. In his mind he gave 69 Homer the highest praise for having sung of such a occurrence as this, so supernatural and divine:

And the gods in the likeness of strangers from far-
    flung places
put on all manner of shapes and wander through the
    cities.[83]

He did indeed believe that he had encountered visitors in human form, but who were in fact gods.[84] While he was 70 engrossed in this incident, sleep took hold of him, and they left the table, and taking the girl with them, they very tenderly and with great care handed over to her the whole array of garments in which she had been initiated, and added certain other instruments and gave orders that she should have it sealed, after they already put some small books into Sosipatra's coffer. And she, no less than her 71 father, took the greatest delight in those men. When the day began to break and the doors were opened, and people began to go to their work, the men also went out with the rest following their routine. Then the girl ran to her father bearing the good news, and one of the servants went with her to carry the coffer. Her father, [collecting] all the 72 money that happened to be available and asking from his

[83] Cf. Hom. *Od.* 17.485–86.
[84] Cf. Hom. *Od.* 9.270–71, cited in Pl. *Soph.* 216a–b.

καὶ παρὰ τῶν οἰκονόμων ὅσον ἦν ἀναγκαῖον αὐτῇ
αἰτήσας, μετεκάλει τοὺς ἄνδρας· οἱ δὲ ἐφάνησαν οὐδαμοῦ. καὶ πρὸς τὴν Σωσιπάτραν εἶπε· "τί δὴ τοῦτό

73   ἐστιν, ὦ τέκνον;" ἡ δὲ ἐπισχοῦσα μικρόν, "ἀλλὰ νῦν
γε," ἔφη, "συνορῶ τὸ λεχθέν. ὡς γὰρ ταῦτα ἐμοὶ δα-
32G κρύοντες | ἐνεχείριζον, 'σκόπει,' ἔφασαν, 'ὦ τέκνον·
ἡμεῖς γὰρ ἐπὶ τὸν ἑσπέριον ὠκεανὸν ἐνεχθέντες,
αὐτίκα ἐπανήξομεν.'" τοῦτο συμφανέστατα δαίμονας

74   εἶναι τοὺς φανέντας ἀπήλεγξε. καὶ οἱ μὲν ἀπιόντες
ᾤχοντο ὁπηδήποτε καὶ ἀπήεσαν· ὁ δὲ πατὴρ τὴν
παῖδα παραλαβὼν τεθειασμένην καὶ σωφρόνως ἐν-
469B θουσιῶσαν, | συνεχώρει τε ζῆν ὅπως βούλεται, καὶ
περιειργάζετο τῶν κατ᾽ ἐκείνην οὐδέν, πλὴν ὅσα γε

75   πρὸς τὴν σιωπὴν αὐτῆς ἐδυσχέραινεν. ἡ δὲ προϊοῦσα
εἰς μέτρον ἀκμῆς διδασκάλων τε ἄλλων οὐ τυχοῦσα,
τά τε τῶν ποιητῶν βιβλία διὰ στόματος εἶχε καὶ φιλοσόφων καὶ ῥητόρων, καὶ ὅσα γε τοῖς πεπονηκόσι
καὶ τεταλαιπωρημένοις μόλις ὑπῆρχε καὶ ἀμυδρῶς
εἰδέναι, ταῦτα ἐκείνη μετ᾽ ὀλιγωρίας ἔφραζεν, εὐκόλως
καὶ ἀλύπως εἰς τὸ σαφὲς ἐπιτρέχουσα.

76   Ἔδοξε γοῦν αὐτῇ καὶ ἀνδρὶ συνελθεῖν. καὶ ἀναμ-
φίλεκτον ἦν ὅτι ἐξ ἁπάντων ἀνδρῶν μόνος Εὐστάθιος
ἄξιος ἦν τοῦ γάμου. ἡ δὲ πρὸς Εὐστάθιον καὶ τοὺς
παρόντας εἰποῦσα· "ἀλλ᾽ ἄκουε μὲν σύ, Εὐστάθιε,
συμμαρτυρούντων δὲ οἱ παρόντες. παῖδας μὲν ὑπὸ
σοὶ τέξομαι τρεῖς, πάντες δὲ τὸ ἀνθρώπινον δοκοῦν

stewards all that was necessary for her, sent to call those men, but they were nowhere to be seen. Then he said to Sosipatra: "What is happening, my child?" After hesitating briefly, she replied: "Now at last I understand what they said. For when they put these things into my hands with tears in their eyes, they said: 'Child, examine these; for we are being taken to the Western Ocean,[85] but we shall return presently.'" This proved very clearly that the men who had appeared were celestial beings. They then went on their way, going off and disappearing into the distance; but her father took charge of the girl, who was fully initiated and filled with divine inspiration in an unassuming way. He permitted her to live as she pleased and did not interfere in any of her affairs, except that sometimes he was ill-pleased with her tendency to remain silent. And as she grew to full maturity, she had no other teachers, but knew by heart the books of the poets, and of philosophers and orators; and all those works that are barely available and difficult to know to those who put in a lot of hard work and painful drudgery, she could expound without paying much attention, serenely and painlessly making their meaning clear with her light touch.

Then she also decided to marry. Now it was beyond dispute that of all living men Eustathius alone was worthy of this marriage. She said to him and to those who were present: "Listen to me, Eustathius, and let those who are here be witnesses with you: I shall bear three children by you, and all of them will be fortunate regarding the human

[85] Homer's ζόφος, "darkness of the West," regarded as consecrated to the heroic dead and supernatural beings.

77 ἀγαθὸν εὐτυχήσουσι,³⁴ πρὸς τὸ θεῖον δὲ εἷς. καὶ σὺ δὲ
προαπολείψεις ἐμέ, καλὴν μεταλαχὼν λῆξιν καὶ πρέπουσαν, ἐγὼ δὲ ἴσως κρείσσονα. σοὶ μὲν γὰρ περὶ
σελήνην ἡ χορεία, καὶ οὐκέτι λατρεύσεις καὶ φιλοσο-
33G φήσεις τὸ πέμπτον, οὕτω γάρ μοί φησι τὸ σὸν | εἴδω-
λον, ἀλλὰ καὶ τὸν ὑπὸ σελήνην παρελεύσῃ τόπον σὺν
78 ἀγαθῇ καὶ εὐηνίῳ φορᾷ· ἐγὼ δὲ καὶ ἐβουλόμην μὲν
εἰπεῖν τὰ κατ' ἐμαυτήν." εἶτα ἐπισιωπήσασα τῷ λόγῳ
βραχύν τινα χρόνον, "ἀλλ' ὁ ἐμός," ἀνεφθέγξατο,
79 "θεός με κωλύει." ταῦτα εἰποῦσα, Μοῖραι γὰρ οὕτως
ἔνευον, τῷ τε Εὐσταθίῳ συνῆλθε καὶ τὰ λεχθέντα οὐδὲν διέφερε τῶν ἀκινήτων μαντειῶν· οὕτω πανταχόσε
ἐγένετο καὶ ἀπέβη καθάπερ ἦν εἰρημένα.

80   Προσιστορῆσαι δὲ τοῖς γεγενημένοις τάδε ἀναγκαίως εἴη. Σωσιπάτρα, μετὰ τὴν ἀποχώρησιν Εὐσταθίου πρὸς τὰ αὑτῆς ἐπανελθοῦσα κτήματα, περὶ τὴν
Ἀσίαν καὶ τὸ παλαιὸν Πέργαμον διέτριβε· καὶ ὁ μέγας Αἰδέσιος θεραπεύων αὐτὴν ἠγάπα καὶ τοὺς παῖ-
81 δας ἐξεπαίδευε. καὶ ἀντεκάθητό γε αὐτῷ φιλοσοφοῦσα κατὰ τὴν ἑαυτῆς οἰκίαν ἡ Σωσιπάτρα, καί,
μετὰ τὴν Αἰδεσίου συνουσίαν, παρ' ἐκείνην φοιτῶντες, οὐκ ἔστιν ὅστις τὴν μὲν ἐν λόγοις ἀκρίβειαν
Αἰδεσίου ὑπερηγάπα καὶ συνεθαύμαζε, τὸν δὲ τῆς
γυναικὸς ἐνθουσιασμὸν <οὐ>³⁵ προσεκύνει καὶ ἐσεβάζετο.

³⁴ εὐτυχήσουσι Go (q.v.): ἀτυχήσουσι A
³⁵ add. Go

good, but as to the happiness that the gods bestow only one will succeed. But you will leave this world before me, and be allotted a fair and fitting end, though I shall perhaps be given a higher one. The orbit around the moon will be yours,[86] and you will not devote your services to philosophy beyond the fifth year from now (for so your aura[87] tells me), but you shall traverse the sublunar region with a blessed and easily guided motion. I would also like to tell you my own fate . . ." Then, after maintaining silence for a short time, she cried aloud: "but my god prevents me!" Having spoken these words—for the Fates approved—she married Eustathius, and her words were no different from unalterable oracles: for everything did come to pass and transpired as had been foretold by her.

I must also relate what happened after these events. After Eustathius had passed away, Sosipatra returned to her own estate, and lived in Asia in the ancient city of Pergamon; and the great Aedesius loved and cared for her and educated her sons. Sosipatra set up a chair, teaching philosophy in her own home opposite to his, and after attending the lectures of Aedesius, the students would go to hear hers; and there was not one person who greatly appreciated and admired the accurate learning of Aedesius, who did not also adore and revere the woman's inspired teaching.

77

78

79

80

81

---

[86] The moon was the home of good demons and heroes. But Sosipatra will attain as high as the ether or the sun.

[87] εἴδωλον must refer to his soul-form, which resembles his physical shape (a Chaldean notion), not his ghost.

82　　Φιλομήτωρ γοῦν τις αὐτῆς ἀνεψιὸς ὤν, τοῦ τε κάλλους ἡττηθεὶς καὶ τῶν λόγων, εἰς ἔρωτα ἀφίκετο, καὶ
τὴν γυναῖκα εἰδὼς θειοτέραν· ἔρως δὲ καὶ συνηνάγ-
καζε καὶ κατεβιάζετο. καὶ ὁ μὲν ἀμφὶ ταῦτα ἦν πολύς
καὶ ἡ γυνὴ συνῃσθάνετο τῆς πείρας· καὶ πρὸς τὸν
Μάξιμον (οὗτος δὲ ἀνὰ τὰ πρῶτα τῆς ὁμιλίας ἐφέρετο
83　　τοῦ Αἰδεσίου, καὶ οὐδὲ συγγενείας κεχώριστο)· "ἀλλὰ
κατάμαθέ γε, ὦ Μάξιμε, ἵνα μὴ πράγματα ἐγὼ ἔχω,
τί τὸ περὶ ἐμὲ πάθος ἐστί." τοῦ δὲ ὑπολαβόντος· "τί
γάρ ἐστι τὸ πάθος;" ἂν μὲν παρῇ Φιλομήτωρ," ἔφη
34G　　πρὸς αὐτόν, "Φιλομήτωρ γέ ἐστι, καὶ | διαφέρει τῶν
84　　πολλῶν ὑμῶν οὐδὲ ἕν· ἂν δὲ ἀποχωροῦντα θεάσωμαι,
δάκνεταί μου καὶ στρέφεταί πως πρὸς τὴν ἔξοδον ἔνδον ἡ καρδία." "ἀλλ' ὅπως ἀθλήσῃς περὶ ἐμοὶ καὶ
θεοφιλὲς ἐπιδείξῃ τι," προσέθηκεν. καὶ ὁ μὲν Μάξιμος
470B　　ἐξῄει τοιαῦτα ἀκηκοώς, | ὑπέρογκος ὤν, ὡς ἂν ἤδη
τοῖς θεοῖς ὁμιλῶν, ὅτι ὑπὸ τοσαύτης γυναικὸς τοιαῦτα
85　　ἐπεπίστευτο. Φιλομήτωρ δὲ τοῖς προτεθεῖσιν ἐνέκειτο.
Μάξιμος δὲ ἀντενέκειτο, διὰ σοφίας μὲν θυτικῆς
καταμαθὼν ῷτινι κέχρηται, βιαιοτέρῳ τε καὶ δυνατω-
τέρῳ καταλύσας τὸ ἔλαττον. καὶ ὁ μὲν ταῦτα συντελέ-
σας ὁ Μάξιμος ἔδραμε παρὰ τὴν Σωσιπάτραν καὶ
παραφυλάττειν ἠξίου μάλα ἀκριβῶς, εἰ τὸ αὐτὸ τοῦ
86　　λοιποῦ πείσεται· ἡ δὲ οὐκέτι πάσχειν ἔφη καὶ τήν τε
εὐχὴν ἀπήγγειλε τῷ Μαξίμῳ καὶ τὴν ἅπασαν πρᾶξιν,
καὶ τήν γε ὥραν προσέθηκεν, ὥσπερ συμπαροῦσα,
καθ' ἣν ταῦτα ἔπραττεν, καὶ τὰ φαν‹θ›έντα[36] ἀνεκά-

458

Now a certain Philometor, a cousin of hers, overcome   82
by her beauty and eloquence, came to desire her passionately, even though he had come to understand that the
woman was of a more divine nature; but passion compelled him and completely overpowered him. And Philometor was totally absorbed by this, and the woman felt
the effect of his advances. So she said to Maximus, who
was one of the most distinguished pupils of Aedesius and
not far removed from him in kinship: "Maximus, please   83
find out what emotion has come upon me, so that I may
not be troubled by it." When he inquired: "What passion
is this?" she replied: "When Philometor is with me, he is
just Philometor, and in no way different from all of you.
But whenever I see him leave, my heart within me aches   84
and somehow tries to find a way out. Please make an effort
on my behalf," she added, "and do something that pleases
the gods." When he had heard this, Maximus went away
puffed up with pride as though he were now associating
with the gods, because so wonderful a woman had entrusted him with such a task. But Philometor pressed on   85
with his plans. Maximus for his part strove to counteract
him and, having discovered through his skill in sacrificial
ritual what kind of power Philometor had used, to dissolve
the weaker spell by one more potent and efficacious.
When Maximus had completed this rite, he hastened to
Sosipatra, and bade her to observe carefully whether she
would have the same sensations in future. But she replied   86
that she no longer felt them, and described to Maximus
his own prayer and the whole ceremony; she also added
the hour at which he had applied this, as though she had

---

36 φαν‹θ›έντα Go (cf. VPS 29.8, 49.20 etc.): φανέντα A

λυψε σημεῖα. τοῦ δὲ πεσόντος ἐπὶ τὴν γῆν ἀχανοῦς
καὶ θεᾶν ἄντικρυς εἶναι τὴν Σωσιπάτραν ὁμολογοῦν-
τος, "ἀνίστω," φησίν, "ὦ τέκνον· θεοί σε φιλοῦσιν,
ἐὰν σὺ πρὸς ἐκείνους βλέπῃς καὶ μὴ ῥέπῃς ἐπὶ τὰ
87   γήϊνα καὶ ἐπίκηρα χρήματα." καὶ ὁ μὲν ταῦτα ἀκούσας, ἐξῄει μεγαλαυχότερος γεγονώς, ὡς καὶ τῆς κατὰ
τὴν γυναῖκα θειότητός γε ἀσφαλῶς πεπειραμένος. ὁ
δὲ Φιλομήτωρ φαιδρὸς ἀπήντα περὶ θύρας αὐτῷ μετὰ
88   πολλῶν ἑταίρων εἰσιών· ὁ δὲ πόρρωθεν μέγα φθεγξά-
μενος εἶπεν ὁ Μάξιμος· "τοὺς θεούς σοι, Φιλομήτωρ
35G   [εἶπε]³⁷ ἑταῖρε, παῦσαι μάτην | κατακαίων τὰ ξύλα,"
ἐνεωρακώς τι τοιοῦτον ἴσως αὐτῷ περὶ ἃ κακουργῶν
89   ἔπραττεν. καὶ ὁ μὲν τὸν Μάξιμον ὑπερευλαβηθεὶς
θεὸν ᾠήθη καὶ τῆς γε ἐπιβουλῆς ἐπαύσατο, καταγελάσας τῆς προθέσεως ὅ τι καὶ ἐνεχείρησεν· ἡ δὲ
Σωσιπάτρα γνησίως καὶ διαφερόντως ἑώρα τοῦ λοιποῦ τὸν Φιλομήτορα, θαυμάζουσα αὐτὸν ὅτι αὐτὴν
ἐθαύμασε.

90   ποτὲ γοῦν συνεληλυθότων ἁπάντων παρ᾽ αὐτῇ
(Φιλομήτωρ δὲ οὐ παρῆν, ἀλλ᾽ ἐν ἀγρῷ διέτριβεν), ἡ
91   μὲν πρόθεσις ἦν καὶ τὸ ζήτημα περὶ ψυχῆς· πολλῶν
δὲ κινουμένων λόγων, ὡς ἤρξατο Σωσιπάτρα λέγειν,
κατὰ μικρὸν ταῖς ἀποδείξεσι διαλύουσα τὰ προβαλ-
λόμενα, εἶτα εἰς τὸν περὶ καθόδου ψυχῆς καὶ τί τὸ
κολαζόμενον καὶ τί τὸ ἀθάνατον αὐτῆς ἐμπίπτουσα
λόγον, μεταξὺ τοῦ κορυβαντιασμοῦ καὶ τῆς ἐκβακ-

³⁷ del. Go

been present, and revealed to him the signs that had appeared. And when he fell to the earth in astonishment and conceded that Sosipatra was an outright goddess, she said: "Rise, my son. The gods love you if you raise your eyes to them and do not lean toward earthly and perishable riches." On hearing this he went away more uplifted with   87
pride than before, having now experienced beyond doubt the woman's divine nature. Near the door he was met by Philometor who, looking pleased with himself, was entering in the company of many friends. Raising his voice   88
Maximus called out to him from some distance: "My dear Philometor, I adjure you by the gods, cease to burn wood to no purpose," perhaps because he had become aware of the suspicious ritual in which the other was engaged. Thereupon Philometor was overawed by Maximus, be-   89
lieved him to be divine, and ceased his plotting, ridiculing the plan and the fact that he had also undertaken it. And ever since Sosipatra beheld Philometor with unaffected and changed eyes, though she admired him for so greatly admiring herself.

Once, for example, when they had all gathered at her   90
house—Philometor however was not present but was staying in the country—the topic of discussion and their inquiry was concerning the soul.[88] Many arguments were   91
propounded, and then Sosipatra began to speak, and gradually by her proofs resolved the points brought forward; then she came to discuss the descent of the soul, and what part of it is subject to punishment, what part immortal, when in the midst of her corybantic and bacchic

[88] Perhaps reading Plato's *Phaedo*.

χεύσεως, ὥσπερ ἀποκοπεῖσα τὴν φωνήν, ἐσιώπησε
καὶ βραχὺν ἐλλιποῦσα χρόνον, "τί τοῦτο;" ἀνεβόησεν
εἰς μέσους· "ὁ συγγενὴς Φιλομήτωρ φερόμενος ἐπ'
ὀχήματος, τό τε ὄχημα κατά τινα δυσχωρίαν περι-
92 τέτραπται, κἀκεῖνος κινδυνεύει περὶ τὼ σκέλη· ἀλλ'
ἐξηρήκασί γε αὐτὸν οἱ θεράποντες ὑγιαίνοντα, πλὴν
ὅσα περὶ τοῖς ἀγκῶσι καὶ χερσὶ τραύματα εἴληφε καὶ
ταῦτά γε ἀκίνδυνα· ἐπὶ φορείου δὲ φέρεται ποτνιώμε-
93 νος." ταῦτα ἔλεγε καὶ εἶχεν οὕτως, καὶ πάντες ᾔδεσαν
ὅτι πανταχοῦ εἴη Σωσιπάτρα, καὶ πᾶσι πάρεστι τοῖς
γινομένοις, ὥσπερ οἱ φιλόσοφοι περὶ τῶν θεῶν λέ-
γουσι.

94   Καὶ ἐτελεύτα γε ἐπὶ τοῖς τρισὶ παισί. καὶ τῶν μὲν
36G δύο τὰ ὀνόματα οὐδὲν δέομαι γράφειν. Ἀντωνῖνος | δὲ
ἦν ἄξιος τῶν πατέρων, ὅς γε τὸ Κανωβικὸν τοῦ Νείλου καταλαβὼν στόμα καὶ τοῖς ἐκεῖ τελουμένοις
προσθεὶς ὅλον ἑαυτόν τήν γε ἀπὸ τῆς μητρὸς πρόρ-
95 ρησιν ἐξεβιάζετο. καὶ ἡ νεότης τῶν ὑγιαινόντων τὰς
ψυχὰς καὶ φιλοσοφίας ἐπιθυμούντων ἐφοίτων πρὸς
471B αὐτόν | καὶ τὸ ἱερὸν νεανίσκων ἱερέων μεστὸν ἦν.
96 αὐτὸς μὲν οὖν ἔτι ἄνθρωπος εἶναι δοκῶν καὶ ἀνθρώποις ὁμιλῶν πᾶσι τοῖς ὁμιληταῖς προὔλεγεν ὡς μετ'
ἐκεῖνον οὐκ ἔτι τὸ ἱερὸν ἔσοιτο, ἀλλὰ καὶ τὰ μεγάλα
καὶ ἅγια τοῦ Σεράπιδος ἱερὰ πρὸς τὸ σκοτοειδὲς καὶ
ἄμορφον χωρήσει καὶ μεταβληθήσεται, καί το μυθῶδες καὶ ἀειδὲς σκότος τυραννήσει τὰ ἐπὶ γῆς κάλλιστα. ὁ δὲ χρόνος ἀπήλεγξεν ἄπαντα καὶ τὸ πρᾶγμά
γε εἰς χρησμοῦ συνετελέσθη βίαν.

trance, she became silent, as though her voice had been cut off, and after letting a short interval pass, she cried aloud in their midst: "What is this? My kinsman Philometor is being carried in a wagon! The wagon has been overturned in a rough place in the road and both his legs are at risk! But wait, his servants have dragged him out unharmed, except that he has received wounds on his elbows and hands, though even these are not dangerous. He is being carried home on a stretcher, groaning loudly." These were her words, and it actually happened this way. All now knew for sure that Sosipatra was everywhere and is present at all things that come about, much like the philosophers assert about the gods.

Sosipatra died leaving the three sons of whom she had spoken. The names of two of them I need not record. But Antoninus was worthy of his parents, for he arrived at the Canobic mouth of the Nile and having devoted himself wholly to the religious rites of that place, strove with all his powers to fulfill his mother's prophecy. To him resorted all the youth whose souls were sane and sound, and who hungered for philosophy, and the temple was filled with young men acting as priests. Though he himself still appeared to be human and mingled with human beings, he foretold to all his followers that after his death[89] the temple would cease to exist, and even the great and holy temples of Serapis would pass into formless darkness and be transformed, and that an unsightly gloom resembling the one from old myths would hold sway over the fairest things on earth. All these prophecies were born out over time, and the event played out with the force of an oracle.

[89] Antoninus died in 390; the temple was destroyed in 391.

97   Τούτου δὲ τοῦ γένους (οὐ γὰρ τὰς Ἡσιόδου κα-
λουμένας Ἠοίας ἔσπευδον γράφειν), ἀπόρροιαί τινες
ὥσπερ ἀστέρων περιελείφθησαν, καὶ εἰς φιλοσοφούντων ἕτερα ἄττα γένη διεσπάρησαν καὶ κατενεμήθη-
98 σαν, οἷς τοῦ φιλοσοφεῖν ἡ συγγένεια κέρδος ἦν. τὰ
πλεῖστα δὲ ἐν δικαστηρίοις, ὥσπερ ὁ Σωκράτης περὶ
τὴν τοῦ βασιλέως στοάν, ἐκινδύνευον· οὕτω περιεφρό-
99 νησαν χρήματα καὶ κατεστύγησαν χρυσίον. ἦν γοῦν
αὐτοῖς φιλοσοφία (τὸ τριβώνιον καὶ τὸ μεμνῆσθαι
τῆς Σωσιπάτρας), καὶ τὸν Εὐστάθιον διὰ στόματος
φέρειν, τὰ δὲ ἐν τοῖς ὁρωμένοις σακκία τε ἁδρὰ καὶ
ὑπόμεστα βιβλιδίων, καὶ ταῦτα ὡς ἂν ἄχθος εἶναι
100 καμήλων πολλῶν. καὶ ἐξηπίσταντό γε πάνυ ἀκριβῶς
τὰ βιβλία· καὶ ταῦτά γε ἦν εἰς οὐδένα φέροντα τῶν
37G παλαιῶν φιλοσόφων, ἀλλὰ | διαθῆκαί τε καὶ ἀντί-
γραφα τούτων, καὶ συμβόλαια περὶ ⟨ὠνῶν καὶ⟩[38]
πράσεων, καὶ ὅσα ὁ κακοδαίμων καὶ ὁ πρὸς τὴν πλα-
νωμένην καὶ ἄτακτον ἄτην ἐπικλίνων βίος ἐπαινεῖν
101 εἴωθεν. οὕτως οὐδὲ ἕν τοῖς μετὰ ταῦτα Σωσιπάτρα ἐς
τὸν χρησμὸν ἀπετύγχανε· καὶ τούτων γε τὰ ὀνόματα
οὐδὲν δέομαι γράφειν—ὁ γὰρ λόγος οὐκ ἐπὶ τοὺς
φαύλους ἀλλ' ἐπὶ τοὺς ἀγαθοὺς φέρειν συνεπείγε-
102 ται—, πλὴν ὅσα εἰς αὐτῆς τῶν παίδων (Ἀντωνῖνος ἦν
ὄνομα αὐτῷ, οὗ καὶ πρὸ βραχέος ἐπεμνήσθην, ὁ διαβαλὼν ἐς τὴν Ἀλεξάνδρειαν, εἶτα τὸ Κανωβικὸν θαυμάσας τε καὶ ὑπεραγασθεὶς τοῦ Νείλου στόμα, καὶ

---

[38] ὠνῶν καὶ περὶ Go (cf. Hdt. 1.135)

From this family—for it is not my purpose to write a poem like the so-called *Eoiae*[90] of Hesiod—certain influential emanations have survived like those from stars.[91] And these went their own way and ended up with various families of philosophers for whom familiarity with philosophizing gave them financial benefit. They spent most of their time in dangerous law cases, like Socrates in the porch of the chief Archon.[92] This is how they despised riches and expressed their disgust of gold! In fact, for them philosophy consisted in wearing the philosopher's cloak, reminiscing about Sosipatra and constantly talking about Eustathius. Moreover, they carried other obvious and external signs, large leather pouches so crammed with small books that would have been quite a load for camels. While they had indeed very accurate knowledge of the books, these had also no bearing on any of the ancient philosophers, but were wills and copies of wills, contracts regarding [purchases and] sales, which that ill-fated life, inclined to aimless and unruly blindness, tends to glorify. Thus it proved that Sosipatra did not get one thing wrong in view of her prediction as to what should happen after these events. But I need not write down even the names of these men, for my narrative is eager to lead on, not to those who are morally inferior, but to those who are morally upright.[93] An exception must be made for one of her sons; his name was Antoninus, and I mentioned him a little earlier; he crossed to Alexandria, and then so greatly admired and preferred the mouth of the Nile at Canobus,

97

98

99

100

101

102

---

90 A genealogical poem not extant (Paus. 2.16.4).
91 See Plot. *Enn*. 2.3.11.   92 Pl. *Euthyphr*. 2a–c, *Tht*. 210d.
93 Restatement of the aim from 1.1–2.

τοῖς ἐκείνῃ θεοῖς τε καὶ ἀρρήτοις ἱεροῖς ἀναθεὶς καὶ
προσαρμόσας ἑαυτόν) ταχὺ μάλα πρὸς τὴν τοῦ θείου
συγγένειαν ἐπέδωκε, σώματός τε περιφρονήσας καὶ
τῶν περὶ τοῦτο ἡδονῶν ἀπολυθείς, σοφίαν τε ἄγνωστον τοῖς πολλοῖς ἐπιτηδεύσας· περὶ οὗ προσῆκε καὶ
103 διὰ μακροτέρων εἰπεῖν. ἐπεδείκνυτο μὲν γὰρ οὐδὲν
θεουργὸν καὶ παράλογον ἐς τὴν φαινομένην αἴσθησιν, τὰς βασιλικὰς ἴσως ὁρμὰς ὑφορώμενος ἑτέρωσε
φερούσας· τοῦ δὲ τὴν καρτερίαν καὶ τὸ ἄκαμπτον καὶ
104 ἀμετάστατον ἐθαύμαζον ἅπαντες. καὶ κατῄεσάν γε
παρ' αὐτὸν ἐπὶ θάλασσαν οἱ κατὰ τὴν Ἀλεξάνδρειαν
τότε σχολάζοντες, (ἡ δὲ Ἀλεξάνδρεια διά γε τὸ τοῦ
105 Σεράπιδος ἱερὸν ἱερά τις ἦν οἰκουμένη·) οἱ γοῦν πανταχόθεν φοιτῶντες ἐς αὐτὴν πλῆθός τε ἦσαν τῷ δήμῳ
παρισούμενοι καὶ μετὰ τὰς θεραπείας τοῦ θείου παρὰ
38G τὸν Ἀντωνῖνον ἔτρεχον, οἱ μὲν διὰ γῆς, ὅσοι γε | ἔτρε-
χον, τοῖς δὲ ἐξήρκει τὰ ποτάμια πλοῖα μετὰ ῥᾳστώνης
106 ἐπὶ τὴν σπουδὴν ὑποφέροντες. συνουσίας δὲ ἀξιωθέν-
τες, οἱ μὲν λογικὸν πρόβλημα προθέμενοι ἀφθόνως
καὶ αὐθωρὸν τῆς Πλατωνικῆς ἐνεφοροῦντο σοφίας, |
472B οἱ δὲ τῶν θειοτέρων τι προβάλλοντες ἀνδριάντι συν-
ετύγχανον· οὐκοῦν ἐφθέγγετο πρὸς αὐτῶν οὐδένα,
ἀλλὰ τὰ ὄμματα στήσας καὶ διαθρήσας εἰς τὸν οὐ-
ρανόν, ἄναυδος ἔκειτο καὶ ἄτεγκτος, οὐδέ τις εἶδεν
αὐτὸν περὶ τῶν τοιούτων ῥᾳδίως εἰς ὁμιλίαν ἐλθόντα
ἀνθρώπων.

466

that he wholly dedicated and applied himself to worship of the gods there, and to their secret rites. He made rapid progress toward affinity with the divine, despised his body, freed himself from its pleasures, and embraced a wisdom that was hidden from the crowd.[94] It is appropriate to speak about him at greater length. He displayed no tendency to anything theurgic and supernatural with regard to perceptible appearances, perhaps because he suspected that the imperial views tended in the opposite direction.[95] But all admired his perseverance, his inflexibility and his steadfastness. Those who were then pursuing their studies at Alexandria used to go down to him to the seashore. For, on account of its temple of Serapis, Alexandria was a sacred world in itself; at any rate those who came there from all directions were a multitude equal in number to its own population, and these, after worship of the divine, used to hasten to Antoninus, some by land, while others were content with river boats, gliding in a leisurely way to their studies. Having been considered worthy to see him, some who propounded a logical problem, filled themselves plentifully and immediately with Platonic wisdom; but others, who put forward a question on more divine topics, encountered a statue. For he would not utter a word to any one of them, but fixing his eyes and gazing up at the sky, he would remain speechless and unrelenting, nor did anyone ever see him lightly enter into conversation with any man on such topics.

103

104

105

106

94 Features that echo Plotinus' lifestyle.
95 Cautious phrasing to avoid persecution; on those suspected of sorcery, see Amm. Marcell. 28.1.

107   Ὅτι δὲ ἦν τι θειότερον τὸ κατ᾽ αὐτόν, οὐκ εἰς μακρὰν ἀπεσημάνθη· οὐ γὰρ ἔφθανεν ἐκεῖνος ἐξ ἀνθρώπων ἀπιών, καὶ ἥ τε θεραπεία τῶν κατὰ τὴν Ἀλεξάνδρειαν καὶ τὸ Σεραπεῖον ἱερῶν³⁹ διεσκεδάννυτο· οὐχ
ἡ θεραπεία μόνον, ἀλλὰ καὶ τὰ οἰκοδομήματα, καὶ
πάντα ἐγίνετο καθάπερ ἐν ποιητικοῖς μύθοις, τῶν Γι-
108   γάντων κεκρατηκότων. καὶ τὰ περὶ τὸν Κάνωβον ἱερὰ
ταὐτὸ τοῦτο ἔπασχον, Θεοδοσίου μὲν τότε βασιλεύοντος, Θεοφίλου δὲ προστατοῦντος τῶν ἐναγῶν, ἀνθρώπου τινὸς Εὐρυμέδοντος

ὅς ποθ᾽ ὑπερθύμοισι Γιγάντεσσιν βασίλευεν,

Εὐαγρίου δὲ τὴν πολιτικὴν ἀρχὴν ἄρχοντος, Ῥωμα-
νοῦ δὲ τοὺς κατ᾽ Αἴγυπτον στρατιώτας πεπιστευμέ-
109   νου· οἵτινες, ἅμα φραξάμενοι κατὰ <τῶν ἱερῶν> λιθ<ί-
ν>ων καὶ λιθοξο<άν>ων,⁴⁰ θυμὸν ἐπὶ ταῦτα βαλλόμενοι,
39G   πολέμου δὲ μήτε | ἀκο<ὴν μήτε παρακο>ὴν⁴¹ ὑφιστά-
μενοι, τῷ τε Σεραπείῳ κατελυμήναντο καὶ τοῖς ἀνα-
θήμασιν ἐπολέμησαν, ἀνανταγώνιστον καὶ ἄμαχον
110   νίκην νικήσαντες. τοῖς γοῦν ἀνδριάσι καὶ ἀναθήμα-
σιν ἐς τοσόνδε γενναίως ἐμαχέσαντο, ὥστε οὐ μόνον
ἐνίκων αὐτά, ἀλλὰ καὶ ἔκλεπτον, καὶ τάξις ἦν αὐτοῖς
111   πολεμικὴ τὸν ὑφελόμενον λαθεῖν. τοῦ δὲ Σεραπείου
μόνον τὸ ἔδαφος οὐχ ὑφείλοντο διὰ βάρος τῶν λίθων,

---

39 ἱερῶν Wytt Vollebr Go: ἱερὸν A Gi
40 λιθ<ίν>ων καὶ λιθοξο<άν>ων coni. Gi, acc. Go: λίθων καὶ
λιθοξόων A Wr   41 inser. Go

Now, not long after, a sign was given that there was in   107
him a more divine element. For as soon as he had left the
world of men, the worship in the temples in Alexandria
and at the shrine of Serapis was disbanded, and not only
the activities of worship but the buildings as well, and everything happened as in the myths of the poets when the
Giants gained the upper hand. The temples at Canobus   108
also suffered the same fate in the reign of Theodosius,
when Theophilus[96] presided over the abominable ones
like a sort of Eurymedon

Who ruled over the proud Giants,[97]

and Evagrius was prefect of the city, and Romanus in command of the legions in Egypt.[98] For these men, having   109
prepared themselves for battle against [the sacred places]
made of stone and adorned with marble statues, setting
their mind on these and with no basis in a pretext nor even
a rumor of war, demolished the temple of Serapis and
made war against the temple offerings, whereby they won
a victory without meeting a foe or fighting a battle. In this   110
fashion they fought so "nobly" against the statues and votive offerings that they not only conquered them, but stole
them as well, and their only military tactics were to ensure
that the thief should escape detection. Only the floor of   111
the temple of Serapis they did not take, simply because of

96 Christian bishop of Alexandria (Zos. v. 28; Theodor. v. 22).
97 Hom. *Od.* 7.59.
98 Sozom. 7.15 gives the Christian account of the conversion
of the Serapeum into a church.

οὐ γὰρ ἦσαν εὐμετακίνητοι· συγχέαντες δὲ ἅπαντα
καὶ ταράξαντες, οἱ πολεμικώτατοι καὶ γενναῖοι, καὶ
τὰς χεῖρας ἀναιμάκτους μέν, οὐκ ἀφιλοχρημάτους δὲ
προτείναντες, τούς τε θεοὺς ἔφασαν νενικηκέναι καὶ
τὴν ἱεροσυλίαν καὶ τὴν ἀσέβειαν εἰς ἔπαινον σφῶν
αὐτῶν κατελογίζοντο.

112   Εἶτα ἐπεισῆγον τοῖς ἱεροῖς τόποις τοὺς καλουμέ-
νους μοναχούς, ἀνθρώπους μὲν κατὰ τὸ εἶδος, ὁ δὲ
βίος αὐτοῖς συώδης, καὶ ἐς τὸ ἐμφανὲς ἔπασχόν τε
καὶ ἐποίουν μυρία κακὰ καὶ ἄφραστα. ἀλλ᾽ ὅμως
τοῦτο μὲν εὐσεβὲς ἐδόκει, τὸ καταφρονεῖν τοῦ θείου·
113   τυραννικὴν γὰρ εἶχεν ἐξουσίαν τότε πᾶς ἄνθρωπος
μέλαιναν φορῶν ἐσθῆτα καὶ δημοσίᾳ βουλόμενος
ἀσχημονεῖν· εἰς τοσόνδε ἀρετῆς ἤλασε τὸ ἀνθρώπινον. ἀλλὰ περὶ τούτων μὲν καὶ ἐν τοῖς καθολικοῖς τῆς
114   ἱστορίας συγγράμμασιν εἴρηται. τοὺς δὲ μοναχοὺς
τούτους καὶ εἰς τὸν Κάνωβον καθίδρυσαν, ἀντὶ τῶν
νοητῶν θεῶν εἰς ἀνδραπόδων θεραπείας, καὶ οὐδὲ
χρηστῶν, καταδήσαντες τὸ ἀνθρώπινον. ὀστέα γὰρ
καὶ κεφαλὰς τῶν ἐπὶ πολλοῖς ἁμαρτήμασιν ἑαλω-
κότων συναλίζοντες, οὓς τὸ πολιτικὸν ἐκόλαζε δικαστήριον, θεούς τε ἀπεδείκνυσαν καὶ προσεκαλιν-
40G   δοῦντο τοῖς ὀστοῖς καὶ κρείττους ὑπελάμβανον | εἶναι
115   μολυνόμενοι πρὸς τοῖς τάφοις. μάρτυρες γοῦν ἐκαλοῦντο καὶ διάκονοί τινες καὶ πρέσβεις τῶν αἰτήσεων

99 Cf. Sozimus, 5.23.4.
100 Cf. Lib. *Or.* 30.8 (*On the Temples*).

470

the weight of the stones that were not easy to move from their place. Then these "great warriors" and "honorable men," after they had thrown everything into confusion and disorder and had stretched out their hands unstained by blood but not free from greed, boasted that they had been victorious over the gods, and counted this sacrilege and impiety among their own praiseworthy deeds.

Next, into the sacred places they imported monks, as 112 they called them, who were men in appearance but swine in lifestyle, and openly did and allowed countless unspeakable acts.[99] Yet this they considered piety, to show contempt for the divine. For in those days every person who 113 wore a black robe and was willing to display unseemly behavior in public,[100] possessed the power of a tyrant; to such a level of "virtue" had the human race advanced! All this however I have described in the comprehensive writings of my *History*.[101] They settled these monks also at 114 Canobus, and thus they fettered the human race to the worship of slaves—and not even honest slaves—instead of the intelligible gods. For they collected the bones and skulls of criminals who had been put to death for numerous crimes, men whom the citizen's law courts had condemned to punishment, made them out to be gods, haunted their sepulchers,[102] and thought that they were better than others while polluting themselves at the graves. "Witnesses" the dead men were called, and "servants" of a sort, and "ambassadors" to carry men's prayers 115

---

[101] Lit., "general writings of history."
[102] Cf. Pl. *Phd.* 81c–d; Julian. *Misop.* 344a; *Adv. Gal.* 335c. Christian churches were built over the graves of martyrs.

παρὰ τῶν θεῶν, ἀνδράποδα δεδουλευκότα κακῶς καὶ
μάστιξι καταδεδαπανημένα καὶ τὰς τῆς μοχθηρίας
116 ὠτειλὰς ἐν τοῖς εἰδώλοις φέροντα· ἀλλ' ὅμως ἡ γῆ
φέρει τούτους τοὺς θεούς. τοῦτο γοῦν εἰς μεγάλην
πρόνοιαν καὶ <εὐστοχίαν>[42] Ἀντωνίνου συνετέλεσεν, |
473B ὅτι πρὸς ἅπαντας ἔφασκε τὰ ἱερὰ τάφους γενήσε-
117 σθαι· (ὥσπερ που καὶ Ἰάμβλιχος ὁ μέγας—ὅπερ ἐν
τοῖς κατ' ἐκεῖνον παραλελοίπαμεν—, ἀνδρός τινος Αἰ-
γυπτίου τὸν Ἀπόλλω καλέσαντος, τοῦ δὲ ἐλθόντος,
καὶ καταπλαγέντων τὴν ὄψιν τῶν παρόντων, "παύσα-
σθε," εἶπεν, "ἑταῖροι, θαυμάζοντες· μονομαχήσαντος
γὰρ ἀνδρός ἐστιν εἴδωλον," οὕτως ἕτερόν τί ἐστι τῷ
νῷ θεωρεῖν καὶ τοῖς τοῦ σώματος ἀπατηλοῖς ὄμμασιν.
ἀλλ' Ἰάμβλιχος μὲν τὰ παρόντα δεινὰ <εἶδεν>,[43] Ἀντωνῖνος δὲ τὰ μέλλοντα προεῖδεν· καὶ τοῦτό γε αὐτοῦ
118 μόνον ἀσθένειαν[44] φέρει. ἄλυπον δὲ αὐτῷ τὸ τέλος εἰς
γῆρας ἄνοσον ἀφικομένῳ καὶ βαθύ, καὶ λυπηρὸν τοῖς
νοῦν ἔχουσι τὸ προεγνωσμένον ἐκείνῳ τῶν ἱερῶν
τέλος.

7. [Μάξιμος][45] Μαξίμου καὶ πρότερον ἐμνήσθημεν,
καὶ ὁ ταῦτα γράφων οὐκ ἦν ἀθέατος τοῦ ἀνδρός,
ἀλλὰ νέος ἔτι γηραιῷ συνετύγχανε καὶ φωνῆς τε
ἤκουσεν, οἵας ἄν τις ἤκουσε τῆς Ὁμηρικῆς Ἀθηνᾶς ἢ
τοῦ Ἀπόλλωνος. τῷ δὲ καὶ πτηναὶ μέν τινες ἦσαν αἱ
τῶν ὀμμάτων κόραι, πολιὸν δὲ καθεῖτο γένειον, τὰς δὲ

[42] καὶ A Civil: καὶ <εὐστοχίαν> Boiss Go Be
[43] εἶδεν add. Wytt Cob; post μὲν add. Go

472

to the gods; these slaves in vilest servitude, who were covered by wounds from the whip and carried on their ghostly shapes the scars of their depravity.[103] But nevertheless, the earth produces these kind of gods. This, then, greatly increased the reputation of Antoninus also for foresight, in that he had foretold to all that the temples would become tombs.[104] In the same way that the great Iamblichus—this I passed over in my account of his life—when a certain Egyptian invoked Apollo, and, to the great amazement of those who saw the vision, Apollo came, said "My friends, cease to wonder; this is only the specter of a gladiator," so different it is to see a thing with the mind or with the deceitful eyes of the body. But while Iamblichus saw the dangers that were present, Antoninus on the other hand foresaw things that were to come. This point at least conveys his only weakness. His end was painless when he had attained to a ripe old age free from sickness, although to all intelligent men the end of the temples that he had predicted was painful.

7. Maximus. I have mentioned Maximus previously and indeed the author of this work actually saw this man with his own eyes, although he met him in his old age when he was still a youth and heard his voice, which was like hearing Homer's Athena or Apollo. The very pupils of his eyes were like wings; he had a long gray beard, and his eyes

116

117

118

103 An echo of Pl. *Grg*. 524e.
104 Cf. Julian. *Or*. 7.228c.

---

44 ἀσθένειαν A Gi Go: εὐσθένειαν coni. Wr
45 In A, f. 232r.

41G
2 ὁρμὰς τῆς ψυχῆς διεδήλου τὰ | ὄμματα. καὶ ἁρμονία
γέ τις ἐπῆν καὶ ἀκούοντι καὶ ὁρῶντι, καὶ δι᾽ ἀμφοῖν
τῶν αἰσθήσεων ὁ συνὼν ἐπλήττετο, οὔτε τὴν ὀξυκινη-
σίαν φέρων τῶν ὀμμάτων οὔτε τὸν δρόμον τῶν λό-
3 γων. ἀλλ᾽ οὐδὲ εἴ τις τῶν ἐμπειροτάτων πάνυ καὶ δει-
νῶν διελέγετο πρὸς αὐτόν, ἀντιλέγειν ἐτόλμα, ἀλλ᾽
ἡσυχῇ παραδόντες αὑτούς, τοῖς λεγομένοις ὥσπερ ἐκ
τριπόδων εἴποντο· τοσαύτη τις ἀφροδίτη τοῖς χείλεσιν ἐπεκάθητο.

4   Ἦν μὲν οὖν τῶν εὖ γεγονότων καὶ πλοῦτος ἁδρότε-
ρος ὑπῆν αὐτῷ, ἀδελφοὺς δὲ εἶχε γνησίους, οὓς
ἐκώλυεν εἶναι πρώτους αὐτὸς ὤν, Κλαυδιανόν τε τὸν
καταλαβόντα τὴν Ἀλεξάνδρειαν κἀκεῖ παιδεύσαντα
καὶ Νυμφιδιανὸν τὸν ἐν Σμύρνῃ περιφανῶς σοφι-
στεύσαντα.

5   Ἦν δὲ ὁ ἀνὴρ οὗτος τῶν διαπλησθέντων τῆς Αἰδεσίου σοφίας. Ἰουλιανοῦ δὲ τοῦ βασιλεύσαντος
ἠξιώθη γενέσθαι διδάσκαλος. οὗτος, πάντων[46] ἀνῃ-
ρημένων ὑπὸ τοῦ Κωνσταντίου (ταῦτα δὲ ἐν τοῖς
κατὰ Ἰουλιανὸν ἀκριβέστερον γέγραπται), καὶ ψιλω-
θέντος τοῦ γένους, [Ἰουλιανὸς][47] περιελείφθη μόνος,
6 δι᾽ ἡλικίαν περιφρονηθεὶς καὶ πρᾳότητα. εὐνοῦχοι δὲ
αὐτὸν ὅμως ἀμφεπόλευον βασιλικοὶ καὶ παραφυλα-
καί τινες ἦσαν, ὅπως εἴη χριστιανὸς βέβαιος· ὁ δὲ
καὶ πρὸς ταῦτα τὸ μέγεθος τῆς φύσεως ἐπεδείκνυτο.

---

[46] πάντων ⟨τῶν οἰκείων⟩ Go
[47] del. Cob Go

brought out the emotions of his soul. There was also a   2
certain inner calmness about him to anyone hearing
or seeing him, and in his presence one would be overwhelmed through both sense organs,[105] unable to endure
his rapid eye movements[106] or the swift flow of his words.
Nor did anyone among the most experienced and most   3
eloquent in discussion with him dare to contradict him,
but they surrendered to him in silence and acquiesced in
what he said as though it came from an oracle; such was
the wonderful charm on his lips.

He came from a respectable family and possessed con-   4
siderable wealth. He also had two brothers. His primacy
kept them from the first rank. Claudian[107] took over Alexandria when he taught there and Nymphidianus was a
renowned public speaker in Smyrna.[108]

Maximus was among those who had been imbued with   5
the wisdom of Aedesius; moreover, he was considered
worthy of being the teacher of the future emperor Julian.
The latter, after all [his relatives] had been put to death by
Constantius (I have recorded this in more detail in my
writings concerning the time of Julian), and having been
robbed of his whole family, he alone survived due to
a disdain for his tender years and his mild disposition.
Nevertheless, eunuchs from the palace took charge of   6
him, and there were some guards to make sure that he
would become a firm Christian. But even in the face of
these difficulties he displayed the greatness of his nature.

---

105 That is, eyes and ears.
106 ὀξυκινησία is rare: cf. Porph. ap. Eus. *PE* 3.1.2.
107 Possibly the father of the poet Claudian (fl. 400).
108 See *VPS* 18.

7 πάντα γοῦν οὕτω διὰ στόματος εἶχε τὰ βιβλία, ὥστε
ἠγανάκτουν ἐκεῖνοι πρὸς τὴν βραχύτητα τῆς παι-
8 δείας, ὡς οὐκ ἔχοντες ὅ τι διδάξουσι τὸ παιδίον. ὡς
δὲ οὔτε ἐκεῖνοι παιδεύειν εἶχον οὔτε Ἰουλιανὸς μανθά-
νειν, ἐξῄτησεν⁴⁸ τὸν ἀνεψιὸν ἐπιτραπῆναί οἱ⁴⁹ καὶ ῥητορικῶν ἀκροάσασθαι καὶ φιλοσόφων λόγων. ὁ δέ,
42G θεοῦ νεύσαντος, | ἐπέτρεψε, περὶ τὰ βιβλία πλανᾶ-
σθαι βουλόμενος αὐτὸν καὶ ἀργεῖν μᾶλλον ἢ τοῦ γένους καὶ τῆς βασιλείας ὑπομιμνήσκεσθαι.

9 Τοῦτο δὲ ἐπιτραπὲν αὐτῷ, πανταχοῦ βαθέων καὶ
474B βαρυτάτων ὑποκειμένων κτημάτων, | μετὰ βασιλικῆς
ὑπονοίας καὶ δορυφορίας περιεφοίτα, καὶ διέστιχεν
ὅπῃ βούλοιτο. καὶ δὴ καὶ εἰς τὸν Πέργαμον ἀφι-
10 κνεῖται κατὰ κλέος τῆς Αἰδεσίου σοφίας. ὁ δὲ ἤδη μὲν
εἰς μακρόν τι γῆρας ἀφῖκτο καὶ τὸ σῶμα ἔκαμνε· τῆς
δὲ ὁμιλίας αὐτοῦ προεστήκεσαν καὶ ἀνὰ τοὺς πρώτους
ἐφέροντο Μάξιμός τε, ὑπὲρ οὗ τάδε γράφεται, καὶ
Χρυσάνθιος ὁ ἐκ Σάρδεων, Πρίσκος τε ὁ Θεσπρωτὸς
ἢ Μολοσσός, Εὐσέβιός τε ὁ ἐκ Καρίας Μύνδου πό-
11 λεως. καὶ συνουσίας ἀξιωθεὶς τῆς Αἰδεσίου, ὁ καὶ ἐν
μειρακίῳ πρεσβύτης Ἰουλιανός, τὴν μὲν ἀκμὴν καὶ
τὸ θεοειδὲς τῆς ψυχῆς καταπλαγείς, οὐκ ἐβούλετο χω-
ρίζεσθαι, ἀλλ᾽, ὥσπερ οἱ κατὰ τὸν μῦθον ὑπὸ τῆς
διψάδος δηχθέντες, χανδὸν καὶ ἀμυστὶ τῶν μαθη-
μάτων ἕλκειν ἐβούλετο, καὶ δῶρά γε ἐπὶ τούτοις βα-

⁴⁸ ἐξῄτησαν A Gi: ἐξῄτησεν Go
⁴⁹ οἱ coni. Go (pro ἑαυτῷ): οἱ A

For he had all books so thoroughly on his lips,[109] that they were irritated over the inadequacy of their own education, since there was nothing that they could teach the boy. Now since they had nothing to teach him and Julian had nothing to learn from them, he asked his cousin's permission to attend lectures of both orators and philosophers. He, with divine consent, permitted this, because he wished Julian to roam among books and to have leisure, rather than leave him to reflect on his own family and [his claim to] the throne.

After he had obtained this permission, Julian, with the enormous wealth from many sources at his disposal,[110] traveled around, accompanied by the emperor's distrust and a bodyguard, and went wherever he pleased. Thus it was that he came to Pergamon, because of the reputation of Aedesius' wisdom. But the latter was by this time far on in years, and his bodily strength was failing. Out of his school the outstanding students were Maximus, about whom I am writing now, Chrysanthius of Sardis, Priscus the Thesprotian or Molossian, and Eusebius who came from the Carian city Myndus. On having been considered worthy to study under Aedesius, Julian, who was very mature for someone his age, awestruck by his vigor and the godlike quality of his soul, did not want to leave him, but like those in the story who had been bitten by the "thirst-snake,"[111] he longed to drink in knowledge open-mouthed and at a gulp, and to that end used to send Aedesius kingly

109 For the expression, cf. *VPS* 6.75, 6.100, 8.1, 10.6.

110 Cf., however, Julian. *Ep. ad Athen.* 273b.

111 This snake bite caused insatiable thirst (implied by its Greek name). Cf. Ael. *NA* 6.51.

12 σιλικὰ διέπεμπεν· ὁ δὲ οὐδὲ ταῦτα προσίετο καὶ μετακαλέσας τὸν νεανίσκον εἶπεν· "ἀλλὰ σὺ μὲν καὶ
τὴν ψυχὴν τὴν ἐμὴν οὐκ ἀγνοεῖς, τηλικαύταις ἀκοαῖς
ἀκροώμενος, τὸ δὲ ὄργανον αὐτῆς συνορᾷς ὅπως διά-
κειται, τῆς γομφώσεως καὶ πήξεως διαλυομένης εἰς

13 τὰ συντιθέντα·⁵⁰ σὺ δέ, εἴ τι καὶ δρᾶν βούλει, τέκνον
σοφίας ἐπήρατον (τοιαῦτα γάρ σου τὰ τῆς ψυχῆς
ἰνδάλματα καταμανθάνω), πρὸς τοὺς ἐμοὺς παῖδας
πορευθεὶς ὄντας γνησίους, ἐκεῖθεν ῥύδην ἐμφοροῦ σοφίας ἁπάσης καὶ μαθημάτων· κἂν τύχῃς τῶν μυστηρίων, αἰσχυνθήσῃ πάντως ὅτι ἐγένου καὶ ἐκλήθης

14 ἄνθρωπος. ἐβουλόμην μὲν ἂν παρεῖναι καὶ Μάξιμον,
43G ἀλλ' ἐπὶ τὴν | Ἔφεσον ἔσταλται. καὶ περὶ Πρίσκου
τὰ ὅμοια διελέχθην ἄν, ἀλλὰ κἀκεῖνος ἐπὶ τῆς Ἑλλάδος πέπλευκε· λοιποὶ δὲ τῶν ἐμῶν ἑταίρων Εὐσέβιός
τε καὶ Χρυσάνθιος, ὡς ἀκροώμενος ἐλάχιστα τὸ ἐμὸν
ἐνοχλήσεις γῆρας."

15 Ὡς δὲ ταῦτα ἤκουσεν Ἰουλιανός, τοῦ φιλοσόφου
μὲν οὐδ' ὡς ἀφίστατο, προσέκειτο δὲ κατὰ τὸν πολὺν
χρόνον Εὐσεβίῳ τε καὶ Χρυσανθίῳ. ἦν δὲ ὁ Χρυσάνθιος ὁμόψυχος Μαξίμῳ, τὰ περὶ θειασμὸν συνενθου-
σιῶν, καὶ ὑφεῖλκεν ἑαυτὸν ἐν τοῖς μαθήμασι, καὶ τὸ

16 ἄλλο ἦθος τοιοῦτον ἔχων. Εὐσέβιος δέ, παρόντος μὲν
Μαξίμου, τὴν ἀκρίβειαν τὴν ἐν τοῖς μέρεσι τοῦ λόγου

---

⁵⁰ coni. Go: τὸ συντιθέν A

gifts. But Aedesius would not accept these, and having   12
summoned the young man he said: "Well, you are not
unfamiliar with my soul, for you have listened many a time
to my teachings; but you see how its instrument is in a state
of disintegration, now that its cohesion and fittings are
dissolving into their constituent parts.[112] But if you desire   13
to accomplish anything at all, beloved child of wisdom (for
I can discern such images of your soul), go to those who
are true sons of mine. From them fill yourself to over-
flowing with every kind of wisdom and learning. Once
admitted to their mysteries you shall be utterly ashamed
to have been born[113] and to be called a human being. I   14
wished that Maximus also were here, but he has been sent
to Ephesus. Of Priscus[114] too I would have said the same,
but he has also departed, sailing to Greece. But of my
companions Eusebius and Chrysanthius remain, and by
studying with them you will trouble my old age the least."

After he had heard this, Julian did not even then leave   15
the philosopher, but devoted the greater part of his time
and attention to Eusebius and Chrysanthius.[115] Chrysanthius had a soul akin to that of Maximus, and like him was
passionately absorbed in rituals that reveal divine power,
and he immersed himself in the study of the science of
divination, and in other respects had a very similar character. But Eusebius, at least when Maximus was present,   16
used to avoid precision in the parts of speech and dialecti-

[112] Echoes Pl. *Phd*. 79c, *Tim*. 43a; Plot. *Enn*. 4.3.21 [16–17].
[113] Cf. Porph *Plot*. 1.
[114] See below. Cf. Amm. Marcell. 25.3; Julian, *Ep*. 2–3.
[115] The two figures represent the two aspects of late Platonism: dialectical and theurgic practice.

479

καὶ τὰς διαλεκτικὰς μηχανὰς καὶ πλοκὰς ὑπέφευγε,
ἀποστάντος δὲ ὥσπερ ἡλιακοῦ φέγγους ἀστὴρ ἀπέ-
λαμπε· τοσαύτη τις εὐκολία καὶ χάρις ἐπήνθει τοῖς
λόγοις. καὶ ὁ Χρυσάνθιος παρὼν ἐπῄνει καὶ συνεπέ-
17 νευεν, ὅ τε Ἰουλιανὸς τὸν ἄνδρα ἐσεβάζετο. προσε-
τίθη δὲ μετὰ τὴν ἐξήγησιν ὁ Εὐσέβιος, ὡς ταῦτα εἴη
τὰ ὄντως ὄντα, αἱ δὲ τὴν αἴσθησιν ἀπατῶσαι μαγγα-
νεῖαι καὶ γοητεύουσαι θαυματοποιῶν ἔργα, καὶ πρὸς
ὑλικάς τινας δυνάμεις παραπαιόντων καὶ μεμηνότων.
18 τοῦτο ἀκούων τὸ ἐπιφώνημα πολλάκις ὁ θειότατος
Ἰουλιανός, ἰδίᾳ τὸν Χρυσάνθιον ἀπολαβών, "εἴ τί σοι
μέτεστιν ἀληθείας, ὦ φίλε Χρυσάνθιε," πρὸς αὐτὸν
ἔφη "φράσον μοι σαφῶς τίς ὁ ἐπίλογος οὗτος τῆς
ἐξηγήσεως." ὁ δὲ βαθέως μάλα καὶ σωφρόνως ἀνενεγ-
κὼν "ἀλλὰ πρᾶγμα ποιήσεις," ἔφη, "σοφόν, μὴ παρ'
19 ἐμοῦ ταῦτα, ἀλλὰ παρ' ἐκείνου πυθόμενος." καὶ μα-
475Β θὼν τοῦτο ἤκουσε καὶ ἐποίησε, | θεόν | τινα νομίσας
44G τὸν Χρυσάνθιον ἐπὶ τῷ λόγῳ. γενομένης δὲ τῆς συνουσίας, ὁ μὲν τὰ αὐτὰ προσεπέραινεν, ὁ δὲ Ἰουλιανὸς
θαρσαλέως ἤρετο τί τοῦτο αὐτῷ βούλεται συνεχῶς
20 ἐπιλεγόμενον. ἐνταῦθα ὁ Εὐσέβιος τὴν ἑαυτοῦ πετά-
σας εὐγλωττίαν καὶ τὸ εὔστομον ἐπὶ τὸ φράζειν
ἀκώλυτον ἀφεὶς φέρεσθαι, "Μάξιμος," εἶπε, "τίς ἐστι
τῶν πρεσβυτέρων ἀκροατῶν καὶ πολλὰ ἐκπεπαιδευ-
21 μένων· οὗτος διὰ μέγεθος φύσεως καὶ λόγων ὑπεροχὴν καταφρονήσας τῶν ἐν τούτοις ἀποδείξεων, ἐπὶ
μανίας τινὰς ὁρμήσας καὶ δραμών, συνεκάλεσεν

cal ploys and complexities;[116] yet when Maximus had gone,
he would shine out like a bright star, with a light like the
sun's; such was the facility and charisma that blossomed in
his discourses. Chrysanthius too was there to applaud and
approve, while Julian idolized the man. But after his inter-   17
pretation Eusebius would add that those [things he spoke
of][117] were the only things that had true existence, whereas
the deceptions that trick and beguile the senses are the
works of conjurors who are insane men led astray into the
exercise of material powers. Because he had heard this   18
final flourish many times, the divinely inspired Julian took
Chrysanthius aside and said to him: "If you have access to
any truth at all, dear Chrysanthius, tell me in clear terms:
what is the meaning of this epilogue concluding his exposition?" The latter replied in a very thoughtful and prudent manner: "The wise thing for you to do will be to ask
this, not of me, but of him." Hearing this Julian listened   19
and acted on it, and regarded Chrysanthius as some divine
being on account of what he had said. Then when the next
lecture took place, Eusebius ended with the same words
as before, and Julian boldly asked him what he was saying
at the end of the lecture. Thereupon Eusebius spread the   20
sails of his natural eloquence and giving free rein to his
powers of speech said: "Maximus is one of the oldest and
most learned students. Because of his lofty character and   21
profuse eloquence he disdained logical proofs in these
subjects and rushed hastily into the acts of a madman.

[116] Cf. Pl. *Symp.* 203d.

[117] Presumably, dialectical discussions. Eusebius was devoted
to philosophical rhetoric, whereas Chrysanthius and Maximus
were thaumaturgists, or miracle-workers.

ἡμᾶς πρώην τοὺς παρόντας εἰς τὸ Ἑκατήσιον καὶ
22 πολλοὺς ἀπεδείκνυ τοὺς καθ' ἑαυτοῦ μάρτυρας. ὡς δὲ
ἀπηντήσαμεν καὶ τὴν θεὸν προσεκυνήσαμεν, 'καθ-
ῆσθε μέν,' εἶπε πρὸς ἡμᾶς, 'ὦ φίλτατοι ἑταῖροι, καὶ
τὸ μέλλον ὁρᾶτε καὶ εἴ τι διαφέρω τῶν πολλῶν ἐγώ.'
23 τοῦτο δὲ εἰπών, καὶ καθεσθέντων ἡμῶν ἁπάντων, χόν-
δρον καθαγίσας λιβανωτοῦ καὶ πρὸς ἑαυτὸν ὄντινα
δήποτε ὕμνον περαίνων, εἰς τοσόνδε παρῆλθεν ἐπιδείξεως, ὥστε τὸ μὲν πρῶτον ἐμειδία τὸ ἄγαλμα, εἶτα
24 καὶ γέλως ἦν τὸ φαινόμενον. θορυβουμένων δὲ ἡμῶν
ὑπὸ τῆς ὄψεως, 'ἀλλὰ ταραχθήτω γε ὑμῶν ὑπὸ τούτων
μηδὲ εἷς, αὐτίκα γὰρ καὶ αἱ λαμπάδες ἀνάψουσιν, ἃς
ἐν ταῖν χεροῖν ἡ θεὸς φέρει·' καὶ τοὺς λόγους ἔφθανε
τὸ φῶς ταῖς λαμπάσι περιφλεγόμενον. ἡμεῖς μὲν οὖν
τὸν θεατρικὸν ἐκεῖνον θαυματοποιὸν πρὸς τὸ παρὸν
25 καταπλαγέντες, ἀνεχωρήσαμεν· σὺ δὲ τούτων μηδὲν
θαυμάσῃς, ὥσπερ οὐδὲ ἐγώ, τὴν διὰ τοῦ λόγου
26 κάθαρσιν μέγα τι χρῆμα ὑπολαμβάνων." ὁ δὲ θειότατος Ἰουλιανὸς τοῦτο ἀκούσας, "ἀλλ' ἔρρωσο," εἶπε,
"καὶ πρόσεχε τοῖς βιβλίοις, ἐμοὶ δὲ ἐμήνυσας ὃν
ἐζήτουν." καὶ ταῦτα εἰπὼν καὶ Χρυσανθίου καταφιλή-
45G σας | τὴν κεφαλήν, ἐπὶ τὴν Ἔφεσον ἐξώρμησε. συν-
τυχὼν δὲ ἐκεῖ Μαξίμῳ, ἐξεκρέματό τε τοῦ ἀνδρὸς καὶ
27 ἀπρὶξ τῆς ὅλης σοφίας εἴχετο. ὁ δὲ Μάξιμος ὑφη-
γεῖται αὐτῷ καὶ τὸν θειότατον μετακαλέσαι Χρυσάνθιον, καί, γενόμενον οὕτως, μόλις ἤρκουν ἄμφω τῇ
τοῦ παιδὸς ἐς τὰς μαθήσεις εὐρυχωρίᾳ.

Soon he invited us to the temple of Hecate and created many witnesses against him. When we had arrived there and had paid our respect to the goddess, he said 'Be seated, my well-beloved friends, and observe what shall come to pass, and see if I distinguish myself in any respect from most [philosophers].' When he had said this, and we had all sat down, he burned a grain of incense[118] and recited to himself the whole of some hymn or other, and was so highly successful in his display that the image of the goddess first began to smile, then even seemed to laugh aloud. We were all much disturbed by this display, but he said: 'Let none of you be terrified by these things, for any moment now even the torches that the goddess holds in her hands shall come alight.' And before he could finish speaking the torches burst into a blaze of light. Admittedly we, at that moment astounded by that theatrical wonder-worker, went away; but you must not admire any of these things, in the same way as I do not; you should rather believe that what matters most is the purification [of the soul] attained by reason." However, when the divinely inspired Julian heard this, he said: "In that case, farewell and devote yourself to your books. You have revealed to me the man I was in search of." After saying this he kissed the head of Chrysanthius and set out for Ephesus. Having met up with Maximus there, he clung to him and completely absorbed all his wisdom. But Maximus persuaded him to summon the divinely inspired Chrysanthius as well, and when this had come to pass, the two of them barely sufficed to satisfy the boy's great capacity for acquiring knowledge.

22

23

24

25

26

27

[118] Cf. Luc. *Sat.* 16; or *gum* of incense, cf. Theophr. *Hist. pl.* 9.4.10.

EUNAPIUS

28　　'Ως δὲ καὶ ταῦτα εἶχε καλῶς, ἀκούσας τι πλέον
εἶναι κατὰ τὴν Ἑλλάδα παρὰ τῷ ταῖν Θεαῖν ἱερο-
φάντῃ, καὶ πρὸς ἐκεῖνον ὀξὺς ἔδραμε. τοῦ δὲ ἱεροφάν-
τος, κατ' ἐκεῖνον τὸν χρόνον ὅστις ἦν, τοὔνομα οὔ
μοι θέμις λέγειν· ἐτέλει γὰρ τὸν ταῦτα γράφοντα καὶ
29　　εἰς Εὐμολπίδας ἦγε· καὶ οὗτός γε ἦν ὁ καὶ τὴν τῶν
ἱερῶν καταστροφὴν καὶ τῆς Ἑλλάδος ἀπώλειαν ἁπάσης προγνούς, τοῦ συγγραφέως παρόντος, καὶ φανερῶς διαμαρτυρόμενος ὡς μεθ' αὑτὸν ἱεροφάντης
γενήσοιτο, ᾧ μὴ θέμις ἱεροφαντικῶν ἅψασθαι θρόνων,
ἐπειδὴ θεοῖς ἑτέροις καθιέρωται καὶ ὀμώμοκεν ἀρ-
30　　ρήτους ὅρκους ἑτέρων ἱερῶν μὴ προστήσεσθαι· προσ-
τήσεσθαι δὲ ἔλεγεν ὅμως αὐτὸν⁵¹ μηδὲ Ἀθηναῖον
ὄντα. καὶ (εἰς τοσόνδε προνοίας ἐξικνεῖτο) ἐπ' αὐτοῦ
τε⁵² τὰ ἱερὰ κατασκαφήσεσθαι καὶ δῃωθήσεσθαι ἔφασκε, κἀκεῖνον ζῶντα ταῦτα ἐπόψεσθαι, διὰ φιλοτιμίαν
476B　περιττὴν ἀτιμαζόμενον, καὶ προτελευτήσειν | γε αὐτοῦ
τὴν θεραπείαν ταῖν Θεαῖν, τὸν δὲ τῆς τιμῆς ἀποστε-
ρηθέντα, μήτε τὸν ἱεροφάντην μήτε τὸν γηραιὸν βίον
31　　ἔχειν. καὶ ταῦτά γε οὕτως· ἅμα τε γὰρ ὁ ἐκ Θεσπιῶν
46G　ἐγίνετο, | πατὴρ ὢν τῆς Μιθριακῆς τελετῆς, καὶ οὐκ

---

⁵¹ αὐτὸν Go: αὐτὸς A
⁵² ἐπ' αὐτοῦ τε Go: ἐφ' αὐτοῦ τε A Civil: alii alia

---

119 That is, Demeter and Persephone worshipped at Eleusis.
120 Lucian, *Lexiphanes* 10, alludes to the crime of naming the
hierophant and torchbearers of the Mysteries.

484

Now when his studies with them were prospering, he   28
heard that there was a higher wisdom in Greece, possessed by the hierophant of the two Goddesses,[119] and
hastened to him with all speed. It is by sacred custom not
for me to tell the name of the person who was hierophant
at that time;[120] for he initiated the author of this work and
introduced him to the Eumolpidae.[121] It was this man who   29
foretold the overthrow of the temples and the ruin of the
whole of Greece (while the author of this book was present), and he clearly testified that after his death there
would be a hierophant who should not be allowed to touch
the hierophant's throne, because he had been consecrated
to the service of other gods and had sworn oaths of the
utmost sanctity that he would not preside over temples
other than theirs. But he foretold that this man would   30
nevertheless preside in this way, though he was not even
an Athenian. And—such was the level of prophetic insight
he reached—that he predicted that in his own lifetime the
sacred temples would be razed to the ground and laid
waste, and that the hierophant would live to see their ruin
and would be despised for his excessive ambition; that the
worship of the Goddesses would come to an end before
his own death, and that deprived of his honor his life
would no longer be that of a hierophant, and that he would
not reach old age. And these things indeed turned out this   31
way. For the moment the citizen of Thespiae was present,
he who was "father" of the Mithras mystery,[122] everything

121 The hereditary priests of Demeter at Eleusis.
122 That is, he had been the priest of Mithras.

εἰς μακρὰν πολλῶν καὶ ἀδιηγήτων ἐπικλύσθη πάντα
κακῶν, ὧν τὰ μὲν ἐν τοῖς διεξοδικοῖς τῆς ἱστορίας
εἴρηται, τὰ δέ, ἐὰν ἐπιτρέπῃ τὸ θεῖον, λελέξεται, ὅ τε
Ἀλλάριχος ἔχων τοὺς βαρβάρους διὰ τῶν Πυλῶν
παρῆλθεν, ὥσπερ διὰ σταδίου καὶ ἱπποκρότου πεδίου

32 τρέχων· τοιαύτας αὐτῷ τὰς πύλας ἀπέδειξε τῆς Ἑλλάδος ἥ τε τῶν τὰ φαιὰ ἱμάτια ἐχόντων ἀκωλύτως
προσπαρεισελθόντων ἀσέβεια καὶ ὁ τῶν ἱεροφαντικῶν θεσμῶν παραρραγεὶς νόμος καὶ σύνδεσμος·
ἀλλὰ ταῦτα μὲν ἐς ὕστερον ἐπράχθη, καὶ ὁ λόγος διὰ
τὴν πρόγνωσιν παρήνεγκεν.

33   Τότε δὲ ὁ μὲν Ἰουλιανὸς τῷ θειοτάτῳ ἱεροφαντῶν
συγγενόμενος καὶ τῆς ἐκεῖθεν σοφίας ἀρυσάμενος
χανδόν, [ὁ μὲν]53 ὑπὸ τοῦ Κωνσταντίου ἀπήγετο σφοδρῶς ὡς παραβασιλεύσων εἰς τὸν Καίσαρα. Μάξιμος
δὲ ἦν κατὰ τὴν Ἀσίαν, Αἰδεσίου δὲ μεταλλάξαντος,

34 πήχεσί γε ἐπὶ πᾶσαν σοφίαν αὐξόμενος, ὥστε ὁ μὲν
Ἰουλιανὸς ἔτυχεν ὧν οὐκ ἐβούλετο μέν, ἀλλ᾽ ἠναγκάζετο. πεμφθεὶς δὲ Καῖσαρ ἐπὶ Γαλατίας οὐχ ἵνα βα-
σιλεύῃ τῶν ἐκείνῃ μόνον, ἀλλ᾽ ἵνα ἐν τῇ βασιλείᾳ
διαφθαρῇ, παρὰ δόξαν ἅπασαν ἐκ τῆς τῶν θεῶν προνοίας ἀνήνεγκεν, πάντας μὲν λανθάνων ὅτι θεραπεύει

53 del. Go.

---

123 Fr. 64.2 Blockley.
124 *Thermo-pylae* (= "Hot Gates," a pass close to hot springs).

was immediately plunged into many inexplicable disasters, of which some have been described in the detailed expositions of my *History*,[123] others, if the divine permits it, will be related [here]. It was the time when Alaric with his barbarians invaded via the Gates,[124] [as easily] as though he was racing through an open stadium or a plain echoing with the sound of hooves. The impiety of the men   32
dressed in black habits, who entered Greece unhindered along with him,[125] opened this gateway of Greece to him, and the fact that the law and restriction on the hierophantic ordinances had been rescinded. But all this happened in later days, and my narrative has digressed because of the prophecy.

At that time, when Julian had become intimate with   33
that most sacred of hierophants and taken deep gulps[126] of his wisdom, he was forcibly removed to rule alongside Constantius at the rank of Caesar.[127] Maximus, however, remained in Asia (Aedesius had now passed away), and progressed by leaps and bounds in every kind of wisdom, which meant that Julian obtained what he did not desire   34
but had thrust upon him. As Caesar he was dispatched to Gaul, not only to rule the peoples there but with the intention that he should perish by violent means while holding his imperial office; but contrary to all expectation, by the providence of the [Hellenic] gods he emerged alive, on the one hand concealing from everyone that he was de-

[125] That is, the Christian monks. This invasion of the Goths in AD 395 is also mentioned in the life of Priscus.
[126] Lit., "with open mouth"; cf. *VPS* 44.1, 48.10–11; *Hist.* fr. 25.1–2, fr. 65.5 Blockley.   [127] Cf. Julian. *Ep. ad Athen.* 271d, 273a and c; Amm. Marcell.; Socrates 2.34.5.

θεούς, πάντας δὲ νικῶν ὅτι ἐθεράπευε θεούς, καὶ τόν
τε Ῥῆνον ἐπεραιώθη, καὶ πάντα ὅσα ὑπὲρ ἐκεῖνον
ἔθνη βάρβαρα συνελὼν καὶ δουλωσάμενος, πολλῶν
ἐπιβουλῶν καὶ μηχανημάτων πλεκομένων αὐτῷ (ὡς
ἐν τοῖς περὶ ἐκεῖνον ἀναγέγραπται), τὸν ἱεροφάντην
47G μετακαλέσας ἐκ τῆς Ἑλλάδος | καὶ σὺν ἐκείνῳ τινὰ
μόνοις ἐκείνοις γνώριμα διαπραξάμενος ἐπὶ τὴν καθ-
35 αίρεσιν ἠγέρθη τῆς Κωνσταντίου τυραννίδος. ταῦτα
δὲ συνῄδεσαν Ὀρειβάσιος ἐκ τοῦ Περγάμου καί τις
τῶν ἐκ Λιβύης, ἣν Ἀφρικὴν καλοῦσι Ῥωμαῖοι κατὰ
τὸ πάτριον τῆς γλώττης, Εὐήμερος. ταῦτα δὲ πάλιν
ἐν τοῖς κατὰ Ἰουλιανὸν βιβλίοις ἀκριβέστερον εἴρη-
36 ται. ὡς δ' οὖν καθεῖλε τὴν τυραννίδα Κωνσταντίου
καὶ τὸν ἱεροφάντην ἀπέπεμψεν ἐπὶ τὴν Ἑλλάδα,
καθάπερ θεόν τινα ἀποπέμπων φανέντα καὶ παρα-
σχόντα ἃ ἐβούλετο—καὶ βασιλικά γε αὐτῷ δῶρα καὶ
θεραπείαν συνέπεμψε πρὸς τὴν ἐπιμέλειαν ⟨τῶν⟩[54]
τῆς Ἑλλάδος ἱερῶν—, τὸν Μάξιμον εὐθὺς μετεπέμ-
37 ψατο καὶ τὸν Χρυσάνθιον. καὶ μία γε ἦν ἐπ' ἀμφοῖν
ἡ κλῆσις. τοῖς δὲ ἐπὶ τοὺς θεοὺς καταφεύγειν ἐδόκει,
καὶ ἄνδρες οὕτω δραστήριοι καὶ πεῖραν ἔχοντες καὶ
συνενεγκόντες εἰς ταὐτὸ τὴν πεῖραν καὶ τὴν περὶ
ταῦτα ὀξυδορκίαν καὶ διάθρησιν τῆς ψυχῆς ἀνεγείραν-
τες καὶ συστησάμενοι, σημείοις ἐγχρίπτουσιν ἀπη-

[54] τῶν add. Go

[128] Cf. Amm. Marcell. 21.2.4.

voted to the [Hellenic] gods,[128] but on the other defeating
everyone because he was devoted to the [Hellenic] gods.
He crossed the Rhine and defeated and subjugated all the
barbarian tribes beyond that river, and this in spite of
numerous intrigues and schemes that were plotted against
him, as I have related in the books about him.[129] Then he
summoned the hierophant from Greece, and having with
the latter's aid performed certain rites known to them
alone, he was roused to abolish the tyrannical rule of Constantius. His accomplices were Oribasius[130] of Pergamon   35
and someone from Libya[131] (which the Romans in their
native tongue call "Africa"),[132] named Euhemerus. But all
this has been described in fuller detail in my books on
Julian. So, after he had abolished the tyranny of Constan-   36
tius,[133] and had sent back the hierophant to Greece, as
though he were sending back some god who had appeared
to him and provided him with what he wanted, and had
sent with him also kingly gifts and attendants to take care
of the temples of Greece, he at once sent for Maximus and
Chrysanthius. There was in fact only one summons to   37
reach them both. They decided to take refuge with the
gods, and even though they both were men of action and
experience, and combined these for this common undertaking, and summoned and brought to bear all their keen
sight and mental astuteness in such matters, they encoun-

129 Cf. *Hist.* fr. 14.2 Blockley.

130 For Oribasius see below, *VPS* 21.

131 Not the modern country.

132 The Roman name for Tunisia.

133 Constantius died in November 361, and Julian entered
Constantinople in triumph in December.

38 νέσι καὶ ἀγρίοις. ἐκεῖνοι ἤδεσαν τὰ φανθέντα σημεῖα.
ὁ μὲν οὖν Χρυσάνθιος εὐθὺς καταπλαγεὶς καὶ πρὸς
τὴν ὄψιν ὑποπτήξας, τὴν γλῶσσαν ἐνδακών, "οὐ με-
νετέον," εἶπεν, "ἐμοὶ μόνον ἐνταῦθα, ὦ Μάξιμε φίλ-
39 τατε, ἀλλὰ καὶ φωλευτέον·" ὁ δὲ ἀναστήσας ἑαυτόν
"ἀλλ᾽ ἐπιλελῆσθαί μοι δοκεῖς," εἶπεν, "ὦ Χρυσάνθιε,
477B | τῆς παιδείας ἣν ἐπαιδεύθημεν, ὡς τῶν ἄκρων γέ
ἐστιν Ἑλλήνων καὶ ταῦτα πεπαιδευμένων μὴ πάντως
εἴκειν τοῖς πρώτως ἀπαντήσασιν, ἀλλ᾽ ἐκβιάζεσθαι
τὴν τοῦ θείου φύσιν ἄχρις ἂν ἐπικλίνῃ πρὸς τὸν θε-
40 ραπεύοντα." Χρυσανθίου δὲ ὑπολαβόντος, "ἴσως σὺ
ταῦτα πράττειν εἶ δεινὸς καὶ τολμηρός, ἐγὼ δὲ τούτοις
οὐκ ἂν μαχεσαίμην τοῖς σημείοις" καὶ μετὰ τοὺς
λόγους ἀποχωρήσαντος, ὁ μὲν Μάξιμος ἐπέμεινεν
ἅπαντα πράττων, ἔστε ἔτυχεν ὧν ἐβούλετο καὶ κατ-
41 επεθύμει· ὁ δὲ | Χρυσάνθιος ἀκινητότερος ἐπέμενεν
48G ἀνδριάντος, τοὺς ἐξ ἀρχῆς πεπηγότας παρ᾽ ἑαυτῷ
λογισμοὺς μηδὲν κινῆσαι διανοούμενος. πάντες οὖν
ἄνθρωποι παρὰ τὸν Μάξιμον ἤδη συνετρόχαζον κατὰ
τὴν Ἀσίαν, ὅσοι τε ἦσαν ἐν ἀρχαῖς καὶ ὅσοι τούτων
42 ἀπελέλυντο, τό τε κρεῖττον τῶν βουλευτηρίων. καὶ
δῆμος ἐστενοχώρει τὰς προόδους τῷ Μαξίμῳ μετὰ
βοῆς πηδῶντες, ἣν δῆμος, ὅταν τινὰ θεραπεύῃ,[55] ἐκ
πολλοῦ μεμελέτηκεν· αἵ τε γυναῖκες παρὰ τὴν γυναῖκα τῇ πλαγίᾳ θύρᾳ παρεισεχέοντο, τὴν εὐδαιμο-
43 νίαν θαυμάζουσαι καὶ μεμνῆσθαι σφῶν ἀξιοῦσαι· ἡ

[55] θεραπεύῃ Boiss Go: θεραπεύειν A Gi Be

tered forbidding and hostile omens. They understood the   38
omens that had appeared. Chrysanthius was immediately
overwhelmed and humbled by what he saw, and he said
while biting his tongue: "Not only must I stay here, my
dear Maximus, but I must also go into hiding." Maximus,   39
however, stood firm and replied: "Chrysanthius, I think
that you have forgotten our education, which has taught
us to believe that it is the duty of the noblest Hellenes,
who have been educated in such matters, not to yield in
any way to the obstacles they encounter at first, but rather
to put forceful pressure on the divine nature until you
cause it to incline toward its worshipper." When Chrysanthius had replied "Perhaps you have the skill and the dar-   40
ing to do this, but I would not fight against these omens,"
and left after speaking these words, Maximus stayed behind, trying every method until he obtained the results
that he wished and desired. Chrysanthius, however, re-   41
mained more immovable than a statue,[134] because he had
decided that he should not change in the least the considerations that had firmly settled in his mind from the start.
As a result all the people of Asia immediately flocked in
haste to Maximus, both those who at the time held office
or who had previously held offices, and the majority of the
city councilors. Common folk also crowded the streets to   42
the house of Maximus, stamping their feet and uttering
shouts, an old custom of the people whenever it would
show its adulation for someone. And the women poured
in by the back door to see his wife, marveling at her felic-
ity, and beseeched her not to forget them: so profound was   43

[134] Cf. *VPS* 6.106, 10.51, 10.73; Pl. *Symp.* 174d, 175b; Epict.
3.9.12.

δὲ φιλοσοφίας ἕνεκεν Μάξιμον οὔτε γράμματα <οὔτε
νεῖν>⁵⁶ εἰδότα ἀπέφαινεν. ὁ μὲν οὖν Μάξιμος ὑπὸ τῆς
Ἀσίας πάσης προσκυνούμενος, ἐπὶ τὴν συντυχίαν
ἀνήει τοῦ βασιλέως, Χρυσάνθιος δὲ ἔμεινε κατὰ χώραν, ἐκεῖνο θεοῦ κατ᾽ ὄναρ, ὡς πρὸς τὸν ταῦτα γράφοντα ἔλεγεν ἐς ὕστερον, εἰπόντος·

ὅς κε θεοῖς ἐπιπείθηται, μάλα τ᾽ ἔκλυον αὐτοῦ.⁵⁷

44   Ὡς δὲ ὁ Μάξιμος μετὰ τοσαύτης πομπείας ἐπὶ τὴν
Κωνσταντινούπολιν ὥρμησέ τε καὶ διὰ ταχέων εἰς
αὐτὴν παρελθὼν ἐξέλαμψεν—ὅ τε γὰρ βασιλεὺς καὶ
οἱ βασιλευόμενοι πάντα ἦσαν ἐπὶ Μαξίμῳ, νὺξ καὶ
ἡμέρα διέφερεν αὐτοῖς οὐδέν, οὕτως ὑπὲρ τῶν παρόν-
45   των ἐπὶ τοὺς θεοὺς ἅπαντα ἀνέφερον—(ἐνταῦθα ὁ μὲν
Μάξιμος βαρὺς ἦν ἤδη περὶ τὰ βασίλεια, στολήν τε
ἁβροτέραν ἢ κατὰ φιλόσοφον περιχεόμενος καὶ πρὸς
49G   τὰς ἐντεύξεις ὢν χαλεπώτερος | καὶ δυσχερέστερος·
46   ὁ δὲ βασιλεὺς ἠγνόει τὰ πραττόμενα.) μεταπέμψα-
σθαι γοῦν αὐτοῖς, ἐκβιασαμένου τοῦ βασιλέως, ἔδοξε
καὶ τὸν Πρίσκον· ὁ δὲ Μάξιμος ἀπήτει προσαναγκά-
47   ζων καὶ τὸν Χρυσάνθιον. καὶ ἄμφω γε ἦσαν μετά-
πεμπτοι, ὁ μὲν Πρίσκος ἐκ τῆς Ἑλλάδος, Χρυσάνθιος
δὲ ἀπὸ Λυδίας καὶ Σάρδεων. καὶ οὕτω γε ἐξεκρέματο
τῆς τοῦ ἀνδρὸς συνουσίας ὁ θεσπέσιος Ἰουλιανός,
ὥστε τοῖς μὲν ὡς φίλοις ἐπέστελλεν, καθάπερ θεοὺς

⁵⁶ οὔτε νεῖν add. Cob Go
⁵⁷ ἐπιπείθηται Junius Gi Go: ἐπιπείθεται A

492

her knowledge of philosophy that she made Maximus seem not to know how to read [or swim].[135] Thus Maximus, adored by all Asia, went on his way to meet the emperor, but Chrysanthius stayed where he was, since a god had appeared to him in a dream, and, as he later on told the author of this narrative, recited the following verse:[136]

He who obeys the gods, they in turn answer his
prayer.

Thus Maximus set out for Constantinople with such a large retinue, and, arriving there he very soon came to shine—for both ruler and ruled were fully focused on Maximus. Whether by day or night made no difference to them, so incessantly did they refer to the gods all questions that arose in their daily life. The result was that at the imperial court Maximus began to grow insolent, wore flowing garments of a stuff too luxurious for a philosopher, and in encounters became more and more difficult and unpleasant; but the emperor was unaware of what was going on. Then they decided, under imperial command, to send for Priscus as well;[137] and Maximus persisted in his demand that Chrysanthius should come as well. So both were summoned, Priscus from Greece, and Chrysanthius from Sardis in Lydia.[138] The divinely inspired Julian was so dependent on the latter's company that he wrote to both men as though they were his intimate friends, and imploring them in the way one would gods, to come and live with

44

45

46

47

135 Cf. Pl. *Leg.* 689d.
136 Hom. *Il.* 1.218.   137 See *VPS* 7.10.
138 For the story cf. *Suda* χ 555.

48 ἱκετεύων ἐλθεῖν καὶ συνεῖναι· τῷ δὲ Χρυσανθίῳ καὶ
γυναῖκα εἶναι πυθόμενος, Μελιτὴν ὄνομα ἔχουσαν καὶ
ὑπ᾽ αὐτοῦ θαυμαζομένην διαφερόντως (τοῦ δὲ ταῦτα
γράφοντος ἀνεψιὰ ἦν), ἰδίᾳ που καθίσας ἑαυτόν, καὶ
πρὸς τὴν γυναῖκα ἐπέστελλεν αὐτὸς γράφων, οὐδενὸς
εἰδότος, καὶ παντοίας ἀφιεὶς φωνάς, τὸν ἄνδρα πείθειν
49 μηδαμῶς ἀπαγορεῦσαι τὴν ἔξοδον· καὶ τὴν πρὸς
Χρυσάνθιον αἰτήσας ἐπιστολήν, εἶτα εἰσβαλὼν ἐκείνην καὶ σφραγῖδα ἀμφοτέραις ἐπιθείς, ὡς ἂν ἦν μία,
τοὺς ἄξοντας ἔστελλεν πολλὰ καὶ ἀπὸ στόματος φρά-
σας ἃ χρήσιμα ἐνόμιζε πρὸς τὸ

ῥηϊδίως πεπιθεῖν μεγάλας φρένας Αἰακίδαο.

50 ὁ μὲν οὖν Πρίσκος ἦλθε, καὶ ἐλθὼν ἐσωφρόνει· καί |
478B τοί γε οὐκ ἐλάττους ἦσαν αὐτὸν οἱ θεραπεύοντες, ἀλλ᾽
ἔμενεν ὅμως ἀκίνητος, οὐχ ὑπὸ τῆς βασιλείας ἐπαι-
ρόμενος, ἀλλὰ τὴν βασιλείαν καταφέρων καὶ ὁμαλί-
ζων ἐς τὸ φιλοσοφώτερον. |

51 Ὁ δὲ Χρυσάνθιος οὐδὲ ταύταις ἑάλω ταῖς ἄρκυσι
50G καὶ μηχαναῖς, ἀλλὰ τοῖς θεοῖς ἐντυχών, ὡς τὰ παρὰ
τῶν θεῶν ἦν ἀμετάβλητα, καὶ αὐτὸς εἵπετο τοῖς θεοῖς
καὶ πρὸς τὸν βασιλέα ἐπέστελλεν, ὡς ὑπὲρ τοῦ βασιλέως ἡ κατὰ Λυδίαν [ὑπὲρ]⁵⁸ αὐτοῦ γίνοιτο μονή,
52 καὶ οἱ θεοὶ ταῦτα ἔφραζον. ὁ δὲ ὑπώπτευσε μὲν τὴν

---

⁵⁸ lac. indic. Gi post Λυδίαν

---

139 These letters (or their precise content) are not extant.

him. But when he learned that Chrysanthius had a wife   48
named Melite whom he admired above all (she was a
cousin of the present author), Julian sat down somewhere
private and wrote (without anyone knowing) with his own
hand to this woman and produced a range of arguments
to persuade the husband not to refuse his departure. Then   49
he asked for the letter addressed to Chrysanthius, next
enclosed this, set his seal on both, as if it were only one
letter,[139] and sent off those who were to bring him back,
having given many personal instructions that he thought
would be useful so as to

> persuade with ease the great heart of the grandson of
> Aeacus.[140]

Priscus accordingly came,[141] and once present he behaved   50
sensibly. And though there were just as many who sought
his favor, he nevertheless remained unmoved, and was not
puffed up by the emperor's court, but rather endeavored
to lower the pride of the court and to bring it to a more
philosophical standard.

Chrysanthius, however, could not even be caught by   51
such snares and devices, but he consulted the gods, and
since the message coming from the gods was unchanged,
he for his part obeyed the gods and wrote to the emperor
that it was in the latter's interest that he should stay in
Lydia, and that the gods had instructed him to do so. The   52
emperor was suspicious of the refusal of his order, but he

[140] Hom. *Il.* 9.184 (like Nestor did for the embassy to Achilles).

[141] Cf. Julian. *Ep. ad Lib.* 52 Wright, written at Antioch early in 363, in which he complains about Priscus' delay.

495

ἀποτυχίαν τῆς κλήσεως, ἀρχιερέα δὲ ἀποδείξας τόν
τε ἄνδρα καὶ τὴν γυναῖκα τῆς Λυδίας, καὶ ὑπ᾽ ἐκείνοις
ἐπιτρέψας εἶναι τῶν ἄλλων τὴν αἵρεσιν, αὐτὸς ἐπὶ τὸν
Περσικὸν συνήγετο πόλεμον, Μαξίμου δὲ καὶ Πρίσκου συνεπομένων. καὶ ἄλλοι δέ τινες συμπαρωμάρ-
τουν εἰς πλῆθος συντελοῦντες, ἑαυτοὺς ἐγκωμιαζόν-
των ἀνθρώπων ὄχλος καὶ σφόδρα γε διογκουμένων
ὅτι ὁ βασιλεὺς ἔφησεν αὐτοῖς συντετυχηκέναι.

53   Ὡς δὲ τὰ πράγματα συντόνως ἀπὸ τῶν μεγάλων
ἐκείνων καὶ λαμπρῶν ἐλπίδων ἐς τὸ ἀφανὲς καὶ ἄμορφον κατερράγη καὶ διωλίσθησεν, ὡς ἐν τοῖς διεξοδικοῖς τοῖς κατὰ Ἰουλιανὸν εἴρηται, ὅ τε Ἰοβιανὸς ἐβα-
54   σίλευσε καὶ τιμῶν τοὺς ἄνδρας διετέλεσεν· εἶτα μάλα
ταχέως καὶ σφοδρῶς συναπῆλθε τῷ προβασιλεύ-
σαντι (εἴ γε μὴν παρὰ τοὺς πλείονας οὗτος ἀπῆλθε),
Βαλεντινιανός τε καὶ Βάλης ἐπέστησαν τοῖς πράγμασιν. ἐνταῦθα συναρπάζονται μὲν Μάξιμος καὶ Πρίσκος, πολὺ τῆς κλήσεως διαφερούσης ἢ ὅτε Ἰου-
55   λιανὸς ἐκάλει. ἐκείνη μὲν γάρ | τις ἦν πανηγυρικὴ καὶ
51G   πρὸς τιμὴν περιττῶς διαλάμπουσα, ταύτης δὲ τῆς
δευτέρας πρὸ τῶν ἐλπιζομένων καὶ τὸ φαινόμενον κίνδυνος ἦν, οὕτως ἀτιμία τις ἁδρὰ καὶ περιφανὴς κατ-
εκέχυτο τῶν ὁρωμένων. ἀλλ᾽ ὁ μὲν Πρίσκος οὐδὲν
ὑποστὰς δεινόν, ἀλλὰ καὶ προσμαρτυρηθεὶς ἀγαθὸς
εἶναι καὶ γεγενῆσθαι κατὰ τὸν καιρὸν ἐκεῖνον,

---

142 Both attended Julian's death (Amm. Marcell. 25.3).
143 Cf. Eunap. *Hist.* fr. 28 Blockley.

appointed Chrysanthius high priest of Lydia, along with his wife, and after having entrusted to them the selection of other priests, he himself was setting out for the war against Persia. Both Maximus and Priscus accompanied him,[142] and certain others joined the expedition, so that they added up to a considerable number; they were, in fact, a mob of men who sang their own praises and were puffed up with pride, because the emperor said that he had encountered them.

But when the enterprise that began with such great and splendid hopes had collapsed into an indistinct and shapeless heap and gone under, as I have described more fully in my detailed accounts of Julian's time,[143] Jovian[144] was made emperor, and he continued to honor these men. Then too swiftly and violently he passed away to join the previous ruler (if we can really say of that predecessor that he joined the majority),[145] and then Valentinian and Valens succeeded to the Imperial throne. Thereupon Maximus and Priscus were both arrested, and this time their summons was very different from the time when Julian invited them. For earlier the summons was of a festive nature and a bright path to honor; but with the second summons, instead of having their hopes up, the danger was apparent, so much did [the fear of] a public and overwhelming disgrace overshadow the whole prospect for them. Priscus, however, suffered no harm, and since evidence was produced that he was a righteous man and had

53

54

55

[144] Upon Julian's death in Persia in June 363, the general Jovian was proclaimed emperor by the army.

[145] Eunapius implies that Julian became a god in the afterlife.

56 ἐπανῆλθεν εἰς τὴν Ἑλλάδα· (καὶ ὁ ταῦτα γράφων
ἐπαιδεύετο κατ᾽ ἐκείνους τοὺς χρόνους, παῖς ὢν καὶ
εἰς ἐφήβους ἄρτι τελῶν.) ὁ δὲ Μάξιμος ⟨πολλὰ
ἔπαθε⟩,[59] πολλοὶ μὲν γὰρ αὐτοῦ κατεβόων δημοσίᾳ τε
ἐν τοῖς θεάτροις καὶ ἰδίᾳ πρὸς τὸν βασιλέα, θαυμα-
στὸς δὲ ἦν καὶ οὕτως, ὅτι πρὸς τοσαύτας ἀνέφερε
συμφοράς, πλὴν ἐς τὸ βαθύτατον αὐτὸν τῆς τιμωρίας
περιάγουσι, τοσούτων τιμήσαντες χρημάτων, ὅσα
μήτε ἀνὴρ ἀκούειν ἐδύνατο φιλοσοφῶν ⟨μήτε ὁρᾶν⟩[60]
(ὑπώπτευον γὰρ αὐτὸν τὰ πάντα ἔχειν), καὶ μετεγίνω-
57 σκον, ὡς ὀλίγου τιμήσαντες αὐτῷ. καὶ ἀνεπέμφθη γε
εἰς τὴν Ἀσίαν ἐπὶ καταβολῇ τῶν χρημάτων, καὶ ὅσα
μὲν ἔπασχεν ὑπὲρ πᾶσάν ἐστι τραγῳδίαν καὶ οὐδεὶς
ἂν εἴη μεγαλόφωνος οὐδὲ ἡδόμενος κακοῖς, ὥστε ἐξ-
αγγέλλειν ἀνδρὸς τοσούτου τηλικαύτας συμφοράς.
58 μικρὰ γὰρ καὶ ἡ Περσῶν λεγομένη σκάφευσις καὶ οἱ
γυναικεῖοι τῶν Ἀρτάβρων σκαλισμοὶ πρὸς τὰς ἐπιφε-
59 ρομένας ὀδύνας τῷ σώματι. | καὶ ἡ θαυμασία γυνὴ
479B παρῆν καὶ ὑπερήλγει. ὡς δὲ ἦν ἄπειρον καὶ ἐπετεί-
νετο, "πριαμένη," φησίν, "ὦ γύναι, φάρμακον, ἐπίδος
60 καὶ ἐλευθέρωσον." ἡ δὲ καὶ ἐπρίατο | καὶ παρῆν
52G ἔχουσα. ἐνταῦθα ὁ μὲν ᾔτει πιεῖν, ἡ δὲ ἠξίωσεν προ-
πιεῖν, καὶ αὐτίκα γε ἀπολομένης· τὴν μὲν οἱ προσήκοντες ἔθαπτον, ὁ δὲ Μάξιμος ἔπιεν οὐκέτι.

[59] inser. Go
[60] add. Go   μήτε ἰδεῖν Gi

498

behaved virtuously during that time, he returned to Greece. It was at the time when the author of this narra- 56 tive was being educated and was still a boy just coming into adolescence. But Maximus [suffered much], while many clamored against him, both in public in the theaters and privately to the emperor, he still won admiration because he bore up against such great misfortunes. Nevertheless, they inflicted on him the severest possible punishment; for they fined him a sum of money so large that it is hardly possible for a philosopher to have either heard of [or seen] such an amount (this was because they suspected that he possessed the whole amount); and then they regretted that they had made his fine too small. He was sent into Asia to 57 arrange for down payment of the money, and what he suffered there was beyond any tragedy, and no one could have the grandiloquence or glee to give a full report of the terrible sufferings of this great man. For even the Persian 58 torture called "The Boat,"[146] or the painful toil of the women with the hoe among the Artabri[147] were insignificant compared with the agonies inflicted on Maximus' body. His wonderful wife was ever by his side and suffered 59 deeply. But when there seemed to be no limit to them and they even grew more intense, he said to her: "wife, buy poison, give it to me and set me free." Accordingly, she 60 bought it and came holding it. Thereupon he asked for it to drink but she insisted on drinking first, and when she had straightaway died, her relatives buried her: but Maximus did no longer drink the poison.

[146] Or "The Trough"; a torture method, cf. Plut. *Artax.* 16.
[147] Strabo 3.220 describes the gold-digging of this tribe in Lusitania. Tzetzes, *Chil.* 10.885, echoes Eunapius.

61   Ἐνταῦθα δὴ πᾶς λόγος ἐλάττων, καὶ πᾶν ὅσον ἂν
τὸ ποιητικὸν ὑμνήσειε γένος, πρὸς τὰς Κλεάρχου
62   πράξεις. ἦν μὲν γὰρ ὁ Κλέαρχος ἐκ Θεσπρωτῶν τῶν
εὐδαιμόνων καὶ διαφερόντως <περιττὸς>[61] περὶ δόξαν
καλὴν γενόμενος· τῶν πραγμάτων ἤδη μεταβεβλη-
μένων, καὶ Βαλεντινιανοῦ μὲν εἰς τὴν ἑσπέραν ἀποκε-
χωρηκότος, τοῦ δὲ βασιλέως Βάλεντος κινδύνοις τοῖς
ἐσχάτοις ἐμβεβηκότος, καὶ οὐ τὸν περὶ βασιλείας,
ἀλλὰ τὸν περὶ τῆς σωτηρίας ἀγῶνα τρέχοντος· ὁ γὰρ
Προκόπιος ἀντανάστας πολλαῖς καὶ ἀπείροις δυνά-
μεσι, πανταχόθεν αὐτὸν περιέκοπτεν εἰς τὸ †συν η
μεναι†,[62] τῆς οὖν Ἀσίας ἁπάσης κατ’ ἐκεῖνον τὸν καιρὸν ὁ Κλέαρχος ἐπεστάτει, ὅση κατὰ τὴν ἐξουσίαν
ἀφ’ Ἑλλησπόντου διὰ Λυδίας καὶ Πισιδίας ἐπὶ Παμ-
63   φυλίαν ἀφορίζεται. καὶ πολλὴν εἰς τὰ πράγματα
συνέφερεν εὔνοιαν, τῷ τε σώματι παραβαλλόμενος ἐς
τοὺς πρώτους κινδύνους καὶ πρὸς τὸν τῆς αὐλῆς
ἔπαρχον ἄντικρυς διαφερόμενος, ὥστε οὐδὲ ὁ βασιλεὺς τὴν διαφορὰν ἠγνόει. καίτοί γε ἦν ἔπαρχος
Σαλούτιος, ἀνὴρ καὶ ἐπὶ τῆς Ἰουλιανοῦ βασιλείας
κοσμήσας τὴν ἑαυτοῦ τυχήν,[63] ἀλλ’ ὅμως τήν τε βλα-

----

[61] περιττὸς inser. Gi (et Be): ἀγωνιστὴς Go
[62] συλληφθῆναι coni. Wr: συν η μεναι A (Go add. cruces)
[63] τύχην A Boiss Go Be: ψυχὴν Cob Wr (cf. VPS 64)

----

[148] Clearchus was a frequent correspondent of Libanius and
prefect of Constantinople (AD 398–402).

Now at this point [in my narrative], any account regard-   61
ing the deeds of Clearchus would prove wanting, even if
every poetic type of poem were to sing his praise.[148]
Clearchus came from a well-to-do family in Thesprotis   62
and had won himself a distinguished reputation when the
political situation had already changed, since Valentinian
had withdrawn to the empire of the West,[149] while emperor Valens had landed into extreme dangers and had to
face a challenge not only for empire but for his very life.
For Procopius had revolted against him with numerous,
even unlimited, forces and was causing damage to him
from all sides to †bring about his capture†. Now at that
time Clearchus was governor of all Asia, the domain that
extends from the Hellespont through Lydia and Pisidia
down to Pamphylia. And he contributed enormous good-   63
will to his governmental affairs and exposed his own person to the greatest risks, and openly had a dispute with the
praetorian prefect, so that not even the emperor could
ignore their quarrel. The prefect's name was Sallust,[150]
and during the reign of the emperor Julian he had adorned
his own fate. Nevertheless, Clearchus exposed his reluc-

[149] In AD 363. The revolt of Procopius (ca. 325–366) was in
365.

[150] Not the prefect of Gaul to whom Julian addressed his *Orations* 4 and 8. The variant spelling "Saloutius," is often used. His
official name, e.g., in inscriptions (PLRE 1 s.v. 3.814–17), was
Secundus (cf. Julian, *Ep. ad Athen.* 282b). After Julian's death he
was offered (but refused) the throne, and again on the death of
Jovian, in 364, he refused it for himself and his son. He seems to
have been prefect of the East in 365 but resigned because of the
hostility of Clearchus, the proconsul of Asia.

κείαν αὐτοῦ διὰ τὸ γῆρας ἀπήλεγχε καὶ Νικίαν |
ἀπεκάλει· καὶ γὰρ ἔμελεν αὐτῷ κατὰ τὸν καιρὸν ἐκεῖνον μοσχεύειν καὶ ῥωννύναι τὴν ψυχὴν ὑπ᾽ ἀναγνώσεώς τε καὶ τῆς ἱστορικῆς ἐμπειρίας.

Χωρησάντων δὲ καλῶς τῶν πραγμάτων, ὁ Βάλης
ὑπερηγάσθη Κλέαρχον καὶ οὐκ ἀπέλυσε τῆς ἀρχῆς,
ἀλλ᾽ εἰς ἀρχὴν μετέστησε μείζονα,[64] ἀνθύπατον αὐτὸν
ἐπιστήσας τῆς νῦν ἰδίως Ἀσίας καλουμένης. (αὕτη δὲ
ἀπὸ Περγάμου τὸ ἀλιτενὲς ἐπέχουσα πρὸς τὴν ὑπερκειμένην ἤπειρον ἄχρι Καρίας ἀποτέμνεται καὶ ὁ
Τμῶλος αὐτῆς περιγράφει τὸ πρὸς Λυδίαν.) ἔστι δὲ
ἀρχῶν ἐνδοξοτάτη, καὶ οὐ κατήκοος τοῦ τῆς αὐλῆς
ἐπάρχου, πλὴν ὅσα γε νῦν πάλιν ἐς τὸν νεώτερον τουτονὶ θόρυβον ἄπαντα συμπέφυρται καὶ ἀνατετά-
ρακται. τότε δὲ τὴν ὑγιαίνουσαν Ἀσίαν ἀπολαβὼν ὁ
Κλέαρχος εὗρεν ἐκεῖ τὸν Μάξιμον κατατεινόμενον
ταῖς βασάνοις καὶ μόλις ἀνέχοντα.

θεῖον δὴ τὸ μετὰ ταῦτά ἐστιν εἰπεῖν ἔργον· οὐ γὰρ
ἄν τις τὸ οὕτως παράλογον ἐς ἄλλον τινὰ ἀναφέροι
δικαίως ἢ θεόν· τούς τε γὰρ στρατιώτας ἄπαντας, οἳ
ταύταις ἐφεστήκεσαν ἀλήκτως ταῖς κολάσεσι, μείζονι
βίᾳ φυγεῖν ἐπηνάγκασε, καὶ τὸν Μάξιμον ἀνῆκε τῶν
δεσμῶν, ἐπιμέλειάν τε ἐποιήσατο τοῦ σώματος καὶ
ὁμοτράπεζον ἔθετο, καὶ πρὸς τὸν βασιλέα τοσαύτῃ
κατεχρήσατο παρρησίᾳ, ὥστε ὁ βασιλεὺς ἤδη καὶ

[64] χείρονα A Be: μείζονα A^ml Wr Go

tance to act due to old age, and disparagingly referred to him as "Nikias."[151] And in fact in those days he [= Sallustius] thought only of nurturing and strengthening his mind by reading and the practice of history. 64

Now when he saw that things went so well, Valens felt 65 enormous admiration for Clearchus and far from removing him from his office he transferred him to a post of greater importance and appointed him proconsul of all territory that is today properly called Asia. This province 66 embraces the sea coast from Pergamon and includes the hinterland of that coast as far as Caria, while Mount Tmolos marks its limits in the direction of Lydia. It is the most illustrious of all the provinces and is outside the jurisdiction of the praetorian prefect, save in so far as everything has been thrown into confusion and disorder in recent troubles.[152] But at that time, when Clearchus took over the 67 government of Asia, then still free from sedition, he discovered Maximus there racked by tortures and barely able to endure them.

Next a divine deed is to be recounted; for no one could 68 justly explain such an unpredictable incident as anything else but a divine intervention. For all the soldiers who had been assigned to punish Maximus without respite, with a superior force he coerced to flee, released Maximus from his shackles, took up the care of his body, and made him sit at his own table. Moreover, he spoke with such frankness to the emperor that the latter not only relaxed his

[151] Nikias, the Athenian general, pursued a policy of "watchful waiting" in the Peloponnesian War.

[152] Perhaps he refers to the supremacy of the Goths about 398, or the sedition of Antioch in 387.

μετεθῆκε τὴν ψυχήν καὶ πάντα γε συνεχώρησεν ὅσα
69 Κλέαρχος ἔπειθεν. τῷ γοῦν Σαλουτίῳ τὴν ἀρχὴν
παραλύσας, Αὐξόνιον ἐπέστησε τοῖς τῆς αὐλῆς ἔρ-
480B γοις. | ὁ δὲ Κλέαρχος τούς τε κολαστῆρας ἐκείνους
στρατιώτας καὶ ὅσον κατὰ τὸν ἀτυχῆ χρόνον ἐκεῖνον
ἦσαν ὑφελόμενοί τι καὶ ὑβρίσαντες, τοὺς μὲν ἠμύ-
70 νετο, | τοὺς δὲ εἰσεπράττετο· καὶ πάντες τοῦτο διὰ
54G στόματος εἶχον ὡς εἴη δεύτερος Ἰουλιανὸς τῷ Μα-
71 ξίμῳ. ἐνταῦθα δὴ καὶ δημοσίας τινὰς ἐπιδείξεις ὁ
Μάξιμος ἐποιήσατο, ἀλλ᾽ (οὐ γὰρ ἐπεφύκει πρὸς θέατρον) τὴν δόξαν εἰς ἐλάχιστον ἤνεγκεν, ἕως[65] ἀνέφε-
ρεν ἑαυτὸν διαλεγόμενος πάλιν. πολλὰ γοῦν τῶν τε
κτημάτων ἀνεκομίζετο καὶ τῶν ἑτέρως πως διακεκλεμ-
μένων, καὶ ἦν ταχὺ μάλα ὄλβιος καὶ ὥσπερ ἄρτι
72 παριὼν εἰς τὴν Ἰουλιανοῦ βασιλείαν. ὁ δὲ καὶ εἰς τὴν
Κωνσταντίνου πόλιν περιφανὴς ὢν ἐπεδήμησε καὶ
πάντες αὐτὸν ἐδεδοίκεσαν, τήν τε τύχην ἀνισταμένην
ὁρῶντες· καὶ τῆς δεινότητος[66] τῆς περὶ θεουργίας ἐστὶ
μὲν πεπειραμένος, †τὴν δὲ ἐς τόνδε†[67] ἐπὶ πλέον ἐδό-
ξαζεν. ἐνταῦθα δὲ αὐτῷ πάλιν διὰ τὸ πολὺ κλέος τρα-
73 χύτερον[68] ἀνέφυ πάθος. οἱ γὰρ περὶ τὰ βασίλεια τοῖς
βασι⟨λεῦσιν ἐπιβουλὴν⟩[69] τινὰ συστησάμενοι καὶ
προστησάμενοι μαντεῖον ἰδιωτικὸν (οὐ παντός ἐστι
καταμαθεῖν ὃ λέγω), χρησμοῦ τινὸς ἐκπεσόντος ἀσα-

---

65 ἕως Gi Civil Go: ὥς A
66 ἀσινότητος A: δεινότητος Go
67 cruces scr. Go; τὴν δὲ ἐς λόγον coni. Gi

state of mind but conceded everything that Clearchus
convinced him to do. Thus, he relieved Sallust of his office   69
and put Auxonius[153] in charge of the duties at the palace.
Then Clearchus proceeded to punish the soldiers who had
tortured Maximus, from all who in that time of misfortune
had stolen anything from him he exacted repayment, and
punished those who had insulted him; and this saying was   70
in the mouths of all: that he was a second Julian to Maximus. Thereupon Maximus even delivered some public   71
declamations, but, lacking the talent for speaking in front
of a large audience, he brought his reputation down to a
low point, until he brought himself back to dialectical debate again. Thus, he restored much of his possessions and
of the items that had been stolen from him in various ways,
and very quickly he became as prosperous as when he first
arrived at Julian's court. He also visited the city of Con-   72
stantine as a distinguished personage, and all men regarded him with awe when they witnessed that his for-
tunes were restored. He even demonstrated his expertise
in theurgy and amplified his reputation [on that score].[154]
Thereupon his widespread renown again gave rise to re-
sentment against him. For those at the court framed a   73
conspiracy against the emperors and put forward a private
oracle of their own (it is not open to everyone to understand what I mean), and when some obscure oracular ut-

---

153 Zos. 4.10: praetorian prefect.
154 The text is very corrupt (see Becker 2013, 400).

---

68 Vollenbr Bo: ταχύτερον A Go
69 add. Gi in lac. [12 litt.]

φεστέρου, τὸν χρησμὸν ἐπὶ τὸν Μάξιμον ἀνήνεγκαν,
τὸ μὲν πρᾶγμα οὐχ ὁμολογήσαντες, ὡς δ' ἂν αὐτοῦ
χρήσαντος καὶ ἀνελόντος τι σαφέστερον βουλόμενοι
μαθεῖν· δέδεικτο γὰρ τότε ⟨πάντων ἀνθρώπων⟩[70] Μάξιμον μόνον τὰ τῶν θεῶν εἰδέναι, κἂν ἐπικεκαλυμμένα

74 πρὸς τοὺς ἄλλους φέρηται. ὁ δὲ τὸν νοῦν ἐπιστήσας
καὶ διαθρῶν τὰ λεγόμενα, τὸ κεκρυμμένον μὲν ἐν τοῖς
λόγοις, ὃν δὲ ἀληθῶς, εἶδεν ὀξέως καὶ μαντείων ἀλη-
θέστερον ἐξήνεγκεν, ὡς τόν τε ἀναγνόντα—λέγων
ἑαυτόν—ἀπώλεσαν καὶ πάντας (οὐ τοὺς εἰδότας τὴν

55G ⟨παρα⟩τάξιν[71] μόνον,| προσέθηκεν, ἀλλὰ καὶ τὸ κολα-
σθησόμενον ἀδίκως πλέον ἀπέφηνατο), ἀνύτων[72] δὲ
ἐπέθηκεν ὅτι "μετὰ τὴν ἁπάντων κοινὴν καὶ πολύτρο-
πον φθοράν, ὁ τὸν φόνον ἐργασάμενος βασιλεὺς[73]
ξένον τινὰ ἀναφθαρήσεται τρόπον, οὐδὲ ταφῆς ἀξιω-

75 θεὶς οὐδὲ ἐνδόξου τάφου." καὶ ταῦτα ἔσχεν οὕτως,
καὶ ἐν τοῖς διεξοδικοῖς ἀκριβέστερον γέγραπται.
ἑαλώκεσαν μὲν γὰρ αὐτίκα οἵ τε συστησάμενοι καὶ
ἀρθμήσαντες· πάντων δὲ πανταχοῦ ἁρπαζομένων καὶ
κατακοπτομένων, ὥσπερ ἀλεκτορίδων ἐν ἑορτῇ καὶ
συμποσίῳ κοινὴν εὐωχίαν ἔχοντι, καὶ ὁ Μάξιμος
συνηρπάσθη μέν, καὶ εἰς τὴν Ἀντιόχειαν ἦλθεν, ἔνθα

76 ὁ βασιλεὺς διέτριβεν· αἰσχυνθέντες δὲ αὐτοῦ τὸν φό-

---

[70] inser. Go pro τὰ τῶν θεῶν (quae post μόνον posuit)
[71] παρα inser. Gi   [72] ἀπέφηνέν τε· ἀδύτων A: ἀπέφηνατο, ἀνύτων Gi Go   [73] Go (cf. VPS 22.14): ἐν ᾗ τοῦ φόνου ἔργον ἐσόμεθα A Gi Be

terance was issued, they referred it to Maximus, without admitting their scheme, under the pretense of wanting to learn its meaning more clearly, as if he himself had given forth and revealed the oracle.[155] For it had been made manifest at that time that of all human beings Maximus alone knew the gods' plans, however obscurely they might be conveyed to other people. So by turning his mind to the 74 oracle and closely observing its wording, he quickly understood the hidden message in the words, but it was the truth, and he revealed it more truthfully than oracles, that is to say, that they had ruined both him who read it (referring to himself), and all men besides—he added, not only those who knew of their plot, but declared that many more would be unjustly chastised. Moreover, he ended by announcing: "After the general and multiform slaughter of all men, the emperor who has brought about the murder will die a strange death, and will not be deemed worthy of burial or the honor of a tomb." And this is how it came to 75 pass, as I have described more accurately in my detailed accounts.[156] For the conspirators who had banded together were immediately arrested and rounded up. While all of them were being dragged to prison from all directions and beheaded, like hens at some festival or banquet to entertain the whole populace, Maximus too was dragged away with them, and so came to Antioch where the emperor[157] was staying at the time. Because they were 76

155 Perhaps the oracle reported in Amm. Marcell. 29.1.33.

156 Cf. *Hist*. fr. 39.7 Blockley.

157 Valens. For the execution of Maximus at Ephesus in 371, cf. Amm. Marcell. 29.1; Zos. 4.1.5.

νον, ὡς πάντα ἐπὶ τῆς κρίσεως ἠλέγχθη καὶ ὅτι κατέγνω τῶν ἐγχειρησάντων καὶ ὅτι προεῖπεν ἀκριβῶς
ἅπαντα, καθάπερ ἐν τῷ Μαξίμου σώματι θεόν τινα
κολάζοντες, φονικήν τινα καὶ μαγειρώδη ψυχὴν τὸν
Φῆστον ἐπὶ τὴν Ἀσίαν αὐτῷ συνεξέπεμψαν, τὴν
77 Ἀσίαν τοιούτου τινὸς ἀξιώσαντες. ὁ δὲ παραγενόμενος τὸ προσταχθὲν ἔπραξε καὶ παρ᾽ ἑαυτοῦ προσέθηκεν, ἄφθονόν τινα χορηγίαν τῷ συώδει καὶ λελυσσηη-
κότι τῆς ψυχῆς νέμων· πολλοὺς γὰρ προκατακόψας
αἰτίους τε καὶ ἀναιτίους, καὶ τὸν μέγαν Μάξιμον
78 αὐτοῖς ἐπέσφαξε. κἀκεῖνο μὲν εἶχεν ἡ μαντεία τέλος,
79 ἀπέβαινε δὲ καὶ τὰ λειπόμενα. ὅ τε γὰρ βασιλεὺς ἐν
μεγάλῃ τῶν Σκυθῶν μάχῃ ξένον τινὰ ἠφανίσθη τρόπον, ὥστε οὐδὲ ὀστέον εἰς ἀναίρεσιν εὑρέθη.

481B   Προσεπέθηκε δὲ ὁ δαίμων καὶ ἕτερόν τι μεῖζον· | ὁ
γὰρ Φῆστος ἐκεῖνος (καὶ ταυτά γε ἀκριβῶς ὁ γράφων
παρὼν συνηπίστατο) παραλυθεὶς τῆς ἀρχῆς καὶ ἀπο-
δημήσας πρὸς τὸν νεωστὶ βασιλεύοντα Θεοδόσιον,
56G   εἶτα ἐπανελθών | (ἐγεγαμήκει γὰρ ἐκ τῆς Ἀσίας
γάμον τυραννίδι πρέπονται), καὶ τὴν τρυφὴν ἐπιδεικνύμενος καὶ τὸ διαπεφευγέναι τὰ ἐγκλήματα, ἑορτήν
τε ἐπήγγελλε πολυτελῆ τοῖς ἐν ἀξιώματι καὶ κατὰ
80   εὐγένειαν προβεβηκόσιν. ἡ τρίτη δὲ ἦν ἡμέρα τῶν
καλανδῶν, ἃς οὕτως Ἰανουαρίας ἡμέρας Ῥωμαῖοι

158 Cf. Amm. Marcell. 29.2.

ashamed to put him to death, both because he had refuted
every charge at the trial and condemned those who had
laid hands on him, and because he had so precisely foretold all that was happening, just as though in the body of
Maximus they were punishing some god, they sent away
with him into Asia a certain Festus,[158] a murderous and
brutal character, judging Asia to be a worthy abode for
such a man. When he arrived, he carried out his orders,   77
and of his own accord even went beyond them, fulfilling
his "public duty" generously through his beastlike and ra-
bid temperament. For he had many beheaded, guilty and
innocent, and next he slaughtered the great Maximus. So   78
the oracle was fulfilled, and the rest of it also came to pass.
The emperor vanished during a fierce battle with the   79
Scythians in a strange fashion,[159] so that not even a bone
was found to recover and bury.

To all this the demon added a still more wondrous
occurrence. For that same Festus (and this the author
learned accurately since he was present), was deprived of
his office, and first he traveled to visit Theodosius who had
lately been made emperor, then he returned (for he had
contracted a marriage from Asia fitting for a tyrant), and
to make a display of his luxurious living and his escape
from all the charges against him, he announced that he
would give a magnificent banquet to those who had risen
to the most distinguished offices or were of the highest
nobility. Now it was the third day after the January Ca-   80
lends, as the Romans call them, and they all paid their

---

[159] Amm. Marcell. 31.13, "nec postea repertus est usquam."
The battle was at Adrianople in 378, against the Goths; late authors often confuse them with the Scythians.

81 προσονομάζουσι, καὶ προσκυνήσαντες πάντες αὐτῷ
ὑπέσχοντο τὴν εὐωχίαν. ὁ δὲ παρῆλθε μὲν εἰς τὸ τῶν
Νεμέσεων ἱερόν (καίτοί γε οὐδέποτε φήσας θεραπεύειν θεούς, ἀλλ᾽ οὓς ἐκόλασεν ἅπαντας διὰ τοῦτο
ἀνῃρηκώς), παρελθὼν δὲ ὅμως, αὐτοῖς ὄναρ ἀπήγ-
82 γειλε καὶ κατεδάκρυε τὴν ὄψιν διηγούμενος. τὸ δὲ
ὄνειρον ἦν· τὸν Μάξιμον ἔφασκε τραχηλάγχην ἐπι-
βαλόμενον ἕλκειν αὐτὸν εἰς τὸν Ἅιδην, ὡς δικασόμε-
νον ἐπὶ τοῦ Πλουτέως. οἱ δὲ παρόντες, καίπερ δεδιότες
καὶ πρὸς τὸν ὅλον τοῦ ἀνδρὸς ἀναφέροντες βίον, τά
τε δάκρυα ἀπέψηχεν ἕκαστος καὶ ταῖν Θεαῖν ἐκέλευον
83 εὔχεσθαι· ὁ δὲ ἐπείθετο καὶ ηὔχετο. ἐξιόντι δὲ αὐτῷ,
τοῖν ποδοῖν ἀμφοῖν ὑπενεχθέντων, ἐπὶ τὰ νῶτα ἐξολι-
σθαίνει τὸ σῶμα καὶ ἄναυδος ἔκειτο· καὶ ἀπενεχθεὶς
αὐτίκα ἐτελεύτησε, καὶ τοῦτο ἔδοξεν εἶναι τῆς προνοίας ἔργον ἄριστον.

8. Πρίσκος. Περὶ δὲ Πρίσκου τὰ μὲν πολλὰ κατὰ
τὴν περιπεσοῦσαν ἀνάγκην καὶ πρότερον εἴρηται
⟨καί⟩[74] ὅθεν τε ἦν· ἴδιον δὲ κατὰ τὸ ἦθος αὐτοῦ τοιοῦτον ἀπομνημονεύεται· κρυψίνους τε ἦν ἄγαν καὶ
βαθυγνώμων, μνήμης τε εἰς ἄκρον ἀφιγμένος, καὶ
τὰς δόξας ἁπάσας τῶν παλαιῶν συνῃρηκὼς καὶ ἐπὶ
2 στόματος ἔχων· κάλλιστος δὲ ὢν καὶ μέγας ὀφθῆναι,
καὶ ἀπαίδευτος ἂν ἔδοξεν εἶναι διὰ τὸ μόλις χωρεῖν
ἐς διάλεξιν, ἀλλ᾽ ὡς θησαυρόν γέ τινα ἐφύλαττε τὰ

[74] inser. Go

respects to him and promised to come to the banquet. Then Festus entered the temple of the Goddesses Nemesis,[160] though he had never professed any reverence for the gods, in fact it was for their worship of the gods that he punished all his victims with death; still he did enter, and related to those present a dream vision he had had, and as he told the tale his face was drenched in tears. Now the dream was as follows: he said that Maximus threw a noose round his neck, seized him, and dragged him down to Hades to have his case tried before Pluto. All those present, although terrified when they recalled the whole life of the man, each of them dried their tears, and advised him to pray to the two Goddesses. He obeyed them and offered up his prayers. But as he came out of the temple he lost his footing, and he fell on his back and lay there speechless. He was carried away and died soon after, an event that was considered to be an excellent outcome of Providence.

8. Priscus. Concerning Priscus I have already related many facts, whenever the need arose, and earlier it was [also] reported where he was from. But of his character the following particular trait is recorded. He was of a too secretive disposition, and his learning was recondite and abstruse; moreover, he had managed to extend his memory to the limit, having collected all the opinions of the ancients and knowing them by heart. In appearance he was very handsome and tall, and he might have seemed uncivilized, because he barely engaged in disputation, but he kept his own convictions hidden as if they were some

81

82

83

2

[160] Two deities called Nemesis were worshipped in Asia, and especially at Smyrna.

δόγματα καὶ τοὺς εὐκόλως περὶ αὐτῶν προϊεμένους
φωνὴν ἀσώτους | ἔφασκεν. οὐ γὰρ τὸν νικώμενον ἐν
ταῖς διαλέξεσιν ἐξημεροῦσθαι μᾶλλον ἔφασκεν, ἀλλὰ
πρὸς τὴν δύναμιν τῆς ἀληθείας ἀντιβαίνοντα, ταῖς τε
ἡδοναῖς καὶ τῷ φιλοσωμάτῳ κατακλώμενον ἀγριοῦ-
σθαι, καὶ μισόλογόν τι ἅμα καὶ μισοφιλόσοφον ἀπο-
τελεῖσθαι καὶ διαπράττεσθαι. διὰ ταύτην οὖν τὴν
αἰτίαν ἐπεῖχε τὰ πολλά. καὶ βαρὺς[75] ἦν καὶ ὀγκώδης
κατὰ τὸ ἦθος, καὶ τὸ ἦθος ἐφύλαττεν οὐ μόνον ὅτε
ἑταίροις καὶ ὁμιληταῖς συνῆν, ἀλλ᾽ ἐκ νεότητος αὐτῷ
τὸ ἀξίωμα συνεγήρασεν. ὁ γοῦν Χρυσάνθιος πρὸς
τὸν ταῦτα γράφοντα ἔλεγεν ὡς ὁ μὲν Αἰδεσίου τρόπος
κοινὸς ἦν καὶ δημοτικός, καὶ μετά γε τοὺς ἄθλους
ὅσοι περὶ λόγους ἦσαν, πρὸς περίπατον ἐξῄει κατὰ
τὸ Πέργαμον καὶ τῶν ἑταίρων παρῆσαν οἱ τιμιώτεροι·
ὁ δὲ διδάσκαλος ἁρμονίαν τινὰ καὶ ἐπιμέλειαν πρὸς
τὸ ἀνθρώπειον ἐμφυτεύων τοῖς μαθηταῖς, ὡς ἀσυ-
φήλους αὐτοὺς ἑώρα καὶ δι᾽ ἀγερωχίαν τῶν δογμάτων
ὑπέρφρονας καὶ τὰ πτερὰ μακρότερα καὶ ἀπαλώτερα
τοῦ Ἰκαρίου, | κατεβίβαζεν αὐτοὺς οὐκ ἐπὶ τὸν πόν-
τον, ἀλλ᾽ ἐπὶ τὴν γῆν καὶ τὸ ἀνθρώπινον. αὐτὸς ὁ
ταῦτα διδάσκων λαχανόπωλίν τε ἀπαντήσας ἡδέως
ἂν εἶδε καὶ τὴν πορείαν ἐπιστήσας προσεφθέγξατο
καὶ περὶ τιμῆς ἂν διελέχθη πρὸς αὐτήν, ὅτι πολὺ τὸ
καπηλεῖον ἐργάζεται, καὶ ἅμα διῄει τὴν γεωργίαν τοῦ
λαχάνου πρὸς αὐτήν. καὶ πρὸς ὑφάντην τοιοῦτον ἄν

[75] Go: βραδὺς A Vollenbr Be

512

kind of treasure, and used to call those who too easily gave
out their views on these matters "spendthrifts." For he   3
used to say that one who is beaten in disputations does not
thereby become civilized, but rather, as he goes up against
the force of the truth and is overwhelmed by the passions
and a love for the body,[161] he becomes more wild, and ends
up hating both reason and philosophy. For this reason he   4
usually held back on many occasions. Also, he had a serious and lofty personality, and he preserved this bearing
not only when he was with his friends and students, and
the dignity of his manner remained with him from youth
to old age. (This is why Chrysanthius used to say to the   5
author of this account that Aedesius' manners were sociable and unassuming, and after their contests in disputation, he would go for a walk in Pergamon accompanied by
the more distinguished of his pupils. And their teacher   6
used to instill in his pupils a feeling of harmony and of
responsibility toward humanity, when he observed that
they were headstrong and arrogant because of their over-
confidence in their own opinions (their wings bigger and
softer than those of Icarus), he would force them back
down, not into the sea, but to earth and to human life.
While he thus instructed them, he himself, if he met a   7
woman selling vegetables, was pleased to see her and
would interrupt his walk to speak to her and discuss the
price she charged, and say that her shop was making a
good profit, while at the same time chatting with her about
the cultivation of vegetables. He would behave in the same

[161] Cf. Pl. *Phd*. 68c; Plu. 2.140c; Porph *De antr. nymph.* 11.

8 τι ἐποίησεν ἕτερον καὶ πρὸς χαλκέα καὶ τέκτονα. οἱ
58G μὲν οὖν | σωφρονέστεροι τῶν ἑταίρων ἐξεπαιδεύοντο
ταῦτα, καὶ μάλιστα Χρυσάνθιος, καὶ εἴ τις ἦν ἐκείνης
τῆς διατριβῆς Χρυσανθίῳ παραπλήσιος.

9   Μόνος δὲ ὁ Πρίσκος οὐδὲ παρόντος ἐφείδετο τοῦ
διδασκάλου, ἀλλὰ προδότην τε αὐτὸν ἐκάλει τοῦ τῆς
φιλοσοφίας ἀξιώματος καὶ ἄνθρωπον λογάρια εἰδότα, κρείττονα μὲν πρὸς ψυχῆς ἀναγωγήν, οὐ φυ-
10 λαττόμενα δὲ ἐπὶ τῶν ἔργων. ἀλλ' ὅμως τοιοῦτος ὤν,
καὶ μετὰ τὴν Ἰουλιανοῦ βασιλείαν ἀμώμητος ἔμεινε
καὶ πολλούς τε νεωτερισμοὺς ἐνεγκὼν κορυβαντιών-
των ἐπὶ σοφίᾳ μειρακίων καὶ ἐπὶ πᾶσι τὸ βαθὺ δια-
φυλάττων ἦθος καὶ γελῶν τὴν ἀνθρωπίνην ἀσθένειαν,
τοῖς τῆς Ἑλλάδος ἱεροῖς, εἰς μακρόν τι γῆρας ἀνύ-
11 σας, ὅς γε ἦν ὑπὲρ τὰ ἐνενήκοντα, συναπώλετο· πολλῶν καὶ ἄλλων ἐν τῷδε τῷ χρόνῳ τῶν μὲν διὰ λύπην
προϊεμένων τὸν βίον, οἱ δὲ καὶ ὑπὸ τῶν βαρβάρων
κατεκόπτοντο· ἐν οἷς Προτέριός τε ἦν τις ἐκ Κεφαλη-
νίας τῆς νήσου, καὶ ἐμαρτυρεῖτο καλὸς καὶ ἀγαθὸς
12 εἶναι. Ἱλάριον δὲ καὶ ὁ ταῦτα γράφων ἠπίστατο, ἄνδρα Βιθυνὸν μὲν τὸ γένος, Ἀθήνησι δὲ καταγηρά-
σαντα, πρὸς δὲ τῷ καθαρῷ τῆς ἄλλης παιδείας, κατὰ
γραφικὴν οὕτω φιλοσοφήσαντα, ὥστε οὐκ ἐτεθνήκει

fashion to a weaver, a smith, or a carpenter. Thus, the more 8
prudent of his pupils were trained in this affability, especially Chrysanthius and all who in that school resembled
Chrysanthius.)[162]

Only Priscus did not spare the feelings of their teacher, 9
but in his presence would call him a traitor to the dignity
of philosophy, a man versed in aphorisms,[163] which, while
quite helpful for elevating the soul,[164] were never observed in practical life. Nevertheless, in spite of his dispo- 10
sition, even after the reign of Julian, Priscus remained
exempt from criticism and supporting many newfangled
ideas among his students, who, like Corybants, were in-
toxicated with the desire for wisdom, and while still maintaining on all occasions his unfathomable character and
smiling at human weakness,[165] he reached an advanced
age (for he was over ninety), and perished at the same time
as the temples of Greece. And, in those days, there were 11
many others who on account of their grief threw away
their lives, while others were slaughtered by the barbarians; among them was Proterius, a native of the island
Cephalonnia whose worth and probity is well evidenced.
The present author also knew Hilarius, by birth a Bithyn- 12
ian; he grew old at Athens, and, besides the whole range
of learning, he had so mastered the art of painting that it
seemed as though in his hands Euphranor was still alive.[166]

162 *VPS* 5–8 digress from the Priscus narrative (Goulet).
163 Echoes Demosthenes, *On the False Embassy* 421; cf. Philostr. *VS* 623.
164 Cf. Iambl. *Myst*. 3.7; Porph. *Sent*. 30.
165 Echoes Pl. *Phd*. 107b.
166 Famous Corinthian sculptor-painter (Plin. *HN* 35.36).

13 ἐν ταῖς ἐκείνου χερσὶν ὁ Εὐφράνωρ. καὶ ὁ ταῦτα γράφων διὰ τοῦτο †αὐτὸ εἴδεσι καλὸν†[76] ἐθαύμαζε καὶ
ὑπερηγάπα. ἀλλ' ὅμως καὶ Ἱλάριος τῶν ἀπολαυσάν-
των ἦν τῆς κοινῆς συμφορᾶς, ἔξω μὲν εὑρεθεὶς τῶν
Ἀθηνῶν (πλησίον γάρ που Κορίνθου διέτριβε), κατα-
κοπεὶς δὲ παρὰ τῶν βαρβάρων ἅμα τοῖς οἰκέταις. καὶ
14 | ταῦτα μὲν ἐν τοῖς διεξοδικοῖς, ἐὰν τῷ δαίμονι δόξῃ,
59G γραφήσεται, οὐ τὸ καθ' ἕκαστον ἔχοντα, ἀλλὰ τὸ κοινὸν ἐκεῖ σαφέστερον λελέξεται· νυνὶ δὲ ὅσον ἐπέβαλε
τὸ καθ' ἕκαστον ἱκανῶς ἐς ἀφήγησιν εἴρηται.

9. Ἰουλιανός. Ἰουλιανὸς δὲ ὁ ἐκ Καππαδοκίας σοφιστὴς εἰς τοὺς Αἰδεσίου χρόνους ἤκμαζε καὶ ἐτυράν-
νει γε τῶν Ἀθηνῶν, καὶ παρὰ τοῦτον ἡ πᾶσα νεότης
πανταχόθεν ἐχώρει, ῥητορικῆς ἕνεκεν τὸν ἄνδρα καὶ
μεγέθους φύσεως σεβαζόμενοι. ἦσαν μὲν γὰρ καὶ
κατὰ ταὐτὸν ἕτεροί τινες παραψαύοντες τοῦ καλοῦ καὶ
πρὸς τὴν ἐκείνου δόξαν διαιρόμενοι, Ἀψίνης τε ὁ ἐκ
Λακεδαίμονος, δόξαν ἔχων τεχνικοῦ τινος, καὶ Ἐπά-
2 γαθος, καὶ τοιαύτη τις ὀνομάτων χορηγία· ὁ δὲ τῷ
μεγέθει τῆς φύσεως ἁπάντων κατεκράτει καὶ τὸ ἔλαττον μακρῷ τινι ἦν ἔλαττον. ὁμιληταὶ δὲ αὐτοῦ πολλοὶ
μὲν καὶ πανταχόθεν, ὡς εἰπεῖν, καὶ πανταχῆ δια-
σπαρέντες καὶ θαυμασθέντες ὅπου ποτὲ ἱδρύθησαν·
3 ἀπόλεκτοι | δὲ τῶν ἄλλων ἁπάντων ὅ τε θειότατος
483B Προαιρέσιος, καὶ Ἡφαιστίων, Ἐπιφάνιός τε ὁ ἐκ

76 A: cruces add. Go: τὸ ἐν εἴδεσι καλῶν Wytt Boiss Wr Gi

516

The author of this narrative used to admire and love him   13
beyond other men, because of the beauty of his portraits.
Nevertheless, even Hilarius could not escape his share in
the general disasters, for he was captured outside Athens
(he was staying somewhere near Corinth), and together
with his slaves was beheaded by the barbarians.[167] And   14
these events, if it pleases the demon, will be recorded
more fully in my historical *Chronicle*, since there they will
be told more clearly, not with reference to the specific
events, but as they concern the interests of the broad
course of history. For the present, however, their bearing
on individuals has been set forth as far as is suitable to my
narrative.[168]

9. Julian.[169] Julian, the sophist from Cappadocia, flourished in the time of Aedesius and held sway over Athens.
For all the youths from all parts flocked to him and revered
the man for his eloquence and his abundant talent. For
there were indeed certain other men, his contemporaries,
who in a limited sense attained to the comprehension of
true beauty and reached the heights of his renown, namely
Apsines of Lacedaemon who was known as a technically
skilled orator, and Epagathus, and a whole host of names
of that sort. But Julian surpassed them all by his abundant   2
talent, and the person coming next was a distant second.
He had numerous pupils who came, so to speak, from all
parts of the world, and when dispersed in every country
were admired wherever and whenever they established
themselves. But most distinguished of them all were the   3
divinely inspired Prohaeresius, and Hephaestion, Epipha-

---

[167] By the Goths in 395.   [168] Cf. fr. 64.3b Blockley.
[169] In this section the lives of sophists start.

EUNAPIUS

Συρίας καὶ Διόφαντος ὁ Ἀράβιος. Τουσκιανοῦ δὲ
μνησθῆναι καλόν, καὶ γὰρ οὗτος ἐκείνου μετέσχε τῆς
ὁμιλίας, ἀλλὰ τούτου μὲν καὶ ἐν τοῖς κατὰ Ἰουλιανὸν
4 ἐμνήσθημεν διεξοδικοῖς. Ἰουλιανοῦ δὲ καὶ τὴν οἰκίαν
ὁ συγγραφεὺς Ἀθήνησιν ἑώρα, μικρὰν μὲν καὶ εὐτελῆ
τινα, Ἑρμοῦ δὲ ὅμως καὶ Μουσῶν περιπνέουσαν,
οὕτως ἱεροῦ τινος ἁγίου διέφερεν οὐδέν· Προαιρεσίῳ
5 δὲ αὐτὴν καταλελοίπει. καὶ εἰκόνες δὲ τῶν ὑπ᾽ αὐτοῦ
θαυμασθέντων ἑταίρων ἀνέκειντο καὶ τὸ θέατρον ἦν
ξεστοῦ λίθου, τῶν δημοσίων θεάτρων εἰς μίμησιν,
6 ἀλλὰ ἔλαττον καὶ ὅσον πρέπειν οἰκίᾳ. τοσαύτη | γὰρ
60G ἦν Ἀθήνησιν ἡ στάσις τῶν τότε ἀνθρώπων καὶ νέων,
καθάπερ τῆς πόλεως, ἐκ τῶν παλαιῶν ἐκείνων πολέμων, τὸν ἐντὸς τείχους ἀσκούσης κίνδυνον, ὥστε οὐδεὶς ἐτόλμα τῶν σοφιστῶν δημοσίᾳ καταβὰς διαλέγεσθαι, ἀλλ᾽ ἐν τοῖς ἰδιωτικοῖς θεάτροις ἀπολαβόντες
τὰς φωνὰς αὐτῶν μειρακίοις διελέγοντο, οὐ τὸν περὶ
ψυχῆς θέοντες, ἀλλὰ τὸν περὶ κρότου καὶ φωνῆς ἀγω-
νιζόμενοι.

7 Πολλῶν δὲ σιωπωμένων, τοῦτο ἀνάγκη περὶ αὐτοῦ
καταβαλεῖν καὶ συνεισενεγκεῖν ἐς τὸν λόγον, δεῖγμα
8 τῆς ὅλης τοῦ ἀνδρὸς παιδείας καὶ συνέσεως. ἔτυχον
μὲν γὰρ οἱ θρασύτατοι τῶν Ἀψίνου μαθητῶν ταῖς
χερσὶ κρατήσαντες τῶν Ἰουλιανοῦ κατὰ τὸν ἐμφύλιον

---

170 See VPS 7.5, 7.35.   171 The antagonism of "Town"
and "Gown" was probably intensified by religious differences,
since most of the students were opposed to Christianity.

518

nius of Syria, and Diophantus the Arab. It is fitting that I
should also mention Tuscianus, since he too was one of
Julian's pupils, but I have already spoken of him in my
detailed writings on the reign of emperor Julian.[170] The 4
author himself saw Julian's house at Athens; it was small
and plain, but its ambiance exuded the presence of Hermes and the Muses, so closely did it resemble a sacred
temple. He had bequeathed it to Prohaeresius. There, too, 5
were erected statues of the pupils whom he had admired
and he had a theater of polished marble made in imitation
of public theaters, but smaller and of a size suitable to a
house. For in those days, so bitter was the feud at Athens 6
between the citizens and the young students,[171] as though
the city after those ancient wars of hers was fostering
within her walls the peril of discord, that not one of the
sophists ventured to go down into the city and hold discourses in public, but they confined their voices to their
private lecture theaters and discoursed there to their students. Thus, they ran no risk of their lives,[172] but competed there for applause and fame for their eloquence.

Though I leave much unsaid, I must set down and in- 7
troduce into this narrative the following illustration of all
of Julian's erudition and intelligence. It so happened that 8
the boldest of Apsines' pupils had beaten Julian's pupils in
a fight during the "war of factions"[173] that they kept up.

[172] Cf. Hom. *Il.* 22.161.
[173] The faction fights of the sophists and their pupils are often
mentioned by Libanius; cf. Himer. *Or.* 4.9 and *Or.* 19 to those
pupils who would neglect their lectures. The incident here described occurred in the 320s.

ἐκεῖνον πόλεμον· χερσὶ δὲ βαρείαις καὶ Λακωνικαῖς
χρησάμενοι, τῶν πεπονθότων καὶ περὶ τοῦ σώματος
9 κινδυνευόντων, ὥσπερ ἀδικηθέντες, κατηγόρουν. ἀνε-
φέρετο δὲ ἐπὶ τὸν ἀνθύπατον ἡ δίκη, καὶ ὃς βαρύς τις
εἶναι καὶ φοβερὸς ἐνδεικνύμενος, καὶ τὸν διδάσκαλον
συναρπασθῆναι κελεύει καὶ τοὺς κατηγορηθέντας
ἅπαντας δεσμώτας, ὥσπερ τοὺς ἐπὶ φόνῳ κατακε-
10 κλεισμένους. ἐῴκει δὲ ὡς Ῥωμαῖός τις οὐκ εἶναι τῶν
ἀπαιδεύτων οὐδὲ τῶν ὑπ' ἀγροίκῳ καὶ ἀμούσῳ τύχῃ
11 τεθραμμένων. ὅ τε γοῦν Ἰουλιανὸς παρῆν, οὕτως ἐπιταχθέν, καὶ ὁ Ἀψίνης συμπαρῆν, οὐκ ἐπιταχθέν, ἀλλ'
ὡς συνηγορήσων τοῖς κατηγορηκόσι. καὶ ἡ μὲν
ἐξέτασις προὔκειτο καὶ τοῖς διώκουσιν εἴσοδος ἐδόθη.
12 προειστήκει δὲ τῆς ἀτάκτου Σπάρτης Θεμιστοκλῆς
τις Ἀθηναῖος, ὃς ἦν καὶ τῶν κακῶν αἴτιος· προπετέ-
στερος δὲ ὢν καὶ θρασύτερος, ἐς τὴν ἐπωνυμίαν ὕβρι-
61G ζεν. εὐθὺς μὲν | οὖν ὁ ἀνθύπατος ταυρηδὸν ὑπιδὼν τὸν
13 Ἀψίνην, "σὲ δὲ τίς," εἶπεν, "ἐλθεῖν ἐκέλευσεν;" ὁ δὲ
ἀπεκρίνατο περὶ τοῖς ἑαυτοῦ τέκνοις ἀγωνιῶν ἐληλυ-
θέναι. καὶ τῇ σιωπῇ κρύψαντος τὴν ἔννοιαν τοῦ ἄρχοντος, εἰσῄεσαν πάλιν οἱ δεσμῶται καὶ ἠδικημένοι
καὶ ὁ διδάσκαλος μετ' αὐτῶν, ⟨ἀργοὺς⟩ κόμας ἔχοντες[77] καὶ τὰ σώματα κεκακωμένοι λίαν, ὥστε οἰκτροὺς

77 ἔχοντες A Wr Gi: αὐχμῶντες Wytt: ⟨ἀργοὺς⟩ κόμας Go

After laying violent hands on them in Spartan fashion,[174] even though the victims of their ill-treatment had been in danger of their lives, they prosecuted them as though they themselves were the injured parties. The lawsuit was referred to the proconsul and he, who turned out to be a stern and intimidating person, ordered that their teacher also be arrested, and that all the accused be thrown into chains, like men imprisoned on a charge of murder. It seems, however, that, for a Roman, he was not uneducated or of the kind who are bred in a boorish and uncultured fashion. Accordingly, Julian was in court, as he had been ordered, and Apsines was there also, not because he had been summoned, but to help the case of the plaintiffs. Now all was ready for the hearing of the case, and the plaintiffs were permitted to enter. The leader of the disorderly Spartan faction was one Themistocles, an Athenian, who was in fact responsible for all the trouble: being a rash and headstrong youth, he put his famous name to shame.[175] The proconsul at once glared fiercely[176] at Apsines, and said: "Who ordered you to come here?" He replied that he had come because he was anxious about his children. The magistrate concealed his real opinion without saying a word and then the prisoners who had been so unfairly treated again came before the court, and with them their teacher. They had their hair [unwashed] and were physically in such discomfort, that they were a

174 Spartan violence (*Laconica manus*), apparently a proverb, here also an allusion to Apsines' place of origin.

175 A reference to Themistocles, the great Athenian of the fifth century BC.

176 An echo of Pl. *Phd.* 117b; cf. Hom. *Il.* 2.245.

14 αὐτοὺς φανῆναι καὶ τῷ κρίνοντι. δοθέντος δὲ τοῦ λόγου τοῖς κατηγοροῦσιν, ἤρξατο μὲν ὁ Ἀψίνης τοῦ λόγου, ἀλλ᾽ ὁ ἀνθύπατος ὑπολαβών, "ἀλλ᾽ οὐ τοῦτό γε,"
εἶπε, "Ῥωμαῖοι δοκιμάζουσιν· ἀλλ᾽ ὁ τὴν πρώτην εἰπὼν κατηγορίαν κινδυνευέτω περὶ τῆς δευτέρας."
ἐνταῦθα παρασκευὴ μὲν οὐκ ἦν πρὸς τὴν τῆς κρίσεως
15 ὀξύτητα· ἦν δὲ ὁ Θεμιστοκλῆς κατηγορηκώς, | καὶ
484B λέγειν ἀναγκαζόμενος χροιάν τε ἤλλαξε καὶ τὰ χείλη
διέδακνεν ἀπορούμενος, καὶ πρὸς τοὺς ἑταίρους ὑπέ-
βλεπε καὶ παρεφθέγγετο τί πρακτέον· εἰσεληλύθεσαν
γὰρ ὡς ἐπὶ τῇ συνηγορίᾳ τοῦ διδασκάλου μόνον κε-
16 κραξόμενοι καὶ βοησόμενοι. πολλῆς οὖν σιωπῆς καὶ
ταραχῆς οὔσης, σιωπῆς μὲν καθ᾽ ὅλον τὸ δικαστήριον, ταραχῆς δὲ περὶ τὸ τῶν διωκόντων μέρος, ἐλε-
εινόν τι παραφθεγξάμενος ὁ Ἰουλιανός, "ἀλλ᾽ ἐμέ γε
17 εἰπεῖν," ἔφη, "κέλευσον·" ὁ δὲ ἀνθύπατος ἀναβοήσας·
"ἀλλ᾽ οὐδεὶς ὑμῶν γ᾽ ἐρεῖ τῶν ἐσκεμμένων διδασκάλων, οὐδὲ κροτήσει τις τῶν μαθητῶν τὸν λέγοντα,
ἀλλ᾽ εἴσεσθέ γε αὐτίκα ἡλίκον ἐστὶ καὶ οἷον τὸ παρὰ
18 Ῥωμαίοις δίκαιον. ἀλλὰ Θεμιστοκλῆς μὲν περαινέτω
τὴν κατηγορίαν, ἀπολογείσθω δὲ ὃν ἂν σὺ ἀποκρίνῃς
ἄριστον." ἐνταῦθα κατηγόρει μὲν οὐδείς, ἀλλὰ Θεμιστοκλῆς ὀνόματος ἦν ὕβρις.

19 Ἀπολογεῖσθαι δὲ πρὸς τὴν προτέραν κατηγορίαν
ὡς ἐκέλευσε τὸν δυνάμενον, ὁ σοφιστὴς Ἰουλιανός
62G "σὺ μέν," εἶπεν, | "ἀνθύπατε, διὰ τὴν ὑπεροχὴν τοῦ

pitiful sight even to the judge. When the plaintiffs were 14
permitted to speak, Apsines began his speech, but the
proconsul interrupted him and said: "No, Romans do not
approve of this approach: instead, let the person who put
forward the first formal accusation try his luck at the second stage." There was now no time for preparation because of the suddenness of the decision. Themistocles had 15
made the speech for the prosecution before, but compelled to speak he turned pale, bit his lips[177] because he
found himself cornered, and looked furtively toward his
comrades and consulted them in whispers as to what was
to be done. For they had come into court intent only on
shouting and applauding loudly their teacher speaking on
their behalf. So now with widespread silence and be- 16
wilderment present—a general silence in the court, but
bewilderment among the accusers—Julian, in a low and
pitiful voice said: "Then allow me to speak." But the pro- 17
consul said in a loud voice: "No, not one of you well-
prepared teachers shall plead, nor shall anyone of your
pupils applaud the speaker; but you shall learn forthwith
how extraordinary is the justice that the Romans dispense.
First, Themistocles is to finish his speech for the prose- 18
cution, and then he whom you think best to speak in
defense." But no one spoke up for the plaintiffs, and
Themistocles was a disgrace to his great name.

When the proconsul next ordered that anyone who 19
could should reply to the earlier speech of the prosecution, the sophist Julian said: "Proconsul, by way of your
superlative justice you have transformed Apsines into a

[177] A sign of anxiety or restrained anger; cf. Hom. *Od.* 1.381;
Eur. *Bacch.* 621 (cf. *VPS* 6.61 above, "bit his tongue").

δικαίου πεποίηκας Πυθαγόραν Ἀψίνην, βραδέως τὸ
20 σιωπᾶν, ἀλλ᾽ ὅμως δικαίως, μαθόντα· ὁ δὲ πάλαι
(τοῦτο γὰρ αὐτὸς καταμανθάνεις) καὶ τοὺς ἑταίρους
πυθαγορίζειν καὶ σιωπᾶν ἐδίδαξεν. εἰ δὲ ἀπολογεῖσθαι κελεύεις τῶν ἐμῶν ἑταίρων τινά, κέλευσον ἀπο-
λυθῆναι τῶν δεσμῶν Προαιρέσιον καὶ δοκιμάσεις
αὐτὸς πότερον ἀττικίζειν ἢ πυθαγορίζειν πεπαίδευ-
21 ται." ὡς δὲ ταῦτα ἐπέτρεψε καὶ μάλα εὐκόλως—ταῦτα
δὲ πρὸς τὸν συγγραφέα Τουσκιανὸς ἐξήγγελλε
παρὼν τῇ κρίσει καὶ εἷς ὢν τῶν κατηγορουμένων—
παρελθὼν εἰς μέσους Προαιρέσιος ἄδεσμος, ἐμβοήσαντος αὐτῷ τοῦ διδασκάλου σφοδρόν τε καὶ διάτο-
νον[78] ὥσπερ ἐπὶ τῶν στεφανιτῶν οἱ παρακελευόμενοι
καὶ προτρέποντες, ἐμβοήσαντος δὲ ὀξέως τό "λέγε,
Προαιρέσιε, νῦν καιρὸς τοῦ λέγειν," ὁ μὲν προοίμιόν
τι, ἔφη—οὐ γὰρ ἠπίστατό γε αὐτὸ Τουσκιανός, τὸν
δὲ νοῦν ἔφραζεν—, ἐξήνεγκεν εἴς τε οἶκτον ὧν ἐπεπόν-
θεσαν ῥέπον, καὶ μεμιγμένον τινὰ εἶχε τὸ προοίμιον
22 ἔπαινον τοῦ διδασκάλου· καί που τις καὶ διὰ λέξεως
μιᾶς διαβολή τις ἐγκατεσπείρετο τῷ προοιμίῳ, προ-
πέτειαν ἐμφαίνουσα τῆς ἀνθυπατικῆς ἀρχῆς, ὡς οὐ
προσῆκον αὐτοῖς οὐδὲ μετὰ τοὺς ἐλέγχους τοιαῦτα
23 ὑποστῆναι καὶ παθεῖν. κάτω δὲ τοῦ ἀνθυπάτου νεύον-
τος καὶ τόν τε νοῦν τῶν λεγομένων καταπεπληγμένου
καὶ τὸ βάθος τῶν λέξεων καὶ τὴν εὐκολίαν καὶ τὸν
κρότον, καὶ πάντων μὲν βουλομένων ἐπαινεῖν, κατα-

---

[78] διάτορον Be; cf. Go ad loc.

Pythagoras, who slowly but still rightly has learned how to
remain silent. Pythagoras long ago (no doubt you know   20
this full well) also taught his pupils to live like a Pythagorean (i.e., be silent). But, if you allow one of my pupils to
make our defense, give orders for Prohaeresius to be released from his bonds, and you shall judge for yourself
whether he was taught to act in the Attic manner or the
Pythagorean manner." The proconsul granted this request   21
very willingly (as Tuscianus,[178] who was present at the trial
and one among the accused, reported to the author), and
Prohaeresius, free from his chains, came forward, after his
master had called out to him in a loud and piercing voice,
such as is used by those who exhort and incite athletes
contending for a garland, and said in a piercing voice:[179]
"Speak, Prohaeresius, the moment to speak is now!" He
then first delivered an introduction (Tuscianus could not
exactly recall it, though he gave me the gist) that took off
and seamlessly moved to a pitiable account of their sufferings, and the introduction included words of praise for
their teacher. He inserted only one complaint (by the use   22
of one word) in this introduction, when he pointed to the
impulsiveness of the proconsular authority, since not even
after sufficient proof of their guilt was it proper for them
to undergo and suffer such treatment. While the procon-   23
sul bowed his head, awestruck by the effect of the arguments and the weight of his words and his facility and
sonorous eloquence, and while they all longed to express

---

[178] Tuscianus, very old when Eunapius knew him, was a correspondent of Libanius; he held various offices in the East and
was for a time a colleague of Anatolius governing Illyricum.

[179] Cf. Hom. *Il*. 17.89.

πτηξάντων δὲ ὥσπερ διοσημείαν καὶ σιωπῆς κατακε-
χυμένης μυστηριώδους, εἰς δεύτερον προοίμιον ὁ
Προαιρέσιος ἐντείνων τὸν λόγον—τοῦτο γὰρ ἐμέ-
μνητο | Τουσκιανός—, ἐνθένδε ἤρξατο· "εἰ μὲν οὖν
ἔξεστι καὶ ἀδικεῖν ἅπαντα καὶ κατηγορεῖν καὶ λέγοντα πιστεύεσθαι πρὸ τῆς ἀπολογίας, ἔστω, γινέ-
σθω Θεμιστοκλέους ἡ πόλις." ἐνταῦθα ἀνά τε ἐπήδη-
σεν ὁ ἀνθύπατος ἐκ τοῦ θρόνου καὶ, τὴν περιπόρφυρον
ἀνασείων ἐσθῆτα (τήβεννον αὐτὴν Ῥωμαῖοι καλοῦσιν), ὥσπερ μειράκιον ὁ βαρὺς ἐκεῖνος καὶ ἀμείλικτος
ἐκρότει τὸν Προαιρέσιον· | συνεκρότει δὲ ὁ Ἀψίνης
οὔτι ἑκών, ἀλλὰ ἀνάγκης βιαιότερον οὐδέν· ὁ διδάσκαλος Ἰουλιανὸς ἐδάκρυε μόνον. ὁ δὲ ἀνθύπατος τὸ
μὲν διωκόμενον μέρος ἐξελθεῖν κελεύσας, τοῦ δὲ δι-
ώκοντος τὸν διδάσκαλον μόνον, εἶτα ἀπολαβὼν τὸν
Θεμιστοκλέα καὶ τοὺς Λάκωνας, τῶν ἐν Λακεδαίμονι
μαστίγων ὑπέμνησε, προσθεὶς αὐτοῖς καὶ τῶν Ἀθηναίων. εὐδοκιμῶν δὲ καὶ αὐτὸς ἄγαν καὶ διὰ τῶν ὁμιλητῶν, Ἀθήνησιν ἐτελεύτα, μέγαν ἐπιτάφιον ἀγῶνα
τοῖς ἑαυτοῦ παραδεδωκὼς ἑταίροις.

10. Προαιρέσιος. Περὶ Προαιρεσίου καὶ ⟨ἐν τοῖς⟩[79]
προλαβοῦσιν ἱκανῶς εἴρηται, καὶ ἐν τοῖς ἱστορικοῖς

[79] add. Go

[180] *Diosêmia*, "sign from Zeus, omen from the sky"; cf. Ar.
Ach. 171, *Plut.* 419e; Philostr. *VA* 2.33; Julian. *Or.* 7.212b.
[181] The phrase μυστηριώδη σιωπή only here and at *VPS* 6.5.

The marginal numbers: 63G, 24, 25, 26, 485B, 27

their admiration, but sat cowering as though forbidden to
do so by a sign from Zeus,[180] and a respectful silence rem-
iniscent of religious initiations[181] pervaded the place, Prohaeresius lengthened his speech into a second prooemium,
as follows (for this part Tuscianus remembered): "If, as it   24
seems, men may commit any injustice with impunity and
bring accusations and win belief for what they say, before
the defense is heard, so be it! Let our city be at the mercy
of Themistocles!" Then up jumped the proconsul and,   25
shaking his purple-edged toga (the Romans call it a "te-
bennos"),[182] this austere and inexorable judge applauded
Prohaeresius like a teenager. Even Apsines joined in the   26
applause, not of his own free will, but because it is pointless to fight the inevitable. His teacher Julian could only
shed tears. The proconsul ordered all the accused, but of
the accusers their teacher only, to withdraw, and then,
taking aside Themistocles and his Spartans, he reminded
them forcibly of the floggings of Lacedaemon, and in addition pointed to the kind of flogging in vogue at Athens.
Julian himself won a great reputation by his own elo-   27
quence, and also through the fame of his students, and
when he died at Athens, he left to his pupils a great occasion for competing over his funeral oration.[183]

10. Prohaeresius. Of Prohaeresius I have spoken sufficiently in the above narrative and have set forth his life

[182] Eunapius gives the Greek word for the Roman toga, or
trabea. For the gesture as a sign of approval, cf. Philostr. *VS* 626.
[183] Cf. Alexander's dying speech, which became a proverb;
Diod. Sic. 17.117; Arr. 7.26; Plu. *Apophth.* 181e. For the prestige
of giving a funeral speech, cf. Thuc. 2.34.

κατὰ τὴν ἐξήγησιν ὑπομνήμασι. καὶ νῦν δὲ ἐπελθεῖν
καιρὸς εἰς τὸ ἀκριβέστερον εἰδότι τε ἀσφαλῶς καὶ
ἀξιωθέντι τῆς ἐκείνου γλώττης καὶ ὁμιλίας· καὶ ταῦτά
γε, εἰ καὶ πάνυ μεγάλα καὶ οὐρανομήκη πρὸς χάριν,
ἐστὶ διδασκάλου, ἀλλ᾽ ὅμως πολλῷ τινι καὶ μακρῷ
τῆς εἰς τὸν συγγραφέα φιλίας ἀφεστήκεσαν αἱ τοσ-
αῦται καὶ ἀδιήγητοι χάριτες.

2   Διέβαλε μὲν γὰρ ὁ ταῦτα συντιθεὶς ἐξ Ἀσίας εἰς
τὴν Εὐρώπην καὶ Ἀθήνας τελῶν εἰς ἕκτον καὶ δέκατον
64G   ἔτος. ὁ δὲ Προαιρέσιος προελήλυθε μὲν ἐπὶ τὸ | ἕβδο-
μον ἐπὶ τοῖς ὀγδοήκοντα ἔτεσιν, ὡς αὐτὸς ἔλεγεν· καὶ
περὶ τὴν ἡλικίαν ταύτην οὔλη τε ἦν αὐτῷ καὶ ἄγαν
συνεχὴς ἡ κόμη, καὶ διὰ πλῆθος πολιῶν τριχῶν
ἀφριζούσῃ θαλάσσῃ προσεμφερὴς καὶ ὑπαργυρί-
3   ζουσα. ἤκμαζε δὲ οὕτω τὰ εἰς λόγους, τῇ νεότητί τε
τῆς ψυχῆς τὸ σῶμα κεκμηκὸς συνηγείρετο, ὥστε ὁ
ταῦτα συγγράφων ἀγήρων τινὰ καὶ ἀθάνατον αὐτὸν
ἐνόμιζε, καὶ προσεῖχεν ὥσπερ αὐτοκλήτῳ καὶ ἄνευ
4   τινὸς πραγματείας φανέντι θεῷ. καίτοι γε ἦν σχὼν
εἰς τὸν Πειραιᾶ περὶ πρώτην φυλακήν, ἐπὶ πυρετῷ
λάβρῳ κατὰ πλοῦν γενομένῳ, καὶ πολλοί τινες ἄλλοι
κατὰ γένος γε αὐτῷ προσήκοντες συνεισπεπλεύκε-
σαν, καὶ περὶ τὴν ὥραν ἐκείνην, πρίν τι γενέσθαι τῶν
εἰωθότων—τὸ γὰρ πλοῖον ἦν τῶν Ἀθήνηθεν, καὶ περὶ
τὰς κατάρσεις οὐκ ὀλίγοι τινὲς ἐναυλόχουν ἀεὶ τῶν

---

184 Cf. *Hist*. fr. 11 Blockley.

still more fully in my historical memoranda in line with my interpretation.[184] Now is the time to go over the facts in more precise detail, given that I had solid knowledge of him and was considered worthy of his inner circle. And if these comments are intended as proof of great, even immense gratitude toward a teacher, nonetheless this great and inexpressible appreciation falls very far short of what the author owes to Prohaeresius for his intimate friendship.[185]

While the compiler of this book had crossed over from Asia to Europe, that is to say to Athens, in the sixteenth year of his life, Prohaeresius had reached his eighty-seventh year, as he himself attested. At this advanced age his hair was curly and very thick, and due to a multitude of gray hairs it looked like sea foam and had a silvery sheen. His powers of oratory were so vigorous, and he so sustained his worn body by the youthfulness of his soul, that the present author considered him as an ageless and immortal being and heeded him as if he was some god who had revealed himself unsummoned and without any ritual. Now it happened that the author had arrived at the Piraeus around the first watch, and during the voyage had been seized by a violent fever; and several other persons, his relatives, had sailed over with him. At that time of night, before any of the usual proceedings could take place[186] (for the ship was among those that came from Athens and many used to lie in wait for her arrival at the dock, each mad enthusiasts for their own particular

2

3

4

---

[185] The meaning is clear, but the grammar is not.

[186] A reference to the fierce competition over recruiting students. Here the captain kidnaps them all for Prohaeresius.

εἰς ἕκαστον διδασκαλεῖον μεμηνότων—, ὁ ναύκληρος
εἰς Ἀθήνας συνέτεινε, τῶν μὲν ἄλλων βαδιζόντων, ὁ
δὲ βαδίζειν ἀδυνάτως ἔχων, ὅμως ἐκ διαδοχῆς ἀνεχό-
5 μενος, ἀνεκομίσθη πρὸς τὴν πόλιν. ἦν τε νυκτὸς τὸ
σταθερώτατον, ἡνίκα ἥλιος μακροτέραν ποιεῖ τὴν νύ-
κτα γινόμενος νοτιώτερος—ἐνεβεβήκει γὰρ τῷ Ζυγῷ,
καὶ τὰ νυκτερεῖα ἔμελλε—καὶ ὁ ναύκληρος ὤν που καὶ
ξένος Προαιρεσίου παλαιός, τοσοῦτον ὄχλον ὁμιλητῶν, ἀράξας τὴν θύραν, εἰσήγαγεν εἰς τὴν οἰκίαν,
ὥστε, ἡνίκα πόλεμοί τινες ἐγίνοντο περὶ ἑνὸς μειρακίου καὶ δυοῖν, πλήρωμα διατριβῆς ὅλους σοφιστικῆς
6 τοὺς ἐληλυθότας φαίνεσθαι. τούτων οἱ μὲν εἰς σώματος ἀλκὴν ἐτέλουν, οἱ δὲ εἰς πλοῦτον ἦσαν ἀβρότεροι,
τὸ δὲ εἶχεν ἀνὰ μέσον· ὁ δὲ συγγραφεὺς ἐλεεινῶς
διακείμενος τὰ πλεῖστα τῶν ἀρχαίων ἐπὶ στόματος |
65G εἶχε μόνον βιβλία. εὐθὺς μὲν οὖν χαρμονή τε ἦν περὶ
7 τὴν οἰκίαν καὶ διαδρομαί τινες ἀνδρῶν τε καὶ γυναι-
8 κῶν, καὶ οἱ μὲν ἐγέλων, οἱ δὲ ἐχλεύαζον. ὁ δὲ Προαιρέσιος συγγενεῖς ἰδίους κατὰ τὴν ὥραν ἐκείνην μετα-
486B πεμψάμενος, | παραλαβεῖν τοὺς ἐλθόντας κελεύει. ἦν
δὲ αὐτός τε ἐξ Ἀρμενίας (ὅσον ἐστὶν Ἀρμενίας Πέρ-
σαις εἰς τὰ βαθύτατα συνημμένον), καὶ Ἀνατόλιος
9 οὗτοι καὶ Μάξιμος ἐκαλοῦντο. καὶ οἱ μὲν ἀπεδέξαντο
τοὺς ἐλθόντας—καὶ ᾖξαν εἰς γειτόνων καὶ περὶ τὰ
λουτρὰ μετὰ πάσης ἐπιδείξεως—ἥ τε νεότης ἐς αὐτοὺς
ἐπεδείκνυτο καὶ χλευασίαν καὶ γέλωτα. καὶ οἱ μὲν

---

187 That is, it was the autumnal equinox.

school), the captain went straight on to Athens. The rest of the passengers walked, and the author, too feeble to walk, was nevertheless supported by them taking turns, and so was brought to the city. It was by then deepest 5 midnight, at the season when the sun makes the nights longer by retiring farther to the South; for he had entered the sign of Libra,[187] and the nightly hunt[188] was about to take place. The captain, who was an old guest-friend of Prohaeresius, knocked at his door and ushered such a large crowd of students into the house, that at a time when battles took place to win only one pupil or two, the newcomers seemed enough in themselves to fill all the schools of the sophists. Some of these youths possessed physical 6 strength, some stood out by their wealth, while the rest remained in between, but the author, who was in a wretched state, possessed little else than the majority of the works of the ancient authors committed to memory.[189] Immediately there was great rejoicing in the house, and a 7 coming and going of men and women, some laughing, others exchanging jests. Prohaeresius at that time of night 8 sent for some of his own relatives and requested that they take in the newcomers. (He was himself a native of Armenia, from the part that borders most closely on Persia, and these kinsmen of his were named Anatolius and Maximus.) They welcomed the new arrivals—they were neigh- 9 bors—and led them to the baths, and showed them off in every way; and the other students made the usual performances with jokes and laughter at their expense.[190] The

---

188 The meaning of νυκτερεῖον is debated (cf. Pl. *Leg.* 824).

189 Cf. *VPS* 6.75, 6.100; Lib. *Or.* 1.8.

190 Part of the regular "hazing" of the novices by the older pupils; cf. Lib. *Or.* 1; Greg. Nazianz. *Or.* 19.328b.

τούτων ποτὲ ἀπηλλάγησαν ἅπαξ λουσάμενοι, ὁ δὲ
συγγραφεύς, ἐντείναντος αὐτῷ τοῦ νοσήματος, δι-
εφθείρετο, μήτε Προαιρέσιον μήτε τὰς Ἀθήνας ἰδών,
ἀλλὰ ὀνειρῶξαι δοκῶν ἐκεῖνα ὧν ἐπεθύμησεν, οἱ δὲ

10 ὁμοεθνεῖς καὶ ἐκ Λυδίας βαρέως ἔφερον. καὶ ὥσπερ
τοῖς κατὰ τήνδε τὴν ἡλικίαν ἀπιοῦσιν ἐπὶ τὸ πλέον
ἅπαντες εἰώθασι χαρίζεσθαι, πολλά τινα καὶ μεγάλα
περὶ αὐτοῦ καταψευσάμενοι καὶ συμφορήσαντες ἐτε-
ρατεύσαντο καὶ πένθος κατεῖχε τὴν πόλιν παράλογον,

11 ὡσὰν ἐπὶ μεγάλῃ συμφορᾷ. Αἰσχίνης δέ τις, (οὐκ
Ἀθηναῖος ἀλλὰ ἡ Χίος ἦν αὐτῷ πατρίς), πολλοὺς
ἀνῃρηκὼς οὐχ ὅσους ἐπηγγείλατο θεραπεύειν, ἀλλὰ
καὶ ὅσους εἶδε μόνον, εἰς μέσους ἀναβοήσας τοὺς
πενθοῦντας, ὡς μετὰ ταῦτα ἐγένετο φανερόν "ἀλλὰ
συγχωρήσατέ γε," εἶπε, "τῷ νεκρῷ με δοῦναι φάρμα-

12 κον." οἱ δὲ συνεχώρησαν Αἰσχίνῃ διαφθεῖραι καὶ
τοὺς ἀπολωλότας. ὁ δὲ ὅ τι μὲν ἐνέχεεν, ὀργάνοις τισὶ
τὸ στόμα διαστήσας, μετὰ ταῦτα ἐξεῖπεν (καὶ ὁ θεὸς
πολλοῖς ὕστερον ἐμαρτύρησε χρόνοις), ἐμβαλὼν δὲ
ὅμως, τοῦ μὲν ἡ γαστὴρ ἀθρόως ἀπελυμάνθη, καὶ τὸν
ἀέρα εἶδε καὶ ἐπέγνω τοὺς οἰκείους. ὁ δὲ Αἰσχίνης ἑνὶ

13
66G τούτῳ γε ἔργῳ θάψας τὰ προγεγενημένα | τῶν ἁμαρ-
τημάτων, ὑπό τε τοῦ σωθέντος προσεκυνεῖτο καὶ τῶν

14 ἡδομένων ὅτι σέσωσται. καὶ ὁ μέν, ἐπὶ τῇ τοιαύτῃ
πράξει πάντων σεβαζομένων αὐτόν, εἰς τὴν Χίον
ἀπῆρε, πλὴν ὅσα γε παραμείνας εἰς ῥῶσιν τοῦ σώματος προσέδωκε πάλιν τῆς δυνάμεως τοῦ φαρμάκου,
καὶ τότε συνῆλθεν ἀκριβῶς ὁ σωθεὶς τῷ σώσαντι.

532

rest, once they had been to the baths, were let off and went
their way, but the author, as his sickness grew more severe,
was wasting away without seeing either Prohaeresius or
Athens, but he seemed to have dreamed all the things he
so desired, while his own relatives and those who had
come from Lydia were greatly concerned. And in the same   10
way as all men are prone to attribute greater talent to
those who are leaving us at such a young age, [so too] they
both told many exorbitant falsehoods about him and con-
spired to invent prodigious fictions, so that the whole city
was overwhelmed by unexpected grief, as though for some
great calamity. But a certain Aeschines (not an Athenian,   11
for his birthplace was Chios), who had killed many, not
only those whom he had been summoned to cure but also
those whom he had merely examined, called out in the
midst of those grieving over me, as became known [to me]
later: "Allow me to give medicine to the corpse." They   12
allowed Aeschines to murder even those who were already
dead. Then he held my lips apart with certain instruments
and poured in a drug; what it was he revealed afterward,
and the god many years later bore witness to it; at any rate
he poured it in, and the patient's stomach was at once
purged, he saw daylight and recognized his own people.
Thus Aeschines by this single act buried his past errors and 13
was admired both by him who had been delivered from
death and by those who rejoiced at his deliverance. For so   14
great an achievement he was worshipped by all, and he
then crossed over to Chios, though he stayed around long
enough to give the patient more of that strong medicine
in order for him to regain his physical strength; and thus
he who had been preserved became the intimate friend of
his preserver.

15 Ὁ δὲ θειότατος Προαιρέσιος οὔπω τὸν συγγραφέα
τεθεαμένος, ἀλλὰ καὶ αὐτὸν ὅσον οὐκ ἤδη κατοδυρό-
μενος, ὡς ἐπύθετο τὴν ἄλογον ταύτην καὶ ἀνεκλάλη-
τον σωτηρίαν, μετακαλέσας τοὺς κρατίστους καὶ γεν-
ναιοτάτους τῶν ὁμιλητῶν καὶ παρ᾽ οἷς ἐπηνεῖτο
χειρῶν ἀλκῆς ἔργον, "πέπονθά τι," πρὸς αὐτοὺς εἶπεν,
"ἐπὶ τῷ σωθέντι παιδίῳ, καίτοί γε οὔπω τεθεαμένος,
16 ἀλλ᾽ ὅμως ἔπασχον ἡνίκα ἀπώλλυτο. εἴ τι δὴ βούλε-
σθε χαρίσασθαί μοι, τῷ δημοσίῳ λουτρῷ τοῦτον καθ-
ήρατε πάσης χλευασίας φεισάμενοι καὶ παιδιᾶς,
17 ὥσπερ ἐμόν τινα παῖδα ψαίροντες." καὶ ταῦτα μὲν
ἔσχεν οὕτως καὶ ἀκριβέστερον ἐν τοῖς κατ᾽ ἐκεῖνον
χρόνοις λελέξεται· ὅμως δὲ ὁ συγγραφεύς, ὁμολογῶν
τὰ ἐς αὐτὸν θεοῦ τινὸς προνοίας τετυχηκέναι ἐκ τῆς
Προαιρεσίου σπουδῆς, οὐδὲν εἰς τὸ καθόλου περὶ τοῦ
ἀνδρὸς ἀποστήσεται τῆς ἀληθείας, εἴ γε πεπηγὼς ὁ
Πλάτωνος λόγος, ὡς ἀλήθεια πάντων μὲν ἀγαθῶν θεοῖς, πάντων δὲ ἀνθρώποις ἡγεῖται.

18 Προαιρεσίῳ δὲ—φερέσθω γὰρ ἐπ᾽ αὐτὸν ὁ λόγος—
τὸ μὲν κάλλος ἦν τοῦ σώματος τοιοῦτον, καίτοι γηραιὸς ὢν [ἦν],[80] ὥστε ἀπορεῖν τε εἴ τις ἐφ᾽ ἡλικίας
487B οὕτω γέγονε καλός, | καὶ θαυμάζειν τὴν τοῦ κάλλους
67G δύναμιν ὅτι πρὸς τοσοῦτον σῶμα | διὰ πάντων εἰς τὴν
19 ἀρίστην πλάσιν ἐξήρκεσε· τὸ δὲ μέγεθος ἦν ἡλίκον
ἄν τις οὐ πιστεύσειεν, ἀλλὰ εἰκάσειεν μόλις. ἀνεστη-
κέναι γὰρ εἰς ἔνατον πόδα κατεφαίνετο, ὥστε κολοσ-

---

[80] ἦν delevi: ὢν del. A^{ml} Go

534

Now the divinely inspired Prohaeresius had not yet 15
seen the author, but he too was saddened [over him] as
though he were on the point of dying, and when he was
told of this hard to explain and indescribable deliverance,
he sent for the best and most distinguished of his pupils
and those who had received praise for the work of their
strong hands, and said to them: "I felt for this boy who has
recovered, and although I have not yet seen him, I still was
aggrieved when he was dying. Now if you wish to do me a 16
favor, initiate him in the public bath, but refrain from all
teasing and joking, and scrub him gently as though he
were my own son." This was how it happened, and a fuller 17
account will be given when the author describes the times
in which Prohaeresius lived.[191] Yet, although the author
asserts that all that happened to that man was under the
direction of some divine providence, he will not in his zeal
for Prohaeresius depart in any way whatsoever from the
truth about him, if at least Plato's statement is firmly fixed,
that truth is the guide to all good for both gods and men.[192]

The physical beauty of Prohaeresius (for my narrative 18
must now return to him) was so striking, even though he
was an old man, that one may well be perplexed whether
anyone had ever been so handsome even in their youth,
and one may marvel also at the power of the beauty that
in view of a body so tall it sufficed to lead to his outstanding shape in all respects. His height was greater than any- 19
one would be inclined to believe, in fact one would hardly
guess it correctly. For he seemed to stand nine feet high,

---

[191] Not in Blockley.
[192] Pl. *Leg*. 730b–c, also quoted by Julian. *Or*. 6.188b.

σὸς ἐδόκει, παρὰ τοὺς μεγίστους ὁρώμενος τῶν καθ᾽
20 ἑαυτὸν ἀνθρώπων. νέον δὲ αὐτὸν ἐξ Ἀρμενίας ἀνα-
στήσαντος τοῦ δαίμονος καὶ πρὸς τὴν Ἀντιόχειαν
διαβάλοντος (οὐ γὰρ ἐπεθύμησεν εὐθὺς τῶν Ἀθηνῶν,
ἥ τε ἔνδεια παρελύπει τῶν χρημάτων· γεγονὼς γὰρ
ἄνωθεν καλῶς, τοῦτο ἠτύχει), καὶ πρὸς τὸν Οὐλπιανὸν
κρατοῦντα τῆς Ἀντιοχείας ἐπὶ λόγοις ὠσθείς, καὶ
21 παρελθὼν εὐθὺς ἀνὰ τοὺς πρώτους ἦν. καὶ χρόνον
οὐκ ὀλίγον ὁμιλήσας ἐκείνῳ, συνέτεινεν ἐπὶ τὰς Ἀθήνας καὶ τὸν Ἰουλιανὸν σφοδρῶς, καὶ πάλιν Ἀθήνησι
πρῶτος ἦν.

22   Ἡφαιστίων δὲ αὐτῷ συνείπετο, φιλοῦντες μὲν ἀλλήλους ἄμφω καὶ πάνυ, φιλονεικοῦντες δὲ ἀλλήλοις
εἰς πενίαν καὶ περὶ τῶν ἐν λόγοις πρωτείων. ἐν γοῦν
αὐτοῖς ὑπῆν ἱμάτιον καὶ τριβώνιον, καὶ πλέον οὐδέν,
καὶ στρώματα τρία που ἢ τέτταρα, τὴν οἴκοθεν βα-
φὴν μετὰ τῆς παχύτητος διὰ χρόνον ἀπαγορεύοντα.
23 περιῆν οὖν αὐτοῖς ἑνί τε ἀνθρώπῳ καὶ δυεῖν εἶναι,
ὥσπερ τὸν Γηρυόνην οἱ μῦθοι φασιν ἐκ τριῶν συντε-
24 θῆναι· κἀκεῖνοι δύο τε ἦσαν καὶ εἷς. Προαιρεσίου μὲν
γὰρ δημοσίᾳ φανέντος, Ἡφαιστίων ἦν ἀφανὴς ἐν
τοῖς στρώμασι κατακείμενος, καὶ συνασκῶν ἑαυτὸν
περὶ τοὺς λόγους· ταὐτὰ δὲ καὶ Προαιρεσίῳ συνέβαινεν Ἡφαιστίωνος φανέντος· τοσαύτη τις εἶχεν αὐτοὺς
ἔνδεια.

25   Ἀλλ᾽ ὅμως Ἰουλιανὸς ἐπὶ τὸν Προαιρέσιον ἐπέκλινε
τὴν ψυχὴν καὶ πρὸς ἐκεῖνον αὐτῷ τὰ ὦτα ἀνειστήκει,
καὶ τὸ μέγεθος κατεδείμαινε τῆς φύσεως. ὡς δέ, ἀπελ-

so that he looked like a colossus when one saw him near
the tallest men of his own time. When he was young, his   20
demon had compelled him to leave Armenia and cross
over to Antioch (for he did not desire to visit Athens immediately, and the lack of funds caused him anguish—a
stroke of bad luck, as he was well born). At Antioch he was
drawn to Ulpian,[193] who was the principal teacher of rhetoric there, and once there he soon ranked among the best
pupils. When he had studied with Ulpian for quite a long   21
time, he made his way to Athens and to Julian (the orator)
with the greatest determination, and again at Athens he
gained first place.

Hephaestion accompanied him, and these two were   22
very devoted friends to each other, but rivaled one another
in their poverty and in the highest honors in rhetoric. For
instance, they had between them only one cloak and one
threadbare mantle and nothing more, and, say, three or
four blankets that over time had lost[194] their original color
as well as their thickness. All they could do therefore was   23
to be both two men and one, just as the myths say that
Geryon was made up of three bodies; they were also two
and one. For when Prohaeresius appeared in public, He-   24
phaestion remained invisible and lay under the blankets in
bed while he did his rhetorical exercises. The same would
happen to Prohaeresius, when Hephaestion appeared in
public: such poverty held them in its grip.

And yet, Julian inclined his soul toward Prohaeresius,   25
readied his ears to listen to him, and he was in awe of his
great talent. And when Julian had departed this life, and

193 Not the famous jurist, but a sophist under Constantine (cf.
Evagr. Schol. *Hist. eccl.* 1.20).   194 Cf. Xen. *Cyr.* 6.2.33.

68G θόντος | Ἰουλιανοῦ, τὰς Ἀθήνας εἶχεν ἔρως τῆς δια-
δοχῆς τῶν ἐπὶ τοῖς λόγοις πλεονεκτημάτων, παραγ-
γέλλουσι μὲν ἐπὶ τῷ κράτει τῆς σοφιστικῆς πολλοὶ

26 καὶ ἄλλοι, ὥστε ὄχλος ἦν καὶ ταῦτα γράφειν. χει-
ροτονοῦνται δὲ δοκιμασθέντες ἁπάσαις κρίσεσι Προ-
αιρέσιός τε καὶ Ἡφαιστίων καὶ Ἐπιφάνιος καὶ
Διόφαντος, καὶ Σώπολις ἐκ [τῆς]81 παραβύστου καὶ
παρημελημένης ἐς τὸν ἀριθμὸν ἐνδείας, καὶ Παρνά-

27 σιός τις ἐκ τῆς εὐτελεστέρας. ἔδει γὰρ πολλοὺς εἶναι
κατὰ τὸν νόμον τὸν Ῥωμαϊκόν, Ἀθήνησι τοὺς μὲν

28 λέγοντας, τοὺς δὲ ἀκούοντας. χειροτονηθέντων δὲ
τούτων, οἱ μὲν εὐτελέστεροι τὸ ὄνομα εἶχον καὶ μέχρι
τῶν σανίδων ἦν τὸ κράτος καὶ τοῦ βήματος ἐφ᾽ ὃ
παρῇεσαν, εἰς δὲ τοὺς δυνατωτέρους ἡ πόλις εὐθὺς
διῄρητο, καὶ οὐχ ἡ πόλις μόνη, ἀλλὰ τὰ ὑπὸ Ῥωμαίοις ἔθνη, καὶ περὶ λόγων οὐκ ἦν αὐτοῖς ἡ στάσις,

29 ἀλλ᾽ ὑπὲρ ἐθνῶν ὅλων ἐπὶ τοῖς λόγοις. ἡ μὲν γὰρ ἑῴα
καθάπερ τι γέρας Ἐπιφανίῳ σαφῶς ἐξῄρητο, τὴν δὲ
Ἀραβίαν εἰλήχει Διόφαντος, Ἡφαιστίων δὲ καταδεί-
σας Προαιρέσιον ἀπῆλθεν ἐξ Ἀθηνῶν τε καὶ ἀνθρώπων, Προαιρεσίῳ δὲ ὁ Πόντος ὅλος καὶ τὰ ἐκείνῃ
πρόσοικα τοὺς ὁμιλητὰς ἀνέπεμπεν, ὥσπερ οἰκεῖον

30 ἀγαθὸν τὸν ἄνδρα θαυμάζοντες· προσετέθη δὲ καὶ
Βιθυνία πᾶσα καὶ Ἑλλήσποντος, ὅσα τε ὑπὲρ Λυδίας

488B διὰ τῆς | καλουμένης νῦν Ἀσίας ἐπὶ Καρίαν καὶ Λυ-
κίαν τείνοντα, πρὸς Παμφυλίαν καὶ τὸν Ταῦρον

81 τῆς del. Go

a yearning for a successor of equal ability to teach rhetoric took hold of Athens, many others put forward their names for this influential chair of rhetoric, so many that it would be a burden to write those also down. But after the count 26 they voted with approval of all in favor of Prohaeresius, Hephaestion, Epiphanius, and Diophantus, next Sopolis, as an add-on and ignoring his lack of means to make up the numbers,[195] and also a certain Parnasius who was of lesser significance. For in accordance with the Roman law, 27 there had to be at Athens many to lecture and many to hear them. Now of those that had been selected, the hum- 28 bler men were sophists in name only, and their power was limited to the walls of their lecture rooms and the platform on which they appeared. But the city at once took sides with the more influential, and not only the city but all the nations under Roman rule, and their quarrel did not concern oratory alone, but whole nations with regard to ora- torical talent. Thus the East[196] manifestly fell to Epipha- 29 nius like a rightful share, Diophantus was awarded Arabia, while Hephaestion, overawed by Prohaeresius, departed from Athens and the society of men; but the whole Pontus and its neighboring peoples sent pupils to Prohaeresius, admiring the man as a homegrown wonder. So, too, did all 30 Bithynia and the Hellespont, and all the region that ex- tends beyond Lydia through what is now called Asia as far as Caria and Lycia, and is bounded by Pamphylia and the

[195] Due to a (Roman) rule that demanded six contenders? The next line does not really answer this question.

[196] That is, Mesopotamia and Syria.

ἀφορίζεται· Αἴγυπτός τε πᾶσα τῆς ἐπὶ τοῖς λόγοις
ἀρχῆς κλῆρος ἦν οἰκεῖος αὐτῷ, καὶ ὅσα ὑπὲρ Αἰγύπτου πρὸς Λιβύην συρόμενα τό τε ἄγνωστον τέλος
31 ἔχει καὶ τὸ οἰκήσιμον. ταῦτα δὲ ὡς ἐπὶ πλέον εἴρηται,
ἐπεί, τό γε ἀκριβῶς, καὶ διαφθορὰς[82] ἔσχε τὰ ἔθνη ἐν
69G ὀλίγοις | τισὶ μειρακίοις, ἢ μετανάστασιν παρ᾽
ἑτέρους ἢ πού τις καὶ κατ᾽ ἀρχὰς ἀπατηθεὶς ἑτέρῳ
προσῆλθε.

32 Πρὸς δὲ τὸ μέγεθος τῆς Προαιρεσίου φύσεως συ-
στάσεως νεανικῆς καὶ μάλα σφοδρᾶς γενομένης, τῶν
ἄλλων ἁπάντων ἐς τοσόνδε ἴσχυσεν ἡ σύστασις,
ὥστε τὸν ἄνδρα ἐξόριστον τῶν Ἀθηνῶν εἰργάσαντο
δεκάσαντες τὸν ἀνθύπατον καὶ τὴν ἐπὶ λόγοις βασι-
33 λείαν εἶχον αὐτοί. ὁ δὲ καὶ πρὸς τὴν φυγὴν μετὰ
πενίας ἰσχυρᾶς ὥσπερ ὁ Πεισίστρατος ἐκπεσὼν κατ-
ῆλθε τὸ δεύτερον· ἀλλ᾽ ὁ μὲν διὰ πλοῦτον, Προαιρεσίῳ δὲ ὁ λόγος ἤρκει μόνος, ὥσπερ ὁ Ὁμηρικὸς Ἑρμῆς ἐπὶ τὴν σκηνὴν τὴν Ἀχιλλέως κἂν τοῖς πολεμίοις
34 παραπέμπων τὸν Πρίαμον. συνῆν δέ τις αὐτῷ καὶ
ἀγαθὴ τύχη νεώτερον ἀνθύπατον κατὰ φήμην ἀγανα-
κτοῦντα ἐπὶ τοῖς γινομένοις ἐπιστήσασα τοῖς πράγ-
35 μασι. καὶ ὁ μέν, οὕτω βασιλέως ἐπιτρέψαντος καὶ
μεταπεσόντος ὀστράκου, κατήει [τὸ δεύτερον][83] εἰς τὰς
Ἀθήνας, οἱ δὲ ἐχθροί, τὸ δεύτερον αὖθις ἑλιχθέντες
καὶ συσπειρασάμενοι καθ᾽ ἑαυτούς, ἀνίσταντο καὶ

---

[82] διαφθορᾶς Gi Go: διαφθορᾶς A: διαφοράς D
[83] del. Wytt Go (omis. Wr Gi)

Taurus. Even the whole of Egypt came into his exclusive possession and under his sway as a teacher of rhetoric, and also the country that stretches beyond Egypt toward Libya and contains the known limit to the inhabited world. All 31 this, however, I have stated with regard to the overall number, for, to speak precisely, some countries lost students in small numbers, because they had either migrated from one teacher to another, or sometimes one had originally been deceived and gone to a teacher other than he had intended.

When a vigorous and violent opposition arose aimed 32 at Prohaeresius' enormous talent, the uprising of all the other sophists so gained the upper hand that they drove him from Athens into exile by bribing the proconsul and so they themselves could seize the crown in oratory. But 33 after being driven into exile along with the utmost poverty, just as Peisistratus, he came to the city once more. While the latter managed it through his wealth, for Prohaeresius his eloquence alone sufficed, much like Homeric Hermes[197] escorting Priam to the hut of Achilles, even though it was in the midst of his foes. Good fortune also was on 34 his side by putting in charge a younger proconsul who was indignant at the report of what had taken place. So, the 35 proverbial tables had turned,[198] and with the emperor's permission he returned to Athens from exile, whereas his enemies for the second time, turning around and reforming their ranks, took a stand and framed other ruses against

[197] See *VPS* 10.51 below (Hermes and rhetoric); for Hermes helping Priam, see Hom. *Il.* 24.440–56.

[198] A proverb (cf. Pl. *Phdr.* 241b) from the game *ostrakinda*.

36 πρὸς τὸ μέλλον ἑτέρας ἐξηρτύοντο μηχανάς. καὶ οἱ
μὲν ἐν τούτοις ἦσαν· προηγουμένων δὲ τῶν εὐτρεπι-
ζόντων τὴν κάθοδον, κατελθὼν ὁ Προαιρέσιος (ταῦτα
δὲ ἀκριβῶς ὁ Λυδὸς παρὼν Τουσκιανὸς ἐξήγγελλεν,
ὃς Προαιρέσιος ἂν ἦν, εἰ μὴ Προαιρέσιος ἦν), κατελθὼν δέ ὅμως, εὑρίσκει μέν, ὥσπερ τις Ὀδυσσεὺς διὰ
μακροῦ παραγενόμενος, ὀλίγους τῶν ἑταίρων, ἐν οἷς
70G καὶ ὁ Τουσκιανὸς ἦν, ὑγιαίνοντας καί ἐπὶ τῷ ἀπίστῳ
37 τοῦ θαύματος [τοὺς]⁸⁴ πρὸς ἐκεῖνον βλέποντας· εὑρὼν
δέ καὶ πληρωθεὶς ἀγαθῶν ἐλπίδων, "περιμένετε,"
φησί, "τὸν ἀνθύπατον"· ὁ δὲ θᾶττον ἦλθεν ἐλπίδος.
ἀφικόμενος δὲ Ἀθήναζε συνεκάλει τε τοὺς σοφιστὰς
38 καὶ διετάραττεν ἅπαντα. οἱ δὲ μόλις μὲν καὶ βάδην
συνῄεσαν, ἀνάγκης δὲ καλούσης, προβλήματά τε
αὐτοῖς προεβλήθη καὶ κατὰ δύναμιν αὐτῶν ἕκαστος
διαλεχθέντες, ἐκ παρακλήσεως καὶ παρασκευῆς τῶν
κρότων συντελουμένων, ἀπηλλάγησαν καὶ τοὺς Προ-
39 αιρεσίου φίλους εἶχεν ἀθυμία. ὁ δὲ ἀνθύπατος αὐτοὺς
τὸ δεύτερον ὡς ἐπὶ τιμαῖς συγκαλέσας, ἅπαντας
κατασχεθῆναι κελεύει καὶ τὸν Προαιρέσιον ἐξαπιναίως εἰσκαλεῖ. οἱ δὲ παρῆσαν ἀγνοοῦντες τὰ μέλλο-
40 ντα. ὁ δὲ ἀνθύπατος "βούλομαι," ἀνέκραγε, "πᾶσιν
ὑμῖν ἓν ζήτημα προβαλών, πάντων ὑμῶν ἀκροάσασθαι σήμερον· ἐρεῖ δὲ μεθ᾽ ὑμᾶς, ἢ ὅπως ἂν βούλη-
41 σθε, καὶ Προαιρέσιος." τῶν δὲ τὸ πρᾶγμα φανερῶς
παραιτησαμένων καὶ τὰ Ἀριστείδου μετὰ πολλῆς

⁸⁴ del. Go

542

him for the near future. They busied themselves with   36
these plots, but meanwhile his friends went ahead and
were smoothing the path of his return, and when Prohaeresius came back (a precise account of all this was given
to me by an eyewitness, Tuscianus of Lydia, who would
have been a Prohaeresius, had not Prohaeresius existed);
when, I say, he did return, like some Odysseus arriving
home after a long absence, he found a few of his friends
safe and sound (among whom was Tuscianus), and these
looked to him for aid after this incredible miracle. Filled   37
with good hopes on finding them there, he said: "Wait for
the proconsul to come." The latter came sooner than could
have been hoped. On his arrival at Athens he called a
meeting of the sophists, and by this means threw all their
plans into confusion. They assembled slowly and reluctantly. Forced by necessity, they discussed, each according   38
to his ability, certain questions that were put to them,
while they were provided with applause by persons who
had received their instructions and had been invited for
the purpose. Then the meeting broke up, and the friends
of Prohaeresius felt discouraged. But the proconsul, after   39
he had summoned them a second time, as though to award
them honors, ordered them all to be detained, and suddenly called in Prohaeresius. So they attended, not knowing what was going to happen. And the proconsul raised   40
his voice and said: "I wish to propose a theme for you all,
and to hear you all declaim on it this very day. And either
after you or in what order you please, Prohaeresius will
also speak." When they openly objected and, after much   41
consideration and effort (for they hardly ever managed to

σκέψεως καὶ πόνου (ἔδει γὰρ μηδὲν ἴδιον αὐτοὺς λέγειν), προενεγκόντων δὲ ὅμως ὡς οὐκ εἰσὶ τῶν ἐμούντων ἀλλὰ τῶν ἀκριβούντων, τὸ δεύτερον ἐμβοήσας
42   ὁ ἀνθύπατος "λέγε," φησίν, "ὦ Προαιρέσιε." | ὁ δὲ
489B   ἀπὸ τῆς καθέδρας εἰς προάγονά τινα διαλεχθεὶς οὐκ
ἀχαρίστως καὶ τὸν σχέδιον ὅσος ἐστὶν ἐξάρας λόγον,
ἀνέστη θαρραλέως ἐπὶ τὸν ἀγῶνα. ἐνταῦθα ὁ μὲν ἀνθύπατος ὅρον τινὰ προβαλεῖν ἕτοιμος ἦν, ὁ δὲ ἀνενεγ-
43   κὼν τὸ πρόσωπον, περιέβλεπε κύκλῳ τὸ θέατρον. ὡς
δὲ πολὺ μὲν ἑώρα τὸ πολέμιον, τὸ δὲ φίλιον μικροῦ
71G   καὶ | διαλανθάνον, ἐγένετο μὲν κατὰ λόγον ἀθυμότε-
44   ρος· ζέοντος δὲ καὶ συγχορεύοντος αὐτῷ δαίμονος,
περισκοπῶν ἅπαντα, συγκεκαλυμμένους ὁρᾷ περὶ τὴν
ἐσχάτην ἄντυγα τοῦ θεάτρου δύο τινὰς ἄνδρας τῶν
περὶ ῥητορικὴν τετριμμένων καὶ ὑφ' ὧν ἐπεπόνθει τὰ
πλεῖστα τῶν κακῶν, καὶ ἀναβοήσας "ὦ θεοί," φησίν,
"ἐνταῦθα οἱ βέλτιστοι καὶ σοφοί.[85] τούτους ἐμοὶ
κέλευσον, ἀνθύπατε, προβαλεῖν· ἴσως γὰρ ὅτι ἠσέβη-
45   σαν πεισθήσονται." οἱ μὲν οὖν, ταῦτα ἀκούσαντες, εἰς
τὸν ὄχλον τε τῶν καθημένων κατεδύοντο καὶ διαλαν-
46   θάνειν ἔσπευδον. ὁ δὲ ἀνθύπατος, διαπέμψας τινὰς
τῶν στρατιωτῶν, εἰς μέσον αὐτοὺς περιήγαγε· καὶ
καταστήσας ἔκ τινος προτροπῆς τὸ προβαλεῖν τὸν
καλούμενον ὅρον, ὡς ἐκεῖνοι, βραχύν τινα χρόνον

---

[85] σοφ⟨ώτατ⟩οι scr. Go (fort. recte): σοφοί A

---

199 For the phrase, cf. Philostr. VS 583, and above, VPS 2.2.

utter anything original), at last produced the words of
Aristeides, that their custom was "not to casually spit out
their words,[199] but to prepare them with care," the proconsul exclaimed again with a loud voice: "Speak, Prohaeresius." Then from his chair the sophist first delivered a 42
not inelegant prelude as opening words, in which he ex-
tolled the greatness of extempore eloquence, then with
the fullest confidence he rose to enter the contest. The
proconsul was ready to propose a defined topic, but Prohaeresius raised his head up high and gazed all around the
theater. And when he saw that his enemies were many, 43
while his friends were of little consequence, and were
trying to escape notice, he was, as one might expect, ap-
prehensive. But as his companion spirit[200] began to warm 44
to the task and got into the rhythm of the performance, he
looked all around, and saw in the most upper row of the
theater, hiding themselves in their cloaks, two men, veter-
ans in the service of rhetoric, at whose hands he had received the worst treatment of all, and he cried out: "By the
gods! There are those most honorable and wise men! Order *them* to propose a theme for me, proconsul. Then
perhaps they will be convinced that they have behaved
impiously." Now the men, on hearing this, submerged 45
themselves in the crowd that was seated there and hastily
tried to avoid detection. But the proconsul sent some of 46
his soldiers and brought them into their midst. With strong
encouragement he ordered them to propose what is called
the definition [of the case].[201] After considering for a short

200 His *demon* (attributed to only him and Julian).
201 Hermogenes, *Inv.* 3.13, gives five kinds of definition, each
kind elaborate and technical (cf. Quint. *Inst.* 7.3).

σκεψάμενοι καὶ πρὸς ἀλλήλους διαλεχθέντες, τὸν
τραχύτατον ὧν ᾔδεσαν καὶ φαυλότατον ἐξήνεγκαν,
ἰδιωτικὸν καὶ τοῦτον καὶ οὐ βάσιμον ῥητορικῇ πομ-
πείᾳ, ταυρηδὸν μὲν αὐτοὺς ὑπέβλεψε, πρὸς δὲ τὸν
ἀνθύπατον· "ἃ πρὸ τοῦ ἀγῶνος αἰτῶ δίκαια, ταῦτά σε
ἱκετεύω δοῦναι·" τοῦ δὲ εἰπόντος ὡς οὐδενὸς ἀτυχήσει

47 δικαίου, "ἀξιῶ," φησί, "δοθῆναί μοι τοὺς ταχέως γράφοντας καὶ στῆναι κατὰ τὸ μέσον οἳ καθ᾽ ἡμέραν μὲν
τὴν τῆς θέμιδος γλῶτταν ἀποσημαίνονται, σήμερον

48 δὲ τοῖς ἡμετέροις ὑπηρετήσονται λόγοις." τοῦ δὲ παρελθεῖν τοὺς ἄκρους τῶν γραφέων ἐπιτρέψαντος, οἱ μὲν
ἑκατέρωθεν ἔστησαν ἐς τὴν γραφὴν ἕτοιμοι, καὶ τὸ
μέλλον οὐδεὶς ἠπίστατο· τοῦ δὲ εἰπόντος ὡς "καὶ ἕτερον αἰτήσω βαρύτερον," εἶτα κελευσθέντος εἰπεῖν,

49 "κροτείτω με," φησί, "μηδὲ εἷς." ὡς δὲ καὶ τοῦτο μετὰ
πολλοῦ πᾶσιν ἐπετέθη φόβου, ἄρχεται μὲν ὁ Προαι-
ρέσιος λέγειν ῥύδην, κατὰ τὸν κρότον ἀναπαύων |

72G ἑκάστην περίοδον, τὸ δὲ ἀναγκαίως Πυθαγορικὸν
θέατρον ὑπὸ τοῦ θαύματος καταρρηγνύμενον, μυκηθ-
μοῦ καὶ στόνου διάμεστον ἦν. ὡς δὲ ὁ λόγος ἐπεδίδου
καὶ ὁ ἀνὴρ ὑπὲρ πάντα ἐφέρετο λόγον καὶ πᾶσαν
δόξαν ἀνθρωπίνην, πρόεισι μὲν εἰς θάτερον μέρος καὶ

50 συμπληροῖ τὴν κατάστασιν· ἐνθουσιῶν δὲ καὶ πηδῶν,
ὥσπερ ἀναπολόγητον τὸ λειπόμενον ἀφιεὶς μέρος, εἰς
τὴν ἐναντίαν ὑπόθεσιν ἐπαφῆκε τὸν λόγον. καὶ οἱ
γράφοντες μόλις εἴποντο καὶ τὸ θέατρον μόλις σιω-

---

202 Lit., "rapid scribes," sometimes called *tachygraphoi*.

time and consulting together, they produced the hardest
and most disagreeable theme that they knew, an amateur-
ish one, moreover, that gave no opening for the solemnity
of rhetoric. Prohaeresius glared at them fiercely and said
to the proconsul: "I implore you to grant me the just de-   47
mands that I make before this contest." On his replying
that Prohaeresius should not fail to have what was just, the
latter said: "I ask to have writers with a fast hand[202] assigned to me, and that they take their place in the center
of the theater; I mean men who every day take down the
words of Themis,[203] but who today shall provide their services to what I have to say." The proconsul gave his permis-   48
sion for the most expert of the scribes to come forward,
and they stood on either side of Prohaeresius ready to
write, but no one knew what was about to happen. Then
he said: "I shall ask for something even more difficult to
grant." He was told to name it and said: "Not one person
should applaud me." When the proconsul had given all   49
present an order reinforced by a serious threat, Prohaeresius began his speech with a flood of eloquence, rounding
every period with a cadenced phrase, while the audience,
which perforce kept a Pythagorean silence, in their amazed
admiration broke through their restraint, and was filled
with groans and sighs. As the speech grew and the man
soared to heights defying human description or belief, he
passed on to the second part of the speech and completed
the exposition of the theme.[204] But then, making a sudden   50
change like one inspired, he abandoned the remaining
part, left it undefended, and turned the flood of his elo-

[203] The goddess of the law courts.
[204] *katastasis* as a part of the speech, like *narratio*.

πᾶν ἠνείχετο καὶ πλῆθος ἦν τῶν εἰρημένων. ὁ δὲ ἐπιστρέψας εἰς τοὺς γράφοντας τὸ πρόσωπον, "ὁρᾶτε
ἀκριβῶς," ἔφη, "εἰ πάντα ταῦτα ἃ προλαβὼν εἶπον
μέμνημαι·" καὶ μηδὲ περὶ μίαν λέξιν σφαλεὶς τὰ αὐτὰ
51 δεύτερον ἀπήγγελλεν. οὔτε ὁ ἀνθύπατος ἐνταῦθα τοὺς
ἑαυτοῦ νόμους ἐφύλαττεν οὔτε τὸ θέατρον τὰς ἀπειλὰς τοῦ ἄρχοντος· καὶ τὰ στέρνα τοῦ σοφιστοῦ περι-
λιχμησάμενοι καθάπερ ἀγάλματος ἐνθέου πάντες οἱ
παρόντες, οἱ μὲν πόδας, οἱ δὲ χεῖρας προσεκύνουν, οἱ
52 δὲ θεὸν ἔφασαν, οἱ δὲ Ἑρμοῦ Λογίου τύπον. | οἱ δὲ
490B ἀντίτεχνοι διὰ φθόνον παρεθέντες ἔκειντο, τινὲς δὲ
αὐτῶν οὐδὲ κείμενοι τῶν ἐπαίνων ἠμέλουν. ὁ δὲ ἀνθύπατος καὶ δορυφόρων μετὰ πάντων [ἢ τῶν δυνατῶν]
53 ⟨αὐτὸν⟩⁸⁶ ἐκ τοῦ θεάτρου παρέπεμψε. μετὰ ταῦτα οὐδεὶς ἀντέλεγεν, ἀλλ᾽ ὥσπερ ὑπὸ σκηπτοῦ πληγέντες,
ἅπαντες συνεχώρησαν αὐτῷ εἶναι κρείττονι. χρόνῳ δὲ
73G ὕστερον ἀναφέροντες, ὥσπερ αἱ τῆς | Ὕδρας κεφαλαί,
πρὸς τὸ οἰκεῖον ἀνωρθοῦντο καὶ διηγείροντο, καὶ τραπέζαις τε πολυτελέσι καὶ θεραπαινιδίοις κομψοῖς τινὰς τῶν ἀκμαζόντων δελεάζοντες, ὥσπερ οἱ τῶν βασιλέων ἔννομον καὶ ὀρθὴν μάχην νενικημένοι, ἐν τοῖς
ἀπόροις εἰς τὸ ἔσχατον συνελθόντες, ἐπὶ ψιλοὺς καὶ
σφενδονήτας καὶ γυμνήτας καὶ τὸ εὐτελὲς ἐπικουρι-

86 [. . .] del. Go et inser. ⟨αὐτὸν⟩ (locus corr.)

205 An attempt to touch was a sign of admiration or respect;
cf. Ar. *Vesp.* 1033, *Pax* 756; Lucian, *Nigr.* 21; Lib. *Or.* 1.89.

quence to defend the contrary hypothesis. The scribes could hardly keep up with him, the audience could hardly endure to remain silent, and an abundance of words flowed. Then, turning his face toward the scribes, he said: "Observe carefully whether I remember all the arguments that I used earlier." And, without faltering over a single word, he began to declaim the same speech for the second time. Neither the proconsul could at this point stick to his own rules nor the audience heed the threats of the magistrate. For all who were present licked the sophist's breast[205] as though it belonged to a statue of some god; some kissed his feet, others his hands, some declared him to be a god, others an exact replica of Hermes Logios, the god of eloquence.[206] His rivals, on the other hand, were brought down, eaten up with envy, though some of them even while beaten could not refrain from applauding; but the proconsul with his whole bodyguard escorted him from the theater. After this no one dared to speak against him, but as though they had been struck by a thunderbolt, they all admitted that he was their superior. However, sometime after, raising themselves up, like the heads of the Hydra, they were restored to their natural disposition and awoke from their inertia; they tempted some of the most powerful men in the city by means of costly banquets and smart maidservants, just as kings do when they have been defeated in a just and regular battle, and in their difficulties are driven to extreme measures, so that they have recourse to light-armed forces and slingers, troops

51

52

53

[206] A sophistic commonplace first used by Aristides to describe Demosthenes; cf. Julian. *Or.* 7.237c.

κὸν καταφεύγουσιν—οὐ ταῦτα τιμῶντες ἐξ ἀρχῆς,
54 ὅμως δὲ δι᾽ ἀνάγκην ταῦτα τιμῶντες—, οὕτω κἀκεῖνοι
πρὸς ἀναγκαῖον συμμαχικὸν ἐπτοημένοι, τοιαύτας
ἐπιβουλὰς ἤρτυον, αἰσχρὰς μέν, ἀνεπίφθονοι δὲ
55 ἦσαν, εἴ τις ἑαυτὸν καὶ κακῶς φιλεῖ. εἶχον γοῦν
ἑταίρων πλῆθος καὶ ἀπῆντα τὸ σόφισμα κατὰ λόγον
αὐτοῖς. τὸ δὲ Προαιρεσίου ⟨κράτος⟩[87] τυραννὶς ἐδόκει
τις εἶναι καὶ εὐτυχεῖν ἡ ἀρετὴ τῶν λόγων ἐδόκει
56 καλῶς· ἢ γὰρ οἱ νοῦν ἔχοντες ἅπαντες αὐτὸν ᾑροῦντο,
ἢ οἱ προσελθόντες εὐθὺς νοῦν εἶχον ὅτι Προαιρέσιον
ᾕρηντο.

57 Κατὰ δὲ τούτους τοὺς χρόνους ἤνεγκεν ὁ βασιλι-
κὸς τῆς αὐλῆς ὅμιλος ἄνδρα καὶ δόξης ἐραστὴν καὶ
λόγων. ἦν μὲν γὰρ ἐκ Βηρυτοῦ πόλεως καὶ Ἀνατόλιος
ἐκαλεῖτο· οἱ δὲ βασκαίνοντες αὐτῷ καὶ Ἀζουτρίωνα
ἐπίκλησιν ἔθεντο, καὶ ὅ τι μὲν τὸ ὄνομα σημαίνειν
58 βούλεται ὁ κακοδαίμων ἴστω τῶν θυμελῶν χορός. δόξης δὲ ἐραστὴς ὁ Ἀνατόλιος καὶ λόγων γενόμενος,
ἀμφοτέρων ἔτυχε· καὶ τῆς τε νομικῆς τελουμένης[88]
παιδείας εἰς ἄκρον ἀφικόμενος, ὡσὰν πατρίδα ἔχων
τὴν Βηρυτὸν ἢ τοῖς τοιούτοις μήτηρ ὑποκάθηται παι-
δεύμασι, καὶ διαπλεύσας εἰς τὴν Ῥώμην καὶ, φρο-
74G νήματος ἐμπλησθεὶς καὶ | λόγων ὕψος ἐχόντων καὶ
βάρος, εἰσφρήσας τε εἰς τὰ βασίλεια, ταχὺ μάλα
πρῶτος ἦν καὶ, διὰ πάσης ἐλθὼν ἀρχῆς ἐν πολλαῖς

[87] inser. Go
[88] τελουμένης A Gi Go: καλουμένης Boiss Wr

without heavy armor and their reserves; for if they valued
these not at all before, they are forced to do so now. Just   54
so those sophists, fleeing in their panic to such allies as
they could muster, framed their plots, disreputable ones,
yet the men were not to be envied, nor are any who love
themselves fatuously. At any rate they had a crowd of ad-   55
herents, and the plot proceeded so that they could reckon
on success. However, the genius of Prohaeresius seemed
to exert a kind of domination [over men's minds], and his
power of eloquence seemed to have extraordinary good
fortune. For either all sensible men chose him as their   56
teacher, or those who had attended his school immediately
saw sense, because they had chosen Prohaeresius.

Now in these days there was a man among those at the   57
imperial court who passionately desired both fame and
eloquence. He came from the city of Berytus and his name
was Anatolius.[207] Those who envied him also called him
Azoutriôn,[208] and what that name is supposed to mean I
leave to that miserable band of the stage! However, Ana-   58
tolius' zeal for fame and eloquence led to success on both
fronts. For not only did he complete, to the highest level,
his law training, [not unexpected] since his birthplace was
Berytus, the foster mother of all such studies,[209] but he
also, after sailing to Rome, made it to the court, since his
wisdom and eloquence were elevated and weighty. He
soon rose to the top, and after holding every high office

207 Himerius addresses a speech, *Ecl.* 32, to this Anatolius, the
prefect of Illyricum; he visited Athens ca. 345.

208 Probably a distorted version of the Roman office of *adiu-
torem* or *adiutrionem* (Goulet 2:257n8).

209 Berytus (Beirut) was famous for its school of Roman law.

τε ἀρχαῖς εὐδοκιμήσας (καὶ γὰρ οἱ μισοῦντες αὐτὸν
ἐθαύμαζον), προϊὼν καὶ εἰς τὸν ἔπαρχον τῆς αὐλῆς
59 ἤλασεν· ἡ δὲ ἀρχὴ βασιλεία ἐστὶν ἀπόρφυρος. τυχὼν
δὲ κατὰ τὴν ἑαυτοῦ φιλοτιμίαν τύχης ἀξίας (τὸ γὰρ
καλούμενον Ἰλλυρικὸν ἐπετέτραπτο), καὶ φιλοθύτης
ὢν καὶ διαφερόντως Ἕλλην (καί τοί γε ἡ κοινὴ κίνη-
σις πρὸς ἄλλας ἔφερε ῥοπάς), ἐξὸν αὐτῷ πρὸς τὰ
καίρια τῆς ἀρχῆς ἐλθεῖν καὶ διοικεῖν ἕκαστα πρὸς ὃ
βούλοιτο, ὁ δέ, χρυσῆς τινος αὐτὸν μανίας ὑπολα-
βούσης ἰδεῖν τὴν Ἑλλάδα καὶ τὰ τῶν λόγων εἴδωλα
διὰ τῆς παιδεύσεως ἐπὶ τὴν αἴσθησιν, μεθ᾽ οὕτως ἀρι-
πρεποῦς ἀξιώματος φερόμενος, συλλαβεῖν, καὶ τὸ
νοούμενον ἐκ τῶν ἀρχαίων ἰνδαλμάτων φάντασμα ἐπὶ
60 τὴν ὄψιν σπάσαι, πρὸς τὴν Ἑλλάδα ἔσπευσεν. καὶ
πρόβλημά γέ τι τοῖς σοφισταῖς προπέμψας (ἐτεθήπεσαν δὲ αὐτὸν ἡ Ἑλλάς, τό τε φρόνημα ἀκούοντες καὶ
491B τὴν παιδείαν, | καὶ ὅτι ἀκλινὴς ἦν καὶ ἀδωροδόκητος),
61 ἐκέλευεν ἅπαντας τὸ αὐτὸ μελετᾶν πρόβλημα. οἱ δὲ
τοῦτο αὐτὸ ἐπιτηδεύοντες καὶ κατὰ τὴν ἑκάστην
ἡμέραν ἀλλήλοις ἐπιβουλεύοντες, ὅμως (ἀνάγκη γὰρ
ἐκέλευε) συνεκρίθησαν, καὶ περὶ τῆς καλουμένης στάσεως τοῦ προβλήματος πολλοὺς ἐν ἀλλήλοις λόγους
ἀντεπιχειρήσαντες—οὐκ ἔγνω τούτου τοῦ πράγματος

210 An allusion to Christianity.   211 *Problêma* (Latin *quaestio*) was a bifurcated question for debating practice; it could be
developed into a speech.   212 *Stasis* is the position one takes
in a debate (Hermog. *Stat.* 2; Cic. *Top.* 25.93).
213 Eunapius never tells us what the topic is.

and winning a great reputation in many official positions
(for even those who disliked him were full of admiration),
he finally attained to the rank of praetorian prefect. The   59
office is an imperial one but lacks the imperial purple. He
had now achieved a station in accord with his ambition (for
the district called Illyricum had been assigned to him),
and since he was devout in offering sacrifices to the gods
and especially committed to Hellenic ways, in spite of the
fact that the main current ran in other directions,[210] instead of choosing as he might have done to visit the most
important places in his dominion and administer everything according to his pleasure, he was overcome by a kind
of golden madness of desire to behold Greece, and, supported by his distinguished reputation, to turn into reali-
ties the mere images of eloquence derived from his learning, and to bring to his own sight what had been a mental
apparition drawn from ancient images, to see for himself
what had been an intellectual concept received from such
presentation of eloquence as ancient writings could give,
he hastened to Greece. Moreover, after sending to the   60
sophists beforehand a dialectical problem[211] for them to
consider (all the Greeks marveled at him when they heard
of his wisdom and learning and that he was unswervingly
upright and incorruptible), he bade them all to practice
declaiming on this same problem. Then they set them-   61
selves to consider his proposition and every day attempted
to outdo each other. Nevertheless, since necessity compelled them, they compared notes, and after bringing forward many opposing theories among themselves with regard to the so-called positing[212] of the problem (the author
never knew of anything more ridiculous than this matter),[213] they were in complete disagreement with each

γελοιότερον ὁ συγγραφεύς—, διεκρίθησαν ἕκαστος,
διὰ φιλοτιμίαν ἕκαστος ἐπαινῶν τὴν ἰδίαν δόξαν καὶ
62 πρὸς τὰ μειράκια φιλοτιμούμενος. ὡς δὲ βαρύτερος
ἦν τῆς Περσικῆς ἐκείνης καὶ πολυυμνήτου στρατιᾶς
ἐπὶ τὴν Ἑλλάδα κατιὼν ὁ Ἀνατόλιος καὶ ὁ κίνδυνος
ἦν παρὰ πόδας οὐ τοῖς Ἕλλησιν ἀλλὰ τοῖς σοφι-
75G στεύουσιν, ἐνταῦθα οἱ μὲν ἄλλοι πάντες[89] | (προσεγε-
γένητο γὰρ αὐτοῖς καὶ Ἱμέριός τις σοφιστὴς ἐκ Βι-
θυνίας· οὐκ ἔγνω τοῦτον ὁ συγγραφεύς, πλὴν ὅσα γε
διὰ συγγραμμάτων), ἐταλαιπωροῦντο δὲ ὅμως ἅπαντες καὶ πολλῷ καμάτῳ παρετείνοντο, τὴν δόξασαν
63 ἕκαστος μελετῶντες στάσιν. ἐνταῦθα ὁ Προαιρέσιος,
θαρσῶν τῇ φύσει, βαρὺς ἦν, οὔτε φιλοτιμούμενος
64 οὔτε ἐκφέρων τὸ ἀπόρρητον. ὁ δὲ Ἀνατόλιος ἐγγύθεν
καὶ εἰσεδήμησεν Ἀθήναζε. θύσας δὲ θαρσαλέως καὶ
περιελθὼν τὰ ἱερὰ πάντα ᾗ θεσμὸς ἱερὸς ἐκέλευεν,
ἐξεκάλει τοὺς σοφιστὰς ἐπὶ τὸν ἀγῶνα. καὶ οἱ παρόντες ἕκαστος πρῶτος ἐς τὴν ἐπίδειξιν ἠπείγετο· οὕτω
65 φίλαυτόν τι χρῆμα ἄνθρωπος· ὁ δὲ Ἀνατόλιος καὶ
τοὺς κροτοῦντας, τὰ μειράκια, ἐγέλα, καὶ τοὺς πατέρας ἠλέει τῆς τῶν παίδων παιδείας ⟨ὅτι⟩[90] ὑπὸ τίσιν
παιδεύονται. ἐκάλει δὲ τὸν Προαιρέσιον· μόνος γὰρ
66 ἀπολέλειπτο· ὁ δὲ θεραπεύσας τινὰ τῶν οἰκείων αὐτοῦ
καὶ πάντα ἐξειδότων, μαθὼν τὴν στάσιν ἣν ἐπαινεῖ
(τοῦτο γὰρ ὁ συγγραφεὺς ἔφη γελοῖον ἐν τοῖς ἄνω
λόγοις· καίτοι γε οὐδενὸς ἦν ἄξιον λόγου, οὐδὲ Ἀνα-

[89] πάντες ⟨ἐταλαιπωροῦντο⟩ Go   [90] add. Go

other, since each man on account of his ambition applauded his own theory and jealously maintained it in the presence of the students. But when Anatolius descended 62 on Greece, more formidable than the famous Persian expedition celebrated in many a song, and the danger was an imminent threat not just to all the Greeks but the sophists,[214] all the others (among whom was included a certain Himerius, a sophist from Bithynia; the author knew him only from his writings) toiled and spared no pains or effort, as each one studied the proposition that he approved. At 63 that stage Prohaeresius, who trusted in his talent, remained confident without showing ambition or revealing his hidden thoughts. But now Anatolius was near and 64 had moved to Athens. When he had courageously[215] performed sacrifices and visited all the temples, in the way a divine ordinance commanded, he summoned the sophists to the competition. When they were in his presence, they one and all strove to be the first to declaim; so prone to self-love are humans! But Anatolius laughed at the young 65 pupils who were applauding them and he felt sorry for the fathers whose sons were being educated by such men. Then he called on Prohaeresius who alone was left. Now 66 he had cultivated the acquaintance of one of Anatolius' friends, who knew all the circumstances, and had learned from him the laying down of the thesis that Anatolius approved. (This is what the author referred to as ridiculous in the comments above.) And even though the theme was unworthy of consideration, and it was not right that [the

---

[214] Hints at the rule of Christian emperors.

[215] Pagan rituals were frowned upon under the Christian emperors Constans (r. 337–350) and Constantius (337–361).

τόλιον ἔδει ταῦτα νικᾶν), ὅμως πρός τε τὴν κλῆσιν
ὑπήκουσεν ἀθρόως, καί, πρὸς ἐκείνην τὴν στάσιν διαθέμενος τὸν ἀγῶνα, ἐς τοσόνδε ἤρκεσε πρὸς τὸ κάλλος τοῦ λόγου, ὥστε ἐπήδα τε ὁ Ἀνατόλιος, καὶ τὸ
θέατρον βοῶν τε ἐρρήγνυτο, καὶ οὐδεὶς ἦν ὃς οὐχὶ
67 θεὸν ὑπελάμβανε. τιμήσας οὖν ἐκεῖνον διαφερόντως
φαίνεται, καίτοι γε τοὺς ἄλλους μόλις ἀξιώσας τῆς
ἑαυτοῦ τραπέζης.

68   Ὁ δὲ Ἀνατόλιος σοφιστὴς ἦν ἐν τοῖς κατ᾽ εὐωχίαν
καὶ πρὸς συμπόσιον· οὐδὲ τὸ συμπόσιον ἦν ἄλογον
καὶ ἀπαίδευτον. ἀλλὰ ταῦτα μὲν ἐγένετο πρὸ πολλῶν
χρόνων καὶ οὕτως ἐξηκρίβου τὴν ἀκοὴν ὁ συγγρα-
69 φεύς. ὁ δὲ Ἀνατόλιος καὶ τὸν Μιλήσιον | ὑπερεθαύμα-
76G ζεν, ὃς ἦν μὲν ἐκ Σμύρνης τῆς Ἰωνικῆς, φύσεως δὲ
ἀρίστης τυχών, ἐς ἀφιλότιμόν τινα καὶ σχολαστὴν
ἑαυτὸν ἐμβαλὼν βίον, πρός τε ἱεροῖς ἦν καὶ γάμων
ἠμέλησε, ποίησίν τε ἅπασαν καὶ μέλος ἐξήσκησε καὶ
ποιήσεως ὅσον ἐπαινοῦσι Χάριτες. οὕτω γοῦν εἷλε
τὸν Ἀνατόλιον, ὥστε καὶ Μοῦσαν ἐκάλει τὸν ἄνθρωπον.

70   Ἐπιφανίου δὲ τοῦ σοφιστεύοντος τὰ ζητήματα δι-
αιρέσεις ἔφασκεν, εἰς μικρολογίαν καὶ περιττὴν ἀκρίβειαν κωμῳδῶν τὸν παιδεύοντα.

71   Περὶ δὲ τῆς διαφωνίας αὐτῶν τῆς κατὰ τὴν στάσιν,
διασιλλαίνων ἅπαντας, "εἰ πλείους," ἔφη, "τῶν δεκα-

216 A pun on *dihaeresis* (cf. below, VPS 11.1). In rhetoric it
refers to subdividing a speech under headings.

view of] Anatolius should prevail, nevertheless Prohaere-sius, when his name was called, obeyed the summons promptly, and, modeling his disputation on the constitu-tion of the theme that I have mentioned, his argument was so able and so elegant that Anatolius jumped up from his seat, the audience erupted in loud approval, and there was not one person who did not regard him as a divine being. Accordingly, Anatolius openly showed him respect above others, but would hardly admit the others worthy to sit at his table.

67

Anatolius was a sophist in the fashion appropriate to feasts and drinking parties; and his drinking party was neither lacking speeches nor devoid of learning. But all this happened many years ago, and therefore the author has been very careful in his report of what he learned from spoken reports. Anatolius felt great admiration for Mile-sius as well, a man who came from Smyrna in Ionia, while endowed with great talent, abandoning himself to an un-ambitious and leisurely life, frequented the temples, he neglected to marry, and cultivated every sort of poetry and lyric and every kind of composition that the Graces ap-prove. By this means, then, he won the favor of Anatolius so that he even called the man a "Muse."

68

69

But Anatolius used to call the investigative questions artfully raised by Epiphanius "dissections,"[216] making fun of that teacher's attention to linguistic detail and excessive precision.

70

He mocked all the sophists for their disagreement over the laying down[217] of a thesis, and said: "If there had been

71

[217] For the rhetorical term, see note 212 to section 61.

τριῶν ἐτύγχανον οἱ σοφιστεύοντες, τάχ᾽ ἂν ἑτέρας
492B προσεξεῦρον στάσεις, | ἵνα διαφόρως ἓν πρόβλημα
μελετήσωσιν." Προαιρέσιον δὲ πάντων ἕνα καὶ μόνον
ὑπερεθαύμαζεν.

72   Ἐτύγχανε δὲ ὁ Προαιρέσιος οὐ πρὸ πολλοῦ χρόνου
μετάπεμπτος ὑπὸ τοῦ βασιλεύοντος γεγονὼς Κών-
σταντος ἐς τὰς Γαλλίας καὶ κρατήσας τοῦ βασιλεύοντος ἐς τοσοῦτον, ὥστε ὁμοτράπεζος ἅμα τοῖς τιμιω-
τάτοις ἦν αὐτῷ, καὶ ὅσον γε τῶν ἐκείνῃ τότε ἀνθρώπων
οὐκ ἐξικνοῦντο τούς τε λόγους ἀναθεωρεῖν καὶ τὰ
ἀπόρρητα τῆς ψυχῆς θαυμάζειν, πρὸς τὴν ὄψιν καὶ τὰ
φαινόμενα μεταφέροντες τὴν ἔκπληξιν, τοῦ τε σώματος αὐτοῦ τὸ κάλλος καὶ τὸ ὕψος ἐτεθήπεσαν, ὥσπερ
ἐς ἀνδριάντα τινὰ καὶ κολοσσὸν μόλις ἀναβλέποντες·
73   οὕτω τὰ πάντα ἦν ὑπὲρ ἄνθρωπον. τήν γε μὴν καρτερίαν ὁρῶντες, ὄντως ἀπαθῆ τινα καὶ σιδήρεον
ὑπελάμβανον, ὅτι λεπτὸν ἔχων τριβώνιον, ἀνυπόδη-
τος, τρυφῆς περιουσίαν ἐτίθετο τοὺς Γαλατικοὺς χει-
74   μῶνας καὶ πεπηγότα σχεδόν τι τὸν Ῥῆνον ἔπινε· καὶ
77G   τόν γε ὅλον | οὕτω διετέλεσε βίον, ἀπείρατος θερμοῦ
γενόμενος ποτοῦ. ἀπέστειλε γοῦν αὐτὸν ὁ βασιλεὺς
εἰς τὴν μεγάλην Ῥώμην, φιλοτιμούμενος οἵων βασιλεύειν ἔλαχεν· οἱ δὲ οὐκ εἶχον ὅ τι θαυμάσουσιν, οὕτω
75   πάντα ἦν παρὰ τὴν ἀνθρωπίνην φύσιν. πολλὰ δὲ ἐπὶ
πολλοῖς ἀγασθέντες, καὶ τυχόντες ἐπαίνων, ἀνδριά-

---

218 Perhaps an echo of Philostr. VS 589, where the sophist
Adrian has a similar effect on audiences with no Greek.

more than thirteen of these professional sophists, they would no doubt have invented still more positions in order to declaim on a single problem from every different angle possible." Prohaeresius was the one and only sophist of them all whom he highly admired.

Now it happened that Prohaeresius had not long be- 72 fore been summoned to the Gallic provinces by Constans, who then held imperial power, and he gained such an influence over Constans that he was a guest at his table along with those whom the emperor most honored. And all the inhabitants of that country who could not attain to a thorough understanding of his lectures and thus admire the innermost secrets of his soul, transferred a sense of awe to what they could see plainly before their eyes, and marveled at his physical beauty and great stature, while they gazed up at him with an effort as though to behold some statue or colossus, so much beyond a human was he in all 73 respects.[218] Moreover, when they observed his endurance, they believed him to be impervious to the elements and as if made of iron; for clad in a threadbare cloak and barefoot[219] he regarded the winters of Gaul as the height of luxury, and he would drink the water of the Rhine when it was almost frozen. And he passed his whole life in this 74 fashion without ever having taken a hot drink. At any rate, Constans dispatched him to mighty Rome, because he was ambitious to show the kind of great men he ruled over. But so entirely did Prohaeresius surpass the ordinary human nature that they were unable to select one quality to admire. They admired his many great qualities one after 75

[219] Cf. above, *VPS* 10.22. Perhaps an allusion to Pl. *Symp.* 220a–b.

ντα κατασκευασάμενοι χαλκοῦν ἰσομέτρητον, ἀνέθη-
καν ἐπιγράψαντες· "ἡ βασιλεύουσα Ῥώμη τὸν βασιλεύοντα τῶν λόγων."

76   Ὁ δὲ βασιλεὺς ἀπιόντι πάλιν Ἀθήναζε καὶ δωρεὰν
αἰτεῖν ἔδωκεν. ὁ δὲ τῆς ἑαυτοῦ φύσεως ἄξιον ᾔτησε,
νήσους οὐκ ὀλίγας οὐδὲ μικρὰς εἰς ἀπαγωγὴν φόρου
κατὰ σιτηρέσιον[91] ταῖς Ἀθήναις. ὁ δὲ καὶ ταῦτα ἔδωκεν καὶ προσέθηκε τὸ μέγιστον τῶν ἀξιωμάτων,
στρατοπεδάρχην ἐπιτρέψας καλεῖσθαι, ὅπως νεμεσῴη
77   μηδεὶς εἰ τοσαῦτα ἐκ τοῦ δημοσίου κομίζοιτο. ταύτην
τὴν δωρεὰν ἔδει βεβαιοῦν τὸν τῆς αὐλῆς ἔπαρχον—
νεωστὶ γὰρ παρῆν ἐκ Γαλατίας ὁ ἔπαρχος— καὶ
μετὰ τοὺς ἐπὶ τοῖς λόγοις ἐκείνους ἀγῶνας, παρὰ τὸν
Ἀνατόλιον ἐλθών, ἠξίου βεβαιοῦν τὴν χάριν, καὶ
συνηγόρους οὐκ ἐκάλεσε μόνους, ἀλλὰ σχεδόν τι
78   πάντας τοὺς πεπαιδευμένους ἐκ τῆς Ἑλλάδος· πάντες
γὰρ ἦσαν Ἀθήνησι διὰ τὴν ἐπιδημίαν. ὡς δὲ ἐπλη-
ρώθη τὸ θέατρον καὶ ὁ Προαιρέσιος ἠξίου τοὺς συνηγόρους λέγειν, παραδραμὼν τὴν ἁπάντων δόξαν ὁ
ἔπαρχος καὶ βασανίζων τὸν Προαιρέσιον ἐς τὸ σχέδιον "λέγε," φησίν, "ὦ Προαιρέσιε· αἰσχρὸν γάρ ἐστι
καὶ λέγειν καὶ βασιλέα ἐπαινεῖν σοῦ παρόντος ἕτε-

91 κατὰ σιτηρέσιον ὄν A: καταστρεψάμενος Gi Go: κατα‹-
στρεψάμενος εἰς› σιτηρέσιον [ὄν] coni. Go in app.

another, and were in turn approved by him, and they cast
and set up in his honor a life-size bronze statue with this
inscription: "Rome the Queen of cities honors the King of
Eloquence."[220]

When he was about to return to Athens, Constans also   76
permitted him to ask for a gift. Thereupon he asked for
something worthy of his character, namely not insignificant number of sizable islands to pay tribute to Athens in
the form of a grain allowance. Constans not only gave
him these, but added the highest possible distinction by
bestowing on him the title of "stratopedarch,"[221] so that
no one would resent his acquisition of so great a fortune
from the public funds. This gift had to be confirmed by   77
the praetorian prefect (the prefect had namely arrived
from Gaul recently). Accordingly, after the competitions
in eloquence that I have described, Prohaeresius approached Anatolius and implored him to confirm the favor
and summoned not only professional advocates for his
cause but almost all the educated men of Greece. For   78
on account of the prefect's visit they were all at Athens.
When the theater had filled up, and Prohaeresius called
on his advocates to speak, the prefect ran counter to
the expectation of all present, because he wished to test
the extempore eloquence of Prohaeresius, and he said:
"Speak, Prohaeresius! For it is unbecoming for any other
man to speak and to praise the emperor when you are

[220] In his *Letter* 278, Libanius mentions this statue at Rome
and another at Athens.

[221] This office, originally military, had become that of a Food
Controller; cf. Julian. *Or.* 1.8c, where he says that Constantine did
not disdain it for himself.

79
78G
ρον." ἐνταῦθα ὁ Προαιρέσιος, ὥσπερ ἵππος εἰς πεδίον
κληθείς, | τοὺς ἐπὶ τῇ δωρεᾷ λόγους <ἐκφέρων>,[92] τόν
τε Κελεὸν καὶ Τριπτόλεμον καὶ τὴν Δήμητρος ἐπιδημίαν ἐπὶ τῇ τοῦ σίτου δωρεᾷ παρήγαγεν, καὶ τὴν τοῦ
βασιλέως χάριν ἐκείνοις προσάπτων τοῖς διηγήμασι,
ταχὺ μάλα μετέστησεν εἰς τὸν ἀρχαῖον ὄγκον τὰ γι-
νόμενα καὶ τοῖς λεγομένοις ἐπεχόρευεν, ἐπιδεικνύμενος εἰς τὴν ὑπόθεσιν· καὶ ὁ τῶν λόγων ἔλεγχος ἦν
αὐτῷ φιλοτιμία.

80
Γάμος δὲ αὐτῷ συνέπεσεν ἐξ Ἀσίας καὶ τῆς Τραλ-
λιανῶν πόλεως· Ἀμφίκλεια μὲν ὄνομα τῇ γυναικί· |
493B
θυγάτρια δὲ αὐτοῖς ἐγενέσθην τοσοῦτον παραλλάτ-
τοντα κατὰ τὴν ἡλικίαν χρόνον, ὅσος ἐς τὸ κύειν καὶ
γίνεσθαι καταναλίσκεται. προελθόντα δὲ εἰς ὥραν ἐν
ᾗ πάγκαλόν τι χρῆμα καὶ μακάριον παιδίον, καὶ τὴν
τοῦ πατρὸς ψυχὴν ὑφ' ἡδονῆς ἀνασείσαντα, ἐν ὀλί-
γαις ἡμέραις ἄμφω τοὺς πατέρας ἀπέλιπεν, ὥστε μι-
81
κροῦ τὸ πάθος καὶ τῶν προσηκόντων ἐκβαλεῖν λογι-
σμῶν τὸν Προαιρέσιον. ἀλλὰ πρὸς τοῦτο μὲν ἤρκεσεν
ἡ Μιλησίου μοῦσα, τὰς ἁρμονικὰς ἀναψαμένη χάρι-
τας καὶ πολλὰ πείθουσα[93] μετ' ἀφροδίτης καὶ τὸν λο-
γισμὸν ἀνακαλουμένη.

Τοῖς δὲ Ῥωμαίοις ἀξιοῦσιν ὁμιλητὴν ἴδιον ἀποπέμ-
πειν ὁ Προαιρέσιος τὸν Εὐσέβιον ἐξέπεμψεν, ὃς ἦν
μὲν ἐξ Ἀλεξανδρείας—, ἐναρμόσειν δὲ ἄλλως ἐδόκει
τῇ πόλει, κολακεύειν τε εἰδὼς καὶ σαίνειν τὸ ὑπερέ-

present." Then Prohaeresius, like a horse summoned to   79
the plain,[222] producing a speech about the imperial gift,
adduced Celeus[223] and Triptolemus and Demeter's sojourn
among men that she might bestow on them the gift of corn,
and linking the generosity of Constans to that famous narrative, he very deftly infused the event with the dignity of
ancient legend, and with his eloquence brought an agile
artistry to the chosen theme. The fact that he obtained the
honor he aspired to was proof of his eloquence.

He had married a woman from Asia and from the city   80
of Tralles; her name was Amphiclea. They had two little
girls, who were so little apart in age as the time needed for
conception and birth. Having reached that time of life
when a child is a wholly lovely and charming thing, and
made their father's heart tremble with joy, they left their
parents desolate, both within a few days, so that his grief
almost shook Prohaeresius from the rational considerations that are appropriate for a philosopher. However, the   81
Muse of Milesius[224] proved able to meet this crisis, and by
composing graceful harmonies and using all her charisma
and persuasion, she recalled him to reason.

When the Romans asked him to send them one of his
own pupils, Prohaeresius sent them Eusebius who was a
native of Alexandria—he seemed to be peculiarly suited
to Rome, because he knew how to flatter and fawn on

222 A proverb: Pl. *Tht.* 183d; Lucian, *Pisc.* 9.
223 King of Eleusis, killed by Erichthonius of Athens.
224 For Milesius see above, *VPS* 10.69.

---

92 add. Go
93 πεσοῦσα A: παίζουσα Boiss Wr: πείθουσα Go

82 χον— · στασιώδης δὲ κατὰ τὰς Ἀθήνας ἐφαίνετο. καὶ
ἅμα ἐβούλετο μεῖζον τὸ καθ᾿ ἑαυτὸν ποιεῖν, ἄνδρα
πέμπων πολιτικῆς κακοτεχνίας οὐκ ἀμύητον· (ἐπεὶ τά
γε κατὰ ῥητορικὴν ἐξαρκεῖ τοσοῦτον εἰπεῖν ὅτι ἦν Αἰ-
83 γύπτιος. τὸ δὲ ἔθνος ἐπὶ ποιητικῇ μὲν σφόδρα μαίνον-
ται, ὁ δὲ σπουδαῖος Ἑρμῆς αὐτῶν ἀποκεχώρηκεν).
84 ἐπανέστη δὲ αὐτῷ ὁ Μουσώνιος, εἰς σοφιστικὴν ὁμι-
79G λητὴς | ὢν αὐτοῦ—περὶ οὗ πολλὰ διὰ τὰς ἄλλας
⟨πράξεις⟩[94] ἐν τοῖς διεξοδικοῖς γέγραπται—, καὶ ὅτε
γε ἀντῆρε, καταμαθὼν πρὸς τίνα ἔχει τὸν ἀγῶνα,
ταχὺ μάλα ἐπὶ τὴν πολιτικὴν κατεπήδησεν.

85 Ἰουλιανοῦ δὲ βασιλεύοντος, νόμῳ[95] τοῦ παιδεύειν
ἐξειργόμενος (ἐδόκει γὰρ εἶναι χριστιανός), συνορῶν
τὸν ἱεροφάντην ὥσπερ Δελφικόν τινα τρίποδα πρὸς
τὴν τοῦ μέλλοντος πρόνοιαν πᾶσι τοῖς δεομένοις ἀνα-
κείμενον, σοφίᾳ τινὶ περιῆλθε ξένῃ τὴν πρόγνωσιν.
86 ἐμέτρει μὲν γὰρ ὁ βασιλεὺς τὴν γῆν τοῖς Ἕλλησιν
εἰς τὸν φόρον, ὅπως μὴ βαρύνοιντο· ὁ δὲ Προαιρέσιος
ἠξίωσεν αὐτὸν ἐκμαθεῖν παρὰ τῶν θεῶν, εἰ βέβαια
μενεῖ τὰ τῆς φιλανθρωπίας. ὡς δὲ ἀπέφησεν, ὁ μὲν
87 ἔγνω τὸ πραχθησόμενον καὶ ἦν εὐθυμότερος. ὁ δὲ
συγγραφεὺς, κατὰ τουτονὶ τὸν χρόνον εἰς ἕκτον που

[94] add. Gi Go
[95] Gi Go: τόπῳ A

those in power, while he was known as a divisive person in
Athens. At the same time Prohaeresius wished to increase   82
his own reputation by sending a man who was not uninitiated in cunning political intrigue. As for his talent for
rhetoric, it is enough to say that he was an Egyptian;
the people from this country rave about the poetic arts,   83
whereas the studious Hermes has abandoned them.
Against him Musonius stood up, a former pupil in the   84
sophistic art. (I have for his other activities written about
him at length in my *historical Chronicle*.) When Musonius
reared his head to oppose him, Eusebius knew well what
sort of man he was up against, so he very quickly came
down from his high horse to take up political oratory.

In the reign of emperor Julian, Prohaeresius was pro-   85
hibited from teaching by law,[225] because he seemed to be
a Christian.[226] When he observed that the hierophant, like
a sort of Delphic tripod, was open to all who had need of
him to foretell future events, he circumvented the prediction with unusual insight. For the emperor was having the   86
land measured for the benefit of the Hellenes, to relieve
them from the weight of taxes. Thereupon Prohaeresius
requested the hierophant[227] to find out from the god
whether this benevolence would be long-lasting. And
when he declared that it would not, Prohaeresius learned
in this way what the future would bring and he took courage. The author, who had nearly reached his sixteenth   87

---

[225] There were two laws (Cod. Theod. 13.3.5; cf. Julian.
Ep. 42 = 61 Bidez). The second was revoked by Jovian (Cod.
Theod. 13.3.6). The first remained in force.

[226] On Prohaeresius as a Christian, see Hieron. *Chron.* 242–
43.   [227] That is, of Eleusis; cf. *VPS* 7.28.

καὶ δέκατον ἔτος τελῶν, παρῆλθέ τε ἐς τὰς Ἀθήνας
καὶ τοῖς ὁμιληταῖς ⟨αὐτοῦ⟩[96] ἐγκατεμίγη· καὶ ἀγαπη-
θεὶς ὑπ᾽ αὐτοῦ καθάπερ παῖς γνήσιος, ἠπείγετο μὲν
μετὰ πέμπτον ἔτος εἰς τὴν Αἴγυπτον, οἱ δὲ πατέρες
καλοῦντες ἐπὶ Λυδίας ἐξεβιάσαντο· κἀκείνῳ μὲν σοφιστικὴ προὔκειτο, καὶ πρὸς τοῦτο ἐξεκάλουν ἅπαντες.

88   Προαιρέσιος δὲ ἐξ ἀνθρώπων ἀνεχώρει μετ᾽ οὐ
πολλὰς ἡμέρας· τοσοῦτος καὶ τοιοῦτος γενόμενος καὶ
διαπλήσας τῶν ἑαυτοῦ λόγων τε καὶ ὁμιλητῶν τὴν
οἰκουμένην.

11. Ἐπιφάνιος· οὗτος ἦν μὲν ἐκ Συρίας, δεινότατος
δὲ εἶναι περὶ τὰς διακρίσεις δόξας τῶν ζητημάτων,
τὸν δὲ λόγον ἀτονώτερος, ὅμως ἀντεσοφίστευσέν τε
Προαιρεσίῳ καὶ εἰς πολὺ δόξης ἐχώρησεν· οὐ γὰρ
φέρει τὸ ἀνθρώπινον ἕνα θαυμάζειν, ἀλλ᾽ ἐγκεκλικὸς
80G   καὶ ἡττώμενον ὑπὸ φθόνου, | τοῖς πολυκρατοῦσι καὶ
ὑπερέχουσιν ἕτερον ἀντικαθίστησιν, ὥσπερ ἐν φυ-
2   σικῇ τὰς ἀρχὰς ἐκ τῶν ἐναντίων λαμβάνοντες. | ἐτε-
494B λεύτα δὲ οὐκ εἰς βαθὺ γῆρας ἀφικόμενος, τὸ αἷμα
νοσήσας· καὶ ἡ γυνὴ ταὐτὸ τοῦτο ἔπαθε, καλλίστη
πασῶν γενομένη. καὶ παιδίον οὐκ ἦν αὐτοῖς. τοῦτον ὁ
ταῦτα γράφων οὐκ ἔγνω, πολὺ προαπελθόντα τῆς ἐπι-
δημίας.

96 add. Go

birthday, arrived at Athens and was enrolled among his pupils; and loved by him as if he was his own son,[228] after five years he felt a pressing desire to go to Egypt, but his parents summoned him and compelled him to return to Lydia. The career of a sophist lay open for him and all were encouraging him in that direction.

A few days later Prohaeresius departed from the human world. He was a man of such stature and talent and he filled the whole known world with his splendid speeches and students.

11. Epiphanius.[229] This man was a native of Syria, and he was reputed to be very skillful in distinguishing positions on investigative questions. Though he was less vigorous as an orator, he still went up against Prohaeresius in the sophistic profession and actually attained to great fame. For human beings are not content to admire one man only, but prone to envy and overcome by it, they set up someone else as rival to those who excel and tower above the rest, in the same way as those in the philosophy of nature derive their fundamental principles from opposites.[230] Epiphanius did not reach a high age, because he suffered from a blood disease, and his wife, who was very beautiful, suffered from the same illness. Also, they left no children. Epiphanius was not personally known to the author, for he died long before the latter's sojourn in Athens.

[228] See above, *VPS* 10.15–16.
[229] Ridiculed by Anatolius for his pedantry; above, *VPS* 10.69–70.
[230] Perhaps a (misplaced) echo of Arist. *Metaph.* 1087a29–30.

EUNAPIUS

12. Διόφαντος. Καὶ Διόφαντος ἦν μὲν ἐξ Ἀραβίας καὶ εἰς τοὺς τεχνικοὺς ἐβιάζετο· ἡ δὲ αὐτὴ δόξα τῶν ἀνθρώπων Προαιρεσίῳ κἀκεῖνον ἀντήγειρεν, ὡσεὶ Καλλίμαχον Ὁμήρῳ τις ἀναστήσειεν. ἀλλ' ἐγέλα ταῦτα ὁ Προαιρέσιος καὶ τοὺς ἀνθρώπους ὅ τι εἰσὶν

2 ἐν διατριβῆς εἶχεν μέρει. τοῦτον ἐγίγνωσκεν ὁ συγγραφεύς καὶ ἠκροάσατό γε πολλάκις δημοσίᾳ λέγοντος. παραθεῖναι δὲ τῇ γραφῇ τῶν λεχθέντων καὶ μνημονευθέντων οὐδὲν ἐδόκει καλῶς ἔχειν· μνήμη γάρ ἐστιν ἀξιολόγων ἀνδρῶν, οὐ χλευασμός, ἡ γραφή.

3 ἀλλ' ὅμως ἐπιτάφιόν τε εἰπεῖν τινα τοῦ Προαιρεσίου λέγεται (προαπῆλθε γὰρ ὁ Προαιρέσιος), καί τι τοιοῦτον ἐπιφθέγξασθαι διαμνημονεύουσιν ἐπὶ τῇ Σαλαμῖνι καὶ τοῖς Μηδικοῖς· "ὦ Μαραθὼν καὶ Σαλαμίν, νῦν σεσίγησθε. οἵαν σάλπιγγα τῶν ὑμετέρων τρο-

4 παίων ἀπολωλέκατε." οὗτος ἀπέλιπε δύο παῖδας ἐπὶ τρυφὴν καὶ πλοῦτον ὁρμήσαντας.

13. Σώπολις. Καὶ Σωπόλιδος ἠκροάσατο πολλάκις ὁ ταῦτα γράφων. καὶ ἦν ἀνὴρ εἰς τὸν ἀρχαῖον χαρακτῆρα τὸν λόγον ἀναφέρειν βιαζόμενος καὶ τῆς ὑγιαινούσης Μούσης ψαύειν ὀριγνώμενος. ἀλλ' ἔκρουε μὲν τὴν θύραν ἱκανῶς, ἠνοίγετο δὲ οὐ πολλάκις· ἀλλ' εἴ πού τι καὶ ψοφήσειεν ἐκεῖθεν, λεπτόν τι καὶ ἀσθενές

2 παρωλίσθαινεν ἔσωθεν τοῦ θείου πνεύματος· τὸ δὲ

81G θέατρον ἐμεμήνεσαν, οὐδὲ τὴν | πεπιεσμένην ῥανίδα τὴν Κασταλίαν φέροντες. τούτῳ παῖς ἐγένετο· καὶ ἐπιβεβηκέναι τοῦ θρόνου τὸν παῖδα φάσκουσιν.

***

231 For the image, cf. Himer. Or. 61.1.

568

12. Diophantus. Diophantus was also a native of Arabia and he forced his way into the circle of specialists in rhetoric. That same envious opinion of mankind of which I have just spoken set him up as another rival of Prohaeresius, as though one could put Callimachus up against Homer. But Prohaeresius laughed about all this, and he regarded human beings and their foibles a trifling thing. The 2 author knew Diophantus and often heard him declaim in public. But he has not considered it appropriate to quote in this work any of his speeches or what he remembers of them. For this document is a record of noteworthy men, not a charade. However, it is said that he delivered a funeral oration in honor of Prohaeresius (for Prohaeresius died before he did), and they record that he concluded with a comment of this sort about Salamis and the war against the Medes: "O Marathon and Salamis, you now have been silenced! What a herald of your glorious victories have you lost!" He left two sons who pursued a life of 4 luxury and moneymaking.

13. Sopolis. The author of this work also often heard Sopolis speak. He was a man who made forced attempts to reproduce an archaic style in his oratory and did his utmost to reach the level of a sane Muse. But though he used to knock diligently at her door, it was seldom opened.[231] If ever it did creak open a little, it was but a thin and feeble spark of the divine inspiration that escaped from within. But his audience would respond with a manic 2 enthusiasm, unable as they were to endure even a single drop squeezed from the Castalian fount.[232] He had a son and they say that he has ascended the professorial chair.[233]

[232] Stream at Delphi and a source of prophecy.
[233] Cf. VPS 6.81, 10.25, and Philostr. VS 566.

14. Ἱμέριος· τὸν ἄνδρα τοῦτον ἤνεγκε μὲν Βιθυνία, οὐκ ἔγνω δὲ αὐτὸν ὁ ταῦτα γράφων· καίτοι γε ἦν κατ᾽ ἐκείνους τοὺς χρόνους. ἀλλὰ πρὸς τὸν αὐτοκράτορα διαβὰς Ἰουλιανὸν κατ᾽ ἐπίδειξιν, ὡς διὰ τὴν ἐς Προαιρέσιον ἀχθηδόνα τοῦ βασιλέως, ἀσμένως ὀφθησόμενος, Ἰουλιανοῦ καταλείποντος τὸ ἀνθρώπινον, ἐνδιέτριψε τῇ ἀποδημίᾳ, καί, Προαιρεσίου τελευτήσαντος,
2 Ἀθήναζε ἠπείγετο. εὔκολος δὲ ἀνὴρ εἰπεῖν καὶ συνηρμοσμένος· κρότον δὲ ἔχει καὶ ἦχον ἡ συνθήκη πολιτικόν· καί που σπάνιος καὶ παρὰ τὸν θεῖον Ἀριστείδην ἵσταται. ἐπὶ θυγατρὶ δὲ τελευτᾷ, τῆς ἱερᾶς νόσου πρὸς γήρᾳ μακρῷ καταλαβούσης αὐτόν.

15. Παρνάσιος. Ἐν τούτοις ἦν τοῖς χρόνοις καὶ Παρνάσιος ἐπὶ τοῦ παιδευτικοῦ θρόνου, ὁμιλητὰς εὐαριθμήτους ἔχων· καὶ τοῦ γε ὀνόματος οὐκ ἀπεστερημένος. |

495B   16. Λιβάνιος. Λιβάνιον δὲ Ἀντιόχεια μὲν ἤνεγκεν ἡ τῆς Κοίλης καλουμένης Συρίας πρώτη πόλεων, Σελεύκου τοῦ Νικάτορος ἐπικληθέντος ἔργον. ἦν δὲ τῶν
2 εὖ γεγονότων καὶ εἰς τοὺς ἄκρους ἐτέλει. νέος δὲ ὢν ἔτι καὶ κύριος ἑαυτοῦ, πατέρων ἀπολελοιπότων, ἀφικόμενος Ἀθήναζε, οὔτε ὡς ἐκ Συρίας Ἐπιφανίῳ προσῆλθε μεγίστην ἔχοντι δόξαν, οὔτε παρὰ Προαιρέσιον ἐφοίτησε, ὡς ἐν τῷ πλήθει τῶν ὁμιλητῶν καὶ τῷ μεγέθει τῆς δόξης τῶν διδασκάλων καλυφθησόμενος.

---

234 The ancient name for epilepsy.
235 For Parnasius see VPS 10.26; he is otherwise unknown.

14. Himerius. This man was a native of Bithynia, yet the author never knew him, though he lived in the same time period. Himerius traveled to the court of the Emperor Julian to declaim before him, in the hope that he would be regarded with favor on account of the emperor's annoyance with Prohaeresius; and when Julian left the human realm, he spent his time abroad. Then, on the death of Prohaeresius, he hastened to Athens. He had an effortless and harmonious ability as a speaker. His style of composition has the sonorous cadences of political oratory. Sometimes, though rarely, he rises as high as the godlike Aristeides. He left a daughter when he died, having suffered a bout of the sacred disease[234] in extreme old age.

15. Parnasius. Parnasius also lived in those days and occupied a teacher's chair. His pupils were not hard to count, and he was still not without a certain reputation.[235]

16. Libanius. Antioch, the capital of Coele Syria as it is called, the creation of Seleucus surnamed Nicator, produced Libanius.[236] He came from a noble family and became very prominent in the community. While he was still a young adult and his own master[237] (since his parents were dead), he came to Athens,[238] and there, though he too came from Syria, he did not attach himself to Epiphanius, who enjoyed the very highest reputation, nor did he attend the school of Prohaeresius, for he expected that he would run the risk of being obscured, partly by so great a crowd of fellow pupils, partly by the celebrity of his teach-

[236] For Libanius' "autobiography," see his *Oration* 1.
[237] Cf. Lib. *Or.* 1.12.
[238] In AD 336.

EUNAPIUS

ἐνεδρευθεὶς δὲ ὑπὸ τῶν Διοφαντείων, Διοφάντῳ προσ-
3 ένειμεν ἑαυτόν· καί, ὡς οἱ πάνυ τὸν ἄνδρα καταμεμα-
θηκότες ἔφασκον, ταῖς μὲν ὁμιλίαις καὶ συνουσίαις,
τὸ γεγονὸς συμμαθών, ἐλάχιστα παρεγίνετο καὶ τῷ
82G διδασκάλῳ τις | ὀχληρὸς οὐκ ἦν· αὐτὸς δὲ ἑαυτὸν ἐπὶ
ταῖς μελέταις συνεῖχεν καὶ πρὸς τὸν ἀρχαῖον ἐξεβιάζετο τύπον, τὴν ψυχὴν διαπλάττων καὶ τὸν λόγον.
4 ὥσπερ οὖν οἱ πολλάκις πέμποντες, ἔστιν ὅτε καὶ τυγ-
χάνοντες τοῦ σκοποῦ, καὶ τὸ συνεχὲς τῆς μελέτης
αὐτοῖς διὰ τῆς γυμνασίας τῶν ὀργάνων ὡς ἐπὶ τὸ
πλεῖστον εὐστοχίας οὐκ ἐπιστήμην ἔφυσεν, ἀλλὰ τὴν
5 τέχνην· οὕτω καὶ Λιβάνιος, ἐκ τοῦ ζήλου καὶ τῆς
παραθέσεως τῆς κατὰ μίμησιν, προσαρτῶν ἑαυτὸν
καὶ παραξέων ἡγεμόσιν ἀρίστοις, τοῖς ἀρχαίοις καὶ
οἷς ἐχρῆν ἑπόμεν+‒ος, ἴχνος τε ἄριστον ἐνέβαινε καὶ
6 ἀπήλαυσε τῆς ὁδοῦ τὰ εἰκότα. θαρσήσας δὲ ἐπὶ τῷ
λέγειν καὶ πείσας ἑαυτὸν ὡς ἐνάμιλλος εἴη τοῖς ἐπὶ
τούτῳ μέγα φρονοῦσιν, οὐχ εἵλετο περὶ μικρὰν πόλιν
κρύπτεσθαι καὶ συγκαταπίπτειν τῷ τῆς πόλεως ἀξιώματι, ἀλλ᾽ ἐπὶ τὴν Κωνσταντίνου πόλιν διαβαλὼν
ἄρτι παριοῦσαν εἰς μέγεθος καὶ ἀκμάζουσαν καὶ δεο-
μένην ἔργων τε ὁμοῦ καὶ λόγων οἳ κατακοσμήσουσι,
ταχὺ μάλα καὶ κατ᾽ αὐτὴν ἐξέλαμψεν, εἰς συνουσίαν
τε ἄριστος καὶ χαριέστατος φανεὶς καὶ εἰς ἐπίδειξιν

239 Cf. Lib. *Or.* 1.16 and 1.20.
240 Cf. Dem. *Or.* 18.149.
241 In 340 (Lib. *Or.* 1.26–29); he left Constantinople in 342

572

ers. But ambushed by the Diophantians,[239] he attached himself to Diophantus. And those who knew the man intimately asserted that, when he learned what had happened to him, he very seldom attended the lectures and meetings of the school and was no burden to his master. But he applied himself to the study of rhetoric and made a strenuous effort to acquire the style of the ancient authors by trying to fashion both his mind and his speech. In the same way as those who, when throwing the javelin often, happen to hit their mark sometimes, and their constant practice and regular exercise with their weapons usually achieves the practical skill in shooting straight over a great distance rather than the proper knowledge; so too Libanius, based on his enthusiasm and comparison so as to emulate, attached himself and stayed close to most excellent guides. Following the ancient authors and those he had to follow, he stepped into the footsteps of the best and benefited from the likely outcomes of that trajectory. As he gained confidence in his eloquence and convinced himself that he could rival those who prided themselves on their own skill, he resolved not to remain invisible in a small town and sink in the esteem of the world to that city's level.[240] Therefore, he crossed over to Constantine's city,[241] which had recently attained to greatness, and, being at the height of her prosperity, needed both deeds and words to adorn her as she deserved.[242] There he very soon became a shining light, since he proved to be an admirable and delightful teacher and his public declamations were

(*Or.* 1.47). The reason for his departure (charge of pederasty) lacks ancient evidence.

[242] Cf. *VPS* 1.1 and contrast 6.14–15 (criticism of its location).

7 λόγων ἐπαφρόδιτος. διαβολῆς δέ τινος αὐτῷ γενομένης περὶ τὰ μειράκια,—θεμιτὸν οὐκ ἦν ἐμοὶ γράφειν, ἐς μνήμην ἀξιολόγων ἀνέντι τὴν γραφήν—,
ἐκπεσὼν τῆς Κωνσταντίνου πόλεως, κατέσχε τὴν Νι-
8 κομήδειαν. κἀκεῖ δέ, τῆς φήμης ἐπισπομένης καὶ
παραθεούσης αὐτῷ, διὰ ταχέων ἀποκρουσθείς, ἐπὶ
τὴν ἑαυτοῦ πατρίδα καὶ πόλιν ἐπανέρχεται, κἀκεῖ τὸν
πάντα ἐβίω χρόνον, μακρὸν καὶ παρατείνοντα γενόμενον.

9 Μνήμην μὲν οὖν αὐτοῦ τὴν πρέπουσαν κἂν τοῖς
βιβλίοις τοῖς κατὰ τὸν Ἰουλιανὸν ἡ γραφὴ πεποίη-
83G ται, τὰ δὲ καθ᾽ ἕκαστον | νῦν ἐπεξελεύσεται. οὐδεὶς
τῶν συλλεγέντων Λιβανίῳ καὶ συνουσίας ἀξιωθέντων
10 ἀπῆλθεν ἄδηκτος· ἀλλὰ τό τε ἦθος εὐθὺς οἷός τις ἦν
ἔγνωστο καὶ συνεῖδεν αὐτοῦ τά τε τῆς ψυχῆς ἐπί τε
τὸ χεῖρον καὶ τὸ κρεῖττον ῥέποντα, καὶ τοσοῦτος ἦν
ἐς τὴν πλάσιν καὶ τὴν εἰς ἑκάτερον ἐξομοίωσιν, ὥστε
ὁ μὲν ⟨πολύπους⟩[97] λῆρος ἦν αὐτῷ, τῶν δὲ συνιόν-
των[98] ἕκαστος ἄλλον ἑαυτὸν ὁρᾶν ὑπελάμβανεν. ἔφασκον γοῦν αὐτὸν οἱ πεπειραμένοι, πίνακά τινα καὶ
11 ἐκμαγεῖον εἶναι παντοδαπῶν ἠθῶν καὶ ποικίλων· οὐδ᾽
496B ἂν | ἥλῳ ποτὲ πολλῶν καὶ διαφόρων συνεληλυθότων

[97] add. Lacapenus (λῆρος in initio lineae in A)
[98] A: συνόντων Vollenbr Go (fort. recte)

[243] Libanius himself says (Or. 1.51) that he was in Nicomedia
for five years, the happiest of his life.

full of charm. But a false charge was brought against him 7
in connection with adolescents. It would not be proper for
me to write about it, because I am determined to record
in this document only what is worthy to be recorded. For
this reason, then, he was expelled from Constantinople,
and settled at Nicomedia. When the scandalous tale fol- 8
lowed him there and kept up with him, he was soon[243]
thrust out of that city as well, and after a time[244] he returned to his native land and the city of his birth, and there
he lived the rest of his life, which lasted a very long time.

Though an account of him was produced as was fitting 9
to my books on the reign of Julian, I will now go through
his activities in detail. Not one of those who associated
with him and were deemed worthy of his teaching left him
without being deeply affected. For he grasped, in the blink 10
of an eye, every man's character for what it was, and understood the proclivities of his soul, whether it was inclined to virtue or vice. And indeed, he was so good at
adapting and assimilating himself to all sorts of men that
the octopus[245] pales into insignificance in comparison,
while everyone interacting with him thought they were
seeing a second self. At any rate, those who had had this
experience used to declare that he was like a canvas or wax
block[246] ready to take on the manifold and varied characteristics of other people. In a gathering of many men of 11
various sorts one could never have guessed who it was that

244 Eunapius does not mention the second sojourn of Libanius at Constantinople.

245 The adaptability of the "polypus" is a favorite commonplace: see Lucian, *Dialogues of the Sea Gods* 4; Philostr. *VS* 486
note 17.   246 A possible echo of Pl. *Tht.* 191c, 196a; *Tim.* 50c.

ᾧ μᾶλλον τέρπεται, ἀλλ᾽ ἐπὶ τοῖς ἐναντίοις ἐπῃνεῖτο
παρὰ τῶν τὸν ἐναντίον ἐλαυνόντων βίον, καὶ πᾶς τις
αὐτὸν τὰ σφέτερα θαυμάζειν ᾤετο· οὕτω πολύμορφόν
12 τι χρῆμα καὶ ἀλλοπρόσαλλον ἦν. γάμου δὲ καὶ οὗτος
ἠμέλησε, πλὴν ὅσα γε αὐτῷ γυνή τις ξυνῆν, οὐκ ἀπὸ
ὁμοίας τῆς ἀξιώσεως.

13 Ὁ δὲ λόγος αὐτῷ, περὶ μὲν τὰς μελέτας, παντελῶς
ἀσθενὴς καὶ τεθνηκὼς καὶ ἄπνους, καὶ διαφαίνεταί γε
οὗτος μὴ τετυχηκέναι διδασκάλου· καὶ γὰρ τὰ πλεῖστα τῶν κοινῶν καὶ παιδὶ γνωρίμων περὶ τὰς μελέτας
14 ἠγνόει· περὶ δὲ ἐπιστολὰς καὶ συνουσίας ἑτέρας
ἱκανῶς ἐπὶ τὸν ἀρχαῖον ἀναφέρει καὶ διεγείρεται τύπον, καὶ χάριτός γε αὐτῷ καὶ κωμικῆς βωμολοχίας
καταπέπλησται τὰ συγγράμματα, καὶ ἡ κομψότης
περιτρέχει πανταχοῦ διακονουμένη τοῖς λόγοις, καὶ ὃ
πάντες οἱ Συροφοίνικες ἔχουσι κατὰ τὴν κοινὴν |
84G ἔντευξιν ἡδὺ καὶ κεχαρισμένον, τοῦτο παρ᾽ ἐκείνου
15 λαβεῖν μετὰ παιδείας ἔξεστιν· οἱ μὲν οὖν Ἀττικοὶ μυ-
κτῆρα καὶ ἀστεϊσμὸν[99] αὐτὸ καλοῦσιν· ὁ δὲ ὥσπερ
κορυφὴν παιδείας τοῦτο ἐπετήδευσεν, ἐκ τῆς ἀρχαίας
κωμῳδίας ὅλος εἰς τὸ ἀπαγγέλλειν εἱλκυσμένος καὶ
τοῦ κατὰ θύραν τερπνοῦ καὶ γοητεύοντος τὴν ἀκοὴν
γενόμενος.

[99] ἀστεϊσμόν coni. Lacapenus: ἀλισμὸν A

247 Cf. Or. 1.12.
248 Cf. Or. 1.20.

he preferred, but individuals who pursued a way of life directly opposed to one another used to applaud in him qualities that were direct opposites, and everyone without exception was convinced that it was their views that Libanius admired—such a malleable and adaptable creature he was! He too did not pursue marriage, while in fact a woman lived with him, though she was not of equal standing.[247]   12

His manner of expression, at least with regard to declamations, was altogether feeble, lifeless, and uninspired, and it is obvious that he had not had the benefit of a teacher;[248] indeed he was unfamiliar with the most common rules of declamation, known to even a schoolboy.[249]   13
But regarding his letters and other interactions he sufficiently manages to bring out and revive the ancient style, and hence his writings are full of grace and lighthearted humor, while a refined elegance pervades the whole and is at the service of his eloquence. Moreover, one can find in him the peculiar allure and sweetness that all Syro-Phoenicians display in everyday encounters, over and above his erudition. The Attic authors call that sarcasm and urbane wit.[250] But he cultivated this as the pinnacle of true education, wholly drawing on ancient comedy for his manner of expression and keen on all that has an outward charm and beguiles the ear.   14

                                                                           15

[249] A puzzling and unfair criticism, inconsistent with Libanius' reputation as a declaimer. Cribiore (2013, 11) thinks Eunapius betrays his partisan support for Prohaeresius' "more turgid style." Cf. above, *VPS* 16.3–5.

[250] Cf. [Longinus], *Subl.* 34.2.

16   Παιδείας δὲ ὑπερβολὴν καὶ ἀναγνώσεώς ἐστιν
εὑρεῖν ἐν τοῖς λόγοις, λέξεσι κατεγλωττισμέναις
ἐντυγχάνοντα. τὰ γοῦν Εὐπόλιδος δένδρα Λαισπο-
δίαν καὶ Δαμασίαν οὐκ ἂν παρῆκεν, εἰ τὰ ὀνόματα
ἔγνω τῶν δένδρων οἷς νῦν αὐτὰ καλοῦσιν οἱ ἄνθρω-
17   ποι. οὗτος λέξιν εὑρών τινα περιττὴν καὶ ὑπ' ἀρ-
χαιότητος διαλανθάνουσαν, ὡς ἀνάθημά τι παλαιὸν
καθαιρῶν,¹⁰⁰ εἰς μέσον τε ἦγεν καὶ διακαθήρας ἐκαλ-
λώπιζεν, ὑπόθεσίν τε αὐτῇ περιπλάττων ὅλην καὶ διανοίας ἀκολουθούσας, ὥσπερ ἄβρας τινὰς καὶ θερα-
παίνας δεσποίνῃ νεοπλούτῳ καὶ τὸ γῆρας ἀπεξεσμένῃ.
18   Ἐθαύμασε μὲν οὖν αὐτὸν ἐπὶ τούτοις καὶ ὁ θειότατος Ἰουλιανός, ἐθαύμασε δὲ καὶ ὅσον ἀνθρώπινον τὴν
ἐν τοῖς λόγοις χάριν. καὶ πλεῖστά γε αὐτοῦ περι-
φέρουσι βιβλία καὶ ὁ νοῦν ἔχων ἀναλεγόμενος ἕκα-
19   στον αὐτῶν εἴσεται. ἱκανὸς δὲ ἦν καὶ πολιτικοῖς ὁμι-
λῆσαι πράγμασι καὶ παρὰ τοὺς λόγους ἕτερά τινα
συντολμῆσαι καὶ ῥᾳδιουργῆσαι πρὸς τέρψιν θεατρι-
20   κωτέραν. τῶν δὲ μετὰ ταῦτα βασιλέων καὶ τῶν ἀξιωμάτων τὸ μέγιστον αὐτῷ προσθέντων (τὸν γὰρ τῆς
αὐλῆς ἔπαρχον μέχρι προσηγορίας ἔχειν ἐκέλευον),
85G   οὐκ ἀπεδέξατο φήσας τὸν σοφιστὴν | εἶναι μείζονα.

¹⁰⁰ καθαιρῶν Go: καθαίρων A

251 Athenian playwright, quoted from his comedy *Demoi* by
the scholiast on Ar. *Av.* 1569, "the stalks L. and D. go with me
knots and all." (For knots, cf. Theophr. *Hist. pl.* 9.13.5).

One can find an abundance of erudition and wide read- 16
ing in his orations, while encountering rare Attic forms
and phrases. For example, he would not have omitted
those "trees" of Eupolis[251]—Laispodias and Dama-
sias[252]—if he had known the names by which everyone
calls the trees nowadays. Whenever he discovered a 17
strange word that, because of its great antiquity had fallen
into oblivion, he would detach it, as though it were an
ancient votive prize [hanging on a wall], and reintroduce
it to the world, embellish it by brushing off the dust and
craft a whole new foundation around it with accompanying
meanings, as if he was adding slave girls and handmaids to
an old mistress who had come into a fortune recently[253]
and had the signs of old age polished away.

For these reasons not only the godlike Julian[254] also 18
admired him, but every human alive admired the appeal
of his oratory as well. Very many of his works are in circulation, and any intelligent man who reads each one of them
will come to know that charm. He was also competent in 19
administering public affairs, and, apart from orations, in
venturing to compose certain other things more suited for
light entertainment in the theater. When the later emper- 20
ors offered him the very highest of all honors—for they
bade him to use the honorary title of praetorian prefect—
he refused, saying that the title of 'sophist' was more dis-

252 Laispodias is an Athenian general (Thuc. 8.86). Both were
ridiculed by the comic poets because of their thin legs.
253 For "nouveau riche," cf. Eunap. *Hist*. fr. 46.1.4–5 Blockley.
254 That is, the emperor (cf. Lib. *Or*. 1.118–33).

EUNAPIUS

21 καὶ τοῦτό ἐστιν οὐκ ὀλίγος ἔπαινος, ὅτι δόξης ἐλάττων ἀνήρ, μόνης ἥττητο τῆς περὶ τοὺς λόγους, τὴν δὲ
22 ἄλλην δημώδη καὶ βάναυσον ὑπελάμβανεν. ἀλλ᾽ ἐτελεύτησε καὶ οὗτος εἰς γῆρας ἀφικόμενος μακρότατον
καὶ θαῦμα οὐκ ὀλίγον ἀπολιπὼν ἅπασιν.

17. Ἀκάκιος. Παλαιστίνης Καισάρεια τὸν Ἀκάκιον
497B ἤνεγκεν, | καὶ ἦν συνανασχὼν τῷ Λιβανίῳ κατὰ τοὺς
αὐτοὺς χρόνους· τόνου δὲ σοφιστικοῦ καὶ πνεύματος,
εἴπερ τις ἄλλος, γέμων, καὶ ἡ λέξις μετὰ κρότου πρὸς
τὸν ἀρχαῖον ἐπέστρεφε τρόπον· συνανασχὼν δὲ Λι-
2 βανίῳ, κατέσεισε τὰ πρῶτα, καὶ περιῆν ἰσχυρῶς. βι-
βλίδιον γοῦν τῷ Λιβανίῳ περὶ εὐφυΐας τι γέγραπται,
πρὸς τὸν Ἀκάκιον ἅπαν ἐκτεθειμένον, ἐν ᾧ δῆλός
ἐστιν ἐπὶ τῷ κρατεῖσθαι τὸ μέγεθος τῆς ἐκείνου φύσεως αἰτιώμενος, αὐτὸς δὲ ἑαυτῷ μαρτυρῶν τὴν περὶ
3 τὰ λεξείδια <ἐπί>στασιν[101] καὶ ἀκρίβειαν· ὥσπερ
ἀγνοῶν ὅτι μήτε Ὁμήρῳ παντὸς ἔμελε μέτρου, ἀλλ᾽
εὐφωνίας τινὸς καὶ μέλους, μήτε Φειδίᾳ τοῦ τὸν δά-
κτυλον παραλαβεῖν καὶ τὸν πόδα πρὸς ἔπαινον τῆς
θεᾶς, ἀλλὰ τυραννεῖν τὸ μὲν κατὰ τὴν ἀκοήν, <τὸ δὲ
κατὰ τὴν ὄψιν>,[102] καὶ τὸ αἴτιον ὑπάρχειν ἀνεύρετον ἢ
δύσκριτον, ὥσπερ ἐν τοῖς καλοῖς καὶ ἐρασμίοις
σώμασιν οὐ πάντες τὸ αὐτὸ θαυμάζουσιν, ὁ δὲ ἁλοὺς

[101] add. Gi Go   [102] add. Wytt Go

255 He was in fact a Phoenician and only taught in Caesarea.

580

tinguished. And it is no faint praise to say that, although   21
he was a man tempted by notoriety, he only gave in to the
sort of renown that an orator can win and held that any
other kind is common and in bad taste. He, too, when he   22
died, had attained to a very great age, and he left in the
minds of all men a profound admiration.

17. Acacius. Caesarea[255] of Palestine produced Acacius, and he rose up in the world around the same time as
Libanius. He was, more than anyone, abundantly endowed
with sophistic force and inspiration, and his diction was
sonorous and also tended to the imitation of the ancient
classical models. Having risen up in the world at the same
time as Libanius, he overthrew his rival's supremacy, and
maintained his superiority with firm hand. In fact, Liba-   2
nius wrote a short book on natural ability,[256] entirely set
out with Acacius in mind, in which he clearly ascribes his
defeat to the man's great natural talent, while at the
same time he gives evidence of his own care and exactitude in
the use of erudite words, as though he did not know that   3
Homer was not worried about every single foot of his
verses,[257] but rather with achieving beauty of expression
and melody, or that Pheidias was not worried about detail-
ing a finger or a foot to honor the goddess Athena, but that
they each exerted their domination over men, the one over
their ears, the other over their eyes; and that the cause of
their success is undiscoverable or hard to define, just as in
fair and lovely bodies not all admire the same feature, and
the captive of that beauty knows not what it was that had

255 This work is lost (cf. Lib. fr. 12, *Ep.* 405), but Eunapius
seems to give us some snippets of its arguments.
257 Cf. Plut. *Quomodo quis suos* 80d.

581

4   οὐκ οἶδεν ὅθεν εἴληπται. ὁ μὲν οὖν Ἀκάκιος ἐς τὸ ἄριστον ἀναδραμών καὶ πολλὴν ἑαυτῷ παρασχὼν δόξαν
86G   ὡς τοῦ | Λιβανίου κρατήσων, ἀπῄει νέος ὢν ἔτι· οἱ δὲ
ἄνθρωποι, ὅσον σπουδαῖον ἐν αὐτοῖς, ἐθαύμαζον αὐτὸν ὥσπερ εἰς γῆρας ἀφιγμένον.

18. Νυμφιδιανός. Νυμφιδιανὸς δὲ ἦν μὲν ἐκ Σμύρνης, Μάξιμος δὲ ἦν ὁ φιλόσοφος ἀδελφὸς αὐτῷ, καὶ
Κλαυδιανὸς ἕτερος, φιλοσοφῶν καὶ αὐτὸς ἄριστα.
ἀνὴρ δὲ τῆς μὲν Ἀθήνησι παιδείας καὶ ἀγωγῆς οὐ
μετεσχηκώς, γεγονὼς δὲ εἰς[103] ῥητορικὴν καὶ τοῦ τῶν
2   σοφιστῶν[104] ὀνόματος ἄξιος. ὁ δὲ αὐτοκράτωρ Ἰουλιανὸς αὐτῷ καὶ τὴν βασιλικὴν γλῶτταν ἐπέτρεψε,
ταῖς ἐπιστολαῖς ἐπιστήσας, ὅσαι διὰ τῶν ἑλληνικῶν
ἑρμηνεύονται λόγων. κρείττων δὲ κατὰ τὰς καλουμέ-
νας μελέτας καὶ τὰ ζητήματα, τὰ δὲ ἐν προάγωσιν
3   καὶ τῷ διαλεχθῆναι οὐκ ἔθ᾽ ὅμοιος. τελευτὴ δὲ αὐτῷ
συνέβη γενομένῳ πρεσβύτῃ καὶ μετὰ τὸν ἀδελφὸν
Μάξιμον.

19. Ζήνων. Ἰατροὶ δὲ κατὰ τούτους ἤκμαζον τοὺς
χρόνους, Ζήνων τε ὁ Κύπριος, διδασκαλίαν τε πολυ-
ύμνητον συστησάμενος, ἀλλ᾽ ἐπέβαλε τοῖς χρόνοις
Ἰουλιανῷ τῷ σοφιστῇ, καὶ μετ᾽ ἐκεῖνον κατὰ τοὺς

103 post εἰς ras. quattuor litt. (Go)
104 post σοφιστῶν ras. fere septem litt. (Go)

258 We know nothing more about this sophist; cf. above, VPS
7.4.

enchanted him. Acacius, then, rising to the first rank in his 4
profession, and after winning a great reputation as one
who would have gone on to excel Libanius, passed away
while still a young man. But all men, at least all who engaged in such pursuits, used to revere him as if he had
already attained to old age.

18. Nymphidianus. Nymphidianus was a native of
Smyrna, whose own brother was Maximus the philosopher, while Claudianus,[258] himself a very distinguished
philosopher, was another brother. He was a man who,
though he never shared in the education and training enjoyed at Athens, with respect to the art of rhetoric still
became worthy of the name "sophist." The emperor Julian 2
entrusted him with the imperial correspondence, and putting him in charge of such letters as were translated into
Greek.[259] The greater among his skills was in the composition of declamations, as they are called, and in handling
problems, but he was not so skillful with opening statements of proof and philosophical disputations. When he 3
died, he was an old man, and he outlived his brother
Maximus.

19. Zeno.[260] Around that time[261] certain physicians
flourished, among them Zeno of Cyprus, who established
a celebrated teaching program. He survived down to the
time of Julian the sophist, and after him, during the life

---

[259] See Philostr. *Life of Antipater*, 607; below, *VPS* 18.2.

[260] Here the account of the "iatrosophists" starts (see Eunapius Introduction). For Zeno's reputation, cf. Julian. *Ep.* 17
(426a–c).

[261] The generation of Nymphidianus and his brother.

2 Προαιρεσίου χρόνους οἱ διάδοχοι Ζήνωνος. ἄμφω δὲ
3 ὁ Ζήνων ἐξήσκητο λέγειν τε καὶ ποιεῖν ἰατρικήν. τῶν
δὲ ὀνομαστῶν ὁμιλητῶν αὐτοῦ διαλαχόντες, οἱ μὲν τὸ
ἕτερον, οἱ δὲ ἀμφότερα, κατελείφθησαν· ἐκράτουν δὲ
ὅμως καὶ καθ᾽ ὅ τις ἐκληρονόμησεν ἔργου τε καὶ λόγου.

20. Μάγνος· οὗτος ἐκ μὲν Ἀντιοχείας ἦν γεγονώς,
τῆς ὑπὲρ τὸν Εὐφράτην, ἣν νῦν Νίσιβιν ὀνομάζουσιν·
2 ἀκροατὴς δὲ γενόμενος Ζήνωνος καὶ τῇ περὶ τῶν σω-
μάτων τῶν προαιρετικῶν φύσει τὸν Ἀριστοτέλην ἐς
87G   τὸ δύνασθαι | λέγειν συνεφελκυσάμενος, | σιωπᾶν μὲν
498B   ἐν τῷ λέγειν τοὺς ἰατροὺς ἠνάγκαζε, θεραπεύειν δὲ
3 οὐκ ἐδόκει δυνατὸς εἶναι καθάπερ λέγειν. ὥσπερ οὖν
οἱ παλαιοί φασιν Ἀρχίδαμον, εἰ Περικλέους εἴη δυνα-
τώτερος ἐρωτώμενον "ἀλλὰ κἂν καταβάλλω Περικλέα," φάναι, "λέγων ἐκεῖνος ὅτι μὴ καταβέβληται,
νενίκηκεν," οὕτω καὶ τοὺς θεραπευθέντας ὑφ᾽ ἑτέρων
4 ἀπεδείκνυ Μάγνος ἔτι νοσοῦντας. οἱ δὲ ὑγιαίνοντες
καὶ ἐρρωμένοι χάριν ὡμολόγουν τοῖς θεραπεύσασιν·
ἀλλ᾽ ἐκράτει τῶν ἰατρῶν μέχρι τοῦ στόματος καὶ τῶν
5 ἐρωτήσεων. καὶ διδασκαλεῖον μὲν ἐξήρητο κοινὸν
αὐτῷ κατὰ τὴν Ἀλεξάνδρειαν, καὶ πάντες ἔπλεον καὶ
παρ᾽ αὐτὸν ἐφοίτων, ὡς θαυμάσαντές τι μόνον ἢ λη-

---

262 The criteria set by Xenophon above (VPS 1.1).
263 Possible reference to Arist. Eth. Nic. 1114a16, on volun-
tary acts and illness. On persuading patients, cf. Pl. Grg. 456b.
264 An echo of Plut. Per. 8, where the anecdote is told of

time of Prohaeresius, came the successors of Zeno. He was 2
trained in both speaking well and practicing medicine.
Having gained their knowledge from him, some of his 3
famous pupils took up the one or the other of these professions, others again took up both; but regardless of which
part of his patrimony they inherited, every one of them
prevailed in deed and word.[262]

20. Magnus. This man was a native of that Antioch
which lies beyond the Euphrates and people now call
Nisibis. Having been a student of Zeno and having drawn 2
on Aristotle with regard to the nature of bodies endowed
with choice in order to give force to his own oratory,[263] he
managed to silence doctors when it came to (theoretical)
discourse, but he was thought to be less able as a healer
than as an orator. In the same way that the ancient authors 3
relate that Archidamus, when asked whether he was stronger than Pericles, replied: "Well, even when I strike Pericles down, he still carries off the victory by declaring that
he has not been thrown at all,"[264] so too Magnus used to
demonstrate that those whom other doctors had cured
were still unwell. And those who had regained their health 4
and strength expressed their gratitude to those who had
healed them, but Magnus still got the better of the doctors
as far as verbal skills and questioning were concerned.[265]
A public school was especially set up for him at Alexandria, 5
and everyone sailed there and attended his lectures, either
only to see and admire him or to enjoy the benefits of his

Pericles and Thucydides (son of Melesias, not the famous historian). The Spartan king Archidamus asked the question of Thucydides, who gave the answer quoted here.

[265] Cf. Hippoc. *Steril.* 213.

6 ψόμενοι τῶν παρ' ἐκείνου καλῶν. καὶ ἀποτυγχάνειν οὐ
συνέβαινεν αὐτοῖς· ἢ γὰρ τὸ λαλεῖν ἐκέρδαινον, ἢ καὶ
τὸ δύνασθαι ποιεῖν τι καὶ ἐνεργεῖν διὰ τῆς σφετέρας
ἐπιμελείας προσελάμβανον.

21. Ὀρειβάσιος. Ὀρειβάσιον δὲ Πέργαμος ἤνεγκε
καὶ τοῦτο εὐθὺς οὕτω συνετέλει πρὸς δόξαν, ὥσπερ
τοῖς Ἀθήνησι γεγονόσιν, ὅταν εὐδοκιμῶσι κατὰ τοὺς
λόγους, πολὺς ἄνω χωρεῖ λόγος ὅτι Ἀττικὴ Μοῦσα
καὶ τὸ ἀγαθὸν οἰκεῖον. ἑκατέρων δὲ εὖ πεφυκώς, ἐκ
παιδὸς ἦν ἐπιφανής, πάσης παιδείας μετεσχηκὼς ἢ
2 πρὸς ἀρετὴν συμφέρει τε καὶ τελεῖ. προϊὼν δὲ ἐς ἡλικίαν, ἀκροατής τε ἐγένετο τοῦ μεγάλου Ζήνωνος καὶ
3 Μάγνου συμφοιτητής. ἀλλὰ τὸν Μάγνον ἀπολιπὼν
παλαίοντα τοῖς νοήμασιν, αὐτὸς καὶ ἐν τούτοις ἄρισ-
88G στος | ὤν, καὶ πρὸς τὸ ἄκρον ἐκδραμὼν τῆς ἰατρικῆς,
τὸν πάτριον ἐμιμεῖτο θεόν, ὅσον ἀνθρώπῳ δυνατὸν ἐς
4 τὴν μίμησιν ὑπελθεῖν τοῦ θείου. ἐκ μειρακίου δὲ ἐπιφανὴς γενόμενος, Ἰουλιανὸς μὲν αὐτὸν εἰς τὸν Καίσαρα προϊὼν συνήρπασεν ἐπὶ τῇ τέχνῃ, ὁ δὲ τοσοῦτον ἐπλεονέκτει ταῖς ἄλλαις ἀρεταῖς, ὥστε καὶ
βασιλέα τὸν Ἰουλιανὸν ἀπέδειξε· καὶ ταῦτά γε ἐν τοῖς
5 κατ' ἐκεῖνον ἀκριβέστερον εἴρηται. ἀλλ' οὐδὲ κορυ-
δαλλίς, ἡ παροιμία φησίν, ἄνευ λόφου, οὐδὲ Ὀρειβά-

---

266 *Anth. Pal.* 11.281 mentions a Magnus who can raise the
dead.

267 Asclepius, who had a temple in Pergamum during the
early empire (cf. Lucian, *Icaromen.* 24).

268 That is, in character and morals.

teaching. And they never failed to succeed, for they either   6
acquired the fluency in medical terminology, or received
the ability to perform hands-on treatment by their own
diligence.[266]

21. Oribasius. Pergamon produced Oribasius, and this
[origin] straightaway contributed to his renown, in the
same way as befalls those who are born at Athens, whenever such men win a name for eloquence, the report
spreads far and wide that their Muse is Attic and that this
paragon is a home product. Oribasius came of a good family on both sides, and from his boyhood he was distinguished because he acquired every kind of learning that
brings benefit to the pursuit of virtue and perfects it.
When he reached early manhood, he became a pupil of   2
the great Zeno and a fellow disciple of Magnus. But leav-   3
ing Magnus to have his tussles over medical theories, an
activity in which he himself also excelled, he raced to first
place in the medical practice and emulated the patron
god[267] of his country, so far as it is possible for a mortal to
advance to the imitation of the divine. Since he achieved   4
distinction even from his earliest youth, Julian, when he
was promoted to the rank of Caesar, snatched him away
with him to practice his art; but he added so much to all
his other good qualities that he actually made Julian into
an emperor.[268] However, these matters have been more
fully described in my books on him.[269] Nevertheless, as the   5
proverb says, "No lark is without a crest,"[270] and so too
Oribasius was not free of envy. For it was because of his

[269] Eunap. *Hist*. fr. 21.2 Blockley.

[270] Cf. Ar. *Av*. 472; Plato Com. 266; Pl. *Euthd*. 291d. For the
proverb, cf. Simonid. fr. 33.1 Page.

σιος ἦν ἄνευ φθόνου. ἀλλὰ διὰ τὴν ὑπεροχὴν τῆς
δόξης οἱ μετὰ Ἰουλιανὸν βασιλεύοντες τῆς τε οὐσίας
ἀφείλοντο, καὶ διαφθεῖραι τὸ σῶμα βουληθέντες, τὸ
μὲν ἔργον ὤκνησαν, ἑτεροίως δὲ ἔπραξαν ὅπερ ᾐσχύν-
6 θησαν· ἐξέθηκαν γὰρ αὐτὸν εἰς τοὺς βαρβάρους,
ὥσπερ Ἀθηναῖοι τοὺς κατ' ἀρετὴν ὑπερέχοντας ἐξω-
7 στράκιζον. ἀλλ' ἐκείνοις μὲν τὸ τῆς πόλεως ἐκβαλεῖν
ὁ νόμος ἔλεγε καὶ προσῆν οὐδέν· οἱ δὲ βασιλεύοντες
καὶ τὸ παραδοῦναι τοῖς ὠμοτάτοις βαρβάροις ἐπέθε-
σαν, ἐκείνους ποιοῦντες κυρίους τοῦ σφετέρου βου-
λεύματος.
8   Ὀρειβάσιος δὲ ἐκτεθεὶς εἰς τὴν πολεμίαν ἔδειξε τῆς
ἀρετῆς τὸ μέγεθος, οὐ τόποις ὁριζομένης, οὐδὲ περι-
γραφομένης ἤθεσιν, ἀλλὰ τὸ στάσιμον καὶ μόνιμον
ἐπιδεικνυμένης κατὰ τὴν ἑαυτῆς ἐνέργειαν, κἂν ἀλλα-
χόθι κἂν παρ' ἄλλοις φαίνηται, ὥσπερ τοὺς ἀριθμούς
9 φασι καὶ τὰ μαθήματα. εὐδοκίμει τε γὰρ εὐθὺς παρὰ
τοῖς βασιλεῦσι τῶν βαρβάρων καὶ ἀνὰ τοὺς πρώτους
ἦν, καὶ κατὰ τὴν Ῥωμαίων ἀρχὴν ἀποβλεπόμενος |
499B παρὰ τοῖς βαρβάροις προσεκυνεῖτο καθάπερ τις |
89G θεός, τοὺς μὲν ἐκ νοσημάτων χρονίων ἀνασώζων,
10 τοὺς δὲ ἀπὸ τῆς τοῦ θανάτου πύλης διακλέπτων. καὶ
ἦν αὐτῷ τὸ τῆς λεγομένης συμφορᾶς εὐδαιμονίας
ἁπάσης πρόφασις, ὥστε καὶ οἱ βασιλεύοντες ἀπαγο-
ρεύσαντες μάχεσθαι πρὸς τὴν διὰ πάντων τοῦ ἀνδρὸς
11 δύναμιν, ἐπανιέναι συνεχώρησαν. ὁ δέ, ὡς ἔτυχε τῆς
ἐπανόδου, μόνον ἑαυτὸν ἔχων ἀντὶ πάσης οὐσίας καὶ
τὸν ἀπὸ τῶν ἀρετῶν πλοῦτον ἐπιδεικνύμενος, γυναικά

extraordinary renown that the emperors who came after Julian took away his livelihood, and while they also wanted to destroy him physically, they shrank from the deed, but carried out by other means the crime that they were ashamed to commit. For they exiled him among the bar- 6 barians, much like the Athenians ostracized men whose virtue stuck out above the rest. However, in their case the 7 law allowed them to exile men from the state, and they added no further penalty, whereas the emperors added to his exile this abandonment to the most savage barbarians, thus making them the executioners of their plan.

But Oribasius, after being thrust out into hostile terri- 8 tory, showed the greatness of his virtue, which has no spatial boundary and is not defined by moral conventions, but ever on display in its stability and constancy in keeping with its natural activity, no matter where or among whom it showed itself, just as some say is the case with numbers and mathematical truths. For he instantly gained great 9 respect from the rulers of the barbarians, and held a posi- tion among the first of them; and while throughout the Roman empire he was highly regarded, among the barbar- ians he was revered like some god, because he restored some from chronic diseases and stole others away from death's door. Thus his so-called misfortune was in fact a 10 cause of his full happiness, so that even the emperors gave up fighting against the man's power so universally dis- played, and permitted him to return from exile. After he 11 had the opportunity to return, with as his only possession his own person, and putting on display the wealth of his virtues instead of worldly goods, he married a wife who

τε ἠγάγετο τῶν κατὰ πλοῦτον ἐπιφανῶν καὶ γένος,
καὶ παῖδας ἔσχε τέτταρας, οἵτινές εἰσί τε καὶ εἴησαν·

12 αὐτὸς δὲ κατὰ τὸν καιρὸν τοῦτον τῆς γραφῆς ἐν ἀνθρώποις ἔστι τε καὶ εἴη, ἀλλὰ τὸν ἀρχαῖον πλοῦτον
ἐκ τῶν δημοσίων ἀνακομισάμενος, τῶν μετὰ ταῦτα
βασιλέων συγκεχωρηκότων ὡς ἐπ᾽ ἀδίκῳ τῇ προτέρᾳ

13 κρίσει. ταῦτα μὲν οὖν ἐστι καὶ οὕτως ἔχει. Ὀρειβασίῳ
τε συντυχεῖν ἀνδρός ἐστι φιλοσοφοῦντος γενναίως,

14 ὥστε εἰδέναι τί πρὸ τῶν ἄλλων θαυμάσει· τοσαύτη τις
ἡ διὰ πάντων ἐστὶ προϊοῦσα καὶ παρατρέχουσα ταῖς
συνουσίαις ἁρμονία καὶ χάρις.

22. Ἰωνικός. Ἰωνικὸς δὲ ἦν μὲν ἐκ Σάρδεων καὶ
πατρὸς ἰατρεύσαντος ἐπιφανῶς· Ζήνωνος δὲ ἀκροατὴς γενόμενος, εἰς ἄκρον τε ἐπιμελείας ἐξίκετο καὶ

2 Ὀρειβάσιός γε αὐτοῦ θαυμαστὴς ἐτύγχανεν. ὀνομάτων δὲ πάντων ἰατρικῆς ἐμπειρότατος γενόμενος καὶ
πραγμάτων, κρείττων ἦν ἐν τῇ καθ᾽ ἕκαστον πείρᾳ,
τῶν τε τοῦ σώματος μορίων ἄκρως δαημονέστερος
γενόμενος καὶ τῆς ἀνθρωπίνης φύσεως ἐξεταστικός.

3 οὐκοῦν οὔτε φαρμάκου τινὸς ἔλαθε κατασκευὴ αὐτὸν
καὶ κρίσις οὐδ᾽ ὅσα ἐμπλάττουσιν οἱ τεχνικώτατοι
τοῖς ἕλκεσι, τὰ μὲν τὴν ἐπιρροὴν ἐπέχοντες, τὰ δὲ τὴν

90G ἐμπεσοῦσαν | διακιδνάντες, ἐκεῖνον ἐλάνθανεν. ἀλλὰ
4 καὶ δῆσαι τὸ πεπονθὸς μόριον, †οὐ σχίσαι τοῖς μέ-
ρεσιν†[105] εὑρετικώτατός τε ἦν καὶ διεξητασμένος.

5 ἔργα τε οὖν καὶ ὀνόματα τούτων ἠπίστατο, ὥστε τοὺς

---

[105] Go: crucibus sign. Gi, in app. [οὐ] σχισμένοις ῥάκεσιν

came of a family illustrious both in wealth and noble stock. By her he had four children who are still alive (and may they live long!). He himself, at this time of writing, is still 12 among the living (and may he remain so!). He did recover his original fortune from the public treasury with the consent of the later emperors, on the ground of the injustice of the earlier verdict. And this is how things stand and the 13 actual situation. Any man who is a genuine philosopher has a chance to meet up with Oribasius, so that he may learn what above all else he ought to admire. So immense 14 are the harmony and the charisma that pervade all things he does and attend all his interactions with others.

22. Ionicus. Ionicus was a native of Sardis and his father had practiced medicine with distinction. Having become a pupil of Zeno, he attained to the highest degree of dedication and as a result Oribasius became an admirer. While 2 he acquired the greatest skill in the theory and practice of medicine in all its branches, he showed peculiar ability in the practice of each individual area, having become thoroughly acquainted with the parts of the body, and also having made researches into the nature of man.[271] Thus 3 neither the composition and mixture of any kind of drug nor the assessment of every sort of plaster and dressing that the most skillful healers apply to wounds, escaped his attention, whether to stop a hemorrhage or to disperse what has gathered there. And he was also most inventive 4 and expert in bandaging the injured body part, †. . .†. In other words, he knew so thoroughly the practice and 5

[271] One of the Hippocratic works was called *On the Nature of Man.*

μέγα φρονοῦντας ἐπὶ τῷ θεραπεύειν ἐξίστασθαι πρὸς
τὴν ἀκρίβειαν, καὶ φανερῶς ὁμολογεῖν ὅτι συντυγχά-
νοντες Ἰωνικῷ, τὰ παρὰ τοῖς παλαιοῖς εἰρημένα μαν-
θάνουσιν ἔργῳ, καὶ πρὸς τὴν χρείαν ἐξάγουσιν,
ὥσπερ ὀνόματα κρυπτόμενα μέχρι τῆς γραφῆς.

6   Τοιοῦτός τε ὢν κατὰ τὴν ἐπιστήμην, καὶ πρὸς
φιλοσοφίαν ἅπασαν ἔρρωτο καὶ πρὸς θειασμόν, ὅσος
τε ἐξ ἰατρικῆς ἐς ἀνθρώπους ἥκει τῶν καμνόντων ἐς
πρόγνωσιν καὶ ὅσος, ἐκ φιλοσοφίας παράβακχος ὤν,
ἐς τοὺς δυναμένους ὑποδέχεσθαι καὶ σώζειν ἀπολήγει
7 καὶ διασπείρεται. ἔμελε δὲ αὐτῷ καὶ ῥητορικῆς ἀκριβείας καὶ λόγων ἁπάντων τέχνης· οὔκουν οὐδὲ ποιήσεως ἀμύητος ἦν. ἀλλ᾽ ἐτελεύτα μικρόν τι πρὸ τῆς
γραφῆς ἐπὶ δύο παισὶν ἀξίοις λόγου τε καὶ μνήμης.

8   Καὶ Θέων δέ τις ἐν Γαλατίᾳ κατὰ τούτους τοὺς
καιροὺς πολλῆς δόξης ἐτύγχανεν.

9   Ἐπανιτέον δὲ ἐπὶ τοὺς φιλοσόφους πάλιν ὅθεν
ἐξέβημεν. |

500B   23. Χρυσάνθιος. Ταυτησὶ τῆς γραφῆς αἴτιος ἐγένετο Χρυσάνθιος, τόν τε γράφοντα ταῦτα πεπαιδευ-
κὼς ἐκ παιδὸς καὶ διασεσωκὼς εἰς τέλος, ὥσπερ
2 νόμον τινά, τὴν περὶ αὐτὸν εὔνοιαν. ἀλλ᾽ οὐδέν γε διὰ
τοῦτο ῥηθήσεται πρὸς χάριν· ἐκεῖνός τε γὰρ ἀλήθειαν
ἐτίμα διαφερόντως καὶ τοῦτο πρῶτον ἐπαίδευεν, ἡμεῖς

272 θειασμός links humans to the divine in different ways.
273 VPS 19–22 dealt with "iatrosophists." It seems to imply
they are not philosophers. Cf. Philostr. VS 479–80.

designations of all these [treatments], that even those who prided themselves on their ability as healers were amazed at his accurate knowledge, and openly admitted that by conversing with Ionicus they really understood the teachings that had been uttered by the physicians of earlier times and could now apply them usefully, though before they had been obscure words on the page.

While he achieved such distinction in this domain of knowledge, he was also exhibiting strengths in every branch of philosophy and in divination;[272] the one kind has been bestowed on humanity for the benefit of the medical science so as to reach a prognosis of the sick, and the other, deriving its inspiration from philosophy, is limited to, and disseminated among, those who have the ability to receive and preserve it. He also studied the art of rhetoric with great precision, and the art of every form of oratory; even in poetry he was not uninitiated. But he died not long before this work was written and left two sons who deserve a mention and remembrance. 6

7

In addition, one Theon acquired a great reputation [as a physician] in Gaul around this time. 8

But it is time to return once more to the philosophers from whom I have digressed.[273] 9

23. Chrysanthius. The reason for writing the present work was Chrysanthius, for he educated the present author from boyhood and to the last upheld, as though it were a decree, his goodwill toward him. Nevertheless, I shall not on that account say anything merely to show my gratitude. For above all else he honored the truth, and taught me this first of all, so that I shall not blemish that 2

τε οὐ διαφθεροῦμεν τὴν δοθεῖσαν δωρεάν, πλὴν ἢ
πού[106] τι καὶ ὑφήσομεν ἐπὶ τὸ καταδεέστερον ἄγοντες,
ἐπειδὴ ταῦτα συνωμολογήσαμεν. |

3
91G
Τῶν μὲν οὖν εἰς βουλὴν τελούντων ἦν ὁ Χρυσάνθιος καὶ τῶν ἀνὰ τοὺς πρώτους ἐπ' εὐγενείᾳ φερο-
μένων· ἐγεγόνει δὲ αὐτῷ πάππος, Ἰνοκέντιός τις, εἴς
τε πλοῦτον ἐλθὼν οὐκ ὀλίγον, καὶ δόξαν ὑπὲρ ἰδιώτην
τινὰ λαχών, ὅς γε νομοθετικὴν εἶχε δύναμιν παρὰ τῶν
4 τότε βασιλευόντων ἐπιτετραμμένος. καὶ βιβλία γε
αὐτοῦ διασώζεται, τὰ μὲν εἰς τὴν Ῥωμαίων γλῶσσαν,
τὰ δὲ εἰς τὴν Ἑλλάδα φέροντα, τό τε ἐξεταστικὸν καὶ
βαθὺ τῆς γνώμης ἑρμηνεύοντα, καὶ τὴν περὶ ταῦτα
κατάληψιν τοῖς ταῦτα βουλομένοις θαυμάζειν συνει-
ληφότα.

5 Χρυσάνθιος δὲ αὐτός, νέος ἀπὸ τοῦ πατρὸς ἀπο-
λειφθεὶς καὶ φιλοσοφίας ἐρασθεὶς διὰ φύσεως θειό-
τητα, πρός τε τὸ Πέργαμον καὶ τὸν μέγαν Αἰδέσιον
6 συνέτεινεν· ἀκμάζοντι δὲ πρὸς μετάδοσιν σοφίας δι-
ψῶν περιτυχών, χανδόν, ἑαυτὸν ὑποθείς, ἐνεφορεῖτο
τῆς τοιαύτης σοφίας <οὐ τῆς συν>τυχούσης,[107] οὔτε
πρὸς ἀκρόασιν ἀπαγορεύων τινά, οὔτε εἰς μελέτην
7 ἐλάττων τινὸς φαινόμενος· καὶ γὰρ ἔτυχεν ἀτρύτου
καὶ ἀδαμαντίνου σώματος, ἐς πᾶσαν ἄσκησιν ὑπουρ-
8 γεῖν εἰωθότος. ὁ δὲ τῶν τε Πλάτωνος καὶ τῶν Ἀριστο-
τέλους λόγων μετασχὼν ἱκανῶς, καὶ πρὸς πᾶν εἶδος

---

106 ἢ πού A Gi Go: εἴ πού A^{m2} Wr
107 <οὐ τῆς συν>τυχούσης in lac. suppl. Be Go

gift that I received at his hands, except that perhaps I may somewhat moderate my statements and say less than the truth, since this was the agreement that we made.

Chrysanthius belonged to the rank of council men and   3 was rated among the most nobly born in his city. His grandfather was a man named Innocentius, who had made a considerable fortune and had acquired a reputation greater than that of an average private citizen, given that the emperors who reigned at that time entrusted him with the task of compiling the legal statutes. And several of his   4 works still survive, some put into the language of the Romans, some into that of Greece, and bear witness to his searching and profound intellect;[274] they encapsulate a firm grasp of these subjects for the benefit of those who are interested in admiring them.

Chrysanthius himself, having been bereaved of his father while he was still a youth, became an ardent lover of   5 philosophy because of its divine nature, and for this reason hastened to Pergamon and the great Aedesius. The latter   6 was at his peak in teaching wisdom when Chrysanthius, thirsty for knowledge, encountered him, and he submitted himself greedily to his influence, gorged on such uncommon wisdom, was untiring in his attendance at lectures, showing himself second to none in his devotion to study. For he possessed an untiring and steely physique, accus-   7 tomed to support him through any severe exercise. When   8 he had had a sufficient share of the doctrines of Plato and

[274] Cf. fr. 29 Blockley.

φιλοσοφίας τρέψας τὴν ψυχήν, καὶ πᾶν εἶδος ἀναλεγόμενος, ὡς περὶ τὴν γνῶσιν τῶν ἐν τοῖς λόγοις
ὑγίαινε καὶ ἔρρωτο, καὶ τῇ συνεχεῖ χρήσει πρὸς τὴν
χρῆσιν[108] αὐτῶν ἕτοιμος ὑπῆρχε, καί, πρὸς ἐπίδειξιν
ἐθάρσει τοῦ κατορθωμένου, τὰ μὲν εἰπεῖν, τὰ δὲ
σιωπῆσαι δυνάμενος, καὶ πρὸς τὸ δύνασθαι κρατεῖν,
εἴ που βιασθείη, τυγχάνων πομπικώτερος, ἐντεῦθεν
92G ἀφῆκεν αὐτὸν ἐπὶ θεῶν γνῶσιν | καὶ σοφίαν ἧς Πυ-
θαγόρας τε ἐφρόντιζεν καὶ ὅσοι Πυθαγόραν ἐζήλω-
σαν, Ἀρχύτας τε ὁ παλαιὸς καὶ ὁ ἐκ Τυάνων Ἀπολλώνιος καὶ οἱ προσκυνήσαντες Ἀπολλώνιον, οἵτινες
9 σῶμά τε ἔδοξαν ἔχειν καὶ εἶναι ἄνθρωποι. καὶ πρὸς
ταῦτά γε Χρυσάνθιος εὐθὺς ἀναδραμὼν καὶ πρώτης
τινὸς λαβῆς ἐπιδραξάμενος, ταῖς ἀρχαῖς αὐταῖς ἡγεμόσι χρώμενος, εἰς τοσοῦτον ἐκουφίσθη τε καὶ ἀνη-
γέρθη παρὰ τοῦ τῆς ψυχῆς τελειώματος,[109] ᾗ φησιν ὁ
Πλάτων, ὥστε πᾶν μὲν εἶδος αὐτῷ παντοίας παιδείας
εἰς ἄκρον ὑπάρχειν καὶ πᾶσαν κατορθοῦσθαι πρό-
10 γνωσιν. ὁρᾶν γοῦν ἄν τις αὐτὸν ἔφησε τὰ ἐσόμενα
μᾶλλον ἢ προλέγειν τὰ μέλλοντα, οὕτως ἅπαντα δι-
ῄθρει καὶ συνελάμβανεν, ὡσανεὶ παρών τε καὶ συνὼν
τοῖς θεοῖς.
11   Χρόνον δὲ ἱκανόν τινα περὶ ταῦτα διατρίψας καὶ
συναθλήσας τῷ Μαξίμῳ πολύ τι, τὸν κοινωνὸν ἀπέλιπεν. ὁ μὲν γὰρ ἔχων τι φιλόνεικον ἐν τῇ φύσει καὶ

108 κρίσιν Boiss: χρῆσιν A Go
109 πτερώματος coni. Wytt Bo: τελειώματος A Go

Aristotle, he also turned his mind to every type[275] of philosophy, and reading in every branch [of knowledge], so
that he had a wholesome and robust grasp of oratory, and
by constant practice began to be equipped for its real-life
application, and became confident in correct judgment,
since he knew what to say and what to leave unsaid, while
he was endowed with magnificent rhetoric that helped
him to win when under pressure. He then applied himself
completely to comprehending the nature of the gods and
that wisdom to which Pythagoras devoted his mind, as did
all those who aimed to emulate Pythagoras, such as Archy-
tas of old, and Apollonius of Tyana, and those who revere
Apollonius [as a god], all of them beings who only seemed
to possess a body and seemed to be mortal men. Chrysan-   9
thius, engaging promptly with these studies and seizing
hold of the first opportunity that offered itself in every
case, while taking solid foundations as his guides, was
lifted up and roused to such a height by the perfection of
his soul, in the way Plato speaks of it,[276] that he arrived at
the pinnacle in every branch of the full range of learning
and had expertise in all kinds of knowledge about the future. Hence one might say of him that he saw, rather than   10
foretold, future events, so accurately did he discern and
comprehend everything, as though he was both alongside,
and in the company of, the gods.

After spending a suitable amount of time on these   11
studies and competing a lot with Maximus, he left this
companion behind. The reason was that Maximus, for his
part, had a jealous and obstinate streak in his character:

[275] Cf. *VPS* 4.4 on Porphyry.
[276] Cf. Pl. *Phdr.* 248c–e (which has πτέρωματος).

δυσεκβίαστον, τοῖς φανθεῖσι σημείοις παρὰ τῶν
θεῶν ἀντιβαίνων, | ἕτερα ᾔτει καὶ προσηνάγκαζεν·
ὁ δὲ Χρυσάνθιος, τοῖς πρώτοις θεωμένοις,[110] κατὰ μικρὸν ἐκ παραγωγῆς ἐπὶ τὴν κίνησιν τῶν δοθέντων
ἐβάδιζε· εἶτα τυχὼν μὲν ἐνίκα, διαμαρτὼν δέ, τῷ φαι-
νομένῳ τὸ παρὰ τῆς ἀνθρωπίνης βουλῆς ἐφήρμοζεν.
οὕτω γοῦν καὶ ἡνίκα ὁ βασιλεὺς Ἰουλιανὸς ἄμφω
μετεκάλει διὰ μιᾶς κλήσεως καὶ οἱ πεμφθέντες στρα-
τιῶται μετὰ τιμῆς τὴν Θετταλικὴν ἐπῆγον πειθανάγ-
κην, | ὡς ἔδοξε κοινώσασθαι τοῖς θεοῖς τὸ ἔργον,
περιφανῶς, ὡς κἂν ἰδιώτην καὶ βάναυσον διακρῖναι
τὰ σημεῖα, τοῦ θεοῦ τὴν ὁδὸν ἀπαγορεύσαντος, ὁ μὲν
Μάξιμος ἐνεφύετο τοῖς ἱεροῖς καὶ ποτνιώμενος ἐπὶ
τοῖς δρωμένοις μετ' ὀλοφυρμῶν ἐνέκειτο, τυχεῖν ἑτέρων σημείων ἱκετεύων τοὺς θεοὺς καὶ μετατεθῆναι τὰ
εἱμαρμένα· καὶ πολλά γε ἐπὶ πολλοῖς αὐτῷ διατεινο-
μένῳ καὶ παρακλίνοντι, ὡς ἐξηγεῖτο Χρυσάνθιος, ἡ
βούλησις τελευτῶντι τὰ φαινόμενα ἔκρινε, καὶ τὸ δοκοῦν ἐν τοῖς ἱεροῖς ἐφαίνετο, οὐ τὸ φανθὲν ἐδοξάζετο.
οὕτως οὖν ὁ μὲν ὥρμησε τὴν ἀρχέκακον ὁδὸν ἐκείνην
καὶ ἀποδημίαν, ὁ δὲ Χρυσάνθιος ἔμεινε κατὰ χώραν.
καὶ τὰ πρῶτα μὲν ὁ βασιλεὺς ἤλγησεν ἐπὶ τῇ μονῇ

---

[110] θεωμένοις ⟨χρώμενος⟩ add. Gi Go

[277] An essential difference between theurgy and magic: the
former communicates with gods, the latter tries to force results
from them. See next note.
[278] Cf. Iambl. Myst. 3.22; Damasc. Pr. 39.

598

resisting the omens revealed by the gods, he would keep demanding further omens and try to force them from them.[277] Chrysanthius, on the contrary, would use the first omens that appeared, then, by gradual derivation,[278] would proceed to alter the signs that had been offered; then, if he got the omens he wanted, he would be the winner, but if he failed, he adapted his human counsel to fit whatever came to light. For instance, at one point the emperor Julian invited them both together to his court by means of a single summons. When the soldiers who had been sent were applying, with respect, the Thessalian style of "forceful persuasion,"[279] Maximus and Chrysanthius decided to communicate with the gods on the matter. With the god warning them against the journey so plainly that any private person, even an ignorant laborer, could have judged the signs, Maximus persisted in using the sacrificial animals, and after the rites had been duly completed, he cried out in indignation with loud lamentations, beseeching the gods to allot him different omens and to alter the course of destiny. And since he persisted in many repeated attempts, and deviated from the interpretation that Chrysanthius gave, he ended up making a personal decision about the portents, and as a result what seemed to him present in the omens was revealed, but he did not form his opinion on what had been revealed.[280] So Maximus for his part set out on that ill-fated path, a journey to another land, whereas Chrysanthius stayed at home. And at first the emperor was upset over the latter's staying put,

12

13

14

15

---

[279] For the tyrannical manners of the Thessalians, cf. Philostr. *VS* 501. It was a proverb: cf. Julian. 31d, 274c.

[280] For these incidents, cf. Philostr. *VS* 476–77.

καί πού τι καὶ τῶν ἀληθῶν προσυπενόησεν, ὡς οὐκ
ἂν ἠρνήσατο Χρυσάνθιος τὴν κλῆσιν εἰ μή τι δυσ-
16 χερὲς ἐνεῖδε τοῖς μέλλουσιν. ἔγραφεν οὖν καὶ πάλιν
μετακαλῶν, καὶ οὐ πρὸς αὐτὸν μόνον αἱ παρακλήσεις
ἦσαν· ὁ δὲ τὴν γυναῖκα συμπείθειν τὸν ἄνδρα διὰ τῶν
γραμμάτων ἐνῆγεν. καὶ πάλιν ἦν πρὸς τὸ θεῖον ἀναφορὰ παρὰ τοῦ Χρυσανθίου καὶ τὰ παρὰ τῶν θεῶν
17 οὐκ ἔληγεν εἰς ταὐτὸ συμφερόμενα. ὡς δὲ πολλάκις
τοῦτο ἦν, [ἔληγεν ὤν]¹¹¹ ὁ μὲν βασιλεὺς ἐπείσθη, ὁ δὲ
Χρυσάνθιος τὴν ἀρχιερωσύνην τοῦ παντὸς ἔθνους
λαβὼν καὶ τὸ μέλλον ἐξεπιστάμενος σαφῶς, οὐ βαρὺς ἦν κατὰ τὴν ἐξουσίαν, οὔτε τοὺς νεὼς ἐγείρων,
ὥσπερ ἅπαντες θερμῶς καὶ περικαῶς ἐς ταῦτα συν-
έθεον, οὔτε λυπῶν τινας τῶν χριστιανῶν περιττῶς·
18 ἀλλὰ τοσαύτη τις ἦν ἁπλότης τοῦ ἤθους, ὡς κατὰ
Λυδίαν μικροῦ καὶ ἔλαθεν ἡ τῶν ἱερῶν ἐπανόρθωσις.
ὡς γοῦν ἑτέρωσε τὰ πρῶτα ἐχώρησεν, οὐδὲν ἐδόκει
πεπρᾶχθαι νεώτερον, οὐδὲ πολύ τι καὶ ἀθρόον κατὰ
94G μεταβολὴν ἐφαίνετο, | ἀλλ' ἐπιεικῶς ἐς ὁμαλότητά
τινα καὶ ἀκινησίαν ἅπαντα συνέστρωντο, καὶ μόνος
ἐθαυμάζετο, τῶν ἄλλων ἁπάντων ὥσπερ ἐν κλύδωνι
κινουμένων, καὶ τῶν μὲν ἐξαπιναίως κατεπτηχότων,
19 τῶν δὲ πρότερον ταπεινῶν ἀνεστηκότων· ἐθαυμάσθη
γοῦν ἐπὶ τούτοις, ὡς οὐ μόνον δεινὸς τὰ μέλλοντα
προνοεῖν, ἀλλὰ καὶ τοῖς γνωσθεῖσι χρήσασθαι.
20   Ἦν δὲ τὸ πᾶν ἦθος τοιοῦτος, ἢ πρὸς τὸν Πλατω-

¹¹¹ inser. Wr Be: omis. Go

and perhaps he even had a suspicion about the truth, that Chrysanthius would not have refused the invitation, unless he had observed some difficulty ahead. So, Julian 16 wrote and summoned him a second time, and his invitations were not addressed to Chrysanthius alone. For in his communications he urged Chrysanthius' wife to help him to persuade her husband. Once more, then, the matter was referred to the divine will by Chrysanthius, and the response coming from the gods amounted to the same outcome. When this had happened several times, even the 17 emperor let up and besieged him no more, while Chrysanthius, after accepting the role of high priest for the whole country and understanding clearly what was about to happen, was not heavy-handed in the exercise of his office, neither reinstating temples, as all other men in their hotheaded and perfervid zeal hastened to do, nor treating any of the Christians very harshly. But such was the liberality 18 of his character that throughout Lydia the restoration of the temples almost escaped notice. At any rate, when those in power pursued a different policy, there proved to have been no serious innovation, nor did there seem to be any great and comprehensive change, but was organized equitably and it was smooth sailing, and he alone won admiration, when all the rest were tossed to and fro as though in a storm; since on a sudden some cowered in consternation, while others, who were humbled before, were once more exalted. For all this, then, he won admira- 19 tion as one who was not only impressive for forecasting the future, but also for using his wide knowledge.

Such was the man's whole character, whether it was 20

νικὸν Σωκράτην ἀναπεφυκώς, ἢ κατά τινα ζῆλον καὶ
μίμησιν ἐκ παιδὸς αὐτῷ γενομένην ἐς ἐκεῖνον συν-
εσχηματισμένος. τό τε γὰρ ἐπιφαινόμενον ἁπλοῦν
καὶ ἀφελὲς καὶ ἀδιήγητον ἐπεκάθητο τοῖς λόγοις, ἥ
τε ἐπὶ τούτοις ἀφροδίτη τῶν ῥημάτων κατέθελγε τὸν
21 ἀκροώμενον. πᾶσίν τε εὔνους ἦν κατὰ τὴν συνουσίαν
καὶ τῶν ἀπιόντων ἕκαστος, ὅτι φιλοῖτο μᾶλλον ἀπῄει
22 πεπεισμένος. ὥσπερ οὖν τὰ κάλλιστα καὶ γλυκύτερα
τῶν μελῶν πρὸς πᾶσαν ἀκοὴν ἡμέρως καὶ πράως
502B καταρρεῖ καὶ | διολισθαίνει καὶ μέχρι τῶν ἀλόγων
διϊκνούμενα, καθάπερ φασὶ τὸν Ὀρφέα, οὕτω καὶ
Χρυσανθίου λόγος πᾶσιν ἦν ἐναρμόνιος καὶ τοσ-
αύταις διαφοραῖς ἠθῶν ἐνέπρεπεν καὶ καθηρμόζετο.
23 δυσκίνητος δὲ ἦν περὶ τὰς διαλέξεις καὶ φιλονεικίας,
ἐν τούτοις μάλιστα τοὺς ἀνθρώπους ὑπολαμβάνων
24 ἐκτραχύνεσθαι· οὐδ᾽ ἂν ῥᾳδίως ἤκουσέ τις αὐτοῦ τὴν
παιδείαν ἣν εἶχεν ἐπιδεικνυμένου καὶ διὰ τοῦτο πρὸς
τοὺς ἄλλους οἰδοῦντος καὶ διογκυλλομένου, ἀλλὰ τά
τε λεγόμενα ὑπ᾽ αὐτῶν. ἐθαύμαζεν, εἰ καὶ φαύλως ἐλέγετο, καὶ τὰ δοξαζόμενα κακῶς ἐπήνει, καθάπερ οὐδὲ
τὴν ἀρχὴν ἀκούων, ἀλλὰ ἐς τὸ συμφατικὸν διὰ τὸ μὴ
25 λυπεῖν γεγονώς. εἰ δέ πού τις, τῶν ἐπὶ σοφίᾳ πρώτων
95G παρόντων, ἐγένετο | κίνησις καὶ συμβαλέσθαι τι τοῖς
λεγομένοις ἔδοξεν αὐτῷ, πάντα ἦν ἡσυχίας μεστά,
26 καθάπερ οὐ παρόντων ἀνθρώπων· οὕτως οὔτε τὰς
ἐρωτήσεις, οὔτε τοὺς διορισμούς, οὔτε τὰς μνήμας
ὑπέμενον τοῦ ἀνδρός, ἀλλ᾽ ἀνέχαζον, ἔξω λόγου καὶ
ἀντιρρήσεως ἑαυτοὺς φυλάττοντες, ὅπως μὴ καταφα-

that in him the Platonic Socrates had come to life again, or that, by some ambition to imitate him, he carefully formed himself from boyhood to be like him. For an unaffected and indescribable simplicity was manifest in his speeches, and the charisma of his words present in them enchanted the person hearing them. In conversation he 21 was amiable to all men, so that everyone leaving went away from him with the conviction that he had been given special attention. And just as the most charming and 22 sweetest songs flow gently and smoothly, as they ease themselves into everyone's ears, even reaching irrational animals, as they say of Orpheus, so too the eloquence of Chrysanthius was agreeable to all ears and he adapted and made it fit all those diverse temperaments. But it was not 23 easy to rouse him to popular lectures or disputations, because he understood that it is especially in such contests that men become embittered. Nor would anyone readily 24 have heard him showing off the erudition he possessed or be insolent and arrogant toward others, or puff himself up because of it; rather he used to admire whatever they said, even though their remarks were trivial, and he would applaud even incorrect conclusions, just as though he had not even heard the basic assumption, but was naturally inclined to assent, because he did not want to aggrieve anyone. And if in a gathering of those most distinguished 25 for learning, a debate was set in motion, and he thought fit to contribute to the discussion, the place became hushed in silence as though no one were there. To such an 26 extent could they face neither his questions nor definitions nor the feats of memory, but they would withdraw into the background and carefully refrain from discussion or dispute, so that their failure would not be too evident.

603

27 νεῖς ἁμαρτάνοντες γίνωνται. καὶ πολλοὶ τῶν μετρίως
ἐγνωκότων αὐτόν, διὰ τοῦ βάθους τῆς ψυχῆς οὐκ
ἀφιγμένων, κατηγορούντων τε ἀλογίαν, καὶ τὴν πρᾳότητα μόνον ἐπαινούντων, ὡς ᾔσθοντο διαλεγομένου
καὶ ἀνελίττοντος ἑαυτὸν εἰς δόγματα καὶ λόγους,
28 ἕτερόν τινα τοῦτον ἐνόμισαν παρ’ ὃν ᾔδεισαν· οὕτως
ἀλλοιότερός τις ἐν ταῖς λογικαῖς κινήσεσιν ἐφαίνετο,
τῆς τε τριχὸς ὑποφριττούσης αὐτῷ, καὶ τῶν ὀφθαλμῶν ἑρμηνευόντων χορεύουσαν ἔνδον τὴν ψυχὴν περὶ
29 τὰ δόγματα. εἰς μακρὸν δὲ γῆρας ἀφικόμενος, τὸν
πάντα διετέλεσε βίον οὐδενὸς τῶν κατ’ ἀνθρώπους
ἑτέρου φροντίσας ἢ οἰκονομίας τινός, ἢ γεωργίας, ἢ
χρημάτων ὅσα δικαίως παραγίνεται. ἀλλὰ πενίαν μὲν
ἔφερε ῥᾷον ἢ πλοῦτον ἕτεροι, διαίτῃ δὲ τῇ παραπε-
σούσῃ προσεκέχρητο, τῶν μὲν ὑείων οὐδέποτε, τῶν
ἄλλων χρεῶν ἐλάχιστα γευόμενος, τὸ δὲ θεῖον θερα-
30 πεύων συντονώτατα. τῆς ⟨τε⟩[112] τῶν ἀρχαίων ἀναγνώ-
σεως ἀπρὶξ εἴχετο, καὶ διέφερεν οὐδὲν νεότης τε καὶ
γῆρας, ἀλλ’ ὑπὲρ ὀγδοήκοντα γεγονὼς ἔτη, τοσαῦτα
ἔγραφεν αὐτοχειρίᾳ, ὅσα μόλις ἀναγινώσκουσι νεά-
31 ζοντες ἕτεροι. τῶν γοῦν γραφόντων τὰ ἄκρα δακτύλων
ὑπὸ τῆς ἀλήκτου μελέτης καὶ χρήσεως ἐνεκέκαμπτο.
ἀναστὰς δὲ ἀπὸ τῆς ἀσκήσεως, ταῖς τε δημοσίαις
προόδοις ἐτέρπετο, καὶ τόν τε ταῦτα γράφοντα παρα-
96G λαβών, μακροὺς | μὲν τοὺς περιπάτους, σχολαίους δὲ
32 ἀπέτεινεν· ἔλαθέν τε ἄν τις περιαλγὴς τοὺς πόδας

[112] add. Gi Go

604

And many of those who knew him only slightly, and therefore had not reached the depths of his soul, held his silence
against him and would praise only his gentle disposition;
but when they heard him maintaining a philosophical
theme and unfolding his teachings and arguments, they
decided that this was a very different person from the man
[they thought] they knew.[281] So transformed did he seem
by the logical force of these views, with his hair standing
on end, and his eyes conveying that the soul within him
was dancing around the teachings that he expressed. He
survived to an advanced old age, and during the whole of
his long life he gave no thought to the ordinary affairs of
human life, except to running a household and agriculture
and just so much money as may be honestly acquired.
Poverty he bore more easily than other men wealth, and
for his daily food he took whatever came to hand, never
eating pork, and only seldom other kinds of meat. He
worshipped the divine with the utmost intensity. He was
steadfast in his reading of the ancient authors, and in old
age he was no different from when he was young, but
when he was over eighty, he wrote as many things with his
own hand as others could barely read in their youth. As a
result the ends of the fingers with which he wrote became
curved and crooked with constant work and use. When he
had ceased his hard work, he enjoyed walking in the public streets with the writer of this narrative to keep him
company; and he would extend these into long walks, but
they were educational. One might forget having very sore

27

28

29

30

31

32

[281] Another Socrates parallel; cf. Pl. *Symp*. 215a4ff. (Silenus).

γενόμενος, οὕτως ὑπὸ τῶν διηγημάτων κατεθέλγετο.
λουτροῖς δὲ ἐλάχιστα ἐκέχρητο, καὶ ὅμως ἐῴκει διὰ
33 παντὸς ἄρτι λελουμένῳ. πρὸς δὲ τὰς τῶν ἀρχόντων
συντυχίας τὸ ὑπερφυὲς οὐκ ἦν δι᾽ ἀλαζονείαν συν-
ιδεῖν ἢ τύφον γινόμενον, ἀλλ᾽ ἁπλότητα ἄν τις ὑπέλα-
βεν ἀγνοοῦντος ἀνδρὸς ὅ τι ἐστὶν ἐξουσία· οὕτω δι-
34 ελέγετο κοινῶς αὐτοῖς καὶ ἐπιδεξίως. τὸν δὲ ταῦτα
γράφοντα ἐκπαιδεύσας νέον ἔτι ὄντα, ἡνίκα ἐπανῆλθεν Ἀθήνηθεν, οὐκ ἔλαττον ἠγάπα, ἀλλὰ καὶ προσ-
ετίθει καθ᾽ ἡμέραν τῷ διαφέροντι τῆς εὐνοίας, ἐς
τοῦτο ἐκνικήσας, ὥστε τὰ ἑωθινὰ μὲν ὁ συγγραφεὺς
503B ἐπὶ ῥητορικοῖς λόγοις <τοῖς> ἑταίροις[113] συνῆν | καὶ
τοὺς δεομένους ἐπαίδευεν, μικρὸν δὲ ὑπὲρ μεσημ-
βρίας ἐπαιδεύετο, παρὰ τὸν ἐξ ἀρχῆς ἰὼν διδάσκαλον, τοὺς θειοτέρους καὶ φιλοσόφους τῶν λόγων·
35 ἡνίκα οὔτε ὁ παιδεύων ἔκαμνεν σοφίας ἐρῶντι συνών,
τῷ τε ἐκδεχομένῳ τὰ μαθήματα τὸ ἔργον ἦν πανήγυρις.

36   Τοῦ δὲ τῶν χριστιανῶν ἐκνικῶντος ἔργου καὶ κατέχοντος ἅπαντα, διὰ μακροῦ τις ἀπὸ τῆς Ῥώμης εἰ-
σεφοίτησεν ἄρχων τῆς Ἀσίας—Ἰοῦστος ὠνομά-
ζετο—, πρεσβύτης μὲν ἤδη κατὰ τὴν ἡλικίαν,
γενναῖος καὶ ἄλλως[114] τὸ ἦθος, καὶ τῆς ἀρχαίας καὶ
πατρίου πολιτείας οὐκ ἀπηλλαγμένος, ἀλλὰ τὸν εὐδαίμονα καὶ μακάριον ἐκεῖνον ἐζηλωκὼς τρόπον, πρός
τε ἱεροῖς ἦν ἀεὶ καὶ μαντείας ἐξεκρέματο πάσης, μέγα

feet, such enchanting stories would he tell. He very seldom went to the baths, and yet he always came across as
freshly bathed. The overpowering impression he made in 33
his conversations with those in authority was not due to
arrogance or pride, but we should regard as the perfect
sincerity of one who was wholly ignorant of the nature of
power; so familiar and so gracious were his conversations
with such persons. He had taught the author of this work, 34
then still a youth, and when the latter returned from Athens Chrysanthius showed him no less kindness, but day
after day he even added to his remarkable goodwill; and
he gained such influence over him that the author in the
early morning used to hold meetings with his companions
in the art of rhetoric and taught those who needed it, but
soon after midday, visiting his master of many years, he
himself would be taught in the more divine and philosophical doctrines. And in this period the teacher never 35
grew weary of instructing his devoted admirer of wisdom,
while the task for him receiving his teaching was a joyful
experience.

Now when the practice of Christianity was gaining 36
ground and held everything in its tight grip, there arrived
from Rome after a long interval a prefect of Asia named
Justus, already well on in years, and in any other way a man
of noble character, who had not cast aside the time-
honored and ancestral mode of living, for he was a keen
follower of that happy and blessed form of worship. He
was constant in his attendance at the temples, wholly under the sway of every kind of divination, and took great

---

113 τοῖς inser. Go   ἑταίροις coni. Penella (1986):
ἑτέροις A Gi   114 καὶ καλὸς Wr: καὶ ἄλλως A Bo Go

φρονῶν ὅτι τούτων ἐπεθύμησέ τε καὶ κατώρθωσεν.
37 οὗτος εἰς τὴν Ἀσίαν διαβὰς ἐκ τῆς Κωνσταντίνου
97G πόλεως καὶ τὸν | ἡγεμόνα τοῦ ἔθνους καταλαβών—
Ἱλάριος ἐκεῖνος ἐκαλεῖτο—συγκορυβαντιῶντα πρὸς
τὴν ἐπιθυμίαν, βωμούς τε ἀνέστησεν αὐτοσχεδίους ἐν
Σάρδεσιν (οὐ γὰρ ἦσαν αὐτόθι), καὶ τοῖς ἴχνεσι τῶν
ἱερῶν, εἴ που τι ἴχνος εὑρέθη, χεῖρα ἐπέβαλεν, ἀνορ-
θῶσαι βουλόμενος.

38 Δημοσίᾳ τε θύσας, ἔπεμπε καὶ συνεκάλει τοὺς
πανταχόθεν ἐπὶ παιδείᾳ δόξαν ἔχοντας. οἱ δὲ παρῆσαν θᾶττον ἢ κληθῆναι, τόν τε ἄνδρα θαυμάζοντες
καὶ καιρὸν τῆς σφῶν αὐτῶν ἐπιδείξεως ἡγούμενοι,
τινὲς δὲ αὐτῶν ἐπὶ τῇ κολακείᾳ θαρροῦντες ὥσπερ
παιδείᾳ καὶ διὰ ταύτης ἐλπίζοντες ἢ τιμὴν ἢ δο-
39 ξάριον[115] ἢ ἀργύριον ἀποκερδαναῖν. ἱερουργίας οὖν
δημοσίᾳ προτεθείσης, παρῆσαν μὲν ἅπαντες, καὶ ὁ
ταῦτα γράφων παρῆν· ὁ δὲ Ἰοῦστος ἐπιστήσας καὶ
τὴν τῶν ὀφθαλμῶν στάσιν ἐπερείσας—ἔκειτο δὲ τὸ
ἱερεῖον ἐν ᾧ δήποτε τῷ σχήματι—, τοὺς παρόντας
ἀνηρώτα· "τί βούλεται τὸ σχῆμα τοῦ πτώματος;" ἔνθα
οἱ μὲν κόλακες παρεφρύγοντο θαυμάζοντες, ὅτι καὶ
ἀπὸ σχημάτων ἐστὶ μαντικός, καὶ μόνῳ παρεχώρουν
40 ἐκείνῳ ταῦτα εἰδέναι· οἱ δὲ σεμνότεροι τὰς ὑπήνας
καταψήσαντες ἄκροις τοῖς δακτύλοις καὶ τὰ πρόσωπα
διαστυγνάσαντες, τάς τε κεφαλὰς βαρύ τι καὶ ἠρε-
μαῖον ἐπισείοντες, παρεθεώρουν ἐς τὸ προκείμενον,

115 δοξαρίδιον corr. A^{m1}, acc. Go

pride in his zeal for these things and his success in restoring them. He crossed over from the city of Constantine to   37
Asia, and when he found that the chief man of the country
(Hilarius was his name) was as enthusiastic as himself in
his zeal, he set up improvised altars at Sardis (for there
were none in that place), and wherever a vestige was to be
found, he set his hand to the remains of the temples with
the intention of reinstating them.

After offering sacrifices in public, he sent to summon   38
the men who were everywhere known for their learning.
And they were in attendance straightaway, both because
they admired the man himself and because they thought
this was an opportunity to show off their own abilities,
while some of them put their confidence as much in their
power to flatter as in their erudition, and hoped by this
means to gain honor or a bit more reputation or money.
Therefore when a public sacrifice was announced they   39
were all present, and so was the author of this work. Then
Justus set himself to the task, and fixing the steady gaze of
his eyes on the victim, which lay in some sort of pose, he
asked the bystanders: "What does the posture of the sacrificial offering indicate?" In response the flatterers for
their part were all fired up in their admiration, because he
was able to divine even from postures, and they deferred
to him as the only person possessing this knowledge. But   40
the more pretentious among them stroked their beards
with the tips of their fingers, and put on a serious expression of face,[282] and shook their heads solemnly and gently
while they gazed at the victim lying there, and each one

---

[282] $\delta\iota\alpha\sigma\tau\nu\gamma\nu\acute{\alpha}\zeta\omega$ (unique verb) used sarcastically.

41 ἄλλος ἄλλο λέγοντες. ὁ δὲ Ἰοῦστος, ὡς μόλις τὸν
γέλωτα ἀνῆκεν, ἐπιστρέψας εἰς τὸν Χρυσάνθιον "σὺ
δὲ τί φής," ἐβόησεν, "ὦ πρεσβύτατε;" καὶ ὁ Χρυσάνθιος οὐδὲν διαταραχθείς, πάντων ἔφησε καταγινώ-
42 σκειν· "ἀλλ' εἴ τι βούλει κἀμέ," ἔφη, "περὶ τούτων
εἰπεῖν, τίς μὲν ὁ τρόπος τῆς μαντείας, εἴ γε τοὺς μαν-
τικοὺς τρόπους ἐπίστασαι, εἰπὲ πρότερον, καὶ ποίου
98G τινὸς εἴδους, τίς | δὲ ἡ πεῦσις, καὶ κατὰ τίνα μέθοδον
43 ἐπηρώτηται. καὶ εἰ ταῦτα λέγοις, εἴποιμ' ἂν ὅπῃ τὸ
φαινόμενον εἰς τὸ μέλλον φέρει. πρὶν δὲ ταῦτα λέγειν,
βάναυσόν ἐστι πρὸς τὴν σὴν ἐρώτησιν, σημαινόντων
τὸ μέλλον τῶν θεῶν, ἐμὲ καὶ περὶ τῆς ἐρωτήσεως καὶ
τοῦ μέλλοντος λέγειν, συνάπτοντα τῷ γεγονότι τὸ
44 ἐσόμενον· δύο γὰρ οὕτως ἂν γίνεσθαι τὰς ἐρωτήσεις.
περὶ δύο δὲ ἢ πλειόνων οὐδεὶς ἐρωτᾷ κατὰ ταὐτόν· τὸ
γὰρ ἐν τοῖς ὡρισμένοις διάφορον ἕνα λόγον οὐκ ἔχει."
ἐνταῦθα Ἰοῦστος ἀνέκραγεν ὡς μανθάνων ὅσα μὴ
504B πρότερον ἠπίστατο, | καὶ τοῦ λοιποῦ γε οὐκ ἐπαύσατο
45 συνὼν ἰδίᾳ καὶ τῆς πηγῆς ἀρνόμενος. καὶ εἴ τινες
ἕτεροι κατ' ἐκείνους τοὺς χρόνους τῶν ἐπὶ σοφίᾳ περι-
βοήτων Χρυσανθίῳ κατὰ κλέος ἦλθον εἰς λόγους,
πεισθέντες ὅτι πόρρω τῆς δεινότητος ἐκείνης εἰσίν,
ἀπιόντες ᾤχοντο. τοῦτο δὲ καὶ Ἑλλησπόντιος ὁ ἐκ
46 Γαλατίας ἔπαθεν, ἀνὴρ διὰ πάντα ἄριστος, καὶ εἰ μὴ

offered a different solution. But Justus, who could hardly   41
contain his laughter, reverted back[283] to Chrysanthius and
said with raised voice: "And what do you say about this,
my honorable friend?" Chrysanthius, who was not the
least intimidated, said that he found all these readings of
little value. "But" said he, "if you wish me to give an opin-   42
ion as well about these matters, if indeed you understand
the modes of divination, tell me first of all, what mode of
divination this is, to what type it belongs, what kind of
question, and according to which method it was investi-
gated. If you were to tell me all this, I would tell you what   43
the bearing on the future of this thing is that we see. But
until you tell me these things, because the gods themselves send signs about the future, it would be meaningless
for me to respond to your question and speak about the
future, thereby connecting the future with what has just
happened. For two different questions would thus arise;   44
but no one asks two or more questions. For when things
have two separate definitions, one explanation does not
suit both." Then Justus exclaimed that he had learned
something that he did not know before, and from now on
he consulted him constantly in private and drank deep
from that fount of knowledge. And if others in those days,   45
renowned for wisdom, came to Chrysanthius on account
of his fame and entered into debates with him, they went
away convinced that they remained far behind his formidable abilities. This also happened to Hellespontius of   46
Galatia, an unusually gifted man in every way, who, if

283 A possible in-joke alluding to the Platonist doctrine that
each thing reverts upon its higher cause (*epistrophê*).

47 Χρυσάνθιος ἦν, πρῶτος ἁπάντων ἂν[116] φανείς. σοφίας
μὲν γὰρ ἐραστὴς οὗτος ὁ ἀνὴρ ἐς τοσόνδε ἐγένετο,
ὥστε ἐπῆλθε μικροῦ καὶ τὴν ἀοίκητον, μαστεύων εἴ
που τινι περιτύχοι πλέον εἰδότι· καλῶν δὲ ἔργων καὶ
λόγων ἀνάπλεως γενόμενος, καὶ εἰς τὰς παλαιὰς Σάρδεις ἀφίκετο διὰ τὴν Χρυσανθίου συνουσίαν. ἀλλὰ
ταῦτα μὲν ὕστερον.

48 Ἐγένετο δὲ Χρυσανθίῳ καὶ παῖς ἐπώνυμος τῷ κατὰ
τὸ Πέργαμον αὐτῷ γενομένῳ διδασκάλῳ—μεμνήμεθα
δὲ πρότερον Αἰδεσίῳ—, καὶ ἦν ὁ παῖς ἐκ παιδὸς ἐπτε-
ρωμένον τι χρῆμα πρὸς ἅπασαν ἀρετήν, καὶ τῶν ἵπ-
99G πων οὐκ εἶχε‹το›[117] | θατέρου, ᾗ φησιν ὁ Πλάτων,
οὐδὲ ἔβριθε τὸ κατανοοῦν[118] αὐτῷ, ἀλλὰ πρός τε μαθήματα σφοδρὸς καὶ ἄγαν ὀξὺς γενόμενος καὶ πρὸς
θεῶν θεραπείαν διαρκέστατος, ἐς τοσόνδε διέφευγε τὸ
ἀνθρώπινον, ὥστε ἄνθρωπος ὢν ἐκινδύνευεν ὅλος εἶ-
49 ναι ψυχή. τὸ γοῦν σῶμα ἐν ταῖς κινήσεσιν οὕτως
αὐτοῦ κοῦφον ἦν, ὥστε ἦν ἀπίθανον γράφειν, καὶ
μάλα ποιητικῶς, εἰς ὅσον ὕψος ἐφέρετο μετάρσιος.
50 ἡ δὲ πρὸς τὸ θεῖον οἰκειότης οὕτως ἦν ἀπραγμάτευτος
καὶ εὔκολος, ὥστε ἐξήρκει τὸν στέφανον ἐπιθεῖναι τῇ
κεφαλῇ καὶ πρὸς τὸν ἥλιον ἀναβλέποντα χρησμοὺς
ἐκφέρειν, καὶ τούτους ἀψευδεῖς καὶ πρὸς τὸ κάλλιστον
51 εἶδος ἐνθέου πνεύματος γεγραμμένους· καίτοι γε οὔτε

---

116 inser. Cob (sic Wr): omis. Gi Go Be
117 εἶχε‹το› Go: εἶχε A
118 ἔβριθε τὸ κατανοοῦν Gi Go: ἐβρίθετο τὸ κατανοοῦν A

Chrysanthius had not existed,[284] would have shown himself first among all. For he was such an ardent lover of learning that he traveled almost to the uninhabited parts of the world in the desire of finding out whether he could meet anyone who knew more than himself.[285] Thus, then, crowned with noble words and deeds he came to ancient Sardis to enjoy the society of Chrysanthius. But all this happened later. 47

Chrysanthius had a son named after his former teacher at Pergamon—I have written about Aedesius above.[286] From his childhood this boy was a creature winged for every excellence, and of the two soul-horses, as Plato puts it,[287] he did not possess the troublesome horse, nor did his intellect get weighed down, but dedicated to his studies and becoming keen-witted, and assiduous in the worship of the gods, he so completely escaped from human nature, that, though a mortal man, he was practically all soul.[288] At any rate his body was so light in its movements that it would seem incredible to describe, even in poetic form, to what a height it rose up. His intimacy with the gods was so effortless and easy that he only had to place the garland on his head and, lifting his gaze up to the sun, to deliver oracles instantly, and these were infallible and were written down after the fairest models of divine inspiration. Yet 48 49 50 51

[284] Cf. Tuscianus in *VPS* 10.36.
[285] Just like Socrates after his oracle (Pl. *Ap.* 21b–22a).
[286] See *VPS* 6.1–6.
[287] Pl. *Phdr.* 246b, 247b.
[288] Also said of Alypius (above, *VPS* 5.25).

μέτρον ἠπίστατο, οὔτε εἰς γραμματικὴν ἐπιστήμην
52 ἔρρωτο, ἀλλὰ θεὸς ἅπαντα ἦν αὐτῷ. νοσήσας δὲ οὐ-
δαμῶς κατὰ τὸν ὡρισμένον βίον, ἀμφὶ τὰ εἴκοσιν ἔτη
μετήλλαξεν. ὁ δὲ πατὴρ καὶ τότε διέδειξεν φιλόσοφος
53 ὤν· ἢ γὰρ τὸ μέγεθος τῆς συμφορᾶς εἰς ἀπάθειαν
αὐτὸν μετέστησεν, ἢ τῷ παιδὶ συγχαίρων τῆς λή-
ξεως, ἔμεινεν ἄτρεπτος· καὶ ἡ μήτηρ δέ, πρὸς τὸν ἄνδρα ὁρῶσα, τὴν γυναικείαν ὑπερήνεγκε φύσιν, πρὸς
τὴν ἀξίαν τοῦ πάθους ὀλοφύρσεις ἐκλύσασα.

54 Τούτων δὲ οὕτω κεχωρηκότων, ὁ Χρυσάνθιος ἦν ἐν
τοῖς συνήθεσι· καὶ πολλῶν καὶ μεγάλων ἐμπιπτόντων
δημοσίων καὶ κοινῶν πραγμάτων, ἃ τὰς ἁπάντων ψυχὰς κατέσεισεν εἰς φόβον, μόνος ἔμεινεν ἀσάλευτος,
ὥστε εἴκασεν ⟨ἂν⟩[119] τις οὐδὲ ἐπὶ γῆς εἶναι τὸν ἄνδρα.
55 κατ᾽ ἐκείνους δὴ τοὺς | χρόνους καὶ Ἑλλησπόντιος
100G παρ᾽ αὐτὸν ἀφικνεῖται καὶ βραδέως μὲν συνῆλθον εἰς
λόγους· ἐπεὶ δὲ εἰς ταὐτὸν συνήντησαν, τοσοῦτον Ἑλλησπόντιος ἑαλώκει, ὥστε, πάντα μεθέμενος, ἕτοιμος
ἦν σκηνοῦσθαι παρὰ Χρυσανθίῳ καὶ νεάζειν ἐν τῷ
56 μανθάνειν· μετεμέλε δὲ αὐτῷ τοσοῦτον πεπλανημένος
χρόνον καὶ εἰς γῆρας ἀφικόμενος πρίν ἤ τι τῶν χρη-
σίμων ἐκμαθεῖν. καὶ ὁ μὲν ἐπὶ τούτῳ τὴν γνώμην
ἔτεινε· τῷ δὲ Χρυσανθίῳ συμβὰν ἔκ τινος συνηθείας
τὴν φλέβα διελεῖν—ὅ τε συγγραφεὺς παρῆν, οὕτω
προστάξαντος—καὶ τῶν ἰατρῶν κενῶσαι βουλομένων

119 add. Go

614

he neither had knowledge of meter nor was he trained in the science of grammar; but god was everything to him. Though he had never been ill during his allotted span of 52 life, he left this world when he was about twenty years of age. On this occasion too his father showed himself to be a true philosopher: whether the magnitude of the calamity 53 made him emotionally invulnerable, or he rejoiced with his son in the latter's destiny, the fact is that he remained untroubled emotionally. Even his mother, observing her husband, rose above the ordinary feminine nature and gave expression to her lamentations of grief in a dignified manner.

After these events had taken place, Chrysanthius pur- 54 sued his usual studies. When both many and great calamities befell public and state affairs, which shook all men's souls into a state of fear, he alone remained unshaken, so much so that one would have imagined that the man did not reside on earth. It was also around this time 55 that Hellespontius came to see him, and after some delay they came to have conversations. When they had an encounter in the same place, Hellespontius was so captivated that he abandoned all else and was ready to live close to Chrysanthius and to live like a youth by studying with him.[289] For he regretted that he had so long wandered in 56 error, and had arrived at old age before learning anything useful. Accordingly he bent his whole mind to this task. But it so happened that Chrysanthius needed to undergo venesection as was his custom, and the author was present in compliance with his request; and when the doctors pre-

[289] As Plato did with Socrates, Plotinus with Ammonius, and Porphyry with Plotinus.

τὸ φερόμενον,[120] αὐτὸς ἐπὶ τὸ συμφέρον σκεψάμε-
505B νος,[121] | παράλογον εἶναι τὸ κενωθὲν ἔφη, καὶ οὕτως
ἐπισχεῖν ἐκέλευσεν· οὐδὲ γὰρ ἄπειρος ἦν ἰατρικῆς ὁ
57 ταῦτα γράφων. Ἑλλησπόντιος δὲ ἀκούσας παρῆν,
ἀγανακτῶν καὶ ποτνιώμενος ὡς μεγάλου κακοῦ γεγο-
νότος εἰ πρεσβύτης οὕτως ἀνὴρ τοσούτου διὰ τῆς
58 χειρὸς αἵματος ἀφῄρηται. ὡς δὲ ἤκουσε τῆς φωνῆς
καὶ ὑγιαίνοντα εἶδε, πρὸς τὸν συγγραφέα τὸν λόγον
ἐπιστρέψας "ἀλλά σέ γε," φησίν, "ἡ πόλις αἰτιῶνται
δεινόν τι δεδρακέναι· νῦν δὲ ἅπαντες σιωπήσουσιν,
59 ὁρῶντες ὑγιαίνοντα." τοῦ δὲ εἰπόντος ὡς οὐκ ἠγνόει
τὸ συμφέρον, ὁ μὲν Ἑλλησπόντιος ὡς συσκευασάμε-
νος τὰ βιβλία καὶ παρὰ τὸν Χρυσάνθιον ἥξων ἐπὶ
60 μαθήσει, τῆς πόλεως ἐξῄει. καὶ ἡ γαστὴρ αὐτοῦ νο-
σεῖν ἤρχετο καὶ παρελθὼν εἰς Ἀπάμειαν τῆς Βιθυνίας
μετήλλαξε ⟨τὸν βίον⟩,[122] τῷ παρόντι τῶν ἑταίρων
Προκοπίῳ πολλὰ ἐπισκήψας μόνον θαυμάζειν Χρυ-
101G σάνθιον. καὶ ὁ | Προκόπιος παραγενόμενος εἰς τὰς
Σάρδεις, ταῦτα ἐποίει τε καὶ ἀπήγγειλεν.
61   Ὁ δὲ Χρυσάνθιος, εἰς τὴν ἐπιοῦσαν ὥραν τοῦ
ἔτους, κατὰ θέρος ἱστάμενον, ἐπὶ τὴν αὐτὴν θεραπείαν ἐλθών, καίτοι τοῦ συγγραφέως προειπόντος
τοῖς ἰατροῖς περιμένειν αὐτὸν κατὰ τὸ σύνηθες, οἱ μὲν

120 A Civil: ⟨ἐπι⟩φερόμενον Gi Be Go
121 Go: σπευσάμενος A: φεισάμενος Gi
122 ⟨τὸν βίον⟩ coni. Junius (sic Go): τὸ ζῆν Wr: lac. 8 litt. A

scribed that the stream of blood should be allowed to flow out,[290] the author in his anxiety to apply the right treatment declared that the bloodletting was unreasonable, and gave orders that it should be stopped immediately; for the author of this work was not without experience in the art of medicine. When he heard what had happened, Hellespontius came at once, upset and loudly expressing his indignation that it was a great calamity that a man of so great an age should lose so much blood from his arm.[291] But when he heard his voice and saw that he was in good health, he directed his remarks to the author and said: "The whole city is accusing you of having done a terrible thing; but now they will all be silenced, when they see that he is in good health." The author replied that he knew what the proper treatment was. Hellespontius, acting as though he would collect his books and go to Chrysanthius for a lesson, in fact left the city. And his stomach too began to cause him ill-health and, changing course to Apamea in Bithynia, he there departed this life, after laying the strictest injunctions on his comrade Procopius, who was present, to venerate no one else but Chrysanthius. And Procopius went to Sardis and did as he said, and reported his death.

Now Chrysanthius, at the same season in the following year, that is at the beginning of summer, had recourse to the same remedy, and though the author of this work had given instructions to the doctors beforehand that they

[290] Verb used of humors in the body: Sor. 1.77; Gal. 1.137.

[291] In medical writings διὰ τῆς χείρος often refers to hand *and* arm or the arm only (cf. Ruf. *Onom*. 11.82; Gal. 2.347; but Pl. *Prt*. 352a differentiates arm and hand).

ἔφθασαν ἐλθόντες, ὁ δὲ ὑπέσχε τὴν χεῖρα, καὶ παρὰ
μέτρον γενομένης τῆς κενώσεως, παρέσεις τε τῶν
μερῶν ἠκολούθησαν καὶ τὰ ἄρθρα συνέκαμνεν καὶ
62 κλινοπετὴς ἦν. καὶ Ὀρειβάσιος ἐνταῦθα παραγίνεται
δι' ἐκεῖνον καθ' ὑπερβολὴν μὲν ἐπιστήμης μικροῦ καὶ
βιασάμενος τὴν φύσιν καὶ χρίσμασι θερμοτέροις καὶ
μαλάττουσι τὰ κατεψυγμένα μικροῦ πρὸς τὸ νεάζειν
63 ἐπήγαγεν. ἀλλ' ἐνίκα τὸ γῆρας· ὀγδοηκοστὸν γὰρ
ὑπελθὸν ἔτος ἐτύγχανε, καὶ τῇ τοῦ θερμοῦ κατὰ τὸ
πλεονάζον ἀλλοτριώσει τὸ γῆρας ἐδιπλασιάσθη· καὶ
τεταρταῖος νοσηλευθείς, εἰς τὴν πρέπουσαν λῆξιν
ἀνεχώρησεν.

24. Ἐπίγονός καὶ Βερονικιανός. Εἰσὶ δὲ μετ' αὐτὸν
διάδοχοι φιλοσοφίας Ἐπίγονός τε ὁ ἐκ Λακεδαίμονος, καὶ Βερονικιανὸς ὁ ἐκ Σάρδεων, ἄνδρες ἄξιοι τοῦ
2 τῆς φιλοσοφίας ὀνόματος· πλὴν ὅσα γε ὁ Βερονικιανὸς ταῖς Χάρισιν ἔθυσε, καὶ ἱκανὸς ἀνθρώποις ὁμιλεῖν ἐστι· καὶ εἴη.

must wait for him as usual, they arrived before him. Chrysanthius offered his arm to them, and there was an excessive loss of blood, with the result that his limbs became
immobile and at the same time his joints were aching, so
that he was bedbound. Then Oribasius attended to him,   62
and he almost succeeded on behalf of Chrysanthius, so
extraordinary was his professional skill, in doing violence
to the laws of nature, and by means of hot and soothing
poultices he almost restored the vigor of youth to those
rigid limbs. Nevertheless, old age was victorious; for as it   63
happens he was coming up to his eightieth year, and the
influence of his age was doubly felt when his temperature
was so greatly changed by the excessive application of
heat. After an illness of four days he departed to a destiny
that was worthy of him.

24. Epigonius and Beronicianus. The successors of
Chrysanthius in the profession of philosophy are Epigonus
of Lacedaemon and Beronicianus of Sardis, men deserving to be associated with philosophy. But Beronicianus has   2
sacrificed [more generously] to the Graces[292] and was
more able to associate with his fellow human beings. Long
may he live to do so!

[292] Compare *VPS* 5.3.

RHETORICAL GLOSSARY

References are to the numbering of Olearius for Philostratus and Goulet for Eunapius.

ἀγωνίζεσθαι: *to deliver an oration in public* (VS 529). Sometimes with the character adopted by the speaker as the verb's object (*VS* 575, of Alexander playing Artabazus; *VS* 514, of playing the Spartans considering whether to build a wall). The sense of *contending*, which the verb carries in its other uses in athletic contexts, suggests the implicitly competitive nature of all sophistic declamation.

ἀκμή: *climactic moment of a speech* (e.g., *VS* 537, of Polemo's habit of leaping up at this point; *VS* 583, of criticism of one of Aristides' ἀκμαί). The adjective ἀκμαῖος is used of themes that call for such an emotional *crescendo* (VS 519).

ἀκρόασις: Used of a *lecture* or *declamation*, especially as something to which one listens, i.e., emphasizing its auditory nature. See for instance VS 491, where the ἀκρόασις of Favorinus delights even those who cannot understand him. Cf. ἀκροατής, used for *student* by Eunapius, *VPS* 4.2 (see also γνώριμοι).

ἀμφιβολία: *ambiguity, double entendre*. Philostratus praises this in the "simulated" speeches of Hermocrates, *VS* 609 (see ἐσχηματισμένη), where this type of doublespeak was especially suitable.

ἀπαγγελία: *style of delivery* (VS 484, 500, 601). The verb ἀπαγγέλλειν, in the sense *deliver a speech*, appears more frequently than does the noun in the *Lives of the Sophists*.

ἀπέριττος: *simple, unaffected* in style (e.g., at VS 514, 527, 544). The opposite of περιττός, which occurs less frequently in Philostratus in the sense *elaborate, highly wrought* (e.g., *VS* 544), but is more often used in nontechnical senses.

ἄπνους: *uninspired*, or more literally, *lacking in inspiration or breath*. Eunapius uses this of the style of Libanius (*VPS* 16.13). See πνεῦμα.

621

ἀπολογέω: *deliver a defense speech* (ἀπολογία). Given the forensic roles of sophists, this group of terms is frequent in both Philostratus (e.g., VS 503, 510) and Eunapius (e.g., VPS 9.20, 9.24).

ἀπόστασις: The exact nature of this Gorgianic figure is still subject to debate, but it appears to be a kind of asyndeton where the new sentence is independent in structure and sometimes in thought. The term appears only twice in Philostratus: once in the *bios* of Gorgias in the *Lives of the Sophists* (VS 492) and once, also in connection with Gorgias, in the letter to Julia Domna (*Letter* 73). See also προσβολή.

ἁρμονία: *harmony* of speech or composition, which Philostratus ascribes to the style of Herodes (VS 564). Though the term is used on only this occasion in the *Lives of the Sophists*, it is a telling instance of the frequent connection of rhetoric to music.

ἀρχαῖος: The concept of the *ancient* is important to Philostratus in several related respects. In the preface to the *Lives of the Sophists*, he divides the Ancient and the Second Sophistics, though insisting at the same time that the second itself is ancient (ἀρχαία). The verbs ἀρχαίζειν and ἀττικίζειν are often near synonyms. See Norden, *Antike Kunstprosa*, p. 357. On ancient authors (ἀρχαιοί), see also Eunapius, VPS 4.3, 10.6, 10.59, 17.1, 20.3, 23.30.

ἀρχή: *basic assumption* in an argument (VPS 23.24).

ἀφέλεια: *simplicity* of style is praised in the *Lives of the Sophists* on several occasions (e.g., VS 487, 564, 624). There are many examples in Greek literature of the Roman era, for instance the opening of Achilles Tatius' *Leucippe and Clitophon* (already cited as an example by Radermacher and Norden). Longus' *Daphnis and Chloe* is the longest sustained composition in this style. Philostratus observes this quality in Aelian (624), whose surviving works do indeed exemplify this quality. For Hermogenes ἀφέλεια was not a separate ἰδέα but one of the means of expression associated with ἦθος.

ἀφροδίτη: *loveliness* or *charm* of style. Used by Eunapius of Plutarch (VPS 5.3) and Libanius (16.14).

γνώριμοι: *pupils*, *students*, apparently of the inner circle of a teaching sophist, by contrast with the ἀκροαταί.

γοργιάζειν: *to write* or *to speak like Gorgias*. In his *bios* of Gorgias, Philostratus claims that Agathon gorgianized in his iambics (VS 493), and at VS 604 Proclus of Naucratis is said to speak in his *dia-*

lexeis like Gorgias and Hippias. *Letter* 73 similarly uses this term to claim Gorgias' influence on a range of people and cities.

δεινότης: The quality of δεινότης appears in the *Lives of the Sophists* primarily in the context of suspicion of the power of sophists. That is, the early sophists' δεινότης, their *cleverness* at speaking, is distrusted by their audiences (see especially *VS* 483 and 499 on Antiphon and his treatment in comedy). By Philostratus' time, δεινότης was both one of the seven qualities (ἰδέαι) of Hermogenes and the last of the four characters or types (χαρακτῆρες) of rhetoric as outlined in Demetrius *De Elocutione*, and had a close association with Demosthenes and with practical rhetoric. His remark that Aeschines combined δεινότης with grace (τὸ ἐπίχαρι, *VS* 510) suggests an understanding of δεινότης similar to that of Demetrius, who states that failure to achieve δεινότης results in a graceless (ἄχαρις) style (*De Elocutione* 302). The ideal kind of δεινότης, for Philostratus, seems to be implicit in his description of Herodes' version of this quality as "creeping up rather than attacking" (564). The adjective δεινός (clever, cunning) also occurs in the context of rhetorical skill (e.g., *VPS* 5.5, 11.1; *VS* 499).

διάλεξις: This word and its cognates appear with two meanings in the *Lives of the Sophists* and other contemporary texts: (1) a *philosophical discourse*. The surviving *dialexis* ascribed to Philostratus (the so-called *Dialexis 2* of Kayser's edition) may well be an example of the genre. In the *Lives of the Sophists* Philostratus employs the related verb (διαλέγεσθαι) of the activity of the philosophizing sophists of the "Ancient Sophistic" (*VS* 480), and Eunapius likewise employs it for dialectical debates (e.g., *VPS* 7.71). (2) It is also the regular term for a relatively informal prooemium prior to the main declamation (the μελετή). See also προοίμιον.

διατίθεσθαι: *perform/compose* a speech. Frequent in Dionysius of Halicarnassus and in the *Lives of the Sophists* (e.g., *VS* 509, 510, 521).

ἔκφυλον: *foreign, outlandish* of words that are not attested in classical Greek authors. See *VS* 578 of a slip by Philagrus of Cilicia with our note *ad loc.* and *VS* 503 of Critias' avoidance of such language. These are the only two occurrences of these terms (the former of the adjective, the latter of the adverb) in the *Lives of the Sophists*, where Philostratus prefers to praise the use of appropriate (but not excessive) Atticizing.

Ἕλληνες: literally, *the Greeks*, but frequently with the connotation of *students of traditional, Hellenic paideia* (e.g., of Herodes' students, at VS 571). By the time of Eunapius the meaning had shifted to mean *followers of the traditional religion* as distinct from Christians (e.g., VPS 7.39).

ἐπεστραμμένη: *vehement* (e.g., VS 504, of the quality of σεμνότης in Demosthenes). Cf. ἐπιστροφή and ἐπιστρεφής. The finite verb (ἐπέστραπται) appears in a similar sense at Longinus, *On the Sublime* 12.3.

ἐπιβολή: *abundance* of language. Dio Chrysostom (18.14) praises Xenophon for this characteristic. Philostratus employs the perfect passive participle ἐπιβεβλημένος to express *ornateness of style* (VS 514, of Isaeus of Assyria). This is distinct from its other, more usual rhetorical meaning, *directness* or *simplicity*, by contrast with πε‐ριβολή. Cf. Hermogenes, *On the Qualities of Oratory* 1.28.

ἐπίδειξις: *display of rhetoric*, *show speech*. The regular term for a public declamation by a sophist. Both Philostratus (e.g., VS 510) and Eunapius (e.g., VPS 7.71) employ this term.

ἐπίκροτος: *resonant*, apparently with a suggestion of a rhythmic or percussive quality (used by Herodes in describing the oratory of Polemo, VS 593).

ἐπὶ πᾶσιν or τὸ ἐπὶ πᾶσιν: *epilogue* or *peroration* of a speech. This is, of course, an important part of a speaker's performance, and comes to be an especial object of controversy in relation to the desirability or undesirability of the singing conclusion (ᾠδή) in the manner of Favorinus (see VS 492).

ἐπιστροφή: *vehemence* or *emphasis*. Cf. ἐπεστραμμένη above.

ἐπίτονος: *intense*. This is identified as a desirable quality on several occasions, e.g., of Polemo at VS 537.

ἐπιφορά: *impetuousness* of rhetorical performance. Mentioned as a quality of Demosthenes (VS 504); of the philosopher Timocrates (VS 536), who impressed Polemo in this regard; as well as of Polemo himself (VS 542) and of Antiochus of Aegae (VS 568).

ἐπιχειρηματικόν: *detailed, technical* argument. Mentioned as a specialty of Lollianus of Ephesus (VS 527).

ἐσχηματισμένη (ὑπόθεσις): *covert allusion* or *veiled speech*. The active verb is used of composing or improvising in this way (σχηματίζειν λόγον). The fuller expression ἐσχηματισμένη ὑπόθεσις κατ᾽ ἔμφασιν appears in Hermogenes (*On Invention*, p. 259 Spengel). This type of expression could be useful in addressing powerful individuals, especially the emperor, on sensitive topics, concealing the meaning sufficiently to avoid outright offense. Rufus of Perinthus showed a preference for employing his intelligence on this type of speech (*VS* 597); Philostratus claims that the impetuous Polemo, despite the opinion of some unnamed people, excelled also in covert arguments (*VS* 542). A distraught Herodes Atticus, however, did not use covert speech in an abusive tirade to Marcus Aurelius (*VS* 561).

εὐγλωττία: *eloquence* or *fluency* of speech. Used as a term of praise in both Philostratus (e.g., of Favorinus and Dio, *VS* 489) and Eunapius (e.g., *VPS* 7.20).

εὐκολία: *flow, facility* (*VPS* 7.16, 9.23). This term, along with the corresponding adjective, εὔκολος, *effortless* (*VPS* 14.2), appears as a term of praise in Eunapius but not in Philostratus.

εὔροια: *fluency* of speech. This is named frequently, and for obvious reasons, as a desirable characteristic of the orator (e.g., *VS* 484, 491, 509).

ἦθος: *character* was one of the qualities of rhetoric in Hermogenes' system of ἰδέαι. The orations of Aeschines, according to Philostratus, are full of character (*VS* 510). Though the term does not occur frequently in its technical sense in the *Lives of the Sophists*, it is noted by Philostratus, as by other writers on epistolary rhetoric, as a desirable quality in letter writing, as for example in the letter of Marcus Aurelius to Herodes Atticus (see *VS* 562 and note).

ἠχώ: *resonant sound* in performance, as for instance of Herodes Atticus at *VS* 563. Performing before Alexander the Clay Plato, Herodes is said to "lift up" or "increase" the ἠχώ of his performance in order to cater to Alexander's tastes (*VS* 573).

θετικός: Used to distinguish themes positing an abstract thesis, as distinct from the those relating to a particular fictional or historical character, which Philostratus claims to be the main focus of the Second Sophistic. At *VS* 576 he remarks that θετικὰς ὑποθέσεις (themes positing an abstract argument) were favored by Quadratus, the teacher of Varus. By contrast, at *VS* 621, Quirinus of Nicomedia was not very good on τὰ θετικὰ τῶν χωρίων, as his succinct and direct style was better suited to more aggressive, forensic oratory. Philostratus does not make use of the distinction between θέσις and ὑπόθεσις, that is, between abstract and specific rhetorical themes, which was current in the ancient rhetorical vocabulary, but uses ὑπόθεσις for both (cf. *VPS* 10.50).

ἰδέα: Like *characters* (see below), the concept of stylistic *qualities* (ἰδέαι) is important in ancient rhetoric and literary criticism. The fullest discussion is Hermogenes' *On Ideas*, which gives a division of eighteen to twenty ἰδέαι. Of these, there are seven primary types (1.105–108), all of which are said by Hermogenes to have been exhibited by Demosthenes: σαφήνεια, μέγεθος, κάλλος, γοργότης, ἦθος, ἀλήθεια, δεινότης. We do not know whether Philostratus knew Hermogenes' works, as he omits any mention of them to focus instead on Hermogenes' short-lived career as a rhetorical performer. Nonetheless, almost all of these terms appear with some frequency in Philostratus' discussion of rhetorical performance, with the exception of γοργότης, which does not appear at all, and κάλλος and ἀλήθεια, which are not used in a technical sense. If Philostratus did not know Hermogenes' formulation of the ἰδέαι, the individual terms must have been in general usage in rhetorical discussion. See also δεινότης; ἦθος; μέγεθος; σαφήνεια.

καιρός: On several occasions Philostratus emphasizes the importance for the sophist of observing the *proper moment* or of suiting his declamation to the *moment* (καιρός). For example, Gorgias "threw himself into speaking about each thing as suited the present moment" (*VS* 482), and Polemo similarly improvised a speech "for the moment" (*VS* 529); Herodes observed a favorable moment for raising a topic before Marcus Aurelius (*VS* 560), and Phoenix the Thessalian never uttered a thought that was not suited to the moment (*VS* 604). This sense of timeliness often relates to verbal wit: Leon of Byzantium improvised with wit "to suit the moment" (*VS* 485) when he persuaded the Athenians to end factional strife, and a philosopher Lucius, friend of Herodes Atticus, employed a wit that was "timely" or again "suited to the moment" (*VS* 556). The longest of Philostratus' brief comments on καιρός are in his praise of As-

RHETORICAL GLOSSARY

pasius of Ravenna for choosing the appropriate moment for his novel inventions. Philostratus here draws a comparison with the supreme importance of timing in music (*VS* 627).

κατηγορία: *accusation*, *indictment*, *prosecution* (e.g., *VPS* 9.18). Primarily used in a legal context, but by extension of other condemnations (e.g., *VS* 488, of Dio's speech condemning Domitian).

κατάστασις: part of a speech that establishes a case (cf. *narratio*) (*VPS* 10.49).

κομψότης: *elegance* of style. Used on one occasion in Eunapius (*VPS* 16.14).

κρότος: On several occasions Philostratus remarks on the κρότος (apparently, *percussive effect*) of a speaker. This effect characterizes both Polemo (*VS* 537) and Herodes Atticus (*VS* 564), the latter of whom combined it with ἀφέλεια. Aristocles of Pergamum lacked both κρότος and ἠχώ (something like rhythm and resonance) in comparison to Herodes (*VS* 568). Though Hadrian of Tyre spoke with ἠχώ rather than κρότος (*VS* 590), Hermocrates was characterized by flow, percussive effect, and rapidity of thought (*VS* 612). The number of references to κρότος indicates its importance for Philostratus, but it appears impossible to be certain of its exact nature in vocal performance. The word is used similarly in Eunapius of *sonorous eloquence* or *rhythmic cadence* (*VPS* 6.14, 9.23, 10.49, 14.2, 17.1.) See also Goulet's note in his edition of Eunapius (vol. 1, 214f. n. 2) and cf. Longinus fr. 42, Philop. *In De an.* P. 376.14–34 Hayduck, and Lucian, *In Praise of Demosth.* 32. Contrary to the use of the noun, Eunapius uses the verb (κροτέω) in the sense *applaud*, *make noise* (*VPS* 9.17, 10.65).

λέξις: *diction* (*VS* 604; *VPS* 5.3).

λευκότης: *lucidity* or *clarity* of expression (*VPS* 5.3).

μέγεθος: *greatness* is one of the qualities (ἰδέαι) of Hermogenes and is used only once in a technical, rhetorical sense in the *Lives of the Sophists*, in the description of Antipater (*VS* 607), who is also credited with the quality of σαφήνεια. On the relation of μέγεθος to related concepts of "fullness" and "abundance," see the *Historisches Wörterbuch der Rhetorik*, s.v. Abundanz.

μελέτη: *declamation*, *speech*. This is, of course, in the world of the

627

Lives of the Sophists the highest cultural activity, and the noun and its cognate verb ($\mu\epsilon\lambda\epsilon\tau\acute{\alpha}\omega$) are consequently of frequent occurrence.

$\acute{o}\mu o\iota o\tau\acute{\epsilon}\lambda\epsilon\upsilon\tau\alpha$: *use of similar endings*. This is especially common in balanced clauses of equal length (see $\pi\acute{\alpha}\rho\iota\sigma\alpha$ below) and is one of the "poetic" effects at the disposal of sophists. The technique is associated especially with Gorgias. See also Philostratus' remarks on the use of *homoioteleuta* by Gorgias' student Polus (VS 497).

$\acute{o}\rho\mu\acute{\eta}$: *energy* or *impetuosity* of style. Philostratus credits Gorgias with discovering this (VS 492); the young Herodes implicitly learns to imitate it from Scopelian, being ignorant of it himself (VS 521). At VS 533 Polemo appears to use it of the *impetus* toward the speech itself, which he claims came from divine inspiration, and at VS 537 it describes the excitement that drove Polemo to leap up from his litter at the height of his declamations. Aristocles of Pergamum is said to be lacking as a forensic orator because his speech lacked bursts of such energy (VS 568). The furious Philagrus of Cilicia is, perhaps unsurprisingly, praised from possessing $\acute{o}\rho\mu\acute{\eta}$ (VS 578). The nontechnical use of this same word for the spring of a lion, in a simile describing the ferocious appearance of Timocrates of Heraclea (VS 536), indicates the energy and vigor that it conveys.

$\pi\alpha\nu\eta\gamma\upsilon\rho\iota\kappa\acute{o}\varsigma$: The term appears in several senses. It can be *panegyrical* in approximately the modern sense (VS 486, of the speech of Philostratus the Egyptian). A $\pi\alpha\nu\eta\gamma\upsilon\rho\iota\kappa\acute{o}\varsigma$ can also be *a speech suited to a religious festival*, as in the instance of Demosthenes' speech at Olympia (VS 505). It is used to describe the general stylistic approach of Euodianus of Smyrna, who is said to follow Aristocles in it (VS 597). Heracleides is praised for "not indulging in Bacchic excesses" ($o\grave{\upsilon}\chi\ \acute{\upsilon}\pi\epsilon\rho\beta\alpha\kappa\chi\epsilon\acute{\upsilon}\omega\nu$) in his panegyrics (VS 613).

$\pi\acute{\alpha}\rho\iota\sigma\alpha$: *clauses of equal length*. As Wright observed (in her glossary s.v. $\pi\acute{\alpha}\rho\iota\sigma\alpha$), these symmetrical clauses are often combined with assonance of endings ($\acute{o}\mu o\iota o\tau\acute{\epsilon}\lambda\epsilon\upsilon\tau\alpha$) and antithesis (citing Aristotle, *Rhetoric* 3.9.9, $\tau\acute{\iota}\ \mathring{\alpha}\nu\ \acute{\epsilon}\pi\alpha\theta\epsilon\varsigma\ \delta\epsilon\iota\nu\acute{o}\nu,\ \epsilon\grave{\iota}\ \mathring{\alpha}\nu\delta\rho'\ \epsilon\mathring{\iota}\delta\epsilon\varsigma\ \mathring{\alpha}\rho\gamma\acute{o}\nu$). Philostratus denies what he says is a common view that Polus of Agrigentum invented $\pi\acute{\alpha}\rho\iota\sigma\alpha$, $\acute{o}\mu o\iota o\tau\acute{\epsilon}\lambda\epsilon\upsilon\tau\alpha$, and $\mathring{\alpha}\nu\tau\acute{\iota}\theta\epsilon\tau\alpha$, saying that he rather abused existing ornaments of speech (VS 497). He also denies that Isocrates invented these devices, but implicitly praises his use of them (*VS* 503). Wright noted the use of πάρισα in the quotation from Isaeus the Assyrian (*VS* 514), but Philostratus does not seem to share her view that this use was excessive.

περιβολή: *fullness of expression, expansion, amplification.* As Wright already observed, Philostratus "uses this term rather vaguely for rhetorical ornament and fulness of statement in general." This, it might be added, is because the *Lives of the Sophists* is a work interested in the effect of rhetorical performance rather than with the technical details of speech construction treated by the handbooks. In the brief notice of Theomnestus of Naucratis, the possession of περιβολή alone was sufficient to make him appear to be a sophist rather than, as he was, a philosopher (*VS* 486). Isocrates, among others, is praised for his attention to περιβολή (*VS* 503).

πνεῦμα, πνεῖν: *inspiration* of a speech (of Gorgias, at *VS* 492); *vigorous energy* (apparently lacking in the speeches of Critias, *VS* 503). Philostratus' remarks on the πνεῦμα of Herodes Atticus are the most detailed: Herodes' πνεῦμα is said not to have been vehement, but smooth and steady, suggesting that there is an overlap here between describing *inspiration* or *vigor* and the physical breath itself (*VS* 564).

πότιμος: *drinkable* or *sweet* style (*VS* 597, 620). This popular image derives from Plato's *Phaedrus* 243d.

προβάλλειν: *to propose a theme* for declamation. Philostratus credits Gorgias with initiating the practice of asking the audience to suggest a subject (*VS* 482). In the school environment, students could suggest a theme, as could distinguished visitors. See, for instance, the students of Polemo turning to Marcus of Byzantium for a theme in their teacher's class (*VS* 529). See also ἀπόστασις.

προλαλία: a less formal discourse delivered prior to a μελέτη. See also διάλεξις.

προοίμιον: *introduction* to a speech (e.g., *VS* 480; *VPS* 9.21). Philostratus reports Herodes Atticus' metaphoric use of this term, when he described the negative impression made on the Athenian sophists by Philagrus of Cilicia as a poorly constructed προοίμιον (*VS* 579). The comparison reveals one of the primary purposes of this part of a speech: getting the audience onto the speaker's side.

προσβολή: This figure does not seem to have been defined by the rhetorical handbooks, as Wright already observed in her glossary, but Philostratus pairs this with ἀπόστασις, a sudden breaking off, in the style of Gorgias (VS 492). This combination also appears, again in relation to Gorgias, in Philostratus' *Letter* 73. Wright noted the related use of the verb προσβάλλειν: "ἀσυνδέτως χωρίῳ προσβάλλειν evidently means an abrupt attachment of clauses or words, a heaping up without connectives."

ῥοῖζος: To judge by its nonrhetorical uses, ῥοῖζος appears to denote *rushing vigor* of sound and expression. It is used twice in the *Lives of the Sophists*, on each occasion of later sophists emulating this quality from Polemo (Hadrian of Tyre, at VS 589; Ptolemy of Naucratis, at 595).

σαφήνεια: *clarity* is one of the qualities of rhetoric in Hermogenes' schema of ἰδέαι. This quality is praised by Philostratus on several occasions: VS 510, of Aeschines; VS 607, of Antipater of Hierapolis; VS 621, of Quirinus of Nicomedia (who made a particular effort for this quality); VS 628, of Philostratus of Lemnos' arguing with Aspasius of Ravenna that σαφήνεια was essential in imperial letter writing. Eunapius likewise remarks on this quality; see his use of σαφής/ἀσαφής (VPS 5.3).

σεμνότης: Etymologically, σεμνότης can convey a sense of *elevation* and *nobility* but also of *arrogance* or *pomposity*. Philostratus uses it of the *dignity* of Gorgias (which is paired with his use of poetic words, VS 492), and of the *grandiloquence* of Protagoras, upon which Plato believed that the sophist relied (VS 494–95). The clearest sense of the word's meaning emerges at VS 504, where Philostratus contrasts the σεμνότης of Demosthenes and Isocrates, demonstrating by examples that the "grand style" of Demosthenes "is more vehement, but that of Isocrates is more graceful and more pleasant." It is telling of the nature of σεμνότης, which is at once a quality of character and of rhetoric, that it is impossible to determine at VS 601 whether Apollonius of Athens is credited with σεμνότης specifically as a rhetorical quality or rather as a more general character trait.

σκηνή: In keeping with the nonrhetorical meaning of this word, the σκηνή of a sophist encapsulated the *theatrical aspects of performance*. The two appearances of this word in relation to declamation in the *Lives of the Sophists* both concern Polemo, who appears to

RHETORICAL GLOSSARY

have been the model for this part of the sophistic art. Polemo's theatrical gestures are described, drawing on a letter of Herodes at *VS* 537. Later, Ptolemy of Naucratis is said to have borrowed his rushing impetus (ῥοῖζος) and use of breath (πνεῦμα) and ornamentation (περιβολή) from the theatrical effects of Polemo (*VS* 595), demonstrating that these, as well as the gestures and habits of delivery discussed at *VS* 537, were part of the sophist's σκηνή.

σοφιστής: *sophist.* This term and the associated words σοφιστεύω (*to be an orator or teacher of rhetoric,* VPS 7.4) and σοφιστικός (*suitable for a sophist, sophistic, related to sophistry,* etc.) are, of course, important to both Philostratus and Eunapius. As Wright observed in her glossary, Philostratus applied the adjective, σοφιστικός, to a speech (λόγος), a theme (ὑπόθεσις), a rhetorical image (εἰκών), and the temperament of an orator. Because, for Philostratus in the *Lives of the Sophists* at least, epideictic oratory is the highest possible achievement, this is unambiguously a term of praise. For Eunapius, sophistic rhetoric occupies a respectable position, though not so elevated as the achievements of his philosophers.

στάσις: This does not occur as a technical term in Philostratus, but it appears in Eunapius in a slightly uncertain sense. It appears to mean *basic premise, proposition* (cf. above, ἀρχή) or more exactly, as Wright already argued, the *stand* or *perspective* that the speaker took to a problem (*VPS* 10.71). Prohaeresius, criticizing the hairsplitting of rhetoricians on the subject, implies that there was a catalog of thirteen στάσεις, when he asserts that if there had been more than thirteen (canonical?) sophists there would have been more στάσεις listed. As Wright also observed, Quintillian (3.6) says that it is the equivalent of Latin *quaestio* or *constitutio* or *status.*

σχέδιος, σχεδιάζειν: *improvised, to improvise* a speech. This group of terms is of great importance to Philostratus, who praises improvisation above all other rhetorical accomplishments. Early in the text he considers, inconclusively, who it was who began the "springs of improvised speeches" (*VS* 482). The same terms are current in Eunapius' discussions of sophistic practice (e.g., *VPS* 10.78).

σχῆμα: See ἐσχηματισμένη.

τερπνός: *charming, graceful, elegant.* This is used by Eunapius of the style of Libanius (*VPS* 16.15).

τόνος: *intensity, elevation* of style. Herodes recognizes this as charac-

631

teristic of Alexander (*VS* 573). In his own voice Philostratus says that it was a feature of Aelian's style (*VS* 624).

τύπος: (rhetorical) *style*. This appears as a semitechnical term in Eunapius (*VPS* 16.3, 16.14) but not in Philostratus.

τυμπανίζειν: *to beat the drum* (metaphorically) in declamation. This appears as part of Philostratus' description of Scopelian's style as Dionysiac (*VS* 520).

ὑπόθεσις: The term ὑπόθεσις appears throughout the *Lives of the Sophists* to denote a rhetorical *theme*, that is, the topic that the speaker must develop and treat in an individual way. In broader rhetorical usage, ὑπόθεσις is often contrasted with θέσις, the former denoting a specific theme, the latter a general one (see in the *Historisches Wörterbuch der Rhetorik*, s.v. These, Hypothese). The form without the prefix (θέσις) does not appear in the *Lives of the Sophists*. In the programmatic passage at *VS* 481, Philostratus states that specific topics were the particular focus of his Second Sophistic, which depicted "poor men and rich and the noble and the tyrants and themes relating to named characters (τὰς ἐς ὄνομα ὑποθέσεις), to which history leads the way."

φορά: *vigor* or *force* of speech. When Herodes is praised for this, he deflects the compliment rather to Polemo's mastery of this quality (*VS* 539). Aristides' φορά proves sufficient to influence Marcus Aurelius to rebuild Smyrna (*VS* 583).

χαρακτήρ: There is some variety between theorists of rhetoric concerning the number of *characters* or *types* of speech. Pseudo-Demetrius (*De Elocutione* 36) states that there are four pure characters, which can be mixed with one another, but adds that some say there are only two (γλαφυρός and δεινός). Pseudo-Plutarch, *Vita Homeri* 72, provides a three-character model (μεγαλοπρεπής, μέσος, ἰσχνός, "magnificent," "middle," and "small" or "lean".) Philostratus does not weigh in on matters of classification, unsurprisingly given the focus and nature of the *Lives of the Sophists*, but does introduce general illustrations and discussion of his sophists' styles by reference to their χαρακτήρ: *VS* 564, 576, 580, 586, 593. Eunapius remarks in a more general way on the χαρακτήρ of some speakers: *VPS* 5.3, 6.43, 7.3, 7.16, 16.6, 16.18.

χάρις: *charm, loveliness* (in style). This does not appear in descriptions of rhetoric in Philostratus but is something of a favorite term of Eunapius: *VPS* 5.3, 6.43, 7.3, 7.16, 16.6, 16.18. See, however, the uses of ἄχαρις and ἐπίχαρις in the *Lives of the Sophists* under δεινότης above.

ᾠδή: *song.* On three occasions in the *Lives of the Sophists*, Philostratus uses this term to refer to a passage, particularly toward the end of a declamation, characterized by a greater exaggeration of the musical qualities of speech. Favorinus' tendency to this is treated critically by Philostratus (*VS* 492), and Isaeus is still more strongly opposed to the habit in his former student, Dionysius of Miletus (*VS* 513). By contrast, Hadrian of Tyre's mastery of the ᾠδή is among the characteristics that Philostratus praises (*VS* 589). A song-like quality could certainly be overdone: Varus of Laodicea (*VS* 620) is condemned for making his speech shameful "with twistings of song" (καμπαῖς ᾀσμάτων).

INDEX TO PHILOSTRATUS

References to page numbers in the introduction and of the notes appear in italics. All other numbers refer to Olearius pages.

638

INDEX TO PHILOSTRATUS

647

INDEX TO EUNAPIUS

References to page numbers in the introduction and of the notes appear in italics. All other numbers refer to Goulet chapters and sections.